Get the eBook FREE!

(PDF, ePub, Kindle, and liveBook all included)

We believe that once you buy a book from us, you should be able to read it in any format we have available. To get electronic versions of this book at no additional cost to you, purchase and then register this book at the Manning website.

Go to https://www.manning.com/freebook and follow the instructions to complete your pBook registration.

That's it!
Thanks from Manning!

Learn Rust in a Month of Lunches

Learn Rust in a Month of Lunches

DAVE MACLEOD
FOREWORD BY ALLEN WYMA

MANNING
SHELTER ISLAND

For online information and ordering of this and other Manning books, please visit
www.manning.com. The publisher offers discounts on this book when ordered in quantity.
For more information, please contact

    Special Sales Department
    Manning Publications Co.
    20 Baldwin Road
    PO Box 761
    Shelter Island, NY 11964
    Email: orders@manning.com

Manning Publications Co.	Development editor:	Ian Hough
20 Baldwin Road	Review editor:	Aleksandar Dragosavljević
PO Box 761	Technical editor:	Jerry Kuch
Shelter Island, NY 11964	Production editor:	Keri Hales
	Copy editor:	Alisa Larson
	Proofreader:	Mike Beady
	Technical proofreader:	Geert Van Laethem
	Typesetter:	Marija Tudor
	Cover designer:	Leslie Haimes

ISBN 9781633438231
Printed in the United States of America

*To MB, Windy, Gomes, and Johnny and to the cloudtops of Venus,
the most Earth-like environment in the solar system.*

brief contents

contents

foreword

The time to learn Rust is now. The sheer amount of C/C++ code written over the past 40 years is mind-boggling. It is used in nearly every operating system and embedded system, even powering some of the most popular programming languages such as Python and JavaScript. It has long been a way to make libraries portable and usable in almost any platform from one to another, even with different CPU architectures. It has also been the source of most hacks and vulnerabilities.

You can think of C/C++ as a katana, but without a handle. You can easily craft what you want, but if you squeeze too tight or aren't very careful, you can cut yourself or others. This has long been the tradeoff that we have made to get the run-time speed and portability that we require when creating software. Thanks to Rust, there's no more need to balance risk and speed, as it addresses most of the safety issues that have long been coupled with traditional C/C++ development.

This book does an excellent job of easing potential Rustaceans into how Rust works in small, easily digestible pieces that any developer can consume and understand. This is the first time I've seen a book start off showing how to comment in the language, which is great because you'll always want to make notes in your code so you can remember what it does! It's stunning that some books don't consider the fundamental needs of a beginner reader; I'm happy to report that this book does. I also enjoy that this book slowly creeps into more advanced topics such as shadowing, which will usually come up in a Rustacean's career before a tutorial mentions it, but it is still important nonetheless.

Learning Rust isn't a simple achievement. There's definitely a rabbit hole of information to burrow through, and that path will change whether you're writing operating systems or a simple web service. This book will give you the basics and ease you into Rust without requiring you to install it until toward the end of the book, which definitely can help you finish within "a month of lunches." You've done yourself a favor in buying this book; now do yourself another favor and read it cover to cover.

—ALLEN WYMA, HOST OF RUSTACEAN STATION PODCAST,
DIRECTOR AT PLANGORA LIMITED

preface

I'll forever be grateful to Rust for solving a paradox in my life, that of having a software-developer-like mind without a place to apply it. I took to programming languages like a duck to water as a child in the 1980s, which at the time meant BASIC, which I liked, and Logo, which I didn't. But truly getting into programming at the time didn't mean taking your fancy laptop to Starbucks every day to interact with people across the globe; it meant spending days inside the computer lab at school with the blinds shut, typing away as the rest of the world went about its business in the sun. Without knowing that programming was much more than working on BASIC and Logo all day (I probably would have loved Ada if I had known about it), I didn't get very far and eventually fell out of love with the idea of programming and moved on to other interests like heavy metal.

Other attempts decades later to learn a few popular programming languages never worked, as they were either too high level, hiding details that I was interested in and lacking in performance for what I really wanted to do (make video games), or too low level, lacking safeguards and outright intimidating. There were no external factors forcing me to learn to code either, as I was already an adult and working full time in other fields.

One day in 2019 I set myself to learn Python, Javascript, and other popular languages for the umpteenth time and thought that I might give this new language called Rust a look. I had heard that it was challenging and incredibly low level and that you needed to be a grizzled old software developer of decades to even hope to make heads or tails of it. Two days later, I was hooked, and my programming language wanderlust was gone. Without getting into too many details, suffice it to say that I had found the language that could make what I wanted to make and that showed me the low-level details I craved to see but with safeguards in place to avoid too many pitfalls.

Learning Rust was a phenomenal experience, and even in 2019, there were sufficient resources to do so. But I think the first encounter with Rust can be even further refined, and that's where this book comes from. If this book ends up being the difference for enough people between giving up on Rust and going all the way, the years put into making it will have all been worth it.

acknowledgments

It takes so many people to put a book like this together. First, I'd like to thank all my family and friends without citing any names in particular, because all of them are fairly private individuals. None of them live nearby, or even on the same continent, but they are an inexhaustible bedrock of support regardless of the physical distance.

As far as years go, I'd like to thank 1999, 2002, and 2017–2018. And, on the subject of years, I'd like to thank Mary Ann Day-Nasr, Mark Lennox, and my other teammates for managing to make 2011 and subsequent years at least pretty OK. I'd also like to thank James Massey for officially turning me from a guy who learned Rust into a professional Rust developer by giving me my first job in the field using the language.

At Manning, I'd like to thank Andy Waldron, my acquisition editor, for seeing the potential of the book and making it happen in the first place; Ian Hough, development editor, for overseeing the entire process and being my main point of contact at Manning from start to finish; and Jerry Kuch, technical editor, for his insightful comments that read much in the same way that the book itself is meant to: an experienced yet friendly hand nudging you in the right direction. Other thanks go to Geert Van Laethem, my technical proofreader, who assisted with checking the code to make sure all the code samples worked as expected. Last, but not least, thanks to the entire Manning production staff who worked behind the scenes to assemble this book into its final form.

To all the reviewers—Adam Wendell, Al Norman, Al Pezewski, Alex Lucas, Alexey Vyskubov, Amit Lamba, Andreas Schroepfer, Antonio Gagliardi, Balasubramanian Sivasankaran, Bikalpa Timilsina, Dan Sheikh, David Jacobs, David White, Francisco Claude, Giovanni Alzetta, Giuseppe Catalano, Helmut Reiterer, Horaci Macias, Ionel Olteanu, Jane Noesgaard Larsen, Jean Lazarou, Jean-Baptiste Bang Nteme, Jeremy Gailor, Joel Kotarski, John Paraskevopoulos, Jonathan Camara, Jonathan Reeves,

Karol Skork, Kent Spillner, Kyle Manning, Laud Bentil, Marcello la Rocca, Marcus Geselle, Marek Petak, Maxim Levkov, Michael Bright, Michael Wright, Mohsen Mostafa Jokar, Olivier Ducatteeuw, Rich Yonts, Richard Meinsen, Rohit Sharma, Rosalyn Williams, Sergio Britos, Seung-jin Kim, Si Dunn, Slavomir Furman, Srikar Vedantam, Thomas Lockney, Thomas Peklak, Tiklu Ganguly, Tim Clark, Tim van Deurzen, and William Wheeler—your suggestions helped make this a better book.

about this book

When Rust was released in 2015, it had to convince the world that it was worth learning. Back then, a lot of books compared Rust to languages like C++ and C because Rust is a good alternative language for C++ and C programmers. Rust books and websites were also written for people coming from Java, C#, and other such languages.

Now, a lot more people are learning Rust as a first language. For those people, a book that starts with examples in other languages is going to be confusing. *Learn Rust in a Month of Lunches* doesn't assume that you know general programming terminology: words like *generics, pointers, stack and heap memory, arguments, expressions, concurrency*, and so on. All of these terms are explained one by one.

Almost all of *Learn Rust in a Month of Lunches* is written using the online Rust Playground, which requires nothing to install. You can, of course, use VS Code or some other IDE you have installed, but you don't need to. The book intends to be easy in this sense, too: you should be able to learn most of the language just by opening up a tab in your browser.

Who should read this book

Learn Rust in a Month of Lunches has a single goal: to be the absolute easiest way for anyone to learn Rust as quickly as possible. I like to think of the book's target audience as these types of people:

- *People who are ambitious and want to learn Rust as quickly as possible*—The simple English used in the book gets out of your way and lets you focus more on Rust itself.
- *People with English as a second language*—Most developers are good enough at English that reading documentation is easy enough, but a full book of wordy and complex English can be a bit of a burden for some.

- *People who are curious but don't have enough time in the day and just want to get to the information*—Maybe you only have 30 minutes a day to devote to Rust. Without any flowery language, you can use those 30 minutes as effectively as possible to get to the information you want.
- *People who have read another introductory Rust book and want to go over the basics again with something new.*
- *People who have tried to learn Rust, but it still hasn't clicked*—Hopefully this book will be the one that does the trick!

How this book is organized: A road map

Learn Rust in a Month of Lunches is organized into 24 separate chapters but not into thematic sections as one often sees in a book of its type. That said, the book could be divided into parts that represent the amount of mental effort required.

Chapters 1 to 6 are a steady progression from Rust's simplest types and concepts to making your own types, working with advanced collection types, and, finally, error handling and some of the first types and concepts that make Rust quite unique. By the end of this section, you will have a feel for what makes Rust the language it is and eager to dive into the rest.

Chapters 7 to 12 are packed to the brim with new concepts and are the chapters where Rust will finally start to click. This is probably the most fascinating yet mentally taxing part of the book. It deals with understanding traits, iterators, closures, lifetimes, interior mutability, multiple threads, and even a type called Cow.

Chapters 13 to 16 are where the pace of learning starts to ease up a bit. Many new concepts are introduced here as well, but they go in hand with beginning to look at how to start building software in Rust, how to test it, and other tips and tricks involving patterns you will use often as a Rust developer.

In Chapters 17 to 19, the book begins to get into external crates: code written by others for you to use in your own programs. This is the point at which we'll begin to assume that you have Rust installed on your computer. It is also the point at which we will learn about async Rust, which is encountered quite a bit in external crates.

Chapters 20 and 21 are a fun tour of the standard library. In these two chapters, we kick back and relax for a bit and see what parts of the standard library we haven't come across yet.

Chapter 22 is about macros, a way to generate code before the compiler begins looking at it. If you walk away from this chapter with a general understanding of how to read macros and when you might use them, it will have done its job.

Chapter 23 and 24 are the last chapters of the book and are a fun send-off. Each of these chapters contains three unfinished projects for you to pick up and develop on your own. Each of the six projects compiles and accomplishes its basic objectives but is left incomplete on purpose to encourage you to make your own changes and add to them.

About the code

This book contains many examples of source code both in numbered listings and in line with normal text. In both cases, source code is formatted in a `fixed-width font like this` to separate it from ordinary text.

In many cases, the original source code has been reformatted; we've added line breaks and reworked indentation to accommodate the available page space in the book. In some cases, even this was not enough, and listings include line-continuation markers (➥). Additionally, comments in the source code have often been removed from the listings when the code is described in the text. Code annotations accompany many of the listings, highlighting important concepts.

You can get executable snippets of code from the liveBook (online) version of this book at https://livebook.manning.com/book/learn-rust-in-a-month-of-lunches. The complete code for the examples in the book is available for download from the Manning website at https://www.manning.com/books/learn-rust-in-a-month-of-lunches.

liveBook discussion forum

Purchase of *Learn Rust in a Month of Lunches* includes free access to liveBook, Manning's online reading platform. Using liveBook's exclusive discussion features, you can attach comments to the book globally or to specific sections or paragraphs. It's a snap to make notes for yourself, ask and answer technical questions, and receive help from the author and other users. To access the forum, go to https://livebook.manning.com/book/learn-rust-in-a-month-of-lunches/discussion. You can also learn more about Manning's forums and the rules of conduct at https://livebook.manning.com/discussion.

Manning's commitment to our readers is to provide a venue where a meaningful dialogue between individual readers and between readers and the author can take place. It is not a commitment to any specific amount of participation on the part of the author, whose contribution to the forum remains voluntary (and unpaid). We suggest you try asking the author some challenging questions lest his interest stray! The forum and the archives of previous discussions will be accessible from the publisher's website as long as the book is in print.

about the author

DAVE MACLEOD is a Canadian who has lived in Korea since 2002, living in Japan a few years before that. As a child in the 1980s, he made small role-playing games in BASIC on the family's ADAM computer, but after a local Logo competition, he decided that programming was not for him. He felt the urge to code again in the early 2010s, but it was not until he came across Rust that he found a language to devote himself to. He speaks a number of natural languages, including Korean and Japanese, as well as the constructed language Occidental. He has worked as an educator, translator, project controller, and copywriter before becoming a full-time Rust developer in Seoul, Korea.

Some basics

1

This first chapter is as easy as Rust gets and has a bit of everything to get started. You'll notice that even in Rust's easiest data types, there's a strong focus on the bits and bytes that make up a computer's system. That means there's quite a bit of choice, even in simple types like integers. You'll also start to get a feel for how strict Rust is. If the compiler isn't satisfied, your program won't run! That's a good thing—it does a lot of the thinking for you.

1.1   *Introducing Rust*

The Rust language was only released in 2015 and, as of 2024, isn't even a decade old. It's quite new but already very popular, appearing just about everywhere you can think of—Windows, Android, the Linux kernel, Amazon Web Services (AWS), Discord, Cloudflare, you name it. It is incredible how popular Rust has become after less than a decade. Rust earned its popularity by giving you almost everything you could want in a language: the speed and control of languages like C or C++, the memory safety of other newer languages like Python, a rich type system that lets you avoid bugs, and a friendly compiler that helps you when you go wrong. It does this with some new ideas that are sometimes different from other languages. That means there are some new things to learn, and you can't just "figure it out as you go along." Rust is a language you have to think about for a while to understand.

So Rust is a language that is famously difficult to learn. But I don't agree that Rust is difficult. Programming itself is difficult. Rust simply shows you these difficulties *when you are writing your code*, not *after* you start running it. That's where this saying comes from: "In Rust, you get the hangover first." In many other languages, the party starts first: your code compiles and looks great! Then you run your code, and there's a lot to debug. That's when you get the hangover.

The hangover in Rust is because you have to satisfy the compiler that you are writing correct code. If your code doesn't satisfy the compiler, it won't run. You can't mix types together, you have to handle possible errors, you have to decide what to do when a value might be missing, etc. But as you do that, the compiler gives you hints and suggestions to fix your code so that it will run. It's tough work, but the compiler tries to guide you along the way. And when your code finally compiles, it works great.

In fact, because of that, Rust was the first language that I was properly able to learn. I loved how friendly the compiler was when my code didn't compile. The compiler felt like a teacher or a co-programmer. It was also interesting how the errors taught me about how computers use memory. Rust wasn't just a language that let me build software; it was a language that taught me details about the inner workings of computers that I never knew before. The more I used it, the more I wanted to know, and that's why I was able to learn Rust as my first language. I hope this book will help others learn it, too, even if Rust is their first programming language.

1.1.1   *A pep talk*

Rust is a fairly easy language. Seriously! Well, sort of. Yes, it's complex and takes a lot of work to learn. Yes, most people who learn Rust have frustrating days (sometimes unbearably frustrating days) where they just want their code to compile and don't understand what to do.

But this period does not last forever. After the period is over, Rust becomes easier because it starts doing a lot of the thinking for you. Rust is the type of language that allows junior developers to start working on an existing code base with confidence because, for the most part, it simply won't compile if there's a problem with your code. Sometimes you hear horror stories about junior developers who join a company and simply aren't able to contribute yet. They see a code base and ask if they can make a change, but the senior developers say not to touch it "because it's working and who knows what will happen if you make a change." Rust isn't like that.

That makes contributing and refactoring code, well, easy. If you watch Rust live streams on YouTube or Twitch, you'll see this happen a lot. The streamer will make a bunch of changes to some existing code and then say, "Okay, let's see what breaks." The compiler then gives a few dozen messages showing what parts don't work anymore, and then the streamer hunts them down one by one and makes the necessary changes until it compiles again—usually in just a few minutes. Not a lot of languages can do that.

1.1.2 Rust is like a critical spouse

A great analogy for Rust is that of a critical but helpful spouse. Imagine you have a job interview and are getting ready to head out the door and ask your spouse how you look. Let's see how two types of spouses treat you: the *lenient language spouse* and the *strict Rust spouse.*

The lenient language spouse sees you going out the door and calls out: "You look great, honey! Hope the interview goes well!" And off you go! You're feeling good. But maybe you don't look great and don't realize it. Maybe you forgot to prepare a number of important things for the interview. If you're an expert in interviews, you'll do fine, but if not, you might be in trouble.

The Rust spouse isn't so lenient and won't even let you out the door: "You're going out wearing that? It's too hot today; you'll be sweating by the time you get in. Put on that suit with the lighter fabric." You change your suit.

The Rust spouse looks at you again and says, "The suit you just changed into doesn't match your socks. You need to change to grey socks." You grumble and go change your socks.

The Rust spouse still isn't satisfied: "It's windy today, and it's at least a quarter-mile walk from the parking lot to the company. Your hair is going to be messy by the time you get there. Put some gel in." You go back to the bathroom and put some gel in your hair.

The Rust spouse says, "You still can't go. The parking lot you'll be using was built a long time ago and doesn't take credit cards. You need $2.50 in change for the machine. Find some change." Sigh. You go and look around for some loose change. Finally, you gather $2.50.

This repeats and repeats another 10 times. You're starting to get annoyed, but you know your spouse is right. You make yet another change. Is it the last one?

Eventually, your Rust spouse looks you up and down, thinks a bit, and says: "Fine. Off you go." Yes! Finally! That was a lot of work.

You head out the door, still a bit frustrated by all the changes you had to make. But you walk by a window and see your reflection. You look great! It's windy today, but your hair isn't being blown around. You pull into the parking lot and put in the $2.50—just the right amount of change.

You look around and see someone else arriving for the interview in a suit that's too heavy and is already sweating. His socks don't match the suit. He only has a credit card and is trying to find a store nearby to get some change. He starts walking to the store, his hair in a mess as the wind blows it every which way. But not you—your spouse did half of the work for you before you even started. So, in that sense, Rust is a really easy language.

If you think about it, *programs* live at run time, but *programmers* can only see up to compile time—the time before a program starts. If your code compiles, you run it and hope for the best. You can't control the program anymore once it starts.

If your language isn't strict at compile time, most of the possible errors will happen at run time instead, and you will have to debug them. Rust is as strict as possible at compile time, where you, the programmer, live. So Rust teaches you as much as it can about your program before you even run it.

Okay, what does this actually look like in practice? Let's take a look at a real example. We'll go to the Rust Playground (https://play.rust-lang.org/), write some incorrect Rust code, and see what happens. We'll try to make a `String` and then push a single character to it and print it out:

```
fn main() {
    let my_name: String = "Dave";
    my_name.push("!");
    println!("{}" my_name);
}
```

This is pretty good for a first try at Rust, but it's not correct yet. What does the Rust compiler have to say about that? Quite a bit, in fact. It gives you three suggestions:

```
error: expected `,`, found `my_name`
  |
4 |     println!("{}" my_name);
  |                   ^^^^^^^ expected `,`

error[E0308]: mismatched types
 --> src/main.rs:2:27
  |
2 |     let my_name: String = "Dave";
  |                  ------   ^^^^^^- help: try using a conversion method:
  |                                  `.to_string()`
  |                  |        |
  |                  |        expected struct `String`, found `&str`
  |                  expected due to this

error[E0308]: mismatched types
 --> src/main.rs:3:18
  |
3 |     my_name.push("!");
  |             ---- ^^^ expected `char`, found `&str`
  |             |
  |             arguments to this function are incorrect
  |
```

```
help: if you meant to write a `char` literal, use single quotes
   |
3  |     my_name.push('!');
   |                  ~~~
```

If you do what the compiler suggests, it will look like this:

```
fn main() {
    let my_name: String = "Dave".to_string();
    my_name.push('!');
    println!("{}", my_name);
}
```

If you click Run again, you'll see the compiler now has a little more to say:

```
error[E0596]: cannot borrow `my_name` as mutable, as it is not declared as
➡mutable
 --> src/main.rs:3:5
  |
2 |     let my_name: String = "Dave".to_string();
  |         ------- help: consider changing this to be mutable: `mut
  |         ➡my_name`
3 |     my_name.push('!');
  |     ^^^^^^^^^^^^^^^^^ cannot borrow as mutable
```

If you follow its advice here, you'll end up with this code:

```
fn main() {
    let mut my_name: String = "Dave".to_string();
    my_name.push('!');
    println!("{}", my_name);
}
```

And it works! That's the combination of strictness and helpfulness that the Rust compiler is famous for. You will understand all of this code within just a few chapters, so don't worry about it too much now.

One final note before we get into chapter 1: the Rust compiler is smart enough to know if you wrote some code you never used. In that case, it will give you a warning so that you will remember that you wrote something you haven't used yet. In this book, many examples have code to teach a concept and never gets used, so don't worry about those warnings.

This code, for example, compiles and runs just fine:

```
fn main() {
    let my_number = 9;
}
```

But when you run it, Rust will generate a warning:

```
warning: unused variable: `my_number`
 --> src/main.rs:2:9
  |
```

```
2 |        let my_number = 9;
  |            ^^^^^^^^^ help: if this is intentional, prefix it with an
  |        ➥underscore: `_my_number`
  |
  = note: `#[warn(unused_variables)]` on by default
```

This is a hint from the compiler to let you know that you created a variable but didn't do anything with it. It doesn't mean there is a problem with your code, so don't worry.

Let's get started!

1.2   Comments

Comments are made for programmers to read, not the computer. It's good to write comments to help other people understand your code. It's also good to help you understand your code later (many people write good code but then forget why they wrote it). To write comments in Rust, you usually use // like in the following example:

```
fn main() {
    // Rust programs start with fn main()
    // You put the code inside a block. It starts with { and ends with }
    let some_number = 100; // We can write as much as we want here and the
    ➥compiler won't look at it
}
```

When you write a // comment, the compiler won't look at anything to the right of the //.

The let some_number = 100; part of the code, by the way, is how you make *variables* in Rust. A variable is basically a piece of data with a name chosen by us—hopefully a good name—so that later on we will remember what sort of data the variable is holding. Here, we are telling Rust to take this piece of data (the number 100) and give it the name some_number so that we can use some_number later to access the number 100 it holds. The variable name could differ depending on the context: we might write let perfect_score = 100;, for example, if the number 100 represented a perfect score on a test.

There is another kind of comment that you write with /* to start and */ to end. A comment wrapped in /* and */ is useful to write in the middle of your code:

```
fn main()
    let some_number/*: i16*/ = 100;
}
```

To the compiler, let some_number/*: i16*/ = 100; looks like let some_number = 100;. The /* */ form is also useful for very long comments of more than one line. In the following example, you can see that you need to write // for every line. But if you type /*, the comment won't stop until you finish it with */:

```
fn main() {
    let some_number = 100; // Let me tell you
    // a little about this number.
```

```
// It's 100, which is my favorite number.
// It's called some_number but actually I think that...

let some_number = 100; /* Let me tell you
a little about this number.
It's 100, which is my favorite number.
It's called some_number but actually I think that... */
}
```

If you see `///` (three slashes), that's a "doc comment" (documentation comment). A doc comment can be automatically made into documentation for your code. Documentation is used to explain how code works, usually for other people to read, but it can be good for you, too, so you won't forget. All the information on documentation pages like http://doc.rust-lang.org/std/index.html is made with doc comments.

So `//` means comments for inside the code, while `///` is for more official information to be shared beyond the code itself. Regular `//` comments can be very informal, like this:

```
// todo: delete this after Fred updates the client.
```

But `///` comments are for outsiders reading your code and tend to be more formal, like:

```
/// Converts a string slice in a given base to an integer. Leading and
    trailing whitespace represent an error.
```

(We'll look at doc comments later in the book. But if you have Rust installed already and are curious, try writing some comments and then typing `cargo doc --open` to see what happens.)

So comments are pretty easy because Rust doesn't notice them at all. Let's move on to another pretty easy subject: Rust's simplest types.

1.3 Primitive types: Integers, characters, and strings

Rust has many types that let you work with numbers, characters, and so on. Some are simple, and others are more complicated; you can even create your own.

The simplest types in Rust are called *primitive types* (primitive = very basic). We will start with two of them: integers and characters. Rust has a lot of integer types, but they all have one thing in common: they are whole numbers with no decimal point. There are two types of integers: signed integers and unsigned integers.

So what does signed mean exactly? It's simple: signed means + (plus sign) and − (minus sign). So, signed integers can be positive or negative (e.g., +8, −8) or zero. But unsigned integers (e.g., 8) can only be nonnegative because they do not have a sign. The signed integer types are `i8`, `i16`, `i32`, `i64`, `i128`, and `isize`. The unsigned integer types are `u8`, `u16`, `u32`, `u64`, `u128`, and `usize`.

The number after the `i` or the `u` means the number of bits for the number, so numbers with more bits can be larger: 8 bits = 1 byte, so `i8` is 1 byte, `i64` is 8 bytes, and so on. Number types with more bits can hold much larger numbers:

- u8 can hold a number as large 255.
- u16 can hold a number as large as 65,535.
- u128 can hold a number as large as 340,282,366,920,938,463,463,374,607,431,768,211,455.

A quick explanation of how integers work: computers use binary numbers, while people use decimals. Binary means 2, and decimal means 10, so you have two possible digits for binary (0 or 1) and 10 possible digits (0 to 9) for decimal.

```
◄─────────────────────────────────────────────────
10000000 | 1000000 | 100000 | 10000 | 1000 | 100 | 10 | 0
```

With decimals, you move up by 10 at a time: 100 is 10 times more than 10, 1,000 is 10 times more than 100, and so on. But computers increase numbers in binary by 2, not 10. Here's what this doubling looks like over the 8 bits of a u8.

```
◄─────────────────────────────────────────
128| 64 | 32 | 16 | 8 | 4 | 2 | 1
┌───┬───┬───┬───┬───┬───┬───┬───┐
|   |   |   |   |   |   |   |   |
└───┴───┴───┴───┴───┴───┴───┴───┘
```

A single digit, either binary or decimal, has to be filled into each box to make a number.

You can see that there are eight spaces for numbers, which are the bits. Each bit is for a number two times larger than the last one. A bit can be a 0 or a 1—nothing else. When a bit shows up as 0, the number isn't counted; if it shows up as 1, it is counted.

If you have a decimal number with eight digits, the highest number you can get is 99,999,999. Reading from right to left, you can think of this number as being made of a 9, a 90, a 900, a 9,000, a 90,000, a 900,000, a 9,000,000, and a 90,000,000. Put them all together, and you get 99,999,999. Now, if you do the same for binary, the highest number you can get over eight digits is 11111111. And if you count up these numbers, you get 1 + 2 + 4 + 8 + 16 + 32 + 64 + 128 = 255. That's why 255 is the largest size for a u8. And if you move to a u16, you have eight more spaces, each one two times larger than the last. So a u16 is all those plus 256, then 512, and so on. Consequently, the highest number for a u16 is 65,535 (a *lot* higher), even though it's only two times the size (16 bits, or 2 bytes).

You can also think of it as this: a human cashier at the grocery who asks you to pay $226 is asking for

- six 1s (6)
- two 10s (20)
- two 100s (200)

But what a "machine cashier" asks you for is 11100010, which is (remember, going from right to left):

- no 1s
- one 2
- no 4s

- no 8s
- no 16s
- one 32
- one 64
- one 128

Putting all that together, you get: 2 + 32 + 64 + 128 = 226. And that's why the u8 for 226 looks like this.

128	64	32	16	8	4	2	1
1	1	1	0	0	0	1	0

Signed integers have a maximum value that is only half that of an unsigned type of the same number of bits because they also have to represent negative numbers. So a u8 goes from 0 to 255 while an i8 goes from −128 to 127.

So what about isize and usize, and why are there no numbers in their name? These two types have a number of bits depending on your type of computer. (The number of bits on your computer is called the *architecture* of your computer.) So isize and usize on a 32-bit computer is like i32 and u32, and isize and usize on a 64-bit computer is like i64 and u64.

There are many reasons why Rust has a lot of integer sizes. One reason is computer performance: a smaller number of bytes can be faster to process. For example, the number −10 as an i8 is 11110110, but as an i64, it is 1111111111111111111111111111111111111111111111111111111111110110. The larger type has a greater maximum number but still uses the same number of bits, even if the number is a small one. But there are quite a few other reasons for having a lot of integer sizes. One is related to the char type, which is related to one of Rust's integer types.

Characters in Rust are called char. Every char has a number: the letter A is number 65, while the character 友 is number 21451. The list of numbers is called Unicode. Unicode uses smaller numbers for basic characters like A through Z, digits 0 through 9, or space. New languages get added to Unicode all the time, and some languages have thousands of characters, which is why 友 is such a high number.

As you can see, a char can be a lot of things, even an emoji:

```
fn main() {
    let first_letter = 'A';
    let space = ' ';            A space inside ' '
                                is also a char.
    let other_language_char = 'Ꮹ';       Thanks to Unicode, other languages
    let cat_face = '😺';                   like Cherokee display just fine, too.
}
                                Emojis are
                                chars, too!
```

So you won't be able to fit all chars into something as small as a u8, for example. But the characters used most (called ASCII) are represented by numbers less than 256, and they *can* fit into a u8. Remember, a u8 is 0 plus all the numbers up to 255, for 256 characters in total. This means that Rust can safely "cast" a u8 into a char, using as. ("Cast a u8 as a char" means "turn a u8 into a char.")

Casting with `as` is useful because Rust is very strict. It always needs to know the type and won't let you use two different types together, even if they are both integers. For example, this will not work:

> main() is where Rust programs start
> to run. Code goes inside {} (known
> as braces or curly brackets).

```
fn main() {
    let my_number = 100;
    println!("{}", my_number as char);
}
```

> We didn't say which integer type it will be, so
> Rust chooses i32. Rust always chooses i32 for
> integers if you don't tell it to use a different type.

Here is the reason:

```
error[E0604]: only u8 can be cast as char, not i32
 --> src\main.rs:3:20
  |
3 |     println!("{}", my_number as char);
  |                    ^^^^^^^^^^^^^^^^^^
```

By the way, you'll see `println!`, `{}`, and `{:?}` in this chapter a bit. Typing `println!` will print and then add a new line, while `{}` and `{:?}` describe what type of printing. `println!` is known as a macro. A macro is a function that writes code for you; all macros have a `!` after them. You don't need to worry about remembering to add the `!` because the compiler will notice if you don't:

```
fn main() {
    let my_number = 100;
    println("{}", my_number);
}
```

The compiler tells us exactly what to do:

```
error[E0423]: expected function, found macro `println`
 --> src/main.rs:3:5
  |
3 |     println("{}", my_number);
  |     ^^^^^^^ not a function
  |
help: use `!` to invoke the macro
  |
3 |     println!("{}", my_number);
  |
```

We will learn more about printing in this and the next chapter.

Now, back to our `my_number as char` problem. Fortunately, we can easily fix this with `as`. We can't cast `i32` as a char, but we can cast an `i32` as a `u8`. Then we can do the same from `u8` to char. So, in one line, we use `as` to make `my_number` a `u8` and again to make it a char. Now it will compile:

```
fn main() {
    let my_number = 100;
    println!("{}", my_number as u8 as char);
}
```

It prints d because that is the `char` in place 100.

So casting can be convenient. But be careful: when you cast a large number into a smaller type, some unexpected things can happen. For example, a `u8` can go up to 255. What happens if you cast the number 256 into a `u8`?

```
fn main() {
    let my_number = 256;
    println!("{}", my_number as u8);
}
```

You might think it would cut it down to 255, the largest possible size, but it returns a 0.

What happens if you cast an `i32` 600 to a `u8`?

```
fn main() {
    let my_number = 600;
    println!("{}", my_number as u8);
}
```

Now it returns an 88. You can probably see what it's doing now: every time it passes the largest possible number, it starts at 0 again. So when you cast a 600 to a `u8`, it passes the largest possible `u8` two times, and then there are 88 left. You can think of it mathematically as 600 − 256 − 256 = 88. So be a little careful when casting into a smaller type! When casting, make sure the old number isn't larger than the new type's largest possible number.

In fact, casting is somewhat rare in Rust because there is usually no need for it. For example, you don't need to use a cast to get a `u8`. You can just tell Rust that `my_number` is a `u8`. Here's how you do it:

```
fn main() {
    let my_number: u8 = 100;
    println!("{}", my_number as char);
}
```
◁─┐ **Change my_number
  │ to my_number: u8.**

So those are two reasons for all the different number types in Rust. Here is another reason: `usize` is the size Rust uses for *indexing*. (Indexing means "which item is first," "which item is second," etc.) A `usize` is the best size for indexing because

- An index can't be negative, so it needs to be an unsigned integer with a u.
- It should have a lot of space because index numbers can get quite large (but it can't be a `u64` because 32-bit computers can't use a `u64`).

So Rust uses `usize` so that your computer can get the biggest number for indexing that it can read.

Let's learn some more about `char`. You saw that a `char` is always one character and uses `' '` (single quotes) instead of `" "` (double quotes).

All `chars` use 4 bytes of memory, since 4 bytes are enough to hold any kind of character:

- Basic letters and symbols usually need 1 byte, (e.g., a b 1 2 + - = $ @).
- Other letters like German umlauts or accents need 2 bytes (e.g., ä ö ü ß è à ñ).
- Korean, Japanese, or Chinese characters need 3 or 4 bytes (e.g., 国 안 녕).

So, to be sure that a `char` can be any of these, it needs to be 4 bytes. With 2 bytes (a `u16`), the largest number you can make is 65,535, which is well below the number of letters in all the languages in the world (Chinese characters alone are more than this!). But a `u32` (4 bytes) offers more than enough space, allowing for up to 4,294,967,295 letters, which is why a `char` is a `u32` on the inside.

But always using 4 bytes is just for the `char` type. Strings are different and don't always use 4 bytes per single character. When a character is part of a string (not the `char` type), the string is encoded to use the least amount of memory needed for each character.

We can use a method called `.len()` to see this for ourselves. Try copying and pasting this and clicking Run:

```
fn main() {
    println!("Size of a char: {}", std::mem::size_of::<char>());
    println!("Size of a: {}", "a".len());
    println!("Size of ß: {}", "ß".len());
    println!("Size of 国: {}", "国".len());
    println!("Size of 𓃒: {}", "𓃒".len());
}
```

(By the way, `std::mem` means the part of the standard library called `mem` where this `size_of()` function is. The `::` symbol is used sort of like a path to an address. It's sort of like writing `USA::California::LosAngeles`. We will learn about this later.)

The previous code prints the following:

```
Size of a char: 4
Size of a: 1
Size of ß: 2
Size of 国: 3
Size of 𓃒: 4
```

You can see that a is 1 byte, the German ß is 2, the Japanese 国 (meaning country) is 3, and the ancient Egyptian 𓃒 (a quail chick) is 4 bytes.

Let's try printing the length of two strings, one with six letters and the other with three letters. Interestingly, the second one is larger:

```
fn main() {
    let str1 = "Hello!";
    println!("str1 is {} bytes.", str1.len());
    let str2 = "안녕!";                          ◁——— Korean
    println!("str2 is {} bytes.", str2.len());         for "Hi"
}
```

This prints

```
str1 is 6 bytes.
str2 is 7 bytes.
```

`str1` is six characters in length and 6 bytes, but `str2` is three characters in length and 7 bytes. So be careful! The `.len()` method returns the number of bytes, not the number of letters or characters.

By the way, the size of a byte is one u8: it's a number that goes from 0 to 255. We can use a method called .as_bytes() to see what these strings look like as bytes:

```
fn main() {
    println!("{:?}", "a".as_bytes());
    println!("{:?}", "ß".as_bytes());
    println!("{:?}", "国".as_bytes());
    println!("{:?}", "𓃻".as_bytes());
}
```

You can see that each one is different and that to show them all in a single type, it needs 4 bytes. And that's why the char type is 4 bytes long:

```
[97]
[195, 159]
[229, 155, 189]
[240, 147, 133, 177]
```

Characters can need up to 4 bytes

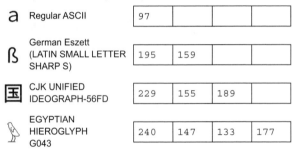

a	Regular ASCII	97			
ß	German Eszett (LATIN SMALL LETTER SHARP S)	195	159		
国	CJK UNIFIED IDEOGRAPH-56FD	229	155	189	
𓃻	EGYPTIAN HIEROGLYPH G043	240	147	133	177

Now, if .len() gives the size in bytes, what about the size in characters? You can find this out by using two methods together. We will learn about these methods in more detail later in the book (especially chapter 8), but for now, you can just remember that .chars().count() will give you the number of characters or letters, not bytes. Calling .chars() first turns a string into a collection of characters, and then .count() counts how many of them there are.

Let's give that a try:

```
fn main() {
    let str1 = "Hello!";
    println!("str1 is {} bytes and also {} characters.", str1.len(),
      str1.chars().count());
    let str2 = "안녕!";
    println!("str2 is {} bytes but only {} characters.", str2.len(),
      str2.chars().count());
}
```

This prints

```
str1 is 6 bytes and also 6 characters.
str2 is 7 bytes but only 3 characters.
```

You might have noticed already that you don't usually need to tell Rust the type of variable you're making. The Rust compiler is happy with `let letter = 'ß'` and doesn't make you type `let letter: char = 'ß'` to declare a `char`. Let's learn why!

1.4   Type inference

The term *type inference* means that Rust can usually decide what type a variable is even if you don't tell it. The term comes from the verb *infer*, which means to make an educated guess.

The compiler is smart enough that it can usually "infer" the types that you are using. In other words, it always needs to know the type of variables you are using, but most of the time, you don't need to tell it. For example, if you type `let my_number = 8`, the variable `my_number` will be an `i32`. That is because the compiler chooses `i32` for integers unless you tell it to choose a different integer type. But if you say `let my_number: u8 = 8`, it will make `my_number` a `u8` because you told it to make a `u8` instead of an `i32`.

So, usually, the compiler can guess. But sometimes you need to tell it, usually for two reasons:

- You are doing something very complex, and the compiler can't determine the type you want.
- You simply want a different type (e.g., you want an `i128`, not an `i32`).

To specify a type, add a colon after the variable name:

```
fn main() {
    let small_number: u8 = 10;
}
```

For numbers, you can add the type after the number. You don't need a space—just type it right after the number:

```
fn main() {
    let small_number = 10u8;        ◁─┐  Same as
}                                      │  u8 = 10
```

You can also add `_` if you want to make the number easy to read:

```
fn main() {
    let small_number = 10_u8;
    let big_number = 100_000_000_i32;
}
```

The `_` is only to make numbers easy for humans to read and does not affect the number. It is completely ignored by the compiler. In fact, it doesn't matter how many `_` you use:

```
fn main() {
    let number = 0_____u8;
    let number2 = 1___6_____2___4_____i32;
    println!("{}, {}", number, number2);
}
```

This prints `0, 1624`.

Interestingly, if you add a decimal point to a number, it won't be an integer (a whole number) anymore. Rust will instead make a float, which is an entirely different type of number. Let's learn how floats work now.

1.5   *Floats*

Floats are numbers with decimal points. `5.5` is a float, and `6` is an integer. `5.0` is also a float, and even `5.` is a float. The variable `my_float` in the following code won't be an `i32` because of the decimal point that follows it:

```
fn main() {
    let my_float = 5.;
}
```

But these types are not officially called *floats*; they are called `f32` and `f64`. As you can imagine, the numbers in their type names show the number of bits needed to make them: 32 and 64 (4 bytes and 8 bytes). In the same way that Rust chooses an `i32` by default, it will also choose `f64` unless you tell it to make an `f32`.

Of course, Rust is strict, so only floats of the same type can be used together. You can't add an `f32` to an `f64`. We can generate an error by telling Rust to make an `f64` and an `f32` and then trying to add them together:

```
fn main() {
    let my_float: f64 = 5.0;
    let my_other_float: f32 = 8.5;

    let third_float = my_float + my_other_float;
}
```

When you try to run this, Rust will say

```
error[E0308]: mismatched types
 --> src\main.rs:5:34
  |
5 |     let third_float = my_float + my_other_float;
  |                                  ^^^^^^^^^^^^^^^ expected `f64`, found
                          `f32`
```

The compiler writes "expected (type), found (type)" when you use the wrong type. It reads your code like this:

- `let my_float: f64 = 5.0;`—Here we specifically tell the compiler that `my_float` must be an `f64`.
- `let my_other_float: f32 = 8.5;`—And here we say that `my_other_float` must be an `f32`. The compiler does what we tell it to do.
- `let third_float = my_float +`—At this point, the variable that follows `my_float` has to be an `f64`. The compiler will expect an `f64` to follow.
- `my_other_float;`—But it's an `f32`, so it can't add them together.

So when you see "expected (type), found (type)", you must find why the compiler expected a different type.

Of course, with simple numbers, it is easy to fix. You *could* cast the f32 to an f64 with as:

```
fn main() {
    let my_float: f64 = 5.0;
    let my_other_float: f32 = 8.5;

    let third_float = my_float + my_other_float as f64;
}
```

my_other_float as f64 = use my_other_float like an f64

But there is an even simpler method: remove the type declarations (to declare a type just means to tell Rust to use a type) and let Rust do the work for us. Rust will choose types that can be added together. In the following code, Rust will make each float an f64:

```
fn main() {
    let my_float = 5.0;
    let my_other_float = 8.5;

    let third_float = my_float + my_other_float;
}
```

The Rust compiler is pretty smart and will not make an f64 if we declare an f32 and try to add it to another float:

```
fn main() {
    let my_float: f32 = 5.0;
    let my_other_float = 8.5;

    let third_float = my_float + my_other_float;
}
```

Usually Rust would choose f64 for my_other_float.

But now it knows you need to add it to an f32 so it chooses f32 for my_other_float, too.

So those are some of the most basic concepts and types in Rust.

You're probably wondering when we're going to look at "Hello, World!," which is usually the first example you see when learning a programming language. That time is now!

1.6   *"Hello, World!" and printing*

When you open a new Rust program in the Playground, it always has this code:

```
fn main() {
    println!("Hello, world!");
}
```

Let's break this code down a bit and see what it means:

- fn means function.
- main() is the function that starts the program.
- () means that we didn't pass the function any *arguments* (an argument is an input to a function). So, that means the function is starting without any variables that it can use.

After that comes {}, which is called a *code block*. Code blocks are spaces where code lives. If you start a variable inside a code block, it will live until the end of the block. This is its *lifetime*. Let's look at the example with floats from before, but we'll put one of them inside its own code block. Now, it won't live until the end of the program:

```
fn main() {
    let my_float = 5.0;          The variable my_float lives
    {                            inside the code block for main().    The variable my_other_float's
        let my_other_float = 8.5; This is where its lifetime starts.  lifetime starts here, but it's
    }                                                                 inside another code block, so
    // let third_float = my_float + my_other_float;                   it doesn't live as long.
}
                                                                      This is where my_other_
         This is the end of the    This won't work anymore, so        float's lifetime ends! After
         block inside which         we commented it out. The          this line, you can't use it.
         my_float lives. This is    variable my_other_float's
         where its lifetime ends.   lifetime is already over.
```

So that's how code blocks with {} work.

A {} doesn't always mean a code block in Rust, though. The following code shows {} being used to change the output in main to add a number 8 after Hello, world:

```
fn main() {
    println!("Hello, world number {}!", 8);
}
```

The {} in println! means "put the variable inside here." In other words, the {} is used to capture the variable. This prints Hello, world number 8!.

We can put more in, just like we did before:

```
fn main() {
    println!("Hello, worlds number {} and {}!", 8, 9);
}
```

This prints Hello, worlds number 8 and 9!.

Did you notice that a ; comes at the end of the line? This is a semicolon, and it has a particular meaning in Rust.

We can see what the semicolon is used for by creating a simple function. We'll call it give_number and put it above main(). (Usually, you put main() on the bottom, but it makes no difference). Then we'll call this function inside main by typing give_number():

```
fn give_number() -> i32 {
    8
}

fn main() {
    println!("Hello, world number {}!", give_number());
}
```

This also prints `Hello, world number 8!`. When Rust looks at `give_number()`, it sees that you are calling a function. This function

- Does not take anything because there's nothing inside `()`.
- Returns an `i32`. The `->` (called a *skinny arrow*) shows what the function returns.

Inside the function is just `8`. Because there is no semicolon at the end of the line, this `8` (an `i32`) is the value the function `give_number()` returns. If it had a semicolon at the end, it would not return anything (it would return a `()`, which is called the unit type and means "nothing").

So here's the important part: Rust will not compile this program if the function's body ends with a `;` because the return type is `i32`, and with `;`, the function returns `()`, not `i32`. Let's try adding `;` to see the error. Now our code looks like this:

```
fn give_number() -> i32 {
    8;
}

fn main() {
    println!("Hello, world number {}", give_number());
}
```

The error looks like this:

```
error[E0308]: mismatched types
 --> src/main.rs:1:21
  |
1 | fn give_number() -> i32 {
  |    -----------          ^^^ expected `i32`, found `()`
  |    |
  |    implicitly returns `()` as its body
  has no tail or `return` expression

2 |     8;
  |      - help: remove this semicolon to return this value
```

This means "you told me that `give_number()` returns an `i32`, but you added a `;` so it doesn't return anything." So, the compiler suggests removing the semicolon.

You can also write `return 8;` to return a value, but in Rust, it is normal to remove the `return`. The last line of the function is what the function returns, and you don't need to type `return` to make the return happen. Of course, if you want to return a value early from the function (before the last line), you'll want to use `return`.

Here is a simple example of a function that returns a value early. Interestingly, the code compiles! It even returns the same `Hello, world number 8` output as before:

```
fn give_number() -> i32 {
    return 8;
    10;
}

fn main() {
```

```
        println!("Hello, world number {}", give_number());
    }
```

It compiles because there is nothing wrong with the code: the `give_number()` function returns an `i32` as it is supposed to. However, Rust does notice that the function will never reach the line below `return 8;` and gives a warning:

```
warning: unreachable expression
 --> src/main.rs:3:5
  |
2 |      return 8;
  |      -------- any code following this expression is unreachable
3 |      10;
  |      ^^ unreachable statement
  |
  = note: `#[warn(unreachable_code)]` on by default
```

So there is no reason for us to use an early return here, but Rust will still run the code for us.

When you want to give variables to a function, put them inside the `()`. You have to give them a name and write the type:

This function will take two i32s, and we will call them number_one and number_two.

```
fn multiply(number_one: i32, number_two: i32) {     ⟵⎯
    let result = number_one * number_two;
    println!("{} times {} is {}", number_one, number_two, result);
}

fn main() {
    multiply(8, 9);              ⟵⎯
    let some_number = 10;        ⟵⎯⎯⎯⎯⎯⎯⎯⎯⎯
    let some_other_number = 2;
    multiply(some_number, some_other_number);     ⟵⎯
}
```

We can pass in the two numbers directly to the function.

Or, we can declare two i32 variables…

…and pass them into the function.

The output for this sample is

```
8 times 9 is 72
10 times 2 is 20
```

We can also return an `i32`. Just take out the semicolon at the end:

```
fn multiply(number_one: i32, number_two: i32) -> i32 {
    let result = number_one * number_two;     ⟵⎯
    result             ⟵⎯
}

fn main() {
    let multiply_result = multiply(8, 9);
    println!("The two numbers multiplied are: {multiply_result}");
}
```

Makes a number called result here

Puts it on the last line to return it

The output will be

```
The two numbers multiplied are: 72
```

In fact, we don't even need to declare a variable before returning it. This code generates the same output:

```
fn multiply(number_one: i32, number_two: i32) -> i32 {
    number_one * number_two        This means "return the result of
}                                   number_one * number_two."

fn main() {
    let multiply_result = multiply(8, 9);
    println!("The two numbers multiplied are: {}", multiply_result);
}
```

One reason that Rust is so fast is that it knows exactly how long variables need to use memory. Once the variables don't need memory, they are dropped, and Rust frees up that memory automatically. Let's now learn about declaring variables and how long they live for.

> **NOTE** How Rust manages memory is different from garbage collection! Most languages have a garbage collector that handles cleaning up memory. In other languages like C and C++, you clean up memory yourself. Rust doesn't have a garbage collector, same as C and C++. But Rust is also different: it is smart enough to know exactly when a variable doesn't need to exist anymore and frees the memory for you.

1.7 *Declaring variables and code blocks*

In Rust, we use the `let` keyword to declare a variable. A variable is just a name that represents some type of information in the same way that a real name represents a person:

```
fn main() {                         Creates the variable my_number
    let my_number = 8;              that is the number 8
    println!("Hello, number {}", my_number);
}
```

Since 2021, you can capture variables inside the {} of `println!`, so you can also do this:

```
fn main() {
    let my_number = 8;
    println!("Hello, number {my_number}");
}
```

In this book, we'll use both methods for printing. Sometimes writing the variable name inside {} looks better:

```
fn main() {
    let color1 = "red";
```

```
    let color2 = "blue";
    let color3 = "green";

    println!("I like {color1} and {color2} and {color3}");
}
```

But sometimes using a comma after {} looks better:

```
fn main() {
    let naver_base_url = "naver";
    let google_base_url = "google";
    let microsoft_base_url = "microsoft";

    println!("The url is www.{naver_base_url}.com");
    println!("The url is www.{google_base_url}.com");
    println!("The url is www.{microsoft_base_url}.com");

    println!("The url is www.{}.com", naver_base_url);
    println!("The url is www.{}.com", google_base_url);
    println!("The url is www.{}.com", microsoft_base_url);
}
```

> **Printing this way is okay.**

> **But this way it lines up much nicer.**

As we saw previously, a variable's lifetime starts and ends inside a code block: {}. This example will generate an error because my_number is inside its own code block and its lifetime ends before we try to print it:

```
fn main() {
    {
        let my_number = 8;
    }
    println!("Hello, number {}", my_number);
}
```

> **The variable my_number starts here but ends just one line later!**

> **Error: there is no my_number for println! to print.**

However, you can return a value from a code block to keep it alive. Take a close look at how this works:

```
fn main() {
    let my_number = {
    let second_number = 8;
        second_number + 9
    };

    println!("My number is: {}", my_number);
}
```

> **No semicolon, so the code block returns 8 + 9. It works just like returning from a function.**

The value of second_number is 8, and we return second_number + 9, so this is like writing let my_number = 8 + 9. And because the block returns the value, my_number never lives inside the block; instead, it gets its value from the return value at the end of the block.

If you add a semicolon inside the block, it will return () (nothing):

```
fn main() {
    let my_number = {
    let second_number = 8;
```

> **Here we declare a variable second_number and add 9 to it.**

```
        second_number + 9;
    };
```
But we added a semicolon, so my_number is not an i32! The block returns a () instead, and second_number dies here.

```
    println!("My number is: {:?}", my_number);
```
my_number is ().

```
}
```

So why did we write {:?} and not {}? We will talk about that now.

1.8   *Display and Debug*

Simple variables in Rust can be printed with {} inside println!. This is called Display *printing.* But some variables won't be able to use {} to print, and you need Debug *printing.* You can think of Debug printing as printing for the programmer because it usually shows more information—and is usually less pretty.

How do you know if you need {:?} and not {}? The compiler will tell you. Let's try printing () with Display to see the error:

```
fn main() {
    let doesnt_print = ();
    println!("This will not print: {}", doesnt_print);
}
```

When we run this, the compiler says

```
error[E0277]: `()` doesn't implement `std::fmt::Display`
  --> src\main.rs:3:41
   |
3  |      println!("This will not print: {}", doesnt_print);
   |                                           ^^^^^^^^^^^^ `()`
   |cannot be formatted with the default formatter
   |
   = help: the trait `std::fmt::Display` is not implemented for `()`
   = note: in format strings you may be able to use `{:?}` (or {:#?}
    for pretty-print) instead
   = note: required by `std::fmt::Display::fmt`
```

This is quite a bit of information. There is also one important word here: trait. Traits are important in Rust, and we will learn about them throughout the book. But for now, you can think of the word *trait* as "what a type can do." So if the compiler says The trait Display is not implemented, it means "the type doesn't have Display capabilities."

Now, here is the important part of the error message:

```
you may be able to use {:?} (or {:#?} for pretty-print) instead.
```

This means that you can try {:?} or {:#?}. {:#?}, is known as "pretty printing." It is the same as Debug with {:?} but prints with different formatting over more lines.

So, with {:?}, you'll see this sort of output:

```
User { name: "Mr. User", user_number: 101 }
```

{:#?} will look more like this, over more lines:

```
User {
    name: "Mr. User",
    user_number: 101,
}
```

One more thing: you can also use `print!` without `ln` if you don't want to add a new line.

```
fn main() {
    print!("This will not print a new line");
    println!(" so this will be on the same line");
}
```

This prints `This will not print a new line so this will be on the same line`.

To sum up, here are the three ways to print that we've learned:

- `{}`—`Display` print. More types have `Debug` than `Display`, so if a type you want to print can't print with `Display`, you can try `Debug`.
- `{:?}`—`Debug` print. If there is too much information on one line, you can try `{:#?}`.
- `{:#?}`—`Debug` print, but pretty. *Pretty* means that each part of a type is printed on its own line to make it easier to read.

There is quite a bit more to printing in Rust, and we will learn more about it in the next chapter. Now, let's get back to some more basic information about Rust's easiest types.

1.9   Smallest and largest numbers

If you want to see the smallest and biggest numbers, you can use MIN and MAX after the name of the type:

```
fn main() {
    println!("The smallest i8: {} The biggest i8: {}", i8::MIN, i8::MAX);
    println!("The smallest u8: {} The biggest u8: {}", u8::MIN, u8::MAX);
    println!("The smallest i16: {} The biggest i16: {}", i16::MIN, i16::MAX);
    println!("The smallest u16: {} and the biggest u16: {}", u16::MIN,
     u16::MAX);
    println!("The smallest i32: {} The biggest i32: {}", i32::MIN, i32::MAX);
    println!("The smallest u32: {} The biggest u32: {}", u32::MIN, u32::MAX);
    println!("The smallest i64: {} The biggest i64: {}", i64::MIN, i64::MAX);
    println!("The smallest u64: {} The biggest u64: {}", u64::MIN, u64::MAX);
    println!("The smallest i128: {} The biggest i128: {}", i128::MIN,
     i128::MAX);
    println!("The smallest u128: {} The biggest u128: {}", u128::MIN,
     u128::MAX);
}
```

This will print the following:

```
The smallest i8: -128 The biggest i8: 127
The smallest u8: 0 The biggest u8: 255
The smallest i16: -32768 The biggest i16: 32767
```

```
The smallest u16: 0 and the biggest u16: 65535
The smallest i32: -2147483648 The biggest i32: 2147483647
The smallest u32: 0 The biggest u32: 4294967295
The smallest i64: -9223372036854775808 The biggest i64: 9223372036854775807
The smallest u64: 0 The biggest u64: 18446744073709551615
The smallest i128: -170141183460469231731687303715884105728 The biggest i128:
➡170141183460469231731687303715884105727 The smallest u128: 0
➡The biggest u128: 340282366920938463463374607431768211455
```

By the way, MIN and MAX are written in all capitals because they are consts (unchangeable global values). In this case, they are consts, which are attached to their types with a :: in between. We will learn more about consts in the next chapter.

1.10 *Mutability (changing)*

When you declare a variable with let, it is immutable (cannot be changed). So this will not work:

```
fn main() {
    let my_number = 8;
    my_number = 10;
}
```

You can't change my_number because variables are immutable if you only write let. The compiler message is pretty detailed:

```
error[E0384]: cannot assign twice to immutable variable `my_number`
 --> src/main.rs:3:5
  |
2 |     let my_number = 8;
  |         ---------
  |         |
  |         first assignment to `my_number`
  |         help: consider making this binding mutable: `mut my_number`
3 |     my_number = 10;
```

But sometimes you want to be able to change your variable, and the compiler has given us some advice if we want to do so. To make a variable that you can change, add mut after let:

```
fn main() {
    let mut my_number = 8;
    my_number = 10;
}
```

Now there is no problem. However, you cannot change the type of a variable even if you declare it as mut. So the following will not work:

```
fn main() {
    let mut my_variable = 8;
    my_variable = "Hello, world!";
}
```

You will see the same "expected" message from the compiler:

```
error[E0308]: mismatched types
 --> src/main.rs:3:19
  |
2 |     let mut my_variable = 8;
  |                                  - expected due to this value
3 |     my_variable = "Hello, world!";
  |                         ^^^^^^^^^^^^^^^^^ expected integer, found `&str`
```

By the way, &str is a string type we will learn soon.

1.11 *Shadowing*

Now that we know the basics of mutability, it's time to learn about shadowing. Shadowing means using let to declare a new variable with the same name as another variable. It looks like mutability, but it is *completely different*. Be sure not to confuse them! Shadowing looks like this:

```
fn main() {
    let my_number = 8;              A regular i32 called
    println!("{}", my_number);      my_number
    let my_number = 9.2;            This is an f64 with the same name.
    println!("{}", my_number);      But it's not the first my_number ;
}                                   it is completely different!
```

Here we say that we "shadowed" my_number with a new "let binding." The variable my_number is now pointing to a completely different value.

So, is the first my_number destroyed? No, but when we call my_number, we now get my_number the f64. Because they are in the same scope block (the same {}), we can't see the first my_number anymore.

But if they are in different blocks, we can see both. Let's take the same example and put the second my_number inside a different block to see what happens:

```
fn main() {
    let my_number = 8;
    println!("{}", my_number);
    {
        let my_number = 9.2;             This prints 9.2 because the second my_number is
        println!("{}", my_number);       shadowing the first my_number. But the second
    }                                    my_number only lives until the end of this block.
    println!("{}", my_number);           The first my_number is still alive!
}                                        Prints 8, not 9.2
```

So, when you shadow a variable with a new variable with the same name, you don't destroy the first one. You *block* it.

Imagine that there's a classroom with a student named Brian who always says true (he's a bool). Every time you call out his name, he tells you his value. Then one day a new student comes in who is also named Brian and sits in front of the other Brian. The second Brian is *shadowing* the first one.

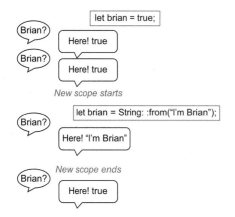

This second Brian is a completely different type: he's a string that says "I'm Brian" every time. Now, every time you call Brian and ask his value, you'll get something completely different. But let's say that the second Brian was only visiting from another school and later leaves—he's in a smaller "scope." Now, when you call out the name Brian, you'll hear `true` again because the first Brian is still there (his scope lasts longer).

What is the advantage of shadowing? Shadowing is good when you need to work on a variable a lot and you don't care about it in between. Imagine that you want to do a lot of simple math with a variable:

```rust
fn times_two(number: i32) -> i32 {
    number * 2
}

fn main() {
    let final_number = {
        let y = 10;
        let x = 9;
        let x = times_two(x);     // Shadows with x: 18   Shadows again with x: 28
        let x = x + y;
        x                          // Returns x: final_number is now the value of x
    };
    println!("The number is now: {}", final_number)
}
```

This prints `The number is now: 28.`

Without shadowing, you would have to think of different names, even though you don't care about x. Let's pretend we wanted to do the same thing, but Rust didn't allow shadowing. We would have to come up with a new variable name each time:

```rust
fn times_two(number: i32) -> i32 {
    number * 2
}

fn main() {
    let final_number = {
        let y = 10;
        let x = 9;
        let x_twice = times_two(x);        // Here we would have to come up with a new variable name.
        let x_twice_and_y = x_twice + y;   // And here again!
        x_twice_and_y
    };
    println!("The number is now: {}", final_number)
}
```

Shadowing can be useful when working with mutability, too. In the following example, we have a number called x again. We'd like to change its value, and we don't care about the original variable called x. In this case, we can shadow it with a new mutable variable that is a float, and now we can change it:

```
fn main() {
    let x = 9
    let mut x = x as f32;    The value
    x += 0.5;                is now 9.5.
}
```

In general, you see shadowing in Rust in cases like these: working quickly with variables we don't care too much about or getting around Rust's strict rules about types, mutability, and so on.

So that's it for the first chapter. If you know another programming language, you might have noticed that Rust is very familiar but quite different in some areas. And if Rust is your first language, that's fine, too. Everything will be new to you, but you won't have any habits to unlearn either.

In the next chapter, we are going to learn about how memory works and how data is owned. Ownership is one of Rust's most unique concepts, so we'll spend a lot of time thinking about it.

Summary

- You can write whatever you want in your comments, and if you write them with ///, Rust can automatically use them to document your code.
- You can tell Rust the type name of a variable you are making, but most of the time, you don't need to.
- Understanding how binary works gives you a sense of which integer type is best to use.
- Variables live inside {} code blocks (scopes). Variables created inside can't leave them unless they are the return value into another larger scope.
- You can change a variable in Rust if you make it mutable with mut. Otherwise, the compiler will give an error if you try.
- Shadowing is completely different from mutability: it's just a variable with the same name that blocks the other one.

Memory, variables, and ownership

2

This chapter covers

- The stack, the heap, pointers, and references
- Strings, the most common way to work with text
- `const` and `static`, variables that last forever
- More on shadowing
- `Copy` types
- More about printing

In this chapter, you'll see how Rust keeps you thinking about the computer itself. Rust keeps you focused on how the computer's memory is being used for your program and what ownership is (who owns the data). Remember this word, *ownership*—it's probably Rust's most unique idea. We'll start with the two types of memory a computer uses: the stack and the heap.

Oh, and there's quite a bit more to learn about printing to build on what you learned in the last chapter. Look for that at the end!

2.1   *The stack, the heap, pointers, and references*

Understanding the stack, the heap, pointers, and references is very important in Rust. We'll start with the stack and the heap, which are two places to keep memory in computers. Here are some important points to keep in mind:

- The stack is very fast, but the heap is not so fast. It's not super slow either, but the stack is usually faster.
- The stack is fast because it is like a stack: memory for a variable gets stacked on top of the last one, right next to it. When a function is done, it removes the value of the variables starting from the last one that was added, and now the memory is freed again. Some people compare the stack to a stack of dishes: you put one on top of the other, and if you want to unstack them, you take the top one off first, then the next top one, and so on. The dishes are all right on top of each other, so they are quick to find. But you can't use the stack all the time.
- Rust needs to know the size of a variable at compile time. So simple variables like `i32` can go on the stack because we know their exact size. You always know that an `i32` is 4 bytes because 32 bits = 4 bytes. So, `i32` can always go on the stack.
- Some types don't know the size at compile time. And yet, the stack needs to know the exact size. So what do you do? First, you put the data in the heap because the heap can have any size of data. (You don't have to do this yourself; the program asks the computer for a piece of memory to put the data in.) And then, to find it, a pointer goes on the stack. This is fine because we always know the size of a pointer. So, then the computer first goes to the pointer, reads the address information, and follows it to the heap where the data is.
- Sometimes you can't even use heap memory! If you are programming in Rust for a small embedded device, you are going to have to use only stack memory. There's no operating system to ask for heap memory on a small embedded device.

Pointers sound complicated, but they don't have to be. Pointers are like a table of contents in a book. Take this book, for example.

This table of contents is like five pointers. You can read them and find the information they are talking about. Where is the chapter "My life"? It's on page 1 (it *points* to page 1). And where is the chapter "My job"? It's on page 23.

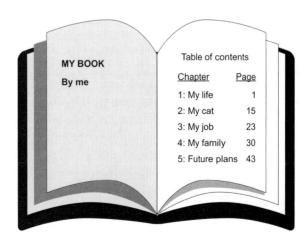

The pointer you usually see in Rust is called a *reference*, which you can think of as a memory-safe pointer: a reference point to owned memory and not just unsafe random memory locations. The important thing to know about a reference is this: a reference points to the memory of another value. A reference means you *borrow* the value, but you don't own it. It's the same as our book: the table of contents doesn't own the information. The chapters own the information. In Rust, references have a `&` in front of them:

- `let my_variable = 8` makes a regular variable.
- `let my_reference = &my_variable` makes a reference to the data held by `my_variable`.

You read `my_reference = &my_variable` like this: "`my_reference` is a reference to `my_variable`" or "`my_reference` refers to `my_variable`." This means that `my_reference` is only looking at the data of `my_variable`; `my_variable` still owns its data.

You can even have a reference to a reference or any number of references:

```
fn main() {                                This is
    let my_number = 15;          ◁──┘ an i32.
    let single_reference = &my_number;         ◁──┤ This is an &i32.        This is
    let double_reference = &single_reference;              ◁──┘ an &&i32.
    let five_references = &&&&&my_number;    ◁──┤ This is an &&&&i32.
}
```

These are all different types, just in the same way that "a friend of a friend" is different from "a friend." In practice, you probably won't see references that are five deep, but you will sometimes see a reference to a reference.

2.2 Strings

Rust has two main types of strings: `String` and `&str`. Why are there two types, and what is the difference?

- A `&str` is a simple string. It's just a pointer to the data plus the length. Usually, you'll hear it pronounced like "ref-stir." With the pointer to the data plus the length, Rust can see where it starts and where it ends. When you write `let my_variable = "Hello, world!"`, you create a `&str`. It is also called a *string slice*. That's because `&str` uses the pointer to find the data and the length to know how much to look at. It might just be a partial view of the data owned by some other variable, so just a *slice* of it.
- `String` is a bit more complicated string. It may be a bit slower, but it has more functionality. A `String` is a pointer with data on the heap. The biggest difference is that a `String` owns its data, while a `&str` is a slice (a view into some data). A `String` is easy to grow, shrink, mutate, and so on.

Also, note that `&str` has the `&` in front of it because you need a reference to use a `str` for the same previously discussed reason: the stack needs to know the size, and a `str` can be of any length. So we access it with a `&`, a reference. The compiler knows the size of a reference's pointer, and it can then use the `&` to find where the `str` data is and read it. Also, because you use a `&` to interact with a `str`, you don't own it. But a `String` is an "owned" type. We will soon learn why that is important to know.

Both `&str` and `String` are encoded with UTF-8, which is the main character-encoding system used worldwide. So the content inside a `&str` or `String` can be in any language:

```
fn main() {
    let name = "자우림";
    let other_name = String::from("Adrian Fahrenheit Țepeș");
}
```

This &str of a Korean rock band's name is no problem; Korean characters are UTF-8, too.

This String holding a famous vampire's name is no problem either: Ț and ș are valid UTF-8.

You can see in `String::from("Adrian Fahrenheit Țepeș")` that it is easy to make a `String` from a `&str`. This second variable is an owned `String`.

You can even write emojis, thanks to UTF-8:

```
fn main() {
    let name = "😂";
    println!("My name is actually {}", name);
}
```

On your computer, that will print `My name is actually 😂` unless your command line can't print it. Then it will show something like `My name is actually` . But Rust itself has no problem with emojis or any other Unicode, even if your command line can't display them.

Let's look at the reason for using a `&` for `str`s again to make sure we understand. A `str` is a dynamically sized type. *Dynamically sized* means that the size can be different. For example, the two names we saw before (자우림 and Adrian Fahrenheit Țepeș) are not the same size. We can see this with two functions: `size_of`, which shows the size of a type, and `size_of_val`, which shows the size of a value pointed to. It looks like this:

```
fn main() {
    let size_of_string = std::mem::size_of::<String>();
    let size_of_i8 = std::mem::size_of::<i8>();
    let size_of_f64 = std::mem::size_of::<f64>();
    let size_of_jaurim = std::mem::size_of_val("자우림");
    let size_of_adrian = std::mem::size_of_val("Adrian Fahrenheit Țepeș");

    println!("A String is Sized and always {size_of_string} bytes.");
    println!("An i8 is Sized and always {size_of_i8} bytes.");
    println!("An f64 is always Sized and {size_of_f64} bytes.");
    println!("But a &str is not Sized: '자우림' is {size_of_jaurim} bytes.");
    println!("And 'Adrian Fahrenheit Țepeș' is {size_of_adrian} bytes - not
      Sized.");
}
```

std::mem::size_of::<Type>() gives you the size of a type in bytes.

std::mem::size_of_val() gives you the size in bytes of a value.

This prints

```
A String is Sized and always 24 bytes.
An i8 is Sized and always 1 bytes.
An f64 is always Sized and 8 bytes.
But a &str is not Sized: '자우림' is 9 bytes.
And 'Adrian Fahrenheit Țepeș' is 25 bytes - not Sized.
```

That is why we need a & because it makes a pointer, and Rust knows the size of the pointer. So, only the pointer goes on the stack. If we wrote `str`, Rust wouldn't know what to do because it doesn't know the size. Actually, you can try it out by telling it to make a `str` instead of a `&str`:

```
fn main() {
    let my_name: str = "My name";
}
```

Here's the error:

```
error[E0308]: mismatched types
 --> src/main.rs:2:24
  |
2 |     let my_name: str = "My name";
  |                  ---   ^^^^^^^^^ expected `str`, found `&str`
  |                  |
  |                  expected due to this

error[E0277]: the size for values of type `str`
cannot be known at compilation time
 --> src/main.rs:2:9
  |
2 |     let my_name: str = "My name";
  |         ^^^^^^^ doesn't have a size known at compile-time
  |
  = help: the trait `Sized` is not implemented for `str`
  = note: all local variables must have a statically known size
  = help: unsized locals are gated as an unstable feature
help: consider borrowing here
  |
2 |     let my_name: &str = "My name";
  |                  +
```

Not a bad error message! The compiler itself seems to enjoy teaching Rust.

There are many ways to make a string. Here are some:

- `String::from("This is the string text");`—This is a method for `String` that takes text and creates a string.
- `"This is the string text".to_string()`—This is a method for `&str` that makes it into a `String`.
- The `format!` macro—This works just like `println!`, except it creates a string instead of printing. So you can do this:

```
fn main() {
    let name = "Billybrobby";
```

```
    let country = "USA";
    let home = "Korea";
    let together = format!("I am {name} from {country} but I live in {home}.");
}
```

Now we have a `String` named `together`, but we have not printed it yet.

Another way to make a `String` is called `.into()`, but it is a bit different because `.into()` isn't for making a string; it's for converting from one type into another type. Some types can easily convert to and from another type using `From::` and `.into()`; if you have `From`, you also have `.into()`. `From` is clearer because you already know the types: you know that `String::from("Some str")` is a `String` from a `&str`. But with `.into()`, sometimes the compiler doesn't know:

```
fn main() {
    let my_string = "Try to make this a String".into();
}
```

> **NOTE** How does this happen? It's thanks to something called a blanket trait implementation. We'll learn about that much later.

Rust doesn't know what type you want because many types can be made from a `&str`. It is saying, "I can make a `&str` into a lot of things, so which one do you want?"

```
error[E0282]: type annotations needed
 --> src\main.rs:2:9
  |
2 |     let my_string = "Try to make this a String".into();
  |         ^^^^^^^^^ consider giving `my_string` a type
```

So, you can do this:

```
fn main() {
    let my_string: String = "Try to make this a String".into();
}
```

And now you get a `String`.

Next up are two keywords that let you make global variables. Global variables last forever, so you don't need to think about ownership for them!

2.3   *const and static*

There are two other ways to declare values without the keyword `let`. These two are known as `const` and `static`. Another difference is that Rust won't use type inference for them: you need to write their type. These are for values that don't change (`const` means constant). Well, technically, `static` can change, but we will learn about that later. The two main differences are

- `const` is for values that don't change and are created at compile time.
- `static` is similar to `const` but has a fixed memory location. It might not be created at compile time.

For the time being, you can think of them as almost the same. For a global variable, Rust programmers will usually use `const`, but there are good reasons for the `static` keyword, too. You'll know about the key differences between the two by the end of chapter 16.

You write them with ALL CAPITAL LETTERS and usually outside of `main` so that they can live for the whole program. Two quick examples are

```
const NUMBER_OF_MONTHS: u32 = 12;
static SEASONS: [&str; 4] = ["Spring", "Summer", "Fall", "Winter"];
```

Because they are global, you can access them anywhere, and they don't get dropped. Here's a quick example. Note that this `print_months()` function has no input, but no problem—NUMBER_OF_MONTHS can be accessed from anywhere:

```
const NUMBER_OF_MONTHS: u32 = 12;
                                              This function
                                              takes no input!
fn print_months() {
    println!("Number of months in the year: {NUMBER_OF_MONTHS}");
}

fn main() {
    print_months();
}
```

That was pretty convenient. So, why not just make everything global? One reason is that these types are made at compile time, before the program runs. If you don't know what a value is during compile time, you can't make it a `const` or `static`. Also, you can't use the heap during compile time because the program needs to perform a memory *allocation* (an allocation is like a reservation for heap memory). Don't worry: you don't need to allocate memory yourself. Rust takes care of memory allocation for you.

`const` and `static` are pretty easy: if the compiler lets you make one, you have it to use anywhere, and you don't have to worry about ownership. So let's move on to references because for those you need to understand ownership, and that takes a bit longer to learn.

2.4 *More on references*

We have learned about references in general, and we know that we use `&` to create a reference. Let's look at an example of some code with references:

```
fn main() {
    let country = String::from("Austria");
    let ref_one = &country;
    let ref_two = &country;
    println!("{}", ref_one);
}
```

This prints `Austria`.

Inside the code is the variable `country`, which is a `String` and, therefore, owns its data. We then created two references to `country`. They have the type `&String`, which is a "reference to a String." These two variables can look at the data owned by country. We could create 3 references or 100 references to country, and it would be no problem because they are just viewing the data.

But this next code is a problem. Let's see what happens when we try to return a reference to a String from a function:

```
fn return_str() -> &String {
    let country = String::from("Austria");
    let country_ref = &country;
    country_ref
}

fn main() {
    let country = return_str();
}
```

Here's what the compiler says:

```
error[E0515]: cannot return value referencing local variable country
 --> src/main.rs:4:5
  |
3 |     let country_ref = &country;
  |                        -------- `country` is borrowed here
4 |     country_ref
  |     ^^^^^^^^^^^ returns a value referencing data owned by the current
    function
```

The function return_str() creates a String, and then it creates a reference to the String. Then it tries to return the reference. But the String called country only lives inside the function, and then it dies (remember, a variable only lives as long as its code block). Once a variable is gone, the computer will clean up the memory so that it can be used for something else. So after the function returns, country_ref would be referring to memory that is already gone. Definitely not okay! Rust prevents us from making a mistake with memory here.

This is the important part about the "owned" type that we talked about previously. Because you own a String, you can pass it around. But a &String will die if its String dies, and you don't pass around ownership with it.

2.5   Mutable references

If you want to use a reference to change data, you can use a mutable reference. For a mutable reference, you write &mut instead of &:

```
fn main() {
    let mut my_number = 8;           ◁──┐  Don't forget to
    let num_ref = &mut my_number;       │  write mut here!
}
```

So what are these two types called? my_number is an i32, and num_ref is &mut i32. In speech, you call this a "mutable reference to an i32" or a "ref mut i32."

Let's use it to add 10 to `my_number`. However, you can't write `num_ref += 10` because `num_ref` is not the `i32` value; it is an `&i32`. There's nothing to add inside a reference. The value to add is actually inside the `i32`. To reach the place where the value is, we use `*`. Using `*` lets you move from the reference to the value behind the reference. In other words, `*` is the opposite of `&`. Also, one `*` erases one `&`.

The following code demonstrates these two concepts. It uses `*` to change the value of a number through a mutable reference and shows that one `*` equals one `&`.

```
fn main() {
    let mut my_number = 8;
    let num_ref = &mut my_number;
    *num_ref += 10;                          Use * to change
    println!("{}", my_number);               the i32 value.

    let second_number = 800;
    let triple_reference = &&&second_number;
    println!("Are they equal? {}", second_number == ***triple_reference);
}
```

This prints

```
18
Are they equal? true
```

Because using `&` is called *referencing*, using `*` is called *de*referencing.

2.5.1   Rust's reference rules

Rust has two rules for mutable and immutable references. They are very important but easy to remember because they make sense:

- *Rule 1 (immutable references)*—You can have as many immutable references as you want: 1 is fine, 3 is fine, 1,000 is fine. It's no problem because you're just viewing data.
- *Rule 2 (mutable references)*—You can only have one mutable reference. Also, you can't have an immutable reference *and* a mutable reference together.

Because mutable references can change the data, you could have problems if you change the data when other references are reading it. A good way to understand is to think of a presentation made with Powerpoint or on Google Docs. Let's look at some ownership situations through a comparison with real life and determine whether they are okay or not.

2.5.2   Situation 1: Only one mutable reference

Say you are an employee writing a presentation using Google Docs online. You own the data. Now you want your manager to help you. You log in with your account on your manager's computer and ask the manager to help by making edits. Now, the manager has a *mutable reference* to your presentation but doesn't own your computer.

The manager can make any changes wanted and then log out after the changes are done. This is fine because nobody else is looking at the presentation.

2.5.3 Situation 2: Only immutable references

Say you are giving the presentation to 100 people. All 100 people can now see your data. They all have an *immutable reference* to your presentation. This is fine because they can see it, but nobody can change the data. One thousand or 1 million more people can come to the presentation, and it wouldn't make any difference.

2.5.4 Situation 3: The problem situation

Say you log in on your manager's computer, as before. The manager now has a mutable reference. Then you give the presentation to 100 people, but the manager hasn't logged out yet. This is definitely not fine because the manager can still do anything on the computer. Maybe the manager will delete the presentation and start typing an email or even something worse! Now, the 100 people have to watch the manager's random computer activity instead of the presentation. That's unexpected behavior and exactly the sort of situation that Rust prevents.

Here is an example of a mutable borrow with an immutable borrow:

```
fn main() {
    let mut number = 10;
    let number_ref = &number;
    let number_change = &mut number;
    *number_change += 10;
    println!("{}", number_ref);
}
```

The compiler prints a helpful message to show us the problem:

```
error[E0502]: cannot borrow `number` as mutable because it is also borrowed
    as immutable
  --> src\main.rs:4:25
  |
3 |     let number_ref = &number;
  |                      ------- immutable borrow occurs here
4 |     let number_change = &mut number;
  |                         ^^^^^^^^^^^ mutable borrow occurs here
5 |     *number_change += 10;
6 |     println!("{}", number_ref);
  |                    ---------- immutable borrow later used here
```

Take a close look at the next code sample. In the sample, we create a mutable variable and then a mutable reference. The code changes the value of the variable through the reference. Finally, it creates an immutable reference and prints the value using the immutable reference. That sounds like a mutable borrow together with an immutable borrow, but the code works. Why?

```
fn main() {
    let mut number = 10;
```

```
    let number_change = &mut number;
    *number_change += 10;
    let number_ref = &number;
    println!("{}", number_ref);
}
```

It prints 20 with no problem. The code works because the compiler is smart enough to understand it. It knows that we used number_change to change number but didn't use it again, so that is the end of the mutable borrow. No problem! We are not using immutable and mutable references together.

Earlier in Rust's history, this kind of code actually generated an error, but the compiler is smarter than it used to be. It can understand not just what we type but when and how we use (almost) everything.

2.6   Shadowing again

Remember when we learned in the last chapter that shadowing doesn't *destroy* a value but *blocks* it? We can prove this now that we know how to use references. Take a look at this code and think about what the output will be. Will it be Austria 8 or 8 8?

```
fn main() {
    let country = String::from("Austria");
    let country_ref = &country;
    let country = 8;
    println!("{country_ref} {country}");
}
```

The answer is Austria, 8. First, we declare a String called country. Then we create the reference country_ref to this string. Then we shadow country with 8, which is an i32. But the first country was not destroyed, so country_ref still points to "Austria", not 8. Here is the same code with some comments to show how it works:

```
fn main() {
    let country = String::from("Austria");        We have a String
    let country_ref = &country;                   called country.        Makes a reference
    let country = 8;                                                      to the String data

    println!("{country_ref}, {country}");       Next, we have a variable called country
}                                               that is an i8. It blocks the original
                                                String, but the String is not destroyed.
            The reference still
            points to the String.
```

References get even more interesting when we pass them into functions because of ownership: functions take ownership, too! The first code example in the next section is a surprise for most people who are learning Rust for the first time. Let's take a look.

2.7   Giving references to functions

One of the rules of values in Rust is that value can only have one owner. This makes references very useful for functions because you can give a function a quick view of some data without having to pass ownership.

The following code doesn't work, but it gives us some insight into how ownership works:

```
fn print_country(country_name: String) {
    println!("{country_name}");
}

fn main() {
    let country = String::from("Austria");       Prints
    print_country(country);                        "Austria".
    print_country(country);        That was fun.
}                                   Let's do it again!
```

It does not work because `country` ends up destroyed, and the memory gets cleaned up after the first calling of the `print_country()` function. Here's how:

- *Step 1*—We create the `String` called `country`. The variable `country` is the owner of the data.
- *Step 2*—We pass `country` to the function `print_country`, which now owns the data. The function doesn't have a `->`, so it doesn't return anything. After `print_country` finishes, our `String` is now dead.
- *Step 3*—We try to give `country` to `print_country`, but we already did that, and it died inside the function! The data that `country` used to own doesn't exist anymore.

This is also called a *move* because the data moves into the function, and that is where it ends. You will see this in the error output, which calls it a `use of moved value`. In other words, you tried to use a value that was moved somewhere else. The compiler is helpful enough to show you exactly which line moved the data:

```
error[E0382]: use of moved value: `country`
  --> src/main.rs:8:19
   |
6  |     let country = String::from("Austria");
   |         ------- move occurs because `country` has type
   `String`, which does not implement the `Copy` trait
7  |     print_country(country);
   |                   ------- value moved here
8  |     print_country(country);
   |                   ^^^^^^^ value used here after move
```

This example shows why software written in Rust is fast. A string allocates memory, and if you do a lot of memory allocation, your program might slow down.

> **NOTE** Of course, a few extra allocations won't slow anything down for the small examples in this book. But sometimes, you need to write software that doesn't use any extra memory at all. For software like multiplayer games and large data processing, you don't want to use any extra memory if you don't have to.

Rust won't allocate new memory for another string unless you want it to. Instead, it just gives ownership of the same data to something else. In this case, the function becomes the owner of the same data. (Also note the part of the error message that says which does not implement the 'Copy' trait. We'll learn about this shortly.)

So what do we do? Well, we could make print_country give the String back, but that would be awkward:

```
fn print_country(country_name: String) -> String {
    println!("{}", country_name);
    country_name
}

fn main() {
    let country = String::from("Austria");
    let country = print_country(country);
    print_country(country);
}
```

> Now this function doesn't just print the String; it prints it and returns it …,

> … which means that we have to grab the return value from the function and assign it to a variable again.

Now it prints

```
Austria
Austria
```

This way is awkward on both sides: you have to make the function return the value, and you have to declare a variable to hold the value that the function returns. Fortunately, there is a better method—just add &:

```
fn print_country(country_name: &String) {
    println!("{}", country_name);
}

fn main() {
    let country = String::from("Austria");
    print_country(&country);
    print_country(&country);
}
```

> Note that you have to pass in &country, not country.

Now print_country() is a function that takes a reference to a String: a &String. Thanks to this, the print_country() function can only view the data but never takes ownership.

Now let's do something similar with a mutable reference. Here is an example of a function that uses a mutable variable:

```
fn add_hungary(country_name: &mut String) {
    country_name.push_str("-Hungary");
    println!("Now it says: {country_name}");
}

fn main() {
    let mut country = String::from("Austria");
    add_hungary(&mut country);
}
```

> This time we are giving a &mut String instead of a &String.

> The push_str() method adds a &str to a String.

> Also note here that we need to pass in a &mut country, not just a &country.

This prints `Now it says: Austria-Hungary`.

So, to conclude,

- `fn function_name(variable: String)` takes a `String` and owns it. If it doesn't return anything, then the variable dies inside the function.
- `fn function_name(variable: &String)` borrows a `String` and can look at it. The variable doesn't die inside the function.
- `fn function_name(variable: &mut String)` borrows a `String` and can change it. The variable doesn't die inside the function.

Pay very close attention to this next example. It looks like a mutable reference, but it is different. There is no `&`, so it's not a reference at all:

```
fn main() {
    let country = String::from("Austria");       ⊲⎯⎤ The variable country is not
    adds_hungary(country);                            mutable, but we are going to
}                                                     print Austria-Hungary. How?

fn adds_hungary(mut string_to_add_hungary_to: String) {   ⊲⎤ Here's how: adds_hungary
    string_to_add_hungary_to.push_str("-Hungary");            takes the String and
    println!("{}", string_to_add_hungary_to);                 declares it mutable!
}
```

The output is `Austria-Hungary`, but that's not the interesting part.

How is this possible? `mut string_to_add_hungary_to` is not a reference: `adds_hungary` owns `country` now. Remember, it takes a `String` and not a `&String`. The moment you call `adds_hungary`, this function becomes the full owner of the data. The variable `string_to_add_hungary_to` doesn't need to care about the variable `country` at all because its data has moved and `country` is now gone. So `adds_hungary` can take `country` as mutable, and it is perfectly safe to do so—nobody else owns it.

Remember our employee and manager situation? In this situation, it is like you just quit your job and gave your whole computer to the manager. You're gone. You won't ever touch it again, so the manager can do anything at all to it.

Even more interesting, if you declare `country` a mutable variable on line 2, the compiler will give you a small warning. Why do you think that is?

```
fn main() {
    let mut country = String::from("Austria");   ⊲⎤ Here we have declared
    adds_hungary(country);                           country as mut.
}

fn adds_hungary(mut string_to_add_hungary_to: String) {
    string_to_add_hungary_to.push_str("-Hungary");
    println!("{}", string_to_add_hungary_to);
}
```

Let's look at the warning:

```
warning: variable does not need to be mutable
 --> src/main.rs:2:9
```

```
  |
2 |        let mut country = String::from("Austria");
  |            ----^^^^^^^
  |            |
  |            help: remove this `mut`
  |
  = note: `#[warn(unused_mut)]` on by default
```

This makes sense because on line 2 we have an owner called `country` that owns this mutable `String`. But it doesn't mutate it! It simply passes it into the `adds_hungary` function. There was no need to make it mutable. But the `adds_hungary` function takes ownership and would like to mutate it, so it declares it as a `mut string_to_add_hungary_to`. (It could have called it `mut country`, but with a different name, we can make it clear that ownership has completely passed to the function.)

To take the employee and manager comparison again, it is as if you started at a new job, got assigned a computer, and then quit and gave it to your manager without even booting it up. There was no need to have mutable access in the first place because you never even touched it.

Also note the position: it's `mut country: String` and not `country: mut String`. This is the same order as when you use `let` like in `let mut country: String`.

2.8   *Copy types*

Rust's simplest types are known as `Copy` types. They are all on the stack, and the compiler knows their size. That means that they are very easy to copy, so the compiler always copies their data when you send these types to a function. `Copy` types are so small and easy that there is no reason not to. In other words, you don't need to worry about ownership for these types.

We saw that in the previous section, too: the compiler said that the data for `String` moved because a `String` isn't a `Copy` type. If it was a `Copy` type, the data would be copied, not moved. Sometimes you'll see this difference expressed as *move semantics* and *copy semantics*. You also see the word *trivial* to talk about `Copy` types a lot, such as "It's trivial to copy them." That means "it's so easy to copy them that there is no reason not to copy them." `Copy` types include integers, floats, booleans (`true` and `false`), `char`, and others.

How do you know if a type "implements" (can use) copy? You can check the documentation. For example, the documentation for `char` can be found at https://doc.rust-lang.org/std/primitive.char.html. On the left in the documentation, you can see `Trait Implementations`. There you can see, for example, `Copy`, `Debug`, and `Display`. With that, you know that a `char`

- is copied when you send it to a function (`Copy`)
- can use {} to print (`Display`)
- can use {:?} to print (`Debug`)

Let's look at a code sample similar to the previous one, except that it involves a function that takes an `i32` (a `Copy` type) instead of a `String`. You don't need to think about

ownership anymore in this case because the i32 simply gets copied every time it passes
into the print_number() function:

```
fn prints_number(number: i32) {
    println!("{}", number);
}
```
There is no -> so the function does not return
anything. If number was not a Copy type, the
function would take it, and we couldn't use it again.

```
fn main() {
    let my_number = 8;
    prints_number(my_number);
    prints_number(my_number);
}
```
prints_number gets a
copy of my_number.

And again here. It's not a problem
because my_number is a Copy type!

But if you look at the documentation for String (https://doc.rust-lang.org/std/
string/struct.String.html), it is not a Copy type.

On the left in Trait Implementations, you can look in alphabetical order (A, B,
C, etc.); there is no Copy in C. But there is one called Clone. Clone is similar to Copy
but usually needs more memory. Also, you have to call it with .clone()—it won't
clone just by itself in the same way that Copy types copy themselves all on their own.

Let's get back to the previous example with the prints_country() function.
Remember that you can't pass the same String in twice because the function takes
ownership:

```
fn prints_country(country_name: String) {
    println!("{country_name}");
}


fn main() {
    let country = String::from("Kiribati");
    prints_country(country);
    prints_country(country);
}
```

But now we understand the message:

```
error[E0382]: use of moved value: `country`
 --> src\main.rs:4:20
  |
2 |     let country = String::from("Kiribati");
  |         ------- move occurs because `country`
  has type `std::string::String`, which does not implement the `Copy` trait
3 |     prints_country(country);
  |                    ------- value moved here
4 |     prints_country(country);
  |                    ^^^^^^^ value used here after move
```

The important part is String, which does not implement the `Copy` trait.

But what if this was someone else's code, and we couldn't change the
prints_country() function to take a &String instead of a String? Or what if we
wanted to take a String by value for some reason? Well, in the documentation, we saw
that String implements the Clone trait. So we can add .clone() to our code. This

creates a clone, and we send the clone to the function. Now `country` is still alive, so we can use it:

```
fn prints_country(country_name: String) {
    println!("{}", country_name);
}

fn main() {
    let country = String::from("Kiribati");
    prints_country(country.clone());
    prints_country(country);
}
```

Makes a clone and gives it to the function. Only the clone goes in, and the country variable is still alive.

Of course, if the `String` is very large, `.clone()` can use a lot of memory. One `String` could be a whole book in length, and every time we call `.clone()`, it will copy the contents of the book. So using `&` for a reference is faster, if you can. For example, the following code pushes a `&str` onto a `String` and then makes a clone every time it gets used in a function:

```
fn get_length(input: String) {
    println!("It's {} words long.",
        input.split_whitespace().count());
}

fn main() {
    let mut my_string = String::new();
    for _ in 0..50 {
        my_string.push_str("Here are some more words ");
        get_length(my_string.clone());
    }
}
```

This function takes ownership of a String.

Here we split to count the number of words. (Whitespace means the space between words.)

It prints

```
It's 5 words long.
It's 10 words long.
...
It's 250 words long.
```

That's 50 clones. Here it is using a reference instead, which is better:

```
fn get_length(input: &String) {
    println!("It's {} words long.", input.split_whitespace().count());
}

fn main() {
    let mut my_string = String::new();
    for _ in 0..50 {
        my_string.push_str("Here are some more words ");
        get_length(&my_string);
    }
}
```

Instead of 50 clones, it's zero.

Here's a good rule of thumb with references and functions: if you can use an immutable reference, go with that. You won't have to worry about a function taking ownership of some data: the function will simply take a look at it and be done. For functions, if you don't need to transfer ownership, a reference is always easiest!

The final memory-related subject in this chapter is pretty short: variables that have a name but no values.

2.9   Variables without values

A variable without a value is called an *uninitialized* variable. Uninitialized means "hasn't started yet." They are simple: just write `let` and then the variable name and (if necessary) the type:

```
fn main() {
    let my_variable: i32;
}
```

You can't use it yet, and Rust won't compile if you try to use a value that isn't initialized. But sometimes they can be useful. Some examples are when

- You have a code block, and the value for your variable is inside it.
- The variable needs to live outside of the code block.
- You want people reading your code to notice the variable name before the block.

Here's a simple example:

```
fn main() {
    let my_number;                  Pretend we need to have
    {                               this code block. We are
                                    writing some complex logic.    Pretend there is
        let calculation_result = {                                 code here, too.
            57
        };                                                  Lots of code and
        my_number = calculation_result;                     then the result
        println!("{my_number}");                                          And, finally, gives
    }                                                                      my_number a value
}
```

This prints 57.

You can see that `my_number` was declared in the `main()` function, so it lives until the end of the function. It gets its value from inside a different block, but that value lives as long as `my_number` because `my_number` holds the value.

Also note that `my_number` is not `mut` and doesn't have to be. We didn't give it a value until we gave it 57, so it never mutated its value. In the end, `my_number` is just a number that finally gets initialized with the value 57.

2.10   More about printing

We learned the basics of printing in the last chapter, but there is quite a bit more to know. You can print in a lot of ways in Rust: complex formatting, printing as bytes, displaying pointer addresses (the part in memory where the pointer is), and a lot more. Let's take a look at all of that now.

Adding \n will make a new line, and \t will make a tab:

```
fn main() {
    print!("\t Start with a tab\nand move to a new line");
}
```

This is print!, not println!

This prints

```
        Start with a tab
and move to a new line
```

Inside a single "" you can write over multiple lines, but be careful with the spacing:

```
fn main() {
    println!("Inside quotes
you can write over
many lines
and it will print just fine.");

    println!("If you forget to write
    on the left side, the spaces
    will be added when you print.");
}
```

After the first line, you have to start on the far left. If you write directly under println!, it will add the spaces.

This prints

```
Inside quotes
you can write over
many lines
and it will print just fine.
If you forget to write
    on the left side, the spaces
    will be added when you print.
```

If you want to print characters like \n, you can add an extra \ (a backslash). This is what is known as an "escape":

```
fn main() {
    println!("Here are two escape characters: \\n and \\t");
}
```

This prints

```
Here are two escape characters: \n and \t
```

Sometimes you end up using too many escape characters and just want Rust to print a string as you see it. To do this, you can add r# to the beginning and # to the end. The r here stands for *raw*.

We had to use \ eight times here—kind of annoying.

```
fn main() {
    println!("He said, \"You can find the file at
    c:\\files\\my_documents\\file.txt.\" Then I found the file.");
```

```
println!(r#"He said, "You can find the file at
    c:\files\my_documents\file.txt." Then I found the file."#);  ⊲——| Much better!
}
```

The output is exactly the same:

```
He said, "You can find the file at c:\files\my_documents\file.txt."
➥Then I found the file.
He said, "You can find the file at c:\files\my_documents\file.txt."
➥Then I found the file.
```

But the code for the second `println!` is easier to read.

But what if # marks the end of the string and you need to print text with a #" inside? In that case, you can start with r## and end with ##. You can keep adding # to the beginning and end if you have longer instances of the # symbol in your text.

This is best understood with a few examples:

```
fn main() {

    let my_string = "'Ice to see you,' he said.";
    let quote_string = r#""Ice to see you," he said."#;
    let hashtag_string = r##"The hashtag "#IceToSeeYou" had become
    ➥very popular."##;
    let many_hashtags = r####""You don't have to type "###" to
    ➥use a hashtag. You can just use #."####;

    println!("{}\n{}\n{}\n{}\n", my_string, quote_string,
    ➥hashtag_string, many_hashtags);
}
```

The output of these four examples is

```
'Ice to see you,' he said.
"Ice to see you," he said.
The hashtag "#IceToSeeYou" had become very popular.
"You don't have to type "###" to use a hashtag. You can just use #.
```

If you want to print the bytes of a `&str` or a `char`, you can write b before the string. This works for all ASCII characters (https://theasciicode.com.ar/).

So when you add a b to print as follows,

```
fn main() {
    println!("{:?}", b"This will look like numbers");
}
```

you will get an output that shows all the bytes:

```
[84, 104, 105, 115, 32, 119, 105, 108, 108, 32, 108, 111, 111, 107, 32, 108,
    105, 107, 101, 32, 110, 117, 109, 98, 101, 114, 115]
```

You can also put b and r together if you need to:

```
fn main() {
    println!("{:?}", br##"I like to write "#"."##);
}
```

That will print [73, 32, 108, 105, 107, 101, 32, 116, 111, 32, 119, 114, 105, 116, 101, 32, 34, 35, 34, 46].

There is also a Unicode escape that lets you print any Unicode character inside a string: \u{}. A hexadecimal number goes inside the {} to print it. Here is a short example of how to get the Unicode number as a u32, which you can then use with \u to print it out again:

```
fn main() {
    println!("{:X}", '행' as u32);        ←┐ Casts char as u32 to get
    println!("{:X}", 'H' as u32);           │ the hexadecimal value
    println!("{:X}", '居' as u32);
    println!("{:X}", 'い' as u32);
                                          ┐ Tries printing them
    println!("\u{D589}, \u{48}, \u{5C45}, \u{3044}");  ←┘ with unicode escape \u
}
```

We know that println! can print with {} for Display and {:?} for Debug, plus {:#?} for pretty printing. But there are many other ways to print.

For example, if you have a reference, you can use {:p} to print the pointer address. *Pointer address* means the location in your computer's memory:

```
fn main() {
    let number = 9;
    let number_ref = &number;
    println!("{:p}", number_ref);
}
```

This prints an address, like 0xe2bc0ffcfc. It might be different every time, depending on how and where your computer stores it. Or you can print binary, hexadecimal, and octal:

```
fn main() {
    let number = 555;
    println!("Binary: {:b}, hexadecimal: {:x}, octal: {:o}", number, number,
      number);
}
```

This prints Binary: 1000101011, hexadecimal: 22b, octal: 1053.

You can also add numbers inside {} to change the order of what gets printed. The first variable following the string will be in index 0, the next in index 1, and so on:

```
fn main() {
    let father_name = "Vlad";
    let son_name = "Adrian Fahrenheit";
    let family_name = "Țepeș";
```

```
    println!("This is {1} {2}, son of {0} {2}.",
    father_name, son_name, family_name);
}
```

Here, `father_name` is in position 0, `son_name` is in position 1, and `family_name` is in position 2. So it prints `This is Adrian Fahrenheit Țepeș, son of Vlad Țepeș`.

You can also use a name instead of an index value to do the same thing. In this case, you have to use the = sign to indicate which name applies to which value:

```
fn main() {
    println!(
        "{city1} is in {country} and {city2}
    is also in {country},
but {city3} is not in {country}.",
        city1 = "Seoul",
        city2 = "Busan",
        city3 = "Tokyo",
        country = "Korea"
    );
}
```

That example prints

```
Seoul is in Korea and Busan is also in Korea,
but Tokyo is not in Korea.
```

Very complex printing is also possible in Rust if you want to use it. Complex printing in Rust is based on this format:

`{variable:padding alignment minimum.maximum}`

Let's look at this one step at a time to understand it:

- Do you want a *variable* name? Write that first, like when we wrote `{country}`. (Then add a `:` after it if you want to do more things.)
- Do you want a *padding* character? For example, 55 with three "padding zeros" looks like 00055.
- What *alignment* (left/middle/right) do you want for the padding?
- Do you want a *minimum* length? (Just write a number.)
- Do you want a *maximum* length? (Write a number with a . in front.)
- Then, at the end, you can add a question mark if you want to `Debug` print.

We use this format every time we print, actually. If you type `println!("{my_type:?}");`, you are choosing the following:

- The variable's name is `my_type`.
- Nothing for padding, alignment, minimum, and maximum.
- Finally, there is a `?` to specify `Debug` printing.

Let's look at some complex printing examples. If you want to write a with five Korean ㅎ characters on the left and five ㅎ characters on the right, you would write this:

```
fn main() {
    let letter = "a";
    println!("{:ㅎ^11}", letter);
}
```

This prints ㅎㅎㅎㅎㅎaㅎㅎㅎㅎㅎ. Let's look at 1 to 5 again to understand how the compiler reads it:

- Do you want a variable name? {:ㅎ^11} No, there is no variable name. There is nothing before the :.
- Do you want a padding character? {:ㅎ^11} Yes, ㅎ comes after the :, so that is the padding character.
- Do you want an alignment? {:ㅎ^11} Yes, the ^ means alignment in the middle, < means alignment on the left, and > means alignment on the right.
- Do you want a minimum length? {:ㅎ^11} Yes, there is an 11 after.
- Do you want a maximum length? {:ㅎ^11} No, there is no number with a . before it.

Here is an example of many types of formatting:

```
fn main() {
    let title = "TODAY'S NEWS";          No variable name; pad with -; ^ to
    println!("{:-^30}", title);          put in center; 30 characters long
    let bar = "|";
    println!("{: <15}{: >15}", bar, bar);   No variable name; pad with space;
    let a = "SEOUL";                        15-character minimum length
    let b = "TOKYO";                        (one to the left, one to the right)
    println!("{city1:-<15}{city2:->15}", city1 = a, city2 = b);
}
```

Variable names city1 and city2; pad
with -; 15 character minimum length
(one to the left, one to the right)

It prints

```
---------TODAY'S NEWS---------
|                            |
SEOUL-------------------TOKYO
```

This chapter had a lot of concepts that are unique to Rust regarding memory and ownership. Let's think of one more comparison to make sure we understand it before we finish the chapter.

Ownership is sort of like how you own your computer. You have

- *Immutable references*—You can show your coworker what's on your screen as many times as you want with no problem.
- *Mutable references*—If your coworker wants to sit down and use your computer for a bit, there should be a good reason for it. And you can't have two coworkers sitting at your computer at the same time typing away—they'll just make a mess.
- *Transferring ownership*—If your coworker wants to own your computer, there better be a good reason for it because you can't ask for it back. They can declare it mutable and do absolutely whatever they want with it.

Finally, there are `Copy` types: they are "trivial" to copy. Think of them as cheap office pens, paperclips, and stickies. If your coworker needs a paperclip, do you care about ownership? No, you just hand it over and forget about it because it's such a trivial item.

Now that you understand ownership, we are going to move on to some more interesting types in Rust. So far, we've only looked at the most primitive types and `String`, but there's a lot more out there. In the next chapter we'll start to look at Rust's collection types.

Summary

- `const` and `static` can be used anywhere and for the whole life of a program.
- You take ownership of data by default in Rust; if you want to borrow, use a reference.
- Even strings in Rust have the concept of ownership: `String` for an owned type, and `&str` for a borrowed string.
- `Copy` types are so cheap that you don't need to worry about ownership. They use "copy semantics," not "move semantics."
- Uninitialized variables are rare, but you can use them as long as the variable is initialized later somewhere.
- The `println!` macro has its own syntax with a surprisingly large amount of functionality.

More complex types

This chapter covers

- Arrays—simple, fast, immutable collections of the same type
- Vectors—similar to arrays but growable and with more functionality
- Tuples (a grouping of various types)
- Control flow—making your code run differently depending on the situation

We're now moving past Rust's simplest types to collection types. Rust has a lot of collection types, and in this chapter, we'll learn three of them: arrays, vectors, and tuples. Unsurprisingly, Rust gives you a lot of options to choose from; this chapter only shows a few. After collection types, we'll learn about control flow, which means telling Rust how to run your code depending on the situation. One of the coolest parts of control flow in Rust is the keyword `match`, so keep an eye out for that.

3.1 Collection types

Rust has a lot of types for making collections. Collections are used when you have more than one value and want to hold them in a single place with some sort of order. For example, you could have information on all the cities in your country inside one collection.

The collection types we are going to look at now are arrays, vectors, and tuples. These are the easiest collection types in Rust to learn. There are other, more complex collection types in Rust, but those won't come up until chapter 6! We will start with arrays. Arrays are simpler types than vectors, so they can be used in places like tiny embedded devices where you can't allocate memory. At the same time, they have the least functionality for the user. They are a little bit like &str in that way.

3.1.1 Arrays

To create an array, just put some data inside square brackets separated by commas. But arrays have some pretty strict rules:

- Arrays must only contain the same type.
- Arrays cannot change their size.

Arrays have a somewhat interesting type: [type; number]. For example, the type of ["One", "Two"] is [&str; 2], while the type of ["One"] is [&str; 1]. This means that even these two arrays are of different types:

```
fn main() {
    let array1 = ["One", "Two"];        ⟵─┤ This one is type [&str; 2].

    let array2 = ["One", "Two", "Five"];    ⟵─┐ But this one is type
}                                             │ [&str; 3]. Different type!
```

Here is a good tip for arrays as well as other types: to find the type of a variable, you can "ask" the compiler by giving it bad instructions, such as trying to call a method that doesn't exist. Take this code for example:

```
fn main() {
    let seasons = ["Spring", "Summer", "Autumn", "Winter"];
    let seasons2 = ["Spring", "Summer", "Fall", "Autumn", "Winter"];
    seasons.ddd();                    ⟵─┤ Compiler: !
    seasons2.thd();   ⟵─┐ Compiler
}                       │ again: !!
```

The compiler says, "What? There's no .ddd() method for seasons and no .thd() method for seasons 2 either!!" as the error output shows us:

```
error[E0599]: no method named `ddd` found for array `[&str; 4]` in the
    current scope
  --> src\main.rs:4:13
   |
4  |     seasons.ddd();
   |             ^^^ method not found in `[&str; 4]`

error[E0599]: no method named `thd` found for array `[&str; 5]`
➥in the current scope
```

```
 --> src\main.rs:5:14
  |
5 |      seasons2.thd();
  |               ^^^ method not found in `[&str; 5]`
```

So when the compiler tells you `method not found in `[&str; 4]``, that's the type.

If you want an array with all the same value, you can declare it by entering the value, then a semicolon, and then the number of times you need it to repeat:

```
fn main() {
    let my_array = ["a"; 5];
    println!("{:?}", my_array);
}
```

This prints `["a", "a", "a", "a", "a"]`.

This method is used a lot to create byte buffers, which computers use when doing operations like downloading data. For example, `let mut buffer = [0u8; 640]` creates an array of 640 `u8` zeroes, which means 640 bytes of empty data. Its type will then be `[u8; 640]`. When data comes in, it can change each zero to a different `u8` number to represent the data. This buffer can change up to 640 of these zeroes before it is "full." We won't try to do any of these operations in Rust in this chapter, but it's good to know what arrays can be used for.

As you can see, you can change the data inside an array as much as you want (if it's `mut`, of course). You just can't add or remove items or change the type of the items inside.

We can use the `b` prefix that we learned in the previous chapter to take a look at an array of bytes. This example won't compile yet, but the error message is interesting:

```
fn main() {
    println!("{}", b"Hello there");
}
```

It says:

```
error[E0277]: `[u8; 11]` doesn't implement `std::fmt::Display`
 --> src/main.rs:2:20
  |
2 |      println!("{}", b"Hello there");
  |                     ^^^^^^^^^^^^^^ `
  |➡ [u8; 11]` cannot be formatted with the default formatter
  |
```

The solution is to use `{:?}` instead of `{}`, but we don't care about that: what's interesting is the type. It's `[u8; 11]`. So when you use `b`, it turns a `&str` into a `byte array`: an array of `u8`.

You can index (get) entries in an array with `[]`. The first entry is `[0]`, the second is `[1]`, and so on:

```
fn main() {
    let my_numbers = [0, 10, -20];
    println!("{}", my_numbers[1]);    ◁─┤ Prints 10
}
```

You can also get a slice (a piece) of an array. First, you need a & because the compiler doesn't know the size (a slice can be any length, so it is not `Sized`). Then you can use `..` to show the range. A range between index 2 and 5, for example, is `2..5`. But remember, in `2..5`, 2 means the third item (because indexes start at 0), and 5 means "up to index 5, but not including it."

This is easier to understand with examples. Let's use the array `[0, 1, 2, 3, 4, 5, 6, 7, 8, 9]` and slice it in different ways:

```
fn main() {
    let array_of_ten = [0, 1, 2, 3, 4, 5, 6, 7, 8, 9];

    let two_to_five = &array_of_ten[2..5];
    let start_at_one = &array_of_ten[1..];
    let end_at_five = &array_of_ten[..5];
    let everything = &array_of_ten[..];

    println!("Two to five: {two_to_five:?},
Start at one: {start_at_one:?},
End at five: {end_at_five:?},
Everything: {everything:?}");
}
```

2..5 means from index 2 up to index 5 but not including index 5.

1.. means from index 1 until the end.

..5 means from the beginning up to but not including index 5.

Using .. means to slice the whole array: beginning to end.

This prints

```
Two to five: [2, 3, 4],
Start at one: [1, 2, 3, 4, 5, 6, 7, 8, 9],
End at five: [0, 1, 2, 3, 4],
Everything: [0, 1, 2, 3, 4, 5, 6, 7, 8, 9]
```

Because a range like `2..5` doesn't include index 5, it's called *exclusive*. But you can also have an *inclusive* range, which means it includes the last number, too. To do this, add = to write `..=` instead of the regular `..` two dots. So instead of `[0..2]` you can write `[0..=2]` if you want the first, second, and third item (these are also called the zeroth, first, and second index).

3.1.2 Vectors

In addition to arrays, we have vectors. The difference between the two is similar to the difference between `&str` and `String`: arrays are simpler, with less flexibility and functionality, and may be faster, while vectors are easier to work with because you can change their size. (Note that arrays are not dynamically sized like a `&str`, so the compiler always knows their size. That's why we didn't need a reference to use them in the previous examples.)

The vector type is written `Vec`, and most people simply call it a *Vec*. It rhymes with *deck*. There are two main ways to declare a vector. One is similar to making a `String` using `new`:

```
fn main() {
    let name1 = String::from("Windy");
    let name2 = String::from("Gomesy");
```

Cat's name

Another cat's name

```
let mut my_vec = Vec::new();
my_vec.push(name1);              Now it knows: it's      If we run the program now, the
my_vec.push(name2);              a Vec<String>           compiler will give an error. It
}                                                        doesn't know the type of Vec.
```

You can see that `Vec` always has something else inside it, and that's what the `<>` (angle brackets) are for. A `Vec<String>` is a vector with one or more `String`s. You can put anything inside a `Vec`—for example:

- `Vec<(i32, i32)>`—This is a Vec where each item is a tuple: `(i32, i32)`. We will learn tuples right after Vecs.
- `Vec<Vec<String>>`—This is a Vec that has `Vec`s of `String`s. Say, for example, you wanted to save the words of your favorite book as a `Vec<String>`. Then you do it again with another book and get another `Vec<String>`. To hold both books, you would put them into another `Vec`, and that would be a `Vec<Vec<String>>`.

Instead of using `.push()` to have Rust decide the type (using type inference), you can declare the type:

```
fn main() {
    let mut my_vec: Vec<String> = Vec::new();      The compiler knows that it
}                                                  is a Vec<String>, so it
                                                   won't generate an error.
```

All items in a Vec must all have the same type, so you can't push an `i32` or anything else into a `Vec<String>`.

Another easy way to create a Vec is with the `vec!` macro. It looks like an array declaration but has `vec!` in front of it. Most people make Vecs this way because it's so easy:

```
fn main() {
    let mut my_vec = vec![8, 10, 10];
}
```

You can slice a vector, too, just like in an array. The following code is the same as the previous array example, except it uses Vecs instead of arrays:

```
fn main() {
    let vec_of_ten = vec![1, 2, 3, 4, 5, 6, 7, 8, 9, 10];
    let three_to_five = &vec_of_ten[2..5];
    let start_at_two = &vec_of_ten[1..];
    let end_at_five = &vec_of_ten[..5];
    let everything = &vec_of_ten[..];

    println!("Three to five: {:?},
start at two: {:?}
end at five: {:?}
everything: {:?}", three_to_five, start_at_two, end_at_five, everything);
}
```

Vecs allocate memory, so they have some methods to reduce memory usage and make them faster. A Vec has a *capacity*, which means the amount of memory given to the Vec to use. As you push new items onto the Vec, it gets closer and closer to the capacity. It won't give an error if you go past the capacity, so don't worry. However, if you go past the capacity, it will double its capacity and copy the items into this new memory space.

For example, imagine that you have a Vec with a capacity of 4 and four items inside it. If you add one more item, it will need a new memory space that can hold all five items. So, it will double its capacity to 8 and copy the five items over into the new memory space. This is called reallocation. You can imagine that this will use extra memory if you keep pushing a lot. We'll use a method called .capacity() to look at the capacity of a Vec as we add items to it, as in the following example:

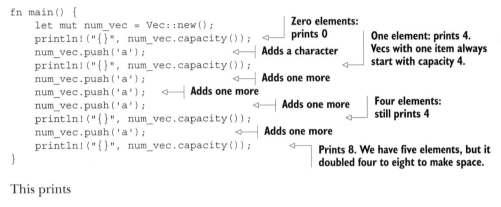

This prints

```
0
4
4
8
```

This vector has two reallocations: 0 to 4 and 4 to 8. We can make it more efficient by giving it a capacity of 8 to start:

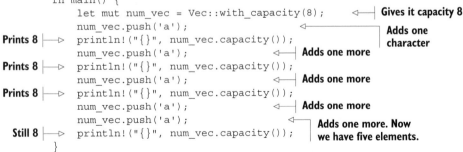

This vector had just a single first allocation, which is much better. If you think you know how many elements you need, you can use Vec::with_capacity() to use less memory and make your program more efficient.

We saw in the previous chapter that you can use .into() to make a &str into a String. You can also use the same method to make an array into a Vec. Interestingly, you have to declare that you want to use `.into()` to make a `Vec`, but you don't have to say which kind! You can simply write `Vec<_>`, and thanks to type inference, Rust will change the array into a `Vec` for you:

```
fn main() {
    let my_vec: Vec<u8> = [1, 2, 3].into();
    let my_vec2: Vec<_> = [9, 0, 10].into();    ⟵     This makes a
}                                                     Vec<i32>.
```

The last collection type in this chapter is called a tuple, which is quite different because it lets you hold a collection of different types together. Internally, tuples are different, too. Let's see how.

3.1.3 *Tuples*

Tuples in Rust use `()`. We have seen many empty tuples already because *nothing* in a function means an empty tuple. The signature

```
fn do_something() {}
```

is short for

```
fn do_something() -> () {}
```

That function gets nothing (an empty tuple) and returns nothing (an empty tuple). We have been using tuples a lot already. When you don't return anything in a function, you return an empty tuple. In Rust, this empty tuple is called the *unit type*. Take a look at the following example and think about what is being returned in both the previous function and inside `main()`:

```
fn just_makes_an_i32() {
    let unused_number = 10;
}

fn main() {
    just_makes_an_i32()
}
```

In the function `just_makes_an_i32()`, we make an `i32` that we never use. It gets declared inside the function and is followed with a semicolon. When you end a line with a semicolon nothing is returned—just an empty tuple. So, the return value for this function is also `()`. Then `main()` starts, and `main()` is also a function that returns nothing—an empty tuple. The interesting part is that `just_makes_an_i32()` isn't followed by a semicolon, but the code still works! That is because `just_makes_an_i32()` returns a `()`, and that becomes the return value for the main function because `just_makes_an_i32()` is on the last line. Of course, it looks much better to write `just_makes_an_i32();` with a semicolon. But this is a good lesson to see that the Rust compiler isn't concerned with whether you use semicolons; it's a compiler, not a formatter. It is only interested in having the expected inputs and outputs match.

Let's go beyond empty tuples and look at tuples that hold values. Items inside a tuple are also accessed with numbers 0, 1, 2, and so on. But to access them, you use a . (dot) instead of a []. There is a good reason for this: tuples are more like objects than indexed collections. In the next chapter, we will learn how to make objects called *structs* that use the same . (dot) notation.

Okay, let's put a whole bunch of types into a single tuple:

```
fn main() {
    let random_tuple = ("Here is a name", 8, vec!['a'], 'b', [8, 9, 10], 7.7);
    println!(
        "Inside the tuple is: First item: {:?}
Second item: {:?}
Third item: {:?}
Fourth item: {:?}
Fifth item: {:?}
Sixth item: {:?}",
        random_tuple.0,
        random_tuple.1,
        random_tuple.2,
        random_tuple.3,
        random_tuple.4,
        random_tuple.5,
    )
}
```

This prints

```
Inside the tuple is: First item: "Here is a name"
Second item: 8
Third item: ['a']
Fourth item: 'b'
Fifth item: [8, 9, 10]
Sixth item: 7.7
```

The type of a tuple depends on the types of the items inside it. So this tuple is of type (&str, i32, Vec<char>, char, [i32; 3], f64).

You can use a tuple to create multiple variables at the same time. Take a look at this code:

```
fn main() {
    let strings = ("one".to_string(),
    "two".to_string(), "three".to_string());
}
```

This strings tuple has three items in it. What if we want to pull them out and use them separately? We can use another tuple for that:

```
fn main() {
    let strings = ("one".to_string(),
    "two".to_string(), "three".to_string());

    let (a, b, c) = strings;
```

```
    println!("{b}");
    // println!("{strings:?}");        ◁──┐  This wouldn't
}                                         └  compile.
```

That prints two, which is the value that b holds. This is known as *destructuring* because the variables are first inside a *structure*, but then we made a, b, and c separately to pull this structure apart. A string is not a Copy type, so the values are moved into a, b, and c, and strings can't be accessed anymore.

Destructuring only works when the pattern matches. The following code works because each side has three items—the patterns match:

```
fn main() {
    let tuple_of_three = ("one", "two", "three");
    let (a, b, c) = tuple_of_three;
}
```

But you can't destructure if the pattern doesn't match. The next code sample is trying to use a tuple of two items to destructure three items, but the patterns don't match, and Rust can't tell what kind of destructuring you are trying to do:

```
fn main() {
    let tuple_of_three = ("one", "two", "three");   │  Should _b_ be "two" or
    let (a, b) = tuple_of_three;            ◁──┘  "three"? Rust can't tell.
}
```

If you write let (a, b, c) instead of let (a, b), then they will match, and you will have the variables a, b, and c to use. But what if you only want to use two items? No problem, just make sure the pattern matches but use _ instead of a variable name:

```
fn main() {
    let tuple_of_three = ("one", "two", "three");
    let (_, b, c) = tuple_of_three;
}
```

Now Rust can tell that you want b and c to have the values "two" and "three", and "one" doesn't get assigned to any variable.

In chapter 6, we'll see more collection types, and we'll see more ways to use them all throughout the book as well. But for the remainder of this chapter, we will learn control flow.

3.2   Control flow

Control flow involves telling your code to do something in a certain situation but to do something else in another situation. What should the code do if a certain condition is true, or a number is even or odd, or some other case? Rust has quite a few ways to manage control flow, and we'll start with the simplest form: the keyword if.

3.2.1   Basic control flow

The simplest form of control flow is if followed by {}. Rust will execute the code inside {} if the condition is true and will do nothing otherwise:

```
fn main() {
    let my_number = 5;
    if my_number == 7 {
        println!("It's seven");
    }
}
```

This code will print nothing because my_number is not 7.

Also note that you use == and not =. Using == is to compare, while = is to *assign* (to give a value). Also note that we wrote if my_number == 7 and not if (my_number == 7). You don't need parentheses with if in Rust. Using if will work with parentheses, but the compiler will tell you that you didn't need to use them.

You can use else if and else to give you more control:

```
fn main() {
    let my_number = 5;
    if my_number == 7 {
        println!("It's seven");
    } else if my_number == 6 {
        println!("It's six")
    } else {
        println!("It's a different number")
    }
}
```

This prints It's a different number because my_number isn't equal to 7 or 6.

You can add more conditions with && (and) and || (or):

```
fn main() {
    let my_number = 5;
    if my_number % 2 == 1 && my_number > 0 {   ◄┐
        println!("It's a positive odd number");  │
    } else if my_number == 6 {                   │
        println!("It's six")                     │
    } else {                                     │
        println!("It's a different number")      │
    }                                            │
}                                                │
```

This % is called modulo and gives the number that remains after dividing. 9 % 3 would give 0, and 5 % 2 would give 1.

This prints It's a positive odd number because when you divide it by 2, you have a remainder of 1, and it's greater than 0.

3.2.2 *Match statements*

You can already see that using if, else, and else if too much can make your code difficult to read. In this case, you can use match instead, which looks much cleaner. But Rust will make you match for every possible situation and won't compile the code otherwise. For example, this will not work:

```
fn main() {
    let my_number: u8 = 5;
    match my_number {
        0 => println!("it's zero"),
```

```
        1 => println!("it's one"),
        2 => println!("it's two"),
    }
}
```

The compiler says

```
error[E0004]: non-exhaustive patterns: `3u8..=std::u8::MAX` not covered
 --> src\main.rs:3:11
  |
3 |      match my_number {
  |            ^^^^^^^^^ pattern `3u8..=std::u8::MAX` not covered
```

The compiler is saying, "You told me about 0 to 2, but u8s can go up to 255. What about 3? What about 4? What about 5?" And so on. In this case, you can add _ (underscore), which means "anything else." This is sometimes called a wildcard:

```
fn main() {
    let my_number: u8 = 5;
    match my_number {
        0 => println!("it's zero"),
        1 => println!("it's one"),
        2 => println!("it's two"),
        _ => println!("It's some other number"),
    }
}
```

That prints It's some other number.

Remember these points for match:

- You write match, then the name of the item to match against, and then a {} code block.
- Write the *pattern* on the left and use a => (fat arrow) to say what to do when the pattern also matches.
- Each line is called an *arm.*
- Put a comma between the arms (not a semicolon).

You can declare a value with a match:

```
fn main() {
    let my_number = 5;
    let second_number = match my_number {
        0 => 0,
        5 => 10,
        _ => 2,
    };
}
```

The variable second_number will be 10. Do you see the semicolon at the end? That is because after the match is over, we told the compiler this: let second_number = 10;.

You can match on more complicated patterns, too. You can use a tuple to do it:

```
fn main() {
    let sky = "cloudy";
    let temperature = "warm";

    match (sky, temperature) {
        ("cloudy", "cold") => println!("It's dark and unpleasant today"),
        ("clear", "warm") => println!("It's a nice day"),
        ("cloudy", "warm") => println!("It's dark but not bad"),
        _ => println!("Not sure what the weather is."),
    }
}
```

This prints It's dark but not bad because it matches "cloudy" and "warm" for sky and temperature.

You can even put if inside of match. This is called a *match guard*:

```
fn main() {
    let children = 5;
    let married = true;

    match (children, married) {
        (children, married) if married == false =>
    println!("Not married with {children} kids"),
        (children, married) if children == 0 && married == true => {
            println!("Married but no children")
        }
        _ => println!("Married? {married}. Number of children: {children}."),
    }
}
```

This will print Married? true. Number of children: 5.

You also don't need to write == true or == false when checking a bool. Instead, you can write the name of the variable by itself (to check if true) or the name of the variable with an exclamation mark in front (to check if false). Here's the same code as before using this shortcut:

```
fn main() {
    let children = 5;
    let married = true;

    match (children, married) {
        (children, married) if !married =>
        ➡println!("Not married with {children} kids"),
        (children, married) if children == 0 && married =>
        ➡println!("Married but no children")
        _ => println!("Married? {married}.
        ➡Number of children: {children}."),
    }
}
```

You can use _ as many times as you want in a match. In this match on colors, we have three to match on, but only check one at a time:

```
fn match_colors(rgb: (i32, i32, i32)) {
    match rgb {
        (r, _, _) if r < 10 => println!("Not much red"),
        (_, g, _) if g < 10 => println!("Not much green"),
        (_, _, b) if b < 10 => println!("Not much blue"),
        _ => println!("Each color has at least 10"),
    }
}

fn main() {
    let first = (200, 0, 0);
    let second = (50, 50, 50);
    let third = (200, 50, 0);

    match_colors(first);
    match_colors(second);
    match_colors(third);
}
```

This prints

```
Not much green
Each color has at least 10
Not much blue
```

This example also shows how `match` statements work because in the first example, it only prints `Not much blue`. But `first` also has "not much green." A match statement always stops when it finds a match and doesn't check the rest. This is a good example of code that compiles well but is probably not the code you want.

You can make a really big `match` statement to fix it, but it is probably better to use a `for` loop. We will learn to use `for` loops very soon.

Each arm of a `match` has to return the same type. So you can't do this:

```
fn main() {
    let my_number = 10;
    let some_variable = match my_number {
        10 => 8,
        _ => "Not ten",
    };
}
```

The compiler tells you that

```
error[E0308]: `match` arms have incompatible types
  --> src\main.rs:17:14
   |
15 |         let some_variable = match my_number {
   |  _____-
16 | |             10 => 8,
   | |                   - this is found to be of type `{integer}`
17 | |             _ => "Not ten",
   | |                  ^^^^^^^^^ expected integer, found `&str`
18 | |         };
   | |_____- `match` arms have incompatible types
```

The following will also not work for the same reason:

```
fn main() {
    let some_variable = if my_number == 10 { 8 } else { "something else "};
    let my_number = 10;
}
```

But the following example using if and else works because if and else are followed by {}, which is a separate scope. The variable some_variable lives and dies inside a separate scope, and so it has nothing to do with if and else:

```
fn main() {
    let my_number = 10;

    if my_number == 10 {
        let some_variable = 8;
    } else {
        let some_variable = "Something else";
    }
}
```

You can also use @ to give a name to the value of a match expression, and then you can use it. In this example, we match an i32 input in a function. If it's 4 or 13, we want to use that number in a println! statement. Otherwise, we don't need to use it:

```
fn match_number(input: i32) {
    match input {
        number @ 4 => println!("{number} is unlucky in China (sounds
        close to 死)!"),
        number @ 13 => println!("{number} is lucky in Italy! In
        bocca al lupo!"),
        number @ 14..=19 => println!("Some other number that ends
        with -teen: {number}"),
        _ => println!("Some other number, I guess"),
    }
}

fn main() {
    match_number(50);
    match_number(13);
    match_number(16);
    match_number(4);
}
```

This prints

```
Some other number, I guess
13 is lucky in Italy! In bocca al lupo!
Some other number that ends with -teen: 16
4 is unlucky in China (sounds close to 死)!
```

Now let's move on to the last part of control flow in this chapter: the loop.

3.2.3   *Loops*

With loops, you can tell Rust to repeat something until you tell it to stop. The keyword `loop` lets you start a loop that does not stop unless you tell the code when to `break`. So this program will never stop:

```
fn main() {
    loop {}
}
```

That's not very helpful, so let's tell the compiler when it can break the loop (and therefore finish the program):

```
fn main() {
    let mut counter = 0;          ◁──┐  Sets a counter
    loop {                            │  to 0
        counter +=1;              ◁──┐  Increases the
        println!("The counter is now: {counter}");  counter by 1
        if counter == 5 {                      ◁──┐  Stops when
            break;                                 │  counter == 5
        }
    }
}
```

This will print

```
The counter is now: 1
The counter is now: 2
The counter is now: 3
The counter is now: 4
The counter is now: 5
```

Rust allows you to give a loop a name, which is helpful when you are within a loop that is inside another loop. You can use a ' (called a *tick*) followed by a colon to give it a name:

```
fn main() {
    let mut counter = 0;
    let mut counter2 = 0;
    println!("Now entering the first loop.");
                                                    Gives the first
    'first_loop: loop {                ◁────────────  loop a name
        counter += 1;
        println!("The counter is now: {}", counter);
        if counter > 5 {
            println!("Now entering the second loop.");
                                                       Starts a second loop
        'second_loop: loop {          ◁────────────  inside the first loop
            println!("The second counter is now: {}", counter2);
            counter2 += 1;
            if counter2 == 3 {
                break 'first_loop;    ◁──┐  Breaks out of 'first_loop so
            }                             │  we can exit the program
```

Now, we are inside 'second_loop. └─▷

```
            }
        }
    }
}
```

If we wrote `break;` or `break second_loop;` inside this code, the program would never end. The loop would keep on entering `'second_loop` and then would exit but stay inside `'first_loop`, enter `'second_loop` again, and continue forever. Instead, the program completes and prints:

```
Now entering the first loop.
The counter is now: 1
The counter is now: 2
The counter is now: 3
The counter is now: 4
The counter is now: 5
The counter is now: 6
Now entering the second loop.
The second counter is now: 0
The second counter is now: 1
The second counter is now: 2
```

Another kind of loop is called a `while` loop. A `while` loop is a loop that continues while something is still `true`. For each loop, Rust will check whether it is still `true`. If it becomes `false`, Rust will stop the loop:

```
fn main() {
    let mut counter = 0;

    while counter < 5 {          Counter < 5` is
        counter +=1;             either true or false.
        println!("The counter is now: {counter}");
    }
}
```

This prints the same result as the previous code sample that used a counter to keep track of the number of loops, but this time it was much simpler to write:

```
The counter is now: 1
The counter is now: 2
The counter is now: 3
The counter is now: 4
The counter is now: 5
```

Another kind of loop is a `for` loop. A `for` loop lets you tell Rust what to do each time. But in a `for` loop, the loop stops after a certain number of times instead of checking to see whether a condition is `true`. `for` loops use *ranges* very often. We learned before that

- `..` *creates an* exclusive *range*—`0..3` gives you `0`, `1`, `2`.
- `..=` *creates an* inclusive *range*—`0..=3` gives you `0`, `1`, `2`, `3`.

So let's use these in a loop!

```
fn main() {
    for number in 0..3 {
        println!("The number is: {}", number);
    }

    for number in 0..=3 {
        println!("The next number is: {}", number);
    }
}
```

This prints

```
The number is: 0
The number is: 1
The number is: 2
The next number is: 0
The next number is: 1
The next number is: 2
The next number is: 3
```

Also notice that `number` becomes the variable name for the numbers from `0..3`. We could have called it `n` or `ntod_het___hno_f` or anything else. We can then use that name to print the number or do some other operation with it.

If you don't need a variable name, use `_` (an underscore):

```
fn main() {
    for _ in 0..3 {
        println!("Printing the same thing three times"); ·
    }
}
```

This prints the same thing three times because there is no number to print each loop anymore:

```
Printing the same thing three times
Printing the same thing three times
Printing the same thing three times
```

If you give a variable name and don't use it, Rust will tell you:

```
fn main() {
    for number in 0..3 {
        println!("Printing the same thing three times");
    }
}
```

This prints the same thing as the previous example. The program compiles fine, but Rust will remind you that you didn't use `number`:

```
warning: unused variable: `number`
 --> src\main.rs:2:9
```

```
2 |      for number in 0..3 {
  |          ^^^^^^ help: if this is intentional,
  ▶prefix it with an underscore: `_number`
```

Rust suggests writing _number instead of _. Putting _ in front of a variable name means "Maybe I will use it later." But using just _ means "I don't care about this variable at all." So you can put _ in front of variable names if you will use them later and don't want the compiler to warn you about them.

You can also use break to return a value. You write the value right after break and use a ;. Here is an example with a loop and a break that gives my_number its value:

```
fn main() {
    let mut counter = 5;
    let my_number = loop {
        counter +=1;
        if counter % 53 == 3 {
            break counter;
        }
    };
    println!("{my_number}");
}
```

This code prints 56. The break counter; code at the end means "Break and return the value of counter." And because the whole block starts with let, my_number gets the value.

Now that we know how to use loops, here is a better solution to our match problem with colors from before. The new solution is better because we want to compare everything instead of matching and breaking out early when a condition matches. A for loop is different, as it looks at every item in the way we tell it to do:

This is a good example of destructuring. We have a tuple called rbg, and instead of using rbg.0, rbg.1, and rbg.2, we can give each item a readable name instead.

```
fn match_colors(rbg: (i32, i32, i32)) {
    let (red, blue, green) = (rbg.0, rbg.1, rbg.2);              ◄─────────┐
    println!("Comparing a color with {red} red, {blue} blue, and
    ▶{green} green:");                                        **Put the colors in a**
    let color_vec = vec![(red, "red"), (blue, "blue"),        **vec. Inside are tuples**
    ▶(green, "green")];                                     ◄── **with the color names.**
    let mut all_have_at_least_10 = true;              ◄─── **Use this variable to track if all colors are**
    for (amount, color) in color_vec {                ◄─── **at least 10. It starts as true and will be**
        if amount < 10 {                                   **set to false if one color is less than 10.**
            all_have_at_least_10 = false;
            println!("Not much {color}.");            **Some more destructuring here,**
        }                                             **letting us give a variable name to**
    }                                                 **the amount and the color name**
    if all_have_at_least_10 {
        println!("Each color has at least 10.")
    }
```

```
    println!();          ←⎯⎤  Adds one
}                            ⎦  more line

fn main() {
    let first = (200, 0, 0);
    let second = (50, 50, 50);
    let third = (200, 50, 0);

    match_colors(first);
    match_colors(second);
    match_colors(third);
}
```

This prints

```
Comparing a color with 200 red, 0 blue, and 0 green:
Not much blue.
Not much green.

Comparing a color with 50 red, 50 blue, and 50 green:
Each color has at least 10.

Comparing a color with 200 red, 50 blue, and 0 green:
Not much green.
```

Hopefully, you are starting to feel excited about Rust by now. In the previous chapter, we learned concepts called *low level*: how computer memory works, ownership of data, and so on. But Rust is also focused on the programmer experience, so the syntax is also very *high level* in places, as we saw in this chapter. Match statements, ranges, and destructuring are three examples: they are very readable and quick to type, yet no less strict than anything else in Rust.

In the next chapter, we are going to start creating our own types. The tuples that you learned about in this chapter will help you there.

Summary

- Arrays are extremely fast but have a set size and a single type.
- Vectors are sort of like `Strings`: they are owned types and very flexible.
- Tuples hold items that can be accessed with numbers, but they act more like new types of their own rather than indexed collections.
- Using `match` can make your code really readable.
- Rust makes sure you match everything in a `match` statement.
- Destructuring is powerful: it lets you pull types apart in almost any way you want.
- Ranges are a nice human-readable way to express when something starts and when it ends.
- If you have a loop inside a loop, you can name the loops to tell the code which one to break out of.

Building your own types

4

This chapter covers

- Structs, which you can use to group values to build your own types
- Enums, which are similar syntax to structs but used for choices, not groupings
- Implementing types, which gives methods to your structs and enums
- More on destructuring and taking types apart
- References and the dot operator

It's now time to look at the main ways to build your own types in Rust: structs and enums. You'll also learn how to implement functions attached to and called on these types, called *methods*. These methods use the keyword `self` a lot, so get ready to see it!

4.1 A quick overview of structs and enums

Structs and enums have a similar syntax and are easiest to learn together, so that's what we'll do here. They also work together because structs can contain enums, and enums can contain structs. Because they look similar, sometimes users new to Rust confuse them. But here's a rule of thumb to start: if you have a lot of things to group together, that's a struct, but if you have a lot of *choices* and need to select *one*, that's an enum.

If this book, *Learn Rust in a Month of Lunches*, were a struct, it would have its own properties, too. It would have a title (that's a String), an author_name (also a String), and a year_of_publication (maybe an i32). But it also has more than one way to buy it: you can choose to buy it either as a printed book or as an eBook. That's an enum! So keep that simple example in mind as we learn how structs and enums work.

4.1.1   *Structs*

With structs, you can create your own type. You can probably guess that the name is short for *structure*; you construct your own type with them. You will use structs all the time in Rust because they are so convenient. Structs are created with the keyword struct, followed by its name. The name of a struct should be in UpperCamelCase (capital letter for each word with no spaces). The code will still work if you write a struct in all lowercase, but the compiler will give a warning recommending that you change its name to UpperCamelCase.

There are three types of structs. One is a unit struct. Unit means "doesn't have anything" (like the unit type). For a unit struct, you simply write the name and a semicolon:

```
struct FileDirectory;
```

The next type is a tuple struct, or an unnamed struct. It is "unnamed" because you only need to write the types inside the tuple, not the field names. Tuple structs are good when you need a simple struct and don't need to remember names. You access their items in the same way as other tuples: .0, .1, and so on:

```
struct ColorRgb(u8, u8, u8);

fn main() {
    let my_color = ColorRgb(50, 0, 50);        ◁──┐ Makes a color out of
    println!("The second part of the color is: {}", my_color.1);   red, green, and blue
}
```

This prints The second part of the color is: 0.

The third type is the named struct, which is the most common struct. In this struct, you declare field names and types inside a {} code block. Note that you don't write a semicolon after a named struct because there is a whole code block after it:

```
struct ColorRgb(u8, u8, u8);        ◁──┐ Declares the same
                                        Color tuple struct
struct SizeAndColor {
    size: u32,
    color: ColorRgb,        ◁──┐ Puts it in our
}                               new named struct
```

```
fn main() {
    let my_color = ColorRgb(50, 0, 50);

    let size_and_color = SizeAndColor {
        size: 150,
        color: my_color
    };
}
```

You separate fields by commas in a named struct, too. For the last field, you can add a comma or not—it's up to you. `SizeAndColor` had a comma after `color`:

```
struct ColorRgb(u8, u8, u8);

struct SizeAndColor {
    size: u32,                      Note the
    color: ColorRgb,     ◁──┘      comma here.
}
```

But you don't need it to compile the program. It can be a good idea to always put a comma because sometimes you will change the order of the fields:

```
struct ColorRgb(u8, u8, u8);

struct SizeAndColor {
    size: u32,                     No comma
    color: ColorRgb    ◁──┘       here
}
```

Then we cut and paste to change the order of the parameters:

```
struct SizeAndColor {
    colour: ColorRgb   ◁──┐    Whoops! Now this
    size: u32,              doesn't have a comma.
}
```

But it is not very important either way.

Now, let's create a `Country` struct as our first concrete example. The `Country` struct has the fields `population`, `capital`, and `leader_name`. To declare a `Country`, we simply give it all the values it needs. Rust won't instantiate (start) a `Country` for us unless we give it a value for each of its three parameters:

```
struct Country {
    population: u32,
    capital: String,
    leader_name: String
}

fn main() {
    let population = 500_000;
    let capital = String::from("Elista");
    let leader_name = String::from("Batu Khasikov");
```

```
    let kalmykia = Country {
        population: population,
        capital: capital,
        leader_name: leader_name,
    };
}
```

Did you notice that we wrote the same thing twice? We wrote `population: popula-tion`, `capital: capital`, and `leader_name: leader_name`. In fact, you don't need to do that. One nice convenience in Rust is that if the field name and variable name are the same, you don't have to write both. Let's give that a try:

```
struct Country {
    population: u32,
    capital: String,
    leader_name: String
}

fn main() {
    let population = 500_000;
    let capital = String::from("Elista");
    let leader_name = String::from("Batu Khasikov");

    let kalmykia = Country {
        population,
        capital,
        leader_name,
    };
}
```

And, of course, you can just put a struct together without making variables first:

```
struct Country {
    population: u32,
    capital: String,
    leader_name: String
}

fn main() {
    let kalmykia = Country {
        population: 500_000,
        capital: String::from("Elista"),
        leader_name: String::from("Batu Khasikov")
    };
}
```

Now, let's say you wanted to add a `climate` (weather) property to `Country`. You would use it to pick a climate type for each country: `Tropical`, `Dry`, `Temperate`, `Continental`, and `Polar` (those are the main climate types). You would write `let kalmkia = Country` and eventually get to `climate` and would write something to choose one of the five. That's what an enum is for! Let's learn them now.

4.1.2   Enums

An enum is short for *enumerations* (we'll find out soon why they are called that). They look very similar to structs but are different:

- Use struct when you want one thing *and* another thing.
- Use enum when you want one thing *or* another thing.

So structs are for *many things* together, while enums are for *many possible choices*.

To declare an enum, write enum and use a code block with the options separated by commas. Just like a struct, the last part can have a comma or not. To make a choice when using an enum, use the enum name, followed by two :: (colons), and then the name of the *variant* (the choice). That means you can choose by typing Climate::Tropical, Climate::Dry, and so on.

Here is our Climate enum, which the Country struct now holds:

```
enum Climate {
    Tropical,
    Dry,
    Temperate,
    Continental,
    Polar,
}

struct Country {
    population: u32,
    capital: String,
    leader_name: String,
    climate: Climate,
}

fn main() {
    let kalmykia = Country {
        population: 500_000,
        capital: String::from("Elista"),
        leader_name: String::from("Batu Khasikov"),
        climate: Climate::Continental,
    };
}
```

As noted before, a struct can hold an enum, and an enum can hold a struct. This is one example of that.

This is the important part: you use :: to make a choice inside an enum.

Now let's change examples and create a simple enum called ThingsInTheSky:

```
enum ThingsInTheSky {
    Sun,
    Stars,
}
```

This, too, is an enum because you can either see the sun *or* the stars: you have to choose one.

Now let's create some functions related to the enum so that we can work with it a bit:

```
enum ThingsInTheSky {
    Sun,
    Stars,
}
```

> This function is pretty simple: it takes a number to represent the hour of the day and returns a ThingsInTheSky based on that. You can see the Sun between 6 and 18 o'clock; otherwise, you can see Stars.

```
fn create_skystate(time: i32) -> ThingsInTheSky {
    match time {
        6..=18 => ThingsInTheSky::Sun,
        _ => ThingsInTheSky::Stars,
    }
}
```

> This second function takes a reference to a ThingsInTheSky and prints a message depending on which variant of ThingsInTheSky it is.

```
fn check_skystate(state: &ThingsInTheSky) {
    match state {
        ThingsInTheSky::Sun => println!("I can see the sun!"),
        ThingsInTheSky::Stars => println!("I can see the stars!")
    }
}
```

```
fn main() {
    let time = 8;
    let skystate = create_skystate(time);
    check_skystate(&skystate);
}
```

> It's 8 o'clock.

> Returns a ThingsInTheSky

This prints I can see the sun!

But what makes Rust's enums special is that they don't just contain choices; they can hold data. A struct can hold an enum, an enum can hold a struct, and an enum can hold other types of data, too. Let's give ThingsInTheSky some data:

```
enum ThingsInTheSky {
    Sun(String),
    Stars(String),
}
```

> Now that the enum variants hold a String, you have to provide a String, too, when creating ThingsInTheSky.

```
fn create_skystate(time: i32) -> ThingsInTheSky {
    match time {
        6..=18 => ThingsInTheSky::Sun(String::from("I can see the sun!")),
        _ => ThingsInTheSky::Stars(String::from("I can see the stars!")),
    }
}
```

> Now, when we match on our reference to ThingsInTheSky, we have access to the data inside (in this case, a String). Note that we can give the inner String any name we want here: description, n, or anything else.

```
fn check_skystate(state: &ThingsInTheSky) {
    match state {
        ThingsInTheSky::Sun(description) =>
    println!("{description}"),
        ThingsInTheSky::Stars(n) => println!("{n}"),
    }
}
```

```
fn main() {
    let time = 8;
    let skystate = create_skystate(time);
    check_skystate(&skystate);
}
```

This prints the same thing: `I can see the sun!`

With the `use` keyword, you can also "import" an enum, so you don't have to type so much. Here's an example with a `Mood` enum where we have to type `Mood::` every time we match on it:

```
enum Mood {
    Happy,
    Sleepy,
    NotBad,
    Angry,
}

fn match_mood(mood: &Mood) -> i32 {
    let happiness_level = match mood {
        Mood::Happy => 10,
        Mood::Sleepy => 6,       Here we type
        Mood::NotBad => 7,       Mood:: every time.
        Mood::Angry => 2,
    };
    happiness_level
}

fn main() {
    let my_mood = Mood::NotBad;
    let happiness_level = match_mood(&my_mood);
    println!("Out of 1 to 10, my happiness is {happiness_level}");
}
```

It prints `Out of 1 to 10, my happiness is 7`. Let's try the `use` keyword to import this enum's variants so that we can type less. To import everything, write `*`:

```
enum Mood {
    Happy,
    Sleepy,
    NotBad,
    Angry,
}                                This imports every variant inside the
                                 Mood enum. Using * is the same as
fn match_mood(mood: &Mood) -> i32 {   writing use Mood::Happy; then use
    use Mood::*;              <——┘     Mood::Sleepy; and so on for each variant.
    let happiness_level = match mood {
        Happy => 10,
        Sleepy => 6,
        NotBad => 7,
        Angry => 2,
    };
    happiness_level
}

fn main() {
    let my_mood = Mood::Happy;
    let happiness_level = match_mood(&my_mood);
    println!("Out of 1 to 10, my happiness is {happiness_level}");
}
```

This use keyword isn't just for enums, by the way: it's used any time you use :: too much and want to type less. Do you remember this example from chapter 2 where we used a function called `std::mem::size_of_val()` to check the size of two names? That was a lot of typing:

```
fn main() {
    let size_of_jaurim = std::mem::size_of_val("자우림");
    let size_of_adrian = std::mem::size_of_val("Adrian Fahrenheit Țepeș");
    println!("{size_of_jaurim}, {size_of_adrian}");
}
```

This prints their size in bytes: 9 and 25 bytes. But we could have gone with use to import the function so that we only have to write `size_of_val` every time we use it:

```
use std::mem::size_of_val;    ⟵┤  The use keyword can be used inside main or inside or outside
                                 another function. If you use it inside a smaller scope, like a
fn main() {                      separate function, then it will only apply inside that scope.
    let size_of_jaurim = size_of_val("자우림");
    let size_of_adrian = size_of_val("Adrian Fahrenheit ?epe?");
    println!("{size_of_jaurim}, {size_of_adrian}");
}
```

4.1.3   *Casting enums into integers*

If an enum doesn't contain any data, then its variants can be cast into an integer. That's because Rust gives each variant of these simple enums a number that starts with 0 for its own use. (That's where the name enum comes from: the num in enum is the same as the num in number.)

Here is a quick example:

```
enum Season {
    Spring,       ⟵┐  If this was Spring(String) or
    Summer,          something it wouldn't work.
    Autumn,
    Winter,
}

fn main() {
    use Season::*;
    let four_seasons = vec![Spring, Summer, Autumn, Winter];
    for season in four_seasons {
        println!("{}", season as u32);
    }
}
```

This prints

```
0
1
2
3
```

However, you can also choose a different number if you like. The compiler doesn't care and can use it in the same way, as long as two variants aren't using the same number. To do this, add an = and your number to the variant that you want to have a number. You don't have to give all of them a number. But if you don't, Rust will add 1 from the variant before to give it a number:

```
enum Star {
    BrownDwarf = 10,
    RedDwarf = 50,
    YellowStar = 100,
    RedGiant = 1000,
    DeadStar,
}
```
> Think about this one.
> What number will it have?

```
fn main() {
    use Star::*;
    let starvec = vec![BrownDwarf, RedDwarf, YellowStar, RedGiant, DeadStar];
    for star in starvec {
        match star as u32 {
            size if size <= 80 => println!("Not the biggest star."),
            size if size >= 80 && size <= 200 =>
            println!("This is a good-sized star."),
            other_size =>
            println!("That star is pretty big! It's {other_size}"),
        }
    }
}
```
> We need to have this final arm of the match so that Rust can decide
> what to do if the u32 it gets is some other value that's not smaller
> than 80, or in between 80 and 200. We called the variable
> other_size here, but we could have called it size or anything else.

This prints

```
Not the biggest star.
Not the biggest star.
This is a good-sized star.
That star is pretty big! It's 1000
That star is pretty big! It's 1001
```

If we hadn't chosen our own numbers, then Rust would have started with 0 for each variant. Thus BrownDwarf would have been a 0 instead of a 10, DeadStar would have been 4 instead of 1001, and so on.

4.1.4   *Enums to use multiple types*

We learned in the last chapter that items in a Vec, array, etc., all need the same type and that only tuples are different. However, enums give us a bit of flexibility here because they can carry data, and that means that you can use an enum to hold different types inside a collection.

Imagine we want to have a Vec that holds either u32s or i32s. Rust will let us create a Vec<u32> or a Vec<i32>, but it won't let us make a Vec<u32 or i32>. However, we can make an enum (let's call it Number) and then put it inside a Vec. That will give us a type `Vec<Number>`. The `Number` enum can have two variants, one of which holds a `u32` and another that holds an `i32`. Here is what it would look like:

```
enum Number {
    U32(u32),
    I32(i32),
}
```

So there are two variants: the `U32` variant with a `u32` inside and the `I32` variant with `i32` inside. `U32` and `I32` are simply names we made. They could have been `UThirtyTwo` and `IThirtyTwo` or anything else.

The compiler doesn't mind that a `Vec<Number>` can hold either a `u32` or `i32` because they are all inside a single type called `Number`. And because it's an enum, you have to pick one, which is what we want. We will use the `.is_positive()` method to pick. If it's `true`, we will choose `U32`, and if it's `false`, we will choose `I32`. Now the code looks like this:

```
enum Number {
    U32(u32),
    I32(i32),
}

fn get_number(input: i32) -> Number {
    let number = match input.is_positive() {
        true => Number::U32(input as u32),        ◁——┐ Changes the number to
        false => Number::I32(input),        ◁——┐     a u32 if it's positive
    };                                          │
    number                                      │ Otherwise, keeps the number as
}                                               │ an i32 because a u32 can't be
                                                │ made from a negative number

fn main() {
    let my_vec = vec![get_number(-800), get_number(8)];

    for item in my_vec {
        match item {
            Number::U32(number) => println!("A u32 with the value {number}"),
            Number::I32(number) => println!("An i32 with the value
    {number}"),
        }
    }
}
```

This prints what we wanted to see:

```
An i32 with the value -800
A u32 with the value 8
```

We used a few functions in our previous samples to match on enums and print out differently depending on which variant the function received. But wouldn't it be nice if we could make functions that are a part of the structs and enums themselves? Indeed, we can: this is called *implementing*.

4.1.5 *Implementing structs and enums*

This is where you can start to give your structs and enums some real power. To write functions for a struct or an enum, use the `impl` keyword and then a scope with {} to write the functions (this is called an *impl block*). These functions are called *methods*. There are two kinds of methods in an `impl` block:

- *Methods*—These take `self` in some form (`&self` or `&mut self` or `self`). Regular methods use a . (a period). `.clone()` is an example of a regular method.
- *Associated functions (known as* static *methods in some languages)*—These do not take `self`. *Associated* means "related to." Associated functions are called differently, by typing `::` in between the type name and the function name. `String::from()` is an associated function, and so is `Vec::new()`. You see associated functions most often used to create new variables.

This simple example shows why associated functions don't use a period:

> The variable my_string doesn't exist yet, so you can't call my_string.some_method_name(). Instead, we use String::from to create a String.

```
fn main() {
    let mut my_string = String::from("I feel excited");
    my_string.push('!');
}
```

> But now the variable my_string exists, so we can use . to call a method on it. One method that we already know is .push(). my_string now holds the value "I feel excited!"

NOTE Actually, you can call all methods using `::` if you want, but methods that take `self` use . for convenience. There is sometimes a good reason to use `::` for a method that takes self, but we will look at that later. It's not very important to know just yet.

One more thing to know before we get to creating an `impl` block: a struct or enum needs to have `Debug` if you want to use `{:?}` to print it. Rust has a convenient way to do this: if you write `#[derive(Debug)]` above the struct or enum, you can print it with `{:?}`. These messages with `#[]` are called *attributes*. You can sometimes use them to tell the compiler to give your struct an ability like `Debug`. There are many attributes, and we will learn about them later. But `derive` is probably the most common, and you see it a lot above structs and enums, so it's good to learn now.

Okay, let's make an enum block now. In the next example, we are going to create animals and print them:

```
#[derive(Debug)]
enum AnimalType {
    Cat,
    Dog,
}

#[derive(Debug)]
struct Animal {
    age: u8,
    animal_type: AnimalType,
}
```

```
impl Animal {
    fn new_cat() -> Self {
        Self {
            age: 10,
            animal_type: AnimalType::Cat,
        }
    }
```

> Here, Self means Animal. You can also write Animal instead of Self. To the compiler, it is the same thing.
>
> **When we write Animal::new(), we always get a cat that is 10 years old.**

```
    fn check_type(&self) {
        match self.animal_type {
            AnimalType::Dog => println!("The animal is a dog"),
            AnimalType::Cat => println!("The animal is a cat"),
        }
    }
```

> Because we are inside impl Animal, &mut self means &mut Animal. Use .change_to_dog() to change the cat to a dog. Taking &mut self lets us change it.

```
    fn change_to_dog(&mut self) {
        self.animal_type = AnimalType::Dog;
        println!("Changed animal to dog! Now it's {self:?}");
    }

    fn change_to_cat(&mut self) {
        self.animal_type = AnimalType::Cat;
        println!("Changed animal to cat! Now it's {self:?}");
    }

}

fn main() {
    let mut new_animal = Animal::new_cat();
    new_animal.check_type();
    new_animal.change_to_dog();
    new_animal.check_type();
    new_animal.change_to_cat();
    new_animal.check_type();
}
```

> **This associated function will create a new Animal for us: a cat, 10 years old**

This prints

```
The animal is a cat
Changed animal to dog! Now it's Animal { age: 10, animal_type: Dog }
The animal is a dog
Changed animal to cat! Now it's Animal { age: 10, animal_type: Cat }
The animal is a cat
```

Remember that Self means the type Self, and self means the variable called self that refers to the object itself. So, in our code, Self means the type Animal. Also, fn change_to_dog(&mut self) means fn change_to_dog(&mut Animal).

Here is one more short example. This time, we will use impl on an enum:

```
enum Mood {
    Good,
    Bad,
    Sleepy,
}
```

```
impl Mood {
    fn check(&self) {
        match self {
            Mood::Good => println!("Feeling good!"),
            Mood::Bad => println!("Eh, not feeling so good"),
            Mood::Sleepy => println!("Need sleep NOW"),
        }
    }
}

fn main() {
    let my_mood = Mood::Sleepy;
    my_mood.check();
}
```

This prints `Need sleep NOW`.

You could take these two examples and develop them a bit if you like. How would you write a function that lets you create a new `Animal` that is an `AnimalType::Dog`? How about letting the user of the function choose an age instead of always generating a `Cat` that is 10 years old? Or how about giving the enum `Mood` to the `Animal` struct, too?

Using structs, enums, and `impl` blocks is one of the most common things you'll do in Rust, so you'll quickly get into the habit of putting them together. In the next section, you'll learn to do the complete opposite! Because if you have a fully constructed struct or other type, you can also destructure it in the same way that we have learned to destructure tuples. Let's take a look at that now.

4.2 *Destructuring*

Let's look at some more destructuring. You can get the values from a struct or enum by using `let` backward. We learned in the last chapter that this is destructuring because it creates variables that are not part of a structure. We'll start with a simple example. You'll recognize the following character if you've seen the movie *8 Mile* before:

```
struct Person {          ⟵⎤ A simple
    name: String,           ⎦ Person struct
    real_name: String,
    height: u8,
    happiness: bool
}

fn main() {                        ⎤ Creates variable
    let papa_doc = Person {    ⟵⎦ papa_doc
        name: "Papa Doc".to_string(),
        real_name: "Clarence".to_string(),
        height: 170,
        happiness: false
    };
                        ⎤ Destructures
    let Person {     ⟵⎦ papa_doc
        name,
```

```
        real_name,
        height,
        happiness,
    } = papa_doc;

    println!("They call him {name} but his real name is {real_name}.
    He is {height} cm tall and is he happy? {happiness}");
}
```

This prints `They call him Papa Doc but his real name is Clarence. He is 170 cm tall and is he happy? false`

You can see that destructuring works backward:

- `let papa_doc = Person { fields };` lets you create a struct.
- `let Person { fields } = papa_doc;` then destructures it.

You can also rename variables as you destructure. The following code is the same as the previous code, except that we chose the name `fake_name` for the `name` parameter and `cm` for the `height` parameter:

```
struct Person {
    name: String,
    real_name: String,
    height: u8,
    happiness: bool
}

fn main() {
    let papa_doc = Person {
        name: "Papa Doc".to_string(),
        real_name: "Clarence".to_string(),
        height: 170,
        happiness: false
    };

    let Person {
        name: fake_name,            ⟵  Here, we choose to call
        real_name,                      the variable fake_name.
        height: cm,             ⟵  And here, we choose
        happiness                   to call the variable cm.
    } = papa_doc;

    println!("They call him {fake_name} but his real name is {real_name}.
    ➡He is {cm} cm tall and is he happy? {happiness}");
}
```

Now, let's look at a bigger example. In this example, we have a `City` struct. We give it a `new` function to make it. Then we have a `process_city_values` function to do things with the values. In the function, we just create a `Vec`, but you can imagine that we can do much more after we destructure it:

```
struct City {
    name: String,
    name_before: String,
```

```
        population: u32,
        date_founded: u32,
}

impl City {
    fn new(
        name: &str,
        name_before: &str,
        population: u32,
        date_founded: u32,
    ) -> Self {
        Self {
            name: String::from(name),
            name_before: String::from(name_before),
            population,
            date_founded,
        }
    }
    fn print_names(&self) {
        let City {
            name,
            name_before,
            population,
            date_founded,
        } = self;
        println!("The city {name} used to be called {name_before}.");
    }
}
fn main() {
    let tallinn = City::new("Tallinn", "Reval", 426_538, 1219);
    tallinn.print_names();
}
```

Now, we have the values to use separately.

This prints `The city Tallinn used to be called Reval`.

You'll notice that the compiler tells us that we didn't use the variables `population` and `date_founded`. We can fix that! If you don't want to use all the properties of a struct, just type `..` after you finish the properties you want to use. The `print_names()` method in the following code will now only destructure with the `name` and `name_before` parameters:

```
struct City {
    name: String,
    name_before: String,
    population: u32,
    date_founded: u32,
}

impl City {
    fn new(
        name: &str,
        name_before: &str,
        population: u32,
        date_founded: u32
    ) -> Self {
```

```
        Self {
            name: String::from(name),
            name_before: String::from(name_before),
            population,
            date_founded,
        }
    }
    fn print_names(&self) {
        let City {
            name,
            name_before,
            ..
        } = self;
        println!("The city {name} used to be called {name_before}.");
    }
}

fn main() {
    let tallinn = City::new("Tallinn", "Reval", 426_538, 1219);
    tallinn.print_names();
}
```

These two dots tell Rust not to care about the other parameters inside City.

Interestingly, you can even destructure inside the signature of a function. Let's give this a try with the same sample with Papa Doc:

```
struct Person {
    name: String,
    real_name: String,
    height: u8,
    happiness: bool,
}

fn check_if_happy(person: &Person) {
    println!("Is {} happy? {}", person.name, person.happiness);
}

fn check_if_happy_destructured(Person { name, happiness, .. }: &Person) {
    println!("Is {name} happy? {happiness}");
}

fn main() {
    let papa_doc = Person {
        name: "Papa Doc".to_string(),
        real_name: "Clarence".to_string(),
        height: 170,
        happiness: false,
    };

    check_if_happy(&papa_doc);
    check_if_happy_destructured(&papa_doc);
}
```

This is the exact same struct as the previous sample—no changes here.

Next is a function that takes a &Person and checks whether the person is happy.

And, finally, a function that does the same thing, except that it destructures the Person struct. This gives direct access to the name and happiness parameters and uses .. to ignore the rest of the struct's parameters.

Here is the output:

```
Is Papa Doc happy? false
Is Papa Doc happy? false
```

So that finishes up the basics of structs and enums. For the final section in this chapter, we'll learn an interesting fact about the . operator: the "dot operator." It has a certain magic to it that keeps syntax clean when using methods for your types.

4.3   *References and the dot operator*

We learned in chapter 2 that when you have a reference, you need to use * to get to the value. A reference is a different type, so the following won't work:

```
fn main() {
    let my_number = 9;
    let reference = &my_number;

    println!("{}", my_number == reference);
}
```

The compiler prints

```
error[E0277]: can't compare `{integer}` with `&{integer}`
 --> src\main.rs:5:30
  |
5 |     println!("{}", my_number == reference);
  |                              ^^ no implementation for
  ╰─ `{integer} == &{integer}`
```

So we changed line 5 to `println!("{}", my_number == *reference);` and now it prints `true` because it's now `i32 == i32`, not `i32 == &i32`. This is called *dereferencing*.

Now let's look at something interesting. First, let's make a simple `String`. We'll see if it's empty:

```
fn main() {
    let my_name = "Billy".to_string();
    println!("{}", my_name.is_empty());
}
```

Easy, right? It just says `false`.

And, just like before, you can't compare a reference to something that's not a reference. So if we try to compare a `String` to a `&String`, we will get an error:

```
fn main() {
    let my_name = "Billy".to_string();
    let other_name = "Billy".to_string();
    println!("{}", my_name == &other_name);
    // println!("{}", &my_name == &&other_name);
}
```

You can't compare a &String with a &&String. Uncommenting this will generate an error, too.

But take a look at this example. Do you think it will compile?

```
fn main() {
    let my_name = "Billy".to_string();
    let double_ref = &&my_name;
    println!("{}", double_ref.is_empty());
}
```

It does! The method .is_empty() is for the String type, but we called it on a &&String. That's because when you use a method, Rust will dereference for you until it reaches the original type. The . in a method is called the dot operator, and it does dereferencing for free. Without it, you would have to write this:

```
fn main() {
    let my_name = "Billy".to_string();
    let double_ref = &&my_name;
    println!("{}", (&**double_ref).is_empty());
}
```

And that compiles, too! That's one * to get to the type itself and then an & to take a reference to it (because .is_empty() takes a &self). But the dot operator will dereference as much as needed, so you don't have to write * and & everywhere just to use the methods for a type. This works just fine, too:

```
fn main() {
    let my_name = "Billy".to_string();
    let my_ref = &my_name;
    println!("{}", &&&&&my_ref.is_empty());
}
```

That was a lot to think about, but, fortunately, the conclusion is easy: when you use the dot operator, you don't need to worry about *.

As a Rust programmer, you are going to use structs and enums everywhere. You'll soon get into the habit of making one, starting an impl block, and then adding methods. It's also nice that you can already see that some of the types you've learned are structs and enums. A String is, in fact, a struct String, a Vec is a struct Vec, and there are impl String and impl Vec blocks, too. There's nothing magic about them, and you're already starting to see how they work. We haven't learned any types in the standard library that are enums yet, but we will in the next chapter! Two of Rust's most famous types are structs and enums, and now you're ready to learn how they work.

Summary

- Structs are a little bit like tuples with names. They can hold all sorts of different types inside.
- Structs can hold enums, and enums can hold structs.
- Usually, after making a struct or enum, you'll start an impl block and give it some methods. Most of the time, they'll take &self or &mut self if you need to change it.
- Not all methods inside an impl block need self: if you want one to start a new struct or enum, it will create a Self and return it. You might even want one without self that returns something else. The compiler doesn't care whether you have self inside an impl block.
- To get data from inside an enum, you'll usually use match or something similar. An enum is about having only one choice, so you have to check which one was chosen!

- Enums are a good way to get around Rust's strict rules. Make one enum and put in as many types as you need!
- Destructuring can look strange at first, but it'll work every time if you take a normal `let` statement and turn the code around.

Generics, option, and result

5

This chapter covers

- Generics—when to use more than one type
- `Option`—when an operation might produce a value but might not
- `Result`—when an operation might succeed but might not

Rust is a strict language with concrete types, but after this chapter, you'll have three important tools to work with. Generics let you describe to Rust "some sort of type" that Rust will turn into a concrete type without you having to do it. After that, we'll learn about two interesting enums called `Option` and `Result`. `Option` tells Rust what to do when there might not be a value, and `Result` tells Rust what to do when something might go wrong.

5.1 Generics

We've known since chapter 1 that Rust needs to know the concrete type for the input and output of a function. The following `return_item()` function has `i32` for both its input and output, and no other type will work—only `i32`:

```
fn return_item(item: i32) -> i32 {
    println!("Here is your item.");
    item
}

fn main() {
    let item = return_item(5);
}
```

But what if you want the function to accept more than i32? It would be annoying if you had to write all these functions:

```
fn return_i32(number: i32) -> i32 {  }
fn return_i16(number: i16) -> i16 {  }
fn return_u8(number: u8) -> u8 {  }
```
⎤ **And so on,**
⎦ **and so on.**

You can use generics for this. Generics basically means "maybe one type, maybe another type."

For generics, you use angle brackets with the type inside, like this: <T>. This means "any type you put into the function." Rust programmers usually use one capital letter for generics (T, U, V, etc.), but the name doesn't matter, and you don't have to use one letter. The only part that matters is the angle brackets: <>.

This is how you change the function to make it generic:

```
fn return_item<T>(item: T) -> T {
    println!("Here is your item.");
    item
}

fn main() {
    let item = return_item(5);
}
```

The important part is the <T> after the function name. Without this, Rust will think that T is a concrete (concrete = not generic) type, like String or i8. When talking about generics, people say that something is "generic over (name of the type)." So, for the return_item function, you would say, "The function return_item is generic over type T."

Type names in generics are easier to understand if we choose a name instead of just T. See what happens when we change T to MyType:

```
fn return_item(item: MyType) -> MyType {
    println!("Here is your item.");
    item
}
```

The compiler gives the error cannot find type `MyType` in this scope. As you can see, MyType is concrete, not generic: the compiler is looking for something called

MyType and can't find it. To tell the compiler that MyType is generic, we need to write it inside the angle brackets:

```
fn return_item<MyType>(item: MyType) -> MyType {
    println!("Here is your item.");
    item
}

fn main() {
    let item = return_item(5);
}
```

Because of the angle brackets, now the compiler sees that this is a generic type that we are calling MyType. Without the angle brackets, it's not generic.

Let's look at the first part of the signature one more time to make sure we understand it. Here is the signature:

```
fn return_item<MyType>(item: MyType)
```

The compiler reads this as

- fn—This is a function.
- <MyType>—Ah, the function is generic! There will be some type in it that the programmer wants to call MyType.
- item: MyType—The function takes a variable called item, which will be of the type MyType that the programmer declared inside the angle brackets.

You could call it anything as long as you put it in angle brackets so the compiler knows that the type is generic. Now, we will go back to calling the type T because Rust code usually uses single letters. You can choose your own names in your own generic code, but it's good to get used to seeing these single letters and recognizing them as a hint that we are dealing with generic types.

You will remember that some types in Rust are Copy, some are Clone, some are Display, some are Debug, and so on. In other words, they implement the traits Copy, Clone, and so on. With Debug, we can print with {:?}.

The following code sample tries to print a generic item called T, but it won't work. Can you guess why?

```
fn print_item<T>(item: T) {
    println!("Here is your item: {item:?}");
}

fn main() {
    print_item(5);
}
```

The function print_item() needs T to have Debug to print item, but is T a type with Debug? Maybe not. Maybe it doesn't have #[derive(Debug)]—who knows? The compiler doesn't know either, so it gives an error:

```
error[E0277]: `T` doesn't implement `Debug`
 --> src/main.rs:2:34
  |
2 |     println!("Here is your item: {item:?}");
  |                                  ^^^^^^^^^ `T` cannot be formatted
  using `{:?}` because it doesn't implement `Debug`
```

There's no guarantee that T implements Debug. Somebody using the function might pass in a type that implements Debug, but also might not! Do we implement Debug for T? No, because we don't know what T is—right now, anyone can use the function and put in any type. Some of them will have Debug; some won't.

However, we can tell the function: "Don't worry, any type T that we pass into this function will implement Debug." It's sort of a promise to the compiler:

```
use std::fmt::Debug;

fn print_item<T: Debug>(item: T) {
    println!("Here is your item: {item:?}");
}

fn main() {
    print_item(5);
}
```

The Debug trait is located at std::fmt::Debug.

<T: Debug> is the important part.

Now the compiler knows: "Okay, this type T is going to have Debug." Now the code works because i32 has Debug. Now, we can give it many types: String, &str, and so on because they all have Debug. The code will now compile, and the compiler won't let any type be the variable item in this function unless it has Debug (you can't trick the compiler).

Now, we can create a struct and give it Debug with #[derive(Debug)], so we can print it, too. Our function can take i32, the struct Animal, and more:

```
use std::fmt::Debug;

#[derive(Debug)]
struct Animal {
    name: String,
    age: u8,
}

fn print_item<T: Debug>(item: T) {
    println!("Here is your item: {item:?}");
}

fn main() {
    let charlie = Animal {
        name: "Charlie".to_string(),
        age: 1,
    };

    let number = 55;

    print_item(charlie);
    print_item(number);
}
```

This prints

```
Here is your item: Animal { name: "Charlie", age: 1 }
Here is your item: 55
```

Sometimes, we need more than one generic type in a generic function. To do this, we have to write out each generic type name and think about how we want to use it. What traits should each type be able to use?

In the following example, we want two types. First, we want a type called T that we would like to print. Printing with {} is nicer, so we will require Display for T.

Next is a generic type that we will call U and two variables, num_1 and num_2, which will be of type U. We want to compare them, so it will need PartialOrd. The PartialOrd trait lets us use comparison operators like <, >, ==, and so on. But we want to print them, too, so we require Display for U as well. You can use + if you want to indicate more than one trait.

To sum up, <U: Display + PartialOrd> means there is a generic type that we are calling U, and it needs to have these two traits:

```
use std::fmt::Display;
use std::cmp::PartialOrd;

fn compare_and_display<T: Display, U: Display + PartialOrd>(statement: T,
➥input_1: U, input_2: U) {
    println!("{statement}! Is {input_1} greater than {input_2}? {}",
        ➥input_1 > input_2);
}

fn main() {
    compare_and_display("Listen up!", 9, 8);
}
```

This prints Listen up!! Is 9 greater than 8? true. So,

```
fn compare_and_display<T: Display, U: Display + PartialOrd>(statement: T,
➥num_1: U, num_2: U)
```

says the following:

- The function name is compare_and_display().
- The first type is T, and it is generic. It must be a type that can print with {}.
- The next type is U, and it is generic. It must be a type that can print with {}. Also, it must be a type that can be compared (so that it can use >, <, and ==).

We can give compare_and_display() different types if we want. The variable statement can be a String, a &str, or anything with Display.

To make generic functions easier to read, we can also use the keyword where right before the code block:

```
use std::cmp::PartialOrd;
use std::fmt::Display;

fn compare_and_display<T, U>(statement: T, num_1: U, num_2: U)
```

Now the part after compare_and_display only has <T, U>, which is a lot cleaner to read.

```
where                        ◁─────┐   Then we use the where keyword
    T: Display,                     │   and indicate the traits needed
    U: Display + PartialOrd,        │   on the following lines.
{
    println!("{statement}! Is {num_1} greater than {num_2}? {}",
    num_1 > num_2);
}

fn main() {
    compare_and_display("Listen up!", 9, 8);
}
```

Using `where` is a good idea when you have many generic types. Also note the following:

- If you have one variable of type `T` and another variable of type `T`, they must be the same type.

- If you have one variable of type `T` and another variable of type `U`, they *can* be different types. But they can also be the same. For example,

```
                                            Types T and U both need to
use std::fmt::Display;                      implement Display, but they
                                                  can be different types.

fn say_two<T: Display, U: Display>(statement_1: T,
➥statement_2: U) {                                        ◁─────────────┐
    println!("I have two things to say: {statement_1} and {statement_2}");
}

fn main() {
    say_two("Hello there!", String::from("I hate sand."));   ◁──────┐
    say_two(String::from("Where is Padme?"),
    String::from("Is she all right?"));   ◁      Type T is a &str, but type U is
}                                                a String. No problem: both of
                            Here both types are String.   these implement Display.
                            No problem: T and U don't
                            have to be different types.
```

This prints

```
I have two things to say: Hello there! and I hate sand.
I have two things to say: Where is Padme? and Is she all right?
```

Now that we understand both enums and generics, we can understand `Option` and `Result`. These are two enums that Rust uses to help us write code that will not crash.

5.2   *Option and Result*

The beginning of the chapter describes `Option` as a type "for when you might get a value, but maybe not," and `Result` as a type "for when an operation might succeed, but maybe not." If you remember that, you should have a good idea of when to use one and when to use the other.

A person in real life, for example, would have an `Option<Spouse>`. You might have one, and you might not. Not having a spouse simply means that you don't have a spouse, but it's not an error—just something that might or might not exist.

But the function `go_to_work()` would return a `Result` because it might fail! Most times `go_to_work()` succeeds, but one day, it might snow too much, and you have to stay home.

Meanwhile, simple functions like `print_string()` or `add_i32()` always produce output and can't fail, so they don't need to deal with `Option` or a `Result`. With that in mind, let's start with `Option`.

5.2.1   *Option*

You use `Option` when something might or might not exist. When a value exists, it is `Some(value)`, and when it doesn't, it's `None`. Here is an example of bad code that can be improved with `Option`:

```
fn take_fifth_item(value: Vec<i32>) -> i32 {
    value[4]
}

fn main() {
    let new_vec = vec![1, 2];
    let index = take_fifth_item(new_vec);
}
```

This code panics when we run it. Here is the message:

```
thread 'main' panicked at 'index out of bounds:
the len is 2 but the index is 4', src\main.rs:34:5
```

Panic means that the program stops before the problem happens. Rust sees that the function wants something impossible and stops. It "unwinds the stack" (takes the values off the stack) and tells you, "Sorry, I can't do that."

To fix this, we will change the return type from `i32` to `Option<i32>`. This means "give me a `Some(i32)` if it's there, and give me `None` if it's not." We say that the `i32` is "wrapped" in an `Option`, which means it's inside an `Option`. If it's `Some`, you have to do something to get the value out:

```
fn try_take_fifth(value: Vec<i32>) -> Option<i32> {
    if value.len() < 5 {
        None
    } else {
        Some(value[4])
    }
}

fn main() {
    let small = vec![1, 2];
    let big = vec![1, 2, 3, 4, 5];
    println!("{:?}, {:?}", try_take_fifth(small), try_take_fifth(big));
}
```

.len() gives the length of the Vec. Here, we are checking that the length is at least 5.

This prints `None, Some(5)`. Our program doesn't panic anymore, so this is better than before. But in the second case, the value `5` is still inside the `Option`. How do we get the `5` out of there?

We can get the value inside an Option with a method called .unwrap(), but be careful with .unwrap(). It's just like unwrapping a present: maybe there's something good inside, or maybe there's an angry snake inside. You only want to .unwrap() if you are sure. If you unwrap a value that is None, the program will panic:

```
fn try_take_fifth(value: Vec<i32>) -> Option<i32> {
    if value.len() < 5 {
        None
    } else {
        Some(value[4])
    }
}

fn main() {
    let small = vec![1, 2];
    let big = vec![1, 2, 3, 4, 5];
    println!("{:?}, {:?}",
        try_take_fifth(small).unwrap(),        ◁——  This one returns None.
        try_take_fifth(big).unwrap()                 .unwrap() will panic!
    );
}
```

The message is

```
thread 'main' panicked at 'called
⟹ `Option::unwrap()` on a `None` value', src\main.rs:14:9
```

But we don't have to use .unwrap(). We can use a match instead. With match, we can print the value if we have Some and not touch it if we have None. For example:

```
fn try_take_fifth(value: Vec<i32>) -> Option<i32> {
    if value.len() < 5 {
        None
    } else {
        Some(value[4])
    }
}

fn handle_options(my_option: &Vec<Option<i32>>) {
    for item in my_option {
        match item {
            Some(number) => println!("Found a {number}!"),
            None => println!("Found a None!"),
        }
    }
}

fn main() {
    let small = vec![1, 2];
    let big = vec![1, 2, 3, 4, 5];
    let mut option_vec = Vec::new();        ◁——  Makes a new Vec to hold our Options.
                                                  The vec is type: Vec<Option<i32>>.
                                                  That means a Vec of Option<i32>.

    option_vec.push(try_take_fifth(small)); ◁——  This pushes None
    option_vec.push(try_take_fifth(big));         into the Vec.
                                                  handle_option() looks at every option
    handle_options(&option_vec);            ◁——  in the Vec. It prints the value if it is
}                                                 Some. It doesn't touch it if it is None.
```

This pushes Some(5) into the vec.

This prints

```
Found a None!
Found a 5!
```

This was a good example of *pattern matching*. Some(number) is a pattern, and None is another pattern. We use match to decide what to do when each of these patterns happens. The Option type has two possible patterns, so we have to decide what to do when we see one pattern and what to do when we see another.

So, what does the actual Option type look like? Because we know generics, we are able to read the code for Option. It is quite simple—just an enum:

```
enum Option<T> {
    None,
    Some(T),
}
```

The important point to remember is with Some, you have a value of type T (any type). Also, note that the angle brackets after the enum name around T tell the compiler that it's generic. It has no trait like Display or anything to limit it; it can be anything. But with None, you don't have any value inside.

So, in a match statement for Option you can't say

```
Some(value) => println!("The value is {}", value),
None(value) => println!("The value is {}", value),
```

because None doesn't hold a T inside it. Only the Some variant will hold a value.

There are easier ways to use Option. In the next code sample, we will use a method called .is_some() to tell us if it is Some. (Yes, there is also a method called .is_none().) Using this means that we don't need handle_option() anymore:

```
fn try_take_fifth(value: Vec<i32>) -> Option<i32> {
    if value.len() < 5 {
        None
    } else {
        Some(value[4])
    }
}

fn main() {
    let small = vec![1, 2];
    let big = vec![1, 2, 3, 4, 5];
    for vec in vec![small, big] {
        let inside_number = try_take_fifth(vec);
        if inside_number.is_some() {
            println!("We got: {}", inside_number.unwrap());
        } else {
            println!("We got nothing.");
        }
    }
}
```

The .is_some() method returns true if we get Some, false if we get None.

We already checked that inside_number is Some, so it is safe to use .unwrap(). There is an easier way to do this called 'if let' that we will learn soon.

This prints

```
We got nothing.
We got: 5
```

Now imagine that we wanted this `take_fifth()` function or some other function to give us a reason for why it fails. We don't want to get `None`; we want to know why it failed. When it fails, we'd like to have some information on what went wrong so we can do something about it. Something like `Error: Vec wasn't long enough to get the fifth item`. That's what `Result` is for! Let's learn that now.

5.2.2   *Result*

`Result` looks similar to `Option`, but here is the difference:

- `Option` holds a `Some` or `None` (value or no value).
- `Result` holds an `Ok` or `Err` (okay result or error result).

You often see both `Option` and `Result` at the same time. For example, you might want to get data from a server. First, you use a function to connect. The connection might fail, so that's a `Result`. And after connecting, there might not be any data. That's an `Option`. So the entire operation would be an `Option` inside a `Result`: a `Result<Option<SomeType>>`.

To compare the two, here are the signatures for `Option` and `Result`:

```
enum Option<T> {
    None,
    Some(T),
}

enum Result<T, E> {
    Ok(T),
    Err(E),
}
```

Note that `Result` has a value inside of `Ok` and inside of `Err`. That is because errors are supposed to contain information that describes what went wrong. Also, note that `Ok` holds a generic type `T`, and `Err` holds a generic type `E`. As we learned in this chapter, they *can* be different types (and usually are) but could be the same.

`Result<T, E>` means you need to think of what you want to return for `Ok` and what you want to return for `Err`. In fact, you can return anything you like. Even returning a `()` in each case is okay:

```
fn check_error() -> Result<(), ()> {
    Ok(())
}

fn main() {
    check_error();
}
```

check_error() says, "Return () if we get Ok, and return () if we get Err." Then we return Ok with a () inside it. The program works with no problem!

The compiler gives us an interesting warning, though:

```
warning: unused `std::result::Result` that must be used
 --> src\main.rs:6:5
  |
6 |     check_error();
  |     ^^^^^^^^^^^^^
  |
  = note: `#[warn(unused_must_use)]` on by default
  = note: this `Result` may be an `Err` variant, which should be handled
```

This is true: we only returned the Result, but it could have been an Err. So, let's handle the error a bit, even though we're still not really doing anything:

```
fn see_if_number_is_even(input: i32) -> Result<(), ()> {
    if input % 2 == 0 {
        return Ok(())
    } else {
        return Err(())
    }
}


fn main() {
    if see_if_number_is_even(5).is_ok() {
        println!("It's okay, guys")
    } else {
        println!("It's an error, guys")
    }
}
```

This prints It's an error, guys. We just handled our first error! Something went wrong, we told Rust what to do in case of an error, and the program didn't panic. That's what Result helps you with.

The four methods to easily check the state of an Option or a Result are as follows:

- Option—.is_some(), .is_none()
- Result—.is_ok(),.is_err()

Sometimes a function with Result will use a String for the Err value. This is not a true error type yet, but it contains some information and is a little better than what we've done so far. Here's a simple example showing a function that expects the number 5 and gives an error otherwise. Using a String now lets us show some extra information:

```
fn check_if_five(number: i32) -> Result<i32, String> {
    match number {
        5 => Ok(number),
        _ => Err(format!("Sorry, bad number. Expected: 5 Got: {number}")),
    }
}
```

```
fn main() {
    for number in 4..=7 {
        println!("{:?}", check_if_five(number));
    }
}
```

Here is the output:

```
Err("Sorry, bad number. Expected: 5 Got: 4")
Ok(5)
Err("Sorry, bad number. Expected: 5 Got: 6")
Err("Sorry, bad number. Expected: 5 Got: 7")
```

Just like unwrapping a `None` for `Option`, using `.unwrap()` on `Err` will panic:

```
fn main() {
    let error_value: Result<i32, &str> =
    ➥Err("There was an error");
    error_value.unwrap();          ←
}
```
Unwraps it. Boom!

A Result is just a regular enum, so we can create one whenever we like. Both Option and Result and their variants are already in scope, so we can just write Err instead of Result::Err.

The program panics and prints

```
thread 'main' panicked at 'called `Result::unwrap()` on an `Err` value:
➥"There was an error"', src/main.rs:3:17
```

This information helps you fix your code. `src\main.rs:3:17` means "go to the folder `src`, then the file `main.rs`, and then to line 3 and column 17 where the error happened." So you can go there to look at your code and fix the problem.

You can also create your own error types. Result functions in the standard library and other people's code usually do this. For example, look at this function from the standard library:

```
pub fn from_utf8(vec: Vec<u8>) -> Result<String, FromUtf8Error>
```

This function takes a vector of bytes (`u8`) and tries to make a `String`. So the success case for the `Result` is a `String`, and the error case is `FromUtf8Error`. You can give your error type any name you want. To make a type into a true error type in Rust, it needs to implement a trait called `Error`. Doing so lets it be used in generic code that expects a type that implements `Error` in the same way that generic code might expect a type to implement `Debug`, `Display`, or `PartialOrd` as we saw in this chapter.

We will start to learn about traits in detail in chapter 7, but we have some more things to learn before then. One of them is more pattern matching, as Rust has a lot of other ways to do pattern matching besides the `match` keyword. Let's see why we might want to use them instead of always using `match`.

5.2.3   *Some other ways to do pattern matching*

IF LET

Using a `match` with `Option` and `Result` sometimes requires a lot of code. For example, take the `.get()` method, which is used on a `Vec` to see whether there is a value at a given index. It returns an `Option`:

```
fn main() {
    let my_vec = vec![2, 3, 4];
    let get_one = my_vec.get(0);          Checks the
    let get_two = my_vec.get(10);         0th index: Some
    println!("{:?}", get_one);            Checks the
    println!("{:?}", get_two);            10th index: None
}
```

This prints

```
Some(2)
None
```

We learned that matching is a safe way to work with an `Option`. Let's do that with a range from indexes 0 to 10 to see whether there are any values:

```
fn main() {
    let my_vec = vec![2, 3, 4];

    for index in 0..10 {
        match my_vec.get(index) {
            Some(number) => println!("The number is: {number}"),
            None => {}
        }
    }
}
```

The code works fine and prints what we expected:

```
The number is: 2
The number is: 3
The number is: 4
```

We weren't doing anything in case of `None` because we were only interested in what happens when we get a `Some`, but we still had to tell Rust what to do in case of `None`. Here we can make the code shorter by using `if let`. Using `if let` means "do something if it matches, and don't do anything if it doesn't." `if let` is for when you don't care about matching for everything:

```
fn main() {
    let my_vec = vec![2, 3, 4];

    for index in 0..10 {
        if let Some(number) = my_vec.get(index) {
            println!("The number is: {number}");
        }
    }
}
```

Two important points to remember:

- `if let Some(number) = my_vec.get(index)` means "if you get the pattern `Some(number)` from `my_vec.get(index)`."
- It uses one `=` and not `==` because it is a pattern match, not a boolean.

LET ELSE

Rust 1.65, released in November 2022, added an interesting new syntax called `let else`. Let's take a look at the same `if let` example but add a `let else` and see what makes it different. First, try reading this sample on your own and think about what is different between `if let` and `let else`:

```
fn main() {
    let my_vec = vec![2, 3, 4];

    for index in 0..10 {
        if let Some(number) = my_vec.get(index) {
            println!("The number is: {number}");
        }
        let Some(number) = my_vec.get(index) else {
            continue;
        };
        println!("The number is: {number}");
    }
}
```

> This is the same if let from the previous example. It only cares about the Some pattern.

> This is the let else syntax. It also is only interested in the Some pattern and doesn't care about None.

The difference between the two is as follows:

- `if let` *checks* to see whether `my_vec.get()` gives the pattern `Some`. If it gets a `Some`, it calls the variable inside it `number` and opens up a new scope inside the `{}` curly brackets. Inside this scope, you are guaranteed to have a variable called `number`. If `.get()` doesn't give the pattern `Some`, it will simply do nothing and go to the next line.
- `let else` *tries* to make a variable `number` from the pattern `Some`. If you take out the `else` part for a moment, you can see that it is trying to do this: `let Some(number) = my_vec.get();`. In other words, it is trying to make this variable called `number`.

  But on the next line, it prints out the variable `number`, so the variable has to exist at this point. So how can this work? It can work thanks to what is called *diverging code*. Diverging code is basically any code that lets you escape before going to the next line. The keyword `continue` will do this, as will the keyword `break`, an early return, and so on.

You can write as much as you want inside the block after `else`, as long as you end with diverging code. For example,

```
fn main() {
    let my_vec = vec![2, 3, 4];

    for index in 0..10 {
        let Some(number) = my_vec.get(index) else {
```

> The block after else starts here. We have a whole block to do whatever we like. We end with break. This means the code will never get to the line below, which needs the variable called number.

```
            println!("Looks like we got a None!");
            println!("We can still do whatever we want inside this block");
            println!("We just have to end with 'diverging code'");
            print!("Because after this block, ");
            println!("the variable 'number' has to exist");
            println!("Time to break the loop now, bye");
            break;
        // return ();
        };
        println!("The number is: {number}");
    }
}
```

This is another example of diverging code. The keyword break; is used to break out of a loop, while return will return early from the function. The function main() returns an empty tuple, as we learned in chapter 3, so using return(); will return a (), the function will be over, and we never got to the line below.

You can see that we printed out quite a bit after we finally got a None. And finally, at the end of all this printing, we use the keyword break to diverge the code, and the program never got down to the next line. Here is the output:

```
The number is: 2
The number is: 3
The number is: 4
Looks like we got a None!
We can still do whatever we want inside this block
We just have to end with 'diverging code'
Because after this block, the variable 'number' has to exist
Time to break the loop now, bye
```

WHILE LET

while let is like a while loop for if let. Imagine that we have weather station data like this, in which we would like to parse certain strings into numbers:

```
["Berlin", "cloudy", "5", "-7", "78"]
["Athens", "sunny", "not humid", "20", "10", "50"]
```

To parse the numbers, we can use a method called parse::<i32>(). First is .parse(), which is the method name, followed by ::<i32>, which is the type to parse into. It will therefore try to turn the &str into an i32 and give it to us if it can. It returns a Result because it might not work (for example, if you wanted it to parse the name "Billy-brobby"—that's not a number).

We will also use .pop(). This takes the last item off of the vector:

```
fn main() {
    let weather_vec = vec![
        vec!["Berlin", "cloudy", "5", "-7", "78"],
        vec!["Athens", "sunny", "not humid", "20", "10", "50"],
    ];
    for mut city in weather_vec {
        println!("For the city of {}:", city[0]);
        while let Some(information) = city.pop() {
```

In our data, every first item is the city name.

while let Some(information) = city.pop() means to keep going until finally city runs out of items and .pop() returns None instead of Some.

```
          if let Ok(number) = information.parse::<i32>() {
              println!("The number is: {number}");
          }
```

> **Nothing happens here because we only care about getting an Ok. We never see anything that returns an Err.**

> **Here we try to parse the variable we called information into an i32. This returns a Result. If it's Ok(number), we will now have a variable called number that we can print.**

This will print

```
For the city of Berlin:
The number is: 78
The number is: -7
The number is: 5
For the city of Athens:
The number is: 50
The number is: 10
The number is: 20
```

This chapter was the most "rusty" one so far. That's because the three concepts you learned, generics, Option, and Result, aren't even in most languages! So you're already learning concepts that many other languages don't even have.

But you probably also noticed that they aren't weird, abstract concepts either. They are real, practical ways to help you write and work with your code. It's nice not to have to write a new function for every type (generics). It's nice to check whether a value is there or not (Option). And it's nice to check whether an error has happened and decide what to do if it does (Result). The creators of Rust took some of these ideas from exotic languages but use them in a practical manner, as you saw in this chapter.

The next chapter isn't too hard compared to this one. In it, you'll learn some more about Result and error handling, and we'll see some more complex collection types than the ones you saw in chapter 3.

Summary

- Generics let you use more than one type in your types or functions. Without them, you would need to repeat your code every time you wanted a different type.
- You can write anything for generic types, but most of the time, people will just write T.
- After T, you write what traits the type will have. Having more traits means T can do more things. But it also means that the function can take fewer types because any type needs all of the traits you wrote.
- Rust is still concrete, though: it turns generic functions into concrete ones at compile time. There's nothing extra that happens at run time.
- If you have a function that could panic, try turning its output into an Option or a Result. By doing so, you can write code that never crashes.
- Don't forget that the Err value of a Result doesn't have to be an official error! If you are still learning Rust, returning a String for the Err value is easier.

More collections, more error handling

This chapter covers

- Other collections—more complex and interesting ones this time
- The question mark operator—just type ? to handle errors
- When panic and unwrap are good

Rust has a *lot* more collection types than the ones we learned in chapter 3. You might not need all of them right away, but be sure to give each collection type a read so that you'll remember when you might need each one of them. This chapter also introduces one of Rust's most loved operators: ? (Yes, it's just a question mark.)

6.1 Other collections

Rust has many more types of collections besides the ones we learned in chapter 3. All of them are contained in the same spot: the `std::collections` module in the standard library. The best way to use them is to bring them into scope with a `use` statement, like we did with our enums in the last chapter. The page for the collections module (http://mng.bz/27yd) on the standard library has a really nice summary of when to use which collection type and for what reasons, so be sure to bookmark it.

We will start with `HashMap`, which is extremely common.

6.1.1 HashMap (and BTreeMap)

A `HashMap` is a collection made out of *keys* and *values*. You use the key to look up the value that matches the key. An example of a key and a value is `email` and `my_email@` `.address.com` (email is the key; the address is the value).

Creating a new `HashMap` is easy: you can just use `HashMap::new()`. After that, you can use the `.insert(key, value)` method to insert items.

The keys of a `HashMap` are not ordered, so if you print every key in a `HashMap` together it will probably print differently. We can see this in an example:

```
use std::collections::HashMap;          This is so we can just write HashMap instead
                                        of std::collections::HashMap every time.
struct City {
    name: String,
    population: HashMap<i32, i32>,       This will have the year and
}                                        the population for the year.

fn main() {

    let mut tallinn = City {
        name: "Tallinn".to_string(),
        population: HashMap::new(),      So far the HashMap
    };                                   is empty.

Inserts
three
dates       tallinn.population.insert(2020, 437_619);      Just so we remember, there is no
            tallinn.population.insert(1372, 3_250);        difference between 24_000 and
            tallinn.population.insert(1851, 24_000);       24000. The _ is just for readability.

    for (year, population) in tallinn.population {
        println!("In {year}, Tallinn had a population of {population}.");
    }                                                  The HashMap is
}                                                       HashMap<i32, i32>, so it
                                                        returns two items each time.
```

Here the three keys are 2020, 1372, and 1851. If a `HashMap` were ordered, the order would be 1372, 1851, and 2020. But because a `HashMap` does not order its keys, we will see them in any order. So, the code might print

```
In 1372, Tallinn had a population of 3250.
In 2020, Tallinn had a population of 437619.
In 1851, Tallinn had a population of 24000.
```

or it might print

```
In 1851, Tallinn had a population of 24000.
In 2020, Tallinn had a population of 437619.
In 1372, Tallinn had a population of 3250.
```

You can see that the keys do not appear in any particular order.

If you want a HashMap that gives you its keys in order, you can use a BTreeMap. Underneath, they are different types, but fortunately, their method names and signatures are very similar. That means we can quickly change our HashMap to a BTreeMap without needing to change almost anything. For our simple example, the code (besides the name BTreeMap) hasn't changed at all:

```
use std::collections::BTreeMap;        ⟵─┐ Changes HashMap
                                          │ to BTreeMap
struct City {
    name: String,
    population: BTreeMap<i32, i32>,     ⟵─┤ Here, too
}

fn main() {

    let mut tallinn = City {
        name: "Tallinn".to_string(),
        population: BTreeMap::new(),    ⟵─┤ And here, too
    };

    tallinn.population.insert(2020, 437_619);
    tallinn.population.insert(1372, 3_250);
    tallinn.population.insert(1851, 24_000);

    for (year, population) in tallinn.population {
        println!("In {year}, Tallinn had a population of {population}.");
    }
}
```

Now, it will always print in this order:

```
In 1372, Tallinn had a population of 3250.
In 1851, Tallinn had a population of 24000.
In 2020, Tallinn had a population of 437619.
```

Now, we will go back to HashMap.

The simplest but least rigorous way to get a value in a HashMap is by putting the key in [] square brackets, similar to typing [0] or [1] to index a Vec. In this next example, we will use this method to look for the value for the key Bielefeld, which is Germany. But be careful because the program will crash if there is no key, just like when indexing a Vec. If you write println!("{:?}", city_hashmap["Bielefeldd"]);, for example, it will panic because Bielefeldd doesn't exist.

If you are not sure there will be a key, you can use .get(), which returns an Option. If it exists, it will be Some(value), and if not, you will get None instead of panicking the program. That's why .get() is the safer way to get a value from a HashMap:

```
use std::collections::HashMap;

fn main() {
    let canadian_cities = vec!["Calgary", "Vancouver", "Gimli"];
    let german_cities = vec!["Karlsruhe", "Bad Doberan", "Bielefeld"];
```

```
    let mut city_hashmap = HashMap::new();

    for city in canadian_cities {
        city_hashmap.insert(city, "Canada");
    }
    for city in german_cities {
        city_hashmap.insert(city, "Germany");
    }

    println!("{:?}", city_hashmap["Bielefeld"]);
    println!("{:?}", city_hashmap.get("Bielefeld"));
    println!("{:?}", city_hashmap.get("Bielefeldd"));
}
```

This prints

```
"Germany"
Some("Germany")
None
```

This is because *Bielefeld* exists, but *Bielefeldd* does not exist.

If a `HashMap` already has a key when you try to put it in, using `.insert()` will over-write its value:

```
use std::collections::HashMap;

fn main() {
    let mut book_hashmap = HashMap::new();

    book_hashmap.insert(1, "L'Allemagne Moderne");
    book_hashmap.insert(1, "Le Petit Prince");
    book_hashmap.insert(1, "섀도우 오브 유어 스마일");
    book_hashmap.insert(1, "Eye of the World");

    println!("{:?}", book_hashmap.get(&1));
}
```

The .get() method takes a reference, which is why we have &1 here.

This prints `Some("Eye of the World")` because it was the last one we used `.insert()` for. It is easy to prevent this by checking whether an entry exists since `.get()` returns an `Option`:

```
use std::collections::HashMap;

fn main() {
    let mut book_hashmap = HashMap::new();
    book_hashmap.insert(1, "L'Allemagne Moderne");

    let key = 1;
    match book_hashmap.get(&key) {
        Some(val) => println!("Key {key} has a value already: {val}"),
        None => {
            book_hashmap.insert(key, "Le Petit Prince");
        }
    }
    println!("{:?}", book_hashmap.get(&1));
}
```

This prints Some("L\'Allemagne Moderne") because there was already a key for 1, so we didn't insert Le Petit Prince.

You might be wondering why we put book_hashmap.insert() inside a {} but didn't do the same for the print statement. That's because .insert() returns a value: an Option that holds the old value if the value was overwritten. And because each arm of a match statement has to return the same type, we can have the part with .insert() return a () by enclosing it in {} and ending it with a semicolon.

Let's try grabbing the old value from the .insert() method and storing it somewhere else so we don't lose it. In this next sample, we will have a Vec that will hold any old values that have been returned by the .insert() method when an existing value has been overwritten:

```
use std::collections::HashMap;

fn main() {
    let mut book_hashmap = HashMap::new();
    let mut old_hashmap_values = Vec::new();

    let hashmap_entries = [
        (1, "L'Allemagne Moderne"),
        (1, "Le Petit Prince"),
        (1, "섀도우 오브 유어 스마일"),
        (1, "Eye of the World"),
    ];

    for (key, value) in hashmap_entries {
        if let Some(old_value) = book_hashmap.insert(key, value) {
            println!("Overwriting {old_value} with {value}!");
            old_hashmap_values.push(old_value);
        }
    }
    println!("All old values: {old_hashmap_values:?}");
}
```

Don't forget to destructure here! You don't have to, but destructuring into (key, value) is much nicer to work with than something like entry.0 and entry.1.

Here's what the output looks like:

```
Overwriting L'Allemagne Moderne with Le Petit Prince!
Overwriting Le Petit Prince with 섀도우 오브 유어 스마일!
Overwriting 섀도우 오브 유어 스마일 with Eye of the World!
All old values: ["L'Allemagne Moderne", "Le Petit Prince", "섀도우 오브 유어 스
    마일"]
```

THE .ENTRY() METHOD

HashMap has a very interesting method called .entry() that you definitely want to try out. It's a little complicated, so let's look at it one bit at a time.

With .entry(), you can try to make an entry and then another method like .or_insert() to insert a default value if there is no key. The interesting part is that the second method also returns a mutable reference, so you can change it if you want. First is an example where we insert true every time we insert a book title into the HashMap.

Let's pretend that we have a library and want to keep track of our books:

```
use std::collections::HashMap;

fn main() {
    let book_collection = vec![
        "L'Allemagne Moderne",
        "Le Petit Prince",
        "Eye of the World",
        "Eye of the World",          ◁────  Note that Eye of the
    ];                                      World appears twice.

    let mut book_hashmap = HashMap::new();

    for book in book_collection {
        book_hashmap.entry(book).or_insert(true);
    }
    for (book, true_or_false) in book_hashmap {
        println!("Do we have {book}? {true_or_false}");
    }
}
```

This prints

```
Do we have Eye of the World? true
Do we have Le Petit Prince? true
Do we have L'Allemagne Moderne? true
```

This worked, but so far, we've only used `.entry()` and `.or_insert()` like the `.insert()` method. Maybe it would be better to count the number of books so that we know that there are two copies of *Eye of the World*.

Here's how it works. Let's look at what `.entry()` does and then what `.or_insert()` does. First is `.entry()`, which only takes a key. It then returns an enum called `Entry`:

```
pub fn entry(&mut self, key: K) -> Entry<K, V>
```

The page for `Entry` can be found at http://mng.bz/1JXV. Here is a simple version of its code. K means key, and V means value:

```
enum Entry<K, V> {
    Occupied(OccupiedEntry<K, V>),
    Vacant(VacantEntry<K, V>),
}
```

So, when you use `.entry()`, the `HashMap` will check the key that it got and return an `Entry` to let you know whether there is a value.

The next method, `.or_insert()`, is a method on the `Entry` enum. This method looks at the enum and decides what to do:

```
fn or_insert(self, default: V) -> &mut V {
    match self {
        Occupied(entry) => entry.into_mut(),
        Vacant(entry) => entry.insert(default),
    }
}
```

The interesting part is that it returns a mutable reference: &mut V. It either returns a mutable reference to the existing value, or it inserts the default value and then returns a mutable reference to it. In either case, it returns a mutable reference.

That means you can use let to attach the mutable reference to a variable name and change the variable to change the value in the HashMap. So let's give that a try. For every book, we will insert a default 0 if there is no entry and then get a mutable reference to the value. We will then increase it by 1. That means that inserting the first book will return a 0, which we will increment to 1: one book. If we insert the same book again, it will return a 1, which we will increment to 2: two books. And so on.

Now the code looks like this:

```
use std::collections::HashMap;

fn main() {
    let book_collection = vec![
        "L'Allemagne Moderne",
        "Le Petit Prince",
        "Eye of the World",
        "Eye of the World",
    ];

    let mut book_hashmap = HashMap::new();

    for book in book_collection {
        let return_value = book_hashmap.entry(book).or_insert(0);
        *return_value += 1;
    }

    for (book, number) in book_hashmap {
        println!("{book}, {number}");
    }
}
```

The variable return_value is a mutable reference. If nothing is there, it will be 0.

Now return_value is at least 1. And if there was another book, the number it returns will now be increased by 1.

The important part is

```
let return_value = book_hashmap.entry(book).or_insert(0);
```

If you take out the let, you get book_hashmap.entry(book).or_insert(0). Without let, it does nothing: it inserts 0, and no variable holds onto the mutable reference to 0. We bind it to return_value so we can keep the 0. Then we increase the value by 1, which gives at least 1 for every book in the HashMap. Then when .entry() looks at *Eye of the World* again, it doesn't insert anything, but it gives us a mutable 1. Then we increase it to 2, and that's why it prints this:

```
L'Allemagne Moderne, 1
Le Petit Prince, 1
Eye of the World, 2
```

You can also do things with .or_insert(), such as insert a Vec and then push a value onto it. Let's pretend that we asked men and women on the street what they think of a politician. They give a rating from 0 to 10. We want to put the numbers together to see whether the politician is more popular with men or women. It can look like this:

```
use std::collections::HashMap;

fn main() {
    let data = vec![            ⊲─────┐  This is the
        ("male", 9),                  │  raw data.
        ("female", 5),
        ("male", 0),
        ("female", 6),
        ("female", 5),
        ("male", 10),
    ];

    let mut survey_hash = HashMap::new();
                                        │  This gives a
                                        │  tuple of (&str, i32).
    for item in data {            ⊲─────┘
        survey_hash.entry(item.0).or_insert(Vec::new()).push(item.1);   ⊲──────┐
    }
                                        Here we push the number into
    for (male_or_female, numbers) in survey_hash {   the Vec inside. This is possible
        println!("{male_or_female}: {numbers:?}");   because after .or_insert(), we
    }                                     have a mutable reference to
}                                         the data, which is a Vec<i32>.
```

This prints

```
"female", [5, 6, 5]
"male", [9, 0, 10]
```

Or it might print `"male"` first—remember, a `HashMap` is unordered. Here as well you could use the same code with a `BTreeMap` if you wanted the keys to be ordered.

The important line is

```
survey_hash.entry(item.0).or_insert(Vec::new()).push(item.1);
```

So if the `HashMap` sees the key `"female"`, it will check to see whether this key is already in the `HashMap`. If not, it will insert a `Vec::new()` and return a mutable reference to it; then we can use `.push()` to push the first number in. If it sees `"female"` already in the `HashMap`, it will not insert a new `Vec`, but it will return a mutable reference to that `Vec`, and then we can push a new number into it.

The next collection type is pretty similar to `HashMap` (even the name is similar) but simpler!

6.1.2 HashSet and BTreeSet

A `HashSet` is actually just a `HashMap` that only has keys. The documentation page for `HashSet` (https://doc.rust-lang.org/std/collections/struct.HashSet.html) has a pretty simple explanation for this: "implemented as a `HashMap` where the value is `()`." That means that a `HashSet` is useful as a collection that lets you know whether a key exists or not.

Imagine that you have 50 random numbers, and each number is between 1 and 50. Some numbers will appear more than once, while some won't appear at all. If you put them into a `HashSet`, you will have a list of all the numbers that appeared:

```
use std::collections::HashSet;

fn main() {
    let many_numbers = vec![
        37, 3, 25, 11, 27, 3, 37, 21, 36, 19, 37, 30, 48, 28, 16, 33, 2,
        10, 1, 12, 38, 35, 30, 21,
        20, 38, 16, 48, 39, 31, 41, 32, 50, 7, 15, 1, 20, 3, 33, 12, 1, 11,
        34, 38, 49, 1, 27, 9,
        46, 33,
    ];

    println!("How many numbers in the Vec? {}", many_numbers.len());

    let mut number_hashset = HashSet::new();

    for number in many_numbers {
        number_hashset.insert(number);
    }

    let hashset_length = number_hashset.len();    ⟵┘ Like a Vec, the other collection types
    println!(                                          have a .len() method, too, that tells
        "There are {hashset_length} unique numbers, so we are missing {}.",  you how many items it holds.
        50 - hashset_length
    );

                                                    ┌ Let's see what numbers
    println!("It does not contain: ");    ⟵──┘ we are missing.
    for number in 0..=50 {
        if number_hashset.get(&number).is_none() {
            print!("{number} ");
        }
    }
}
```

This prints

```
How many numbers in the Vec? 50
There are 31 unique numbers, so we are missing 19.
It does not contain:
0 4 5 6 8 13 14 17 18 22 23 24 26 29 40 42 43 44 45 47
```

A `BTreeSet` is similar to a `HashSet` in the same way that a `BTreeMap` is similar to a `HashMap`. If we print each item in the `HashSet`, we don't know what the order will be:

```
for entry in number_hashset {
    print!("{} ", entry);
}
```

Maybe it will print

```
48, 27, 36, 16, 32, 37, 41, 20, 7, 25, 15, 35, 3, 33, 21, 39, 12,
2, 46, 19, 31, 30, 10, 49, 28, 34, 50, 11, 1, 38, 9.
```

But it will almost never print these numbers in the same way again.

Here as well, it is easy to change your `HashSet` to a `BTreeSet` if you decide you need ordering. In our code, we only need to make two changes to switch from a `HashSet` to a `BTreeSet`.

Instead of just printing out the numbers in a `BTreeSet`, let's demonstrate that each number is greater than the last. To do this, we can keep track of the latest number and then compare it to the next number the `BTreeSet` contains. What do you think the following code will print?

```
use std::collections::BTreeSet;

fn main() {
    let many_numbers = vec![37, 3, 25, 11, 27, 3, 37, 21, 36, 19, 37, 30, 48,
        28, 16, 33, 2, 10, 1, 12, 38, 35, 30, 21, 20, 38, 16, 48, 39, 31, 41,
        32, 50, 7, 15, 1, 20, 3, 33, 12, 1, 11, 34, 38, 49, 1, 27, 9, 46, 33];

    let mut current_number = i32::MIN;
    let mut number_set = BTreeSet::new();
    for number in many_numbers {
        number_set.insert(number);
    }
    for number in number_set {
        if number < current_number {
            println!("This will never happen");
        }
        current_number = number;
    }
}
```

We are going to compare increasingly large numbers, so the best way to start is with a number that is lower than any number in the BTreeSet. We could have gone with -1, but another interesting way is to pick the lowest number possible for an i32.

For each number, we will check to see whether it is less than the last number. That will never happen, though, because each number will be larger than the last.

Don't forget to set current_number to the most recent number that we saw.

This code should print nothing at all because each number is greater than the last.

Two more collection types left! The next one is more rarely used than the others so far but has a very clear purpose.

6.1.3   *BinaryHeap*

A `BinaryHeap` is an interesting collection type because it is mostly unordered but has a bit of order. It keeps the item with the greatest value in the front, but the other items are in any order. Some languages call this a *priority queue*. We will use another list of items for an example, but this time, smaller:

```
use std::collections::BinaryHeap;

fn main() {
    let many_numbers = vec![0, 5, 10, 15, 20, 25, 30];
    let mut heap = BinaryHeap::new();
    for num in many_numbers {
        heap.push(num);
    }
    println!("First item is largest, others are out of order: {heap:?}");
    while let Some(num) = heap.pop() {
```

Note that these numbers are in order. They won't be in the same order once we put them inside our BinaryHeap, though.

The .pop() method returns Some(number) if a number is there, and None if not. It pops from the front, which is where the item with the greatest value is.

```
        println!("Popped off {num}. Remaining numbers are: {heap:?}");
    }
}
```

This prints

```
First item is largest, others are out of order: [30, 15, 25, 0, 10, 5, 20]
Popped off 30. Remaining numbers are: [25, 15, 20, 0, 10, 5]
Popped off 25. Remaining numbers are: [20, 15, 5, 0, 10]
Popped off 20. Remaining numbers are: [15, 10, 5, 0]
Popped off 15. Remaining numbers are: [10, 0, 5]
Popped off 10. Remaining numbers are: [5, 0]
Popped off 5. Remaining numbers are: [0]
Popped off 0. Remaining numbers are: []
```

You can see that the number in the 0th index is always largest: 30, 25, 20, 15, 10, 5, and then 0. But the other items are all in random order.

A good way to use a `BinaryHeap` is for a collection of things to do. Here we create a `BinaryHeap<(u8, &str)>` where the u8 is a number for the importance of the task. The &str is a description of what to do:

```
use std::collections::BinaryHeap;

fn main() {
    let mut jobs = BinaryHeap::new();

    jobs.push((100, "Reply to email from the CEO"));    ←  Adds jobs to do
    jobs.push((80, "Finish the report today"));             throughout the day
    jobs.push((5, "Watch some YouTube"));
    jobs.push((70, "Tell your team members thanks for always working hard"));
    jobs.push((30, "Plan who to hire next for the team"));

    for (_, job) in jobs {          ←  Here's a nice example of destructuring
        println!("You need to: {job}");    again. We don't care to print out the
    }                                      number, just the description.
}
```

Because the largest item always shows up first, this will always print

```
You need to: Reply to email from the CEO
You need to: Finish the report today
You need to: Tell your team members thanks for always working hard
You need to: Plan who to hire next for the team
You need to: Watch some YouTube
```

Finally, we have the famous VecDeque, a sort of special Vec that also has a very clear purpose.

6.1.4   *VecDeque*

A VecDeque (pronounced "vec-deck") is a Vec that is optimized for (i.e., good at) popping items both off the front and the back. Rust has VecDeque because Vecs are great for popping off the back (the last item) but not so great off the front. When you use

.pop() on a Vec, it just takes off the last item on the right, and nothing else is moved. But if you remove an item from anywhere else inside a Vec, all the items to the right of it are moved over one position to the left. You can see this in the description for .remove():

Removes and returns the element at position index within the vector, ➥shifting all elements after it to the left.

Take this example:

```
fn main() {
    let mut my_vec = vec![9, 8, 7, 6, 5];
    my_vec.remove(0);
}
```

What happens when we remove the number 9 from index 0? Well, all the other elements have to move one step left. The 8 in index 1 will move to index 0, the 7 in index 2 will move to index 1, and so on. It's sort of like a traffic jam. If you remove one car from the front, then all the rest have to move forward a bit.

With a big Vec, this is a *lot* of work for the computer. In fact, if you run it on the Playground, it will probably just give up because it's too much work. And if you run this on your own computer, it should take about a minute to finish:

```
fn main() {
    let mut my_vec = vec![0; 600_000];
    for _ in 0..600000 {
        my_vec.remove(0);
    }
}
```

It's easy to imagine why. We start with a Vec of 600,000 zeros. Every time you use remove(0) on it, it moves each remaining zero one space to the left. And then it does it 600,000 times. So that's 599,999 items moved, then 599,998 items moved, then 599,997 moves, and so on—600,000 times in total.

You don't have to worry about that with a VecDeque (it uses something called a ring buffer to make this possible). In general, it is a bit slower than a Vec, but if you have to do things on both ends, it is *much* faster, thanks to the buffer. You can use VecDeque::from() with a Vec to make one. Our previous code then looks like this:

```
use std::collections::VecDeque;

fn main() {
    let mut my_vec = VecDeque::from(vec![0; 600000]);
    for i in 0..600000 {
        my_vec.pop_front();      ◁─┐  pop_front is like .pop
    }                              │  but for the front.
}
```

It is now much faster, and the code on the Playground should finish in under a second.

That's the last collection type we have to learn in this book. For the rest of the chapter, we're going to change subjects a bit and learn some tips about error handling.

6.2   *The ? operator*

There is an even shorter way to deal with `Result`, shorter than `match` and even shorter than `if let`. It is called the "question mark operator," and you simply type `?` to use it. After anything that returns a `Result`, you can add `?`. This will

- Give what is inside the `Result` if it is `Ok`.
- Pass the error back if it is `Err` (this is called an early return).

In other words, it does almost everything for you.

> **NOTE**   The `?` operator works with `Option`, too, although the majority of the time you see it used to handle a `Result`.

We can try this with `.parse()` again. We will write a function called `parse_and_log_str` that tries to turn a `&str` into an `i32`, prints a message, and returns the number. It looks like this:

```
use std::num::ParseIntError;    ⟵┤ How did we know where to find this error
                                   type? We'll find out in just a moment.

fn parse_and_log_str(input: &str) -> Result<i32, ParseIntError> {
    let parsed_number = input.parse::<i32>()?;    ⟵
    println!("Number parsed successfully into {parsed_number}");
    Ok(parsed_number)
}
```

This is the key line in the function. If the &str parses successfully, you will have a variable called parsed_number that is an i32. If it doesn't parse successfully, the function ends here and returns an error.

This function takes a `&str`. If it is `Ok`, it gives an `i32` wrapped in `Ok`. If it is an `Err`, it returns a `ParseIntError`, and the function is over. So when we try to parse the number, we add `?`, which means "check whether it is an error, and give what is inside the `Result` if it is `Ok`." If it is not `Ok`, it will return the error, and the function ends. But if it is `Ok`, it will go to the next line, and the function will not need to return early. This is why we can then type `println!("Number parsed successfully into {parsed_number}");` because if it had returned an `Err`, the function would have already returned, and we never would have reached this line.

On the last line is the number inside of `Ok()`. We need to wrap it in `Ok` because the return value is `Result<i32, ParseIntError>`, not `i32`.

By the way, the `?` operator is just short for a `match`. You could write the `parse_str()` function without `?`, but it is a lot more typing. Here is what `?` does:

```
use std::num::ParseIntError;

fn parse_and_log_str(input: &str) -> Result<i32, ParseIntError> {
    let parsed_number = match input.parse::<i32>() {
        Ok(number) => number,
        Err(e) => return Err(e),
    };
    println!("Number parsed successfully into {parsed_number}");
    Ok(parsed_number)
}
```

Now, we can try out our function. Let's see what it does with a Vec of &strs.

```
use std::num::ParseIntError;

fn parse_and_log_str(input: &str) -> Result<i32, ParseIntError> {
    let parsed_number = input.parse::<i32>()?;
    println!("Number parsed successfully into {parsed_number}");
    Ok(parsed_number)
}

fn main() {
    let str_vec = vec!["Seven", "8", "9.0", "nice", "6060"];
    for item in str_vec {
        let parsed = parse_and_log_str(item);
        println!("Result: {parsed:?}");
    }
}
```

This prints

```
Result: Err(ParseIntError { kind: InvalidDigit })
Number parsed successfully into 8
Result: Ok(8)
Result: Err(ParseIntError { kind: InvalidDigit })
Result: Err(ParseIntError { kind: InvalidDigit })
Number parsed successfully into 6060
Result: Ok(6060)
```

You might be wondering how we know to use `std::num::ParseIntError`. One easy way
is to "ask" the compiler again (although if you have Rust installed and an IDE like Visual
Studio, then hovering your mouse over the type will show what the signature is):

```
fn main() {
    let failure = "Not a number".parse::<i32>();       Compiler: "What
    failure.rbrbrb();                            ◁┘    is rbrbrb()???"
}
```

The compiler doesn't understand why we are trying to call a method called `.rbrbrb()`
on a `Result` enum, and tells us what type we are trying to use this method on:

```
error[E0599]: no method named `rbrbrb` found for enum
➥`std::result::Result<i32, std::num::ParseIntError>` in the current scope
 --> src\main.rs:3:13
  |
3 |     failure.rbrbrb();
  |             ^^^^^^ method not found in `std::result::Result<i32,
 ➥std::num::ParseIntError>`
```

So `std::result::Result<i32, std::num::ParseIntError>` is the signature we need.
   We don't need to write `std::result::Result` because `Result` is always in scope
(in scope = ready to use). Rust does this for all the types we use a lot, so we don't have
to write `std::result::Result`, `std::collections::Vec`, etc. This full path is known
as the fully qualified path.

In our example with our `parse_int()` function, we are handling the result of the function inside `main()`. But is it possible to use the question mark inside `main()`? After all, `main` is expecting a return type of `()`, but the question mark operator here returns a `Result`, not `()`. The answer is yes: `main` can return a few other things besides `()`, one of which is `Result` (see https://doc.rust-lang.org/std/process/trait.Termination .html). Let's try parsing some numbers in `main()` and see what happens:

```
use std::num::ParseIntError;

fn main() -> Result<(), ParseIntError> {
    for item in vec!["89", "8", "9.0", "eleven", "6060"] {
        let parsed = item.parse::<u32>()?;      ◁─┐   Here we use the question mark operator.
        println!("{parsed}");                      │   What do you think will happen when
    }                                              │   we get a number that fails to parse?
    Ok(())      ◁─┐   Now main() expects a Result. If all of the
}               │   numbers parse, we will reach this line
                │   and now simply wrap an () inside of Ok.
```

Here is the output:

```
89
8
Error: ParseIntError { kind: InvalidDigit }
```

As you can see, the third item failed to parse and `main()` returned early instead of trying to parse the rest. Note that this was not a panic: the `main()` function simply returned early with an `Err` value.

So using the question mark operator in `main` should be used when you don't mind ending the whole program early when there is an error. One good example of this is if you are starting up an app that has a lot of components that all need to work properly: a certain file needs to be found, a connection to the database needs to be set up, and so on. In that case, you definitely want the program to end early if any of these go wrong so you can find the problem and fix it.

The `?` operator becomes even more useful once we know how to deal with multiple error types because you can use one `?` after another in a single line. At this point in the book, we don't know how to work with multiple error types at the same time, but we can put together a useless but quick example that will at least give you a taste. Instead of making an `i32` with `.parse()`, we'll do a lot more. We'll make a `u16`, then turn it to a `String`, then a `u32`, then to a `String` again, and finally to an `i32`:

```
use std::num::ParseIntError;

fn parse_str(input: &str) -> Result<i32, ParseIntError> {
    let parsed_number = input
        .parse::<u16>()?
        .to_string()
        .parse::<u32>()?
        .to_string()
        .parse::<i32>()?;
    println!("Number parsed successfully into {parsed_number}");
```

```
        Ok(parsed_number)
}

fn main() {
    let str_vec = vec!["Seven", "8", "9.0", "nice", "6060"];
    for item in str_vec {
        let parsed = parse_str(item);
        println!("{parsed:?}");
    }
}
```

The output is the same as the example before:

```
Err(ParseIntError { kind: InvalidDigit })
Number parsed successfully into 8
Ok(8)
Err(ParseIntError { kind: InvalidDigit })
Err(ParseIntError { kind: InvalidDigit })
Number parsed successfully into 6060
Ok(6060)
```

At the moment, we only know how to use ? when returning a single error type. Here is why. Imagine that you want to take some bytes, turn them into a String, and then parse it into a number. First, you need to successfully create a String from the bytes using a method called String::from_utf8(). And then it needs to successfully parse into a number. We could write it like this:

```
fn turn_into_string_and_parse(bytes: Vec<u8>) -> i32 {
    let as_string = String::from_utf8(bytes).unwrap();
    let as_num = as_string.parse::<i32>().unwrap();
    as_num
}

fn main() {
    let num = turn_into_string_and_parse(vec![49, 53, 53]);
    println!("{num}");
}
```

Fortunately, we give it an input that worked: the bytes 49, 53, and 53 turn into the String "155", which parses successfully into a 155. But this is bad error handling (actually, it's *no* error handling). If any input returns an Err, the whole program will panic. It would be nice to use the ? operator here in both cases. But as we start writing the code, we get to this point and stop:

```
use std::num::ParseIntError;
use std::string::FromUtf8Error;

fn turn_into_string_and_parse(bytes: Vec<u8>) ->
➡Result<i32, ????> {                              ◄────── What will the error type be? Two
    let num = String::from_utf8(bytes)?.parse::<i32>()?;  ◄── possible errors can be returned, but
    Ok(num)                                                   we only know how to return one.
}
```

This is what we would like to write if we only knew how. Then we could handle the error and do everything we want on a single line.

The problem is the return type. If `String::from_utf8()` fails, it will return `Err<FromUtf8Error>`. And if `.parse()` fails, it will return an `Err<ParseIntError>`. But we can't return a `Result<i32, ParseIntError or FromUtf8Error>`—the errors are completely different types. To solve this requires learning a lot more about traits. We will start to learn about traits in the next chapter, and by chapter 13, we will finally know enough to solve this problem. In the meantime, let's think about `panic!` and `.unwrap()` some more.

6.3   *When panic and unwrap are good*

Rust has a `panic!` macro that you can use to make it panic. It is easy to use:

```
fn main() {
    panic!();
}
```

Easy! The program panics and gives us this output:

```
thread 'main' panicked at 'explicit panic', src/main.rs:2:5
```

Or you can panic with a message:

```
fn main() {
    panic!("Time to panic!");
}
```

This time, the message `Time to panic!` displays when you run the program:

```
thread 'main' panicked at 'Time to panic!', src/main.rs:2:5
```

You will remember that `src/main.rs` is the directory and filename, and `2:3` is the line and column name. With this information, you can find the code and fix it.

`panic!` is a good macro to use to make sure that you know when something changes in your code. For example, the function called `print_all_three_things` always prints index `[0]`, `[1]`, and `[2]` from a vector. It is okay at the moment because we always give it a vector with three items:

```
fn print_all_three_things(vector: Vec<i32>) {
    println!("{}, {}, {}", vector[0], vector[1], vector[2]);
}

fn main() {
    let my_vec = vec![8, 9, 10];
    print_all_three_things(my_vec);
}
```

It prints `8, 9, 10`, and everything is fine.

But imagine that later on we write more and more code and forget that `my_vec` can only be three things. Now `my_vec` in this part has six things:

```
fn main() {
  let my_vec = vec![8, 9, 10, 10, 55, 99];
```

Now my_vec has six things.

```
    print_all_three_things(my_vec);
}

fn print_all_three_things(vector: Vec<i32>) {
  println!("{}, {}, {}", vector[0], vector[1], vector[2]);
}
```

No error happens because `[0]`, `[1]`, and `[2]` are all inside this longer vector. But what if it was really important to only have three items in the `Vec`? We wouldn't know that there was a problem because the program doesn't panic. This is known as a logic bug: the code runs fine, but the logic is wrong. Telling the code to panic in certain cases is a good way to watch out for logic bugs:

```
fn print_all_three_things(vector: Vec<i32>) {
    if vector.len() != 3 {
        panic!("my_vec must always have three items");
    }
    println!("{}, {}, {}", vector[0], vector[1], vector[2]);
}

fn main() {
    let my_vec = vec![8, 9, 10, 10, 55, 99];
    print_all_three_things(my_vec);
}
```

And now this code will panic as we told it to:

```
thread 'main' panicked at 'my_vec must always have three items',
  src/main.rs:3:9
```

Thanks to `panic!`, we now remember that `my_vec` should only have three items. So `panic!` is a good macro to create reminders in your code.

There are three other macros that are similar to `panic!` that you use a lot in testing. They are `assert!`, `assert_eq!`, and `assert_ne!`. Here is what they mean:

- `assert!`—If the part inside `()` is not true, the program will panic.
- `assert_eq!`—The two items inside `()` must be equal.
- `assert_ne!`—The two items inside `()` must not be equal (`ne` means "not equal").

Some examples are as follows:

```
fn main() {
    let my_name = "Loki Laufeyson";

    assert!(my_name == "Loki Laufeyson");
    assert_eq!(my_name, "Loki Laufeyson");
    assert_ne!(my_name, "Mithridates");
}
```

This will do nothing because all three assert macros are okay (this is what we want).

You can also add a message to these methods if you want:

```
fn main() {
    let my_name = "Loki Laufeyson";

    assert!(
        my_name == "Loki Laufeyson",
        "Name {my_name} is wrong: should be Loki Laufeyson"
    );
    assert_eq!(
        my_name, "Loki Laufeyson",
        "{my_name} and Loki Laufeyson should be equal"
    );
    assert_ne!(
        my_name, "Mithridates",
        "You entered {my_name}. Input must not equal Mithridates"
    );
}
```

These messages will only display if the program panics. So, if you run

```
fn main() {
    let my_name = "Mithridates";

    assert_ne!(
        my_name, "Mithridates",
        "You entered {my_name}. Input must not equal Mithridates"
    );
}
```

it will display

```
thread 'main' panicked at 'assertion failed: `(left != right)`
  left: `"Mithridates"`,
  right: `"Mithridates"`: You entered Mithridates. Input must not equal
➥Mithridates', src\main.rs:4:5
```

The output is telling us, "You said that left != right, but left == right." And it displays our custom message that says You entered Mithridates. Input must not equal Mithridates.

Unwrapping is also good when you are first writing your program and you want it to crash when there is a problem. Later, when your code is finished, it is good to change unwrap() to something else that won't crash. (You don't want a program to panic while a customer is using it.)

You can also use expect, which is like unwrap but a bit better because you give it your own message. Textbooks usually give this advice: "If you use unwrap a lot, at least use expect for better error messages."

This will crash:

```
fn get_fourth(input: &Vec<i32>) -> i32 {
    let fourth = input.get(3).unwrap();
    *fourth
}
```

```
fn main() {
    let my_vec = vec![9, 0, 10];
    let fourth = get_fourth(&my_vec);
}
```

The error message is

```
thread 'main' panicked at 'called Option::unwrap() on a None
➡value', src\main.rs:7:18.
```

Now we write our own message with `expect`:

```
fn get_fourth(input: &Vec<i32>) -> i32 {
    let fourth = input.get(3).expect("Input vector needs at least 4 items");
    *fourth
}

fn main() {
    let my_vec = vec![9, 0, 10];
    let fourth = get_fourth(&my_vec);
}
```

It crashes again, but the error is better:

```
thread 'main' panicked at 'Input vector needs at least 4 items',
        src\main.rs:7:18
```

So `expect` is a little better than `unwrap`, but it will still panic on `None`. The `.expect()` method is also good for documentation because it allows anyone reading your code to have an idea of what could go wrong and where.

Now, here is an example of a bad practice: a function that tries to unwrap two times. It takes a `Vec<Option<i32>>`, so maybe each part will have a `Some<i32>` or maybe a `None`:

```
fn try_two_unwraps(input: Vec<Option<i32>>) {
    println!("Index 0 is: {}", input[0].unwrap());
    println!("Index 1 is: {}", input[1].unwrap());
}

fn main() {
    let vector = vec![None, Some(1000)];        ⬅┐ This vector has a
    try_two_unwraps(vector);                      │ None, so it will panic.
}
```

The message is

```
thread 'main' panicked at 'called Option::unwrap() on a None
➡value', src\main.rs:2:32
```

We're not sure if it was the first `unwrap` or the second `unwrap` until we check the line, and in a large codebase, it can take a bit of time to find the exact file and line where a panic occurred. It would be better to check the length and also not to unwrap. But with `expect`, at least it will be a *little* better. Here it is with `expect`:

```
fn try_two_unwraps(input: Vec<Option<i32>>) {
    println!(
        "Index 0 is: {}",
        input[0].expect("The first unwrap had a None!")
    );
    println!(
        "Index 1 is: {}",
        input[1].expect("The second unwrap had a None!")
    );
}

fn main() {
    let vector = vec![None, Some(1000)];
    try_two_unwraps(vector);
}
```

So that is a bit better:

```
thread 'main' panicked at 'The first unwrap had a None!', src\main.rs:2:32
```

We have the line number as well so we can find it.

There is another method called .unwrap_or() that is useful if you want to always have a value that you want to choose. If you do this, it will never panic, which is good because your program won't panic, but maybe not good if you want the program to panic if there's a problem.

But usually, we don't want our program to panic, so .unwrap_or() is a good method to use:

```
fn main() {
    let my_vec = vec![8, 9, 10];

    let fourth = my_vec.get(3).unwrap_or(&0);
    println!("{fourth}");
}
```

If .get doesn't work, we will make the value &0. .get() returns a reference, so we need &0 and not 0 to match it. You can also write "let *fourth" with a * if you want fourth to be a 0 and not a &0.

This prints 0 because .unwrap_or(&0) gives a zero even if it is a None. It will never panic.

This chapter was a lot of expansion of what you already know, so it probably wasn't too hard. You learned some extra collection types on top of the ones you already know, and we learned more about error handling. The question mark operator is new, but it's still based on what you already know: matching on a Result. But in the next chapter, we will learn something new: how traits work and how to write our own traits.

Summary

- For keys and values, usually use HashMap. Change Hash to BTree if you need alphabetical order.
- If you want to know whether something exists or not, use a HashSet. Change Hash to BTree if you need an ordered collection.

- `VecDeque` is slower than `Vec` unless you need to work from both the front and back. In that case, `VecDeque` is a *lot* faster.
- A `BinaryHeap` always has the largest value at the front. Everything else is unsorted.
- Using `?` is convenient because it automatically pulls out the `Ok` value from a `Result`. If the value is an `Err`, it will exit the function early and return the `Err`.
- With `Result` and `Option`, you can avoid the program panicking, but sometimes a panic can make sense.

Traits: Making different
types do the same thing

This chapter covers

- The basics of how to write your own traits
- Method signatures in traits
- More complex trait examples
- The `From` trait
- The orphan rule—what you're allowed to implement a trait on
- Taking a `String` or a `&str` in a function

We've touched on traits a little bit here and there in the book so far, but now it's time to give them some needed attention. Understanding traits and how they work will let us give traits to our own types and even make our own.

7.1 Traits: The basics

We have seen traits before: `Debug`, `Copy`, and `Clone` are all traits. The easiest way to think of traits is as *powers* or *qualifications*. If a type has a trait, it can do things it couldn't do before. Also, if a type has a trait, you can guarantee to the compiler that it can do something—no matter what type it is.

To give a trait to a type, you have to implement that trait for that type. "Type X implements Trait Y" means that Type X definitely has the methods of Trait Y. Type X can have its own separate methods, too, and Type X might implement other traits as well. A human equivalent would be that Person X might decide to take the bar exam to become a lawyer. But Person X might have other qualifications, too, and might have other personal skills, such as being able to type really fast.

Rust uses a special syntax called attributes to automatically implement traits like `Debug` because they are so common. That's what happens when you write `#[derive(Debug)]`: you are automatically implementing the `Debug` trait. So, all you need to do to implement that trait is this:

```
#[derive(Debug)]
struct MyStruct {
    number: usize,
}
```

You can manually implement `Debug` yourself, too, if you want to, but most of the time, people are happy with using `derive` to do it.

But other traits are more difficult for the compiler to guess, so you can't use `derive` to implement them. Those traits need to be manually implemented with the `impl` keyword. A good example is the `Add` trait (found at `std::ops::Add`), which is used to add two things. Any type that implements the `Add` trait can use the + operator to add. But Rust can't guess how you want to add things, so you have to tell it. Take this struct, for example:

```
struct ThingsToAdd {
    first_thing: u32,
    second_thing: f32,
}
```

It has a `u32` and an `f32` inside it. If you want to add a `ThingsToAdd` to another `ThingsToAdd`, how do you want to do it? Do you want to

- Add `first_thing` to the other `first_thing` and `second_thing` to the other `second_thing` to return a new `ThingsToAdd`?
- Add both properties together and return a `u32`?
- Add both properties together and return an `f32`?
- Turn both properties into a `String` and stick them next to each other?
- Do something else?

Rust can't guess what you want, which is why there is no way to use `#[derive(Add)]` to give a type the `Add` trait.

Before we derive other traits, let's first look at how to make a trait. The important thing to remember about traits is that they are about behavior. To make a trait, write `trait` and then create some methods for it:

```
struct Dog {                         A simple struct—an Animal
    name: String,                    only has a name
}

struct Parrot {          Another simple struct
    name: String,
}
                              The dog trait gives
trait DogLike {           some functionality
    fn bark(&self) {               It can bark.
        println!("Woof woof!");
    }
    fn run(&self) {                And it can run.
        println!("The dog is running!");
    }
}
                                   Now, Animal has
impl DogLike for Dog {}            the trait DogLike.
impl DogLike for Parrot {}         Anything else can
                                   implement DogLike, too.
fn main() {
    let rover = Dog {
        name: "Rover".to_string(),
    };

    let brian = Parrot {
        name: "Brian".to_string(),
    };
                             Now Dog can
    rover.bark();           use bark()    And it can
    rover.run();                          use run(),
    brian.bark();           Brian the parrot
}                           learned to bark, too.
```

This prints

```
Woof woof!
The dog is running!
Woof woof!
```

Now, if we were to call `brian.run();` on the previous code, it would print `The dog is running!` even though we are calling the method on a `Parrot`. What if you don't want to print `The dog is running`? Can you do that?

The answer is yes, but you have to have the same signature. That means it needs to take the same things and return the same things. For example, we can change the method `.run()`, but we have to follow the signature. The signature says

```
fn run(&self) {
    println!("The dog is running!");
}
```

`fn run(&self)` means "fn run() takes &self and returns nothing." So you can't return something different like this:

```
fn run(&self) -> i32 {
    5
}
```

Rust will tell you that the signature is wrong. The method always has to return nothing, but now it's returning an i32:

```
= note: expected fn pointer `fn(&Animal)`
            found fn pointer `fn(&Animal) -> i32`
```

But we can do this:

```
struct Parrot {
    name: String,
}

trait DogLike {
    fn bark(&self) {                    ◁── It can bark.
        println!("Woof woof!");
    }
    fn run(&self) {                     ◁── And it can run.
        println!("The dog is running!");
    }
}                                       We're implementing the trait
                                        ourselves and writing the run
impl DogLike for Parrot{   ◁────────── method the way we want to.
    fn run(&self) {
        println!("{} the parrot is running!", self.name);   ◁─────────┐
    }
}
                                This is the interesting part. The trait itself can't
                                call self.name because it doesn't know which
fn main() {                     types will implement it and whether they have a
    let brian = Parrot {        name property or not. But we know that Parrot
        name: "Brian".to_string(),   has a name property, so we can use it here.
    };

    brian.bark();
    brian.run();
}
```

Now it prints Brian the parrot is running! This is okay because we are returning ()
or nothing, which is what the method signature tells us to do.

7.1.1 All you need are the method signatures

You need to be able to write your own methods for a trait because you never know
what type might use it. In fact, you can just write the function signature when making
a trait. Many traits write most of their methods like this.

Now, when you do that, the user will have to write the function. Let's try that. We
will change .bark() and .run() to fn bark(&self); and fn run(&self);. These
methods are now incomplete, which means that any type implementing them must
write out the methods themselves:

```
struct Animal {
    name: String,
}

trait DogLike {
    fn bark(&self);
    fn run(&self);
}

impl DogLike for Animal {
    fn bark(&self) {
        println!("{}, stop barking!!", self.name);
    }
    fn run(&self) {
        println!("{} is running!", self.name);
    }
}

fn main() {
    let rover = Animal {
        name: "Rover".to_string(),
    };

    rover.bark();
    rover.run();
}
```

The method .bark() says it needs a &self and returns nothing. .run() says it needs a &self and returns nothing. So now we have to write them ourselves.

So when you create a trait, you must think: "Which methods should I write? And which ones should the user write?" If you think most users will use the methods the same way every time, it makes sense for you to write a default method inside the trait. But if you think that users will use the methods differently every time, write the signature.

So now that you know how to impl a trait, let's try implementing someone else's trait for your own type: the Display trait. First, we will make a simple struct:

```
struct Cat {
    name: String,
    age: u8,
}

fn main() {
    let mr_mantle = Cat {
        name: "Reggie Mantle".to_string(),
        age: 4,
    };
}
```

Now we want to print mr_mantle. The Debug trait is easy to derive:

```
#[derive(Debug)]
struct Cat {
    name: String,
    age: u8,
}
```

```
fn main() {
    let mr_mantle = Cat {
        name: "Reggie Mantle".to_string(),
        age: 4,
    };
    println!("Mr. Mantle is a {mr_mantle:?}");
}
```

But Debug print is not exactly the prettiest way to print. Here is what the output for our `Cat` struct looks like:

```
Mr. Mantle is a Cat { name: "Reggie Mantle", age: 4 }
```

So we should implement `Display` for `Cat` if we want to display it exactly the way we want. In the documentation for the Display trait (https://doc.rust-lang.org/std/fmt/trait.Display.html), we can see the general information for `Display`, along with one example. Here is the example that it gives:

```
use std::fmt;

struct Position {
    longitude: f32,
    latitude: f32,
}

impl fmt::Display for Position {
    fn fmt(&self, f: &mut fmt::Formatter<'_>) -> fmt::Result {
        write!(f, "({}, {})", self.longitude, self.latitude)
    }
}
```

Some parts of the previous code we don't understand yet, like what `<'_>` and this `f` variable are doing. But the `Position` struct is pretty easy to understand: it is just two `f32`s. We also understand that `self.longitude` and `self.latitude` are the fields in the struct.

   Maybe we can take this code for our struct and change the code to `self.name` and `self.age`. Also, the `write!` macro looks a lot like `println!`, so it is pretty familiar. Let's steal the code and change it a bit. We'll change

```
write!(f, "({}, {})", self.longitude, self.latitude)
```

to

```
write!(f, "{} is a cat who is {} years old.", self.name, self.age)
```

Now the code to implement `Display` for our `Cat` struct looks like this:

```
use std::fmt;

struct Cat {
    name: String,
    age: u8,
}
```

```
impl fmt::Display for Cat {
    fn fmt(&self, f: &mut fmt::Formatter<'_>) -> fmt::Result {
        write!(f, "{} is a cat who is {} years old", self.name, self.age)
    }
}
```

Let's add a `fn main()` and print our `Cat` out:

```
use std::fmt;

struct Cat {
    name: String,
    age: u8,
}

impl fmt::Display for Cat {
    fn fmt(&self, f: &mut fmt::Formatter<'_>) -> fmt::Result {
        write!(f, "{} is a cat who is {} years old", self.name, self.age)
    }
}

fn main() {
    let mr_mantle = Cat {
        name: "Reggie Mantle".to_string(),
        age: 4,
    };
    println!("{mr_mantle}");
}
```

Success! We can use {} to print our `Cat`, which gives us the output `Reggie Mantle is a cat who is 4 years old`. This looks much better.

Sometimes implementing a trait gives you some extra, unexpected benefits. For example, if you implement `Display` for a type, you get the `ToString` trait for free, which gives you the `.to_string()` method that we already know. If you want to turn your type into a `String`, simply implement `Display`. (The reason is that `ToString` uses a *blanket implementation*, which means that it implements itself on any type that has `Display`. We'll learn how to do blanket implementations later.)

We could do something like this, where we pass `reggie_mantle` to a function that wants a `String` or anything else:

```
use std::fmt;
struct Cat {
    name: String,
    age: u8,
}

impl fmt::Display for Cat {
    fn fmt(&self, f: &mut fmt::Formatter<'_>) -> fmt::Result {
        write!(f, "{} is a cat who is {} years old", self.name, self.age)
    }
}
```

```
fn print_excitedly(input: String) {
    println!("{input}!!!!!");
}

fn main() {
    let mr_mantle = Cat {
        name: "Reggie Mantle".to_string(),
        age: 4,
    };

    print_excitedly(mr_mantle.to_string());
    println!(
        "Mr. Mantle's String is {} letters long.",
        mr_mantle.to_string().chars().count()
    );
}
```

Turns Mr. Mantle into a String and passes it into this function

Turns Mr. Mantle into chars and counts them. Be sure to use .chars().count() and not .len() unless you know each character will only be 1 byte in length!

This prints

```
Reggie Mantle is a cat who is 4 years old!!!!!
Mr. Mantle's String is 41 letters long.
```

The thing to remember about traits is that they are about the shared behavior of something. How does your struct or enum act? What can it do? And how can you easily show that your type, and other types, all have this behavior? That's what traits are for. If you think of some of the traits we've seen so far, they are all about behavior: Copy is something that a type can do. Display is also something that a type can do. ToString is another trait, and it's also something that a type can do: it can change into a String. And with these traits, we can prove that any type that implements them will all have these abilities.

The trait examples have been pretty simple so far. Let's look at some examples of where we might actually want to make our own traits.

7.1.2 More complex examples

Let's look at another example that is even more connected to just behavior. We'll imagine a fantasy game with some simple characters. One is a Monster; the other two are Wizard and Ranger. There is a Monster that just has health so we can attack it, and the other two don't have anything yet. But we made two traits. One is called Fight-Close and lets you fight up close. The other is FightFromDistance, which lets you fight from far away. Only Ranger can use FightFromDistance. Let's try putting that together to see what it looks like:

```
trait FightClose {
    fn attack_with_sword(&self, opponent: &mut Monster) {
        opponent.health -= 10;
        println!(
            "Sword attack! Your opponent has {} health left.",
            opponent.health
        );
```

```
    }
    fn attack_with_hand(&self, opponent: &mut Monster) {
        opponent.health -= 2;
        println!(
            "Hand attack! Your opponent has {} health left.",
            opponent.health
        );
    }
}
impl FightClose for Wizard {}
impl FightClose for Ranger {}

trait FightFromDistance {
    fn attack_with_bow(&self, opponent: &mut Monster, distance: u32) {
        if distance < 10 {
            opponent.health -= 10;
            println!(
                "Bow attack! Your opponent has {} health left.",
                opponent.health
            );
        }
    }
    fn attack_with_rock(&self, opponent: &mut Monster, distance: u32) {
        if distance < 3 {
            opponent.health -= 4;
        }
        println!(
            "Rock attack! Your opponent has {} health left.",
            opponent.health
        );
    }
}impl FightFromDistance for Ranger {}

fn main() {
    let radagast = Wizard {};
    let aragorn = Ranger {};

    let mut uruk_hai = Monster { health: 40 };

    radagast.attack_with_sword(&mut uruk_hai);
    aragorn.attack_with_bow(&mut uruk_hai, 8);
}
```

This prints

```
Sword attack! Your opponent has 30 health left.
Bow attack! Your opponent has 20 health left.
```

We pass &self inside traits all the time, but we can't do much with it right now. That's because Rust doesn't know what type is going to use it. It could be a Wizard, it could be a Ranger, it could be a new struct called Toefocfgetobjodd, or anything else. So far, these traits are better as regular methods because at least we would have access to a *concrete* &self and not just a &self that represents *some* type that will implement the trait.

If the type inside a trait's definition can be anything, what can we do to make `&self` more useful? It would be nice to get *some* idea of what types will use it and what they can do. To give it some functionality, we can add *trait bounds* (necessary traits) to the signature. If we want to print with `{:?}`, for example, we need `Debug`. You can add it to the trait by writing it after `:` (a colon). Now our code looks like this:

```
use std::fmt::Debug;

struct Monster {
    health: i32,
}

#[derive(Debug)]
struct Wizard {
    health: i32,
}
#[derive(Debug)]
struct Ranger {
    health: i32,
}

trait DisplayHealth {
    fn health(&self) -> i32;
}

trait FightClose: Debug {
    fn attack_with_sword(&self, opponent: &mut Monster) {
        opponent.health -= 10;
        println!(
            "Sword attack! Opponent's health: {}. You are now at: {:?}",
            opponent.health, self
        );
    }
    fn attack_with_hand(&self, opponent: &mut Monster) {
        opponent.health -= 2;
        println!(
            "Hand attack! Opponent's health: {}. You are now at: {:?}",
            opponent.health, self
        );
    }
}
impl FightClose for Wizard {}
impl FightClose for Ranger {}

trait FightFromDistance: Debug {
    fn attack_with_bow(&self, opponent: &mut Monster, distance: u32) {
        if distance < 10 {
            opponent.health -= 10;
            println!(
                "Bow attack! Opponent's health: {}. You are now at: {:?}",
                opponent.health, self
            );
        }
    }
}
```

Wizard and Ranger implement Debug. They also have a property called health now.

With this bound, any type needs Debug first to implement FightClose. They are guaranteed to have the Debug trait.

With that guarantee, we can use {:?} to print out &self.

```
    fn attack_with_rock(&self, opponent: &mut Monster, distance: u32) {
        if distance < 3 {
            opponent.health -= 4;
        }
        println!(
            "Rock attack! Opponent's health: {}.  You are now at: {:?}",
            opponent.health, self
        );
    }
}
impl FightFromDistance for Ranger {}

fn main() {
    let radagast = Wizard { health: 60 };
    let aragorn = Ranger { health: 80 };

    let mut uruk_hai = Monster { health: 40 };

    radagast.attack_with_sword(&mut uruk_hai);
    aragorn.attack_with_bow(&mut uruk_hai, 8);
}
```

This prints

```
Sword attack! Opponent's health: 30. You are now at: Wizard { health: 60 }
Bow attack! Opponent's health: 20. You are now at: Ranger { health: 80 }
```

In a real game, it might be better to rewrite this for each type because You are now at: Wizard { health: 60 } looks funny. Or you could require Display instead of just Debug. Methods inside traits are usually simple because you don't know what type is going to use it. You can't write things like self.0 += 10, for example. But this example shows that we can use other traits inside a trait we are writing, and that helps.

You might have noticed that the trait methods need a Monster, which is a concrete type. That might be a bit limiting unless we only have a single Monster struct for our whole game. You could rewrite the methods so that instead of a Monster, it takes any type that implements a trait called TakeDamage, for example.

Let's do that with generics. We'll make a trait called MonsterBehavior. We'll give it a method .take_damage(), and another one called .display_self(). It looks like this:

```
trait MonsterBehavior: Debug {
    fn take_damage(&mut self, damage: i32);
    fn display_self(&self) {
        println!("The monster is now: {self:?}");
    }
}
```

You'll notice three things here:

- It's written MonsterBehavior: Debug, so to implement this trait, a type needs to have Debug. That's because we want to Debug print it.

- The `.take_damage()` method isn't written out because we have no idea how to do it. Will a struct have a `.health` parameter or something else to do this? No idea. But it takes a `&mut self` so it can be changed and a `damage: i32`, which shows what the damage is. With that information, we can implement it for `Monster`, and others can implement it for their types, too.

- We write out the `.display_self()` method because we know a type will at least have `Debug`. But if you implement it for a type that has `Display`, you can print it out that way. Or maybe you want to implement it differently, too—it's your choice.

The code looks like this:

```
use std::fmt::Debug;

trait MonsterBehavior: Debug {
    fn take_damage(&mut self, damage: i32);
    fn display_self(&self) {
        println!("The monster is now: {self:?}");
    }
}

#[derive(Debug)]
struct Monster {
    health: i32,
}

impl MonsterBehavior for Monster {          We implement the
    fn take_damage(&mut self, damage: i32) {   trait for Monster.
        self.health -= damage;
    }
}

#[derive(Debug)]
struct Wizard {
    health: i32,
}
#[derive(Debug)]
struct Ranger {
    health: i32,
}                       And now the opponents are all
                        &mut T, and T is guaranteed to
trait FightClose {      implement MonsterBehavior.
    fn attack_with_sword<T: MonsterBehavior>(&self, opponent: &mut T) {
        println!("You attack with your sword!");
        opponent.take_damage(10);
        opponent.display_self();       And we can call
    }                                  this one, too.

    fn attack_with_hand<T: MonsterBehavior>(&self, opponent: &mut T) {
        println!("You attack with your hand!");
        opponent.take_damage(2);
        opponent.display_self();                     And so on, for the
    }                                                rest of the code
```

So we can call this method.

```
}
impl FightClose for Wizard {}
impl FightClose for Ranger {}

trait FightFromDistance: Debug {
    fn attack_with_bow<T: MonsterBehavior>(&self, opponent: &mut T,
    ➡distance: u32) {
        println!("You attack with your bow!");
        if distance < 10 {
            opponent.take_damage(10);
        } else {
            println!("Too far away!");
        }
        opponent.display_self();
    }
    fn attack_with_rock<T: MonsterBehavior>(&self, opponent: &mut T,
    ➡distance: u32) {
        println!("You attack with a rock!");
        if distance < 3 {
            opponent.take_damage(4);
        } else {
            println!("Too far away!");
        }
        opponent.display_self();
    }
}
impl FightFromDistance for Ranger {}

fn main() {
    let radagast = Wizard { health: 60 };
    let aragorn = Ranger { health: 80 };

    let mut uruk_hai = Monster { health: 40 };

    radagast.attack_with_sword(&mut uruk_hai);
    aragorn.attack_with_bow(&mut uruk_hai, 8);
}
```

This prints

```
You attack with your sword!
The monster is now: Monster { health: 30 }
You attack with your bow!
The monster is now: Monster { health: 20 }
```

7.1.3   *Traits as bounds*

Interestingly, a trait doesn't need to have any methods at all. That's because even a trait that doesn't have any methods can still be used as a trait bound. In other words, the trait must be implemented even though it doesn't add any new functionality.

Imagine you are going to court, and you need a good lawyer to do fn argue_in_court() for you. Your bounds for this function would probably be Lawyer and Experienced. Any type of person could do the function as long as they have these two traits: they are "bound" to have them. That means that any type that you want to pass into argue_in_court() will need to impl Lawyer and impl Experienced first. This is basically the same as the bar exam in real life: courts have the "trait bound" that only people who have passed the bar exam can act as lawyers. And any "type" (any person) who wants to be one will have to "implement" this before they can argue as lawyers in a court.

So trait bounds can be really easy because a trait doesn't need any methods or anything at all. Let's rewrite our previous code in a somewhat different way. (We'll use the concrete Monster struct again to make it simple.) This time, our trait doesn't have any methods, but instead, we have other functions that require traits to use:

```rust
use std::fmt::Debug;

struct Monster {
    health: i32,
}

#[derive(Debug)]
struct Wizard {
    health: i32,
}
#[derive(Debug)]
struct Ranger {
    health: i32,
}

trait Magic {}                        // No methods for any of these
trait FightClose {}                   //    traits! They are just trait bounds.
trait FightFromDistance {}            // Each type gets
                                      //    FightClose.

impl FightClose for Ranger {}
impl FightClose for Wizard {}         // But only Ranger gets
impl FightFromDistance for Ranger {}  //    FightFromDistance.
impl Magic for Wizard {}              // And only Wizard
                                      //    gets Magic.
fn attack_with_bow<T>(pc: &T, opponent: &mut Monster, distance: u32)
where
    T: FightFromDistance + Debug,
{
    if distance < 10 {
        opponent.health -= 10;
        println!(
            "Bow attack! Opponent's health: {}.  You are now at: {pc:?}",
            opponent.health
        );
    }
}

fn attack_with_sword<T>(pc: &T, opponent: &mut Monster)
where
    T: FightClose + Debug,
{
    opponent.health -= 10;
    println!(
```

```
            "Sword attack! Opponent's health: {}. You are now at: {pc:?}",
            opponent.health
        );
}

fn fireball<T>(pc: &T, opponent: &mut Monster, distance: u32)
where
    T: Magic + Debug,
{
    if distance < 15 {
        opponent.health -= 20;
        println!(
            "A massive fireball! Opponent's health: {}. You are now at:
            ➥{pc:?}",
            opponent.health
        );
    }
}

fn main() {
    let radagast = Wizard { health: 60 };
    let aragorn = Ranger { health: 80 };

    let mut uruk_hai = Monster { health: 40 };

    attack_with_sword(&radagast, &mut uruk_hai);
    attack_with_bow(&aragorn, &mut uruk_hai, 8);
    fireball(&radagast, &mut uruk_hai, 8);
}
```

This prints almost the same thing:

```
Sword attack! Opponent's health: 30. You are now at: Wizard { health: 60 }
Bow attack! Opponent's health: 20.  You are now at: Ranger { health: 80 }
```

A massive fireball! Opponent's health: 0. You are now at: `Wizard { health: 60 }` So you can see there are many ways to do the same thing when you use traits. It all depends on what makes the most sense for the program that you are writing.

7.1.4   *Traits are like qualifications*

The more examples of traits you see, the easier it is to get a feel for how they work. So let's finish up the overview of traits in this chapter by imagining a whole bunch of imaginary traits and how they might work. We'll look at their names and then think about which types should implement them.

First, sometimes, people who use other languages look at traits and think that they are just like classes or interfaces. (If you don't know what classes or interfaces are, don't worry—Rust doesn't have them.) And while traits do look like classes, it's easier to think of them as qualifications. Let's think of a few:

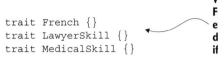

```
trait French {}
trait LawyerSkill {}
trait MedicalSkill {}
```

With effort, anyone can learn French, anyone can take the bar exam, anyone can get a medical degree. You can even get all three if you work for it.

Now let's imagine some structs. Which of those three traits does it make sense for them to implement?

```
struct FrenchCitizen;
struct ExchangeStudentInFrance;
struct AmericanLawyer;
struct AmericanDoctor;
struct FrenchLawyer;
struct FrenchDoctor;
struct MrKnowsEverything;
```

Some structs. Based on their name, what trait(s) do you think they should have?

Let's start implementing the French trait for the following types.

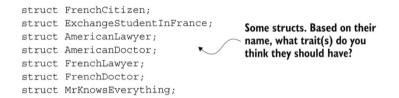

```
impl French for FrenchCitizen {}
impl French for ExchangeStudentInFrance {}
impl French for FrenchLawyer {}
impl French for FrenchDoctor {}
impl French for MrKnowsEverything {}
```

Lots of them speak French...

Next is the trait called LawyerSkill. Which types should implement it?

```
impl LawyerSkill for AmericanLawyer {}
impl LawyerSkill for FrenchLawyer {}
impl LawyerSkill for MrKnowsEverything {}
```

Some of them took the bar exam...

Can some of them work as doctors? Looks like it. So let's give the MedicalSkill trait to those types.

```
impl MedicalSkill for AmericanDoctor {}
impl MedicalSkill for FrenchDoctor {}
impl MedicalSkill for MrKnowsEverything {}
```

And some of them got a medical degree. (MrKnowsEverything really knows everything!)

Now let's make some functions and use these traits as bounds. We don't care what type goes in, as long as it implements the right trait (or traits).

Now time for some generic functions. They can take any type, as long as they are qualified to go in.

```
fn speak_french<T: French>(speaker: T) {}
fn enter_court<T: LawyerSkill>(lawyer: T) {}
fn cure_patient<T: MedicalSkill>(doctor: T) {}
fn enter_french_court<T: LawyerSkill + French>(lawyer: T) {}
fn cure_french_patient<T: MedicalSkill + French>(doctor: T) {}
fn present_medical_case_in_french_court<T: MedicalSkill + French +
➥ LawyerSkill>(lawyer: T) {}
```

Now everything will match up, and the compiler won't complain.

Now we'll start main() and call some of these functions.

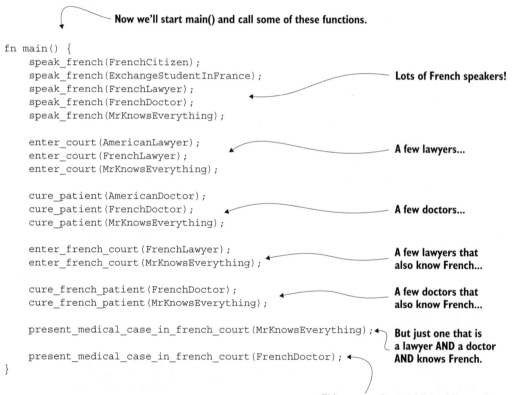

```
fn main() {
    speak_french(FrenchCitizen);
    speak_french(ExchangeStudentInFrance);          Lots of French speakers!
    speak_french(FrenchLawyer);
    speak_french(FrenchDoctor);
    speak_french(MrKnowsEverything);

    enter_court(AmericanLawyer);
    enter_court(FrenchLawyer);                        A few lawyers...
    enter_court(MrKnowsEverything);

    cure_patient(AmericanDoctor);
    cure_patient(FrenchDoctor);                       A few doctors...
    cure_patient(MrKnowsEverything);

    enter_french_court(FrenchLawyer);                 A few lawyers that
    enter_french_court(MrKnowsEverything);            also know French...

    cure_french_patient(FrenchDoctor);                A few doctors that
    cure_french_patient(MrKnowsEverything);           also know French...

    present_medical_case_in_french_court(MrKnowsEverything);   But just one that is
                                                               a lawyer AND a doctor
    present_medical_case_in_french_court(FrenchDoctor);        AND knows French.
}
```

This one won't work! FrenchDoctor has French and MedicalSkill but not LawyerSkill.

That was a lot of comparisons and examples! Traits can take a long time to get used to, so the more comparisons and examples, the better. Now that you have an idea of how traits work, the next step is to start looking at real traits you'll use a lot in your code. Let's start by looking at how to implement one of the main traits you will use in Rust.

7.2   *The From trait*

From is a very convenient trait to use, and you know this because you have seen it so much already. With From, you can make a String from a &str, but you can make many types from many other types. For example, Vec uses From for 18 (!) types. Here are the ones we know:

```
From<&'_ [T]>
From<&'_ mut [T]>
From<&'_ str>
From<&'a Vec<T>>
From<[T; N]>
From<BinaryHeap<T>>
From<String>>
From<Vec<T>>
From<VecDeque<T>>
```

You can see these implementations on the left side of the documentation for Vec (https://doc.rust-lang.org/std/vec/struct.Vec.html). That's a lot of Vec::from() that we haven't tried yet! Let's experiment with some of these and see what happens. We will try making a Vec from [T; N], the generic name for an array (the technical term is *const generics.*, which we will learn more about in chapter 16). T stands for type, and N stands for number), plus a String and a &str:

```
fn main() {
    let array_vec = Vec::from([8, 9, 10]);
    println!("Vec from array: {array_vec:?}");

    let str_vec = Vec::from("What kind of Vec am I?");
    println!("Vec from str: {str_vec:?}");

    let string_vec = Vec::from("What will a String be?".to_string());
    println!("Vec from String: {string_vec:?}");
}
```

It prints

```
Vec from array: [8, 9, 10]
Vec from str: [87, 104, 97, 116, 32, 107, 105, 110, 100, 32, 111, 102, 32,
➡86, 101, 99, 32, 97, 109, 32, 73, 63]
Vec from String: [87, 104, 97, 116, 32, 119, 105, 108, 108, 32, 97, 32, 83,
➡116, 114, 105, 110, 103, 32, 98, 101, 63]
```

The first one is no surprise: a Vec from an array of three numbers shows the three numbers. But the Vecs from &str and String are all bytes! If you look at the signature for `Vec` from `&str` and `String`, you can see that they return a `Vec<u8>`. Here is the full code, which is quite simple:

```
fn from(string: String) -> Vec<u8> {
    string.into_bytes()
}
```

You can see that `From` is quite simple: all you have to do is choose two types and decide which one you want to turn into the other. After that, it's completely up to you how to make it happen. In this case, the creators of the standard library decided that it would be convenient to implement `From<String>` for `Vec<u8>`. Let's try implementing `From` with our own types.

We'll make two structs and then implement `From` for one of them. One struct will be `City`, and the other will be `Country`. We want to be able to write this code: `let country_name = Country::from(vector_of_cities)`.

It looks like this:

```
#[derive(Debug)]
struct City {
    name: String,
    population: u32,
}

impl City {
    fn new(name: &str, population: u32) -> Self {        ◁─── Nothing special here—just a
        Self {                                                 convenience function that will
            name: name.to_string(),                            do the .to_string() part for us
            population,
        }
    }
}
#[derive(Debug)]
struct Country {                    ┐ Our cities
    cities: Vec<City>,      ◁───────┘ go in here.
}

impl From<Vec<City>> for Country {
    fn from(cities: Vec<City>) -> Self {      ┐ And here is our implementation
        Self { cities }                ◁──────┘ of From. Pretty simple!
    }
}
impl Country {                              ┐ Prints the cities
    fn print_cities(&self) {      ◁─────────┘ in a Country      ┐ Here we use & because
        for city in &self.cities {                    ◁────────┘ City isn't a Copy type.
            println!(
                "{:?} has a population of {:?}.",
                city.name, city.population
            );
        }
    }
}
fn main() {
    let helsinki = City::new("Helsinki", 631_695);
    let turku = City::new("Turku", 186_756);
```

```
let finland_cities = vec![helsinki, turku];
let finland = Country::from(finland_cities);

finland.print_cities();
}
```

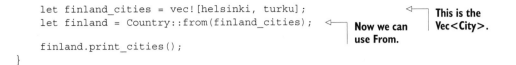

Now we can use From.

This is the Vec<City>.

This prints

```
"Helsinki" has a population of 631695.
"Turku" has a population of 186756.
```

While reading this section, you might have gotten some ideas for implementing `From` on some other types you know in the standard library. But you're not always allowed to! Let's find out why.

7.3   *The orphan rule*

You can imagine that `From` would be easy to implement on types you didn't create like `Vec`, `i32`, and so on. But hold on, there's one rule that Rust has about this. It's called the *orphan rule*:

- You can implement *your* trait on someone else's type.
- You can implement *someone else's* trait on your type.
- However, you can't implement *someone else's* trait on *someone else's* type.

That's because if anyone could implement anyone's trait on anyone's type, you could never keep a single type consistent. Maybe you created a type for others to use that you planned to `impl Display` on later, but someone else already did it in their own way! Now, other people are using your code in a way you didn't intend. If one person imports it from your code, it will display in one way, but if imported from somewhere else, it will display in another. Or it could be a much more serious problem, like if your type is used for cryptographic security and you want very tight control over how it is used. A company might use your type, thinking it is the one you made, but it was actually your type plus a number of changes made by other people without asking you. The orphan rule prevents that.

So what's the best way to get around the orphan rule? The easiest way is to wrap someone else's type in a tuple struct, thereby creating an entirely new type. This is called the newtype idiom, and we will learn that now.

7.4   *Getting around the orphan rule with newtypes*

Let's look at the so-called newtype idiom. It is actually quite simple: wrap someone else's type in a tuple struct. Let's imagine that we want a type called `File`, which, for the moment, will only contain a `String`:

```
struct File(String);
```

File is a wrapper around String.

```
fn main() {
    let my_file = File(String::from("I am file contents"));
    let my_string = String::from("I am file contents");
}
```

Because this is now a new type, it doesn't have any of the traits that `String` has. So the compiler will refuse to compare a `File` with a `String`, even though `File` has a `String` inside:

```
struct File(String);

fn main() {
    let my_file = File(String::from("I am file contents"));
    let my_string = String::from("I am file contents");
    println!("{}", my_file == my_string);          ⟵┐ Cannot compare
}                                                      │ File with String.
```

If you want to compare the `String` inside, you can use `my_file.0`:

```
struct File(String);

fn main() {
    let my_file = File(String::from("I am file contents"));
    let my_string = String::from("I am file contents");
    println!("{}", my_file.0 == my_string);          ⟵
}
```

This time we are comparing a String with a String, so the code compiles and prints true.

This type doesn't have any traits, so you can implement them yourself in the same way you do for any of your types—with `#[derive]` or manually using an `impl` block:

```
#[derive(Clone, Debug)]
struct File(String);

impl std::fmt::Display for File {
    fn fmt(&self, f: &mut std::fmt::Formatter<'_>) -> std::fmt::Result {
        let as_bytes = format!("{:?}", self.0.as_bytes());          ⟵┐
        write!(f, "{as_bytes}")
    }
}
```

Maybe we'd like a File by default to print by showing the bytes inside. We can make a String using the format! macro and then use that as output.

```
fn main() {
    let file = File(String::from("I am file contents"));
    println!("{file:?}");
    println!("{file}");
}
```

Now, our new type has its own traits, and it's sort of like implementing our own traits on `String` itself, since `File` is just a wrapper around a `String`. Here is the output:

```
File("I am file contents")
[73, 32, 97, 109, 32, 102, 105, 108, 101, 32, 99, 111, 110, 116, 101, 110,
➥116, 115]
```

So when you use the `File` type here, you can clone it and `Debug` print it, but it doesn't have the methods of `String` unless you use `.0` to get to the `String` inside it. We can use `.0` to access the `String` inside here, but that's because we are making the `File` type ourselves. In other people's code, you could only access `.0` if it's marked `pub` for public, and most of the time, people don't make everything `pub`. We will learn more about structuring code and using the `pub` keyword in chapter 14.

There is also a trait called `Deref` that lets you automatically use all the methods of the type inside, which, in this case, would be a convenient way to let people use the *methods* for the `String` inside without using `pub` to give them access to the `String` itself. We will learn about this in chapter 15.

Finally, let's finish off the chapter with another trait you'll find useful: `AsRef`.

7.5   Taking a String and a &str in a function

Sometimes you want a function that can take both a `String` and a `&str`. You can do this with the `AsRef` trait, which is used to give a reference from one type to another type. You can think of it as a sort of cheap version of `From`: instead of converting from one type to another, you do a cheap conversion from one reference to another. Here is how the standard library describes it:

```
Used to do a cheap reference-to-reference conversion. [...] If you need to do
    a costly conversion it is better to implement From with type &T or write
    a custom function.
```

We don't need to think too deeply about this trait now (we aren't going to implement it for anything), but here is the important part: both `String` and `str` implement `AsRef<str>`. Here is how they do it:

```
impl AsRef<str> for str {
    fn as_ref(&self) -> &str {
        self
    }
}

impl AsRef<str> for String {
    fn as_ref(&self) -> &str {
        self
    }
}
```

You can see that it takes `&self` and gives a reference to the other type, and in this case, they both return a `&str`. This means if you have a generic type `T` in your function, you can say that it needs `AsRef<str>` and then treat it as a `&str` inside the function.

Let's start thinking about using it with a generic function. We'll start with a function that tries to print its input but won't work yet:

```
fn print_it<T>(input: T) {
    println!("{}", input);
}

fn main() {
    print_it("Please print me");
}
```

Rust gives an error: `error[E0277]: T doesn't implement std::fmt::Display`. So we will require `T` to implement `Display`:

```
use std::fmt::Display;

fn print_it<T: Display>(input: T) {
    println!("{}", input);
}

fn main() {
    print_it("Please print me");
}
```

Now the function works and prints `Please print me`. That works well enough, but `T` can still be too many things. It can be an `i8`, an `f32`, and anything else with `Display`. We would rather take something that is a `String` or a `&str`, not just anything that implements `Display`. So we change `T: Display` to `T: AsRef<str>`. Now the function won't accept types like `i8`, and it almost works:

```
fn print_it<T: AsRef<str>>(input: T) {
    println!("{}", input)
}

fn main() {
    print_it("Please print me");
    print_it("Also, please print me".to_string());
    // print_it(7);              ⟵┐  This will
}                                 └  not print.
```

Here is the error: `error[E0277]: `T` doesn't implement `std::fmt::Display``.

We got this error because `T` is a type that implements `AsRef<str>`, but `T` itself isn't a type that implements `Display`. But we can turn it into a reference to a `str`, thanks to the `AsRef` trait. To do that, call the trait's method: `.as_ref()`. Because it is being given a `&str`, and `&str` implements `Display`, the compiler is happy with our code:

```
fn print_it<T: AsRef<str>>(input: T) {
    println!("{}", input.as_ref())
}

fn main() {
    print_it("Please print me");
    print_it("Also, please print me".to_string());
}
```

This prints what we wanted to see:

```
Please print me
Also, please print me
```

You can see that traits are a big subject in Rust—we spent the whole chapter on them! They always require some thought. If Rust is your first programming language, you will need to learn how they work and when to use them. But you may need to do almost as much work if Rust isn't your first programming language because there might be some unlearning involved. Many people from other languages look at traits and think, "Oh, this is the same as a class" or "Oh, this is the same as an interface." But traits are different and require you to sit down and think about them for a while.

The next chapter has a lot of new concepts to learn, too. You'll learn about iterators, which let you operate on every item in a collection. And you'll learn about closures, which are quick functions that don't need to have a name.

Summary

- If you have a lot of types and want them all to have the same methods, write a trait.
- Types that implement a trait will all be different. But they are all guaranteed to have the trait's methods.
- In the same way, every person who speaks a language will be different. But they are all guaranteed to know the language.
- You can implement your traits on other people's types. You can implement other people's traits on your types. But you can't implement other people's traits on other people's types.
- The `From` trait is pretty easy, and you see it everywhere. Check the code source if you're curious how it's done for any particular type.
- Taking an `AsRef<str>` is a convenient way to take both a `String` and a `&str` in a function.

Iterators and closures

This chapter covers

- Using method chaining to call one method after another after another
- Using iterators, which are the most convenient way to work with collections
- Using closures, which are functions that don't need names and can capture variables in their scope

In this chapter, we're going to see a lot of Rust's functional style, which is based on expressions. This style lets you use a method that gives an output, that output becomes the next method's input, and you repeat until you have the final output that you want. It works like a chain of methods, which is why people call it *method chaining*. Method chaining is a lot of fun once you get used to it; it lets you do a lot of work with not very much code. Iterators and closures are a big help here, so they are the main focus of this chapter.

8.1   *Chaining methods*

Rust is a systems programming language like C and C++, and its code can be written as separate commands in separate lines, but it also has a functional style. Both styles are okay, but functional style is usually shorter.

Here is an example of the nonfunctional style (called *imperative style*) to make a Vec from 1 to 10:

```
fn main() {
    let mut new_vec = Vec::new();
    let mut counter = 1;
    loop {
        new_vec.push(counter);
        counter += 1;
        if counter == 10 {
            break;
        }
    }
    println!("{new_vec:?}");
}
```

This prints [1, 2, 3, 4, 5, 6, 7, 8, 9, 10].

Imperative means to give orders or instructions, and that's what this example shows. (Indeed, the word *imperative* and *emperor* are related: an emperor is the person who gives orders to everyone else.) The code is being instructed to do a lot of individual things: start a loop, push into a Vec, increase a variable called counter, check the value of counter, and break out of the loop at a certain point.

But functional style is more about expressions: taking the output of an expression, putting that into a new *function*, taking that output, putting it into yet another function, and so on until finally you have the result that you want.

Here is an example of Rust's functional style that does the same as the previous code:

Or you can write it like this: let new_vec: Vec<i32> = (1..).take(10).collect();.

```
fn main() {
    let new_vec = (1..).take(10).collect::<Vec<i32>>();
    println!("{new_vec:?}");
}
```

This code starts with a range (an iterator) that goes up from 1. It has a method called .take(), which we can use to take the first 10 items. After that, you can call another method, .collect(), to turn it into a Vec. .collect() can make collections of many types, so we have to tell .collect() the type here.

With functional style, you can chain as many methods as you want. Here is an example of many methods chained together:

```
fn main() {
    let my_vec = vec![0, 1, 2, 3, 4, 5, 6, 7, 8, 9, 10];
```

```
    let new_vec = my_vec.into_iter().skip(3).take(4).collect::<Vec<i32>>();
    println!("{new_vec:?}");
}
```

This creates a `Vec` with `[3, 4, 5, 6]`. This is a lot of information for one line, so it can help to put each method on a new line. Doing that makes it easier to read and demonstrates the functional style a lot better. Read the following code line by line and try to guess what the output of the code will be:

```
fn main() {
    let my_vec = vec![0, 1, 2, 3, 4, 5, 6, 7, 8, 9, 10];
    let new_vec = my_vec
        .into_iter()          ◁──────────────────────────  Iterates over the items (iterate = work
                                                            with each item inside it). into_iter()
        .skip(3)                                            gives us owned values, not references.
        .take(4)              ◁────────────────
        .collect::<Vec<i32>>(  ◁──   Puts them
    println!("{new_vec:?}");        in a new        Takes the next
}                                   Vec<i32>        four: 3, 4, 5, and 6
```

Skips over three items: 0, 1, and 2

The output will be a `Vec` that holds the values `[3, 4, 5, 6]`.

We can use this functional style best once we understand what exactly iterators and closures are. So we will learn them next.

8.2   Iterators

An iterator is sort of like a collection type that gives you its items one at a time. It's a little bit like someone dealing a deck of cards. You can take one card at a time until the deck runs out. Or you can draw the fifth card. Or you can skip 10 cards and take the next 10. Or you can ask for the 60th card and be told that there is no 60th card in the deck.

We have already used iterators a lot because the `for` loop gives you an iterator. When you want to use an iterator other times, you have to choose what kind:

- `.iter()`—For an iterator of references
- `.iter_mut()`—For an iterator of mutable references
- `.into_iter()`—For an iterator of values (not references)

A `for` loop is an iterator of values, so typing `for item in iterator` is the same as typing `for item in iterator.into_iter()`. Let's look at a quick example of these three types of iterators:

```
fn main() {
    let vector1 = vec![1, 2, 3];
    let mut vector2 = vec![10, 20, 30];

    for num in vector1.iter() {
        println!("Printing a &i32: {num}");
    }
    for num in vector1 {
        println!("Printing an i32: {num}");
    }
}
```

First, we use .iter() so that vector1 is not destroyed.

This is the same as writing "for num in vector1.into_iter()." It owns the values, and vector1 no longer exists after this for loop is done.

```
    for num in vector2.iter_mut() {
        *num *= 10;
        println!("num is now {num}");
    }
    println!("{vector2:?}");
    // println!("{vector1:?}");
}
```

This for loop takes mutable references, so vector2 still exists after it is over.

We can still print vector2, but vector1 is gone. The compiler will give an error if you uncomment this last line.

Here is the output:

```
Printing a &i32: 1
Printing a &i32: 2
Printing a &i32: 3
Printing an i32: 1
Printing an i32: 2
Printing an i32: 3
num is now 100
num is now 200
num is now 300
[100, 200, 300]
```

You don't need to use `for` to use an iterator, though. Here is another way to use them:

```
fn main() {
    let vector1 = vec![1, 2, 3];
    let vector1_a = vector1
        .iter()
        .map(|x| x + 1)
        .collect::<Vec<i32>>();
    let vector1_b = vector1
        .into_iter()
        .map(|x| x * 10)
        .collect::<Vec<i32>>();
    let mut vector2 = vec![10, 20, 30];
    vector2.iter_mut().for_each(|x| *x +=100);

    println!("{:?}", vector1_a);
    println!("{:?}", vector1_b);
    println!("{:?}", vector2);
}
```

Here as well, we are using .iter() first so that vector1 is not destroyed.

This prints

```
[2, 3, 4]
[10, 20, 30]
[110, 120, 130]
```

For the first two, we used a method called `.map()`. This method lets you do something to every item (including turning it into a different type) and then pass it on to make a new iterator. The last one we used is one called `.for_each()`. This method lets you do something with every item without creating a new iterator. `.iter_mut()` plus `.for_each()` is basically a `for` loop. Inside each method, we can give a name to every item (we called it x) and use that to change it. These are called *closures*, and we will learn about them in the next section. For now, just remember that a closure uses | | where a regular function uses (), so |x| means "x gets passed into the closure (the function)."

Let's go over them again, one at a time. First, we used .iter() on vector1 to get references. We added 1 to each and passed it on with .map(). Then we collected it into a new Vec:

```
let vector1_a = vector1.iter().map(|x| x + 1).collect::<Vec<i32>>();
```

The original vector1 is still alive because we only used references: we didn't take by value. Now we have vector1, and a new Vec called vector1_a. Because .map() just passes it on, we needed to use .collect() to make it into a Vec.

Then we used .into_iter() to get an iterator by value from vector1:

```
let vector1_b = vector1.into_iter().map(|x| x * 10).collect::<Vec<i32>>();
```

This destroys vector1 because that's what .into_iter() does. Therefore, after we make vector1_b, we can't use vector1 again.

Finally, we used .iter_mut() for vector2:

```
let mut vector2 = vec![10, 20, 30];
vector2.iter_mut().for_each(|x| *x +=100);
```

It is mutable, so we don't need to use .collect() to create a new Vec. Instead, we change the values in the same Vec with mutable references. Thus, vector2 is still there after the iterator is over. We want to modify each item but don't need to make a new Vec, so we use the .for_each() method.

The core of every iterator is a method called .next(), which returns an Option. When you use an iterator, it calls .next() over and over again to see whether there are more items left. If .next() returns Some, there are still items left, and the iterator keeps going. If None is returned, the iteration is finished. (Well, usually. You can actually make iterators that never return None, only return None, and so on. We'll see some of those soon.) But generally, an iterator gives out a bunch of Somes until it runs out, and then it only gives None. This is how the for loops in the previous examples knew when to stop looping. If you wish, you can also manually call .next() on an iterator if you want more control, as the next example shows.

Do you remember the assert_eq! macro? You see it all the time in documentation. Here it is showing how an iterator works:

```
fn main() {
    let my_vec = vec!['a', 'b', '거', '柳'];        ◁──┐ Just a regular
                                                        Vec<char>.

    let mut my_vec_iter = my_vec.iter();    ◁──┤ The Vec is an Iterator type now, but
                                                 we haven't called .next() on it yet.
                                                 It's an iterator waiting to be called.

    assert_eq!(my_vec_iter.next(), Some(&'a'));    ◁──┐ Calls the first item with .next()
    assert_eq!(my_vec_iter.next(), Some(&'b'));        and then again and again. Each
    assert_eq!(my_vec_iter.next(), Some(&'거'));       time the iterator will return
    assert_eq!(my_vec_iter.next(), Some(&'柳'));       Some with the value inside.
```

```
        assert_eq!(my_vec_iter.next(), None);
        assert_eq!(my_vec_iter.next(), None);
}
```

Now the iterator is out of items, so it returns None.

You can keep calling .next() on the iterator, and it will simply return None every time.

The previous code will output absolutely nothing! That's because the output of the iterator matched our assertion, and so nothing happened (the code didn't panic). This is an interesting, indirect way to show what is happening in code without printing.

Implementing `Iterator` for your own types is not too difficult. First, let's make a book library struct and think about how we might want to use an iterator there. The code is pretty simple:

```
#[derive(Debug)]
struct Library {
    name: String,
    books: Vec<String>,
}

impl Library {
    fn add_book(&mut self, book: &str) {
        self.books.push(book.to_string());
    }

    fn new(name: &str) -> Self {
        Self {
            name: name.to_string(),
            books: Vec::new(),
        }
    }
}

fn main() {
    let my_library = Library::new("Calgary");
    println!("{my_library:?}");
}
```

So far, it just prints `Library { name: "Calgary", books: [] }`. It's a new library, empty and ready to put some books in. When you add books to the library, they will be inside a `Vec<String>`. You can turn a `Vec` into an iterator whenever you want, as we just saw. But what if you want to change the behavior a bit? Then you can implement `Iterator` for your own type. Let's look at the `Iterator` trait in the standard library (https://doc.rust-lang.org/std/iter/trait.Iterator.html) and see whether we can figure it out.

The top left of the page has the most important information we need to know:

- Required Associated Types: `Item`
- Required Methods: `next`

An *associated type* means "a type that goes together" (it goes together with the trait). Returning a `String` sounds like a good idea for our iterator, so we will choose `String` for the association type. And we want to implement it on this type of our own because of the orphan rule we learned in the last chapter. You can't implement `Iterator` for

Vec<String> because we didn't create the Vec type, and we didn't create the String type. But we can put a Vec<String> inside our own type, and now we can implement traits on it.

First, we'll change our Library a bit. The books are now a struct called Book-Collection, which holds a Vec<String>. And we'll add a method that clones it so we can do what we want with it without touching the original Library. Now it looks like this:

```
#[derive(Debug)]
struct Library {
    name: String,
    books: BookCollection,
}

#[derive(Debug, Clone)]
struct BookCollection(Vec<String>);    ◁──┐  BookCollection is just a Vec<String>
                                          │  on the inside, but it's our type, so we
impl Library {                            └─ can implement traits on it.
    fn add_book(&mut self, book: &str) {
        self.books.0.push(book.to_string());
    }

    fn new(name: &str) -> Self {
        Self {
            name: name.to_string(),
            books: BookCollection(Vec::new()),
        }
    }
    fn get_books(&self) -> BookCollection {
        self.books.clone()
    }
}
```

How do we implement Iterator on this BookCollection type? Let's look at the page in the standard library on the Iterator trait again. That page has a simple example of an iterator that looks like this:

```
struct Alternate {      ◁──┐  An iterator which alternates
    state: i32,            │  between Some and None
}

impl Iterator for Alternate {
    type Item = i32;

    fn next(&mut self) -> Option<i32> {
        let val = self.state;
        self.state = self.state + 1;

        if val % 2 == 0 {      ◁──┐  If it's even, Some(i32),
            Some(val)            │  else None
        } else {
            None
        }
    }
}
```

You can see that under `impl Iterator for Alternate` it says `type Item = i32`. This is the associated type. Our iterator will be for our list of books, which is a `BookCollection`. When we call `.next()`, it will give us a `String`. We will copy this code except we will use `type Item = String;`. That is our associated item.

To implement `Iterator`, you also need to write the `.next()` method. This is where you decide what the iterator should do. For `BookCollection` in our `Library`, we will do something simple: give us the last books first. We will also imagine that we want to print the output every time an item is found so that we can log it somewhere, so we will stick a `println!` inside the `.next()` method to log this information. (Maybe the library council wants to keep track of what each library is doing.) So we will `match` with `.pop()`, which takes the last item off if it is `Some`. Now it looks like this:

```rust
#[derive(Debug)]
struct Library {
    name: String,
    books: BookCollection,
}

#[derive(Clone, Debug)]
struct BookCollection(Vec<String>);

impl Library {
    fn add_book(&mut self, book: &str) {
        self.books.0.push(book.to_string());
    }

    fn new(name: &str) -> Self {
        Self {
            name: name.to_string(),
            books: BookCollection(Vec::new()),
        }
    }
    fn get_books(&self) -> BookCollection {
        self.books.clone()
    }
}

impl Iterator for BookCollection {
    type Item = String;

    fn next(&mut self) -> Option<String> {
        match self.0.pop() {
            Some(book) => {
                println!("Accessing book: {book}");
                Some(book)
            }
            None => {
                println!("Out of books at the library!");
                None
            }
        }
    }
}
```

```
fn main() {
    let mut my_library = Library::new("Calgary");
    my_library.add_book("The Doom of the Darksword");
    my_library.add_book("Demian - die Geschichte einer Jugend");
    my_library.add_book("구운몽");
    my_library.add_book("吾輩は猫である");

    for item in my_library.get_books() {
        println!("{item}");
    }
}
```

This prints

```
Accessing book: 吾輩は猫である
吾輩は猫である
Accessing book: 구운몽
구운몽
Accessing book: Demian - die Geschichte einer Jugend
Demian - die Geschichte einer Jugend
Accessing book: The Doom of the Darksword
The Doom of the Darksword
Out of books at the library!
```

You can see that .next() did indeed return None once because we told the code to print out Out of books at the library! if None is returned from the function.

In this example, we just popped off each item and printed it out before we passed it off as Some, but you can implement an iterator in very different ways. You don't ever need to return None if you want an iterator that never ends. Here's an iterator that just gives the number 1 forever:

```
struct GivesOne;

impl Iterator for GivesOne {
    type Item = i32;
    fn next(&mut self) -> Option<i32> {
        Some(1)
    }
}
```

If you use a while loop that continues as long as the iterator returns Some, the program will never stop. But you can use the .take() method we learned before to only call it five times and then collect that into a Vec:

```
struct GivesOne;

impl Iterator for GivesOne {
    type Item = i32;
    fn next(&mut self) -> Option<i32> {
        Some(1)
    }
}
```

```
fn main() {
    let five_ones: Vec<i32> = GivesOne.into_iter().take(5).collect();
    println!("{five_ones:?}");
}
```

This prints out [1, 1, 1, 1, 1].

Note that the GivesOne struct doesn't hold anything! It's a good example of one of the ways that an iterator differs from a collection type. In this case, the GivesOne struct is just an empty struct that implements the Iterator trait.

There is quite a bit more to know about iterators, but now we understand the basics. You see closures a lot when using the iterators in Rust's standard library, so let's learn about them now.

8.3   *Closures and closures inside iterators*

Closures are quick functions that don't need a name—in other words, anonymous functions. Sometimes they are called *lambdas* in other languages. It's easy to notice where closures are because they use || instead of (). They are very common in Rust, and once you learn to use them, you will wonder how you lived without them.

You can bind a closure to a variable, and then it looks exactly like a function when you use it:

```
fn main() {
    let my_closure = || println!("This is a closure");
    my_closure();
}
```

This closure takes nothing: || and prints a message: This is a closure.

In between the ||, we can add input variables and types in the same way that we put them inside () for regular functions. This next closure takes an i32 and prints it out:

```
fn main() {
    let my_closure = |x: i32| println!("{x}");

    my_closure(5);
    my_closure(5+5);
}
```

This prints

```
5
10
```

For longer closures, you need to add a code block. Then it can be as long as you want:

```
fn main() {
    let my_closure = || {
        let number = 7;
        let other_number = 10;
```

```
        println!("The two numbers are {number} and {other_number}.");
    };
    my_closure();    ◁──┐ This closure can be as long as
}                       │ we want, just like a function.
```

One thing that makes closures special is that they can take variables from their environment that are *outside* the closure, even if you only write ||. You can think of a closure as a standalone type that can hold references in the same way that a struct can.

> **NOTE** If you're curious about the details of closure types, see the page in the reference here: https://doc.rust-lang.org/reference/types/closure.html.

So you can do this:

```
fn main() {
    let number_one = 6;
    let number_two = 10;
    let my_closure = || println!("{}", number_one + number_two);
    my_closure();
}
```

Calling the closure `my_closure` prints 16. You didn't need to put anything in || because it can just take `number_one` and `number_two` and add them. If you want to be very correct:

- A || that doesn't enclose a variable from outside is an *anonymous function*. Anonymous means "doesn't have a name." It works more like a regular function and can be passed into places where a function is required if the signature is the same.
- A || that encloses a variable from outside is also anonymous but called a *closure*. It "encloses" the variables around it to use them.

But people will often call all || functions closures, so you don't have to worry about the name too much. We will call anything with a || a *closure*, but remember that it can mean an *anonymous function*.

Let's look at some more things that closures can do. You can do this:

```
fn main() {
    let number_one = 6;
    let number_two = 10;

    let my_closure = |x: i32| println!("{}", number_one + number_two + x);
    my_closure(5);
}
```

This closure takes `number_one` and `number_two`. We also gave it the new variable x and said that x is 5. Then it adds all three together to print 21.

8.3.1 *Closures inside of methods*

Usually you see closures in Rust inside of methods because it is very convenient to have a closure inside. The convenience comes from the fact that the user can write the body of the closure differently each time, depending on the situation. We saw closures in the last section with `.map()` and `.for_each()`. The closure inside `.for_each()`, for example, simply takes a mutable reference to the item and returns nothing, and with that freedom, the user of the `.for_each()` method can do anything inside as long as the signature matches. Here is a quick example:

```
fn main() {
    (1..=3).for_each(|num| println!("{num}"));
    (1..=3).for_each(|num| {
        println!("Got a {num}!");
        if num % 2 == 0 {
            println!("It's even")
        } else {
            println!("It's odd")
        };
    });
}
```

The output is

```
1
2
3
Got a 1!
It's odd
Got a 2!
It's even
Got a 3!
It's odd
```

Here is another example: remember the `.unwrap_or()` method that we learned that you can use to return a default value if an `Option` is a `None` or `Result` is an `Err`? The following code will print `0` instead of panicking because we gave it the default value `0`:

```
fn main() {
    let nothing: Option<i32> = None;
    println!("{}", nothing.unwrap_or(0));
}
```

There is another similar method called `.unwrap_or_else()`. This method also allows us to give a default value, except that it passes on a closure that we can use to write some more complex logic. See whether you can guess what the output for this code sample will be:

```
fn main() {
    let my_vec = vec![8, 9, 10];

    let fourth = my_vec.get(3).unwrap_or_else(|| {     ◁── First, we try to get
                                                            an item at index 3.
        if let Some(val) = my_vec.get(2) {     ◁──
            val                                      If it doesn't work, maybe we have a
        } else {     ◁──                             good reason to look for an item one
            &0             And then finally we will return   index back. Inside the closure we
        }              a &0 in case no items have     can try .get() again! And then return
    }                  been found at either index.    that value if it's found at index 2.
```

```
    });

    println!("{fourth}");
}
```

The output is 10 because there was no item at index 3, but an item was then found at index 0, which was a 10.

A closure can, of course, be very simple. For example, you can write `let fourth = my_vec.get(3).unwrap_or_else(|| &0);`. You don't always need to use a `{}` and write complicated code just because there is a closure.

There are a lot of methods for iterators that enhance the iterator in a certain way. For example, let's say that you have an iterator that holds the chars `'z'`, `'y'`, and `'x'`. An iterator will return `Some('z')`, then `Some('y')`, and finally `Some('x')` before starting to return `None`. But what if you wanted to also see the index of each item along with the item itself?

Well, it turns out that all you have to do is add `.enumerate()` to an iterator to make this happen. (You might see this called *zip with index* in other languages.)

```
fn main() {
    let char_vec = vec!['z', 'y', 'x'];

    char_vec                    Makes char_vec
        .iter()      ←——┘       into an iterator            Now, each item is (usize,
        .enumerate()                                    ←——┘ char) instead of just char.
        .for_each(|(index, c)| println!("Index {index} is: {c}"));
}
```

This prints

```
Index 0 is: 'z'
Index 1 is: 'y'
Index 2 is: 'x'
```

In this case, we use `.for_each()` instead of `.map()` because we didn't need to collect `char_vec` into a new iterator.

Meanwhile, `.map()` is for *doing something to* each item and passing it on, as we previously saw.

8.3.2 *Closures: Lazy and fast*

One interesting thing about `.map()` is that it doesn't do anything unless you use a method like `.collect()`. Let's take a look at `.map()` again, first with `collect`. Here is a classic example of using `.map()` to make a new `Vec` from an existing `Vec`:

```
fn main() {
    let num_vec = vec![2, 4, 6];
                                                                   Takes
Makes into    let double_vec: Vec<i32> = num_vec       ←——————————— num_vec
an iterator └—→  .iter()                            Multiplies each item
                 .map(|num| num * 2)            ←——┘ by 2 and passes it on
```

```
        .collect();
    println!("{:?}", double_vec);
}
```
<--- **And collects into a new Vec**

That was pretty easy and prints [4, 8, 12]. But let's see what happens when we don't collect into a Vec. The code won't panic, but the compiler will tell you that you didn't do anything:

```
fn main() {
    let num_vec = vec![2, 4, 6];

    num_vec
        .iter()
        .enumerate()
        .map(|(index, num)| format!("Index {index} is {num}"));
}
```

It says

```
warning: unused `Map` that must be used
  --> src/main.rs:4:5
   |
4  | /       num_vec
5  | |           .iter()
6  | |           .enumerate()
7  | |           .map(|(index, num)| format!("Index {index} is {num}"));
   | |_____^
   |
   = note: iterators are lazy and do nothing unless consumed
```

This is a *warning*, so it's not an error: the program runs fine. But why doesn't num_vec do anything? We can look at the types to see:

- let num_vec = vec![10, 9, 8];—Right now it is a Vec<i32>.
- .iter()—Now it is an Iter<i32>, so it is an iterator with items of i32.
- .enumerate()—Now it is an Enumerate<Iter<i32>>, so it is a type Enumerate of type Iter of i32s.
- .map()—Now it is a type Map<Enumerate<Iter<i32>>>, so it is a type Map of type Enumerate of type Iter of i32s.

All we did was make a more and more complicated structure. So this Map<Enumerate <Iter<i32>>> is a structure that is ready to go, but only when we tell it what to do. This is one of the ways that Rust keeps even fancy functional-looking code as fast as any other kind of code. Rust avoids this sort of operation:

1 Iterate over all the i32s in the Vec.
2 Enumerate over all the i32s from the iterator.
3 Map over all the enumerated i32s.

Instead, an iterator with a method and another method and another method simply creates a single structure and waits until we decide what to do with it. If we add

`.collect::<Vec<i32>>()`, it knows what to do. This is what `iterators are lazy and do nothing unless consumed` means. The iterators don't do anything until you "consume" them (use them up).

This is an example of an idea in Rust called *zero-cost abstractions*. The idea behind zero-cost abstractions is that complicated code might or might not take longer to compile, but at run time, they will be the same speed. Your program won't be any slower if you use a complicated iterator than if you wrote everything by hand.

You can even create complicated things like `HashMap` using `.collect()`, so it is very powerful. Here is an example of how to put two `Vec`s into a `HashMap`. First, we make two vectors, one for the keys and the other for the values. We will then use `.into_iter()` on each of them to get an iterator of values. Then we use the `.zip()` method. This method takes two iterators and attaches them together, like a zipper. Finally, we use `.collect()` to make the `HashMap`. Here is the code:

```
use std::collections::HashMap;

fn main() {
    let some_keys = vec![0, 1, 2, 3, 4, 5];
    let some_values = vec!["zero", "one", "two", "three", "four", "five"];

    let number_word_hashmap = some_keys
        .into_iter()                           ⟵—  Now it is an iter.
        .zip(some_values.into_iter())          ⟵⎤  On this line, .zip() takes our iterator
        .collect::<HashMap<_, _>>();              ⎦  and zips it together with the second.

    println!(
        "The value at key 2 is: {}",
        number_word_hashmap.get(&2).unwrap()
    );
}
```

This prints `The value at key 2 is: two`.

You can see that we wrote `<HashMap<_, _>>` because that is enough information for Rust to decide on the type `HashMap<i32, &str>`. You can write `.collect::<HashMap<i32, &str>>();` if you want, or you can declare the type up front like this if you prefer:

```
use std::collections::HashMap;

fn main() {
    let some_numbers = vec![0, 1, 2, 3, 4, 5];
    let some_words = vec!["zero", "one", "two", "three", "four", "five"];
    let number_word_hashmap: HashMap<_, _> = some_numbers   ⟵⎤  We specified
        .into_iter()                                           ⎦  the type here ...
        .zip(some_words.into_iter())
        .collect();                         ⟵⎤  ... so we don't have to type anything after .collect()
}                                              ⎦  here: Rust already knows the type to collect into.
```

Or you can turn the `Vec`s into iterators right away! This code also does the exact same thing as the previous two samples:

```
use std::collections::HashMap;

fn main() {
    let keys = vec![0, 1, 2, 3, 4, 5].into_iter();
    let values = vec!["zero", "one", "two", "three", "four",
    ➥"five"].into_iter();

    let number_word_hashmap: HashMap<i32, &str> = keys.zip(values).collect();

    println!(
        "The value at key 2 is: {}",
        number_word_hashmap.get(&2).unwrap()
    );
}
```

> **Both some_keys and some_values are now iterators. Now, the first lines are a bit longer but the .zip() method looks cleaner.**

There is another method that is like .enumerate() for char: .char_indices(). (Indices means "indexes.") You use it in the same way. Let's take a big string of numbers and print them three characters at a time with a tab-length space between them:

```
fn main() {
    let numbers_together = "1403999234818006226232180009598281";

    for (index, num) in numbers_together.char_indices() {
        match (index % 3, num) {
            (0 | 1, num) => print!("{num}"),
            _ => print!("{num}\t"),
        }
    }
}
```

> **We'll use the index number modulo 3 to get the remainder after dividing by 3.**
>
> **You can also use | in match statements, meaning "or"—in this case, 0 or 1.**
>
> **The only other possible remainder after dividing by 3 is 2, but Rust doesn't know that, so we'll use a _ wildcard.**

This prints

```
140     399     923     481     800     622     623     218     009     598
➥281
```

8.3.3 |_| *in a closure*

Sometimes you see |_| in a closure. It's not a special syntax, though. It only means that the closure needs to take an argument that you give a name to (like x or num), but you don't want to use it. |_| means "okay, this closure takes an argument, but I won't give it a name because I won't bother to use it."

Here is an example of an error when you don't do that:

```
fn main() {
    let my_vec = vec![8, 9, 10];
    my_vec
        .iter()
        .for_each(|| println!("We didn't use the variables at all"));
}
```

Rust says

```
error[E0593]: closure is expected to take 1 argument, but it takes 0 arguments
 --> src/main.rs:5:10
```

```
     |
5    |              .for_each(|| println!("We didn't use the variables at all"));
     |              ^^^^^^^^^^ -- takes 0 arguments
     |              |
     |              expected closure that takes 1 argument
```

It then continues with some pretty good advice:

```
help: consider changing the closure to take and ignore the expected argument
     |
5    |              .for_each(|_| println!("We didn't use the variables at all"));
     |                        ~~~
```

Sounds good. If you change || to |_|, it will work because it takes the argument but then ignores it.

That should be enough for an introduction to iterators and closures. Hopefully, you enjoyed learning about what they are and how they work because they are everywhere in Rust and very convenient. We only took a quick look in this chapter, and there's a lot more to learn. If you don't feel like you understand iterators and closures yet, don't worry—we aren't changing subjects yet. The next chapter is also about the same thing! In chapter 9, we will take a look at some of the most common methods for iterators and closures.

Summary

- Method chaining can be unfamiliar at first, but it is so convenient that people tend to use it more and more as they become familiar with Rust.
- The core method in iterators is .next(), which returns an Option. Almost all iterators return Some until they run out of items, and after that, None.
- Iterators are lazy. To use one, call .next() or use a method like .collect() to turn it into another type (usually a Vec).
- You can give a closure a name if you want to use the name to call the closure later. But most of the time, you don't give names to closures.
- A closure can capture variables in its scope. You don't need to pass the variables in as arguments—the closure can just grab them.
- An associated type is the type that goes with a trait. Most traits don't have them, but some do.
- You, as the user, decide what the concrete type of an associated type will be when you implement a trait.

Iterators and closures again!

Iterators and closures in Rust have so many methods that we need another full chapter to go over them. There are a lot of these methods, but it's worth the effort to learn them because they do a lot of work for you. You might not memorize them all during your first reading, but if you remember their names and what they do, you can look them up later when you need them.

9.1 *Helpful methods for closures and iterators*

Rust becomes an even more fun language once you become comfortable with closures. As we saw in the last chapter, with closures you can "chain" methods to each other and do a lot of things with very little code. And the more of them you know, the more you can chain together. This chapter is mostly going to show you how to use certain common iterator methods that work conveniently with closures.

9.1.1 *Mapping and filtering*

Besides mapping, another common use case for using an iterator is filtering. While mapping lets you do something to and pass on each item in an iterator, filtering lets you keep only items that match a certain condition. There is even a method that enables you to do both at the same time. Let's look at the main methods to do these operations, starting with the `.filter()` method.

The `.filter()` method allows you to keep the items in an iterator that you want based on an expression that returns a `bool`. Let's give this a try by filtering the months of the year:

```
fn main() {
    let months = vec!["January", "February", "March", "April", "May",
    ➡"June", "July", "August", "September", "October", "November",
    ➡"December"];

    let filtered_months = months
        .into_iter()
        .filter(|month| month.len() < 5)        ⬅
        .filter(|month| month.contains("u"))    ⬅
        .collect::<Vec<&str>>();

    println!("{:?}", filtered_months);
}
```

> For some reason, we don't want months more than 5 bytes in length. We know that each letter is 1 byte, so using .len() is fine.

> Also, we only like months with the letter u. You can .filter() and .filter() again as many times as you like.

This prints `["June", "July"]`.

Of course, you could also type `.filter(|month| month.len() < 5 && month.contains("u"))` to filter over one line. But this example shows that you can filter and filter again as much as you want.

The next method with a closure in it that we'll learn has a pretty similar name: `filter_map()`. You can probably guess that its name is `.filter_map()` because it does both `.filter()` and `.map()`. Instead of a `bool`, the closure must return an `Option<T>`, and then `.filter_map()` takes the value out of each `Option` if it is `Some`. For example, if you were to `.filter_map()` and then `collect()` on a Vec holding `Some(2)`, `None`, `Some(3)]`, it would return `[2, 3]`. So that is why it uses `Option`: it filters out everything that is `None`. But it also maps because it passes the value on.

We will write an example with a `Company` struct. Each company has a `name` of type `String`, but the CEO might have recently quit, leaving the company without a leader. To represent this we can make the `ceo` field an `Option<String>`. We will `.filter_map()` over some companies to just keep the CEO names:

```
struct Company {
    name: String,
    ceo: Option<String>,
}

impl Company {
    fn new(name: &str, ceo: &str) -> Self {
        let ceo = match ceo {
            "" => None,
            ceo => Some(ceo.to_string()),
        };
        Self {
            name: name.to_string(),
            ceo,
        }
    }

    fn get_ceo(&self) -> Option<String> {
        self.ceo.clone()
    }
}

fn main() {
    let company_vec = vec![
        Company::new("Umbrella Corporation", "Unknown"),
        Company::new("Ovintiv", "Brendan McCracken"),
        Company::new("The Red-Headed League", ""),
        Company::new("Stark Enterprises", ""),
    ];

    let all_the_ceos = company_vec
        .iter()
        .filter_map(|company| company.get_ceo())
        .collect::<Vec<String>>();

    println!("{:?}", all_the_ceos);
}
```

ceo is decided, so now we return Self.

Just returns a clone of the CEO (struct is not Copy)

filter_map needs Option<T>.

This prints `["Unknown", "Brendan McCracken"]`.

Since the closure inside `.filter_map()` needs to return an `Option`, what if you have a function that returns a `Result`? No problem: there is a method called `.ok()` that turns `Result` into `Option`. This method is probably called `.ok()` because all that can be passed on from a `Result` to an `Option` is the information inside an `Ok` result, as `None` doesn't hold any information (thus, any `Err` information is gone). We can see this in the documentation for the `.ok()` method:

Converts from Result<T, E> to Option<T>.

Since you start out with a `Result<T, E>`, `.ok()` drops the `E` to turn it into an `Option<T>`, and any `Err` information that `E` had is now gone. If you had an `Ok(some_variable)` and called `.ok()`, it would turn into a `Some(some_variable)`; if you had an `Err(some_err_variable)`, it would turn into `None`.

Using .parse() is an easy example of this, where we try to parse some user input into a number. In the next example, .parse() takes a &str and tries to turn it into an f32. It returns a Result, but we would like to use .filter_map() to filter out any parsing that didn't work. Anything that returns an Err becomes None after the .ok() method and then gets filtered out by .filter_map().

```
fn main() {
let user_input = vec![
        "8.9",
        "Nine point nine five",
        "8.0",
        "7.6",
        "eleventy-twelve",
    ];

    let successful_numbers = user_input
        .iter()
        .filter_map(|input| input.parse::<f32>().ok())
        .collect::<Vec<f32>>();

    println!("{:?}", successful_numbers);
}
```

This prints [8.9, 8.0, 7.6].

On the opposite side of .ok() is .ok_or() and .ok_or_else(). Both of these methods turn an Option into a Result. This method is called .ok_or() because a Result gives an Ok *or* an Err, so you have to let it know what the Err value will be if it doesn't return an Ok. After all, None in an Option doesn't have any information to pass on, so we have to provide it.

In the last chapter, we saw the methods .unwrap_or() and .unwrap_or_else(), in which the _or_else method took a closure. You can see the same thing here: .ok_or_else() also takes a closure. This is the way a lot of methods in the standard library are named.

We can take our Option from the Company struct and turn it into a Result this way. For long-term error handling, it is good to create your own type of error. But for now, we will type a quick error message, which means that the method will return a Result<String, &str>:

```
struct Company {                    ⟵──┐  Everything before main() in
    name: String,                       │  this example is exactly the
    ceo: Option<String>,                │  same as the last example.
}

impl Company {
    fn new(name: &str, ceo: &str) -> Self {
        let ceo = match ceo {
            "" => None,
            ceo => Some(ceo.to_string()),
        };
        Self {
            name: name.to_string(),
```

```
            ceo,
        }
    }

    fn get_ceo(&self) -> Option<String> {
        self.ceo.clone()
    }
}

fn main() {
    let company_vec = vec![
        Company::new("Umbrella Corporation", "Unknown"),
        Company::new("Ovintiv", "Brendan McCracken"),
        Company::new("The Red-Headed League", ""),
        Company::new("Stark Enterprises", ""),
    ];

    let results: Vec<Result<String, &str>> = company_vec
        .iter()
        .map(|company| company.get_ceo().ok_or("No CEO found"))
        .collect();

    for item in results {
        println!("{:?}", item);
    }
}
```

The following line is the biggest change:

```
.map(|company| company.get_ceo().ok_or("No CEO found"))
```

The line means "for each company, use `.get_ceo()` and turn it into a `Result`. If `.get_ceo()` returns a `Some`, pass on the value inside `Ok`. If `.get_ceo()` returns a `None`, pass on `"No CEO found"` inside `Err`."

When we print the `Vec` results, we get this:

```
Ok("Unknown")
Ok("Brendan McCracken")
Err("No CEO found")
Err("No CEO found")
```

Now we have all four entries. Let's use `.ok_or_else()` so we can use a closure and get a better error message since having a closure gives us the space to do whatever we want. We can use `format!` to create a `String` and put the company name in that. Then we return the `String`. (We could do anything else, too, because we have a whole closure to work with.) This is starting to look a bit more like real production code:

```
struct Company {
    name: String,
    ceo: Option<String>,
}

fn get_current_datetime() -> String {
    "2024-01-27T23:11:23".to_string()
}
```

> We haven't learned to work with dates yet, so we'll use a dummy function that gives a single date.

```
impl Company {
    fn new(name: &str, ceo: &str) -> Self {
        let ceo = match ceo {
            "" => None,
            name => Some(name.to_string()),
        };
        Self {
            name: name.to_string(),
            ceo,
        }
    }

    fn get_ceo(&self) -> Option<String> {
        self.ceo.clone()
    }
}

fn main() {
    let company_vec = vec![
        Company::new("Umbrella Corporation", "Unknown"),
        Company::new("Ovintiv", "Brendan McCracken"),
        Company::new("The Red-Headed League", ""),
        Company::new("Stark Enterprises", ""),
    ];

    let results: Vec<Result<String, String>> = company_vec
        .iter()
        .map(|company| {
            company.get_ceo().ok_or_else(|| {
                let err_message = format!("No CEO found for {}",
company.name);
                    println!("{err_message} at {}",
get_current_datetime());
                    err_message
            })
        })
        .collect();

    results
        .iter()
        .filter(|res| res.is_ok())
        .for_each(|res| println!("{res:?}"));
}
```

This time we are using ok_or_else, which gives a lot more room.

First, we'll construct an error message.

Then we'll log the message as well as the date and time that the error happened . . .

. . . and pass on err_message in case of an Err.

We've already logged the errors, so let's just print out the Ok results this time. A quick .filter() and .for_each() will do the trick.

This gives us the following input:

```
No CEO found for The Red-Headed League at 2024-01-27T23:11:23
No CEO found for Stark Enterprises at 2024-01-27T23:11:23
Ok("Unknown")
Ok("Brendan McCracken")
```

9.1.2 *Some more iterator and related methods*

There are some methods that are commonly used inside iterators that work on `Option` and `Result`. You'll see these inside methods like `.map()` a lot.

One of them is called `.and_then()`. This method is a helpful one that takes an `Option` and lets you do something to the value inside in case it is a `Some` and pass it on. Meanwhile, a `None` holds no value, so it will just be passed on. This method's input is an `Option`, and its output is also an `Option`. It is sort of like a safe "unwrap if `Some`, do something to the value, and wrap again."

The following code shows an array that holds some `&str` values. We'll check the first five indexes in the array by using `.get()` to see whether there is an item at that index. We will try to parse the `&str` into a `u32` and then make the `u32` into a `char`. Because `.and_then()` expects an `Option` and not a `Result`, we can use `.ok()` to turn each `Result` into an `Option` along the way:

```
fn main() {
    let num_array = ["8", "9", "Hi", "9898989898"];
    let mut char_vec = vec![];            <──┐ Results go
                                             │ in here.
    for index in 0..5 {
        char_vec.push(
            num_array                  ┌── .get() returns
                .get(index)        <───┘    an Option
                .and_then(|number| number.parse::<u32>().ok())   <──────────
                .and_then(|number| char::try_from(number).ok()),
        );
    }                                        Next, we try to parse the
    println!("{:?}", char_vec);              number into a u32 and then use
}                                            .ok() to turn it into an Option.
```

We do the same here. (annotations pointing to `.and_then` lines)

The previous code prints

```
[Some('\u{8}'), Some('\t'), None, None, None]
```

Notice that `None` isn't filtered out; it's just passed on. Also, all the `Err` information has been removed, so

- The `"Hi"` value couldn't be turned into a `u32`.
- The `"9898989898"` value turned into a `u32` but was too large to turn into a `char`.
- There was no value at index 4.

Each of these parts failed for different reasons, but all we see at the end is `None`.

Another method is `.and()`, which is sort of like a `bool` for `Option`. You can match many `Option`s to each other, and if they are all `Some`, it will give the last one. But if one of them is a `None`, it will give `None`.

Here is a `bool` example to help you imagine. You can see that if you are using `&&` (ampersands), even one `false` makes everything `false`:

```
fn main() {
    let one = true;
    let two = false;
    let three = true;
    let four = true;
```

```
println!("{}", one && three);
println!("{}", one && two && three && four);
}
```

true and true:
prints true

true and false and true
and true: prints false

Here is something similar using the `.and()` method. Imagine we did five operations and put the results in an array that holds `Option<&str>` values. If we get a value, we push `Some("Okay!")` into the array. We do this two more times. After that, we use `.and()` to show only the indexes that got `Some` every time:

```
fn main() {
    let try_1 = [Some("Okay!"), None, Some("Okay!"), Some("Okay!"), None];
    let try_2 = [None, Some("Okay!"), Some("Okay!"), Some("Okay!"),
    ➥Some("Okay!")];
    let try_3 = [Some("Okay!"), Some("Okay!"), Some("Okay!"),
    ➥Some("Okay!"), None];

    for i in 0..try_1.len() {
        println!("{:?}", try_1[i].and(try_2[i]).and(try_3[i]));
    }
}
```

This prints

```
None
None
Some("Okay!")
Some("Okay!")
None
```

The first attempt (index 0) is `None` because there is a `None` for index 0 in `try_2`. The second is `None` because there is a `None` in `first_try`. The next is `Some("Okay!")` because there is no `None` for `try_1`, `try_2`, or `try_3`.

The `.flatten()` method is a convenient way to ignore all `None` or `Err` values in an iterator and only return the successful values. Let's try parsing some strings into numbers again:

```
fn main() {
    for num in ["9", "nine", "ninety-nine", "9.9"]
        .into_iter()
        .map(|num| num.parse::<f32>())
    {
        println!("{num:?}");
    }
}
```

The output shows both the `Ok` and `Err` values:

```
Ok(9.0)
Err(ParseFloatError { kind: Invalid })
Err(ParseFloatError { kind: Invalid })
Ok(9.9)
```

That works great! However, if we don't care about the `Err` values, we can add `.flatten()` to directly access the values inside `Ok` and ignore the rest:

```
fn main() {
    for num in ["9", "nine", "ninety-nine", "9.9"]
        .into_iter()
        .map(|num| num.parse::<f32>())
        .flatten()
    {
        println!("{num}");
    }
}
```

Now the output is much simpler—just the two successful `f32` values:

```
9
9.9
```

Some more common methods tell you whether an iterator contains a certain item or whether all of the items satisfy a condition. Or you might want to know where a certain item is so you can access it later. Let's look at those methods now.

9.1.3 *Checking and finding items inside iterators*

The next two iterator methods to learn are `.any()` and `.all()`, which simply return a `bool` depending on whether a condition is true for *any* of the items or *all* of the items.

In the following example, we'll make a large `Vec` (about 20,000 items) with all the chars from `'a'` to `'働'`. Next, we will make a smaller `Vec` and ask it whether it is all alphabetic (with the `.is_alphabetic()` method). Then we will ask it whether all the characters are less than the Korean character `'행'`.

Also, note that you put a reference in because `.iter()` gives a reference, and you need an `&` to compare with another `&`:

```
fn in_char_vec(char_vec: &Vec<char>, check: char) {
    println!(
        "Is {check} inside? {}",
        char_vec.iter().any(|&char| char == check)
    );
}

fn main() {
    let char_vec = ('a'..'働').collect::<Vec<char>>();
    in_char_vec(&char_vec, 'i');
    in_char_vec(&char_vec, '뷁');
    in_char_vec(&char_vec, '鑿');

    let smaller_vec = ('A'..'z').collect::<Vec<char>>();
    println!(
        "All alphabetic? {}",
        smaller_vec.iter().all(|&x| x.is_alphabetic())
    );
    println!(
```

```
        "All less than the character 행? {}",
        smaller_vec.iter().all(|&x| x < '행')
    );
}
```

This prints

```
Is i inside? true
Is 붱 inside? false
Is 鬀 inside? false
All alphabetic? false
All less than the character 행? true
```

> **NOTE** All alphabetic? returns false because there are a few nonalphabetic
> characters in between the last capital letter and the first lowercase letter.

As you might have guessed, .any() only checks until it finds one matching item, and
then it stops—there's no need to check the rest of the items at this point. This early
stop is sometimes called a *short circuit*. That means that if you are going to use .any()
on a Vec, it might be a good idea to push the items that might return true near the
front. Or you can use .rev() after .iter() to reverse the iterator if you think that
items that could return true might be closer to the end. Here's one such Vec:

```
fn main() {
    let mut big_vec = vec![6; 1000];
    big_vec.push(5);
}
```

This Vec has a thousand 6s followed by one 5. Let's pretend we want to use .any() to
see whether it contains 5. First, let's make sure that .rev() is working. Remember, an
Iterator always has .next() that lets you check what it returns each time:

```
fn main() {
    let mut big_vec = vec![6; 1000];
    big_vec.push(5);

    let mut iterator = big_vec.iter().rev();
    assert_eq!(iterator.next(), Some(&5));
    assert_eq!(iterator.next(), Some(&6));
}
```

The code doesn't panic, so we were right that a 5 is returned first, followed by a 6. So,
if we were to write this:

```
fn main() {
    let mut big_vec = vec![6; 1000];
    big_vec.push(5);

    println!("{:?}", big_vec.iter().rev().any(|&number| number == 5));
}
```

because we used .rev(), it only calls .next() one time and stops. If we don't use
.rev(), it will call .next() 1,001 times before it stops. This code shows it:

```
fn main() {
    let mut big_vec = vec![6; 1000];
    big_vec.push(5);

    let mut num_loops = 0;                               Starts
    let mut big_iter = big_vec.into_iter();              counting
    loop {                                               Makes it
        num_loops +=1;                                   an iterator
        if big_iter.next() == Some(5) {
            break;                                       Keeps calling .next()
        }                                                until we get Some(5)
    }
    println!("Number of loops: {num_loops}");
}
```

This prints `Number of loops: 1001`, so we know that it had to call `.next()` 1,001 times before it found 5.

The next two iterator methods we will look at are called `.find()` and `.position()`. The `.find()` method returns an item if it can, while `.position()` simply tells you where it is. `.find()` is different from `.any()` because it returns an `Option` with the value inside (or `None`). Meanwhile, `.position()` is also an `Option` with the position number or `None`:

- `.find()`—"I'll try to get it for you."
- `.position()`—"I'll try to find where it is for you."

Here is a simple example that tries to find numbers that can be divided by 3, followed by numbers divided by 11:

```
fn main() {
    let num_vec = vec![10, 20, 30, 40, 50, 60, 70, 80, 90, 100];

    println!("{:?}", num_vec.iter().find(|number| *number % 3 == 0));
    println!("{:?}", num_vec.iter().position(|number| *number % 3 == 0));
    println!("{:?}", num_vec.iter().find(|number| *number % 11 == 0));
    println!("{:?}", num_vec.iter().position(|number| *number % 11 == 0));
}
```

This prints

```
Some(30)
Some(2)
None
None
```

The first `Some(30)` and `Some(2)` are saying the following:

- `Some(30)`—"I found an item that matches; it's the number 30."
- `Some(2)`—"I found an item that matches; it's at index 2."

Finally, we'll take a look at a whole bunch of other iterator methods. You can make iterators that run forever, zip two iterators together, cut them into pieces, add the items together, and more.

9.1.4   *Cycling, zipping, folding, and more*

With the `.cycle()` method, you can create an iterator that loops forever. This type of iterator works well with `.zip()` to create something new, like this example, which creates a `Vec<(i32, &str)>`:

```
fn main() {
    let even_odd_iter = ["even", "odd"].into_iter().cycle();

    let even_odd_vec: Vec<(i32, &str)> = (0..=5)
        .zip(even_odd_iter)
        .collect();
    println!("{:?}", even_odd_vec);
}
```

This iterator will first return Some("even") and Some("odd") forever. It will never return None.

Even though `even_odd_iter` will never end, the other iterator only runs six times and thus the final `Vec` also only has six items. The output is

```
[(0, "even"), (1, "odd"), (2, "even"), (3, "odd"), (4, "even"), (5, "odd")]
```

Something similar can be done with a range that doesn't have an ending. If you write `0..`, you create a range (which is also an iterator) that never stops. This is pretty easy to use:

```
fn main() {
    let ten_chars: Vec<char> = ('a'..).take(10).collect();
    let skip_then_ten_chars: Vec<char> =
      ('a'..).skip(1300).take(10).collect();

    println!("{ten_chars:?}");
    println!("{skip_then_ten_chars:?}");
}
```

Both print 10 characters, but the second one skips 1,300 places and prints 10 letters in Armenian:

```
['a', 'b', 'c', 'd', 'e', 'f', 'g', 'h', 'i', 'j']
['յ', 'ս', 'շ', 'ո', 'շ', 'պ', 'ջ', 'ռ', 'ս', 'վ']
```

Another popular method is called `.fold()`. This method is often used to add together the items in an iterator, but you can also do a lot more. The `.fold()` method is somewhat similar to `.for_each()` except that it returns a final value at the end. When using `.fold()`, you first add a starting value, then a comma, and then the closure. The closure gives you two items: the total so far and the next item. Here is a simple example showing `.fold()` to add items together:

```
fn main() {
    let some_numbers = vec![9, 6, 9, 10, 11];

    println!("{}", some_numbers
        .iter()
        .fold(0, |total_so_far, next_number| total_so_far + next_number)
    );
}
```

These steps explain the logic:

1 Starts with 0 and adds the next number: 9
2 Takes that 9 and adds the 6: 15
3 Takes that 15 and adds the 9: 24
4 Takes that 24 and adds the 10: 34
5 Takes that 34 and adds the 11: 45
6 Prints 45

But .fold() isn't just useful for adding numbers. Here is another example where we use .fold() to aggregate (combine) some events into a single struct:

```
#[derive(Debug)]
struct CombinedEvents {
    num_of_events: u32,
    data: Vec<String>,
}

fn main() {
    let events = [
        "Went to grocery store",
        "Came home",
        "Fed cat",
        "Fed cat again",
    ];

    let empty_events = CombinedEvents {
        num_of_events: 0,
        data: vec![]
    };

    let combined_events =
        events
            .iter()
            .fold(empty_events, |mut total_events, next_event| {
                total_events.num_of_events += 1;
                total_events.data.push(next_event.to_string());
                total_events
            });
    println!("{combined_events:#?}");
}
```

We'll start with an empty CombinedEvents struct. You could also use #[derive(Default)] on top and then write CombinedEvents::default() to do the same thing.

.fold() needs a default value, which is the empty struct. Then, for every item in our events array, we get access to the CombinedEvents struct and the next event (a &str).

We increase the number of events by 1 every time, push the next event to the data field and pass on the struct so it is available for the next iteration.

This prints

```
CombinedEvents {
    num_of_events: 4,
    data: [
        "Went to grocery store",
        "Came home",
        "Fed cat",
        "Fed cat again",
    ],
}
```

There really are a lot of convenient methods for iterators. Here is a quick introduction to a few more:

- `.take_while()`—Takes into an iterator as long as it gets `true`. `.take_while(|x| x < &5)` is one example.
- `.cloned()`—Makes a clone inside the iterator. This turns a reference into a value.
- Many other `_while` methods—`.skip_while()`, `.map_while()`, and so on
- `.sum()`—Adds everything together.
- `.by_ref()`—Makes an iterator take by reference.

`.by_ref()` is good if you want to use part of an iterator for something but leave the rest of it alone. For example, the `.take()` method takes a `self`, so it takes the whole iterator if you use it. But if you only want to take two items and leave the iterator alone, you can use `.into_iter().by_ref().take(2)`. Here's a quick example that fails to compile:

```
fn main() {
    let mut number_iter = [7, 8, 9, 10].into_iter();
    let first_two = number_iter.take(2).collect::<Vec<_>>();
    let second_two = number_iter.take(2).collect::<Vec<_>>();
}
```

Oops! `.take()` took ownership of the data:

```
error[E0382]: use of moved value: `number_iter`
  --> src\main.rs:4:22
   |
2  |     let mut number_iter = [7, 8, 9, 10].into_iter();
   |         --------------- move occurs because `number_iter` has type
 ➡`std::array::IntoIter<i32, 4>`, which does not implement the `Copy`
 ➡trait
3  |     let first_two = number_iter.take(2).collect::<Vec<_>>();
   |                                 ------- `number_iter` moved due to
 ➡this method call
4  |     let second_two = number_iter.take(2).collect::<Vec<_>>();
   |                      ^^^^^^^^^^^ value used here after move
   |
```

So we'll use `.by_ref()` to fix it. Now `.take()` won't take ownership anymore:

```
fn main() {
    let mut number_iter = [7, 8, 9, 10].into_iter();

    let first_two = number_iter.by_ref().take(2).collect::<Vec<_>>();
    let second_two = number_iter.take(2).collect::<Vec<_>>();
}
```

You can also create iterators made out of cut-up pieces of a `Vec` or array. The `.chunks()` and `.windows()` methods will let you do that. To use them, write the number of items you want in each piece inside the parentheses. Let's say you have a vector with 10 items, and you want each piece to have a size of 3. Here is the difference between the two methods:

- `.chunks()` will give you four slices: `[0, 1, 2]`, `[3, 4, 5]`, `[6, 7, 8]`, and `[9]`. Note, at the end, it tries to make a slice of three items but doesn't panic if it doesn't have three items left—it just returns one.
- `.windows()` will first give you a slice of `[0, 1, 2]`. Then it will move over one and give you `[1, 2, 3]`. It will do that until it finally reaches the last slice of three and stops.

So let's use them on a simple vector of numbers. It looks like this:

```
fn main() {
    let num_vec = vec![1, 2, 3, 4, 5, 6, 7];

    for chunk in num_vec.chunks(3) {
        println!("{:?}", chunk);
    }
    println!();
    for window in num_vec.windows(3) {
        println!("{:?}", window);
    }
}
```

This prints

```
[1, 2, 3]
[4, 5, 6]
[7]

[1, 2, 3]
[2, 3, 4]
[3, 4, 5]
[4, 5, 6]
[5, 6, 7]
```

By the way, `.chunks()` will panic if you give it a zero. You can write `.chunks(1000)` for a vector with one item, but you can't make a `.chunks(0)` with a length of 0. You can see that right in the function if you look at its source code (clicking on `[src]` will let you see this):

```
pub fn chunks(&self, chunk_size: usize) -> Chunks<'_, T> {
    assert!(chunk_size != 0, "chunk size must be non-zero");
    Chunks::new(self, chunk_size)
}
```

There are a few parts of this code that we don't understand yet, but this line is pretty clear: it will panic if given a 0.

The `.match_indices()` method is sort of like a combination of `.find()` and `.position()`, except that it doesn't involve returning an `Option`. Instead, it returns a tuple of the index and the item that matches.

`.match_indices()` lets you pull out everything inside a `String` or `&str` that matches your input and gives you the index, too. It is similar to `.enumerate()` because it returns a tuple with two items. This method is interesting because it allows you to insert anything that matches a trait called `Pattern`. We don't need to think too much about this trait here—just remember that `&str`, `char`, and even closures can be passed into this method. Here is a quick example:

```
fn main() {
    let some_str = "Er ist noch nicht erklärt. Aber es gibt Krieg. Verlaß
    ➥dich drauf.";
    for (index, item) in some_str.match_indices(|c| c > 'z') {
        println!("{item} at {index}");
    }
    for (index, item) in some_str.match_indices(". ") {
        println!("'{item}' at index {index}");
    }
}
```

This prints

```
ä at 22
ß at 53
'. ' at index 26
'. ' at index 46
```

The `.peekable()` method lets you make an iterator where you can see (peek at) the next item. It's like calling `.next()` (it gives an `Option`) except that the iterator doesn't move, so you can use it as many times as you want. You can think of peekable as "stoppable" because you can stop for as long as you want. The next example is a simple one that shows that we can use `.peek()` forever until it is time to call `.next()` to move on to the next item:

> This creates a type of iterator called Peekable, which has the .peek() method. Regular iterators can't use .peek().

```
fn main() {
    let just_numbers = vec![1, 5, 100];
    let mut number_iter = just_numbers.iter().peekable();

    for _ in 0..3 {
        println!("I love the number {}", number_iter.peek().unwrap());
        println!("I really love the number {}", number_iter.peek().unwrap());
        println!("{} is such a nice number", number_iter.peek().unwrap());
        number_iter.next();
    }
}
```

This prints

```
I love the number 1
I really love the number 1
1 is such a nice number
I love the number 5
I really love the number 5
5 is such a nice number
I love the number 100
I really love the number 100
100 is such a nice number
```

That should be enough iterator methods for one chapter. This covers the majority of the ones you'll use daily. But what if you wanted to see a method for an iterator that you didn't see here? First, take a look in the standard library (https://doc.rust-lang .org/std/iter/trait.Iterator.html) to see whether a method there fits what you need. If that doesn't have what you want, check out the `itertools` crate (https://docs.rs/iter tools/latest/itertools/), which has a ton of other methods that might fit your needs. (We will learn how to use external crates in chapter 16.)

With iterator methods covered, we'll finish off the chapter with something easy: a macro and a method that will help you with quick and easy debugging of your code.

9.2 *The dbg! macro and .inspect*

The `dbg!` macro is a very useful one that prints quick information. It is a good alternative to `println!` because it is faster to type and gives more information:

```
fn main() {
    let my_number = 8;
    dbg!(my_number);
}
```

This prints `[src\main.rs:4] my_number = 8`.

You can put `dbg!` in many other places and even wrap code in it. Look at this code for example:

```
fn main() {
    let mut my_number = 9;
    my_number += 10;
    let new_vec = vec![8, 9, 10];
    let double_vec = new_vec.iter().map(|x| x * 2).collect::<Vec<i32>>();
}
```

This code creates a new mutable number and changes it. Then it creates a `Vec` and uses `.iter()`, `.map()`, and `.collect()` to create a new `Vec`. Interestingly, we can put `dbg!` almost everywhere in this code. `dbg!` essentially asks the compiler: "What are you doing at this moment, and what expression is being returned?" This next code sample is the same as the previous one except we have put `dbg!` everywhere:

```
fn main() {
    let mut my_number = dbg!(9);
    dbg!(my_number += 10);
    let new_vec = dbg!(vec![8, 9, 10]);
    let double_vec = dbg!(new_vec.iter().map(|x| x *
      2).collect::<Vec<i32>>());
    dbg!(double_vec);
}
```

Each line of the code, followed by the output from the `dbg!` macro, is

```
let mut my_number = dbg!(9);
[src\main.rs:3] 9 = 9
```

and

```
dbg!(my_number += 10);
[src\main.rs:4] my_number += 10 = ()
```

and

```
let new_vec = dbg!(vec![8, 9, 10]);
[src\main.rs:6] vec![8, 9, 10] = [
    8,
    9,
    10,
]
```

and

```
let double_vec = dbg!(new_vec.iter().map(|x| x * 2).collect::<Vec<i32>>());
[src\main.rs:8] new_vec.iter().map(|x| x * 2).collect::<Vec<i32>>() = [
    16,
    18,
    20,
]
```

which shows you the value of the expression, and

```
dbg!(double_vec);
[src\main.rs:10] double_vec = [
    16,
    18,
    20,
]
```

Another method called .inspect() is similar to dbg!, but it is used in iterators in a similar fashion to .map(). This method simply gives you the item to look at, which lets you print it or do whatever you want. For example, let's look at our double_vec again:

```
fn main() {
    let new_vec = vec![8, 9, 10];

    let double_vec = new_vec
        .iter()
        .map(|x| x * 2)
        .collect::<Vec<i32>>();
}
```

We want to know more information about what the code is doing, so we add .inspect() in two places:

```
fn main() {
    let new_vec = vec![8, 9, 10];

    let double_vec = new_vec
        .iter()
        .inspect(|first_item| println!("The item is: {first_item}"))
        .map(|x| x * 2)
```

```
        .inspect(|next_item| println!("Then it is: {next_item}"))
        .collect::<Vec<i32>>();
}
```

This prints

```
The item is: 8
Then it is: 16
The item is: 9
Then it is: 18
The item is: 10
Then it is: 20
```

Because .inspect() takes a closure, we have as much space as we like to work with the item:

```
fn main() {
    let new_vec = vec![8, 9, 10];

    let double_vec = new_vec
        .iter()
        .inspect(|first_item| {
            println!("The item is: {first_item}");
            match **first_item % 2 {          ⟵┐  The first item is a
                0 => println!("It is even."),    │  &&i32 so we use **.
                _ => println!("It is odd."),
            }
            println!("In binary it is {:b}.", first_item);
        })
        .map(|x| x * 2)
        .collect::<Vec<i32>>();
}
```

This prints

```
The item is: 8
It is even.
In binary it is 1000.
The item is: 9
It is odd.
In binary it is 1001.
The item is: 10
It is even.
In binary it is 1010.
```

This chapter probably gave you a feel for why Rust code looks so functional some-times. The reason is that the more you know about iterators and closures, the more you want to use them, so code written by experienced Rust users tends to have a lot of these. As you use Rust, you'll begin to think of chains of one method after another, much in the same way you think in English or your native language. Take this human-readable example of an operation we might want to do: "Make an iterator, keep every-thing greater than 5, multiply each item by 2, reverse the iterator, pull off the first 10 items, and collect them into a Vec." You can do that with one method for each. This is pretty close to the way we think as humans and probably another reason why iterator methods are used so much in Rust.

The next chapter has two important concepts. The first is lifetimes, which you use to tell Rust how long a reference will live. The next is interior mutability, which lets you (safely!) mutate variables without needing to use the `mut` keyword.

Summary

- Mapping, filtering, and collecting is probably the most common use of iterators. As you get more used to them, you can start trying out related methods like `.filter_map()` and `.and_then()`.
- Instead of looping over the items in an iterator, see whether there's a `_while` method for what you want to do: `.take_while()`, `.map_while()`, and so on.
- The most common methods for finding items are `.any()`, `.all()`, `.find()`, and `.position()`. Methods like `.any()` short-circuit, so be sure to `.rev()` the iterator if you think an item might be closer to the end of your iterator.
- While iterators usually return `Some` until they return `None`, there's no rule that you have to do so. They can return only `Some`, only `None`, or anything else you can imagine.
- The `.fold()` method is usually used to sum numbers, but there's no rule about that either. You can find a lot of other uses for it, too.
- Some methods like `.zip()` and `.enumerate()` let you combine or expand on the existing items in an iterator.
- You can quickly debug your code with the `dbg!` macro and the `.inspect()` method when using iterators.

Lifetimes and interior mutability

It is now time to learn about Rust's famous *lifetimes,* used by the compiler to know when variables can be dropped and how long references last. Usually, you don't need to specify lifetimes in your code, but sometimes the compiler needs a bit of help and will ask you to tell it how long something should last. We are also going to learn how to (safely!) mutate values without needing a mutable reference to do it!

10.1 Types of &str

We've been using `&str` for most of the book so far. But here's an interesting fact about them: there is actually more than one type of `&str`. The two ways you'll see a `&str` are as follows:

- *String literals*—You make these when you write `let my_str = "I am a &str";`. They last for the whole program because they are written directly into the binary. They have the type `&'static str`. The `'` means its lifetime, and string literals have a lifetime called `static`.
- *Borrowed* `str`—This is the regular `&str` form without a `'static` lifetime. If you have a `String` and pass a reference to it (a `&String`), Rust will convert it to a `&str` when you need it. This is thanks to a trait called `Deref`. We will learn to use `Deref` in chapter 15, but, for the moment, just remember that you can pass in a `&String` to a function that takes a `&str`.

Here is an example of a borrowed `str`:

```
fn prints_str(my_str: &str) {
    println!("{my_str}");
}

fn main() {
    let my_string = String::from("I am a string");
    prints_str(&my_string);
}
```

We know that you can't return a reference from something that only lives inside a function because it dies as soon as the function is over. When the variable dies, you don't want to have a reference pointing to where the data was. That's unsafe, so Rust doesn't allow it. But when using a `str` with a `'static` lifetime, the data never disappears. So, you can return a reference to it! In the following code, the first function will work, but the second will not:

```
fn works() -> &'static str {
    "I live forever!"
}

// fn does_not_work() -> &'static str {
//     &String::from("Sorry, I only live inside the fn. Not 'static")
// }
```

You are probably getting the feeling that lifetimes are a pretty big subject in Rust. They definitely are. Let's start learning how they work.

10.2 *Lifetime annotations*

We already learned that a lifetime means "how long the variable or reference lives." Most of the time, Rust takes care of lifetimes for you, but sometimes, it needs a bit of extra help. This extra help is called a *lifetime annotation*, which means "extra lifetime information." You only need to think about lifetimes with references. References aren't allowed to live longer than the object they come from because references point to the same memory, and this memory gets freed up when the object is gone. It would be a big problem if references could live longer because then they could point to memory that is already cleaned up and used by something else. You see lifetime annotations in a lot of places. We'll start with lifetime annotations in functions.

10.2.1 *Lifetimes in functions*

Lifetimes are not too hard to work with in functions because functions have a nice clear start and end. Here's an example of a function that doesn't work:

```
fn returns_reference() -> &str {
    let my_string = String::from("I am a string");
    &my_string
}
```

The problem is that `my_string` only lives inside `returns_reference`. We try to return `&my_string`, but `&my_string` can't exist without `my_string`. So the compiler says no.

Writing the code this way doesn't fix the problem, either:

```
fn returns_str() -> &str {
    let my_string = String::from("I am a string");
    "I am a str"
}

fn main() {
    let my_str = returns_str();
    println!("{my_str}");
}
```

In both cases, it *almost* works. Each time we try, the compiler says

```
error[E0106]: missing lifetime specifier
 --> src\main.rs:6:21
  |
6 | fn returns_str() -> &str {
  |                     ^ expected named lifetime parameter
  |
  = help: this function's return type contains a borrowed value, but there
 ➡ is no value for it to be borrowed from
help: consider using the `'static` lifetime
  |
6 | fn returns_str() -> &'static str {
  |                     ^^^^^^^^
```

This `missing lifetime specifier` means that we need to add a ' to the lifetime. The next part of the error message says that it `contains a borrowed value, but there is no value for it to be borrowed from`. This message means that the return value for the function is `&str`, which is a borrowed `str`, but `I am a str` isn't borrowed from a variable. However, the compiler guesses at what we are trying to do by suggesting `consider using the 'static lifetime` by writing `&'static str`, which is a string literal.

If we try the compiler's suggestion, the code will now compile:

```
fn returns_str() -> &'static str {
    let my_string = String::from("I am a string");
    "I am a str"
}
```

```
fn main() {
    let my_str = returns_str();
    println!("{my_str}");
}
```

Of course, the code only worked because we were outright ignoring my_string and letting it die inside the function. But you can see that the compiler is satisfied that we returned a &str with a lifetime of 'static. Meanwhile, my_string can only be returned as an owned String: we can't return a reference to it because it is going to die after the next line.

Now, fn returns_str() -> &'static str tells Rust: "Don't worry; we will only return a string literal." String literals live for the whole program, so the compiler is now happy with this.

You might notice that lifetime annotations work in a similar way to generic annotations. When we tell the compiler something like <T: Display>, we promise that we will only use something that implements Display. The compiler will understand this and reject anything that doesn't implement Display. And when we tell the compiler that a function returns a &'static str, it will understand and reject anything that doesn't have this lifetime. But writing &'static str doesn't give anything a 'static lifetime in the same way that writing T: Display doesn't give anything the trait Display.

However, 'static is not the only lifetime: every variable has a lifetime, but we don't usually have to write it. The compiler is pretty smart and can usually figure it out for itself. We only have to write the lifetime for references when the compiler can't decide on its own.

10.2.2 *Lifetime annotations in types*

Here is an example of another lifetime. Imagine we want to create a City struct and try to give it a &str for the name instead of a String. Interestingly, if we write &str instead of String, the code won't compile:

```
#[derive(Debug)]
struct City {
    name: &str,              ◁——┐  Here's the
    date_founded: u32,           │  problem.
}

fn main() {
    let my_city = City {
        name: "Ichinomiya",
        date_founded: 1921,
    };
}
```

The compiler says:

```
error[E0106]: missing lifetime specifier
 --> src\main.rs:3:11
  |
```

```
3 |     name: &str,
  |               ^ expected named lifetime parameter
  |
help: consider introducing a named lifetime parameter
  |
2 | struct City<'a> {
3 |     name: &'a str,
  |
```

Rust needs a lifetime for `&str` because `&str` is a reference. What happens when the value that `name` points to is dropped? Its memory would be cleaned up, and the reference would point to nothing or even someone else's data. That would be unsafe, so Rust doesn't allow it.

What about `'static`? Will that work? We used it before. Let's try:

```
#[derive(Debug)]
struct City {
    name: &'static str,        ⟵┐ Changes
    date_founded: u32,              &str to &'static str
}

fn main() {
    let my_city = City {
        name: "Ichinomiya",
        date_founded: 1921,
    };

    println!("{} was founded in {}", my_city.name, my_city.date_founded);
}
```

Okay, that works. Maybe this is what you wanted for the struct. However, note that now we can only take string literals, not references to something else. That's because we told the compiler that we would only give it something that can live for the whole life of the program. So, this will not work:

```
#[derive(Debug)]
struct City {
    name: &'static str,        ⟵┐ The parameter name is 'static, so it must
    date_founded: u32,            be able to live for the whole program.
}

fn main() {
    let city_names = vec!["Ichinomiya".to_string(),    │ However, city_names does not
    "Kurume".to_string()];                          ⟵ live for the whole program.

    let my_city = City {                 │ This is a &str, not a &'static str. It is a
        name: &city_names[0],        ⟵ reference to a value inside city_names.
        date_founded: 1921,
    };

    println!("{} was founded in {}", my_city.name, my_city.date_founded);
}
```

The compiler says:

```
error[E0597]: `city_names` does not live long enough
  --> src\main.rs:12:16
   |
12 |          name: &city_names[0],
   |                ^^^^^^^^^^^^
   |                |
   |                borrowed value does not live long enough
   |                requires that `city_names` is borrowed for `'static`
...
18 | }
   | - `city_names` dropped here while still borrowed
```

This is important to understand because the reference we gave it *does* live long enough for us to print the struct `City`. But we promised that we would only give it a `&'static str`, and that is what it expects.

Now, we will try what the compiler suggested before. It said to try writing `struct City<'a>` and `name: &'a str`. This means that it will only take a reference for `name` if it lives as long as `City`.

You can read the `<'a>` and `name: &'a str` in the code as "The `City` struct has a lifetime that we will call `'a`, and its `name` property must also live at least as long as `'a`. Other shorter lifetimes will not be accepted."

```
#[derive(Debug)]                    | City has
struct City<'a> {            ⟵──┘   lifetime 'a.
    name: &'a str,               ⟵┐ Name also has
    date_founded: u32,             | lifetime 'a.
}

fn main() {
    let city_names = vec!["Ichinomiya".to_string(), "Kurume".to_string()];

    let my_city = City {
        name: &city_names[0],
        date_founded: 1921,
    };

    println!("{} was founded in {}", my_city.name, my_city.date_founded);
}
```

Also, remember that you can write anything instead of `'a` if you want. This is also similar to generics, where we write `T` and `U` but can write anything.

```
#[derive(Debug)]                    | The lifetime is
struct City<'city> {         ⟵──    now called 'city.
    name: &'city str,            ⟵┐ Name has the
    date_founded: u32,             | 'city lifetime.
}
```

Usually, you will write `'a`, `'b`, `'c`, etc., because it is quick and the usual way to write. But you can change it if you want. One good tip is that changing the lifetime to a human-readable name can help you read code if it is very complicated.

Let's look at the comparison to traits for generics again with this example:

```
use std::fmt::Display;

fn prints<T: Display>(input: T) {
    println!("T is {input}");
}
```

When you write `T: Display`, it means "Please only take `T` if it has the trait `Display`." It does not mean "I am giving the trait `Display` to `T`."

The same is true for lifetimes. Take a close look at `'a` here:

```
#[derive(Debug)]
struct City<'a> {
    name: &'a str,
    date_founded: u32,
}
```

The `'a` means "Please only take an input for `name` if it lives at least as long as `City`." It does not mean, "This will make the input for `name` live as long as `City`."

10.2.3 *The anonymous lifetime*

Do you remember seeing a `<'_>` back in chapter 7 when we implemented `Display` for our `Cat` struct? Here's what we wrote:

```
impl fmt::Display for Cat {
    fn fmt(&self, f: &mut fmt::Formatter<'_>) -> fmt::Result {
        write!(f, "{} is a cat who is {} years old.", self.name, self.age)
    }
}
```

Now, we can finally learn what this `<'_>` means. This is called the *anonymous lifetime* and is an indicator that references are being used. Rust will suggest it to you when you are implementing structs, for example. Here is one struct that almost works but not yet:

```
struct Adventurer<'a> {
    name: &'a str,
    hit_points: u32,
}

impl Adventurer {
    fn take_damage(&mut self) {
        self.hit_points -= 20;
        println!("{} has {} hit points left!", self.name, self.hit_points);
    }
}
```

We did what we needed to do for the struct: we said that `name` comes from a `&str`. That means we need to indicate a lifetime, so we gave it `<'a>`. But then Rust tells us to indicate a lifetime again inside the `impl` block:

```
error[E0726]: implicit elided lifetime not allowed here
 --> src\main.rs:6:6
  |
6 | impl Adventurer {
  |      ^^^^^^^^^^- help: indicate the anonymous lifetime: `<'_>`
```

It wants us to add that anonymous lifetime to show that there is a reference being used. If we write that, it will be happy:

```
struct Adventurer<'a> {
    name: &'a str,
    hit_points: u32,
}

impl Adventurer<'_> {
    fn take_damage(&mut self) {
        self.hit_points -= 20;
        println!("{} has {} hit points left!", self.name, self.hit_points);
    }
}
```

This lifetime was made so that you don't always have to write things like `impl<'a> Adventurer<'a>`, because the struct already shows the lifetime.

Hold on, though. Why does the `impl` block need to talk about lifetimes, too? Let's pretend there is a trait that needs to deal with two lifetimes. It might look like this:

```
trait HasSomeLifeTime<'a, 'b> {}
```

You might also have a struct that also has two references, and each one has its own lifetime for some reason. (Don't worry, this isn't something you usually see in Rust. It's just to explain.)

```
struct SomeStruct<'a, 'b> {
    name: &'a str,
    other: &'b str
}
```

Imagine you want to implement `HasSomeLifeTime` for `SomeStruct`. The trait has its own lifetimes to deal with, and the struct has its own lifetimes to deal with. Both the struct and the trait choose to call them `'a` and `'b`, but `'a` and `'b` in the struct `Some-Struct` have nothing to do with `'a` and `'b` in the trait `HasSomeLifeTime`. Therefore, when you use `impl`, you declare some lifetimes, and that's when you can decide how long one lifetime must be compared to the other.

You might implement the trait like this:

```
impl <'a, 'b> HasSomeLifeTime<'a, 'b> for SomeStruct<'a, 'b> {}
```

This means "We are talking about two different lifetimes here, `'a` and `'b`." Now, the `'a` and `'b` for the trait and the struct are the same lifetime.

But maybe you don't want to say that they will all be the same, and maybe you don't want to use the same names either. You could even write this:

```
impl <'one, 'two, 'three, 'four> HasSomeLifeTime<'one, 'three> for
➟SomeStruct<'two, 'four> {}
```

This means "There are four lifetimes involved here," and the trait has its own two while the struct has its own two. The four lifetimes can now all be separate from each other.

But you almost never need to worry about lifetimes to this point in Rust, so don't worry. Even in this complex example, you can just elide the lifetimes and let Rust figure it out:

```
impl HasSomeLifeTime<'_, '_> for SomeStruct<'_, '_> {}
```

That means "Each one has its own two lifetimes; you figure it out." To emphasize this point again: it is very rare to deal with this many lifetimes in Rust!

Lifetimes can be difficult in Rust, but here are some tips to avoid getting too stressed about them:

- You can stay with owned types, use clones, etc., if you want to avoid lifetimes for the time being. If you get a `&'a str` in a function, you can just turn it into a `String` and put that on your struct! Rust is extremely fast, even when you do this.
- Much of the time, when the compiler wants a lifetime, you will just end up writing `<'a>` in a few places, and then it will work. It's just a way of saying, "Don't worry, I won't give you anything that doesn't live long enough."
- You can explore lifetimes just a bit at a time. Write some code with owned values and then make one a reference. The compiler will start to complain but also give some suggestions. If it gets too complicated, you can undo it and try again next time.

Let's do this with our code and see what the compiler says. We'll go back and take the lifetimes out and implement `Display`. `Display` will just print the `Adventurer`'s name. Here is the code again that won't compile:

```
struct Adventurer {
    name: &str,
    hit_points: u32,
}

impl Adventurer {
    fn take_damage(&mut self) {
        self.hit_points -= 20;
        println!("{} has {} hit points left!", self.name, self.hit_points);
    }
}
```

```
impl std::fmt::Display for Adventurer {
        fn fmt(&self, f: &mut std::fmt::Formatter<'_>) -> std::fmt::Result {
            write!(f, "{} has {} hit points.", self.name, self.hit_points)
        }
}
```

The first complaint is this:

```
error[E0106]: missing lifetime specifier
 --> src\main.rs:2:11
  |
2 |     name: &str,
  |           ^ expected named lifetime parameter
  |
help: consider introducing a named lifetime parameter
  |
1 | struct Adventurer<'a> {
2 |     name: &'a str,
  |
```

It suggests what to do: `<'a>` after `Adventurer` and `&'a str`. So we do that. The code is closer to compiling but not quite:

```
struct Adventurer<'a> {
    name: &'a str,
    hit_points: u32,
}

impl Adventurer {
    fn take_damage(&mut self) {
        self.hit_points -= 20;
        println!("{} has {} hit points left!", self.name, self.hit_points);
    }
}

impl std::fmt::Display for Adventurer {
        fn fmt(&self, f: &mut std::fmt::Formatter<'_>) -> std::fmt::Result {
            write!(f, "{} has {} hit points.", self.name, self.hit_points)
        }
}
```

The compiler is now happy with our changes, but it is wondering about the `impl` blocks. It wants us to mention that it's using references:

```
error[E0726]: implicit elided lifetime not allowed here
 --> src\main.rs:6:6
  |
6 | impl Adventurer {
  |      ^^^^^^^^^^- help: indicate the anonymous lifetime: `<'_>`

error[E0726]: implicit elided lifetime not allowed here
  --> src\main.rs:12:28
  |
12 | impl std::fmt::Display for Adventurer {
  |                            ^^^^^^^^^^- help: indicate the anonymous
                                  ➡lifetime: `<'_>`
```

Okay, so we add the anonymous lifetime as it suggests, and now it works! Now, we can make an `Adventurer` and do some things with it:

```
struct Adventurer<'a> {
    name: &'a str,
    hit_points: u32,
}

impl Adventurer<'_> {
    fn take_damage(&mut self) {
        self.hit_points -= 20;
        println!("{} has {} hit points left!", self.name, self.hit_points);
    }
}

impl std::fmt::Display for Adventurer<'_> {

        fn fmt(&self, f: &mut std::fmt::Formatter<'_>) -> std::fmt::Result {
            write!(f, "{} has {} hit points.", self.name, self.hit_points)
        }
}

fn main() {
    let mut billy = Adventurer {
        name: "Billy",
        hit_points: 100_000,
    };
    println!("{}", billy);
    billy.take_damage();
}
```

This prints

```
Billy has 100000 hit points.
Billy has 99980 hit points left!
```

You can see that lifetimes are often the compiler wanting to make sure. It is usually smart enough to almost guess at what lifetimes you want and just needs you to tell it so that it can be certain.

10.3   *Interior mutability*

Interior mutability means having a little bit of mutability on the inside (the interior). Remember, in Rust, you need to use mut to change a variable. But there are also some ways to change them without the word mut. This is because Rust has some ways to let you safely change values inside of a struct that is itself immutable. Each way of doing so follows some rules that make sure that changing the values is still safe.

Let's look at a simple example where we would want this. Imagine a struct called `PhoneModel` with many fields:

```
struct PhoneModel {
    company_name: String,
    model_name: String,
    screen_size: f32,
```

```
        memory: usize,
        date_issued: u32,
        on_sale: bool,
    }

    impl PhoneModel {
        fn method_one(&self) {}
        fn method_two(&self) {}
    }

    fn main() {
        let super_phone_3000 = PhoneModel {
            company_name: "YY Electronics".to_string(),
            model_name: "Super Phone 3000".to_string(),
            screen_size: 7.5,
            memory: 4_000_000,
            date_issued: 2020,
            on_sale: true,
        };

    }
```

These methods are unfinished so they don't do anything, but imagine we have a lot of methods that all take &self but that we'd like to mutate some data inside PhoneModel.

Maybe we want the fields in `PhoneModel` to be immutable because we don't want the data to change. The `date_issued` and `screen_size` never change, for example, and the methods we have for `PhoneModel` use `&self` and not a `&mut self`, which is more convenient for us. We'd rather not have to use `&mut self` if we don't have to.

But inside is one field called `on_sale`. A phone model will first be on sale (`true`), but later, the company will stop selling it. Can we make just this one field mutable? We don't want to write `let mut super_phone_3000;`. If we do, the whole struct will become mutable. Maybe there is a function we need to use that takes a `&PhoneModel` as an input, not a `&mut Phonemodel`, but we'd still like to mutate some data inside it.

Fortunately, there is a way to do this. Rust has four main ways to allow some safe mutability inside of something that is immutable: `Cell`, `RefCell`, `Mutex`, and `RwLock`. Let's look at them now.

10.3.1 *Cell*

The simplest way to use interior mutability in Rust is called `Cell`, which its documentation describes as a "mutable memory location." The signature of `Cell` is just `Cell<T>`, the `T` being the data type you want it to hold. Let's use `Cell` for our previous Phone-Model.

First, we write `use std::cell::Cell;`, so we can just write `Cell` instead of `std::cell::Cell` every time. Then we change `on_sale: bool` to `on_sale: Cell<bool>`. Now, it isn't a `bool`: it's a `Cell` that holds a `bool`.

`Cell` has a method called `.set()` where you can change the value. We use `.set()` to change `on_sale: true` to `on_sale: Cell::new(false)`:

```
use std::cell::Cell;

#[derive(Debug)]
struct PhoneModel {
```

```
        company_name: String,
        model_name: String,
        screen_size: f32,
        memory: usize,
        date_issued: u32,
        on_sale: Cell<bool>,
}

impl PhoneModel {
    fn make_not_on_sale(&self) {
        self.on_sale.set(false);
    }
}

fn main() {
    let super_phone_3000 = PhoneModel {
        company_name: "YY Electronics".to_string(),
        model_name: "Super Phone 3000".to_string(),
        screen_size: 7.5,
        memory: 4_000_000,
        date_issued: 2020,
        on_sale: Cell::new(true),
    };
```

Ten years later, `super_phone_3000` is not on sale anymore:

```
    super_phone_3000.make_not_on_sale();
    println!("{super_phone_3000:#?}");
}
```

The input shows that the value for `on_sale` has changed to `false` without us needing to use any mutable references:

```
PhoneModel {
    company_name: "YY Electronics",
    model_name: "Super Phone 3000",
    screen_size: 7.5,
    memory: 4000000,
    date_issued: 2020,
    on_sale: Cell {
        value: false,
    },
}
```

`Cell` works for all types, but it works best for simple `Copy` types because it gives values, not references. `Cell` has a method called `.get()`, for example, that only works when the inner type implements `Copy`.

Another type that you can use is `RefCell`.

10.3.2 *RefCell*

A `RefCell` is another way to change values without needing to declare `mut`. It means "reference cell" and is a bit similar not only to a `Cell` but also to regular references.

Let's make a `User` struct for the next example that holds a `RefCell`. So far, you can see that it is similar to `Cell` in that it holds a value, and you use a method called `new()` to create it:

```
use std::cell::RefCell;

#[derive(Debug)]
struct User {
    id: u32,
    year_registered: u32,
    username: String,
    active: RefCell<bool>,
}

fn main() {
    let user_1 = User {
        id: 1,
        year_registered: 2020,
        username: "User 1".to_string(),
        active: RefCell::new(true),
    };

    println!("{:?}", user_1.active);
}
```

In real life, this would have a lot more fields, but we'll just include a few to keep it short.

This prints `RefCell { value: true }`.

There are many methods for `RefCell`. Two of them are `.borrow()` and `.borrow_mut()`. With these methods, you can do the same thing you do with `&` and `&mut`. The rules are the same:

- Having many immutable borrows is fine.
- One mutable borrow is fine.
- Mutable and immutable borrows together is not fine.

Changing the value in a `RefCell` feels pretty much the same as using a mutable reference. You can create a variable that can be used to mutate the value and then change the value that way:

```
let user_1 = User {
    id: 1,
    year_registered: 2020,
    username: "User 1".to_string(),
    active: RefCell::new(true),
};
let mut borrow = user_1.active.borrow_mut();
*borrow = false;
```

Note how similar this is to using a mutable reference without a `RefCell` if `user_1` itself had been declared as `mut`:

```
let borrow = &mut user_1.active;
*borrow = false;
```

Or you can change the value without declaring a variable to do it with:

```
let user_1 = User {
    id: 1,
    year_registered: 2020,
    username: "User 1".to_string(),
    active: RefCell::new(true),
};
*user_1.active.borrow_mut() = false;
```

But you have to be careful with a `RefCell` because it checks borrows at run time, not compilation time. So the following will compile, even though it is wrong:

```
use std::cell::RefCell;

#[derive(Debug)]
struct User {
    id: u32,
    year_registered: u32,
    username: String,
    active: RefCell<bool>,
}

fn main() {
    let user_1 = User {
        id: 1,
        year_registered: 2020,
        username: "User 1".to_string(),
        active: RefCell::new(true),
    };

    let borrow_one = user_1.active.borrow_mut();     ⟵  First mutable
    let borrow_two = user_1.active.borrow_mut();     ⟵  borrow—okay
}                                                        Second mutable
                                                         borrow—not okay
```

But if you run it, it will immediately panic:

```
thread 'main' panicked at 'already borrowed: BorrowMutError',
➥src\main.rs:21:36
Note: run with `RUST_BACKTRACE=1` environment variable to display a
➥backtrace
```

There are two ways to be sure that your code won't panic when using a `RefCell`:

- Always immediately change the value with `.borrow_mut()` without assigning this to a variable. If no variables are holding on to the output of `.borrow_mut()`, there is no way the code will panic.
- Use the `.try_borrow_mut()` method instead of `borrow_mut()` if there is a chance of a double borrow. This will return an error if the `RefCell` is already borrowed.

So that was a quick introduction to `Cell` and `RefCell`, the two simplest types for interior mutability in Rust. The next two are known as `Mutex` and `RwLock` and will seem sort of similar to `RefCell`. So why do they exist? They exist because of multiple threads, which are used to do two things at once in your code. `Cell` and `RefCell` don't have any guards in place to make sure that data isn't being changed at the same time, so Rust won't let you use them in multiple threads. Here is a quick teaser:

```
use std::cel::RefCell;

fn main() {
    let bool_in_refcell = RefCell::new(true);

    std::thread::spawn(|| {
        *bool_in_refcell.borrow_mut() = false;
    });
}
```

> Here, we try to start a new thread to do something at the same time as the rest of the code. But Rust won't let us use a RefCell inside it.

Rust tells us exactly why it won't let the code compile:

```
error[E0277]: `RefCell<bool>` cannot be shared between threads safely
```

We will learn to use multiple threads in the next chapter, but, for now, just remember that this is why the next two types exist. So let's move on to the next one!

10.3.3 *Mutex*

`Mutex` is another way to change values without declaring `mut`. Mutex means "mutual exclusion," which means "only one at a time." This is why a `Mutex` is safe because it only lets one thread change it at a time. To do this, it uses a method called `.lock()`, which returns a struct called a `MutexGuard`. This `MutexGuard` is like locking a door from the inside. You go into a room and lock the door, and now you can change things inside the room. Nobody else can come in and stop you because you locked the door.

A `Mutex` is easier to understand through examples. In this example, note that `Mutex` is located at `std::sync::Mutex`. Inside the standard library, `sync` is for types that are thread-safe, meaning they can be used in multiple threads:

```
use std::sync::Mutex;

fn main() {
    let my_mutex = Mutex::new(5);

    let mut mutex_changer = my_mutex.lock().unwrap();

    println!("{my_mutex:?}");

    println!("{mutex_changer:?}");

    *mutex_changer = 6;

    println!("{mutex_changer:?}");
}
```

> A new Mutex<i32>. We don't need to declare it as mut.

> mutex_changer is a MutexGuard, which gives access to the Mutex. It has to be mut because we will change it. The Mutex itself is now locked.

> This prints 5. Let's change it to 6.

> Here we can see that the Mutex is locked as it prints "Mutex { data: <locked> }". The only way to access and change the data is through mutex_changer.

> And now it prints 6.

> mutex_changer is a MutexGuard<i32>, but we want to change the i32 itself. We can use * to change the i32 (the inner value).

Here is the output:

```
Mutex { data: <locked>, poisoned: false, .. }
5
6
```

But `mutex_changer` still holds a lock after it is done changing the value. How do we stop it and unlock the `Mutex`? A `Mutex` is unlocked when the `MutexGuard` goes out of scope (when it is dropped). One way to do this is to put the `MutexGuard` into its own scope:

```
use std::sync::Mutex;

fn main() {
    let my_mutex = Mutex::new(5);
    {
        let mut mutex_changer = my_mutex.lock().unwrap();
        *mutex_changer = 6;
    }

    println!("{my_mutex:?}");
}
```

At this point, mutex_changer goes out of scope and is now gone, and my_mutex isn't locked anymore.

Note that the output now shows us the data inside because we print `my_mutex` when it isn't locked anymore:

```
Mutex { data: 6, poisoned: false, .. }
```

There is an easier way to unlock a `Mutex`, though, thanks to a convenient function called `drop()`, which automatically makes an object go out of scope. We can simply stick `mutex_changer` inside `drop()`, and it will cease to exist:

```
use std::sync::Mutex;

fn main() {
    let my_mutex = Mutex::new(5);
    let mut mutex_changer = my_mutex.lock().unwrap();
    *mutex_changer = 6;
    drop(mutex_changer);

    println!("{my_mutex:?}");
}
```

This drops mutex_changer. It is now gone, and my_mutex is unlocked.

Output:
Mutex { data: 6 }

You have to be careful with a `Mutex` because if another variable tries to `.lock()` it, it will wait forever. This is known as a deadlock:

```
use std::sync::Mutex;

fn main() {
    let my_mutex = Mutex::new(5);
    let mut mutex_changer = my_mutex.lock().unwrap();
    let mut other_mutex_changer = my_mutex.lock().unwrap();

    println!("This will never print...");
}
```

mutex_changer has the lock after this line.

But other_mutex_changer wants the lock, too. The program will wait forever.

This behavior makes sense because Mutexes are made for usage across multiple threads, and if you have two threads doing two things at the same time, any call to .lock() to a Mutex that is already locked should wait until the other thread is done. But it also means that you have to be a bit careful with your code to avoid deadlocks.

The solutions to this are similar to the solutions mentioned in section 10.3.2 on RefCell. Instead of .lock(), you can use a method called .try_lock(). This method will try once, and if it doesn't get the lock, it will give up. You can use if let or match for this:

```
use std::sync::Mutex;

fn main() {
    let my_mutex = Mutex::new(5);
    let mut mutex_changer = my_mutex.lock().unwrap();
    let mut other_mutex_changer = my_mutex.try_lock();

    if let Ok(value) = other_mutex_changer {
        println!("The MutexGuard has: {value}")
    } else {
        println!("Didn't get the lock")
    }
}
```

This code will print Didn't get the lock instead of deadlocking and holding up the program.

Same as with a RefCell, you don't need to make a variable to change the Mutex. You can just use .lock() to change the value right away:

```
use std::sync::Mutex;

fn main() {
    let my_mutex = Mutex::new(5);
    *my_mutex.lock().unwrap() = 6;
}
```

When you type *my_mutex.lock().unwrap() = 6;, you never create a variable that holds the lock, so you don't need to call drop(). You can do it 100 times if you want, and it doesn't matter because no variable ever holds the lock:

```
use std::sync::Mutex;

fn main() {
    let my_mutex = Mutex::new(5);
    for _ in 0..100 {
        *my_mutex.lock().unwrap() += 1;
    }
}
```

10.3.4 RwLock

RwLock stands for "read–write lock." It is not only like a Mutex because it is thread-safe, but it is also similar to a RefCell in the way it is used: you can get mutable or immutable references to the value inside. You use `.write().unwrap()` instead of `.lock().unwrap()` to change it. You can also use `.read().unwrap()` to get read access. `RwLock` is similar to `RefCell` because it follows the same rules that Rust uses for references:

- Many variables with `.read()` access is okay.
- One variable with `.write()` access is okay.
- You can't hold anything else on top of a variable returned from `.write()`. You can't have an extra variable made with `.write()` or even with `.read()`.

But `RwLock` is also similar to `Mutex` in that the program will deadlock instead of panicking if you try to use `.write()` when you can't get access:

```
use std::sync::RwLock;

fn main() {
    let my_rwlock = RwLock::new(5);
    let read1 = my_rwlock.read().unwrap();          One .read()
    let read2 = my_rwlock.read().unwrap();          is fine.        Another .read()—
    println!("{read1:?}, {read2:?}");                               also fine
    let write1 = my_rwlock.write().unwrap();        Uh oh, now
}                                                   we're deadlocked.
```

This code will print 5, 5 and then deadlock forever.

To solve this, we can use `drop()` (or a new scope) just like in a `Mutex`:

```
use std::sync::RwLock;

fn main() {
    let my_rwlock = RwLock::new(5);
    let read1 = my_rwlock.read().unwrap();
    let read2 = my_rwlock.read().unwrap();
    println!("{read1:?}, {read2:?}");
    drop(read1);                                We dropped both,
    drop(read2);                                so we can use .write().

    let mut write1 = my_rwlock.write().unwrap();
    *write1 = 6;
    drop(write1);
    println!("{:?}", my_rwlock);
}
```

This time, there is no deadlock, and the output shows the changed value:

```
5, 5
RwLock { data: 6, poisoned: false, .. }
```

`RwLock` has the same `.try_` methods as well to help ensure that you'll never have a deadlock: `.try_read()` and `.try_write`:

```
fn main() {
    let my_rwlock = RwLock::new(5);
```

```
let read1 = my_rwlock.read().unwrap();
let read2 = my_rwlock.read().unwrap();

if let Ok(mut number) = my_rwlock.try_write() {
    *number += 10;
    println!("Now the number is {}", number);
} else {
    println!("Couldn't get write access, sorry!")
};
}
```

Once again, the code gives up with the message `Couldn't get write access, sorry!` instead of deadlocking forever.

You learned in this chapter that sometimes the compiler doesn't know, or can't decide, how long a reference lives. In those rare cases, you have to tell it which lifetime to use. But the good news is that you can just use owned types in the meantime if you find lifetimes too annoying to use. You can always get used to lifetimes a bit at a time.

Also, hopefully, you enjoyed learning that Rust has some more flexibility than you thought. Rust is strict, but it's not strict just to be strict. As long as there is a safe way to mutate a value, Rust has no problem with it.

The next chapter has a bunch of interesting stuff all together. You'll learn how to use a `Cow` (yes, that's a type in Rust) and reference counters and start learning about multiple threads to do many things at the same time.

Summary

- If you don't want to think too much about lifetime annotations yet, you can mostly avoid them by using owned data as much as possible.
- A lifetime annotation is another type of generic annotation. They tell the compiler what lifetimes to expect, but they don't change how long references live.
- If you are using a `&str` in one of your types but will only give it string literals, you can avoid lifetime annotations by having it take a `&'static str` instead of a `&'a str`.
- If you need mutability but can't or don't want to use a `&mut`, try one of the four interior mutability types. `Cell` is best for `Copy` types, `RefCell` is similar to regular references, and `Mutex` and `RwLock` can be passed between threads.
- When changing values inside a `RefCell`, `Mutex`, and `RwLock`, it's easiest to change the values outright without making a variable that holds a borrow or a lock. Then, you won't have to think about whether the variable that holds the borrow or lock is dropped or not.
- If you need to use variables that hold a borrow or a lock, you can use methods like `.try_borrow()` and `.try_lock()` to make sure that there won't be a deadlock.

Multiple threads
and a lot more

This chapter covers

- The `todo!` macro to make the compiler quiet for a while
- Type aliases to create different names but not new types
- The `Cow` enum, which allows you to choose to borrow or own data however you want
- `Rc`, which allows shared instead of unique ownership
- Using multiple threads to run many things at the same time

You're getting pretty good at Rust by now, so it's time to take a look at some more advanced types. This chapter doesn't really have a single theme. Instead, we'll look in turn at some advanced subjects: `Cow`, type aliases, `Rc`, and multiple threads. Understanding how multiple threads work is probably the hardest part of this chapter. The famous `Cow` type (yes, that's its real name) is a little bit tricky, too. You'll probably like the `Rc` (reference counter) type as it gives you a bit of extra flexibility when it comes to Rust's ownership rules.

11.1   *Importing and renaming inside a function*

Usually, you write `use` at the top of the program like this:

```
use std::cell::{Cell, RefCell};
```

But we saw that you can do this anywhere, especially in functions with enums that have long names. Here is an example:

```
enum MapDirection {
    North,
    NorthEast,
    East,
    SouthEast,
    South,
    SouthWest,
    West,
    NorthWest,
}

fn give_direction(direction: &MapDirection) {
    match direction {
        MapDirection::North => println!("You are heading north."),
        MapDirection::NorthEast => println!("You are heading northeast."),
    }
}
```

So much more left to type before the code will compile.

So now we will import `MapDirection` inside the function. That means that inside the function, you can simply write `North` , `NorthEast`, and so on:

```
enum MapDirection {
    North,
    NorthEast,
    East,
    SouthEast,
    South,
    SouthWest,
    West,
    NorthWest,
}

fn give_direction(direction: &MapDirection) {
    use MapDirection::*;

    match direction {
        North =>
    }
}
```

Imports everything in MapDirection

And so on for each variant until the code compiles.

We've seen that `::*` means "import everything after the `::`." In our case, that means `North, NorthEast`, and so on—all the way to `NorthWest`. When you import other people's code, you can do that, too, but if the code is very large, you might have problems. What if it has some items that have the same name as those in your code? It's usually best not to use `::*` all the time unless you're sure. A lot of times you see a section called `prelude` in other people's code with all the main items you probably need. Then you will usually use it like this: `name::prelude::*`. We will talk about this more in the sections for modules and crates.

If you have duplicate names or you have some reason to change a type name, you can use `as` to do it. This can be done with any type:

```
fn main() {
    use String as S;
    let my_string = S::from("Hi!");
}
```

You might find this useful when using someone else's code and aren't satisfied with the naming. This enum is a bit awkwardly named:

```
enum FileState {
    CannotAccessFile,
    FileOpenedAndReady,
    NoSuchFileExists,
    SimilarFileNameInNextDirectory,
}
```

Let's try importing this enum's variants and giving them all a different name. Since 2021, in Rust, you can even change their names to another language:

```
enum FileState {
    CannotAccessFile,
    FileOpenedAndReady,
    NoSuchFileExists,
    SimilarFileNameInNextDirectory,
}

fn give_filestate(input: &FileState) {
    use FileState::{
        CannotAccessFile as NoAccess,                    Korean for
        FileOpenedAndReady as 잘됨,          ⟵         "works great."
        NoSuchFileExists as NoFile,
        SimilarFileNameInNextDirectory as OtherDirectory
    };
    match input {
        NoAccess => println!("Can't access file."),
        잘됨 => println!("Here is your file"),
        NoFile => println!("Sorry, there is no file by that name."),
        OtherDirectory => println!("Please check the other directory."),
    }
}
```

Using imports in this way lets you type `OtherDirectory` instead of `FileState::SimilarFileNameInNextDirectory`.

Very handy! Having learned about importing and renaming, let's move on and take a look at the `todo!` macro next.

11.2   *The todo! macro*

Rust users love the `todo!` macro because it lets you tell the compiler to be quiet for a bit. Sometimes, you want to write the general structure of your code to help you imagine your project's final form (writing the general structure of your code is called *prototyping*). For example, imagine a simple project to do something with books. The comments in the code show what you might be thinking as you write it:

```
// Okay, first I need a book struct.
// Nothing in there yet - will add later
struct Book;

// A book can be hardcover or softcover, so add an enum…
enum BookType {
    HardCover,
    SoftCover,
}

// should take a &Book and return an Option<String>
fn get_book(book: &Book) -> Option<String> {}

// should take a ref Book and return a Result...
fn delete_book(book: &Book) -> Result<(), String> {}

// TODO: impl block and make these functions methods…
// TODO: make this a proper error
fn check_book_type(book_type: &BookType) {

// Let's make sure the match statement works
    match book_type {
        BookType::HardCover => println!("It's hardcover"),
        BookType::SoftCover => println!("It's softcover"),
    }
}

fn main() {
    let book_type = BookType::HardCover;
    // Okay, let's check this function!
    check_book_type(&book_type);
}
```

Unfortunately, Rust is not happy with `.get_book()` and `.delete_book()` and won't even compile the code:

```
error[E0308]: mismatched types
  --> src\main.rs:32:29
   |
32 | fn get_book(book: &Book) -> Option<String> {}
   |    --------                 ^^^^^^^^^^^^^^ expected enum
   |➥ `std::option::Option`, found `()`
   |    |
   |    implicitly returns `()` as its body has no tail or `return`
   |➥ expression
   |
```

```
    = note:   expected enum `std::option::Option<std::string::String>`
              found unit type `()`

error[E0308]: mismatched types
  --> src\main.rs:34:31
    |
34 | fn delete_book(book: Book) -> Result<(), String> {}
    |    -----------                ^^^^^^^^^^^^^^^^^^^ expected enum
    ⇒`std::result::Result`, found `()`
    |     |
    |     implicitly returns `()` as its body has no tail or `return`
    ⇒expression
    |
    = note:   expected enum `std::result::Result<(), std::string::String>`
              found unit type `()`
```

But maybe you don't feel like finishing the `.get_book()` and `.delete_book()` functions right now because you want to finish the code's general structure first. This is where you can use `todo!()`. If you add that to the function, Rust will stop complaining and compile your code:

```
struct Book;

enum BookType {
    HardCover,
    SoftCover,
}

fn get_book(book: &Book) -> Option<String> {
    todo!();
}

fn delete_book(book: &Book) -> Result<(), String> {
    todo!();
}

fn check_book_type(book_type: &BookType) {
    match book_type {
        BookType::HardCover => println!("It's hardcover"),
        BookType::SoftCover => println!("It's softcover"),
    }
}

fn main() {
    let book_type = BookType::HardCover;
    check_book_type(&book_type);
}
```

Now the code compiles, and you can see the result of `.check_book_type()`:

```
It's hardcover
```

Make sure that you don't call the functions that have `todo!` inside. Rust will compile our code and let us use it, but if it comes across a `todo!`, it will automatically panic.

Also, `todo!` functions still need signatures that Rust can understand. Code that uses undeclared types, like the next example, won't work even if you put a `todo!` inside the code:

```
struct Book;

fn get_book(book: &Book) -> WorldsBestType {
    todo!()
}
```

It will say

```
error[E0412]: cannot find type `WorldsBestType` in this scope
  --> src\main.rs:32:29
   |
32 |  fn get_book(book: &Book) -> WorldsBestType {
   |                              ^^^^^^^^^^^^^^^ not found in this scope
```

You can use `todo!` in other places, too, like struct parameters:

```
struct Book {
    name: String,
    year: u8
}

fn make_book() -> Book {
    Book {
        name: todo!(),
        year: todo!()
    }
}

fn main() {}
```

Here, too, the `.make_book()` function never gets called so the code will compile and run without panicking.

One final note: `todo!` is the same as another macro called `unimplemented!`. Rust users originally only had `unimplemented!` to use, but it was a bit too much to type, so the macro `todo!` was created, which is shorter.

11.3   *Type aliases*

A type alias means "giving a new name to another type." Type aliases are very easy because they don't change the type at all (just the name). Usually, you use them when you have a long type name that makes your code difficult to read or when you want to describe an existing type in a different way. Here are two examples of type aliases.

First, say you have a type that is not difficult to read, but you want to make your code easier to understand for other people (or for you):

```
type CharacterVec = Vec<char>;
```

When you have a type that makes your code difficult to read:

```
fn returns_some_chars(input: Vec<char>) ->
➥std::iter::Take<std::iter::Skip<std::vec::IntoIter<char>>> {
    input.into_iter().skip(4).take(5)
}
```

You can change it to this:

```
type SkipFourTakeFive =
➥std::iter::Take<std::iter::Skip<std::vec::IntoIter<char>>>;

fn returns_some_chars(input: Vec<char>) -> SkipFourTakeFive {
    input.into_iter().skip(4).take(5)
}
```

You could also import items to make the type shorter instead of using a type alias:

```
use std::iter::{Take, Skip};
use std::vec::IntoIter;

fn returns_some_chars(input: Vec<char>) -> Take<Skip<IntoIter<char>>> {
    input.into_iter().skip(4).take(5)
}
```

You can decide what looks best in your code depending on what you like.

Keep in mind, however, that a type alias doesn't create an actual new type. It's just a name to use instead of an existing type. So if you write `type File = String;`, the compiler just sees a `String`. So this will print `true`:

```
type File = String;

fn main() {
    let my_file = File::from("I am file contents");
    let my_string = String::from("I am file contents");
    println!("{}", my_file == my_string);
}
```

Because a type alias isn't a new type, it doesn't violate the orphan rule. You can use them on anybody's type with no problem because you're not touching the original type.

11.4   Cow

`Cow` is a very convenient enum. It means "clone on write" and lets you return a `&str` if you don't need an owned `String` or a `String` if you do. It can also do the same with any other types that you might want to borrow but also might want to own.

To understand it, let's look at the signature. It's a bit complicated, so we'll first start with a very simplified version:

```
enum Cow {
    Borrowed,
    Owned
}
```

Okay, so a `Cow` offers two choices.

Next is the generic part: Cow is generic over a single type called B (it could have been called anything, but the creators of the standard library chose B). Both Borrowed and Owned have it:

```
enum Cow<B> {
    Borrowed(B),
    Owned(B),
}
```

Now, let's take a look at the real signature, which involves lifetimes:

```
enum Cow<'a, B>
where
    B: 'a + ToOwned + ?Sized,
  {
    Borrowed(&'a B),
    Owned(<B as ToOwned>::Owned),
}
```

We already know that 'a means that Cow can hold a reference. The ToOwned trait means that B must be a type that can be turned into an owned type. For example, str is usually a reference (&str), and you can turn it into an owned String.

Next is ?Sized. This means "maybe Sized, but maybe not." Remember the term *dynamically sized*? Almost every type in Rust is Sized, but types like str are not. That is why we need an & for a str because the compiler doesn't know the size. If you want a trait that can use something like a str, you add ?Sized, which means "might be dynamically sized."

Now, let's look at the enum's variants, Borrowed and Owned. Imagine that you have a function that returns Cow<'static, str>. If you tell the function to return "My message".into(), it will look at the type: "My message" is a str. This is a Borrowed type, so it chooses Borrowed(&'a B). It becomes Cow::Borrowed(&'static str).

If you give it a format!("{}", "My message").into(), it will look at the type. This time, it is a String because format!() makes a String. This time it will select "Owned" and return that.

Let's put together a quick example that shows how Cow might be useful and how to match on a Cow. We'll have a function called generate_message() that generates messages, which are usually a &'static str. But when an error happens, we can add some more information with a struct called ErrorInfo:

```
use std::borrow::Cow;

#[derive(Debug)]
struct ErrorInfo {
    error: LocalError,
    message: String,
}

#[derive(Debug)]
enum LocalError {
```

No surprises in these two structs. LocalError is an enum, and ExtraInfo holds a LocalError and a String.

```
    TooBig,
    TooSmall,
}

fn generate_message(
    message: &'static str,
    error_info: Option<ErrorInfo>
) -> Cow<'static, str> {
    match error_info {
        None => message.into(),
        Some(info) => format!("{message}: {info:?}").into(),
    }
}
```

If we only pass in a &'static str and no extra info, we won't need an allocation, so the Cow will be a Cow::Borrowed. But if we need the extra info, we will need an allocation, and it will be a Cow::Owned that owns its data.

```
fn main() {
    let msg1 = generate_message(
        "Everything is fine",
        None
    );
```

Now, let's make two messages: one that won't need an allocation and one that will.

```
    let msg2 = generate_message(
        "Got an error",
        Some(ErrorInfo {
            error: LocalError::TooBig,
            message: "It was too big".to_string(),
        }),
    );
```

And since Cow is just a simple enum, we can always match on it to see if it's a Cow::Borrowed or a Cow::Owned.

```
    for msg in [msg1, msg2] {
        match msg {
            Cow::Borrowed(msg) => {
                println!("Borrowed, didn't need an allocation:\n  {msg}")
            }
            Cow::Owned(msg) => {
                println!("Owned, because we needed an allocation:\n  {msg}")
            }
        }
    }
}
```

Here is the output:

```
Borrowed message, didn't need an allocation:
  Everything is fine
Owned message because we needed an allocation:
  Got an error: ExtraInfo { error: TooBig, message: "It was too big" }
```

Cow has some other methods, like into_owned or into_borrowed, so you can change it if you need to.

Cow is a convenient type to place on your structs and enums, too, and is another method to take both &str and String if you want. Imagine you have a User struct that you would like to take either &str or String, but you don't want to clone or use .to_string() if you don't have to. You can use a Cow here, too:

```
use std::borrow::Cow;

struct User {
    name: Cow<'static, str>,
}

fn main() {
    let user_name = "User1";
    let other_user_name = "User10".to_string();

    let user1 = User {
        name: user_name.into(),
    };

    let user2 = User {
        name: other_user_name.into(),
    };

    for name in [user1.name, user2.name] {
        match name {
            Cow::Borrowed(n) => {
                println!("Borrowed name, didn't need an allocation:\n  {n}")
            }
            Cow::Owned(n) => {
                println!("Owned name because we needed an allocation:\n  {n}")
            }
        }
    }
}
```

Once again, both borrowed and owned values work just fine:

```
Borrowed name, didn't need an allocation:
  User1
Owned name because we needed an allocation:
  User10
```

Both `"User1"` and `"User10".to_string()` work! Of course, if you also want to take in a nonstatic `&str`, you would write `User<'a>` and name: `Cow<'a, str>` instead of `'static` to let Rust know that the reference will live long enough. So this code would work, too:

```
use std::borrow::Cow;

struct User<'a> {          ◁─┐  Here we are using the lifetime
    name: Cow<'a, str>,      │  <'a> instead of 'static . . .
}

fn main() {                                      . . . which means that we can now
    let user_name = "User1";                     use a reference to a String that
    let other_user_name = &"User10".to_string(); ◁─┘ doesn't have a 'static lifetime.

    let user1 = User {
        name: user_name.into(),
    };
```

```
    let user2 = User {
        name: other_user_name.into(),
    };

    for name in [user1.name, user2.name] {
        match name {
            Cow::Borrowed(n) => {
                println!("Borrowed name, didn't need an allocation:\n  {n}")
            }
            Cow::Owned(n) => {
                println!("Owned name because we needed an allocation:\n  {n}")
            }
        }
    }
}
```

The output shows that both names were used as a `Cow::Borrowed` because they are both borrowed values:

```
Borrowed name, didn't need an allocation:
  User1
Borrowed name, didn't need an allocation:
  User10
```

We've had a good look at the `Cow` type; let's move on to the next advanced Rust concept, `Rc`, a useful type that provides some flexibility in a language as strict as Rust.

11.5 *Rc*

`Rc` stands for "reference counter" (or "reference counted," depending on who you ask). `Rc` is used a lot as a way to get around Rust's strict rules on ownership—without actually breaking them—by allowing shared ownership and by keeping a careful eye on how long the data is being shared. Let's learn what makes `Rc` useful.

11.5.1 *Why Rc exists*

We know that in Rust, every variable can only have one owner. That is why this doesn't work:

```
fn takes_a_string(_unused_string: String) {}

fn main() {
    let user_name = String::from("User MacUserson");
    takes_a_string(user_name);
    takes_a_string(user_name);
}
```

After `takes_a_string` takes `user_name`, you can't use it anymore. For us, this is no problem: you can give it `user_name.clone()`. However, sometimes, a variable is part of a struct, and maybe you can't clone the struct. Or maybe the `String` is really long, and you don't want to clone it. An `Rc` gets around this by letting you have more than one owner. An `Rc` is like a good office worker: it writes down who has ownership and how many of them there are. Once the number of owners goes down to 0, the value can be dropped.

One interesting thing about Rc has to do with garbage collection. Rust doesn't use garbage collection, which is why you have to think about things like references and lifetimes. But most other languages use garbage collection invisibly in a manner similar to Rc: the language keeps track of where memory is being shared and later cleans it up when nobody is using it anymore. That's why a lot of new programmers to Rust use Rc a lot because it lets them not worry about references and lifetimes so much.

11.5.2 Using Rc in practice

Here is how you use an Rc. First, imagine two structs: one called City and another called CityData. City has information for one city, and CityData puts all the cities together in Vecs:

```
#[derive(Debug)]
struct City {
    name: String,
    population: u32,
    city_history: String,
}

#[derive(Debug)]
struct CityData {
    names: Vec<String>,
    histories: Vec<String>,
}

fn main() {
    let calgary = City {
        name: "Calgary".to_string(),
        population: 1_200_000,
        city_history: "Calgary began as a fort called Fort Calgary
        ➥that...".to_string(),
    };
    let canada_cities = CityData {
        names: vec![calgary.name],
        histories: vec![calgary.city_history],
    };
    println!("Calgary's history is: {}", calgary.city_history);
}
```

> **Pretend that this string is very, very long.** (points to `city_history: "Calgary began as a fort called Fort Calgary that...".to_string()`)

> **This uses calgary.name, which is short.** (points to `names: vec![calgary.name],`)

> **But this String is long.** (points to `histories: vec![calgary.city_history],`)

Of course, it doesn't work because canada_cities owns the data and calgary doesn't. It says

```
error[E0382]: borrow of moved value: `calgary.city_history`
  --> src\main.rs:27:42
   |
24 |         histories: vec![calgary.city_history],
   |                         -------------------- value moved here
...
27 |     println!("Calgary's history is: {}", calgary.city_history);
```

> **But this String is very long.** (points to line 24 `histories: vec![calgary.city_history],`)

```
    |                                            ^^^^^^^^^^^^^^^^^^^^ value
⇒ borrowed here after move
    |
    = note: move occurs because `calgary.city_history` has type
    ⇒ `std::string::String`, which does not implement the `Copy` trait
```

You can easily clone the `String`s, but you can also wrap everything that you want to share inside an `Rc`. Here's how to do it. First, add the `use` declaration:

```
use std::rc::Rc;
```

Then, put `Rc` around everything we want to share:

```
use std::rc::Rc;

#[derive(Debug)]
struct City {
    name: Rc<String>,
    population: u32,
    city_history: Rc<String>,
}

#[derive(Debug)]
struct CityData {
    names: Vec<Rc<String>>,
    histories: Vec<Rc<String>>,
}
```

To add a new reference, you have to clone the `Rc`.

But, hold on! Didn't we want to avoid using `.clone()`? Not exactly—we didn't want to clone the whole `String`. But a clone of an `Rc` just clones the pointer: it's basically free. It's like putting a name sticker on a box of books to show two people own it instead of making a whole new box.

You can clone an `Rc` called `item` with `Rc::clone(&item)` or `item.clone()`. Usually, `Rc::clone(&item)` is better because an `Rc` holds a type that might have its own methods (including `.clone()`!). Thus, it's a good way to show that you are cloning the `Rc`, not the object inside it.

There is also a method for `Rc` called `strong_count()` that shows you how many owners there are for a piece of data. We will use this method in the following code, too. How many owners do you think there are for Calgary's city history?

```
use std::rc::Rc;

#[derive(Debug)]
struct City {
    name: Rc<String>,
    population: u32,
    city_history: Rc<String>,       ⟵⎤  A String
}                                        inside an Rc

#[derive(Debug)]
struct CityData {
```

```
    names: Vec<Rc<String>>,
    histories: Vec<Rc<String>>,        ◄─┐  A Vec of Strings
}                                         │  inside Rcs

fn main() {

    let calgary_name = Rc::new("Calgary".to_string());
    let calgary_history = Rc::new("Calgary began as a fort called Fort
    ➡Calgary that...".to_string());

    let calgary = City {
        name: Rc::clone(&calgary_name),
        population: 1_200_000,
        city_history: Rc::clone(&calgary_history)
    };
                                               │ .clone() will increase
    let canada_cities = CityData {             │ the count.
        names: vec![Rc::clone(&calgary_name)],  ◄─┘
        histories: vec![Rc::clone(&calgary_history)],
    };

    println!("Calgary's history is: {}", calgary.city_history);
    println!("{}", Rc::strong_count(&calgary.city_history));
}
```

The answer is 3, as the output shows:

```
Calgary's history is: Calgary began as a fort called Fort Calgary that...
3
```

First, we made a `String` inside an `Rc`: one owner. Then, we cloned the `Rc`, and the `City` struct is using it: two owners. Finally, we cloned it again, and the `CityData` struct is using it: three owners.

If there are strong pointers, are there also weak pointers? Yes, there are. Weak pointers are useful because if two `Rc`s point at each other, they can't die (to be precise, they can't drop their values). This is called a *reference cycle*. If item 1 has an `Rc` to item 2 and item 2 has an `Rc` to item 1, they can't get to 0 and will never be able to drop their values. In this case, you want to use weak references. Weak references still maintain a memory allocation but allow the `Rc` to drop its value. `Rc` will count both strong and weak references, but strong references are the only references that keep an `Rc` from dropping its value. You use `Rc::downgrade(&item)` instead of `Rc::clone(&item)` to make weak references. Also, you use `Rc::weak_count(&item)` to see the weak count.

Remember the quick example with the two functions that each take a `String`? Solving it with reference counters is easy now that you know how: wrap a `String` in an `Rc` and then clone it with `Rc::clone()`. Change the function signatures from `String` to `Rc<String>`, and you're done! Now it looks like this:

```
use std::rc::Rc;

fn takes_a_string(input: Rc<String>) {
    println!("It is: {input}")
}
```

```
fn main() {
    let user_name = Rc::new(String::from("User MacUserson"));

    takes_a_string(Rc::clone(&user_name));
    takes_a_string(Rc::clone(&user_name));
}
```

Finally, we have the output we wanted:

```
It is: User MacUserson
It is: User MacUserson
```

11.5.3 *Avoiding lifetime annotations with Rc*

Rc has been interesting so far, but the two examples haven't really given us an overwhelming reason to use them. If you search online, you'll see that Rc is really popular with new Rust users. The reason is that using Rc lets you avoid writing lifetimes while not needing to use .clone(). Let's look at our example from the last chapter with the City struct, which holds a &'a str for its name. But this time, we have added two more structs: a Country struct that holds a Vec<City> and a World struct that holds a Vec<Country>. We write this, but it won't compile yet:

```
#[derive(Debug)]
struct City<'a> {
    name: &'a str,
    date_founded: u32,
}

#[derive(Debug)]
struct Country {
    cities: Vec<City>
}

#[derive(Debug)]
struct World {
    countries: Vec<Country>
}

fn main() {
    let city_names = vec!["Ichinomiya".to_string(), "Kurume".to_string()];
    let my_city = City {
        name: &city_names[0],
        date_founded: 1921,
    };
    println!("{} was founded in {}", my_city.name, my_city.date_founded);
}
```

Here is the error:

```
error[E0106]: missing lifetime specifier
 --> src/main.rs:9:17
  |
9 |     cities: Vec<City>
  |                 ^^^^ expected named lifetime parameter
```

```
   |
help: consider introducing a named lifetime parameter
   |
8 ~ struct Country<'a> {
9 ~     cities: Vec<City<'a>>
   |
```

City has a lifetime of `<'a>`, and so the compiler wants to know how long `Country` will live in relation to `City`. Will they both share the same lifetime?

Fine, we will give them the same lifetime:

```
#[derive(Debug)]
struct Country<'a> {
    cities: Vec<City<'a>>
}
```

The compiler gives the same error message again because `World` holds a `Vec<Country>`, and `Country` has the lifetime `<'a>`. We indicate the lifetime again in the same way and now the code compiles:

```
#[derive(Debug)]
struct World<'a> {
    countries: Vec<Country<'a>>
}
```

That works just fine, but it took a lot of typing. It is starting to feel a bit awkward to keep writing this lifetime just because we don't want to clone a `String` inside the `city_names` Vec. Every time a `City`, `Country`, or `World` gets used anywhere, we will need to specify the lifetime again.

Let's try an `Rc` instead: we'll make `city_names` a `Vec<Rc<String>>` instead of a `Vec<String>` and clone the `Rc`. City will take an `Rc<String>` for its name instead of a `&'a str`, and we can get rid of all the lifetime annotations everywhere else. Now the code looks like this:

```
use std::rc::Rc;

#[derive(Debug)]
struct City {
    name: Rc<String>,
    date_founded: u32,
}

#[derive(Debug)]
struct Country {
    cities: Vec<City>,
}

#[derive(Debug)]
struct World {
    countries: Vec<Country>,
}

impl World {}
```

If we were still using lifetimes, you would need to write impl World<'_> here.

```
fn main() {
    let city_names = vec![
        Rc::new("Ichinomiya".to_string()),
        Rc::new("Kurume".to_string()),
    ];

    let my_city = City {
        name: Rc::clone(&city_names[0]),
        date_founded: 1921,
    };

    println!("{} was founded in {}", my_city.name, my_city.date_founded);
}
```

This compiles fine and prints `Ichinomiya was founded in 1921`.

Hopefully, you'll get some good use out of the `Rc` type. Let's move on to the final topic in this chapter: multiple threads.

11.6 Multiple threads

Using multiple threads allows us to do many things at the same time. Modern computers have multiple cores and multiple threads, so they can do more than one thing at the same time, and Rust lets you use them. Rust uses threads that are called *OS threads*, each of which gets its own state stack and local state, making OS threads both efficient and independent. (Some other languages use what are known as *green threads*, which need a run time and are less powerful.)

11.6.1 Spawning threads

You create threads with `std::thread::spawn` and a closure to tell it what to do. Threads are interesting because they run at the same time, and it can be fun to run your code to see what happens as they all operate at the same time. What do you think the output of this simple example will be?

```
fn main() {
    std::thread::spawn(|| {
        println!("I am printing something");
    });
}
```

In fact, the output will be different every time. Sometimes it will print, and sometimes it won't (this depends on your computer, too, and usually, it won't print in the Playground). That is because sometimes `main()` finishes before the thread finishes, and when `main()` finishes, the program is over. This is easier to see in a `for` loop:

```
fn main() {
    for _ in 0..10 {              ◁─┤ Sets up 10 threads
        std::thread::spawn(|| {
            println!("I am printing something");   ◁─┤ Now the threads start.
        });
    }                  ┤ How many can finish
}                      ┘ before main() ends here?
```

The code goes as follows:

- The main thread loops once, starting an independent thread. This thread is going to try to print a message.
- This loop repeats nine more times. Now a total of ten threads are independently trying to print a message. But they might not all get the chance to print, because…
- …the main thread quickly reaches the end of fn main() and shuts down the program.

Usually, about four threads will print before main() ends, but it is always different. If your computer is faster, it might not print any. Also, sometimes the threads will panic:

```
thread 'thread 'I am printing something
thread '<unnamed><unnamed>thread '' panicked at '<unnamed>I am printing
➥something
' panicked at 'thread '<unnamed>cannot access stdout during shutdown'
➥panicked at '<unnamed>thread 'cannot access stdout during
shutdown
```

This error occurs when the thread tries to do something just when the program is shutting down.

You could, of course, give the computer something to do after starting the threads so that the program won't shut down right away:

```
fn main() {
    for _ in 0..10 {
        std::thread::spawn(|| {
            println!("I am printing something");
        });
    }
    let mut busy_work = vec![];
    for _ in 0..1_000_000 {          ⟵   Makes the program push 9 into a Vec and then
        busy_work.push(9);                 removes it 1 million times. It has to finish
        busy_work.pop();                   this before it can exit the main function.
    }
}
```

That will guarantee that all 10 threads have time to print their messages. But that's a pretty silly way to give the threads time to finish. The better way is to tell the code to stop until the threads are done. The cool thing here is that the spawn() function actually returns something called a JoinHandle that lets us do exactly this. You can see this in the signature for spawn():

```
pub fn spawn<F, T>(f: F) -> JoinHandle<T>
where
    F: FnOnce() -> T,
    F: Send + 'static,
    T: Send + 'static,
```

Here are two notes on the signature:

- f is the closure. We will learn how to put closures into our functions later.

- Did you notice that both of them need a `'static` lifetime? The page in the documentation explains why (https://doc.rust-lang.org/std/thread/fn.spawn.html): "`'static` means that the closure and its return value must have a lifetime of the whole program. That's because threads can outlive the lifetime they have been created in. . . . Since we can't know when it will return, we need to have them as long as possible, so until the end of the program."

NOTE In Rust 1.63, in August 2022, Rust got a new type of thread that doesn't need `'static`! We'll look at that in the next chapter.

11.6.2 Using JoinHandles to wait for threads to finish

Okay, back to the `JoinHandle` returned by the `spawn()` function. Let's make a variable to hold a `JoinHandle` every time a thread is spawned:

```
fn main() {
    for _ in 0..10 {
        let handle = std::thread::spawn(|| {
            println!("I am printing something");
        });
    }
}
```

The variable `handle` is now a `JoinHandle`, but we aren't doing anything with it yet, and the main program is still finishing before the threads have had time to print their messages. To use the `JoinHandle` to tell the program to wait for the threads to finish, we call a method called `.join()`. This method means "wait until the thread is done" (it waits for the thread to "join" it). Write `handle.join()`, and it will wait for each of the threads to finish:

```
fn main() {
    for _ in 0..10 {
        let handle = std::thread::spawn(|| {
            println!("I am printing something");
        });
        handle.join();        ◁── Waits for the
    }                             threads to finish
}
```

So now we won't leave `main()` until all 10 threads are done. But, actually, we aren't using threads exactly the way we want yet. We start a thread, do something, and then call `.join()` to wait—and only then we start a new thread. What we want instead is for `main()` to start all the threads at the same time, get them to start working, and only then call `.join()` on the threads.

To solve this, we can create a `Vec` that will hold all of the `JoinHandles`. Then we can call `.join()` on them once all 10 of the threads are up and running:

```
fn main() {
    let mut join_handles = vec![];      ◁── Here is the Vec that will hold
    for _ in 0..10 {                        each of the JoinHandles. It
                                            stands outside the for loop.
```

```
let handle = std::thread::spawn(|| {
    println!("I am printing something");
});
join_handles.push(handle);
}
for handle in join_handles {
    handle.join().unwrap();
}
}
```

We are pushing each JoinHandle into the Vec and haven't called them to .join() yet. This will let all 10 threads start working without waiting.

Now that all 10 threads are working, we can finally call .join() on each of the threads to make sure that they are done. Now all 10 threads are working, and main() will not finish until they are all done.

The code successfully prints I am printing something 10 times, showing us that main() is indeed waiting for all 10 threads to finish. Success!

Now, let's make a small change to the code. Every thread is working on its own, so it would be interesting to print out the thread number instead of just printing I am printing something every time. We could do this by making a variable called num inside the for loop and printing that out. Surprisingly, however, the code doesn't work:

```
fn main() {
    let mut join_handles = vec![];
    for num in 0..10 {
        let handle = std::thread::spawn(|| {
            println!("Inside thread number: {num}");
        });
        join_handles.push(handle);
    }
    for handle in join_handles {
        handle.join().unwrap();
    }
}
```

We write for num instead of for _, so we can print out the thread number . . .

. . . and print it out here.

The error message is pretty long:

```
error[E0373]: closure may outlive the current function, but it borrows
➥ `num`, which is owned by the current function
  --> src\main.rs:4:41
   |
4  |         let handle = std::thread::spawn(|| {
   |                                         ^^ may outlive borrowed value
➥ `num`
5  |             println!("Inside thread number: {num}");
   |                                              --- `num` is borrowed here
   |
note: function requires argument type to outlive `'static`
  --> src\main.rs:4:22
   |
4  |         let handle = std::thread::spawn(|| {
   |  _____^
5  | |             println!("Inside thread number: {num}");
6  | |         });
   | |_____^
```

```
help: to force the closure to take ownership of `num` (and any other
   referenced variables), use the `move` keyword
   |
4  |          let handle = std::thread::spawn(move || {
   |                                           ++++
```

Wow. That is quite the error message. But at least the end of the error message gives us some advice: add the `move` keyword. Indeed, adding this keyword fixes the problem, and we can see the thread numbers in random order:

```
Inside thread number: 0
Inside thread number: 1
Inside thread number: 4
Inside thread number: 2
Inside thread number: 5
Inside thread number: 6
Inside thread number: 7
Inside thread number: 8
Inside thread number: 9
Inside thread number: 3
```

But what did this keyword do exactly, and why did we need it? To understand this, we need a small detour to learn about the three types of closures. Understanding the behavior of the three types of closures is a big help in understanding how multiple threads work.

11.6.3 *Types of closures*

We will take a longer look at closures in the next chapter, but here is a quick introduction. Remember the `F: FnOnce() -> T` part in the `spawn()` function? `FnOnce` is the name of one of the three traits implemented by closures. The following three are the traits implemented by closures:

- `FnOnce`—Takes by value
- `FnMut`—Takes a mutable reference
- `Fn`—Takes a regular reference

When a closure captures a variable from its environment, it will try to use `Fn` if it can. But if it needs to change the value, it will use `FnMut`, and if it needs to take by value, it will use `FnOnce`. `FnOnce` is a good name because it explains what it does: it takes the value once, and then it can't take it again.

Here is an example:

```
fn main() {
    let my_string = String::from("I will go into the closure");
    let my_closure = || println!("{my_string}");
    my_closure();
    my_closure();
}
```

The closure `my_closure()` doesn't need to change or take by value, so it implements `Fn`: it takes a reference. Therefore, the code compiles.

If we change `my_string`, the closure will implement `FnMut`.

```
fn main() {
    let mut my_string = String::from("I will be changed in the closure");
    let mut my_closure = || {
        my_string.push_str(" now");
        println!("{my_string}");
    };
    my_closure();
    my_closure();
}
```

This prints

```
I will be changed in the closure now
I will be changed in the closure now now
```

If you take by value, it implements `FnOnce`:

```
fn main() {
    let my_vec: Vec<i32> = vec![8, 9, 10];
    let my_closure = || {
        my_vec.into_iter().for_each(|item| println!("{item}"));
    };
    my_closure();
    // my_closure();
}
```

into_iter takes ownership, and my_vec is pulled into my_closure.

This won't work because the closure, FnOnce, took ownership of my_vec, and my_vec is already gone.

We took by value, so we can't run `my_closure()` more than once. That is where the name `FnOnce` comes from.

We will learn a lot more about these three closure types in the next chapter, but these basics are enough to help us solve our problem with the `move` keyword.

11.6.4 *Using the move keyword*

Let's return to threads. Let's try to use a value from outside:

```
fn main() {
    let my_string = String::from("Can I go inside the thread?");
    let handle = std::thread::spawn(|| {
        println!("{my_string}");
    });
    handle.join().unwrap();
}
```

As before, the compiler says that this won't work:

```
error[E0373]: closure may outlive the current function, but it borrows
➡`my_string`, which is owned by the current function
  --> src\main.rs:28:37
   |
28 |     let handle = std::thread::spawn(|| {
   |                                     ^^ may outlive borrowed value
   ➡`my_string`
```

```
29 |            println!("{}", my_string);
   |                     --------- `my_string` is borrowed here
   |
note: function requires argument type to outlive `'static`
  --> src\main.rs:28:18
   |
28 |        let handle = std::thread::spawn(|| {
   | _____^
29 | |              println!("{}", my_string);
30 | |          });
   | |_____^
help: to force the closure to take ownership of `my_string` (and any other
➡referenced variables), use the `move` keyword
   |
28 |        let handle = std::thread::spawn(move || {
   |                                        ^^^^^^
```

This time, we can understand the message and why move will solve the problem. In this case, the closure wants to use Fn because it only wants to use my_string as a reference to print it. As we saw in the last section, a closure will use Fn if it can because it prefers to only use a reference. However, the spawn() method requires an FnOnce to be used, which means to take by value. The move keyword lets us force the closure to take by value instead of reference, and now that it owns the String, there are no lifetime problems anymore.

Now the code works:

```
fn main() {
    let mut my_string = String::from("Can I go inside the thread?");
    let handle = std::thread::spawn(move || {
        println!("{my_string}");
    });
    handle.join().unwrap();
}
```

That was the problem with our former code, too. Let's look at it again:

```
fn main() {
    let mut join_handles = vec![];
    for num in 0..10 {
        let handle = std::thread::spawn(|| {
            println!("Inside thread number: {num}");
        });
        join_handles.push(handle);
    }
    for handle in join_handles {
        handle.join().unwrap();
    }
}
```

You can see that num is being declared outside of the thread, and then the println! statement is trying to borrow num. However, the spawn() method holds an FnOnce closure, which needs to take num by value, not by reference. That's why the move keyword was needed here, too.

That was a lot of work! You can see that the compiler is watching your back when you use multiple threads to make sure that no data is being borrowed in the wrong way. In the meantime, you now have some tools that give you extra flexibility: Rc for multiple ownership, Cow to take in either owned or borrowed data, and more knowledge of how closures work to help you further understand Rust's rules on borrowing. Chapter 13 is going to be a relaxing chapter, but we have some hard work yet to do in chapter 12. We will continue to learn to understand threads, closures, and related types.

Summary

- If you feel like you are using .clone() too much, maybe think about using an Rc (reference counter).
- If you like sketching out a high-level view of your code before you begin, use todo! everywhere, and the compiler will leave you alone.
- Once you understand its signature, Cow is a pretty convenient type that lets you take in both owned and borrowed values.
- If you make a new type, you can implement any traits on it you like. This is the most common way to get around the orphan rule. But type aliases are just new names for existing types, so using them doesn't change their underlying behavior.
- Because threads are independent, another thread might not be finished by the time main() finishes. If you want to wait for a thread to finish, use the Join-Handle that you get from the spawn() function.
- The compiler seems extra strict when using multiple threads because a thread might live longer than the data it borrows. Usually, you use the move keyword to solve this.

More on closures,
generics, and threads

12

This chapter covers

- Closures in functions
- `impl Trait` as another way to use generics
- `Arc`, which is like `Rc` but thread-safe
- Scoped threads, threads that only live inside a scope
- Using channels to send messages, even across threads

This chapter is a bit like the last one: lots of new ideas that are tricky to understand at first. The first section on closures as arguments in functions is probably the hardest but continues what we learned in the last chapter about the three types of closures. Fortunately, the rest of the chapter is made up of similar things to what you've learned before. `impl Trait` is like regular generics but easier to write, `Arc` is like `Rc`, and scoped threads are like threads but easier to use; you'll understand the channel examples fairly easily too because you already know how multiple threads work.

12.1   *Closures as arguments*

Closures are great. We know how to make our own, but what about closures as arguments in functions? Arguments need to have a type, but what exactly is a closure's type?

So far, we've seen that there are three types of closures, and we know that they can capture variables that are in the same scope. We also know that when a closure accesses a variable in Rust, it can take by value, by reference, or by mutable reference. As we saw in the last chapter, a closure is able to choose on its own between `Fn`, `FnMut`, and `FnOnce` when capturing variables. However, as a function argument or return value, you have to choose one of these three. This is pretty similar to regular type inference. When you write `let my_num = 9` or `let my_num = 9.0`, the compiler can determine the type, but in a function signature, you have to choose the exact type it will be: an `i32`, a `u8`, and so on.

A good way to get a feel for closures is by looking at a few function signatures. Here is the one for the `.all()` method. We saw before that `.all()` checks an iterator to see whether everything is `true` (depending on how you decide to return `true` or `false`). Part of its signature says this:

```
fn all<F>(&mut self, f: F) -> bool
where
    F: FnMut(Self::Item) -> bool,
```

Let's look at this signature bit by bit:

- `fn all<F>` tells you that the function involves a generic type that here is called `F`.
- `&mut self` is pretty easy: this is a method that takes a `&mut self` (a mutable reference to `self`, which is the iterator).
- `f: F` is usually what you see for a closure: this is the variable name and the generic type. There is nothing special about `f` and `F`, and they could be different names. You could write `my_closure: Closure` or `func: Function` or anything else if you wanted—it doesn't matter. But, in signatures, you almost always see `f: F`. In fact, up to this line, there is nothing that tells us that `f` is a closure. It could still be any other generic type.
- `F: FnMut(Self::Item) -> bool` is the part that tells us that the function takes a closure. This closure implements `FnMut`, so it can change the values by mutable reference. It takes a `Self::Item` (the associated type of the iterator), and it has to return `true` or `false`.

You see this sort of signature a lot in the iterator methods that take closures. For example, this is the signature for `.map()`:

```
fn map<B, F>(self, f: F) -> Map<Self, F>
    where
        Self: Sized,
        F: FnMut(Self::Item) -> B,
    {
        Map::new(self, f)
    }
```

The signature `fn map<B, F>(self, f: F)` means that the function takes two generic types. `F` is a function that takes one item from the container implementing `.map()`, and `B` is the return type of that function (the item that you pass on). After the `where`, we see the trait bounds. One is `Sized`, and the next is the closure signature. It must be an `FnMut` and do the closure on `Self::Item`, which is the next item from the iterator. It returns `B`, which is whatever you choose to pass on. If you look at the iterator methods that we learned in chapter 9, you will see `FnMut` everywhere.

Now, let's relax a bit with maybe the simplest possible function that takes a closure:

```
fn do_something<F>(f: F)
where
    F: FnOnce(),
{
    f();
}
```

The function signature here simply says that it takes a closure that takes by value (`FnOnce`) and doesn't return anything. Now, we can write this closure that takes nothing and put whatever we like inside it. We will create a `Vec` and then iterate over it just to show what we can do now:

```
fn do_something<F>(f: F)
where
    F: FnOnce(),
{
    f();
}

fn main() {
    let some_vec = vec![9, 8, 10];
    do_something(|| {
        some_vec
            .into_iter()
            .for_each(|x| println!("The number is: {x}"));
    });
}
```

Here is the output:

```
The number is: 9
The number is: 8
The number is: 10
```

Because the closure is an `FnOnce()` (and because `.into_iter()` inside takes by value), you can't call it with `some_vec` again—it was taken by value and is now gone. Give it a try! The code won't compile now because we are calling `do_something` twice:

```
fn do_something<F>(f: F)
where
    F: FnOnce(),
{
    f();
}
```

```
fn main() {
    let some_vec = vec![9, 8, 10];
    do_something(|| {
        some_vec
            .into_iter()
            .for_each(|x| println!("The number is: {x}"));
    });
    do_something(|| {
        some_vec
            .into_iter()
            .for_each(|x| println!("The number is: {x}"));
    });
}
```

The error message is exactly the same as when a value moves in other cases: the value is "moved into" somewhere else and can't be used again:

```
9  |       let some_vec = vec![9, 8, 10];
   |           -------- move occurs because `some_vec` has type `Vec<i32>`,
   which does not implement the `Copy` trait
10 |       do_something(|| {
   |                    -- value moved into closure here
11 |           some_vec
   |           -------- variable moved due to use in closure
...
15 |       do_something(|| {
   |                    ^^ value used here after move
16 |           some_vec
   |           -------- use occurs due to use in closure
```

Now, let's try a closure that takes by reference. To do so, we can say that the closure is an Fn(). This closure will call some_vec as many times as we like, and the variable will still be alive:

```
fn do_something<F>(f: F)
where
    F: Fn(),
{
    f();
}

fn main() {
    let some_vec = vec![9, 8, 10];
    do_something(|| {
        some_vec.iter().for_each(|x| println!("The number is: {x}"));
    });

    do_something(|| {
        some_vec.iter().for_each(|x| println!("The number is: {x}"));
    });
}
```

The output will be the same as the last sample, just printed two times.

But here is something that might seem odd: try changing the `F: Fn()` on line 3 to `F: FnOnce()`. The code compiles! This might be unexpected. Let's find out why.

12.1.1 Some simple closures

To understand how the three closure traits work, let's take a look at some super-simple functions that each takes a closure. First, we have a function that takes an `Fn()` closure and calls it two times:

```
fn takes_fn<F: Fn()>(f: F) {
    f();
    f();
}
```

As you can see, it's not `FnOnce`, so it can be called twice (or three times or more).

Up next is a function that takes an `FnMut()` closure and calls it twice. This one can also be called more than once:

```
fn takes_fnmut<F: FnMut()>(mut f: F) {
    f();
    f();
}
```

Finally, we have a function that takes an `FnOnce()` closure. It won't compile if you call it a second time:

```
fn takes_fnonce<F: FnOnce()>(f: F) {
    f();
    // f();      ⊲——| This won't work.
}
```

You'll notice that functions that take closures can look extremely simple. This is because closures can capture variables from their environment, so often you don't need to pass any arguments in. Each of our closures (`Fn()`, `FnMut()`, and `FnOnce()`) takes no arguments and returns nothing, but they can capture variables around them.

Let's make some actual closures to pass into these functions. Inside `main()`, we will have a mutable `String` and three types of closures that capture it. Then we will call each of them:

```
fn takes_fnonce<F: FnOnce()>(f: F) {
    f();
}
fn takes_fnmut<F: FnMut()>(mut f: F) {
    f();
    f();
}
fn takes_fn<F: Fn()>(f: F) {
    f();
    f();
}
```

```
fn main() {
    let mut my_string = String::from("Hello there");

    let prints_string = || {                ◄─┐  This closure only needs to capture by
        println!("{my_string}");               │  reference, so it will be an Fn closure.
    };
    takes_fn(prints_string);                ◄──│  The takes_fn function takes the closure
                                               │  as an argument and calls it two times.
    let adds_exclamation_and_prints = || {  ◄──┐  This next closure needs to
        my_string.push('!');                   │  capture by mutable reference,
        println!("{my_string}");               │  so it will be an FnMut closure.
    };
    takes_fnmut(adds_exclamation_and_prints);  ◄──┐  The takes_fnmut function takes
                                                  │  the closure as an argument
    let prints_then_drops = || {            ◄──   │  and calls it two times.
        println!("Now dropping {my_string}");
        drop(my_string);                       Finally, we have a closure that captures
    };                                         by value, so it will be an FnOnce closure.
    takes_fnonce(prints_then_drops);
    // takes_fnonce(prints_then_drops);     ◄──┐  The takes_fnonce function takes
}                                              │  prints_then_drops but can't do it again.
```

Here is the output:

```
Hello there
Hello there
Hello there!
Hello there!!
Now dropping Hello there!!
```

You don't have to name a closure, though, and it's usually more common to just write the closure out inside the function that uses it as an argument. The following code is the exact same as the code we just saw, except we are just writing the closures instead of giving them names first:

```
fn takes_fnonce<F: FnOnce()>(f: F) {
    f();
}
fn takes_fnmut<F: FnMut()>(mut f: F) {
    f();
    f();
}
fn takes_fn<F: Fn()>(f: F) {
    f();
    f();
}

fn main() {
    let mut my_string = String::from("Hello there");
    takes_fn(|| {
        println!("{my_string}");
    });
    takes_fnmut(|| {
        my_string.push('!');
        println!("{my_string}");
```

```
    });
    takes_fnonce(|| {
        println!("Now dropping {my_string}");
        drop(my_string);
    });
}
```

Hopefully, that makes sense: when we write a closure we are just writing another kind of function. The regular functions call those closures once or twice. When we call those regular functions, they call the closures once or twice, and our code inside the closures is executed.

Now that we have these basics down, let's take a look at the signatures for each of the three closure types and see what they can tell us.

12.1.2 The relationship between FnOnce, FnMut, and Fn

There is an interesting relationship among the three closure traits, which we can see from their signature. Let's take a look at the signature for Fn first. Here is the important part:

```
pub trait Fn: FnMut
```

Just as in any other trait, the trait after : is the trait that must be implemented first. This means that a closure needs to implement FnMut before it can implement Fn. So let's take a look at FnMut:

```
pub trait FnMut: FnOnce
```

Interesting! A closure needs FnMut to implement Fn, but before it implements FnMut, it needs FnOnce. Finally, let's check FnOnce:

```
pub trait FnOnce
```

So, FnOnce doesn't need any other traits to be implemented first. To sum up:

- Fn must implement the other two traits (FnMut and FnOnce).
- FnMut must implement one other trait (FnOnce).
- FnOnce doesn't need any other traits to be implemented.

That means that *all* closures implement FnOnce.

The trait after the : is known as a *supertrait*. FnOnce is a supertrait of FnMut, and FnMut is a supertrait of Fn. The word *super* is just the Latin word meaning "over," so you can think of it as this:

- First, start at the top and implement FnOnce.
- With FnOnce implemented, FnMut can now be implemented.
- Finally, Fn can be implemented.

The opposite of this is *subtrait*, which just means *under*. Supertrait and subtrait are easy to remember if you imagine implementing the first trait needed (the line above, so *super*) and going down to the next line to implement the next trait (the line below, so *sub*).

Why is this useful? Well, it means that if a function takes an FnOnce as an argument, it can also take an Fn instead (because Fn also implements FnOnce) or an FnMut (because FnMut also implements FnOnce). If a function takes an FnMut, it can also take an Fn (because Fn implements FnMut).

We can show this with our previous example. We will get rid of the function takes_fn() and keep takes_fnonce() and takes_fnmut(). It still works:

```
fn takes_fnonce<F: FnOnce()>(f: F) {
    f();
}
fn takes_fnmut<F: FnMut()>(mut f: F) {
    f();
    f();
}

fn main() {
    let mut my_string = String::from("Hello there");
    let prints_string = || {
        println!("{my_string}");
    };
    takes_fnonce(prints_string);          ⟵  takes_fnonce takes an
    takes_fnmut(prints_string);           ⟵  FnOnce, and Fn implements
    let adds_exclamation_and_prints = || {    FnOnce. No problem.
        my_string.push('!');              ⟵  takes_fnmut takes an FnMut,
        println!("{my_string}");              and Fn implements FnMut.
    };                                        Once again, no problem.
    takes_fnonce(adds_exclamation_and_prints);   ⟵  takes_fnonce takes an FnOnce,
    let prints_then_drops = || {                     and FnMut implements FnOnce.
        println!("Now dropping {my_string}");
        drop(my_string);                      Finally, takes_fnonce takes
    };                                        an FnOnce, and FnOnce (of
    takes_fnonce(prints_then_drops);     ⟵   course) implements FnOnce.
}
```

This is why you sometimes see books say that Fn is the "most powerful" of the three closure traits because it can be passed in no matter which closure trait is written. At the same time, having a function that takes an Fn is the most restrictive because an Fn closure must implement all three traits. No FnMut or FnOnce can be an argument in a function that wants an Fn.

12.1.3 *Closures are all unique*

One interesting fact about closures is that one closure is never the same type as another closure, even if the signature is the same. The types are always different because Fn, FnMut, and FnOnce are traits, not concrete types.

Let's look at an example to prove this. Here is a function that takes a closure of type Fn() -> i32. We'll make a closure and give it to the function. The function does nothing, so there is no output from the example, but the compiler is happy with this:

```
fn takes_a_closure_and_does_nothing<F>(f: F)
where
    F: Fn() -> i32,
{}

fn main() {
    let my_closure = || 9;
    takes_a_closure_and_does_nothing(my_closure);
}
```

Takes nothing,
returns an i32

Now, let's try having it take two closures with the exact same signature to pass them in:

```
fn takes_two_closures_and_does_nothing<F>(first: F, second: F)
where
    F: Fn() -> i32,
{
}

fn main() {
    let first_closure = || 9;
    let second_closure = || 9;
    takes_two_closures_and_does_nothing(first_closure, second_closure);
}
```

Interestingly, it doesn't work! Fortunately, the compiler gives us a fantastic error that tells us exactly what the problem is:

```
error[E0308]: mismatched types
  --> src/main.rs:10:56
   |
8  |         let first_closure = || 9;
   |                             -- the expected closure
9  |         let second_closure = || 9;
   |                              -- the found closure
10 |         takes_two_closures_and_does_nothing(first_closure,
   second_closure);                                           ^^^^^^^^^^^^^^
   |         ----------------------------------
   expected closure, found a different closure
   |         |
   |         arguments to this function are incorrect
   |
   = note: expected closure `[closure@src/main.rs:8:25: 8:27]`
              found closure `[closure@src/main.rs:9:26: 9:28]`
   = note: no two closures, even if identical, have the same type
   = help: consider boxing your closure and/or using it as a trait object
```

This makes sense because these closures are unique types that implement the trait `Fn`, not a concrete type `Fn`. From the compiler's point of view, the two arguments look like this:

- *Argument 1*—Some type that implements `Fn`, takes no arguments, and returns an i32.

- *Argument 2*—Some other type that implements `Fn`, takes no arguments, and returns an `i32`.

Since `first_closure` is some type that implements a trait, and `second_closure` is some other type that implements a trait, they are not the same type.

The last part of the error message is interesting: `consider boxing your closure`. We will learn what this message is talking about in the next chapter. (If you are curious about this right away, try doing a search for the term *trait object*.)

Now, if we just wanted this code to compile, we could inform the compiler that the closures are different types by calling them `F` and `G` instead of just `F`. The compiler will be happy with this:

```
fn takes_two_closures_and_does_nothing<F, G>(first: F, second: G)
where
    F: Fn() -> i32,
    G: Fn() -> i32,
{
}

fn main() {
    let first_closure = || 9;
    let second_closure = || 9;
    takes_two_closures_and_does_nothing(first_closure, second_closure);
}
```

Hopefully, this clears up some of the mysteries about closures. Let's finish up with an example that is a little more interesting than the simple ones we have looked at so far.

12.1.4　*A closure example*

Now let's put together a closure example that actually does something interesting. In this example, we will create a `City` struct again. This time, the `City` struct has more data about years and populations. It has a `Vec<u32>` for all the years and another, `Vec<u32>`, for all the populations.

`City` has a single method called `.change_city_data()`, which takes a closure. When we use `.change_city_data()`, it gives us the years and the populations and a closure, so we can do what we want with the data. The closure type is `FnMut`, so we can change the data without taking ownership. In the following example, we will just have some fun with the closure by making some random changes to the `City` data. It looks like this:

```
#[derive(Debug)]
struct City {
    name: String,
    years: Vec<u32>,
    populations: Vec<u32>,
}

impl City {
    fn change_city_data<F>(&mut self, mut f: F)
```

We bring in self, and f is a generic type F. You could write it "mut closure: GenericClosure" or any other names you choose, but f and F are most common in Rust.

The closure takes mutable vectors of u32, which are the year and population data. How do we make sure that the year and population data get passed in? Well . . .

. . . we do it by calling the closure in and passing in these parameters as the arguments. Now, a user of the function gets access to these parameters and can do whatever they want with the closure every time we use it as long as the signature matches.

```rust
    where
        F: FnMut(&mut Vec<u32>, &mut Vec<u32>),
    {
        f(&mut self.years, &mut self.populations)
    }
}

fn main() {
    let mut tallinn = City {
        name: "Tallinn".to_string(),
        years: vec![1372, 1834, 1897, 1925, 1959, 1989, 2000, 2010, 2020],
        populations: vec![3_250, 15_300, 58_800,
            119_800, 283_071, 478_974,
            400_378, 406_703, 437_619,
        ],
    };

    tallinn.change_city_data(|x, y| {
        x.push(2030);
        y.push(500_000);
    });

    tallinn.change_city_data(|years, populations| {
        let new_vec = years
            .iter_mut()
            .zip(populations.iter_mut())
            .take(3)
            .collect::<Vec<(_, _)>>();
        println!("{new_vec:?}");
    });

    tallinn.change_city_data(|x, y| {
        let position_option = x.iter().position(|x| *x == 1834);
        if let Some(position) = position_option {
            println!(
                "Going to delete {} at position {:?} now.",
                x[position], position
            );
            x.remove(position);
            y.remove(position);
        }
    });

    println!(
        "Years left are {:?}\nPopulations left are {:?}",
        tallinn.years, tallinn.populations
    );
}
```

We'll choose x and y for the two variables and can use them to add some data for the year 2030.

Or we can choose the names' years and populations. Let's put the data for three years together and print it.

Zips the two together and only takes the first three

Tells Rust to decide the types inside the tuple

For our final random change to the data, let's delete the data for 1834 if the .position() method finds it.

Running this code will print the result of all the times we called .change_city_
data():

```
[(1372, 3250), (1834, 15300), (1897, 58800)]
Going to delete 1834 at position 1 now.
Years left are [1372, 1897, 1925, 1959, 1989, 2000, 2010, 2020, 2030]
Populations left are [3250, 58800, 119800, 283071, 478974, 400378, 406703,
↪437619, 500000]
```

This might be a good example for you to pick up and experiment for a bit. One idea
you could try would be changing the closure inside change_city_data() to take a
mutable reference to all of self (the City struct) instead of the two parameters. How
would you change the signature? And what changes would you then have to make to
the rest of the code to have it compile again?

That's enough learning about closures for a while! You'll see closures enough anyway as you start to use Rust more and more. Now, let's take a look at something else
you'll see: another way to use generics.

12.2   impl Trait

It turns out that Rust has other ways to use generics, and now it's time to learn the
next one: impl Trait. Don't worry; there are good reasons for having multiple types
of generics. We first learned that generics use a type T (or any other name), which
then gets decided when the program compiles. Let's do a quick review of the generics
we already know so that we can understand how impl Trait generics are different.

12.2.1   Regular generics compared to impl Trait

Let's look at a concrete function to start, a very simple one that compares two numbers:

```rust
fn print_maximum(one: i32, two: i32) {
    let higher = if one > two { one } else { two };
    println!("{higher} is higher");
}

fn main() {
    print_maximum(8, 10);
}
```

This prints 10 is higher.

But this only takes an i32, so now we will make it generic so we can take in more
than just i32s. We need to compare, and we want to print with {}. To do that, our type
T will need to have PartialOrd and Display. Remember, this means "only take types
that already have PartialOrd and Display." Here it is as a generic function:

```rust
use std::fmt::Display;

fn print_maximum<T: PartialOrd + Display>(one: T, two: T) {
    let higher = if one > two { one } else { two };
    println!("{higher} is higher.");
}
```

```
fn main() {
    print_maximum(8, 10);
}
```

Now let's look at `impl Trait`, which is similar. Instead of a type `T`, we can bring in an `impl Trait`. The function will then accept a type that implements that trait. You'll notice that it involves less typing but otherwise looks pretty similar:

```
use std::fmt::Display;

fn prints_it(input: impl Into<String> + Display) {        ◄─────────┐
    println!("You can print many things, including {input}");       │
}                                                                   │
                                               Takes anything that can
fn main() {                                     turn into a String and
    let name = "Tuon";                          also implements Display │
    let string_name = String::from("Tuon");
    prints_it(name);
    prints_it(string_name);
}
```

There are a few differences and limitations when you use `impl Trait` compared to regular generics. One difference is that for `impl Trait` you can't decide the type—the function decides it. Take a look at this example:

```
use std::fmt::Display;

fn prints_it_impl_trait(input: impl Display) {
    println!("You can print many things, including {input}");
}

fn prints_it_regular_generic<T: Display>(input: T) {
    println!("You can print many things, including {input}");
}
                                  You can specify
fn main() {                       u8 if you want.        Here you can't—it'll be
    prints_it_regular_generic::<u8>(100);    ◄───┘       an i32 because Rust
    prints_it_impl_trait(100);                   ◄───    chooses i32 by default.
    prints_it_impl_trait(100u8);                      ◄─  Well, we could pass in a u8 in this way.
    // prints_it_impl_trait::<u8>(100);       ◄───┐       But we're not telling the function what
}                                                 │       concrete type to choose; we're just giving
              This last one won't work for just   │       it a concrete type that it will react to.
              this reason: you can't decide the
              type when calling the function.
```

The difference between the two gets even clearer when we look at the `impl Trait` version of our first example, the `gives_higher()` function. Interestingly, this code won't work:

```
use std::fmt::Display;

fn gives_higher(one: impl PartialOrd + Display, two: impl PartialOrd +
➡Display) {
    let higher = if one > two { one } else { two };
```

```
        println!("{higher} is higher.");
}

fn main() {
    gives_higher(8, 10);
}
```

The code doesn't work because regular generics specify a type name, like T. Writing T: PartialOrd + Display means, "There is a single type named T, and it will implement PartialOrd and Display." But writing impl PartialOrd + Display means, "This argument will be *some* type that implements PartialOrd and Display." But there is nothing to say that they will be the same type, and PartialOrd is used to compare two variables of the same type! There is no type T to tell the compiler that we are talking about a single type.

The compiler error is pretty funny and one of the rare examples where the compiler is confusing to the reader:

```
4 |        let higher = if one > two { one } else { two };
  |                          ---      ^^^ expected type parameter `impl PartialOrd
  ➥+ Display`, found a different type parameter `impl PartialOrd +
  ➥Display`
  |                          |
  |                          |
  |                      expected because this is `impl PartialOrd + Display`
  |
  = note: expected type parameter `impl PartialOrd + Display` (type
  ➥parameter `impl PartialOrd + Display`)
            found type parameter `impl PartialOrd + Display` (type
  ➥parameter `impl PartialOrd + Display`)
```

Hopefully, this compiler message will be improved in the future.

Another limitation is that impl Trait can only be a parameter or return type of a regular function (http://mng.bz/46mj). It cannot appear when implementing traits. It can't be the type of a let binding. And it can't appear inside a type alias.

So far, we've only talked about the disadvantages of impl Trait! But it has a big advantage: we can return impl Trait from a function, and that lets us return closures because their function signatures are traits. In other words, you can write functions that return functions! Let's see how that works.

12.2.2 Returning closures with impl Trait

Since we can return impl Trait from a function, we can also use it to return a closure. To return a closure, use impl and then the closure signature. Once you return it, you can use it just like any other closure.

Here is a small example of a function that gives you a closure depending on the text you put in. If you put "double" or "triple" in, it multiplies it by 2 or 3; otherwise, it gives you the same number. Let's also print a message while we're at it:

```
fn returns_a_closure(input: &str) -> impl FnMut(i32) -> i32 {
    match input {
```

```
        "double" => |mut number| {
            number *= 2;
            println!("Doubling number. Now it is {number}");
            number
        },
        "triple" => |mut number| {
            number *= 3;
            println!("Tripling number. Now it is {number}");
            number
        },
        _ => |number| {
            println!("Sorry, it's the same: {number}.");
            number
        },
    }
}

fn main() {
    let my_number = 10;

    let mut doubles = returns_a_closure("double");       │ Makes three closures
    let mut triples = returns_a_closure("triple");       │
    let mut does_nothing = returns_a_closure("HI");      │

    let doubled = doubles(my_number);
    let tripled = triples(my_number);
    let same = does_nothing(my_number);
}
```

The output is

```
Doubling number. Now it is 20
Tripling number. Now it is 30
Sorry, it's the same: 10.
```

So you can see that `returns_a_closure()` is just like any other function: it has a return type that you have to follow. Except that its return type is not a number or some other type but a closure of `FnMut(i32) -> i32`. And if that's what the closure returns, the compiler will let your code compile.

Here is a bit longer example. Let's imagine a game where your character is facing monsters that are stronger at night. We can make an enum called `TimeOfDay` to keep track of the day. Your character is named Simon and has a number called `character_fear`, which is an `f64`. It goes up at night and down during the day. We will make a `make_fear_closure()` function that not only changes his fear but also does other things like write messages. It could look like this:

```
enum TimeOfDay {
    Dawn,
    Day,
    Sunset,
    Night,
}
```

```
fn make_fear_closure(input: TimeOfDay) ->
   impl FnMut(&mut f64) {
    match input {
        TimeOfDay::Dawn => |x: &mut f64| {
            *x *= 0.5;
            println!(
                "The morning sun has vanquished the horrible night.
You no longer feel afraid.\n  Fear: {x}"
            );
        },
        TimeOfDay::Day => |x: &mut f64| {
            *x *= 0.2;
            println!("What a nice day!\n  Fear: {x}");
        },
        TimeOfDay::Sunset => |x: &mut f64| {
            *x *= 1.4;
            println!("The sun is almost down! Oh dear.\n Fear: {x}");
        },
        TimeOfDay::Night => |x: &mut f64| {
            *x *= 5.0;
            println!("What a horrible night to have a curse.\n Fear: {x}");
        },
    }
}
```

The function takes a TimeOfDay and returns a closure. We use impl FnMut(&mut f64) to say that it needs to change the value.

```
fn main() {
    use TimeOfDay::*;
    let mut fear = 10.0;

    let mut make_daytime = make_fear_closure(Day);
    let mut make_sunset = make_fear_closure(Sunset);
    let mut make_night = make_fear_closure(Night);
    let mut make_morning = make_fear_closure(Dawn);

    make_daytime(&mut fear);
    make_sunset(&mut fear);
    make_night(&mut fear);
    make_morning(&mut fear);
}
```

Starts Simon with 10

Makes four closures to call every time we want to change Simon's fear

Calls the closures on Simon's fear. They give a message and change the fear number.

This prints

```
What a nice day!
 Fear: 2
The sun is almost down! Oh dear.
 Fear: 2.8
What a horrible night to have a curse.
 Fear: 14
The morning sun has vanquished the horrible night.
You no longer feel afraid.
 Fear: 7
```

Is that the best way to write this code for a video game? Probably not. But it's good practice for returning closures because being able to return a function like this can be very powerful.

12.3 Arc

You may remember in the previous chapter we used an `Rc` to give a variable more than one owner. If we are doing the same thing in a thread, we need an `Arc`. `Arc` stands for *atomic reference counter*. *Atomic* means that it uses atomic operations. Atomic operations are called *atomic* because they are indivisible (cannot be divided). For computer operations, this means that atomic operations can't be seen in progress—they are either completed or not completed. This is why they are thread-safe because no other threads can interfere when an atomic operation is happening. Each computer processor does atomic operations in its own way. We don't need to think about those details, but you might be wondering: If atomic operations happen on the processor level, are there processors that don't have them? The answer is yes, but they are very rare. We can see a few of them in the documentation on Rust's atomic types (https://doc.rust -lang.org/std/sync/atomic/index.html):

> *The atomic types in this module might not be available on all platforms. The atomic types here are all widely available, however, and can generally be relied upon existing. Some notable exceptions are:*
>
> – PowerPC and MIPS platforms with 32-bit pointers do not have `AtomicU64` or `AtomicI64` types.
> – ARM platforms like `armv5te` that aren't for Linux only provide load and store operations, and do not support Compare and Swap (CAS) operations... (and so on and so on).

So, as long as you are not building your Rust code on a very old or rare computer, you will have access to thread-safe types like `Arc`.

Atomic operations are important because if two threads write data at the same time, you will get an unexpected result. For example, imagine if you could do something like this in Rust without a thread-safe type like `Arc`:

```
let mut x = 10;

for i in 0..10 {      ◁─┤ Inside thread 1
    x += 1;
}
for i in 0..10 {      ◁─┤ Inside thread 2
    x += 1;
}
```

If thread 1 and thread 2 start together, maybe this will happen:

- Thread 1 sees 10 and adds 1; now it's 11. Then, thread 2 sees 11 and adds 1; now it's 12. No problem so far.
- Thread 1 sees 12. At the same time, thread 2 sees 12. Thread 1 adds 1, and now it's 13. But thread 2 still thinks it's 12 and writes 13. Now we have 13, but it should be 14. That's a big problem.

An `Arc` uses atomic operations to make sure this doesn't happen (atomic operations don't allow more than one access at one time), so it is the method you must use when you have threads. You don't want an `Arc` for just one thread, though, because `Rc` is a bit faster. So stick with an `Rc` unless you have multiple threads.

You can't change data with just an `Arc`, though—it's just a reference counter. You must wrap the data in a `Mutex`, and *then* you wrap the `Mutex` in an `Arc`. Now it can have multiple owners (because it's a reference counter); it's thread-safe (because it's atomic); and it's changeable (because it's inside a `Mutex`).

So, let's use a `Mutex` inside an `Arc` to change the value of a number. First, let's set up one thread:

```
fn main() {

    let handle = std::thread::spawn(|| {        Just testing
        println!("The thread is working!")      the thread
    });
                                        With .join(), we wait here
    handle.join().unwrap();             until the thread is done.
    println!("Exiting the program");
}
```

So far, this prints

```
The thread is working!
Exiting the program
```

Good. Now let's put it in a `for` loop for `0..5`:

```
fn main() {

    let handle = std::thread::spawn(|| {
        for _ in 0..5 {
            println!("The thread is working!")
        }
    });

    handle.join().unwrap();
    println!("Exiting the program");
}
```

This works, too. We get the following:

```
The thread is working!
The thread is working!
The thread is working!
The thread is working!
The thread is working!
Exiting the program
```

Now, let's make one more thread. Each thread will do the same thing. You can see that the threads are working at the same time. Sometimes, it will say `Thread 1 is working!`

first, but other times `Thread 2 is working!` is first. This is called *concurrency*, which comes from a Latin word meaning "running together."

```
fn main() {
    let thread1 = std::thread::spawn(|| {
        for _ in 0..5 {
            println!("Thread 1 is working!")
        }
    });

    let thread2 = std::thread::spawn(|| {
        for _ in 0..5 {
            println!("Thread 2 is working!")
        }
    });

    thread1.join().unwrap();
    thread2.join().unwrap();
    println!("Exiting the program");
}
```

Now, we want to change the value of `my_number`. Right now, it is an `i32`. We will change it to an `Arc<Mutex<i32>>`, an `i32` that can be changed, wrapped in an `Arc`:

```
let my_number = Arc::new(Mutex::new(0));
```

Now that we have this, we can clone it, and each clone can go into a different thread. We have two threads, so we will make two clones. One will go into the first thread, and the second, into the second thread:

```
let my_number = Arc::new(Mutex::new(0));

let cloned_1 = Arc::clone(&my_number);
let cloned_2 = Arc::clone(&my_number);
```

Now that we have thread-safe clones attached to `my_number`, we can move them into other threads with no problem:

```
use std::sync::{Arc, Mutex};

fn main() {
    let my_number = Arc::new(Mutex::new(0));

    let cloned_1 = Arc::clone(&my_number);
    let cloned_2 = Arc::clone(&my_number);

    let thread1 = std::thread::spawn(move || {       ◁─┐  The thread uses the move
        for _ in 0..10 {                                   keyword to take ownership,
            *cloned_1.lock().unwrap() += 1;      ◁─┐     but it's only taking ownership
        }                                            │     of a clone of the Arc, so
    });                                              │     my_number is still around.
                                                     │
                                          Locks the Mutex and
                                          changes the value here
    let thread2 = std::thread::spawn(move || {       ◁─┐  Only the clone goes
        for _ in 0..10 {                                   into thread 2.
```

```
            *cloned_2.lock().unwrap() += 1;
        }
    });

    thread1.join().unwrap();
    thread2.join().unwrap();
    println!("Value is: {my_number:?}");
    println!("Exiting the program");
}
```

The program prints this every time:

```
Value is: Mutex { data: 20, poisoned: false, .. }
Exiting the program
```

It was a success!

We can then join the threads together in a single `for` loop, which lets us use many more threads without having to write a lot of extra code. We need to save the handles somewhere so we can call `.join()` on each one outside of the loop, as we learned before:

```
use std::sync::{Arc, Mutex};

fn main() {
    let my_number = Arc::new(Mutex::new(0));      Our JoinHandles
    let mut handle_vec = vec![];              ◁──  will go inside here.
                                       Let's use 10
    for _ in 0..10 {              ◁──  threads this time.              Makes a clone before
        let my_number_clone = Arc::clone(&my_number);  ◁──  starting the thread
        let handle = std::thread::spawn(move || {     ◁──
            for _ in 0..10 {                            Uses move to make the
                *my_number_clone.lock().unwrap() += 1;  thread own the clone
            }
        });
        handle_vec.push(handle);  ◁──  Saves the JoinHandle so we can call
    }                                  .join() on it outside of the loop

    handle_vec.into_iter().for_each(|handle| handle.join().unwrap());  ◁──
    println!("{my_number:?}");
}                                                          Finally, calls .join()
                                                           on all the handles
```

Finally, this prints `Mutex { data: 100, poisoned: false, .. }`.

This looks complicated, but `Arc<Mutex<SomeType>>>` is used very often in Rust, and using this pattern quickly becomes natural. In the meantime, you could also rewrite your code to make it easier for you to read while you are still getting used to the syntax. Here is the same code with one more `use` statement and two functions. The functions don't do anything new, but they move some code out of `main()` and might make reasoning about the code a little easier:

```
use std::sync::{Arc, Mutex};         We can write spawn
use std::thread::spawn;         ◁──  to start a new thread.
```

```
fn make_arc(number: i32) -> Arc<Mutex<i32>> {
    Arc::new(Mutex::new(number))
}
```

A function that makes a Mutex wrapped in an Arc. We're using it to shrink the code a bit and make it easier to understand.

```
fn new_clone(input: &Arc<Mutex<i32>>) -> Arc<Mutex<i32>> {
    Arc::clone(&input)
}
```

Same here—just a function to make this thread example easier to read.

```
fn main() {
    let mut handle_vec = vec![];
    let my_number = make_arc(0);

    for _ in 0..10 {
        let my_number_clone = new_clone(&my_number);
        let handle = spawn(move || {
            for _ in 0..10 {
                let mut value_inside = my_number_clone.lock().unwrap();
                *value_inside += 1;
            }
        });
        handle_vec.push(handle);
    }
    handle_vec.into_iter().for_each(|handle| handle.join().unwrap());
    println!("{my_number:?}");
}
```

After all this learning about threads, we have another kind of thread to learn. But don't worry, this one is actually easier to use! Let's take a look.

12.4 Scoped threads

Scoped threads are a fairly recent addition to Rust, as they were only stabilized in August 2022 when Rust 1.63 was released. Remember in the last example how you had to clone the Arc for regular threads and use move to take ownership because regular threads need a 'static guarantee? Scoped threads don't need this because they are guaranteed to live inside a single scope (inside the {} curly brackets). Here's what the documentation says (http://mng.bz/5onD): "Unlike non-scoped threads, scoped threads can borrow non-'static data, as the scope guarantees all threads will be joined at the end of the scope."

Nice! That means you don't need to use .join() either because the threads will be automatically joined at the end of the scope. Let's look at the difference. With a regular thread, you use thread::spawn() to start a thread:

```
use std::thread;

fn main() {
    thread::spawn(|| {
```
Do more thread stuff.
```
    });
    thread::spawn(|| {
```
Do more thread stuff.
```
    });
```
Don't forget to join them here; otherwise, main() might end before the threads do.
```
}
```

With scoped threads, you start with a scope, using `thread::scope()`. The threads will only live inside there. Then you use the closure that `scope` gives you to spawn the threads:

```
use std::thread;

fn main() {
    thread::scope(|s| {          ◁─┐  We are just calling it "s" here.
        s.spawn(|| {                │  You could call it anything.
                        ◁───┤ Do thread stuff.
        });
        s.spawn(|| {
                        ◁───┤ Do thread stuff.
        });#
    });          ◁──┐  The threads automatically join here, so
}                   │  there's no need to think about JoinHandles.
```

Now, let's take our previous example and put it in scoped threads instead. Look at how much simpler the code is. You still need a `Mutex` because more than one thread is changing `my_number`, but you don't need an `Arc` anymore. You don't need to use `move` because the threads aren't forced to take ownership: they can just borrow the values because the threads are guaranteed to not exist after the scope is over:

```
use std::sync::Mutex;
use std::thread;

fn main() {
    let my_number = Mutex::new(0);
    thread::scope(|s| {
        s.spawn(|| {
            for _ in 0..10 {
                *my_number.lock().unwrap() += 1;
            }
        });
        s.spawn(|| {
            for _ in 0..10 {
                *my_number.lock().unwrap() += 1;
            }
        });
    });
}
```

In fact, you don't need a `Mutex` at all if only one thread is using your data. Scoped threads follow all the regular borrowing rules in Rust, so if only one has a mutable borrow, there will be no problem. Let's add two regular numbers (one mutable, one immutable) to our scoped threads and take a look:

```
use std::sync::Mutex;
use std::thread;

fn main() {
    let mutex_number = Mutex::new(0);     ◁─┐  Both threads use this, so we
                                             │  use a thread-safe Mutex.
```

```
let mut regular_mut_number = 0;
let regular_unmut_number = 0;

thread::scope(|s| {
    s.spawn(|| {
        for _ in 0..3 {
            *mutex_number.lock().unwrap() += 1;
            regular_mut_number += 1;
            println!("Multiple immutable borrows is fine!
{regular_unmut_number}");
        }
    });
    s.spawn(|| {
        for _ in 0..3 {
            *mutex_number.lock().unwrap() += 1;
            // regular_mut_number += 1;
            println!("Borrowing {regular_unmut_number} here too, it's
➥just fine!");
        }
    });
});

println!("mutex_number: {mutex_number:?}");
println!("regular_mut_number: {regular_mut_number}");
}
```

Callout (top): **Only one thread will modify this, so there's no need for a Mutex.**

Callout: **This variable isn't variable, so both threads can borrow it.**

Callout: **This part is commented out because it won't work: it's two mutable references at the same time, which is never allowed in Rust.**

The output will look different each time because of the multiple threads working at the same time but will be something similar to this:

```
Borrowing 0 here too, it's just fine!
Multiple immutable borrows is fine! 0
Multiple immutable borrows is fine! 0
Borrowing 0 here too, it's just fine!
Multiple immutable borrows is fine! 0
Borrowing 0 here too, it's just fine!
mutex_number: Mutex { data: 6, poisoned: false, .. }
regular_mut_number: 3
```

If you want to see a busier (but easier to read) example, just try something like this:

```
use std::thread;

fn main() {
    thread::scope(|s| {
        for thread_number in 0..1000 {
            s.spawn(move|| {
                println!("Thread number {thread_number}");
            });
        };
    });
}
```

If you run this, you will see that there are, indeed, a lot of threads running at the same time. The output will be different every time. One example while writing the book looked like this:

```
Thread number 2
Thread number 305
Thread number 176
Thread number 50
Thread number 175
Thread number 3
Thread number 4
Thread number 5
Thread number 6
Thread number 7
```

So, if you are okay with your threads only living inside a single scope, be sure to check out scoped threads. Regular threads have the advantage of living forever as long as your program is running, but scoped threads are easy to spawn and use if you have a task to accomplish and don't need them after the task is done.

12.5 Channels

Using a channel in the Rust standard library is an easy way to send information to one receiver, even between threads. Channels are fairly popular because they are thread-safe but pretty simple to put together. The flexibility of channels is another reason for their popularity. A channel has one or more senders and one receiver, which you can put wherever you want, such as on other structs and inside other functions. But once you have opened a channel between them, you can send from a sender to the receiver no matter where they are located.

12.5.1 Channel basics

You can create a channel in Rust with the `channel()` function in `std::sync::mpsc`. The letters `mpsc` stand for "multiple producer, single consumer"—in other words, "many senders sending to one place." The name *channel* is well chosen because an `mpsc` channel is like the channels of a river: you can have many small streams, but they all flow into the same larger river downstream. To start a channel, use the `channel()` function, which creates a `Sender` and a `Receiver`. These two are tied together, and both hold the same generic type. You can see this in the function signature:

```
pub fn channel<T>() -> (Sender<T>, Receiver<T>)
```

One sends a `T`; the other receives a `T`. Simple!

The output of the `channel()` function is a tuple, so the best way to start out is to choose one name for the sender and one for the receiver (destructuring). Usually, you see something like `let (sender, receiver) = channel();` to start. Because the function is generic, Rust won't know the type if all you do is type `channel()`:

```
use std::sync::mpsc::channel;

fn main() {
    let (sender, receiver) = channel();
}
```

The compiler says

```
error[E0282]: type annotations needed for `(std::sync::mpsc::Sender<T>,
std::sync::mpsc::Receiver<T>)`
  --> src\main.rs:30:30
   |
30 |     let (sender, receiver) = channel();
   |         ------------------   ^^^^^^^ cannot infer type for type
   parameter `T` declared on the function `channel`
   |             |
   |         consider giving this pattern the explicit type
   `(std::sync::mpsc::Sender<T>, std::sync::mpsc::Receiver<T>)`,
   where the type parameter `T` is specified
```

It suggests adding a type for the `Sender` and `Receiver`. You could specify the type if you want:

```
use std::sync::mpsc::{channel, Sender, Receiver};

fn main() {
    let (sender, receiver): (Sender<i32>, Receiver<i32>) = channel();
}
```

But you don't have to. Once you start using the `Sender` and `Receiver`, Rust will be able to infer the type.

12.5.2 Implementing a channel

Let's look at the simplest way to use a channel:

```
use std::sync::mpsc::channel;

fn main() {
    let (sender, receiver) = channel();

    sender.send(5);          recv stands for
    receiver.recv();    ◁─┘  "receive," not "rec v."
}
```

We have sent a 5, which is an `i32`, from the `Sender` to the `Receiver`, so now Rust knows the type.

Each of these methods might fail, so they each return a `Result`. The `.send()` method for `sender` returns a `Result<(), SendError<i32>>` and the receiver's method returns a `Result<i32, RecvError>`. You can use `.unwrap()` to see whether the sending works or use better error handling. Let's add `.unwrap()` and also `println!` to see what we get:

```
use std::sync::mpsc::channel;

fn main() {
    let (sender, receiver) = channel();

    sender.send(5).unwrap();
    println!("{}", receiver.recv().unwrap());
}
```

This prints 5, showing that we successfully sent the value from the Sender to the Receiver.

A channel is like an Arc because you can clone it and send the clones into other threads. Let's make two threads and send values to receiver:

```
use std::sync::mpsc::channel;

fn main() {
    let (sender, receiver) = channel();
    let sender_clone = sender.clone();

    std::thread::spawn(move || {
        sender.send("Send a &str this time").unwrap();       | Moves sender in
        sender.send("Send a &str this time").unwrap();
    });

    std::thread::spawn(move || {
        sender_clone.send("And here is another &str").unwrap();   | Moves
        sender_clone.send("And here is another &str").unwrap();   | sender_clone in
    });

    while let Ok(res) = receiver.recv() {
        println!("{res}");
    }
}
```

This will print those four &strs in the order the Receiver gets them.

Be careful, though: .recv() is a blocking function. A Sender gets dropped at the end of its scope (same as any other variable in Rust), but the Receiver using .recv() will keep blocking if the Sender is still alive. So, if a Sender thread is taking a long time to process before sending, the Receiver will just keep waiting.

In fact, our Receiver does wait quite a bit in this example. If you change the last part to while let Ok(res) = receiver.try_recv(), you probably won't see any output because the Receiver will quickly see whether there is anything to receive, see that nothing has been sent yet, and give up right away.

In addition, if you change .recv() to .try_recv(), you might get a panic because the Receiver gets dropped after trying just once while the Senders are still trying to send. That's because we're using .unwrap() here, of course. In real code, you don't want to .unwrap() everywhere.

Let's finish up by quickly looking at how the .send() and .recv() methods can fail. The .send() method will always fail if the Receiver has been dropped. We can easily try this out by dropping the Receiver and trying to send:

```
use std::sync::mpsc::channel;

fn main() {
    let (sender, receiver) = channel();

    drop(receiver);
    if let Err(e) = sender.send(5) {
        println!("Got an error: {e}")
    }
}
```

This will print

```
Got an error: sending on a closed channel
```

That's easy enough. Meanwhile, `.recv()` will return an `Err` if the `Sender` has been dropped *and* there is no more data to receive. However, if there is still sent data for the `Receiver` to receive, it will return `Ok` with the data inside even if the `Sender` has been dropped.

For example, if the `Sender` sends twice and the `Receiver` tries to receive three times, it will keep blocking and the program will never end:

```
use std::sync::mpsc::channel;

fn main() {
    let (sender, receiver) = channel();

    sender.send(5).unwrap();
    sender.send(5).unwrap();

    println!("{:?}", receiver.recv());
    println!("{:?}", receiver.recv());
    println!("{:?}", receiver.recv());
}
```

But if the `Sender` is first dropped, the `.recv()` method will not block anymore on the third try. Instead, it will recognize that the data has all been received and the channel has been closed, so it returns an `Err` instead of blocking:

```
use std::sync::mpsc::channel;

fn main() {
    let (sender, receiver) = channel();

    sender.send(5).unwrap();
    sender.send(5).unwrap();
    drop(sender);

    println!("{:?}", receiver.recv());
    println!("{:?}", receiver.recv());
    println!("{:?}", receiver.recv());
}
```

The output is

```
Ok(5)
Ok(5)
Err(RecvError)
```

This chapter was a lot of work. We learned how to pass closures into your own functions by picking among `Fn`, `FnMut`, and `FnOnce` and writing the closure's signature. We also learned about `impl Trait` and how it differs from regular generics. Finally, we got to some more thread-related functionality: `Arc` (like `Rc` but thread-safe), scoped threads as an alternative to regular threads, and channels as another thread-safe way to pass information from one end to another.

After all the hard work in the latest chapters, we are now a little bit more than halfway through the book. Here is a pleasant surprise: you've already covered a lot of Rust's most difficult concepts. Good work! There is a lot more content to learn as we move toward the end of the book, but the learning curve will not be as steep. The next chapter will be easy compared to this one, as we learn to read documentation and about the smart pointer known as a `Box` and what makes it so useful.

Summary

- One closure will never be the same type as another closure. The only thing they have in common is which trait (`Fn`, `FnMut`, and `FnOnce`) they implement and the rest of their signature.

- When using a closure as an input, first imagine it as a function: what arguments will it take, and what will it return? After that, change `fn` to whichever of the three closure traits you need: `Fn` to take by reference, `FnMut` to take by mutable reference, or `FnOnce` to take by value.

- `impl Trait` is more flexible than regular generics in some areas and less flexible in others. The best way to get a feel for the difference is practice: if you are using regular generics somewhere, see whether you can use `impl Trait` in its place, and vice versa. The compiler will tell you if you can't.

- When regular threads capture items, they need to have a `'static` lifetime. That lets you spawn a thread and forget about it, or you can use `.join()` to wait for a thread to end.

- Channels in the standard library let you make as many senders as you like. To get a feel for this, try making a channel and putting senders everywhere you can think of: as parameters of structs, in function inputs, in their own threads, and so on. This will give you a feel for just how useful they can be.

- Scoped threads let you use threads without having to think about the `'static` lifetime. Just make sure that your threads eventually end because if they don't, their scope will also never end (and then your program will never end).

Box and Rust
documentation

This chapter is a bit of a break after the last two, with `Box` being the only really new concept. But `Box` is one of the most important types in Rust because it makes a lot of things possible that otherwise wouldn't be, especially when working with traits. You'll be glad to know it! To start off the chapter, though, we will relax a bit and learn how to read documentation, which in Rust is always generated in the same way. This is nice because once you get used to reading documentation in Rust, you will be able to understand the documentation for anyone else's code. We'll also learn about attributes, which are the small pieces of code that start with a # that you see above a type (like `#[derive(Debug)]`, for example) or at the beginning of a file.

13.1 Reading Rust documentation

It's important to know how to read documentation in Rust so you can understand what other people write. As the saying goes, reading other people's code is just as important as writing your own. Fortunately, Rust excels here, too, because Rust documentation is always put together in the same way. In chapter 18, we'll look at the tool that makes documentation in more detail, but if you have Rust installed and can't wait to try it out, type `cargo doc --open` in any directory that has your Rust code. It will put the documentation together and open it up in your browser like magic! If you have Cargo installed already, check out the documentation (https://doc.rust-lang.org/cargo/commands/cargo-doc.html) for other flags to add to the `cargo doc` command.

The `cargo doc` tool is used to make the documentation for the standard library and just about everything else, so you only need to learn how to read Rust documentation once. Let's look at some things you need to know when reading Rust documentation.

13.1.1 assert_eq!

We previously saw that `assert_eq!` is used when adding guarantees inside your code. If you put two items inside the macro, the program will panic if they are not equal. Here is a simple example where we need an even number:

```
fn main() {
    prints_number(56);
}

fn prints_number(input: i32) {
    assert_eq!(input % 2, 0);
    println!("The number is not odd. It is {input}");
}
```

The variable number must be even. If the number % 2 is not 0, it panics.

The output is

```
The number is not odd. It is 56,
```

which shows that it satisfied the `assert_eq!` macro by returning `true`, and thus, the program did not panic.

Maybe you don't have any plans to use `assert_eq!` in your code, but it is everywhere in Rust documentation. Otherwise, you would need to use `println!` and have readers actually run your code to see the output. Plus, you would require `Display` or `Debug` for anything you needed to print. That's why documentation has `assert_eq!` everywhere. The following example comes from the `std::vec::Vec` documentation (https://doc.rust-lang.org/std/vec/struct.Vec.html), which shows how to use a `Vec`:

```
fn main() {
    let mut vec = Vec::new();
    vec.push(1);
    vec.push(2);

    assert_eq!(vec.len(), 2);
    assert_eq!(vec[0], 1);
```

```
        assert_eq!(vec.pop(), Some(2));
        assert_eq!(vec.len(), 1);

        vec[0] = 7;
        assert_eq!(vec[0], 7);

        vec.extend([1, 2, 3].iter().copied());

        for x in &vec {
            println!("{}", x);
        }
        assert_eq!(vec, [7, 1, 2, 3]);
}
```

In such examples, you can think of assert_eq!(a, b) as saying, "At this point, a and b will be the same." Now, look at the same example with annotations on the right that show what it actually means:

```
fn main() {
    let mut vec = Vec::new();
    vec.push(1);
    vec.push(2);
                                        Now the length
    assert_eq!(vec.len(), 2);     ←┘    of vec is 2.      Now the value
    assert_eq!(vec[0], 1);        ←                       of vec[0] is 1.

    assert_eq!(vec.pop(), Some(2));    ←                When you use .pop() here,
    assert_eq!(vec.len(), 1);     ←┐   Now vec contains  it returns Some(2).
    vec[0] = 7;                        one item.
    assert_eq!(vec[0], 7);        ←                    Now the value
                                                       of vec[0] is 7.
    vec.extend([1, 2, 3].iter().copied());

    for x in &vec {
        println!("{}", x);
    }                                  Now vec contains
    assert_eq!(vec, [7, 1, 2, 3]); ←┘  [7, 1, 2, 3].
}
```

Because assert_eq! will panic if the two items aren't equal, you can also run the code, and if it doesn't panic, you know that the items inside are correct. We will see a lot more of this macro in chapter 15, which is devoted to testing.

13.1.2 Searching

The search bar always shows up at the top of the page in Rust documentation and shows you results as you type. When you go down a page, you can't see the search bar anymore, but if you press the S key on the keyboard, it will take you back up to the top. So, pressing S anywhere lets you search right away (see figure 13.1).

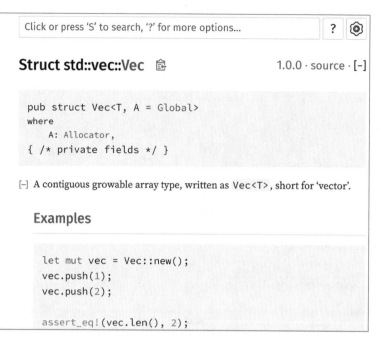

Figure 13.1
Just press S to
jump to the top.

13.1.3 *The [src] button*

Usually, the code for a method, struct, etc., will not be shown in full. You don't usually need to see the full source to know how it works, and the full code can be confusing. Also, items that aren't `pub` won't show up in the documentation. But if you do want to see everything, you can always click `[src]`. For example, on the page for `String`, you can see this signature for `with_capacity()`:

```
pub fn with_capacity(capacity: usize) -> String
```

Okay, so you put a number in, and it gives you a `String`. That's easy, but maybe we are curious and want to see more. How does it actually work? If you click `[src]`, you can see the full code:

```
pub fn with_capacity(capacity: usize) -> String {
    String { vec: Vec::with_capacity(capacity) }
}
```

Interesting! This shows us that `String` is a kind of `Vec`. Actually, the type `String` is a vector of `u8` bytes, which is interesting to know. You didn't need to know that to use the `with_capacity()` method, so the entire code is only shown if you click `[src]`. Thus, clicking `[src]` is a good idea if the document doesn't have much detail and you want to know more.

Let's take a look at the source code for another type we recently learned, `Cell`. In chapter 10, we learned that the `.get()` method for `Cell` only works when the inner type implements `Copy`. It's fine to remember this directly, but if we look at the documentation (https://doc.rust-lang.org/src/core/cell.rs.html#435), it becomes even clearer:

```
impl<T: Copy> Cell<T> {
    pub fn get(&self) -> T {
        // Function details…
    }

    pub fn update<F>(&self, f: F) -> T
    where
        F: FnOnce(T) -> T,
    {
        // Function details…
    }
}
```

`Cell` also only lets you `.clone()` if the inner type is `Copy`:

```
impl<T: Copy> Clone for Cell<T> {
    fn clone(&self) -> Cell<T> {
        Cell::new(self.get())
    }
}
```

Interesting! So these methods don't exist if the inner type doesn't implement `Copy` because they are written in separate `impl` blocks that start with `impl<T: Copy>`, thus requiring `T` to be `Copy` to be used.

Looking at the source details of the code can help you remember in a more interesting and effective way than just repeating that "`Cell`'s `.get()` and `.update()` and `.clone()` methods only work if the inner type implements `Copy`."

13.1.4 *Information on traits*

The important part of the documentation for a trait is "Required Methods" on the left. If you see that a trait has required methods, you will probably have to write the method yourself. For example, for `Iterator`, you need to write the `.next()` method. For `From`, you need to write the `from()` method. However, some traits can be implemented with just an attribute, as we see in `#[derive(Debug)]`. `Debug` needs the `.fmt()` method, but usually, you just use `#[derive(Debug)]` unless you want to do it yourself. That's why the page on `std::fmt::Debug` says, "Generally speaking, you should just derive a Debug implementation."

13.1.5 *Attributes*

Let's look at attributes in more detail. An attribute is a small piece of code that the compiler interprets in different ways. They are not always easy to create, but they are very easy to use. Some attributes are built into the language, some are used to derive traits (like `#[derive(Debug)]`), and some are for configuring tools (the previously mentioned cargo doc is one example of a tool).

If you write an attribute with just #, it will affect the code on the next line. But if you write it with #!, it will affect everything in the file.

An attribute with a # is called an *outer attribute* because it stands *outside* of the item that follows it. An attribute with a #! is called an *inner attribute* because it affects everything *inside* its file. An inner attribute needs to be placed at the very top of the file or module it is used in. Files and modules are another subject we will learn in chapter 15. For now, just remember this easy rule: put inner attributes at the very top!

And in any case, the compiler will complain if you don't put inner attributes above everything else. For example, if you run

```
fn empty_function() {}

#![allow(dead_code)]
```

the compiler will tell you exactly what is wrong and the reason why:

```
error: an inner attribute is not permitted in this context
  --> src/lib.rs:3:1
   |
 3 | #![allow(dead_code)]
   | ^^^^^^^^^^^^^^^^^^^^
   |
   = note: inner attributes, like `#![no_std]`, annotate the item enclosing
   ➡them, and are usually found at the beginning of source files
   = note: outer attributes, like `#[test]`, annotate the item following them
```

Let's look at some attributes you will see a lot.

#[allow(dead_code)] and #[allow(unused_variables)]. If you write code that you don't use, Rust will still compile, but it will let you know. For example, here is a struct with nothing in it and one variable. We don't use either of them:

```
struct JustAStruct {}

fn main() {
    let some_char = 'ん';
}
```

If you write this, Rust will remind you that you didn't use them:

```
warning: unused variable: `some_char`
  --> src\main.rs:4:9
   |
 4 |     let some_char = 'ん';
   |         ^^^^^^^^^ help: if this is intentional, prefix it with an
   ➡underscore: `_some_char`
   |
   = note: `#[warn(unused_variables)]` on by default

warning: struct is never constructed: `JustAStruct`
  --> src\main.rs:1:8
   |
```

```
1 | struct JustAStruct {}
  |        ^^^^^^^^^^^
  |
  = note: `#[warn(dead_code)]` on by default
```

We know that you can write an _ before the name to make the compiler be quiet:

```
struct _JustAStruct {}

fn main() {
    let _some_char = 'ん';
}
```

But you can also use attributes. You'll notice in the message that it uses `#[warn(unused_variables)]` and `#[warn(dead_code)]`. In our code, `JustAStruct` is dead code, and `some_char` is an unused variable. The opposite of `warn` is `allow`, so we can write this and it will not say anything:

```
#![allow(dead_code)]
#![allow(unused_variables)]

struct Struct1 {}
struct Struct2 {}            Creates five structs
struct Struct3 {}
struct Struct4 {}
struct Struct5 {}

fn main() {
    let char1 = 'ん';                                  Creates four variables. We
    let char2 = ';';                                   don't use any of them but
    let some_str = "I'm just a regular &str";          the compiler is quiet.
    let some_vec = vec!["I", "am", "just", "a", "vec"];
}
```

You can combine these two into a single attribute if you want the compiler to be quiet about everything that isn't being unused: `#![allow(unused)]`.

Of course, dealing with dead code and unused variables is important. But sometimes, you want the compiler to be quiet for a while. Or you might need to show some code or teach people Rust and don't want to confuse them with compiler messages.

`#[derive(TraitName)]` lets you derive some traits for structs and enums that you create. This works with many common traits that can be automatically derived. Some, like `Display`, can't be automatically derived because `Display` is meant for a nice, human-readable display, and that requires a human to decide how to do it. So this won't work:

```
#[derive(Display)]
struct HoldsAString {
    the_string: String,
}
```

```
fn main() {
    let my_string = HoldsAString {
        the_string: "Here I am!".to_string(),
    };
}
```

The error message will tell you that:

```
error: cannot find derive macro `Display` in this scope
 --> src\main.rs:2:10
  |
2 | #[derive(Display)]
  |
```

For traits that you can automatically derive, you can put in as many as you like. Let's give HoldsAString seven traits in a single line, just for fun, even though at the moment it only needs one. You see this practice a lot in Rust:

```
#[derive(Debug, PartialEq, Eq, Ord, PartialOrd, Hash, Clone)]
struct HoldsAString {
    the_string: String,
}

fn main() {
    let my_string = HoldsAString {
        the_string: "Here I am!".to_string(),
    };
    println!("{:?}", my_string);
}
```

Also, you can make a struct Copy if (and only if) it also implements Clone and if fields all implement Copy. HoldsAString has String, which is not Copy, so you can't use #[derive(Copy)] for it. But for this struct, you can:

```
#[derive(Clone, Copy)]
struct NumberAndBool {
    number: i32,              ◁──┤ i32 is Copy.
    true_or_false: bool          ◁──┐ bool is also Copy,
}                                   │ so no problem.

fn does_nothing(input: NumberAndBool) {}

fn main() {
    let number_and_bool = NumberAndBool {
        number: 8,
        true_or_false: true
    };

    does_nothing(number_and_bool);
    does_nothing(number_and_bool);   ◁──┐ This would Err if it
}                                       │ didn't have Copy.
```

`#[cfg()]` is another attribute that stands for *configuration* and tells the compiler things like whether to run code or not. You usually see it like this: `#[cfg(test)]`. You use that when writing test functions so that it knows not to compile and run them unless you are testing. Then you can have tests next to your code, but the compiler will ignore them unless you tell it not to. We will learn about testing in the next chapter.

One other example of the `cfg` attribute is `#[cfg(target_os = "windows")]`. With that, you can tell the compiler to run the code only on Windows, or Linux, or anything else.

`#![no_std]` is an interesting attribute that tells Rust not to bring in the standard library. That means you don't have `Vec`, `String`, and anything else in the standard library. You will see this in code for small devices that don't have much memory or space and thus can only use the stack, never the heap.

`#[non_exhaustive]`, when placed above a type, lets the compiler know that it may have more variants or fields in the future. This is used almost entirely with enums. These enums can still be used by anyone, but when matching on a `#[non_exhaustive]` enum created by someone else, you will have to include a final check after all the variants just in case a new one is added in the future.

`#[deprecated]` lets you mark an item, usually a function, as deprecated (not used anymore). This attribute won't stop people from using the function, but it will give a warning. Letting people still use the old item makes sense because a new item or type might be completely different, and people using your code might have to do some work to figure it out. Here is the easiest way to give this attribute a try:

```
#[deprecated]
fn deprecated_function() {}

fn main() {
    deprecated_function();
}
```

As expected, we get a warning that the function is deprecated, but the code compiles and runs:

```
warning: use of deprecated function `deprecated_function`
  --> src/main.rs:17:5
   |
17 |     deprecated_function();
   |     ^^^^^^^^^^^^^^^^^^^^
   |
   = note: `#[warn(deprecated)]` on by default
```

Inside an IDE you'll probably see special highlighting for these functions, like a strikethrough, to make it clear that they are deprecated. Figure 13.2 shows what the previous code looks like inside Visual Studio Code.

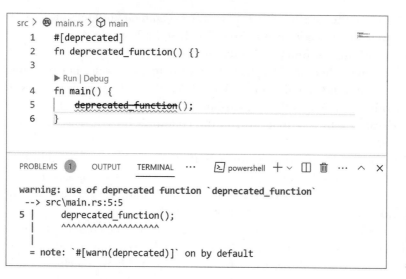

Figure 13.2 Many IDEs will recognize the #[deprecated] attribute.

You can add a note inside the `deprecated` attribute to give some more information. Usually, such a note is used to advise the user which function to use instead or to warn that it will be entirely removed later. Here is a quick example of a deprecated function with a note:

```
#[deprecated(note = "Always panics for some reason, not sure why. Please
use new_function instead")]
fn old_function() {
    panic!();
    println!("Works well");
}

fn new_function() {
    println!("Works well");
}

fn main() {
    old_function();
}
```

As expected, the program gives the full message and then panics:

```
warning: use of deprecated function `old_function`: Always panics for some
reason, not sure why. Please use new_function instead
  --> src/main.rs:14:5
   |
14 |       old_function();
   |       ^^^^^^^^^^^^
   |
   = note: `#[warn(deprecated)]` on by default
```

You can see many more attributes in the documentation (https://doc.rust-lang.org/reference/attributes.html).

So far, this chapter has been fairly passive, with learning about reading documentation and using attributes that are already built in. We will now turn to a type that you will use actively and probably quite frequently: Box. Let's see what makes a Box special and often even necessary.

13.2 *Box*

A Box is a type of pointer and a very convenient type in Rust. When you use a Box, you can put a variable's data on the heap instead of the stack. To make a new Box, use Box::new() and put the item inside. Let's put an i32 inside a Box and see what happens:

```
fn just_takes_a_variable<T>(item: T) {}        Takes anything
                                               and drops it
fn main() {
    let my_number = 1;                  This is an i32.
    just_takes_a_variable(my_number);          Using this function twice is not
    just_takes_a_variable(my_number);          a problem because it's Copy.

    let my_box = Box::new(1);          This is a Box<i32>.
    just_takes_a_variable(my_box.clone());       Without .clone(), the second function
    just_takes_a_variable(my_box);               would produce an error because
}                                                Box does not implement Copy.
```

Hmm, so what's the point of that? Let's find out.

13.2.1 *Some Box basics*

At first, it is hard to imagine where to use it, but let's start with the basics of how Box works. You can think of a Box as sort of like a reference, except that it owns its data.

We learned that & is used for str because the compiler doesn't know the size of a str: it can be any length. But the & reference is always the same length, so the compiler can use it. Box is similar, but it owns the data. Also, you can use * on a Box to get to the value, just like with &:

```
fn main() {                         This is a
    let my_box = Box::new(1);       Box<i32>.
    let an_integer = *my_box;       This is an i32.
}
```

A Box is called a "smart pointer" because it is like a & reference (a kind of pointer) but can do more things.

You can also use a Box to create structs with the same struct inside. These are called *recursive*, which means that inside struct A is maybe another struct A. You can't do this in Rust (the compiler will tell you).

But if you want to create a recursive struct, you can use a Box. Let's make a simple struct called a Holder that might hold another Holder inside itself. Here's what happens if you try without a Box:

```
struct Holder {
    next_holder: Option<Holder>,
}
```

You can see that when making a Holder, you can choose to give it a `Some<Holder>` (another `Holder`) or `None`. Because you can choose `None`, you can make a Holder that doesn't always need another Holder inside. For example, you might want to make a Holder that has a `Some(Holder)`, which itself holds a `Some(Holder)`, but finally ends with `None`. However, this won't compile!

```
struct Holder {
    next_holder: Option<Holder>
}


fn main() {
    let x = Holder {
        next_holder: Some(Holder {
            next_holder: Some(Holder { next_holder: None }),
        }),
    };
}
```

It won't compile because the compiler doesn't know the size:

```
error[E0072]: recursive type `Holder` has infinite size
 --> src/main.rs:1:1
  |
1 | struct Holder {
  | ^^^^^^^^^^^^^
2 |     next_holder: Option<Holder>,
  |                         ------ recursive without indirection
  |
help: insert some indirection (e.g., a `Box`, `Rc`, or `&`) to break the
➡cycle
  |
2 |     next_holder: Option<Box<Holder>>,
  |                         ++++     +
```

You can see that the error even suggests trying a Box and shows us exactly how to write it. So, let's put a Box around `Holder`:

```
struct Holder {
    item: Option<Box<Holder>>,
}
fn main() {}
```

The compiler is now fine with the Holder because everything is behind a Box, and the compiler knows the size of a Box. Now we can use `Box::new()` to put the next Holder inside, and the code we tried previously will now work:

```
#[derive(Debug)]
struct Holder {
    next_holder: Option<Box<Holder>>
}

fn main() {
    let x = Holder {
```

```
        next_holder: Some(Box::new(Holder {
            next_holder: Some(Box::new(Holder { next_holder: None })),
        })),
    };

    println!("{x:#?}");
}
```

Here is the output:

```
Holder {
    next_holder: Some(
        Holder {
            next_holder: Some(
                Holder {
                    next_holder: None,
                },
            ),
        },
    ),
}
```

Even with a type as simple as this, the code looks a bit complicated, and Rust does not use recursiveness very much.

If you are coming from another programming language, you may now be thinking that a Box can help you make a linked list in Rust, but be warned: Rust's strict rules on borrowing and ownership make this a pain. In fact, there is a whole book online (https://rust-unofficial.github.io/too-many-lists/) that explains just what a pain it is to write a linked list in Rust. Nevertheless, if you are curious, give the book a read. It is a good example of a common pattern in other languages that simply does not work in Rust without a lot of pain.

A Box also lets you use `drop()` on it because it's on the heap. That can be convenient sometimes.

So, Boxes let you put data on the heap, and you can make recursive types with them, and you could use one to make a data structure (that doesn't fit Rust very well). But none of this explains why Boxes are so popular in Rust. Let's finally get to the main reason, which is that Boxes are very useful, even necessary sometimes, when dealing with traits. Let's see how that works.

13.2.2 *Putting a Box around traits*

We know that we can write traits in generic functions like in this example:

```
use std::fmt::Display;

struct DoesntImplementDisplay {}

fn displays_it<T: Display>(input: T) {
    println!("{}", input);
}
```

This code only takes something with `Display`, so it can't accept our struct `Doesnt-ImplementDisplay`. But it can take in a lot of others like `String` that do implement `Display`.

You also saw that we can use `impl Trait` to return other traits or closures. A Box can be used in a similar way. You can use a Box because, otherwise, the compiler won't know the size of the value. This example with a bunch of different structs and enums shows that a trait can be used on something of any size:

```
use std::mem::size_of;                    ◄──────────────┐ This function gives
                                                          │ the size of a type.
trait JustATrait {}      ◄──────┐
                                │ We will implement
                                │ this on everything.
enum EnumOfNumbers {
    I8(i8),
    AnotherI8(i8),
    OneMoreI8(i8),
}
impl JustATrait for EnumOfNumbers {}

struct StructOfNumbers {
    an_i8: i8,
    another_i8: i8,
    one_more_i8: i8,
}
impl JustATrait for StructOfNumbers {}

enum EnumOfOtherTypes {
    I8(i8),
    AnotherI8(i8),
    Collection(Vec<String>),
}
impl JustATrait for EnumOfOtherTypes {}

struct StructOfOtherTypes {
    an_i8: i8,
    another_i8: i8,
    a_collection: Vec<String>,
}
impl JustATrait for StructOfOtherTypes {}

struct ArrayAndI8 {
    array: [i8; 1000],      ◄──────┐ This one will
    an_i8: i8,                     │ be very large.
    in_u8: u8,
}
impl JustATrait for ArrayAndI8 {}

fn main() {
    println!(
        "{}, {}, {}, {}, {}",
        size_of::<EnumOfNumbers>(),
        size_of::<StructOfNumbers>(),
        size_of::<EnumOfOtherTypes>(),
```

```
            size_of::<StructOfOtherTypes>(),
            size_of::<ArrayAndI8>(),
    );
}
```

When we print the size of these, we get 2, 3, 32, 32, 1002. Each one of these clearly has a different size. So, if you were to write a function that returns a JustATrait, it would give an error:

```
fn returns_just_a_trait() -> JustATrait {
    let some_enum = EnumOfNumbers::I8(8);
    some_enum
}
```

It says

```
error[E0746]: return type cannot have an unboxed trait object
  --> src\main.rs:53:30
   |
53 | fn returns_just_a_trait() -> JustATrait {
   |                              ^^^^^^^^^^ doesn't have a size known at
   compile-time
```

And this is true because the size could be 2, 3, 32, 1002, or anything else. So, we put it in a Box instead. Here we also add the keyword dyn. dyn shows that you are talking about a trait, not a struct or anything else.

The technical term is *dynamic dispatch*, which is like generics, except Rust accesses the type at run time, not compile time. That's where the dyn comes from.

Dynamic means "moving," and dispatch means "sending" or "passing on." The opposite of dynamic dispatch is static (i.e., not moving) dispatch. Static dispatch happens when the compiler turns a generic type into a concrete type before run time, so nothing is moving: the types have been made concrete before the program even started. So, you can change the function to this:

```
trait JustATrait {}

enum EnumOfNumbers {
    I8(i8),
    AnotherI8(i8),
    OneMoreI8(i8),
}
impl JustATrait for EnumOfNumbers {}


fn returns_just_a_trait() -> Box<dyn JustATrait> {
    let some_enum = EnumOfNumbers::I8(8);
    Box::new(some_enum)
}
```

And now it works because on the stack is a Box, and the compiler knows the size of a Box.

NOTE Box<T> is 8 bytes, Box<&T> (a reference) is also 8 bytes, but a Box<[T]> (a slice) is 16 bytes. Why is that? It's because a slice can be any size (any length), so the Box needs to store the length, too, and that takes 8 more bytes. If it doesn't need to know the length, it just stores the memory address, and that's just 8 bytes, not 16. In either case, the compiler knows the size and will be happy with it.

You see dynamic dispatch a lot in the form Box<dyn Error> because, as we saw in previous chapters, sometimes you have to work with more than one possible error. Let's learn about how that works now.

13.2.3 *Using a Box to handle multiple error types*

To make an official error type, you have to implement std::error::Error. That part is easy because the Error trait doesn't have any required methods: just write impl std::error::Error {}. But errors also need Debug and Display so they can give information about the problem. You can see this in the signature for the trait, which is pub trait Error: Debug + Display.

Debug is easy with #[derive(Debug)], but Display needs the fmt() method. We learned how to implement Display back in chapter 7.

Let's quickly create two error types to explore how implementing Error works. The code looks like this:

```
use std::error::Error;
use std::fmt;

#[derive(Debug)]
struct ErrorOne;

impl Error for ErrorOne {}    ◁

impl fmt::Display for ErrorOne {
    fn fmt(&self, f: &mut fmt::Formatter) -> fmt::Result {
        write!(f, "You got the first error!")
    }
}


#[derive(Debug)]
struct ErrorTwo;

impl Error for ErrorTwo {}

impl fmt::Display for ErrorTwo {
    fn fmt(&self, f: &mut fmt::Formatter) -> fmt::Result {
        write!(f, "You got the second error!")
    }
}

fn returns_errors(input: u8) -> Result<String, Box<dyn Error>> {    ◁
    match input {
```

ErrorOne is now an error type with Debug as long as it has Display as well. Now it's time to implement Display.

This function will return either a String or an Error. By returning a Box<dyn Error>, we can return a Box that holds anything that implements the Error trait.

```
                      0 => Err(Box::new(ErrorOne)),
                      1 => Err(Box::new(ErrorTwo)),
                      _ => Ok("Looks fine to me".to_string()),
                  }

          }

fn main() {

    let vec_of_u8s = vec![0_u8, 1, 80];

    for number in vec_of_u8s {
        match returns_errors(number) {
            Ok(input) => println!("{}", input),
            Err(message) => println!("{}", message),
        }
    }
}
```

Don't forget to put it in a Box.

This is the success type.

Three numbers to try out

This will print

```
You got the first error!
You got the second error!
Looks fine to me
```

If we didn't have a `Box<dyn Error>` and wrote this, we would have a problem:

```
fn returns_errors(input: u8) -> Result<String, Error> {
    match input {
        0 => Err(ErrorOne),
        1 => Err(ErrorTwo),
        _ => Ok("Looks fine to me".to_string()),
    }.
}
```

It will tell you

```
21 | fn returns_errors(input: u8) -> Result<String, Error> {
   |                                        ^^^^^^^^^^^^^^^^^^^^^^^ doesn't have a
   ⇒size known at compile-time
```

This is not surprising because we know that a trait can be implemented on many things, and chances are the error types will have different sizes. Even in this case, where `ErrorOne` and `ErrorTwo` have the same size, it still isn't allowed because Rust is concerned with type safety, not just size.

NOTE When you use types behind a trait in this way, they are called *trait objects*. A trait object represents *some* type that implements a trait but does not show you what the concrete object is. In other words, you have access to the type's implementation of a trait but not the concrete type itself. Not knowing the concrete type is called *type erasure* because the concrete type is erased: the function only says it's *some* type that has this trait. It could be almost anything.

Sometimes, you don't care to know the exact type. All errors can be printed, so you can, of course, just print them out:

```
fn handle_error_inside_function() {
    println!("{:?}", "seven".parse::<i32>());
}

fn main() {
    handle_error_inside_function();
}
```

This says `Err(ParseIntError { kind: InvalidDigit })`. Good enough.

Or you might know the error type if it panics. The following example shows a function with two types of possible errors: an error when parsing into an `i32` and an error when parsing into an `f64`. Then we try to add them together and return them as an `f64`. But two possible errors could happen, so we will return a `Result<f64, Box<dyn Error>>`. Then we use the question mark operator, see what happens, and then unwrap:

```
use std::error::Error;

fn parse_numbers(int: &str, float: &str) -> Result<f64, Box<dyn Error>> {
    let num_1 = int.parse::<i32>()?;
    let num_2 = float.parse::<f64>()?;
    Ok(num_1 as f64 + num_2)
}

fn main() {
    let my_number = parse_numbers("8", "ninepointnine").unwrap();
}
```

The error message tells us what it is:

```
thread 'main' panicked at 'called Result::unwrap() on an Err value:
➡ParseFloatError { kind: Invalid }', src/main.rs:10:57.
```

But what if you have some `dyn Error` trait objects and don't know their exact type but want to know? Let's imagine the worst error possible. We'll derive `Error` for it, as well as `Debug` and `Display`, but make the error messages tell the user nothing about what actually went wrong. We can even make `Debug` extra terrible by implementing it manually. Implementing `Debug` in this way looks a bit similar to `Display` but uses a method called `.debug_struct()` to do it. Just like `Display`, you can find an example in the documentation and just change it a bit, which is what we will do here:

```
use std::fmt;

enum MyError {
    TooMuchStuff,
    CantConnect,
    NoUserRegistered,
    SomethingElse,
}
```

```
impl std::error::Error for MyError {}

impl fmt::Display for MyError {
    fn fmt(&self, f: &mut fmt::Formatter<'_>) -> Result<(), fmt::Error> {
        write!(f, "Wouldn't you like to know...")
    }
}

impl fmt::Debug for MyError {
    fn fmt(&self, f: &mut fmt::Formatter<'_>) -> fmt::Result {
        f.debug_struct("Lol not telling you what went wrong").finish()
    }
}

fn main() {
    let err = MyError::TooMuchStuff;
    println!("{err}");
    println!("{err:?}");
}
```

This prints

```
Wouldn't you like to know...
Lol not telling you what went wrong
```

If this were a `dyn Error` trait object, you'd never know what it was. Even if the messages were good, you still might want to get the concrete type back and do a match over the enum: `TooMuchStuff`, `CantConnect`, and so on. Just having a `String` printed out sometimes isn't enough. Fortunately, there is a method called *downcasting* that lets us try to turn a trait object back into a concrete type.

13.2.4 *Downcasting to a concrete type*

The `Error` trait lets us downcast through a method called `.downcast()` (and `.downcast_ref()` and `.downcast_mut()`). You can use this method to try to turn a `dyn Error` trait object back into an error type. We'll use our unhelpful error and pick one more at random from the standard library. Let's go with `RecvError`, which can be returned from the channels that we learned to use in the last chapter. Then we'll try downcasting them.

In this example, we'll make a function that gives a boxed `MyError` if it gets `true` and a boxed `RecvError` if it gets `false`. But these two error types will show up as trait objects with the signature `Box<dyn Error>`, and you won't know the exact error type unless you downcast (or `.downcast_ref()` or `.downcast_mut()`) them:

```
use std::sync::mpsc::RecvError;
use std::error::Error;
use std::fmt;

enum MyError {
    TooMuchStuff,
    CantConnect,
```

```
        NoUserRegistered,
        SomethingElse,
}

impl std::error::Error for MyError {}

impl fmt::Display for MyError {
    fn fmt(&self, f: &mut fmt::Formatter<'_>) -> Result<(), fmt::Error> {
        write!(f, "Wouldn't you like to know...")
    }
}

impl fmt::Debug for MyError {
    fn fmt(&self, f: &mut fmt::Formatter<'_>) -> fmt::Result {
        f.debug_struct("Lol not telling you what went wrong")
            .finish()
    }
}

fn give_error_back(is_tru: bool) -> Box<dyn Error> {
    if is_true {
        Box::new(MyError::TooMuchStuff)
    } else {
        Box::new(RecvError)
    }
}
```

Here again, MyError is the worst error type possible. Neither Display nor Debug have any useful information at all. As a Box<dyn Error> trait object, you won't even know that the type name is MyError.

This function returns one of the two errors as a Box<dyn Error> trait object. The concrete types aren't known.

Make a vec of these errors:

```
fn main() {
    let errs = [true, false, false, true]
        .into_iter()
        .map(|boolean| give_error_back(boolean))
        .collect::<Vec<_>>();
```

Then print them out:

```
        println!("{errs:#?}");

        for err in errs.iter() {
            if let Some(my_error) = err.downcast_ref::<MyError>() {
                println!("Got a MyError!");
            } else if let Some(parse_error) = err.downcast_ref::<RecvError>() {
                println!("Got a RecvError!");
            }
        }
}
```

We'll use the .downcast_ref() method because .iter() gives us references.

Now that the error types are concrete again, we could match on the enum or do anything we want with it—same as with any other concrete type. It's not a trait object anymore.

Here's the output:

```
[
    Lol not telling you what went wrong,
    RecvError,
    RecvError,
    Lol not telling you what went wrong,
```

```
]
Got a MyError!
Got a RecvError!
Got a RecvError!
Got a MyError!
```

You can see that the first time we printed the errors, they were `Box<dyn Error>` trait objects, which means that they have the `Error` trait and `Debug` and `Display` (because `Error` requires these two), but we don't know anything more about them. After that, we used `.downcast_ref()` to try to turn them into a `MyError` and a `RecError` and got the concrete objects back.

Hopefully, Rust feels a lot friendlier to you by the end of this chapter. We've learned to read Rust's documentation and can now look through the source code in the standard library to find extra information on the types we already know. We also now have a general sense for attributes, including some of the most widely used ones. Maybe most importantly, we now understand why `Box` is used so much in Rust. The next chapter builds on this one as we learn to structure our code and test it to prove that it does what it should. Get ready to see the `assert_eq!` macro a lot!

Summary

- Clicking on the `[src]` button in documentation is a great habit to get into. You'll get more insight into how other code works even if you don't understand everything yet.
- The `assert_eq!` macro is everywhere in documentation to show the reader the values of variables at certain points in the code.
- A Box is a smart pointer that points to data on the heap. A Box owns its data.
- Using a `Box<dyn trait>` lets you "erase" a type. The type inside the Box is still concrete, but when inside the Box, it can only be used as a trait object. In other words, you can only use its trait methods.
- You can downcast a trait object back to a concrete type as long as you know what concrete type it might be. You can only try downcasting to one type at a time.
- Static dispatch happens at compile time, during which the compiler turns generic types into concrete ones. Dynamic dispatch happens during run time.
- Any type can implement `Error`, but a type can be of any size. To satisfy the compiler when returning errors, you can return a `Box<dyn Error>` instead.

Testing and building your code from tests

This chapter covers

- Using crates and modules to structure your code and limit how others can use it
- Using testing to prove that your code runs as it should
- Using test-driven development by writing the tests first and then the code

As your code grows, you're going to want to think about its structure. The more you write, the more you'll find that some code belongs in its own space, separate from other bits of code. You'll also want to start testing your code as it grows because even Rust's strict compiler can't protect you from logic errors. Tests also help to remind you when you change your code if something has gone wrong. Writing tests can be a bit boring at times, but, in general, the more tests you have to catch problems, the better. We'll also learn test-driven development (TDD), which means to write the tests before you write any code! In TDD, you write your tests, which will all fail. Only then, you write your code to make the tests pass one by one until finally everything works the way you intended.

14.1   Crates and modules

First, we are going to learn about where to put your code, what parts to make `pub` (available to others to use), and so on. Every time you write code in Rust, you are writing it in a `crate`. A `crate` is the file, or files, that go together for your code. (It also has a few other files to manage the project, but we'll look at those later.) Inside the file you write, you can also make modules using the keyword `mod`. In other programming languages, a module is often known as a *namespace*. A module is a space for functions, structs, and anything else that you think belongs inside its own space. Here are some reasons to use a module:

- *Building your code*—It helps you think about the general structure of your code and remember what code goes where. This can be important as your code gets larger and larger.
- *Defining names and keeping types from conflicting with other types with similar or the same names*—One good example is the standard library that has three traits that are each called `CommandExt`. But looking at the modules they belong to, it is quite clear why they all have the same name: they end with `linux::process::Command-Ext`, `unix::process::CommandExt`, and `windows::process::CommandExt`.
- *Reading your code*—People can understand your code more easily. For example, the name `std::collections::HashMap` tells you that it's in `std` inside the module `collections`. This gives you a hint that maybe there are more collection types inside `collections` that you can try.
- *Privacy*—Everything inside a module starts out as private. Modules themselves are also private unless you make them public. Doing this lets you keep users from using types and functions directly. This idea is sometimes called *encapsulation*: keeping things that are private in their own "capsules" and limiting access to them.

You can probably see already why you might want to use modules as your code grows. So let's make one and see what it looks like.

14.1.1   Module basics

To make a module, just write `mod` and start a code block with `{ }`. We will make a module called `print_things` that has some printing-related functions:

```
mod print_things {
    use std::fmt::Display;

    fn prints_one_thing<T: Display>(input: T) {
        println!("{input}");
    }
}

fn main() {}
```

You can see that we wrote use std::fmt::Display; inside print_things because a module is a separate space. If you wrote use std::fmt::Display; on the very top outside of the print_things module, the code wouldn't compile because it wouldn't be able to find the path to the Display trait.

We also can't call this function from main() yet. Without the pub keyword in front of fn it will stay private and inaccessible, so the code will not compile:

```
mod print_things {
    use std::fmt::Display;

    fn prints_one_thing<T: Display>(input: T) {
        println!("{}", input)
    }
}

fn main() {
    use print_things::prints_one_thing;

    prints_one_thing(6);
    prints_one_thing("Trying to print a string...".to_string());
}
```

Here's the error:

```
error[E0603]: function `prints_one_thing` is private
  --> src\main.rs:10:30
   |
10 |     use crate::print_things::prints_one_thing;
   |                              ^^^^^^^^^^^^^^^^^ private function
   |
note: the function `prints_one_thing` is defined here
  --> src\main.rs:4:5
   |
4  |     fn prints_one_thing<T: Display>(input: T) {
   |     ^^^^^^^^^^^^^^^^^^^^^^^^^^^^^^^^^^^^^^^^^^^
```

It's easy to understand that the function prints_one_thing is private. The error message helpfully shows us with src\main.rs:4:5 where to find the function. This is helpful because you can write mods not just in one file but over a lot of files as well.

The solution to this is easy: we can just write pub fn instead of fn and now everything works:

```
mod print_things {
    use std::fmt::Display;

    pub fn prints_one_thing<T: Display>(input: T) {
        println!("{}", input)
    }
}

fn main() {
    use print_things::prints_one_thing;
```

```
    prints_one_thing(6);
    prints_one_thing("Trying to print a string...".to_string());
}
```

This prints

```
6
Trying to print a string...
```

The pub keyword works a little differently depending on what you are making public. Let's see what the differences are.

14.1.2 *More on how the pub keyword works*

There are small differences in what the pub keyword does depending on whether it is in front of a struct, enum, trait, or module. These differences make sense when you think about them. They are as follows:

- pub *for a struct*—pub makes the struct public, but the parameters are still private. To make a parameter public, you have to write pub for it, too. The same rule applies to tuple structs, too, so to make a pub Email(String) fully public, you would have to write pub Email(pub String). So a pub Email(String) is a type called Email which the user can use, but they can't use .0 to access the String inside. (In the next chapter, we will learn about a popular trait called Deref that lets you use inner methods, like all the methods for String in this case, while keeping a type's parameters private.)
- pub *for an enum or trait*—Everything becomes public. For a trait, this means every method in the trait, and for an enum, this means every variant of the enum. This makes sense because traits are about giving the same behavior to something. And enums are about choosing between variants, and you need to see them all to choose them.
- pub *for a module*—A top-level module will be pub by default inside its own crate (as we saw in the previous example) but won't be accessible from outside without pub. And modules inside modules all need pub to be public.

The Rust reference (http://mng.bz/XqGa) sums this up quite well in a single sentence: "By default, everything is private, with two exceptions: items in a pub Trait are public by default; Enum variants in a pub enum are also public by default."

To demonstrate, let's make a struct called Billy inside print_things. This struct will be almost all public, but not quite. The struct itself is public, so it will say pub struct Billy. Inside, it will have a name and times_to_print. The parameter name will not be public because we don't want the user to be able to choose any name but Billy. But the user can select the number of times to print, so that part will be public. It looks like this:

```
mod print_things {

    #[derive(Debug)]
    pub struct Billy {       ⟵┐ Billy, the struct, is public, but the
        name: String,             parameter name inside it is private.
```

```
        pub times_to_print: u32,
    }

    impl Billy {
        pub fn new(times_to_print: u32) -> Self {
            Self {
                name: "Billy".to_string(),
                times_to_print,
            }
        }
        pub fn print_billy(&self) {
            for _ in 0..self.times_to_print {
                println!("{}", self.name);
            }
        }
    }
}

fn main() {
    use print_things::*;

    let my_billy = Billy::new(3);
    my_billy.print_billy();
}
```

The user needs to use new() to create a Billy. The user can only change the number of times_to_print.

We choose the name; the user can't. No Billy struct can have any name but Billy.

Now we use *, which imports everything from the module print_things.

This will print

```
"Billy"
"Billy"
"Billy"
```

By the way, the * to import everything is called the *glob operator*. Glob stands for *global*—in other words, everything.

14.1.3 Modules inside modules

Inside a mod, you can create other modules. A child module (a module inside a module) can always use anything inside a parent module. You can see this in the next example where we have a mod city inside a mod province inside a mod country.

You can think of the structure like this: even if you are in a country, you might not be in a province (or state, or prefecture). And even if you are in a province, you might not be in a city. But if you are in a certain city, you are guaranteed to be in its province and in its country.

Two other things to pay attention to here are crate:: and super::. If you start a path to a type or function with crate::, it starts from the beginning—from the outside to the inside. But if you are inside a module, you can use super:: to move up one module. (As we learned before, the word *super* itself means "above," like in "superior.") Pay close attention to the city module. Inside this module, we are calling the same function twice, one using the path that starts from crate:: and the other using super:: two times to go up two modules. Those are simply two ways to call the same thing:

```
        mod country {
This  ┌──▷  fn print_country(country: &str) {        ◁──────────────────  The top level module
function             println!("We are in the country of {country}");      doesn't need pub.
isn't pub.        }
            pub mod province {                    ◁──┤  Makes this module pub
                fn print_province(province: &str) {      ◁──┐
                    println!("in the province of {province}");   │  This function
                }                                                   isn't pub either.
This module and  ┌──▷  pub mod city {
the function            pub fn print_city(country: &str, province: &str, city: &str) {
it holds
are both pub. │
                        crate::country::print_country(country);      ◁──────────
                        super::super::print_country(country);

                        crate::country::province::print_province(province);   ◁──
                        super::print_province(province);
                        println!("in the city of {city}");
                    }                                      Here's one more example
                }                                          of writing the same thing
            }                                              either from the crate level
        }                                                  down or current level up.

        fn main() {
            country::province::city::print_city("Canada", "New Brunswick",
              "Moncton");
        }                              The path to the print_country function can be written
                                       from the crate level moving down or from the current
                                       location moving up using the keyword super.
```

Try to follow the flow of the code and imagine what the output will be if you run this code sample.

The interesting part is that print_city() can access print_province() and print_country(). That's because mod city is inside the other modules. It doesn't need pub in front of print_province() to use it. And that makes sense: a city doesn't need to do anything to be inside a province and inside a country.

Here is the output (see figure 14.1):

```
We are in the country of Canada
We are in the country of Canada
in the province of New Brunswick
in the province of New Brunswick
in the city of Moncton
```

When putting together your own project, the general setup looks like this: a main.rs file for the main function and related code and a lib.rs file. which is the library to hold types, functions, and so on that aren't related to the main running of the software you are building. Of course, nothing is stopping you from putting everything inside main.rs if you really want.

Something interesting happens when creating separate files (for example, a file called functions.rs): Rust won't even notice them! You can write all sorts of garbage inside this new file and—although your IDE might notice—the program will compile without any problems.

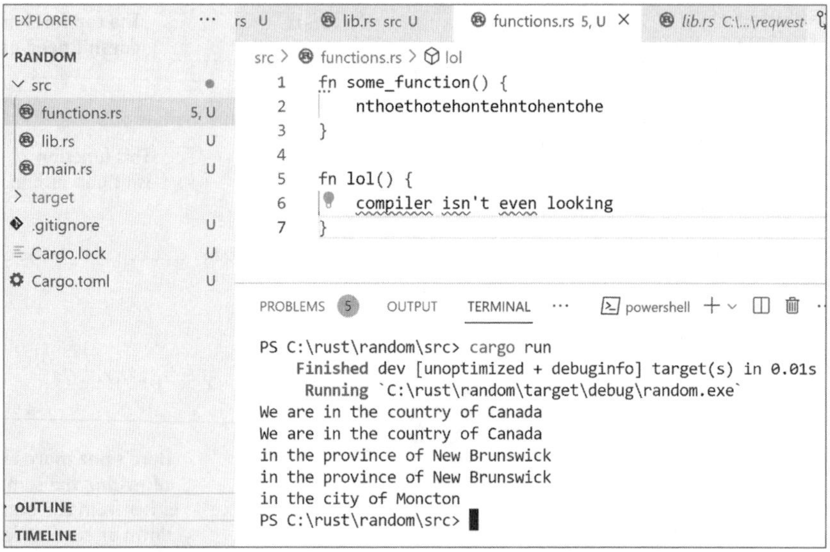

Figure 14.1   Files that aren't declared don't exist as far as Rust is concerned...

To have Rust notice them, go to `lib.rs` and declare them using the `mod` keyword. So if you make a `functions.rs` file, you have to type `mod functions;` inside `lib.rs`. Otherwise, Rust won't see it. But once the file has been declared, Rust will see it, and it won't compile the code anymore if there is a problem with it (see figure 14.2).

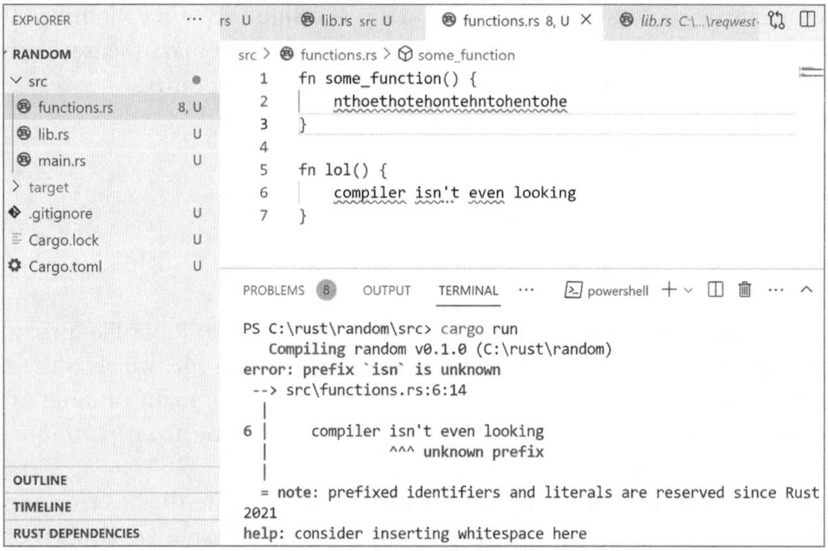

Figure 14.2   ...but declare the file and Rust will snap to attention.

We will look more at structuring a project in chapter 18, where we will learn about Rust on the computer instead of just in the Playground. But, for now, let's leave it at that and learn how to write tests.

14.2 Testing

Testing is a good subject to learn now that we understand modules. Testing your code is easy in Rust because you can write tests right next to your code. You can create separate test files if you want, but you don't have to if you don't want to. Let's look at the easiest way to start testing.

14.2.1 Just add #[test], and now it's a test

The easiest way to start testing is to add #[test] above a function. Here is a simple one:

```
#[test]
fn two_is_two() {
    assert_eq!(2, 2);
}
```

But if you try to run it in the Playground with the Run button, it gives an error: error[E0601]: `main` function not found in crate `playground`. That's because you don't use Run for tests; you use Test. To run this in the Playground, click on ··· next to RUN on the top left and change it to TEST. Now if you click on it, it will run all of your tests. In this case, it will just be one. (If you have Rust installed already, you will type cargo test to do this instead of cargo run or cargo check.)

Also, you don't use a main() function for tests: they go outside. You can outright delete the main() function and still run tests.

Here is the output of the previous test:

```
running 1 test
test two_is_two ... ok

test result: ok. 1 passed; 0 failed; 0 ignored; 0 measured; 0 filtered out
```

One other point to note: test functions can't take any arguments. So this won't compile:

```
#[test]
fn test_that_wont_work(input: i32) {}
```

The compiler message is as clear as day: error: functions used as tests can not have any arguments. A test function is pretty similar to main() in this way.

So, how does the compiler know that the test passed? It's pretty simple: if a test function does not panic, then it is a pass, and if it does panic, then it's a failure. The assert_eq! macro will panic if the two arguments inside it don't match, or you can use other ways to panic upon failure: .unwrap(), .expect(), the panic! macro, and so on.

The output for a passing test is pretty boring, so let's see what happens when it panics.

14.2.2 What happens when tests fail

Let's change `assert_eq!(2, 2)` to `assert_eq!(2, 3)` and see what we get. When a test fails, you get a lot more information:

```
running 1 test
test two_is_two ... FAILED

failures:

---- two_is_two stdout ----
thread 'two_is_two' panicked at src/lib.rs:3:5:
assertion `left == right` failed
  left: 2
 right: 3
note: run with `RUST_BACKTRACE=1` environment variable to display a backtrace


failures:
    two_is_two

test result: FAILED. 0 passed; 1 failed; 0 ignored; 0 measured; 0 filtered
➥out; finished in 0.00s
```

`assert_eq!(left, right)` and `assert!(bool)` are probably the most common ways to test a function in Rust. For `assert_eq!`, if the left and right sides don't match, it will panic and show that the values are different: left has 2 but right has 3.

The output for the `assert!` macro is almost the same:

```
#[test]
fn two_is_two() {
    assert!(2 == 3);
}
```

The output is

```
running 1 test
test two_is_two ... FAILED

failures:

---- two_is_two stdout ----
thread 'two_is_two' panicked at src/lib.rs:3:1:
assertion failed: 2 == 3
note: run with `RUST_BACKTRACE=1` environment variable to display a backtrace


failures:
    two_is_two

test result: FAILED. 0 passed; 1 failed; 0 ignored; 0 measured; 0 filtered
➥out; finished in 0.00s
```

So what does RUST_BACKTRACE=1 mean? This is a setting on your computer that you can use to get a lot more detail when an assertion fails. These settings are known as environment variables. We will learn more about them in chapter 18, but, in the meantime, just remember that they can be found using the function std::env::var(). Let's use this function to take a look at the default value for RUST_BACKTRACE:

```
fn main() {
    println!("{:?}", std::env::var("RUST_BACKTRACE"));
}
```

By default, that will print Err(NotPresent). But in the Playground, it's easy to enable: click ⋯ next to STABLE and set backtrace to ENABLED. Or you can use the function set_var() to do the same thing: std::env::set_var("RUST_BACKTRACE", "1"); If you do that, it will give you a lot more information:

```
running 1 test
test two_is_two ... FAILED

failures:

---- two_is_two stdout ----
thread 'two_is_two' panicked at src/lib.rs:3:5:
assertion failed: 2 == 3
stack backtrace:
   0: rust_begin_unwind
             at /rustc/a28077b28a02b92985b3a3faecf92813155f1ea1/library/std/
            ➥src/panicking.rs:597:5
   1: core::panicking::panic_fmt
             at /rustc/a28077b28a02b92985b3a3faecf92813155f1ea1/library/core/
            ➥src/panicking.rs:597:5src/panicking.rs:72:14
   2: core::panicking::panic
             at /rustc/a28077b28a02b92985b3a3faecf92813155f1ea1/library/core/
            ➥src/panicking.rs:597:5src/panicking.rs:127:5
   3: playground::two_is_two
             at ./src/lib.rs:3:5
   4: playground::two_is_two::{{closure}}
             at ./src/lib.rs:2:17
   5: core::ops::function::FnOnce::call_once
             at /rustc/a28077b28a02b92985b3a3faecf92813155f1ea1/library/core/
            ➥src/panicking.rs:597:5src/ops/function.rs:250:5
   6: core::ops::function::FnOnce::call_once
             at /rustc/a28077b28a02b92985b3a3faecf92813155f1ea1/library/core/
            ➥src/panicking.rs:597:5src/ops/function.rs:250:5
note: Some details are omitted, run with `RUST_BACKTRACE=full` for a verbose
➥src/panicking.rs:597:5 backtrace.


failures:
    two_is_two

test result: FAILED. 0 passed; 1 failed; 0 ignored; 0 measured; 0 filtered
➥src/panicking.rs:597:5 out; finished in 0.05s
```

You don't need to use a backtrace unless you really can't find where the problem is. But, luckily, you don't need to understand it all either. If you read from the bottom to the top, you will soon come across where the error happens: it's on line 4 where it says playground—that's where it talks about your code. Here's that part again:

```
4: playground::two_is_two
        at ./src/lib.rs:3:5
5: playground::two_is_two::{{closure}}
            at ./src/lib.rs:2:1
```

You'll also notice that the message tells us that we can set `"RUST_BACKTRACE=full"` for a "verbose backtrace" (a detailed backtrace). This used to be the default backtrace on Rust until it was improved with the less complicated output we just saw.

The verbose backtrace output is so verbose that it would take up a full page in this book. The Playground doesn't have a button to enable a verbose backtrace, but we can use `std::env::set_var()` to set it. Give this code a try if you want to see just how verbose it is:

```rust
#[test]
fn two_is_two() {
    std::env::set_var("RUST_BACKTRACE", "full");
    assert!(2 == 3);
}
```

The output is indeed verbose: it's about four times longer!

Now let's turn backtrace off again and return to regular tests.

14.2.3 *Writing multiple tests*

Now, we'll start writing multiple tests. Let's put a few simple functions together, followed by test functions to make sure that they work. Here are a few:

```rust
fn return_two() -> i8 {
    2
}
#[test]
fn it_returns_two() {
    assert_eq!(return_two(), 2);
}

fn return_six() -> i8 {
    4 + return_two()
}
#[test]
fn it_returns_six() {
    assert_eq!(return_six(), 6)
}
```

Now it runs both:

```
running 2 tests
test it_returns_two ... ok
```

```
test it_returns_six ... ok
```

```
test result: ok. 2 passed; 0 failed; 0 ignored; 0 measured; 0 filtered out
```

That's not too hard.

Rust programmers often put their tests in their own modules. To do this, use the mod keyword to create a new module and add #[cfg(test)] above it (remember: cfg means "configure"). This attribute tells Rust not to compile it unless you are testing. You also need to continue to write #[test] above each test. This is because later on, when you install Rust, you can do more complicated testing. You will be able to run one test, or all of them, or run a few. Also, don't forget to write use super::*; because the test module needs access to the functions above it. Now, it will look like this:

```
fn return_two() -> i8 {
    2
}
fn return_six() -> i8 {
    4 + return_two()
}

#[cfg(test)]
mod tests {
    use super::*;

    #[test]
    fn it_returns_six() {
        assert_eq!(return_six(), 6)
    }
    #[test]
    fn it_returns_two() {
        assert_eq!(return_two(), 2);
    }
}
```

This is the way you will usually see testing done in Rust and in other languages, too. You write your code first, then want to make sure that it behaves in the way it should, and then write some tests. This is probably human nature since the desire to create and the desire to get work done is so strong. But you can also do it the other way around by writing the tests first! Let's take a look at how that works.

14.3   *Test-driven development*

You might see the words *test-driven development* (TDD) when reading about Rust or another language. TDD is a bit unique, and some people like it while others prefer something else (so it's up to you how to test your own code).

TDD means writing tests first, all of which will fail! Only then you start writing the code. Then you start writing the code and keep doing that until all the tests pass. The tests then stay to show you if something goes wrong when you add to and rewrite your code later on. This is pretty easy in Rust because the compiler gives a lot of information about what to fix. Let's write a small example of test-driven development and see what it looks like.

14.3.1 *Building a calculator: Starting with the tests*

Let's imagine a calculator that takes user input as a `String`. To make the example as simple as possible, we'll only let the calculator subtract (we'll call it the `Subtractor`). If the user writes `"5 - 6"`, it should return -1; if the user writes `"15 - 6 - 7"`, it should return 2; if the user writes `"1 -- 1"`, it should return 2, and so on. And because we are using TDD, we will start with test functions before a single line of code is written.

We won't write the `Subtractor` yet, but we still need to give it a bit of thought so we can write tests that it will need to pass. The plan is to use a single function called `math()` to do everything. It will return an `i32` (we won't use floats).

For our `Subtractor`, the following five tests seem reasonable:

- Simple operation with one minus sign: `"1 - 2"` should return -1.
- Simple operation with two minus signs: `"1 - - 1"` should return 2.
- More complex operation: `"3-3-3--3"` should return 0.
- Spaces and characters after the last number should be ignored: `"18 - 9   -9-- ---"` should return 0.
- If the input doesn't contain a number, a space, or a minus sign, the program should panic: `"7 - seven"` should panic.

The absolute minimum code to make the tests is to have an empty `Subtractor` struct and a `.math()` method that returns an `i32`. For the `.math()` method, we'll just have it return a random number like 6—we'll think about it later. The first code looks like this:

```
struct Subtractor;

impl Subtractor {
    fn math(&mut self, input: &str) -> i32 {
        6
    }
}

#[test]
fn one_minus_two_is_minus_one() {
    let mut calc = Subtractor;              ◁─── So far, there's nothing to mutate in
    assert_eq!(calc.math("1 - 2"), -1);          Subtractor, but we plan to have it
}                                                hold input and parse numbers, so
#[test]                                          it will be mutable from the start.
fn one_minus_minus_one_is_two() {
    let mut calc = Subtractor;
    assert_eq!(calc.math("1 - -1"), 2);
}
#[test]
fn three_minus_three_minus_three_minus_minus_three_is_zero() {
    let mut calc = Subtractor;
    assert_eq!(calc.math("3-3-3--3"), 0);
}
```

```
#[test]
fn eighteen_minus_nine_minus_nine_is_zero_even_with_characters_on_the_end() {
    let mut calc = Subtractor;
    assert_eq!(calc.math("18   - 9       -9-----"), 0);
}
#[test]
#[should_panic]
fn panics_when_characters_not_right() {
    let mut calc = Subtractor;
    calc.math("7 - seven");
}
```

> Note that this test is annotated with #[should_panic]. If it doesn't panic, that's a failure.

The first part of the test output simply tells us which tests passed or not:

```
running 5 tests
test eighteen_minus_nine_minus_nine_is_zero_even_with_characters_on_the_end
... FAILED
test nine_minus_three_minus_three_minus_three_is_zero ... FAILED
test one_minus_two_is_minus_one ... FAILED
test one_minus_minus_one_is_two ... FAILED
test panics_when_characters_not_right - should panic ... FAILED
```

Along with that is information per failed test on why it failed, such as `thread 'tests
::one_minus_two_is_minus_one'` panicked at `src/lib.rs:10:5: assertion left ==
right` failed. We haven't started the `.math()` method yet, so this output is still of no use to us.

You can also see that function names in tests are usually quite descriptive, like `one_minus_two_is_minus_one`. You can probably imagine why: as your code grows, you might end up making 10s or even 100s of tests, and descriptive test names let you understand right away which tests have failed.

Now it's time to think about how to make the `Subtractor`. First, we will accept any number, the minus symbol, and empty spaces. We can represent this with a const called `OKAY_CHARACTERS` that contains all the possible input. To check input, we can use `.chars()` on the const to make an iterator of characters and `.any()` to panic with an error message if any characters aren't contained in `OKAY_CHARACTERS`.

Now, the code before the tests looks like this:

```
const OKAY_CHARACTERS: &str = "1234567890- ";

struct Subtractor;

impl Subtractor {
    fn math(&mut self, input: &str) -> i32 {
        if input
        .chars()
        .any(|character| !OKAY_CHARACTERS.contains(character))
    {
        panic!("Please only input numbers, -, or spaces.");
    }
        6
    }
}
```

Running the tests gives us this result:

```
running 5 tests
test one_minus_minus_one_is_two ... FAILED
test one_minus_two_is_minus_one ... FAILED
test panics_when_characters_not_right - should panic ... ok
test six_minus_three_minus_three_minus_minus_three_is_zero ... FAILED
test eighteen_minus_nine_minus_nine_is_zero_even_with_characters_on_the_end
➡️... FAILED
```

One test succeeded! Our `.math()` method will only accept proper input now. That was the easiest part. Now it's time to actually put the `Subtractor` together.

14.3.2 *Putting the calculator together*

The first step in putting the `Subtractor` together is to think about what the `.math()` method should return and how. Instead of returning a `6` every time, it should return some total. To start, we'll concentrate on the following:

- We'll give the `Subtractor` struct a parameter called `total`, which starts at zero.
- First, we'll remove any spaces from the input and trim the input string so that any spaces or minus signs at the end are ignored. That leaves only numbers and the minus sign as possible characters.
- We'll then go through each character and match on it. If it's a number, we'll push it into a parameter (a `String`) called `num_to_parse`. If we see a minus sign, we will know that the number is done. For example, for the input `"55-7"`, we would push a `5`, then push another `5`, and then see a minus sign and know that the number is done. In that case, we'll parse `num_to_parse` into an `i32` and subtract it from the total.
- Since `total` starts at 0 and `num_to_parse` is an empty `String`, we might as well implement `Default` for our `Subtractor`.
- As for double minus signs, we'll think about that later. Let's just try to get one more test to pass.

Here is our new code:

```rust
const OKAY_CHARACTERS: &str = "1234567890- ";

#[derive(Default)]
struct Subtractor {
    total: i32,
    num_to_parse: String,
}

impl Subtractor {
    fn math(&mut self, input: &str) -> i32 {
            if input
            .chars()
            .any(|character| !OKAY_CHARACTERS.contains(character))
        {
            panic!("Please only input numbers, -, or spaces.");
        }
```

```
        let input = input
            .trim_end_matches(|x| "- ".contains(x))
            .chars()
            .filter(|x| *x != ' ')
            .collect::<String>();
```

.trim_end_matches()
removes anything that
matches at the end of a &str.

```
        for character in input.chars() {
            match character {
                '-' => {
                    let num = self.num_to_parse.parse::<i32>().unwrap();
                    self.total -= num;
                    self.num_to_parse.clear();
                }
                number => self.num_to_parse.push(number),
            }
        }
        self.total
    }
}
```

The tests are the same except
that we are using Default to
make the Subtractor now.

```
#[test]
fn one_minus_two_is_minus_one() {
    let mut calc = Subtractor::default();
    assert_eq!(calc.math("1 - 2"), -1);
}
#[test]
fn one_minus_minus_one_is_two() {
    let mut calc = Subtractor::default();
    assert_eq!(calc.math("1 - -1"), 2);
}
#[test]
fn three_minus_three_minus_three_minus_minus_three_is_zero() {
    let mut calc = Subtractor::default();
    assert_eq!(calc.math("3-3-3--3"), 0);
}
#[test]
fn eighteen_minus_nine_minus_nine_is_zero_even_with_characters_
➥on_the_end() {
    let mut calc = Subtractor::default();
    assert_eq!(calc.math("18  - 9     -9-----"), 0);
}
#[test]
#[should_panic]
fn panics_when_characters_not_right() {
    let mut calc = Subtractor::default();
    calc.math("7 - seven");
}
```

NOTE .trim_end_matches() and .trim_start_matches() used to be .trim_
right_matches() and .trim_left_matches(). But people noticed that some
languages go from right to left (Persian, Hebrew, etc.) so right and left didn't
always mean end and start. You might still see the other names in really old
Rust code.

The tests won't change from here on, so we won't include the test code in the code samples anymore. Happily, one more test passes!

```
running 5 tests
test eighteen_minus_nine_minus_nine_is_zero_even_with_characters_on_the_end
➥... FAILED
test one_minus_minus_one_is_two ... FAILED
test panics_when_characters_not_right - should panic ... ok
test three_minus_three_minus_three_minus_minus_three_is_zero ... FAILED
test one_minus_two_is_minus_one ... ok
```

We still haven't made the `Subtractor` smart enough to know that a minus sign can also mean to add, so three tests have still failed. But interestingly, two of the tests have given us an unexpected hint for what to do next. Here is the error:

```
---- one_minus_minus_one_is_two stdout ----
thread 'one_minus_minus_one_is_two' panicked at src/lib.rs:22:44:
called `Result::unwrap()` on an `Err` value: ParseIntError { kind: Empty }
```

The code is still simple enough that we can imagine what is happening here. In this test, the input is `"1 - -1"`. The spaces and needless input at the end are removed, turning the input to `"1--"`. If we follow the logic, here is what the program is doing:

- Sees 1, pushes 1 to `num_to_parse`.
- Sees a minus sign, parses `num_to_parse`, adds it to the total.
- Sees a minus sign, parses `num_to_parse`...ah ha! It's trying to parse a number that doesn't exist.

We can fix this with a quick check to see whether `num_to_parse` is empty or not. Change the scope that starts with `for character in input.chars()` to the following:

```
for character in input.chars() {
    match character {
        '-' => {
            if !self.num_to_parse.is_empty() {
                let num = self.num_to_parse.parse::<i32>().unwrap();
                self.total -= num;
                self.num_to_parse.clear();
            }
        }
        number => self.num_to_parse.push(number),
    }
}
```

With that done, three tests still fail. But at least we are not trying to parse an empty string anymore, and the `ParseIntErrors` are gone. And it was thanks to the tests that we noticed this.

Up next, we will tell the `Subtractor` when it should add and when it should subtract. Fortunately, this isn't too hard: one minus sign means subtract, two minus signs means to add, three means to subtract, and so on. We could count the number of minus signs, but there is a way that is both easier to use and to read: use an enum. We will make an enum called `Operation` with two variants: `Add` and `Subtract`. The `Subtractor` will default to `Add`, and every time it sees a minus sign, it will simply switch.

Let's give this a try:

```rust
const OKAY_CHARACTERS: &str = "1234567890- ";

#[derive(Default)]
struct Subtractor {
    total: i32,
    num_to_parse: String,
    operation: Operation,
}

#[derive(Default)]
enum Operation {
    #[default]
    Add,
    Subtract,
}
```

> Since Rust 1.62 (released July 2022), you can now pick a default variant for an enum, as long as it is a "unit enum variant" (has no data in it). You do it by using the #[derive(Default)] attribute on top and then #[default] over the default variant.

```rust
impl Subtractor {
    fn switch_operation(&mut self) {
        self.operation = match self.operation {
            Operation::Add => Operation::Subtract,
            Operation::Subtract => Operation::Add,
        }
    }
    fn math(&mut self, input: &str) -> i32 {
        if input
            .chars()
            .any(|character| !OKAY_CHARACTERS.contains(character))
        {
            panic!("Please only input numbers, -, or spaces.");
        }

        let input = input
            .trim_end_matches(|x| "- ".contains(x))
            .chars()
            .filter(|x| *x != ' ')
            .collect::<String>();

        for character in input.chars() {
            match character {
                '-' => {
                    if !self.num_to_parse.is_empty() {
                        let num = self.num_to_parse.parse::<i32>().unwrap();
                        match self.operation {
                            Operation::Add => self.total += num,
                            Operation::Subtract => self.total -= num
                        }
                        self.operation = Operation::Add;
                        self.num_to_parse.clear();
                    }
                    self.switch_operation();
```

> These two lines restore the Subtractor to the default now that the operation is over.

```
                }
            number => self.num_to_parse.push(number),
        }
    }
    self.total
}
}
```

Interestingly, now only one test passes! Let's look at the failures closely (left = test output, right = expected output). See whether you can tell what they all have in common:

```
Input: "18  - 9      -9--  ---"
left: 9, right: 0

Input: "1 - 2"
left: 1, right: -1

Input: "1 - -1"
left: 1, right: 2

"3-3-3--3"
left: -3, right: 0
```

Ah, yes, they are all ignoring the last number. At the very end of our iterator through self.input, we always have a final number but just push it to self.num_to_parse and end the program without adding or subtracting it. To fix this, we can just check at the end whether num_to_parse is empty or not, and if it isn't empty, we can add to or subtract from the total. Since that operation will use the same code as before, we can make a method called .do_operation() so that we aren't duplicating code.

And after doing this, the tests pass. Here is the final code:

```
const OKAY_CHARACTERS: &str = "1234567890- ";

#[derive(Default)]
struct Subtractor {
    total: i32,
    num_to_parse: String,
    operation: Operation,
}

#[derive(Default)]
enum Operation {
    #[default]
    Add,
    Subtract,
}

impl Subtractor {
    fn switch_operation(&mut self) {
        self.operation = match self.operation {
            Operation::Add => Operation::Subtract,
            Operation::Subtract => Operation::Add,
        }
    }
```

```
fn do_operation(&mut self) {
    let num = self.num_to_parse.parse::<i32>().unwrap();
    match self.operation {
        Operation::Add => self.total += num,
        Operation::Subtract => self.total -= num,
    }
    self.operation = Operation::Add;
    self.num_to_parse.clear();
}

fn math(&mut self, input: &str) -> i32 {
    if input
        .chars()
        .any(|character| !OKAY_CHARACTERS.contains(character))
    {
        panic!("Please only input numbers, -, or spaces.");
    }

    let input = input
        .trim_end_matches(|x| "- ".contains(x))
        .chars()
        .filter(|x| *x != ' ')
        .collect::<String>();

    for character in input.chars() {
        match character {
            '-' => {
                if !self.num_to_parse.is_empty() {
                    self.do_operation();
                }
                self.switch_operation();
            }
            number => self.num_to_parse.push(number),
        }
    }
    if !self.num_to_parse.is_empty() {
        self.do_operation();
    }
    self.total
}
}
```

Success! And now that the tests pass, we could start refactoring the code a bit. We could return a `Result` instead of panicking or make some small methods to make the code cleaner. But this section is only about testing, so we'll leave it the way it is.

You can see that there is a back-and-forth process in TDD. It's something like this:

- First, you write all the tests you can think of. They will all fail because you haven't written the code yet to make them pass.
- Then you start writing the code. The tests will start to pass, and eventually, they will all pass.
- As you write the code, you get ideas for other tests.

- You add the tests, and your tests grow as you go. The more tests you have, the more times your code gets checked.

Of course, tests don't check everything, and it is wrong to think that "passing all tests" equals "the code is perfect." At the end of the day, a test only checks what the human programmer thinks should be checked. But tests are also great for when you change your code. Say you change your code later on and run the tests. If one of them doesn't work, you will know what to fix. This is especially important when working on a team or writing code that someone else might have to manage one day.

In this chapter, we've learned about structuring and testing your project, and we haven't even needed to install Rust yet! This will be good practice for later on in the book when it's time to move on to Rust installed on your computer. But in the meantime, we have a lot of Rust left that can be learned on the Playground. In the next chapter, we will learn some interesting patterns, plus a popular trait called `Deref` that gives you all the methods from someone else's type inside your types for free!

Summary

- Putting your code into modules is a good way to start thinking about what parts of your types should be made public.
- Since Rust makes everything private by default, you can simply use the `pub` keyword whenever you need it to compile your code. Or you can rewrite your code if you don't want to give access to your type's parameters.
- A test function is similar to `main()` because it takes no arguments.
- Use `#[cfg(test)]` over test code to let the compiler know that it doesn't need to compile it unless you are doing tests. You can still keep the test code close to your other code, just don't forget the annotation.
- Test-driven development is great if you already know what you want your final product to look like. It can also help if you sort of know what you want your final product to look like. As you write the tests, you will get a clearer and clearer picture of what you are trying to make.
- With TDD, all tests will fail in the beginning. Write as many as you can think of and then start writing the code to make them pass.

Default, the builder pattern, and Deref

This chapter is a fun one. You'll learn the builder pattern, which lets you declare variables by chaining method after method instead of writing all the parameters for a struct. It's especially good for writing code that other people might use because you can control which parts they can touch and which they can't. The `Deref` trait that you'll learn later in the chapter lets you make your own types that hold all the methods of another type for free. This allows you to easily make types that hold someone else's type inside, to which you can add your own methods on top.

15.1 Implementing Default

You can implement the `Default` trait to give values to a struct or enum that you think will be most common or represent the type's base state. The builder pattern

303

in the next section works nicely with this to let users easily make any changes after starting with default values.

Most frequently used types in the Rust standard library already implement `Default`. You can see which types implement `Default` in the documentation (http:// mng.bz/yZgd) if you are curious. Default values are not surprising, such as 0, "" (empty strings), `false`, and so on, which makes sense (you wouldn't want defaults to be something like `"Smurf"` for `String` or some random number like 576 for an `i32`!). We can see some default values in a quick example:

```
fn main() {
    let default_i8: i8 = Default::default();
    let default_str: String = Default::default();
    let default_bool: bool = Default::default();

    println!("'{default_i8}', '{default_str}', '{default_bool}'");
}
```

This prints `'0'`, `''`, `'false'`.

So `Default` is sort of like a `new()` method that can't take any arguments. Let's try it with our own type. First, we will make a struct that doesn't implement `Default` yet. It has a `new` function, which we use to make a character named Billy with some stats:

```
struct Character {
    name: String,
    age: u8,
    height: u32,
    weight: u32,
    lifestate: LifeState,
}

enum LifeState {
    Alive,
    Dead,
    NeverAlive,
    Uncertain
}

impl Character {
    fn new(name: String, age: u8, height: u32, weight: u32, alive: bool) ->
    ➥Self {
        Self {
            name,
            age,
            height,
            weight,
            lifestate: if alive {
                LifeState::Alive
            } else {
                LifeState::Dead
            },
        }
    }
}
```

```
fn main() {
    let character_1 = Character::new("Billy".to_string(), 15, 170, 70, true);
}
```

But maybe in our world, we want most of the characters to be named Billy, age 15, height 170, weight 70, and alive. We can implement `Default` so that we can just write `Character::default()` and won't need to enter any arguments. It looks like this:

```
#[derive(Debug)]
struct Character {
    name: String,
    age: u8,
    height: u32,
    weight: u32,
    lifestate: LifeState,
}

#[derive(Debug)]
enum LifeState {
    Alive,
    Dead,
    NeverAlive,
    Uncertain,
}

impl Default for Character {
    fn default() -> Self {
        Self {
            name: "Billy".to_string(),
            age: 15,
            height: 170,
            weight: 70,
            lifestate: LifeState::Alive,
        }
    }
}

fn main() {
    let character_1 = Character::default();

    println!(
        "The character {:?} is {:?} years old.",
        character_1.name, character_1.age
    );
}
```

It prints `The character "Billy" is 15 years old`. Much easier!

But not having to enter arguments isn't the main reason for implementing `Default`. After all, you could just come up with any other function that returns a `Character` with these parameters. So why implement `Default` instead of writing a `new()` or some other function? Here are a few good reasons why you might want to implement `Default`:

- `Default` is a trait, so if you implement `Default`, you can pass your type into anything that requires it. Sometimes, you will come across functions or traits that require `Default` to be implemented, such as the `.unwrap_or_default()` method.
- Your type might need to be a parameter in another struct or enum that wants to implement `Default`. To implement `Default` using `#[derive(Default)]`, all of a type's parameters need to implement it, too.
- Having `Default` gives users of your types a general idea of how to use them. For example, you might want to have a method called `new()` or `create()` to make a type with lots of customization. But you could also implement `Default` so the user can just create one without thinking about all the settings.
- Default is really convenient when working with parameters in a struct.

This last point is easiest to explain using an example. Consider this simple struct:

```
#[derive(Default)]
struct Size {
    height: f64,
    length: f64,
    width: f64,
}
```

Each of the struct's parameters is `f64`, which implements `Default`, so we can easily use `#[derive(Default)]` for it, too. That lets us write `Size::default()` if we want each parameter to be 0.0, but it also lets us do something like this:

```
#[derive(Debug, Default)]
struct Size {
    height: f64,
    length: f64,
    width: f64,
}

fn main() {
    let only_height = Size {
        height: 1.0,            ⟵  Makes height 1.0
        ..Default::default()    ⟵  For the rest, uses their default
    };                               values. Typing .. means "for
    println!("{only_height:?}");     each remaining parameter."
}
```

The output is

```
Size { height: 1.0, length: 0.0, width: 0.0 }
```

You also see `Default` a lot in a pattern known as the builder pattern, which we will take a look at now.

15.2 The builder pattern

The builder pattern is an interesting way to build a type (usually a struct). Some people like this pattern because it is quite readable, as it lets you chain method after method for all the parameters you want to change. For example, if we used the builder pattern on the `Size` struct we just looked at, it might look something like this, which is quite readable:

```
let my_size = Size::default().height(1.0).width(5.0);
```

The readability comes from being pretty close to how you would explain this in regular conversation: "Make a struct `Size` called `my_size` with default values but change `height` to `1.0` and `width` to `5.0`."

But the builder pattern isn't just for readable syntax: it also gives you more control over how other people use your types. Generally, the builder pattern makes the most sense when you have a type with a lot of fields, most of which are default values. A good example would be a database client with a lot of fields like `username`, `password`, `connect_timeout`, `port_address`, and so on. In most cases, a user will prefer default values, but the builder pattern allows some of these values to be changed when necessary.

To keep our examples short, though, we'll keep using the previous `Character` struct whose default name was Billy, so we will start with that as the default as we learn this pattern. As before, most of our characters will be named Billy, but we also want to give people the option to make some changes. Let's learn how to do that.

15.2.1 *Writing builder methods*

Let's imagine that we have a `Character` struct and would like to type `.height()` after declaring it to change the height. How would we do that? One way is to take the whole struct by value, change one value, and pass it back. In other words, each builder method will return `Self`. Here is what it would look like:

```
fn height(mut self, height: u32) -> Self {
    self.height = height;
    self
}
```

Notice that it takes a `mut self`, which is an owned `self`—not a mutable reference (`&mut self`). It takes ownership of `Self`, and with `mut`, it will be mutable, even if it wasn't mutable before. That's because `.height()` has full ownership, and nobody else can touch it, so it is safe to be mutable. Then the method just changes `self.height` and returns `Self` (which, in this case, is `Character`).

Let's have three of these builder methods. They are exceptionally easy to write. Just take a `mut self` and a value, change a parameter to the value, and return `self`:

```
fn height(mut self, height: u32) -> Self {
    self.height = height;
    self
}

fn weight(mut self, weight: u32) -> Self {
    self.weight = weight;
    self
}
```

```
fn name(mut self, name: &str) -> Self {
    self.name = name.to_string();
    self
}
```

Because each of these methods gives a `Self` back, we can now chain methods to write something like this to make a character:

```
let character_1 = Character::default().height(180).weight(60).name("Bobby");
```

So far, our code looks like this:

```
#[derive(Debug)]
struct Character {
    name: String,
    age: u8,
    height: u32,
    weight: u32,
    lifestate: LifeState,
}

#[derive(Debug)]
enum LifeState {
    Alive,
    Dead,
    NeverAlive,
    Uncertain,
}

impl Character {
    fn height(mut self, height: u32) -> Self {
        self.height = height;
        self
    }

    fn weight(mut self, weight: u32) -> Self {
        self.weight = weight;
        self
    }

    fn name(mut self, name: &str) -> Self {
        self.name = name.to_string();
        self
    }
}

impl Default for Character {
    fn default() -> Self {
        Self {
            name: "Billy".to_string(),
            age: 15,
            height: 170,
            weight: 70,
            lifestate: LifeState::Alive,
        }
```

```
        }
    }

fn main() {
    let character_1 =
     Character::default().height(180).weight(60).name("Bobby");
    println!("{character_1:?}");
}
```

This prints `Character { name: "Bobby", age: 15, height: 180, weight: 60, life-state: Alive }`.

That's the first part of the builder pattern, but what about the part about giving you greater control over how people use your types? At the moment, height is a `u32`, so nothing is stopping people from making a character with a height up to 4294967295 (the highest possible number for `u32`). Let's think about how to keep people from doing that.

15.2.2 *Adding a final check to the builder pattern*

One last method to add in the builder pattern is usually called `.build()`. This method is a sort of final check. When you give a user a method like `.height()` you can make sure that they only put in a `u32`, but what if they enter `5000` for height? That might not be okay in the game you are making. For our final `.build()` method, we will have it return a `Result`. Inside the method, we will check whether the user input is okay, and if it is, we will return an `Ok(Self)`.

This raises a question: How do we force a user to use this `.build()` method? Right now, a user can write `let x = Character::new().height(76767);` and get a `Character`. There are many ways to do this. First, let's look at a quick and dirty method. We'll add a `can_use: bool` value to `Character`:

```
#[derive(Debug)]
struct Character {
    name: String,
    age: u8,
    height: u32,
    weight: u32,
    lifestate: LifeState,      Sets whether the user
    can_use: bool,        ←┘   can use the character
}
```

Next, skipping over the code in between, the implementation for `Default` will now look like this:

```
impl Default for Character {
    fn default() -> Self {
        Self {
            name: "Billy".to_string(),
            age: 15,
            height: 170,
            weight: 70,
```

```
                lifestate: LifeState::Alive,
                can_use: true,                    ◁──┐ Default::()default() always gives
            }                                        │ a good character, so it's true.
        }
    }
}
```

For the other methods, like `.height()`, we will set `can_use` to `false`. Only `.build()` will set it to `true` again, so now the user has to do a final check with `.build()`. We will make sure that `height` is not above 200 and `weight` is not above 300. Also, in our game, there is a bad word called `smurf` that we don't want characters to use.

Our `.build()` method looks like this:

```
fn build(mut self) -> Result<Character, String> {
    if self.height < 200
        && self.weight < 300
        && !self.name.to_lowercase().contains("smurf")
    {
        self.can_use = true;
        Ok(self)
    } else {
        Err("Could not create character. Characters must have:
1) Height below 200
2) Weight below 300
3) A name that is not Smurf (that is a bad word)"
            .to_string())
    }
}
```

Using `!self.name.to_lowercase().contains("smurf")` makes sure that the user doesn't write something like `"SMURF"` or `"IamSmurf"`. It makes the whole `String` lowercase (small letters) and checks for `.contains()` instead of `==`.

If everything is okay, we set `can_use` to `true` and give the character to the user inside `Ok`.

Now that our code is done, we will create three characters that don't work and one character that does work. The code now looks like this:

```
#[derive(Debug)]
struct Character {
    name: String,
    age: u8,
    height: u32,
    weight: u32,
    lifestate: LifeState,
    can_use: bool,
}

#[derive(Debug)]
enum LifeState {
    Alive,
    Dead,
    NeverAlive,
    Uncertain,
}
```

```
impl Default for Character {
    fn default() -> Self {
        Self {
            name: "Billy".to_string(),
            age: 15,
            height: 170,
            weight: 70,
            lifestate: LifeState::Alive,
            can_use: true,
        }
    }
}

impl Character {

    fn height(mut self, height: u32) -> Self {
        self.height = height;
        self.can_use = false;        ◁─── Set this to false every time
        self                               a parameter changes.
    }

    fn weight(mut self, weight: u32) -> Self {
        self.weight = weight;
        self.can_use = false;
        self
    }

    fn name(mut self, name: &str) -> Self {
        self.name = name.to_string();
        self.can_use = false;
        self
    }

    fn build(mut self) -> Result<Character, String> {
    if self.height < 200
        && self.weight < 300
        && !self.name.to_lowercase().contains("smurf")
            self.can_use = true;     ◁─── At this point, everything is okay, so set
            Ok(self)                       it to true and return the character.
        } else {
            Err("Could not create character. Characters must have:
1) Height below 200
2) Weight below 300
3) A name that is not Smurf (that is a bad word)"
                .to_string())
        }
    }
}

let character_with_smurf = Character::default()     This one contains
    .name("Lol I am Smurf!!").build();         ◁─┘ "smurf"—not okay.
Too tall— ┌─▷ let character_too_tall = Character::default()
not okay  │      .height(400)
          │      .build();                          Too heavy—
          └─  let character_too_heavy = Character::default() ◁─── not okay
```

```
                .weight(500)
                .build();
        let okay_character = Character::default()
                .name("Billybrobby")
                .height(180)
                .weight(100)          This character is okay. Name is
                .build();             fine; height and weight are fine.

        let character_vec = vec![          Each of these is a
                character_with_smurf,      Result<Character, String>.
                character_too_tall,        Let's put them in a Vec so
                character_too_heavy,       we can see them.
                okay_character,
        ];

        for character in character_vec {
                match character {
                        Ok(character) => println!("{character:?}\n"),
                        Err(err_info) => println!("{err_info}\n"),
                }
        }
    }
```

This will print

```
Could not create character. Characters must have:
1) Height below 200
2) Weight below 300
3) A name that is not Smurf (that is a bad word)

Could not create character. Characters must have:
1) Height below 200
2) Weight below 300
3) A name that is not Smurf (that is a bad word)

Could not create character. Characters must have:
1) Height below 200
2) Weight below 300
3) A name that is not Smurf (that is a bad word)

Character { name: "Billybrobby", age: 15, height: 180, weight: 100,
lifestate: Alive, can_use: true }
```

So that's not bad as long as our code checks whether can_use is true or not. But what if we are writing a library for other people to use? We can't force them to check can_use, so we can't keep them from making a Character that is wrong. Is there a way to not even generate a Character struct in the first place if it shouldn't be built? Let's look at that pattern now.

15.2.3 *Making the builder pattern more rigorous*

The main way to make sure nobody can generate a Character struct on their own is to start with a different type. This type will look similar, but can't be used anywhere—it can only be used to turn into a Character if the parameters are okay. We'll call it

CharacterBuilder. Any functions that take a `Character` require a `Character` and nothing else, so even though `CharacterBuilder` has the same properties, it's not the same type. And to turn a `CharacterBuilder` into a `Character`, we'll make a method called `.try_build()`.

To make this last example more readable, let's simplify the `Character` struct. It might look something like this:

```
#[derive(Debug)]
pub struct Character {          This is fine because we control both
    name: String,              name and age. We know that these
    age: u8,                   two parameters are acceptable.
}
impl Default for Character {
    fn default() -> Self {
        Self {
            name: "Billy".to_string(),
            age: 15,
        }
    }
}
#[derive(Debug)]
pub struct CharacterBuilder {
    pub name: String,
    pub age: u8,                              This returns a CharacterBuilder, so
}                                             we can give the user full control over
                                              the parameters. A CharacterBuilder
impl CharacterBuilder {                       on its own is useless except to try
    fn new(name: String, age: u8) -> Self {  ← to turn into a Character.
        Self { name, age }
    }

    fn try_build(self) -> Result<Character, &'static str> {   ←
        if !self.name.to_lowercase().contains("smurf") {
            Ok(Character {
                name: self.name,          A proper error type would be nice here,
                age: self.age,             but we'll keep it simple for now and
            })                             return a &'static str for the Err case.
        } else {
            Err("Can't make a character with the word 'smurf' inside it!")
        }
    }                                        This function does nothing yet;
}                                            it only accepts a Character, not
                                                        a CharacterBuilder.
fn do_something_with_character(character: &Character) {}   ←

fn main() {
    let default_character = Character::default();
    do_something_with_character(&default_character);
    let second_character = CharacterBuilder::new("Bobby".to_string(), 27)
        .try_build()
        .unwrap();
    do_something_with_character(&second_character);
    let bad_character = CharacterBuilder::new("Smurfysmurf".to_string(), 40)
        .try_build();
```

```
        println!("{bad_character:?}");
        // do_something_with_character(&bad_character);
    }
```

This bad_character variable is a Result::Err. It failed to turn into a Character, so it can't be used in this function.

In this case, everything works out except `bad_character`. We didn't unwrap it, but it looks like this: `Err("Can't make a character with the word 'smurf' inside it!")`.

By now, we should have a pretty good idea of how to use the builder pattern. What's most interesting about this pattern is not that you can use slick names like `.name()` but that it makes you think about how others will use your types. Starting with `Default` and then adding these small methods makes it really easy to predict how people will use your types because you have complete control over them.

Up next, we will learn the `Deref` trait, which lets you make your own types that you control and also have quick access to the methods in other people's types.

15.3   Deref and DerefMut

Way back in chapter 7, we saw the word `Deref` when learning the newtype pattern. Here is the tuple struct we used to make a new type:

```
struct File(String);

fn main() {
    let my_file = File(String::from("I am file contents"));
    let my_string = String::from("I am file contents");
}
```

We noted that the `File` struct holds a `String`, but it can't use any of `String`'s methods. If you are just writing a bit of code in a single file, then you can, of course, use `.0` to access the `String` inside. But if `File` is inside another mod and isn't written `struct File(pub String);`, you won't be able to use `.0` to access `String`, and you won't be able to use any of `String`'s methods. This is where the `Deref` trait comes in, so let's take a look at how that works.

15.3.1 Deref basics

`Deref` is the trait that lets you use `*` to dereference something, which we learned pretty early on in the book. For example, we know that a reference is not the same as a value:

```
fn main() {
    let value = 7;          ⟵──  This is an i32.
    let reference = &7;              ⟵──  This is a &i32.
    println!("{}", value == reference);
}
```

This code doesn't even return `false` because Rust refuses to even compare the two—they are different types:

```
error[E0277]: can't compare `{integer}` with `&{integer}`
 --> src\main.rs:4:26
```

```
  |
4 |     println!("{}", value == reference);
  |                          ^^ no implementation for `{integer} ==
  ➡&{integer}`
```

As we saw before, the solution here is to use * to dereference. Now, this will print true:

```
fn main() {
    let value = 7;
    let reference = &7;
    println!("{}", value == *reference);
}
```

Now, let's imagine a simple type that only holds a number. It would be nice if we could use it like a Box by using * to dereference, and we have some ideas for some extra functions for it. But there isn't much we can do yet with a struct that only holds a number.

For example, we can't use * as we could with Box:

```
struct HoldsANumber(u8);

fn main() {
    let boxed_number = Box::new(20);
    println!("This works fine: {}", *boxed_number);
    let my_number = HoldsANumber(20);
    println!("This fails though: {}", *my_number + 20);
}
```

The error is

```
error[E0614]: type `HoldsANumber` cannot be dereferenced
  --> src\main.rs:24:22
   |
24 |     println!("{:?}", *my_number + 20);
```

We can, of course, do this: `println!("{:?}", my number.0 + 20);`. But then we are just manually adding the u8 to the 20. Plus, it is likely that we don't want to make the u8 inside it pub when other people use our code. It would be nice if we could add them together somehow.

The message `cannot be dereferenced` gives us a clue: we need to implement Deref. Something simple that implements Deref is sometimes called a "smart pointer." A smart pointer can point to its item, might have information about it (metadata; one example of metadata in a smart pointer is Vec, which holds information on its length), and can use its methods. Right now, we can add my_number.0, which is a u8, but we can't do much else with a HoldsANumber—all it has so far is Debug.

Interestingly, String is a smart pointer to &str, and Vec is a smart pointer to array (or other types). Box, Rc, RefCell, and so on are smart pointers too. So, we have actually been using smart pointers all this time. Let's implement Deref now and make our HoldsANumber struct into a smart pointer, too.

15.3.2 *Implementing Deref*

Implementing `Deref` is not too hard, and the examples in the standard library are easy. Let's take a look at the sample code from the standard library (http://mng.bz/M94B):

```
use std::ops::Deref;

struct DerefExample<T> {
    value: T
}

impl<T> Deref for DerefExample<T> {
    type Target = T;

    fn deref(&self) -> &Self::Target {
        &self.value
    }
}

fn main() {
    let x = DerefExample { value: 'a' };
    assert_eq!('a', *x);
}
```

We can follow this code and change it to fit our `HoldsANumber` type. With `Deref`, it now looks like this:

```
impl Deref for HoldsANumber {
    type Target = u8;

    fn deref(&self) -> &Self::Target {
        &self.0
    }
}
```

Remember, this is the associated type—a type that goes together with a trait. The return value is Self::Target, which we decided will be a u8.

We chose &self.0 because it's a tuple struct. In a named struct, it would be something like &self.number.

Rust calls .deref() when you use * or use the dot operator when using a method. We just defined Target as a u8, so this &Self::Target is easy to understand: it's a reference to a u8. If Self::Target is a u8, then &Self::Target is a &u8.

With these changes, we can now use the `*` operator:

```
use std::ops::Deref;
#[derive(Debug)]
struct HoldsANumber(u8);

impl Deref for HoldsANumber {
    type Target = u8;

    fn deref(&self) -> &Self::Target {
        &self.0
    }
}

fn main() {
    let my_number = HoldsANumber(20);
    println!("{:?}", *my_number + 20);
}
```

That will print 40 without us needing to write my_number.0.

And here's the interesting part: Deref gives us access to the methods of u8, and on top of that, we can write our own methods for HoldsANumber. Let's write our own simple method for HoldsANumber and use another method we get from u8 called .checked_sub(). The .checked_sub() method is a safe subtraction that returns an Option. If it can do the subtraction within the bounds of a number, it returns the value inside Some, and if it can't do it, it returns a None. Remember, a u8 can't be negative, so it's safer to do .checked_sub() so we don't panic:

```rust
use std::ops::Deref;

struct HoldsANumber(u8);

impl HoldsANumber {
    fn prints_the_number_times_two(&self) {
        println!("{}", self.0 * 2);
    }
}

impl Deref for HoldsANumber {
    type Target = u8;

    fn deref(&self) -> &Self::Target {
        &self.0
    }
}

fn main() {
    let my_number = HoldsANumber(20);
    println!("{:?}", my_number.checked_sub(100));    // A method from u8
    my_number.prints_the_number_times_two();         // Our own method
}
```

This prints

```
None
40
```

Deref alone doesn't give mutable access to the inner type, though, so this won't work:

```rust
use std::ops::Deref;

struct HoldsANumber(u8);

impl Deref for HoldsANumber {
    type Target = u8;

    fn deref(&self) -> &Self::Target {
        &self.0
    }
}

fn main() {
    let mut my_number = HoldsANumber(20);
    *my_number = 30;
}
```

Here, we try to dereference and turn the number inside from 20 to 30, but the compiler won't let us:

```
error[E0594]: cannot assign to data in dereference of `HoldsANumber`
  --> src/main.rs:21:5
   |
21 |     *my_number = 30;
   |     ^^^^^^^^^^^^^^^ cannot assign
   |
   = help: trait `DerefMut` is required to modify through a dereference, but
     it is not implemented for `HoldsANumber`
```

But no problem! Implementing DerefMut after we've already implemented Deref is incredibly easy. Let's do that now.

15.3.3 *Implementing DerefMut*

We can also implement DerefMut if we need mutable access, but you need Deref before you can implement DerefMut, as the signature shows:

```
pub trait DerefMut: Deref
```

The signatures for Deref and DerefMut are very similar, so let's compare the two and see which parts are different. First, Deref:

```
pub trait Deref {
    type Target: ?Sized;

    fn deref(&self) -> &Self::Target;
}
```

Then DerefMut:

```
pub trait DerefMut: Deref {
    fn deref_mut(&mut self) -> &mut Self::Target;
}
```

Here are some items to note:

- Deref has an associated type. DerefMut *looks* like it doesn't involve an associated type, but note that it says DerefMut: Deref. That means that you need Deref to implement DerefMut, so anything that implements DerefMut will have the associated type Self::Target. So you don't need to declare the associated type again for DerefMut; it's already there.
- That's why you see &mut Self::Target as the output for the deref_mut() method. If you see an associated type in a signature without an associated type in the trait, check to see whether another required trait made the associated type.
- The function signatures are exactly the same, except they are mutable versions. We have &mut self instead of &self, deref_mut() instead of deref(), and &mut Self::Target instead of &Self::Target.

In other words, to implement `DerefMut` after `Deref`, you copy and paste the `Deref` implementation, delete the first line, and add a bunch of `mut`s everywhere.

Knowing this, we can now implement both `Deref` and `DerefMut` for our `Holds-ANumber`:

```rust
use std::ops::{Deref, DerefMut};

struct HoldsANumber(u8);

impl HoldsANumber {
    fn prints_the_number_times_two(&self) {
        println!("{}", self.0 * 2);
    }
}

impl Deref for HoldsANumber {
    type Target = u8;

    fn deref(&self) -> &Self::Target {
        &self.0
    }
}

impl DerefMut for HoldsANumber {
    fn deref_mut(&mut self) -> &mut Self::Target {
        &mut self.0
    }
}

fn main() {
    let mut my_number = HoldsANumber(20);        // DerefMut lets
    *my_number = 30;                             // ◁── us do this.
    println!("{:?}", my_number.checked_sub(100));
    my_number.prints_the_number_times_two();
}
```

You can see that `Deref` gives your type a lot of power. Just implement `Deref`, and you get all the methods for the type inside!

Probably the most common use for `Deref` in everyday code is when you want type safety. Let's say you have an `Email` type that is an `Email(String)` or a `Quantity` type that is a `Quantity(u32)`. If you implement `Deref`, you get the methods of the type inside. But at the same time, nobody can just use a `String` and a `u32` where your function calls for an `Email` or a `Quantity` because they are not the same type.

After reading this, `Deref` might now be your favorite new trait. It's best to use `Deref` only when it makes sense, though. Let's see why.

15.3.4 *Using Deref the wrong way*

The standard library has a strong recommendation on how `Deref` should be used, which says, `Deref should only be implemented for smart pointers to avoid confusion`. That's because you can do some strange things with `Deref` for a type that doesn't really have any relation with what it dereferences to. (Well, the compiler won't consider it strange, but anyone reading the code will!)

Let's try to imagine the worst possible way to use `Deref` to understand what they mean. We'll start with `Character` struct for a game. A new `Character` needs some stats like intelligence and strength. Here is our first character:

```
struct Character {
    name: String,
    strength: u8,
    dexterity: u8,
    intelligence: u8,
    hit_points: i8,
}

impl Character {
    fn new(
        name: String,
        strength: u8,
        dexterity: u8,
        intelligence: u8,
        hit_points: i8,
    ) -> Self {
        Self {
            name,
            strength,
            dexterity,
            intelligence,
            hit_points,
        }
    }
}

fn main() {
    let billy = Character::new("Billy".to_string(), 9, 12, 7, 10);
}
```

Now, let's imagine that we'd like to modify the character's hit points when they get hit (the hit points will go down) or when they heal (like when they drink a potion; the hit points will go up). And maybe we'd like to keep character hit points in a big `Vec`. Maybe we'll put monster data in there, too, and keep it all together and do some calculations later. Since `hit_points` is an `i8`, we implement `Deref` so we can do all sorts of math on it. And to change the hit points, we'll implement `DerefMut`, too. But look at how strange it looks in our `main()` function now:

```
use std::ops::{Deref, DerefMut};

struct Character {
    name: String,
    strength: u8,
    dexterity: u8,
    intelligence: u8,
    hit_points: i8,
```

```
    }

impl Character {
    fn new(
        name: String,
        strength: u8,
        dexterity: u8,
        intelligence: u8,
        hit_points: i8,
    ) -> Self {
        Self {
            name,
            strength,
            dexterity,
            intelligence,
            hit_points,
        }
    }
}

impl Deref for Character {
    type Target = i8;

    fn deref(&self) -> &Self::Target {
        &self.hit_points
    }
}

impl DerefMut for Character {

    fn deref_mut(&mut self) -> &mut Self::Target {
        &mut self.hit_points
    }
}
fn main() {
    let mut billy = Character::new("Billy".to_string(), 9, 12, 7, 10);
    let mut brandy = Character::new("Brandy".to_string(), 10, 8, 9, 10);

    *billy -= 10;
    *brandy += 1;

    let mut hit_points_vec = vec![];
    hit_points_vec.push(*billy);
    hit_points_vec.push(*brandy);
}
```

> **With impl Deref for Character, we can do any integer math we want on their hit points! And with DerefMut, we can change their hit points, too.**

> **We'll start main() by creating two characters.**

> **Changes their hit points. It's starting to look weird.**

> **Starts our hit points analysis. We push *billy and *brandy into the Vec. Or, rather, we push their hit points in.**

Our code is now very strange for someone to read. Can a reader of the code understand what happens when you `-= 10` on a `Character`? And how could anyone know that using `.push()` on a `Character` struct is pushing an `i8`? You'd have to go to the `Deref` implementation to see what's going on.

We can read `Deref` just above `main()` and figure out that `*billy` means `i8`, but what if there was a lot of code? Maybe our program is 2,000 lines long, and we have to do a lot of searching through the code to find out why we are `.push()`ing `*billy`. `Character` is certainly more than just a smart pointer for `i8`.

Of course, it is not illegal to write `hit_points_vec.push(*billy)`, and the compiler is happy to run this code, but it makes the code look weird. A simple `.get_hp()` or `.change_hp()` method would be much better. `Deref` gives a lot of power, but it's good to make sure that the code is logical.

Hopefully, this chapter has given you a lot of ideas for how to put your types together. Rust's rich type system and traits like `Default` and `Deref` give you a lot of options and a great deal of control. The builder pattern we learned is not a built-in Rust type or trait but is commonly used for all the good reasons we saw in this chapter. In the next chapter, we will learn the final type of Rust generics called *const generics* and begin looking at external crates (code written by others for us to use). We will also look at unsafe Rust, a type of Rust that you may never need to use but that exists for very good reasons. Unsafe Rust also serves as a good reminder of why Rust was created in the first place.

Summary

- Implementing `Default` for your types has some nice benefits. Among other benefits, it makes your code cleaner and lets your type be used wherever there is a `Default` trait bound.

- The builder pattern has a lot of flexibility. You can use it just because you like the syntax, or you can use it to give a lot of control over how your types are used.

- Making a separate type that can only be used as a builder to turn into another type is a great way to make sure that your types don't get misused.

- With `Deref` and `DerefMut`, you can make your own types that have access to the methods of other types they hold.

- Implementing `DerefMut` after `Deref` is easy: simply copy and paste the code, remove the line with the associated type, and add the word `mut` everywhere.

- `Deref` is best used for simple types like smart pointers. Using it for more complex types can make your code difficult to understand.

Const, "unsafe" Rust, and external crates

16

This chapter covers

- Const generics, or generics over const values
- Const functions that you can always call at compile time
- Mutable statics, the unsafe way to change static variables
- Unsafe Rust
- External crates, including `rand`

It's now time to learn about Rust's third generic type (const generics) and all the other things to do with const and static in Rust. Const generics let you be generic over const values, which is most useful when working with arrays. Const functions are similar to regular functions, but they can be called at compile time before your program starts. We will also start to learn about the unsafe side of Rust, starting with `static mut`, a `static` that is unsafe to use. We'll also learn about why unsafe Rust even exists and why you might never even need to touch it. Then we will start moving into external crates, which, thanks to Cargo, are extremely easy to use.

16.1 *Const generics*

Up to now, we have learned two types of generic parameters in Rust:

- *Generic over types*—These are the generics we are most familiar with, as we learned them back in chapter 5. A generic `T: Debug` means any type that implements the `Debug` trait. When Rust users say *generics*, they are usually talking about type generics.
- *Generic over lifetimes*—Lifetimes are actually another sort of generics. For example, when you have a `'static` lifetime in a function, it means any type that has a `'static` lifetime. We began learning about lifetimes in chapter 10.

With const generics, we will now encounter the third and final generic parameter used in Rust. Const generics let items be generic over *const* values. Const generics were implemented fairly recently in Rust, in 2021. A lot of people wanted to see const generics because of difficulties with arrays.

> **NOTE** The three types of generics can be seen in the Rust Reference here: https://doc.rust-lang.org/reference/items/generics.html. They are officially known as `LifetimeParam`, `TypeParam`, and `ConstParam`.

Let's look at what the pain point was when working with arrays before const generics. We learned that one array can only be the same type as another array if it holds both the same type and the same number of items. So, an `[i32; 3]` is not the same type as an `[i32; 4]` even though the second one only has one more item. This strictness in arrays made them quite difficult to work with before const generics were introduced.

To get a feel for this strictness, let's imagine a struct with two arrays. These two arrays contain some `u8`s and are probably byte buffers used to hold some data. Without const generics, you have to say exactly how many items it will have:

```
struct Buffers {
    array_one: [u8; 640],
    array_two: [u8; 640]
}
```

This works, but what if we want a larger buffer, such as 1,280 bytes instead of 640? That would require a new struct. Let's put one in:

```
struct Buffers {
    array_one: [u8; 640],
    array_two: [u8; 640]
}

struct BigBuffers {
    array_one: [u8; 1280],
    array_two: [u8; 1280]
}
```

Any other array size will require a new struct, too. Now, let's think about implementing a trait for our `Buffers` or `BigBuffers` struct. What if we want to implement a trait like `Display`? We would have to implement the trait for each one. What if we want a lot of different array sizes? We'd need a different struct for each, and each struct would need to implement the traits.

> **NOTE** Rust users had to use macros a lot for these types of structs before const generics were implemented. One Reddit user noted back in 2019: "By far the single biggest pain point is const_generics. It can't be implemented and stabilized fast enough. I wrote an elaborate system of macros to solve the issue for our particular system" (http://mng.bz/eE8V).

Let's look at how const generics make this easy. We'll turn the `Buffers` struct into this:

```
struct Buffers<T, const N: usize> {
    array_one: [T; N],
    array_two: [T; N]
}
```

Now, we only need a single struct to do what we were attempting to do before. Our `Buffers` struct is generic in two ways. First, it is generic over a type `T`, and this will be a `u8` or an `i32` or something like that. And the second generic is a const generic, which we are calling `N`, and it's a `usize`. The `const` keyword here shows us that it is a const generic. Only `usize` will work here because Rust uses `usize` to index arrays. So the type here is fixed, but the number is not: it's `N` and can be any number.

Let's give it a try with some really small arrays so we can print them out here:

```
#[derive(Debug)]                              ◁─┐  Now Debug works for any size array,
struct Buffers<T, const N: usize> {              │  just like for any other struct!
    array_one: [T; N],
    array_two: [T; N],
}

fn main() {
    let buffer_1 = Buffers {
        array_one: [0u8; 3],
        array_two: [0; 3],
    };

    let buffer_2 = Buffers {
        array_one: [0i32; 4],
        array_two: [10; 4],
    };

    println!("{buffer_1:#?}, {buffer_2:#?}");
}
```

The code gives us the following output:

```
Buffers {
    array_one: [
        0,
        0,
        0,
    ],
```

```
        array_two: [
            0,
            0,
            0,
        ],
    }, Buffers {
        array_one: [
            0,
            0,
            0,
            0,
        ],
        array_two: [
            10,
            10,
            10,
            10,
        ],
    }
}
```

Const generics are used for more than just arrays, but working with arrays is the main pain point that it solves.

16.2 Const functions

On top of fn, Rust also has a const fn. Rust's documentation defines a const fn as a function that is "permitted to call from a const context" and adds that in this case "the function is interpreted by the compiler at compile time" (http://mng.bz/g78v). Note the word *permitted* in the wording: a const fn doesn't *have* to be called during compile time, but it always *can* be. So a const fn can be called anywhere, not just in const contexts. As the reference states, "you can freely do anything with a const function that you can do with a regular function."

Here's a quick example:

```
const NUMBER: u8 = give_eight();

const fn give_eight() -> u8 {
    8
}

fn main() {
    let mut my_vec = Vec::new();
    my_vec.push(give_eight());
}
```

This give_eight() function is used to make a const, which is used by NUMBER at compile time to get its value. But then down in main(), the same function is being used to push a number to a Vec, which is an allocation (allocations aren't allowed at compile time). The function is being used both at compile time and after compile time.

Now, if we change const fn give_eight() to a regular fn give_eight(), it won't work. Rust complains that our function isn't const, so it can't guarantee that it can be called:

```
error[E0015]: cannot call non-const fn `give_eight` in constants
 --> src/main.rs:1:20
  |
1 | const NUMBER: u8 = give_eight();
  |                    ^^^^^^^^^^^^
  |
  = note: calls in constants are limited to constant functions, tuple structs
    and tuple variants
```

That's why not all functions are const: not all things are allowed in a const context (like allocations).

If you want to give a const fn a try, add const to your function and see what the compiler says. You might be able to find a way to make it work.

This is a bit vague, but that's because what you can do in a const fn in Rust can be a bit vague and is always improving. Const functions were quite limited in the beginning, but the Rust team continues to work on them to allow more and more functionality inside. For example, Rust 1.61 in 2022 added the following:

> *Several incremental features have been stabilized in this release to enable more functionality in const functions:*
>
> – *Basic handling of* fn *pointers*—You can now create, pass, and cast function pointers in a const fn. For example, this could be useful to build compile-time function tables for an interpreter. However, it is still not permitted to call fn pointers.
>
> – *Trait bounds*—You can now write trait bounds on generic parameters to const fn, such as T: Copy, where previously only Sized was allowed.
>
> – dyn Trait *types*—Similarly, const fn can now deal with trait objects, dyn Trait.
>
> – impl Trait *types*—Arguments and return values for const fn can now be opaque impl Trait types.
>
> *Note that the trait features do not yet support calling methods from those traits in a* const fn. *(http://mng.bz/amAm)*

By the time you start learning Rust, there might be more and more things allowed in const fn than when this book was published.

On top of that, each Rust version will usually have a list of functions that are now const. Taking a look at version 1.61 again (http://mng.bz/wjM2), you can see that these functions are const. So they wouldn't have worked in a const context before, but do now:

```
The following previously stable functions are now const:

<*const T>::offset and <*mut T>::offset
<*const T>::wrapping_offset and <*mut T>::wrapping_offset
<*const T>::add and <*mut T>::add
<*const T>::sub and <*mut T>::sub
<*const T>::wrapping_add and <*mut T>::wrapping_add
<*const T>::wrapping_sub and <*mut T>::wrapping_sub
```

Okay, those are some pretty obscure functions. Let's look at some key functions that were made const fairly recently (as of Rust 1.63) because they are pretty useful!

16.3 *Mutable statics*

Mutable global variables are used a lot in other languages, but in Rust, they are a lot harder. You can imagine why: first, Rust has strict rules on borrowing and mutating data. Second, global variables (consts and statics) are initialized in a const context, which means only a const fn can be used. There are external crates that can help work around this, but in Rust 1.63, a nice change happened: `Mutex::new()` and `RwLock::new()` became const functions! With that, you can stick anything inside them that can be made in a const context. That even includes some types we know on the heap because their `new()` functions don't allocate. For example, `String::new()`, `Vec::new()` became const fns in Rust 1.39, so those are just fine.

Let's give this a try with a super-simple global logger that is just a `Vec<Log>`, in which a `Log` is just a struct with two fields. This code wasn't possible in Rust before August 2022, so it's a very nice change to have:

```
use std::sync::Mutex;

#[derive(Debug)]
struct Log {
    date: &'static str,        ◄── Timestamps are usually i64, but we'll just use a &str here.
    message: String,
}

static GLOBAL_LOGGER: Mutex<Vec<Log>> = Mutex::new(Vec::new());    ◄──

fn add_message(date: &'static str) {
    GLOBAL_LOGGER.lock().unwrap().push(Log {    ◄──
        date,
        message: "Everything's fine".to_string(),
    });
}

fn main() {
    add_message("2022-12-12");
    add_message("2023-05-05");
    println!("{GLOBAL_LOGGER:#?}");
}
```

Nothing is inside, so no allocations; thus, it's fine as a static. And it's a Mutex, so we can change what's inside it. Pretty convenient!

GLOBAL_LOGGER is global, so we don't have to pass it in as a function argument.

This prints

```
Mutex {
    data: [
        Log {
            date: "2022-12-12",
            message: "Everything's fine",
        },
        Log {
            date: "2023-05-05",
            message: "Everything's fine",
```

```
        },
    ],
    poisoned: false,
    ..
}
```

As you can see, there is nothing new for us to learn here: we are just using a regular `Mutex` with a regular `Vec`. As long as they are empty to start with, they can be used as a `static` and then modified at run time.

16.4   Unsafe Rust

Statics in Rust have another interesting property that brings us to a new subject of discussion: they can actually be mutable. Making a `static` mutable is as easy as making anything else mutable: just declare a `static mut` instead of a `static`. This is another property of statics that makes them much different from a const. And once you have declared a `static` as mutable, it can be changed by *anything* at *any time* throughout the program.

Hopefully, this is already setting off warning bells inside your head! It seems a little too convenient, doesn't it?

Indeed, mutable statics haven't been mentioned in the book yet because a `static mut` can only be used with the `unsafe` keyword, and Rust has many safer ways to modify static variables compared to the early days of the language. On that note, what is unsafe Rust, and why is the `unsafe` keyword needed when using a `static mut`?

16.4.1   Overview of unsafe Rust

So what's unsafe Rust? Isn't Rust supposed to be safe?

It is, but Rust is also a systems programming language. That means that you can use it to build an operating system, you can use it for robotics, or anything like that. As an example, hardware often requires sending a signal to a certain memory address to start up or accomplish some other task. The Rust compiler has no idea what is at these memory addresses, so you need to use the `unsafe` keyword for that.

> **TIP**   The Writing an OS in Rust blog has many good examples of the `unsafe` keyword used for such cases: https://os.phil-opp.com/testing/.

You can also use Rust to work with other languages like C and Javascript. Here again, the Rust compiler has no idea whether their functions are safe or not, as they are entirely different languages. So you use `unsafe` here, too. For example, in the bindings between Rust and libc (the standard library for the C language), every function (https://docs.rs/libc/latest/libc/#functions) is an unsafe function. A lot of work has been done to make sure that they are as safe as possible, but Rust still can't make any guarantees because it's a different language.

There is a lot of discussion about the word "unsafe" because the keyword itself can be a bit shocking, and the keyword `unsafe` does not necessarily mean that there is anything wrong with a piece of code. After all, anyone can see that this code (100% safe code just wrapped in an unsafe block) is perfectly safe:

```
fn main() {
    let my_name = unsafe { "My name" };
    println!("{my_name}");
}
```

But the unsafe keyword was chosen to be shocking on purpose to ensure that people know that the developer now bears more responsibility because the compiler allows some code inside an unsafe block to compile when it would not compile otherwise. In essence, an unsafe block is more like a trust_me_i_know_what_im_doing block.

Outside of the previously mentioned contexts, unsafe is extremely rare. If you are not working with low-level system resources or directly connecting to functions in other languages, you might never use unsafe. Many Rust programmers have never even had to use a single unsafe block of code.

Having said that, let's take a look at some unsafe for fun. You'll see this word in unsafe blocks and unsafe fns. A function with unsafe code will need to be called an unsafe fn, and to access it, you'll need an unsafe block. So this won't quite work:

```
unsafe fn uh_oh() {}

fn main() {
    uh_oh();
}
```

The compiler says:

```
error[E0133]: call to unsafe function is unsafe and requires unsafe
➥function or block
 --> src/main.rs:6:5
  |
6 |     uh_oh();
  |     ^^^^^^^ call to unsafe function
  |
```

That's easy to fix; just add an unsafe block:

```
unsafe fn uh_oh() {}

fn main() {
    unsafe {
        uh_oh();
    }
}
```

Done!

> **NOTE**   If you find yourself enjoying this section on unsafe Rust, you might also be pleased to know that there is a whole book on unsafe code! It's called *The Rustonomicon* and can be read here: https://doc.rust-lang.org/nomicon/index.html.

16.4.2 Using static mut in unsafe Rust

Now let's look at what a static mut is. As the name suggests, it is simply a static that can be directly changed—no need for a Mutex or any other sort of wrapper to do so. Let's give one a try. This code almost compiles:

```
static mut NUMBER: u32 = 0;

fn main() {
    NUMBER += 1;
    println!("{NUMBER}");
}
```

However, the compiler won't let us modify or even print NUMBER unless we put it in a block marked unsafe. It also tells us why mutable statics are unsafe:

```
error[E0133]: use of mutable static is unsafe and requires unsafe function
or block
 --> src/main.rs:4:5
  |
4 |     NUMBER += 1;
  |     ^^^^^^^^^^^ use of mutable static
  |
  = note: mutable statics can be mutated by multiple threads: aliasing
violations or data races will cause undefined behavior
```

So the reason is "aliasing violations or data races will cause undefined behavior." You'll see the term "undefined behavior" a lot, sometimes abbreviated as UB, when people discuss unsafe Rust. Avoiding undefined behavior is the reason why we use types like Arc<Mutex> to ensure that access happens the way we expect it to. Let's see whether we can make some undefined behavior with this static mut. We will spawn some threads, modify NUMBER, and see what happens.

In this example, we will spawn 10 threads, and each one will have a for loop that loops 10 times, increasing NUMBER by 1 each time. With each of the 10 threads incrementing NUMBER 10 times, we are expecting to see a final result of 100:

```
static mut NUMBER: u32 = 0;

fn main() {
    let mut join_handle_vec = vec![];
    for _ in 0..10 {
        join_handle_vec.push(std::thread::spawn(|| {
            for _ in 0..10 {
                unsafe {
                    NUMBER += 1;
                }
            }
        }));
    }
    for handle in join_handle_vec {
        handle.join().unwrap();
    }
```

```
    unsafe {
        println!("{NUMBER}");
    }
}
```

And the result is 100! No problem yet. Let's bump the numbers up. Now, we will use 1,000 threads, and each thread will loop 1,000 times. The code will be the same as the previous code; we are just changing each `for _ in 0..10` to `for _ in 0..1000`. Because 1,000 times 1,000 is 1,000,000, we now expect to see 1,000,000 as the final number.

But the output is 959,696. Or 853,775. Or 825,266. Or anything else. Now we can see why `static mut` is unsafe. Each thread is adding 1 to NUMBER for each loop, but sometimes a thread is accessing NUMBER at the same time as another one. If you add `println!("{NUMBER}");` just after `NUMBER += 1;`, you will see this sort of output in the middle of all the incrementing:

```
225071        Adds 1.
225072    ⊲──┘ Looks good.       Adds 1.
225073               ⊲──┘ Looks good.
225073    ⊲──┤ Uh oh . . .
```

In this example, NUMBER had the value 225,072, two threads accessed it, each added 1, and gave NUMBER the new value 225,073. The threads each did what they were supposed to do, but nothing was keeping them from accessing NUMBER at the same time.

And with this, we can now understand another big difference between `const` and `static`: a `const` is an unchangeable value that is evaluated at compile time, while a `static` is a static location in memory. There is technically no rule that a `static` cannot be `mut`.

16.4.3 *Rust's most famous unsafe method*

Now, let's look at Rust's most famous unsafe function, `transmute()`. The documentation for the function explains it as follows: "Reinterprets the bits of a value of one type as another type. Both types must have the same size" (https://doc.rust-lang.org/std/mem/fn.transmute.html).

So with `transmute()`, you essentially take the bits of one type and tell the compiler: "take these bits and use them as a different type." Here's the function signature:

```
fn transmute<T, U>(e: T) -> U
```

So you tell it which two types (`T`, `U`) it will work on and give it a `T`, and it returns it as a `U`.

Let's try something simple. We'll make an `i32` and tell Rust that it's now a `u32`. Both `i32` and `u32` have a length of 4 bytes, so the code will compile:

```
use std::mem::transmute;

fn main() {
    let x = 19;
    let y = unsafe { transmute::<i32, u32>(x) };
    println!("{y}");
}
```

That prints 19, simple enough. What if we make x a -19 instead? A u32 can't be nega-tive, so it can't possibly end up as the same -19 value. Let's try that again and see what happens:

```
use std::mem::transmute;

fn main() {
    let x = -19;
    let y: u32 = unsafe { transmute::<i32, u32>(x) };
    println!("{y}");
}
```

Now it prints 4294967277. Quite different! Remember how to format println! to dis-play bytes that we learned near the beginning of the book? You use {:b} to do it. If transmute() is just reinterpreting the same bytes, then -19 and 4294967277u32 should look the same as bytes. Let's give it a try:

```
fn main() {
    println!("{:b}\n{:b}", -19, 4294967277u32);
}
```

Indeed they do! We get the following output, which shows, indeed, that transmute() is taking the same bytes and treating them differently:

```
11111111111111111111111111101101
11111111111111111111111111101101
```

Okay, let's see whether we can be even more unsafe by transmuting something more complex. Let's make a User struct with a bit of basic info and see what its size is:

```
struct User {
    name: String,
    number: u32,
}

fn main() {
    println!("{}", std::mem::size_of::<User>());
}
```

It's 32 bytes. So what happens if we give Rust an array of eight i32s and tell it to make a User? Both of these are 32 bytes in length, so the program will compile, and transmute() will simply tell Rust to treat these bytes as a User. Let's see what happens:

```
use std::mem::transmute;

struct User {
    name: String,
    number: u32,
}

fn main() {
    let some_i32s = [1, 2, 3, 4, 5, 6, 7, 8];
    let user = unsafe { transmute::<[i32; 8], User>(some_i32s) };
}
```

Whoops! We got a segmentation fault:

```
timeout: the monitored command dumped core
/playground/tools/entrypoint.sh: line 11:        8 Segmentation fault
➥timeout --signal=KILL ${timeout} "$@"
```

The `transmute()` documentation (https://doc.rust-lang.org/std/mem/fn.transmute .html) puts it this way:

> *Both the argument and the result must be valid at their given type. The compiler will generate code assuming that you, the programmer, ensure that there will never be undefined behavior. It is therefore your responsibility to guarantee that every value passed to* `transmute` *is valid at both types* `Src` *and* `Dst`*. Failing to uphold this condition may lead to unexpected and unstable compilation results. This makes* `transmute` *incredibly unsafe.* `transmute` *should be the absolute last resort.*

Any programmer choosing to use `transmute()` has been warned in advance!

16.4.4   *Methods ending in _unchecked*

The most common and "safest" form of `unsafe` is probably seen in the `_unchecked` methods that a lot of types have. For example, `Option` and `Result` have unsafe `.unwrap_unchecked()` methods that assume you have a `Some` or an `Ok` and will unwrap without checking. But if you don't have a `Some` or an `Ok`, then undefined behavior will happen. People will sometimes try these methods to see whether there is any performance improvement in their code. In that case, you will usually see a note like this to explain why `unsafe` is being used:

```
fn main() {
    let my_option = Some(10);
    // SAFETY: my_option is declared as Some(10). It will never be None
    let unwrapped = unsafe {
        my_option.unwrap_unchecked()
    };
    println!("{unwrapped}");
}
```

This will print `10`, and no problems will happen. But once again, using an unsafe function means that all the responsibility is on you. In the previous example, if you change the first line to `let my_option: Option<i32> = None;` and run it on the Playground, it will dump the core:

```
   Running `target/debug/playground`
timeout: the monitored command dumped core
/playground/tools/entrypoint.sh: line 11:        8 Illegal instruction
➥timeout --signal=KILL ${timeout} "$@"
```

That's pretty bad.

And there is no guarantee that the `_unchecked` methods will be faster either. Sometimes, the compiler can use information from the checks in the non-unsafe methods to speed up your code, resulting in _unchecked being slower than the regular safe methods. It can be fun to experiment, but when in doubt, don't use unsafe!

To sum up:

- You can spend your whole life as a Rust programmer without using unsafe. You don't need it to build software.
- However, if you are a low-level systems programmer or need to directly link to other languages (like C libraries, for example), this is the way you can get the flexibility you need.

In the early days of Rust, users of the language emphasized how easy it was to link it to C and C++ libraries. (Here is one example from 2015: http://mng.bz/qjnJ). But as time has gone by, more and more libraries have been written in pure Rust, and it has become quite rare to see unsafe in a Rust external crate. And a lot of other interesting developments are going on to help use unsafe even less frequently. There is even a working group to make the transmute() function safe (http://mng.bz/7vwe)!

On that note, it's time to turn our attention to external crates.

16.5 Introducing external crates

An external crate simply means a crate that isn't the one that you are working on and is usually someone else's crate. We learned in chapter 14 about modules and structuring your code for others to use, which is the first step to creating an external crate. When people write crates they think might be useful for others, they publish them on https://crates.io/, and those become usable by anyone else. As of early 2024, over 130,000 crates have been published!

For this section, you *almost* need to install Rust, but we can still use just the Playground. That's because the Playground has all the most-used external crates already installed. Using external crates is important in Rust for two reasons: it is incredibly easy to import other crates, and the Rust standard library is quite small.

That means that it is normal in Rust to bring in an external crate for a lot of basic functions, and that's why the Playground includes so many. The idea is that if it is easy to use external crates, you can choose the best one. Often, one person will make a crate that provides some functionality, and then someone else will make a similar and possibly better one.

In this book, we will only look at the most popular crates, the crates that everyone who uses Rust knows. To begin learning external crates, we will start with a pretty simple one: rand.

16.5.1 Crates and Cargo.toml

Have you noticed that we haven't used any random number functions yet in this book? That's because random numbers aren't in the standard library. But there are a lot of crates that are "almost standard library" because everybody uses and trusts them. These crates are also nicknamed Rust's "blessed crates," and there is even a website (https://blessed.rs/crates) that lists them (called blessed.rs!). The crate rand is one of these "blessed crates."

In any case, it's very easy to bring in a crate. If you have a Cargo (Rust) project on your computer, you should notice a file called Cargo.toml that has this information. The Cargo.toml file looks like this when you start:

```
[package]
name = "rust_book"
version = "0.1.0"
authors = ["David MacLeod"]
edition = "2021"

# See more keys and their definitions at https://doc.rust-
➥ lang.org/cargo/reference/manifest.html

[dependencies]
```

Now, if you want to add the rand crate, go to https://crates.io. Search for rand and click on it. Now you are at https://crates.io/crates/rand. Click in the box under Or Add the Following Line to Your Cargo.toml, which is located on the right-hand side of the page, to copy it. Then just add it under [dependencies] like this:

```
[package]
name = "rust_book"
version = "0.1.0"
authors = ["David MacLeod"]
edition = "2021"

# See more keys and their definitions at https://doc.rust-lang.org/cargo/
        reference/manifest.html

[dependencies]
rand = "0.8.5"
```

Cargo will do the rest for you. Or you can use the command cargo add rand on the command line, and it will do the same thing. Then, when you type cargo run to run your program, it will automatically bring in the code to use rand, and you will be able to use this crate in the same way that we've been using code from the standard library. The only difference is that the first part of the path will be rand instead of std.

To get to the documents for rand, you can click on the docs button on its page on crates.io, which will take you to the documentation (https://docs.rs/rand/latest/rand/). Fortunately the documentation looks the same as that in the standard library! Thanks to a standardized layout for documentation, you won't have any trouble looking around the rand crate to see what it holds. Now let's give rand a try.

16.5.2 *Using the rand crate*

We are still using the Playground by default, which fortunately already has the top 100 crates installed. On the Playground, you can imagine that it has a long list like this with 100 crates:

```
[dependencies]
rand = "0.8.5"
some_other_crate = "0.1.0"
another_nice_crate = "1.7"
```

And so on. So that means we don't need to look at Cargo.toml again until a bit later in the book. So, to use rand, you can just do this:

```
use rand::random;       ◁─┐   This means the whole crate rand. On your
                          │   computer, you can't simply write this; you
fn main() {               │   need to write in the Cargo.toml file first.
    for _ in 0..5 {
        let random_u16 = random::<u16>();
        print!("{random_u16} ");
    }
}
```

This code will print a different u16 number every time, like 42266 52873 56528 46927 6867.

The main functions in rand are random() and thread_rng() (rng means "random number generator"). If you look at random(), it says: "This is simply a shortcut for thread_rng().gen()." So, it's actually thread_rng() that does almost everything.

Here is a simple example of numbers from 1 to 10. To get those numbers, we use .gen_range() between 1 and 11.

```
use rand::{thread_rng, Rng};

fn main() {                                            ┌ Or we can just use
    let mut number_maker = thread_rng();    ◁─┘  rand::*; if we are lazy.
    for _ in 0..5 {
        print!("{} ", number_maker.gen_range(1..11));
    }
}
```

This will print something like 7 2 4 8 6.

16.5.3 *Rolling some dice with rand*

With random numbers, we can do fun things like make characters for a game. In this game, our characters have six stats, and you use a d6 for them. A d6 is a die (a cube) that gives 1, 2, 3, 4, 5, or 6 when you throw it. Each character rolls a d6 three times, so each stat is between 3 and 18.

But sometimes it can be unfair if your character has a really low stat, like a 3 or 4. If your strength is 3, you can't carry anything, for example. And a character that rolls 3 for intelligence won't even be smart enough to know how to speak. Because of this, there is one more dice rolling method that rolls a d6 four times and throws away the lowest number. So, if you roll 3, 3, 1, and 6, you throw out the 1 and keep 3, 3, and 6, giving a value of 12 (instead of 7). This method keeps characters from having stats that are too low while still keeping 18 as the maximum.

We will make a simple character creator that lets you choose between rolling three times and rolling four times. We create a `Character` struct for the stats and have a function to roll the dice that takes an enum to choose between rolling three or four times:

```rust
use rand::{thread_rng, Rng};

#[derive(Debug)]
struct Character {
    strength: u8,
    dexterity: u8,
    constitution: u8,
    intelligence: u8,
    wisdom: u8,
    charisma: u8,
}

#[derive(Copy, Clone)]
enum Dice {
    Three,
    Four,
}
```

Dice doesn't hold any data so we might as well make it both Copy and Clone.

```rust
fn roll_dice(dice_choice: Dice) -> u8 {
    let mut generator = thread_rng();
    let mut total = 0;
    match dice_choice {
        Dice::Three => {
            for _ in 0..3 {
                total += generator.gen_range(1..=6);
            }
        }
        Dice::Four => {
            let mut results = vec![];
            (0..4).for_each(|_| results.push(generator.gen_range(1..=6)));
            results.sort();
            results.remove(0);
            total += results.into_iter().sum::<u8>();
        }
    }
    total
}
```

We can't just add the numbers to the total when rolling four dice, so we will first put them all in a Vec. Then we'll use .sort() and remove the 0th item (the smallest).

```rust
impl Character {
    fn new(dice_choice: Dice) -> Self {
        let mut stats = (0..6).map(|_| roll_dice(dice_choice));
        Self {
            strength: stats.next().unwrap(),
            dexterity: stats.next().unwrap(),
            constitution: stats.next().unwrap(),
            intelligence: stats.next().unwrap(),
            wisdom: stats.next().unwrap(),
            charisma: stats.next().unwrap(),
        }
```

We're confident that our stats iterator is six items in length so we'll just unwrap for each.

```
        }
    }

fn main() {
    let weak_billy = Character::new(Dice::Three);
    let strong_billy = Character::new(Dice::Four);
    println!("{weak_billy:#?}");
    println!("{strong_billy:#?}");
}
```

It will print something like this:

```
Character {
    strength: 11,
    dexterity: 9,
    constitution: 9,
    intelligence: 8,
    wisdom: 7,
    charisma: 13,
}
Character {
    strength: 15,
    dexterity: 13,
    constitution: 5,
    intelligence: 13,
    wisdom: 14,
    charisma: 15,
}
```

As you can see, the character with four dice rolls is usually a bit better at most things.

That was easy! We've learned that with a single line in `Cargo.toml` you can use external crates in the same way that we've been using the standard library. We also learned about const generics, which you won't see as much as regular generics and lifetimes but is good to understand. And we now have an idea of why Rust as a language needs `unsafe` in certain situations and why you almost never need to use it unless you are working with rare cases like embedded software or calling into other languages.

We have only scraped the surface of the fantastic external crates that Rust has to offer, so in the next chapter, we will look at some more of the "blessed" ones. Even though they are technically external crates, you can almost think of them as extensions of the standard library. You will definitely want to be familiar with their names and what they do.

Summary

- Const generics let you be generic over const values. These generics are most useful in arrays due to the unique type signature arrays have: both a type and a length.
- More and more methods in the standard library are becoming const fn, which lets you, as a Rust user, more easily make your own functions into const fns if you want.

- Unsafe Rust has good reasons to exist, especially because the Rust compiler isn't able to understand other languages and determine whether they are safe or not.

- The word `unsafe` is meant to be a bit shocking so that people will not use it too much. In reality, it is sort of a `trust_me_I_know_what_Im_doing` block (if you know what you're doing).

- To do anything with an unsafe function in Rust, you will need to put it inside an `unsafe` block. The same goes for anything else that is `unsafe` like a `static mut`, even if you just want to print it.

- To add an external crate if Rust is installed, go to `Cargo.toml` and type the crate name and the version number. If you are using the Playground, you won't even need to do that if the crate is popular enough.

Rust's most popular crates

This chapter is sort of a cookbook of some of the most popular external crates. These crates are so common that you can almost think of them as extensions of the standard library—they're not just random crates sitting around that nobody uses. Learning just these few crates will allow you to turn data like JSON into Rust structs, work with time and time zones, handle errors with less code, speed up your code, and work with global statics.

You'll also learn about blanket trait implementations, which are extremely fun. With those, you can give your trait methods to other people's types even if they didn't ask for them!

17.1   *serde*

The `serde` crate is an extremely popular crate that lets you convert to and from formats like JSON, YAML, and so on. In fact, it's so popular that it's rare to find a Rust programmer who has never heard of it.

JSON is one of the most common ways to send requests and receive information online, and it's is pretty simple, being made up of keys and values. Here is what it looks like:

```
{
    "name":"BillyTheUser",
    "id":6876
}
```

Here's a longer example:

```
[
    {
        "name":"BobbyTheUser",
        "id":6877
    },
    {
        "name":"BillyTheUser",
        "id":6876
    }
]
```

So how do you turn something like `"name"`: `"BillyTheUser"` into a Rust type of your own? JSON only has seven(!) data types, while Rust has a nearly unlimited number. In your own data type in Rust, you might want `"BillyTheUser"` to be a `String`, a `&str`, a `Cow`, your own type such as a `UserName(String)`, or almost anything else. Doing this conversion between Rust and other formats like JSON is what serde is for.

The most common way to use it is by creating a struct with serde's `Serialize` and/or `Deserialize` attributes on top. To work with the data from the previous example, we could make a struct like this with serde's attributes to let us convert between Rust and JSON:

```
use serde::{Serialize, Deserialize};

#[derive(Serialize, Deserialize, Debug)]
struct User {
    name: String,
    id: u32,
}
```

`Serialize` is used to turn your Rust type into another format like JSON, while `Deserialize` is the other way around: it's the trait to turn another format into a Rust type. That's also where the name comes from: "Ser" from *serialize* and "De" from *deserialize* make the name *serde*. If you are curious about how serde does this, take a look at the page on the Serde data model at https://serde.rs/data-model.html.

If you are using JSON, you will also need to use the `serde_json` crate; for YAML, you will need `serde_yaml`, and so on. Each of these crates works on top of the serde data model for its own separate data format.

Here's a really simple example where we imagine that we have a server that takes requests to make new users. The request needs a user name and a user ID, so we make a struct called `NewUserRequest` that has these fields. As long as these fields are in the request, it will deserialize correctly, and our `NewUserRequest` will work. To do this, we use `serde_json`'s `from_str()` method:

```
use serde::{Deserialize, Serialize};
use serde_json;

#[derive(Debug, Serialize, Deserialize)]
struct User {
    name: String,
    id: u32,
    is_deleted: bool,
}

#[derive(Debug, Serialize, Deserialize)]
struct NewUserRequest {
    name: String,
    id: u32,
}

impl From<NewUserRequest> for User {
    fn from(request: NewUserRequest) -> Self {
        Self {
            name: request.name,
            id: request.id,
            is_deleted: false,
        }
    }
}

fn handle_request(json_request: &str) {
    match serde_json::from_str::<NewUserRequest>(json_request) {
        Ok(good_request) => {
            let new_user = User::from(good_request);
            println!("Made a new user! {new_user:#?}");
            println!(
                "Serialized back into JSON: {:#?}",
                serde_json::to_string(&new_user)
            );
        }
        Err(e) => {
            println!("Got an error from {json_request}: {e}");
        }
    }
}
```

```
fn main() {
    let good_json_request = r#"
    {
        "name": "BillyTheUser",
        "id": 6876
    }
    "#;

    let bad_json_request = r#"
    {
        "name": "BobbyTheUser",
        "idd": "6877"
    }
    "#;

    handle_request(good_json_request);
    handle_request(bad_json_request);
}
```

Here's the output:

```
Made a new user! User {
    name: "BillyTheUser",
    id: 6876,
    is_deleted: false,
}
Serialized back into JSON: Ok(
    "{\"name\":\"BillyTheUser\",\"id\":6876,\"is_deleted\":false}",
)
Got an error from
    {
        "name": "BobbyTheUser",
        "idd": "6877"
    }
    : missing field `id` at line 5 column 5
```

And because `User` implements `Serialize`, it could then be turned back into JSON if we needed to send it somewhere else in that format.

Serde has a lot of customizations depending on how you want to serialize or deserialize a type. For example, if you have an enum that you need to be in all capitals when serialized, you can stick this on top: `#[serde(rename_all = "SCREAMING_SNAKE_CASE")]`, and serde will do the rest. The serde documentation has information on these attributes (https://serde.rs/container-attrs.html).

17.2   *Time in the standard library*

The next crate we are going to look at is called chrono (https://crates.io/crates/chrono), which is the main crate for those who need functionality for time, such as formatting dates, setting time zones, and so on. But you might be wondering: Why not just use the `time` module in the standard library? The answer is simple: `std::time` is minimal, and there isn't much you can do with `std::time` alone. It does have some useful types, though, so we will start with this module before we move on to chrono.

The simplest way to start with the `time` module is by getting a snapshot of the present moment with `Instant::now()`. This returns an `Instant` that we can print out:

```
use std::time::Instant;

fn main() {
    let time = Instant::now();
    println!("{:?}", time);
}
```

However, the output of an `Instant` is maybe a bit surprising. On the Playground, it will look something like this:

```
Instant { tv_sec: 949256, tv_nsec: 824417508 }
```

If we do a quick calculation, 949,256 seconds is just under 11 days. There is a reason for this: an `Instant` shows the time since the system booted up, not the time since a set date. Obviously, this won't be able to help us know today's date, or the month or the year. The page on `Instant` tells us that it isn't supposed to be useful on its own, describing it as

```
Opaque and useful only with Duration.
```

The page explains that `Instant` is "often useful for tasks such as measuring benchmarks or timing how long an operation takes." And a `Duration`, as you might guess, is a struct that is used to show how much time has passed.

We can see how `Instant` and `Duration` work together if we look at the traits implemented for `Instant`. For example, one of them is `Sub<Instant>`, which lets us use the minus symbol to subtract one `Instant` from another. Let's click on the `[src]` button to see the source code. It's not too complicated:

```
impl Sub<Instant> for Instant {
    type Output = Duration;

    fn sub(self, other: Instant) -> Duration {
        self.duration_since(other)
    }
}
```

It looks like `Instant` has a method called `.duration_since()` that produces a `Duration`. Let's try subtracting one `Instant` from another to see what we get. We'll make two of them by using the `Instant::now()` function twice, and then we'll make the program busy for a while. Then we'll make one more `Instant::now()`. Finally, we'll see how long it took:

```
use std::time::Instant;

fn main() {
    let start_of_main = Instant::now();
    let before_operation = Instant::now();   ◄─┐ Nothing happened between these
                                               │ two variables, so the Duration
                                               │ should be extremely small.
```

```
        let mut new_string = String::new();
        loop {
            new_string.push('ჶ');
            if new_string.len() > 100_000 {
                break;
            }
        }
        let after_operation = Instant::now();
        println!("{:?}", before_operation - start_of_main);
        println!("{:?}", after_operation - start_of_main);
    }
```

Now we'll give the program some busy work. It has to push this Georgian letter onto new_string until it is 100000 bytes in length.

Then we'll make a new Instant after the busy work is done and see how long everything took.

This code will print something like this:

```
1.025µs
683.378µs
```

So that's just over 1 microsecond versus 683 microseconds. Subtracting one `Instant` from another `Instant` shows us that the program did indeed take some time to work on the task that we gave it.

There is also a method called `.elapsed()` that lets us do the same thing without creating a new `Instant` every time. The following code gives the same output as the previous example, except that it just calls `.elapsed()` to see how much time has gone by since the first `Instant`:

```
use std::time::Instant;

fn main() {
    let start = Instant::now();
    println!("Time elapsed before busy operation: {:?}", start.elapsed());

    let mut new_string = String::new();
    loop {
        new_string.push('ჶ');
        if new_string.len() > 100_000 {
            break;
        }
    }
    println!("Operation complete. Time elapsed: {:?}", start.elapsed());
}
```

The output is the same as before.

By the way, the `Opaque and useful only with Duration` comment feels like a challenge. Surely we can find some use for this. Let's have some fun by implementing a really bad random number generator. We saw that an `Instant` when printed using `Debug` has a lot of numbers that are different each time. We can use `.chars()` to turn this into an iterator and `.rev()` to reverse it and then filter out chars that aren't digits. Instead of `.parse()`, we can use a convenient `.to_digit()` method that `char` has that returns an `Option`. The code looks like this:

```
use std::time::Instant;
```

```
fn bad_random_number(digits: usize) {
    if digits > 9 {
        panic!("Random number can only be up to 9 digits");
    }
    let now_as_string = format!("{:?}", Instant::now());

    now_as_string
        .chars()
        .rev()
        .filter_map(|c| c.to_digit(10))
        .take(digits)
        .for_each(|character| print!("{}", character));
    println!();
}

fn main() {
    bad_random_number(1);
    bad_random_number(1);
    bad_random_number(3);
    bad_random_number(3);
}
```

> **The .to_digit() method here is taking a 10 because we want a decimal number (0–9). We could have used .to_digit(2) for binary, .to_digit(16) for hexadecimal, and so on.**

The code will print something like the following:

```
6
4
967
180
```

The function is called `bad_random_number()` for a good reason. For example, if we choose to print nine digits, the final numbers won't be very random anymore:

```
855482162
155882162
688592162
```

That's because after a few digits we have printed out all the nanoseconds and are now printing out the seconds, which will not change much during this short code sample. So definitely stick with crates like `rand` and `fastrand`.

The `time` module has two more items to note: a struct called `SystemTime` and a const called `UNIX_EPOCH`, the Unix epoch representing midnight on the 1st of January, 1970. The `SystemTime` struct can be used to get the current date or at least the number of seconds that have passed since 1970. The page on `SystemTime` (https://doc.rust-lang.org/std/time/struct.SystemTime.html) has a nice clear explanation of what makes it different from `Instant`, so let's just read what is written there:

> *A measurement of the system clock, useful for talking to external entities like the file system or other processes.*
>
> *Distinct from the* `Instant` *type, this time measurement is not monotonic. This means that you can save a file to the file system, then save another file to the file system, and the second file has a* `SystemTime` *measurement earlier than the first. In*

other words, an operation that happens after another operation in real time may have an earlier `SystemTime`!

Knowing this, let's do a quick comparison of the two by printing each one out:

```
use std::time::{Instant, SystemTime};

fn main() {
    let instant = Instant::now();
    let system_time = SystemTime::now();
    println!("{instant:?}");
    println!("{system_time:?}");
}
```

The output will look something like this:

```
Instant { tv_sec: 956710, tv_nsec: 22275264 }
SystemTime { tv_sec: 1676778839, tv_nsec: 183795450 }
```

And if we do the math, 95,6710 seconds (from `Instant`) turns out to be about 11 days. But 1,676,778,839 seconds (from `SystemTime`) turns out to be a bit over 53 years, which is exactly how much time has passed since 1970 when this code was run.

For a more readable output, we can use `.duration_since()` and put `UNIX_EPOCH` inside:

```
use std::time::{SystemTime, UNIX_EPOCH};

fn main() {
    println!("{:?}", SystemTime::now().duration_since(UNIX_EPOCH).unwrap());
}
```

This will print something like `1676779741.912581202s`. And that's pretty much all the standard library has for printing out dates. It doesn't have anything to turn 1,676,779,741 seconds into a human-readable date, apply a time zone, or anything like that.

We have one last item in `std::time` before moving on to chrono: putting threads to sleep by passing in a `Duration`. Inside a thread, you can use `std::thread::sleep()` to make the thread stop for a while. If you aren't using multiple threads, this function will make the entire program sleep, as there are no other threads to do anything while the main thread is asleep. To use this function, you have to give it a `Duration`. Creating a `Duration` is fairly simple: pick the method that matches the unit of time you want to use and give it a number. `Duration::from_millis()` is used to stop for a number of milliseconds, `Duration::from_secs()` for seconds, and so on. Here's one example:

```
use std::time::Duration;
use std::thread::sleep;

fn main() {
    let three_seconds = Duration::from_secs(3);
    println!("I must sleep now.");
```

```
    sleep(three_seconds);
    println!("Did I miss anything?");
}
```

The output is just the first line followed by the second line 3 seconds later:

```
I must sleep now.
Did I miss anything?
```

Enough waiting, let's move on to chrono!

17.3 chrono

Time is a pretty complex subject, thanks to a combination of astronomy and history. Astronomically, time basically has to do with measuring the rotation of the Earth around the Sun, the spinning of the Earth around itself, and cutting the Earth into time zones so that everyone can have a similar idea when they see the time on the clock (figure 17.1). With this, 12 pm means noon when the Sun is high (well, usually), 6 am is early morning, 12 am is midnight when the day changes, and so on, no matter where you are on the planet.

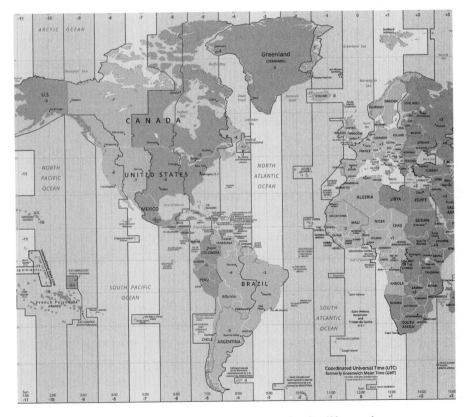

Figure 17.1 Code dealing with time is complex because time itself is complex.

Historically, time is just as complex. We have a lot of different calendars. One year has 365 days, one day has 24 hours (thanks to the Egyptians), and months have different lengths (thanks to the Roman emperors), and we count using 60 instead of 100 (thanks to the Sumerians). Plus, we have leap years and even leap seconds! It's probably not surprising that the types inside the chrono crate can be complex, too.

But there are some fairly simple types inside chrono, which start with Naive: NaiveDate, NaiveDateTime, and so on. Naive here means that they don't have any time zone info. The easiest way to create them is with the methods that start with from_ and end with _opt. A quick example will be the easiest way to demonstrate this:

```
use chrono::naive::{NaiveDate, NaiveTime};

fn main() {
    println!("{:?}", NaiveDate::from_ymd_opt(2023, 3, 25));
    println!("{:?}", NaiveTime::from_hms_opt(12, 5, 30));
    println!("{:?}", NaiveDate::from_ymd_opt(2023, 3,
      25).unwrap().and_hms_opt(12, 5, 30));
}
```

The output is

```
Some(2023-03-25)
Some(12:05:30)
Some(2023-03-25T12:05:30)
```

Here, ymd stands for "year month day," and hms stands for "hour minutes seconds." The first println! shows an Option<NaiveDate>; the second, an Option<NaiveTime>; and the third, an Option<NaiveDateTime>. The .and_hms_opt() method turns a NaiveDate into a NaiveDateTime by giving it the hour, minutes, and seconds needed to know the time of day.

You might be wondering: Why do all these methods have an _opt at the end? This brings us to an interesting discussion. Let's change the subject just a little bit.

17.3.1 Checking the code inside external crates

The simple answer to the previous question is that the _opt at the end of these methods is because they return an Option. But then again, none of the other methods we have seen in this book that return an Option have an _opt at the end. Why are these method names so long?

It's an interesting story. If you take a look at the history of the chrono crate, you can see a change made as recently as November 2022 to deprecate the methods without _opt, because inside there was a chance that they could panic. For example, the from_ymd() method simply calls from_ymd_opt() with .expect(), and "panics on out-of-range date, invalid month and/or day":

```
/// Makes a new `NaiveDate` from the [calendar date](#calendar-date)
/// (year, month and day).
///
/// Panics on the out-of-range date, invalid month and/or day.
```

```
#[deprecated(since = "0.4.23", note = "use `from_ymd_opt()` instead")]
pub fn from_ymd(year: i32, month: u32, day: u32) -> NaiveDate {
    NaiveDate::from_ymd_opt(year, month, day).expect("invalid or out-
➥of-range date")
}
```

Perhaps too many people were using methods like .from_ymd() without reading the note on possible panics, and the crate authors decided to make it clear that the method could fail.

In fact, the chrono crate is planning to change these methods again (https://github.com/chronotope/chrono/issues/970) to return a Result instead of an Option with a different name that begins with try_, such as try_from_ymd(). So, by the time you read this book, the chrono crate might have changed the methods a little bit.

In any case, the small lesson here is that you should click on the source for methods you use in other crates and do a quick check for possible panics. Sometimes crate authors decide that a small chance of panic is worth it in exchange for extra convenience or if it makes sense to panic. For example, every thread made by the thread::spawn() method in the standard library is given a certain amount of memory to use, and the program will panic if the operating system is unable to create a thread, which usually comes from running out of memory. (The documentation for spawn() mentions this possibility, by the way.)

We can give this a try ourselves! Let's spawn 100,000 threads and see whether the Playground runs out of memory:

```
fn main() {
    for _ in 0..100000 {
        std::thread::spawn(|| {});
    }
}
```

Here is the output:

```
thread 'main' panicked at 'failed to spawn thread: Os { code: 11, kind:
➥WouldBlock, message: "Resource temporarily unavailable" }',
```

In any case, it was probably a good idea for the authors of chrono to make it clearer to users that these methods may fail. Now, let's return to the crate again.

17.3.2 *Back to chrono*

We will finish up our quick look at the chrono crate with an example that shows the following:

- Using SystemTime and the UNIX_EPOCH const to get the number of seconds since 1970
- Using a NaiveDateTime that uses these seconds to display the date and time without a time zone
- Creating a DateTime<Utc> from a NaiveDateTime

- Creating a `FixedOffset` to create a time zone that differs from `Utc`
- Turning the `DateTime<FixedOffset>` back into a `NaiveDateTime`

This is generally the sort of tinkering you will do when working with chrono. Here is the code:

We learned to use SystemTime and .duration_since() with the UNIX_EPOCH just above, and this will give us a Duration to work with.

To construct a NaiveDateTime, we need to give it seconds and nanoseconds. We could also use as_nanos() to get the nanoseconds in the Duration, but we don't care about being that exact.

```
use std::time::SystemTime;
use chrono::{DateTime, FixedOffset, NaiveDateTime, Utc};

fn main() {
    let now = SystemTime::now().duration_since(SystemTime::
    ➥UNIX_EPOCH).unwrap();
    let seconds = now.as_secs();
    println!("Seconds from 1970 to today: {seconds}");

    let naive_dt = NaiveDateTime::from_timestamp_opt
    ➥(seconds as i64, 0).unwrap();
    println!("As NaiveDateTime: {naive_dt}");
```

The .as_secs() method gave us a u64. NaiveDateTime::from_timestamp_opt() takes an i64, and we're pretty sure that we are living after 1970 when the Unix epoch began, so the number won't be negative.

You can make a time zone-aware DateTime from NaiveDateTime if you give it a time zone. The Utc time zone is its own type in chrono, so we can just stick it in.

For other time zones, we have to make an offset. Kyiv is three hours east of Utc, which is 3 hours * 60 minutes per hour * 60 seconds per minute.

```
    let utc_dt = DateTime::<Utc>::from_utc(naive_dt, Utc);
    println!("As DateTime<Utc>: {utc_dt}");

    let kyiv_offset = FixedOffset::east_opt(3 * 60 * 60)
    ➥.unwrap();
    let kyiv_dt: DateTime::<FixedOffset> = DateTime::from_utc(naive_dt,
    ➥kyiv_offset);
    println!("In a timezone 3 hours from UTC: {kyiv_dt}");

    let kyiv_naive_dt = kyiv_dt.naive_local();
    println!("With timezone information removed: {kyiv_naive_dt}");
}
```

Then we can construct a DateTime in basically the same way as the Utc DateTime above.

And we can turn it back into a NaiveDateTime, removing the time zone information.

The output will look something like this:

```
Seconds from 1970 to today: 1683253399
As NaiveDateTime: 2023-05-05 02:23:19
As DateTime<Utc>: 2023-05-05 02:23:19 UTC
In a timezone 3 hours from UTC: 2023-05-05 05:23:19 +03:00
With timezone information removed: 2023-05-05 05:23:19
```

That should give us some idea of how to work with time using chrono. It requires reading the documentation thoroughly and finding the right way to convert from one type into another.

For our final example, let's think of something a bit closer to what we might build ourselves. The following code imagines that we are working with a service that receives events with a UTC timestamp and some data. We then need to turn these timestamps into the Korea/Japan time zone (9 hours ahead of UTC) and make them into a KoreaJapanUserEvent struct. This time, we'll also create two small tests to confirm that the data is what we expect it to be:

```rust
use chrono::{DateTime, FixedOffset, Utc};
use std::str::FromStr;
```

This use statement lets us use the DateTime::from_str() method. You'll learn how this works in the section on blanket trait implementations just below.

```rust
const SECONDS_IN_HOUR: i32 = 3600;
const UTC_TO_KST_HOURS: i32 = 9;
const UTC_TO_KST_SECONDS: i32 = UTC_TO_KST_HOURS * SECONDS_IN_HOUR;

#[derive(Debug)]
struct UtcUserEvent {
    timestamp: &'static str,
    data: String,
}
```

This UtcUserEvent struct represents data that we get from outside the service.

Nine hours is 32,400 seconds. We could write 32,400, but having const values makes the code easy for others to follow.

```rust
#[derive(Debug)]
struct KoreaJapanUserEvent {
    timestamp: DateTime<FixedOffset>,
    data: String,
}
```

This KoreaJapanUserEvent is what we want to turn the UtcUserEvent into.

We construct a DateTime<Utc>, bring in the Offset to change the time zone, and make a DateTime<FixedOffset> out of it.

```rust
impl From<UtcUserEvent> for KoreaJapanUserEvent {
    fn from(event: UtcUserEvent) -> Self {
        let utc_datetime: DateTime<Utc> =
            DateTime::from_str(event.timestamp).unwrap();
        let offset = FixedOffset::east_opt(UTC_TO_KST_SECONDS).unwrap();
        let timestamp: DateTime<FixedOffset> =
            DateTime::from_utc(utc_datetime.naive_utc(), offset);
        Self {
            timestamp,
            data: event.data,
        }
    }
}

fn main() {
    let incoming_event = UtcUserEvent {
        timestamp: "2023-03-27 23:48:50 UTC",
        data: "Something happened in UTC time".to_string(),
    };
    println!("Event as Utc:\n{incoming_event:?}");

    let korea_japan_event = KoreaJapanUserEvent::from(incoming_event);

    println!("Event in Korea/Japan time:\n{korea_japan_event:?}");
}
```

```
#[test]
fn utc_to_korea_output_same_evening() {
    let morning_event = UtcUserEvent {
        timestamp: "2023-03-27 09:48:50 UTC",
        data: String::new(),
    };
    let to_korea_japan = KoreaJapanUserEvent::from(morning_event);
    assert_eq!(
        &to_korea_japan.timestamp.to_string(),
        "2023-03-27 18:48:50 +09:00"
    );
}
```

> Finally, two short tests with one assertion in each. This is a nice way to show expected behavior to people reading your code without needing to print things out in main().

```
#[test]
fn utc_to_korea_output_next_morning() {
    let evening_event = UtcUserEvent {
        timestamp: "2023-03-27 23:59:59 UTC",
        data: String::new(),
    };
    let korea_japan_next_morning = KoreaJapanUserEvent::from(evening_event);
    assert_eq!(
        &korea_japan_next_morning.timestamp.to_string(),
        "2023-03-28 08:59:59 +09:00"
    );
}
```

Here is the output for this final example:

```
Event as Utc:
UtcUserEvent { timestamp: "2023-03-27 23:48:50 UTC", data: "Something
➥happened in UTC time" }
Event in Korea/Japan time:
KoreaJapanUserEvent { timestamp: 2023-03-28T08:48:50+09:00, data:
➥"Something happened in UTC time" }
```

That should be enough to get you started on using chrono to work with time. To finish things off, here are two other crates to take a look at:

- The `time` crate (https://docs.rs/time/latest/time/), which is similar to chrono but smaller and simpler. Both chrono and time are on the list of Rust's "blessed" crates.
- `chrono_tz` (https://docs.rs/chrono-tz/latest/chrono_tz/), which makes working with time zones in chrono much easier.

The next crate, Rayon, also has something to do with time: it's about reducing the time it takes for your code to run! Let's take a look at how it works.

17.4   *Rayon*

Rayon is a popular crate that lets you speed up your Rust code by automatically spawning multiple threads when working with iterators and related types. Instead of using `thread::spawn()` to spawn threads, you can just add `par_` to the iterator methods you already know.

For example, Rayon has `.par_iter()` for `.iter()`, while the methods `.iter_mut()`, `.into_iter()`, and `.chars()` in Rayon are simply `.par_iter_mut()`, `.par_into_iter()`, and `.par_chars()`. (You can probably imagine that `par` means *parallel* because it uses threads working in parallel.)

Here is an example of a simple piece of code that might be making the computer do a lot of work:

```
fn main() {
    let mut my_vec = vec![0; 2_000_000];
    my_vec
        .iter_mut()
        .enumerate()
        .for_each(|(index, number)| *number += index + 1);
    println!("{:?}", &my_vec[5000..5005]);
}
```

It creates a vector with 2,000,000 items: each one is 0. Then it calls `.enumerate()` to get the index for each number and changes the 0 to the index number plus 1. It's too long to print, so we only print items from index 5000 to 5004 (the output is `[5001, 5002, 5003, 5004, 5005]`). To potentially speed this up with Rayon, you can write almost the same code:

```
use rayon::prelude::*;          ◁─┤ Imports Rayon

fn main() {
    let mut my_vec = vec![0; 2_000_000];
    my_vec
        .par_iter_mut()
        .enumerate()                                                     │ Adds
        .for_each(|(index, number)| *number += index + 1);   ◁─┤ par_ to iter_mut
}
```

And that's it! Rayon has many other methods to customize what you want to do, but at its simplest, it is "add _par to make your program faster."

But how much faster? And why did we say the first code sample *might* be a lot of work for a computer and that Rayon can *potentially* speed it up?

We can do a simple test to see how much faster Rayon is. First, we will use a method inside the `std::thread` module called `available_parallelism()` to see how many threads will be spawned. Rayon uses a method similar to this to decide on the best number of threads. Then we will create an `Instant`, change the Vec as in the previous example, and then use `.elapsed()` to see how much time went by. We will do this 10 times and stick the result in microseconds each time into a Vec, and then print out the average at the end:

```
use rayon::prelude::*;
use std::thread::available_parallelism;

fn main() {
    println!(
        "Estimated parallelism on this computer: {:?}",
```

```
        available_parallelism()
    );
    let mut without_rayon = vec![];
    let mut with_rayon = vec![];

    for _ in 0..10 {
        let mut my_vec = vec![0; 2_000_000];
        let now = std::time::Instant::now();
        my_vec.iter_mut().enumerate().for_each(|(index, number)| {
            *number += index + 1;
            *number -= index + 1;
        });
        let elapsed = now.elapsed();
        without_rayon.push(elapsed.as_micros());

        let mut my_vec = vec![0; 2_000_000];
        let now = std::time::Instant::now();
        my_vec
            .par_iter_mut()
            .enumerate()
            .for_each(|(index, number)| {
                *number += index + 1;
                *number -= index + 1;
            });
        let elapsed = now.elapsed();
        with_rayon.push(elapsed.as_micros());
    }
    println!(
        "Average time without rayon: {} microseconds",
        without_rayon.into_iter().sum::<u128>() / 10
    );
    println!(
        "Average time with rayon: {} microseconds",
        with_rayon.into_iter().sum::<u128>() / 10
    );
}
```

> Inside these Vecs, we will push the time that elapsed during each test.

> There are other methods too like .as_nanos() and .as_millis(). Microseconds should be precise enough for us.

The speedup that Rayon gives will depend a lot on your code and the number of threads on your computer. This is quite clear when using the Playground, where the available parallelism is only 2. Surprisingly, the output will usually show only a moderate benefit:

```
Estimated parallelism on this computer: Ok(2)
Average time without rayon: 64570 microseconds
Average time with rayon: 56822 microseconds
```

And using Rayon will sometimes be slower in this case. On my computer, however, and probably on your computer, Rayon will use more threads and thus will show a much larger improvement. Here is one output from my computer:

```
Estimated parallelism on this computer: Ok(12)
Average time without rayon: 27633 microseconds
Average time with rayon: 9661 microseconds
```

And here is another surprise: if you click on `Debug` in the Playground and change it to `Release`, the code will take longer to compile but will run faster. In this case, Rayon is incredibly slow in comparison:

```
Estimated parallelism on this computer: Ok(2)
Average time without rayon: 0 microseconds
Average time with rayon: 87 microseconds
```

In fact, the code without Rayon is so fast that we would need to use the `.as_nanos()` method instead of `.as_micros()` even to see how long it took. Then, it will produce an output similar to this:

```
Estimated parallelism on this computer: Ok(2)
Average time without rayon: 74 microseconds
Average time with rayon: 113832 microseconds
```

That is a huge slowdown! This is because during release mode, the compiler tries to compute the result of methods ahead of time—especially for one as simple as this where we are just changing a few numbers. In effect, it just generates code to return the result without calculating anything at run time. (This is called optimization, and we will learn more about it in the next chapter.) But the Rayon code involves a lot of threading that makes the code more complex. That means that the compiler isn't able to know the result until the code runs, so it ends up being slower. In short, Rayon *might* speed up your code. But be sure to check!

17.5   Anyhow and thiserror

These two crates are used to help you with error handling. They are actually both made by the same person (David Tolnay) and are somewhat different.

Let's imagine why someone might use these crates. Much of the time, Rust code is written in the following way:

- A developer starts writing some code and uses `.unwrap()` or `.expect()` everywhere. This is fine at the beginning because you want to compile now and think about errors later. And it doesn't matter if the program panics at this point—nobody else is using it.
- The code starts to work, and you want to start handling errors properly. But it would be nice to have a single error type that's easy to use. This is what Anyhow is used for. (A `Box<dyn Error>` is another common way to do this, as we have seen.)
- Maybe later on, you decide you want your own error types, but implementing them manually is a lot of typing, and you want something more ergonomic. This is what thiserror is used for (although a lot of people just stick with Anyhow if it gets the job done).

17.5.1   Anyhow

Let's think about a quick example where we might want to deal with multiple errors. This code won't compile yet, but you can see the idea. We would like to take a slice of bytes and turn it into a &str. Then we'll try to parse it into an i32. After that, we'll send it to another function of ours that will send an Ok if the number is under 1 million. So, that's three types of errors that could happen.

Also note that we are using std::io::Error as the return type in one of our functions. That error type is a fairly convenient one because it has an ErrorKind enum inside it with a huge number of variants. However, in this code sample, we are trying to use the question mark operator for methods that may return a different of error kind, so we can't choose std::io::Error as a return value:

```
use std::io::{Error, ErrorKind};

fn parse_then_send(input: &[u8]) {          ◁──┐  What's the
    let some_str = std::str::from_utf8(input)?;    return type?
    let number = some_str.parse::<i32>()?;
    send_number(number)?;
}

fn send_number(number: i32) -> Result<(), Error> {
    if number < 1_000_000 {
        println!("Number sent!");
        Ok(())
    } else {
        Err(Error::new(ErrorKind::InvalidData))
    }
}

fn main() {}
```

This is where Anyhow comes in handy. Let's see what Anyhow's documentation says:

Use Result<T, anyhow::Error>, or equivalently anyhow::Result<T>, as the
▬▶return type of any fallible function.

Looks good. We can also bring in the anyhow! macro, which makes a quick anyhow::Error from a string or an error type. Let's give it a try:

```
use anyhow::{anyhow, Error};          ◁────────────┐  Error now means Anyhow's
                                                    Error type, not std::io::Error
fn parse_then_send(input: &[u8]) -> Result<(), Error> {   as in the previous example.
    let some_str = std::str::from_utf8(input)?;           We could also write `use
    let number = some_str.parse::<i32>()?;               anyhow::Error as
    send_number(number)?;                                AnyhowError` to give it a
    Ok(())                                               different name if we wanted.
}

fn send_number(number: i32) -> Result<(), Error> {
    if number < 1_000_000 {
        println!("Number sent!");
        Ok(())
    } else {
        println!("Too large!");
        Err(anyhow!("Number is too large"))
    }
}
```

```
fn main() {
    println!("{:?}", parse_then_send(b"nine"));
    println!("{:?}", parse_then_send(b"10"));
}
```

Nice! Now anyhow's `Error` is our single error type. The code gives this output:

```
Err(invalid digit found in string)
Number sent!
Ok(())
```

That's not too bad. Note, though, that the first error is a little vague. Anyhow has a number of methods for its `Error` type that can help here, but a particularly easy one is `.with_context()`, which takes something that implements `Display`. You can use that to add some extra info. Let's add some context:

```
use anyhow::{anyhow, Context, Error};

fn parse_then_send(input: &[u8]) -> Result<(), Error> {
    let some_str = std::str::from_utf8(input)
    .with_context(|| "Couldn't parse into a str")?;
    let number = some_str
        .parse::<i32>()
        .with_context(|| format!("Got a weird str to parse: {some_str}"))?;
    send_number(number)?;
    Ok(())
}

fn send_number(number: i32) -> Result<(), Error> {
    if number < 1_000_000 {
        println!("Number sent!");
        Ok(())
    } else {
        println!("Too large!");
        Err(anyhow!("Number is too large"))
    }
}

fn main() {
    println!("{:?}", parse_then_send(b"nine"));
    println!("{:?}", parse_then_send(b"10"));
}
```

Now the output is more helpful:

```
Err(Got a weird str to parse: nine

Caused by:
    invalid digit found in string)
Number sent!
Ok(())
```

So that's Anyhow. One thing Anyhow isn't, however, is an actual error type (a type that implements `std::error::Error`). Anyhow (https://docs.rs/anyhow/latest/anyhow/) suggests using thiserror if we want an actual error type:

Anyhow works with any error type that has an impl of `std::error::Error`, *including ones defined in your crate. We do not bundle a* `derive(Error)` *macro but you can write the impls yourself or use a standalone macro like thiserror.*

So let's look at that crate now.

17.5.2 *thiserror*

The main convenience in thiserror is a derive macro called `thiserror::Error` that will quickly turn your type into one that implements `std::error::Error`. If we imagine that we want to make our code into a library and have a proper error type, we could use `thiserror` to do this. In this small example we have three possible errors, so let's make an enum:

```
enum SystemError {
    StrFromUtf8Error,
    ParseI32Error,
    SendError
}
```

Now we'll use thiserror to turn it into a proper error type. You use `#[derive(Error)]` on top and then another `#[error]` attribute above each variant if we want a message. This will automatically implement `Display`. Note that if you print using `Debug`, you won't see these extra messages.

You can also use another attribute called `#[from]` to automatically implement `From` for other error types. A type created from thiserror usually ends up looking something like this:

```
#[derive(Error, Debug)]

enum SystemError {
    #[error("Couldn't send: {0}")]

    SendError(String),
    #[error("Couldn't parse into a str: {0}")]

    StringFromUtf8Error(#[from] Utf8Error),
    #[error("Couldn't turn into an i32: {0}")]
    ParseI32Error(#[from] ParseIntError),
    #[error("Wrong color: Red {0} Green {1} Blue {2}")]

    ColorError(u8, u8, u8),
    #[error("Something happened")]
    OtherError,
}
```

This here is thiserror's Error macro. Easy to miss!

First is a variant unrelated to any other external error types. The zero in these attribute macros means .0 used when accessing a tuple.

These next two will hold the information from the Utf8Error and ParseIntError types in the standard library, so we will use #[from].

We'll throw in a ColorError while we're at it to really make it clear that we are accessing the inner value in the same way we access any other tuple.

You can see that the error attribute has the same format as when you use the `format!` macro.

Now let's look at almost the same example we used previously with thiserror instead of Anyhow:

```
use std::{num::ParseIntError, str::Utf8Error};

use thiserror::Error;

#[derive(Error, Debug)]
enum SystemError {
    #[error("Couldn't send: {0}")]
    SendError(String),
    #[error("Couldn't parse into a str: {0}")]
    StringFromUtf8Error(#[from] Utf8Error),
    #[error("Couldn't turn into an i32: {0}")]
    ParseI32Error(#[from] ParseIntError),
    #[error("Wrong color: Red {0} Green {1} Blue {2}")]
    ColorError(u8, u8, u8),
    #[error("Something happened")]
    OtherError,
}

fn parse_then_send(input: &[u8]) -> Result<(), SystemError> {
    let some_str = std::str::from_utf8(input)?;     ◁──┐  Having a From impl makes the
    let number = some_str.parse::<i32>()?;                code pretty nice here—just use
    send_number(number)?;                                the question mark operator.
    Ok(())
}

fn send_number(number: i32) -> Result<(), SystemError> {
    match number {
        num if num == 500 => Err(SystemError::OtherError),                    ◁──────
        num if num > 1_000_000 => Err(SystemError::SendError(format!(
            "{num} is too large, can't send!"
        ))),                                          This is just an excuse to use the
        _ => {                                        OtherError variant. 500 is a bad
            println!("Number sent!");                    number for some reason.
            Ok(())
        }
    }                                            The .unwrap_err() method is like .unwrap()
}                                                   except it panics upon receiving an Ok
                                                 instead of when receiving an Err. It's a quick
fn main() {                                           way to get to the error type inside.
    println!("{}", parse_then_send(b"nine").unwrap_err());           ◁──────
    println!("{}", parse_then_send(&[8, 9, 0, 200]).unwrap_err());
    println!("{}", parse_then_send(b"109080098").unwrap_err());
    println!("{}", SystemError::ColorError(8, 10, 200));
    parse_then_send(b"10098").unwrap();
}
```

Now the output is

```
Couldn't turn into an i32: invalid digit found in string
Couldn't parse into a str: incomplete utf-8 byte sequence from index 3
Couldn't send: 109080098 is too large, can't send!
Wrong color: Red 8 Green 10 Blue 200
Number sent!
```

Pretty slick! With not too many lines of code, we have a proper error enum with all the info we need.

So thiserror lets us implement `From` for certain other error types to bring into our error enum. What if we wanted to make a variant that implements `From` for all types that implement `std::error::Error`? Let's take a small detour and talk about blanket trait implementations.

17.6 *Blanket trait implementations*

A blanket trait implementation lets you implement your trait for other people's types. Usually, it's used for every type that implements certain other traits, but you can also implement it on any and all other types if you want.

Let's start by making a trait that says "Hello":

```rust
trait SaysHello {
    fn hello(&self) {
        println!("Hello");
    }
}
```

It would be nice to let every other type in the world have this trait. How do we do that? Pretty easy—just give it to a generic type `T`:

```rust
trait SaysHello {
    fn hello(&self) {
        println!("Hello");
    }
}

impl<T> SaysHello for T {}
```

This generic type `T` doesn't have any bounds like `Display` or `Debug`, so every Rust type in the whole world counts as a type `T`. And now every type in our code can call `.hello()`. Let's give it a try! Now every type everywhere implements `SaysHello`:

```rust
trait SaysHello {
    fn hello(&self) {
        println!("Hello");
    }
}

impl<T> SaysHello for T {}

struct Nothing;

fn main() {
    8.hello();
    &'c'.hello();
    &mut String::from("Hello there").hello();
    8.7897.hello();
    Nothing.hello();
    std::collections::HashMap::<i32, i32>::new().hello();
}
```

All of these print `Hello`.

Now, usually, a blanket trait implementation is implemented for a certain type with a trait of its own, such as `<T: Debug>`. We are quite familiar with this already: with a `Debug` trait bound, we know that the type will implement `Debug` and thus can be printed with `{:?}`, used as a function parameter that needs `Debug`, and so on.

In our case, we can make a trait and implement it for anything that implements `std::error::Error`. We can then use a blanket implementation on anything that implements `Error` and, if it does, to put it into a variant of our enum. This lets us have our own proper error type while keeping a place to put all the possible errors from external crates. Here's what it could look like:

```
use std::error::Error as StdError;      ⟵   Gives Error (in the standard
use thiserror::Error;                        library) and Error (in the
                                             thiserror crate) different names
#[derive(Error, Debug)]
enum SystemError {                           This variant will hold
    #[error("Couldn't send: {0}")]           all the external errors.
    SendError(String),
    #[error("External crate error: {0}")]                  This function will turn a
    ExternalCrateError(String),    ⟵                        Result<T, E> to a Result
}                                                          <T, SystemError>. Anything
                                                            with std::error::Error will
trait ToSystemError<T> {                                    implement Display, so
    fn to_system_error(self) -> Result<T, SystemError>;      we can call .to_string()
}                                                           and put it inside the
                                                           ExternalCrateError variant.
impl<T, E: StdError> ToSystemError<T> for Result<T, E> {    ⟵
    fn to_system_error(self) -> Result<T, SystemError> {
        self.map_err(|e| SystemError::ExternalCrateError(e.to_string()))
    }
}
```

This uses a blanket implementation for anything that is an `Error` type, turns it into a `String`, and sticks it into a variant called `ExternalCrateError`. With this trait, you can then just type `.to_system_error()?` every time you have code from another source that you want to put into the `SystemError` enum. Then it looks like this:

```
use std::error::Error as StdError;
use thiserror::Error;

#[derive(Error, Debug)]
enum SystemError {
    #[error("Couldn't send {0}")]
    SendError(i32),
    #[error("External crate error: {0}")]
    ExternalCrateError(String),
}

trait ToSystemError<T> {
    fn to_system_error(self) -> Result<T, SystemError>;
}

impl<T, E: StdError> ToSystemError<T> for Result<T, E> {
```

```
    fn to_system_error(self) -> Result<T, SystemError> {
        self.map_err(|e| SystemError::ExternalCrateError(e.to_string()))
    }
}

fn parse_then_send(input: &[u8]) -> Result<(), SystemError> {
    let some_str = std::str::from_utf8(input).to_system_error()?;
    let number = some_str.parse::<i32>().to_system_error()?;
    send_number(number).to_system_error()?;
    Ok(())
}

fn send_number(number: i32) -> Result<(), SystemError> {
    if number < 1_000_000 {
        println!("Number sent!");
        Ok(())
    } else {
        println!("Too large!");
        Err(SystemError::SendError(number))
    }
}

fn main() {
    println!("{}", parse_then_send(b"nine").unwrap_err());
    println!("{:?}", parse_then_send(b"nine"));
    println!("{:?}", parse_then_send(b"10"));
}
```

> **We are calling the function twice to compare the Display and Debug output.**

This prints

```
External crate error: invalid digit found in string
Err(ExternalCrateError("invalid digit found in string"))
Number sent!
Ok(())
```

The standard library has a lot of other blanket implementations that you can find by looking for impl on generic types (usually T). Let's take a look at a few.

This first one is familiar: with Display, we get the .to_string() method from the ToString trait for free:

```
impl<T> ToString for T
where T: Display + ?Sized,
```

This next one is also familiar. If you implement From, you get Into for free:

```
impl<T, U> Into<U> for T
where
    U: From<T>,
```

This next one is interesting. If you have From, you get Into for free, and if you have Into, you also get TryFrom for free:

```
impl<T, U> TryFrom<U> for T
where
    U: Into<T>,
```

This also makes sense because it would be weird to have a function or parameter that requires a `TryFrom<T>` but refuses a type that implements `From<T>`!

Here is the simplest possible example showing these two blanket traits:

```
#[derive(Debug)]
struct One;
#[derive(Debug)]
struct Two;

impl From<One> for Two {          ◁─┐  We implement
    fn from(one: One) -> Self {      │  From<One>.
        Two
    }
}

fn main() {
    let two: Two = One.into();      ◁─┐  Now we get both Into<Two>
    let try_two = Two::try_from(One); │  and TryFrom<One> for free!
    println!("{two:?}, {try_two:?}");
}
```

This prints `Two, Ok(Two)`.

There are tons and tons of blanket implementations for `From`. Let's pick a fancy one. But if you read it slowly, you'll be able to figure it out:

```
impl<K, V, const N: usize> From<[(K, V); N]> for BTreeMap<K, V>
  where
    K: Ord,
```

Let's break this down:

- The implementation involves a `K` (a key) and a `V` (a value), which makes sense—a `BTreeMap` uses keys and values.
- There is also a `const N: usize`. That's const generics! We learned them just in the last chapter.
- The `[(K, V); N]` signature means an array of length `N` (in other words, any length) that holds tuples of `(K, V)`.
- `BTreeMap`s order their contents, so their keys need to implement `Ord`.

So, it looks like this is a blanket implementation to construct a `BTreeMap` from an array of tuples of keys and values, where the keys can be ordered. Let's try this out to see whether we can make a `BTreeMap` straight from an array:

```
use std::collections::BTreeMap;

fn main() {
    let my_btree_map = BTreeMap::from([
        ("customer_1_money".to_string(), 10),
        ("customer_2_money".to_string(), 200),
    ]);
}
```

It works! The array here is of type `[(String, i32); 2]`.

It's time to get back to external crates with our last two: `lazy_static` and `Once-Cell`.

17.7 *lazy_static and once_cell*

Remember the section in the last chapter on mutable static variables? We saw that starting in Rust 1.63 (summer 2022), this sort of expression became possible because all of these functions are `const fns`:

```
static GLOBAL_LOGGER: Mutex<Vec<Log>> = Mutex::new(Vec::new());
```

Before Rust 1.63, you needed either the crate `lazy_static` or the crate `once_cell` to do this.

However, there are still a lot of other static variables you might want to have but can't initialize with a `const fn`, and that is what these two crates allow you to do. They are called *lazily initiated statics*, meaning that they are initiated at run time instead of compile time. `lazy_static` is the older and simpler crate, so we'll look at it first.

17.7.1 *Lazy static: Lazily evaluated statics*

Let's imagine that our `GLOBAL_LOGGER` also wants to send data to a server somewhere else over HTTP. It would be nice to give it a `Vec<Log>` for the info, a `String` for the URL to send the requests to, and a Client that will post the data. So something like this would be good to start:

```
use reqwest::Client;

#[derive(Debug)]
struct Logger {
    logs: Vec<Log>,
    url: String,
    client: Client,
}

#[derive(Debug)]
struct Log {
    message: String,
    timestamp: i64,
}
```

By the way, `reqwest` (note the spelling) is the next external crate that we will look at. For this code sample, we won't do anything with it, but just remember that `reqwest::Client` is used for POST, GET, and all other HTTP actions.

But making it a static like this won't work for us:

```
use reqwest::Client;
use std::sync::Mutex;

#[derive(Debug)]
struct Logger {
```

```
    logs: Mutex<Vec<Log>>,
    url: String,
    client: Client,
}

#[derive(Debug)]
struct Log {
    message: String,
    timestamp: i64,
}

static GLOBAL_LOGGER: Logger = Logger {
    logs: Mutex::new(vec![]),
    url: "https://somethingsomething.com".to_string(),
    client: Client::default()
};

fn main() {

}
```

The compiler lets us know that this `Logger` struct involves functions that aren't `const` and thus can't be called:

```
error[E0015]: cannot call non-const fn `<str as ToString>::to_string` in
➡statics
error[E0015]: cannot call non-const fn `<reqwest::Client as
➡Default>::default` in statics
```

Even if we change the URL to a `Mutex<String>`, the Client itself is a `non-const fn`, so no luck there. And we might want to add more parameters to our `Logger` struct anyway.

This is where `lazy_static` comes in. It's pretty easy. Here's how its crate describes it (https://docs.rs/lazy_static/latest/lazy_static/):

> *Using this macro, it is possible to have* `statics` *that require code to be executed at runtime in order to be initialized. This includes anything requiring heap allocations, like vectors or hash maps, as well as anything that requires function calls to be computed.*

To initiate a lazy static, you can use the `lazy_static!` and declare a `static ref` instead of a `static`. Note that `static ref` is a term only used by this crate: there's nothing in Rust itself called a `static ref`. But it's called a `static ref` because of the following:

> *For a given static* `ref` `NAME: TYPE = EXPR;`, *the macro generates a unique type that implements* `Deref<TYPE>` *and stores it in a static with name* `NAME`. *(Attributes end up attaching to this type.)*

Cool. But we don't even need to think about that if we don't want to. Just make a `lazy_static!` block and put statics in there that we now call `static ref` instead of `static`. This part of the code is almost identical to before:

```
lazy_static! {
    static ref GLOBAL_LOGGER: Logger = Logger {
        logs: Mutex::new(vec![]),
        url: "https://somethingsomething.com".to_string(),
        client: Client::default()
    };
}
```

> **We call the lazy_static! macro.**

> **We call it a static ref instead of a static. Everything else is the same.**

And with just those two changes, we have a static that can be called anywhere from the program. Here is what the code looks like now:

```rust
use lazy_static::lazy_static;
use reqwest::Client;
use std::sync::Mutex;

#[derive(Debug)]
struct Logger {
    logs: Mutex<Vec<Log>>,
    url: String,
    client: Client,
}

#[derive(Debug)]
struct Log {
    message: String,
    timestamp: i64,
}

lazy_static! {
    static ref GLOBAL_LOGGER: Logger = Logger {
        logs: Mutex::new(vec![]),
        url: "https://somethingsomething.com".to_string(),
        client: Client::default()
    };
}

fn main() {
    GLOBAL_LOGGER.logs.lock().unwrap().push(Log {
        message: "Everything's going well".to_string(),
        timestamp: 1658930674
    });
    println!("{:#?}", *GLOBAL_LOGGER.logs.lock().unwrap());
}
```

So that's `lazy_static`. The other one is called `once_cell` and is a bit harder to use but more flexible. `OnceCell` is also in the process of being added to the standard library, so it's good to know. In fact, it might even be done by the time you read this book. As of June 2023, parts of the `once_cell` crate can be used in the standard library (http://mng.bz/mj84). Even after the rest of the functionality is ported to the standard library, we will probably see the `once_cell` crate in use in Rust code for many years to come.

17.7.2 OnceCell: A cell to only write to once

As the name suggests, a `OnceCell` is a cell that is written to once. You start it off as a `OnceCell::new()` of some type (like a `OnceCell<String>` or `OnceCell<Logger>`) and then call `.set()` to initialize the type that it holds.

A `OnceCell` feels pretty similar to a `Cell` and has similar method names, too, such as `.set()` and `.get()`.

So what makes a `OnceCell` more flexible than `lazy_static`? Here are some highlights:

- A `OnceCell` can hold a whole type (like our whole `Logger`), or it can be a parameter inside another type.
- You can use a `OnceCell` with variables that we don't know until much later in the program. Maybe we don't know our `Logger`'s URL yet and need to get it somewhere. We can start `main()`, get the URL much later, and then stick it inside our `Logger` using `.set()`.
- For a `OnceCell`, you can choose a sync or unsync version. If you don't need to send it between threads, just choose unsync.

Let's give `OnceCell` a try with the same `Logger` struct as before. We'll make the same `GLOBAL_LOGGER`, but this time, it will be a `OnceCell<Logger>`. To start a `OnceCell`, just use `OnceCell::new()`. It looks like this:

```
static GLOBAL_LOGGER: OnceCell<Logger> = OnceCell::new();
```

This gives us an empty cell that is ready for us to call `.set()` to initialize the value inside. The whole thing looks like this:

```
use once_cell::sync::OnceCell;
use reqwest::Client;
use std::sync::Mutex;

#[derive(Debug)]
struct Logger {
    logs: Mutex<Vec<Log>>,
    url: String,
    client: Client,
}

#[derive(Debug)]
struct Log {
    message: String,
    timestamp: i64,
}

static GLOBAL_LOGGER: OnceCell<Logger> = OnceCell::new();

fn fetch_url() -> String {

    "http://somethingsomething.com".to_string()
}
```

We'll pretend that this function needs to do something at run time to find the url.

Pretend that there is a lot of code here.

Finally returns the URL

```
fn main() {
    let url = fetch_url();
    GLOBAL_LOGGER
        .set(Logger {
            logs: Mutex::new(vec![]),
            url,
            client: Client::default(),
        })
        .unwrap();

    GLOBAL_LOGGER
        .get()
        .unwrap()
        .logs
        .lock()
        .unwrap()
        .push(Log {
            message: "Everything's going well".to_string(),
            timestamp: 1658930674,
        });

    println!("{GLOBAL_LOGGER:?}");
}
```

The program has started, and we got the URL. Now it's time to set the GLOBAL_LOGGER by putting a Logger struct inside.

.set() returns a Result but will return an error if the cell has already been set.

GLOBAL_LOGGER is initialized. Let's get a reference to it.

.get() returns a None if the cell hasn't been set yet. We'll unwrap here, too.

Finally, we are accessing .logs inside the Logger struct, which is a Mutex. The rest of the code involves locking the Mutex and pushing a message to the Vec<Log> that it holds.

Done!

This prints out everything inside our GLOBAL_LOGGER. It works! You can see the message inside it:

```
OnceCell(Logger { logs: Mutex { data: [Log { message: "Everything's going
well", timestamp: 1658930674 }], poisoned: false, .. }, url:
"http://somethingsomething.com", client: Client { accepts: Accepts,
proxies: [Proxy(System({}), None)], referer: true, default_headers:
{"accept": "*/*"} } })
```

And don't worry about the porting of OnceCell to the standard library, as the code is almost exactly the same. Here is the same example as before except that we are using the standard library instead. The only difference here is that a std::cell::OnceCell in the standard library is not thread-safe, while the thread-safe version is called a std::sync::OnceLock. Other than that, though, the code is exactly the same!

```
use reqwest::Client;
use std::sync::Mutex;
use std::sync::OnceLock;

#[derive(Debug)]
struct Logger {
    logs: Mutex<Vec<Log>>,
    url: String,
    client: Client,
}

#[derive(Debug)]
struct Log {
    message: String,
```

```
    timestamp: i64,
}

static GLOBAL_LOGGER: OnceLock<Logger> = OnceLock::new();

fn fetch_url() -> String {
    "http://somethingsomething.com".to_string()
}

fn main() {
    let url = fetch_url();

    GLOBAL_LOGGER
        .set(Logger {
            logs: Mutex::new(vec![]),
            url,
            client: Client::default(),
        })
        .unwrap();

    GLOBAL_LOGGER
        .get()
        .unwrap()
        .logs
        .lock()
        .unwrap()
        .push(Log {
        message: "Everything's going well".to_string(),
        timestamp: 1658930674,
    });
    println!("{GLOBAL_LOGGER:?}");
}
```

So that's how `OnceCell` works. You must be curious about the `reqwest` crate by now, but we won't see it in detail until chapter 19 because there are a few items to take care of first. One of them is installing Rust on your computer because the Rust Playground won't let people use `reqwest` to make HTTP requests. (Who knows what people would use that for . . .)

This means that we've finally reached the part of the book that deals with Rust on your computer (although you've probably already installed Rust if you've read this far in the book). In the next chapter, we'll go over the basics of using Rust on your computer: installing Rust, setting up a project using Cargo, using Cargo doc to automatically generate your documentation, and all the other nice things that come with using Cargo to set up a project and run your code instead of just the Playground.

Summary

- External crates are used all the time in Rust, even for key functionality like dealing with time.
- If you are doing a lot of heavy computing with iterators (and don't feel like spawning extra threads yourself), try bringing in the `rayon` crate.

- Anyhow is the most frequently used external crate for dealing with multiple errors, while thiserror can be used to easily create your own error types.
- The `lazy_static` and `once_cell` crates are used for creating global variables that can't be constructed at compile time.
- The functionality of both `lazy_static` and `once_cell` are being ported to the standard library, so eventually you may not need to use any external crates at all to create any global variables.
- Blanket implementations let you give trait methods to any types you want. These are used everywhere in the standard library, too, such as when you get the `.to_string()` method for free for anything that implements `Display`.

Rust on your computer

We have seen that it is possible to learn almost anything in Rust just using the Playground. But if you have read this far in the book, you probably already have Rust installed on your computer. And there are always things that you can't do with the Playground, such as working with files or writing code in more than just one file. Some other things that are best done on your computer for are user input and command-line arguments. But most important is that with Rust on your computer, you can use external crates. We have already learned a few crates, but the Playground only has access to the most popular ones. With Rust on your computer, you can use any external crate at all. The tool that binds this all together is called Cargo, Rust's package manager.

18.1 Cargo

One of the largest selling points of Rust is that pretty much everyone uses Cargo to build and manage their projects. Using Cargo gives Rust projects a common structure that makes it easy to work with external code written by multiple people at the same time. To understand why Cargo is found almost everywhere in Rust code, let's first see what writing Rust is like without it.

18.1.1 Why everyone uses Cargo

The Rust compiler is called `rustc` and is what does the actual compiling. A Rust file ends with an `.rs`. Technically, you can compile programs on your own with commands like `rustc main.rs`, but it quickly gets annoying.

But let's give it a try. Make a new directory and create a new file called test.rs. Then put something simple in like this:

```
fn main() {
    println!("Does this work?");
}
```

After that, type `rustc test.rs`. You should see a file called test.exe. That's your program! Now just type `test`, and you should see something like this:

```
c:\nothing>test
Does this work?

c:\nothing>
```

Not bad! But how do you handle bringing in external code? If we want a random number, we will probably use the `rand` crate:

```
use rand::{thread_rng, Rng};

fn main() {
    let mut rng = thread_rng();
    println!("Today's lucky number: {}", rng.gen::<u8>());
}
```

But no luck. A lonely compiler doesn't know what to do with this sudden `rand` keyword:

```
error[E0432]: unresolved import `rand`
 --> test.rs:1:5
  |
1 | use rand::{thread_rng, Rng};
  |     ^^^^ maybe a missing crate `rand`?
  |
  = help: consider adding `extern crate rand` to use the `rand` crate
```

It is just as confused even if we add `extern crate rand` as it suggests:

```
error[E0463]: can't find crate for `rand`
 --> test.rs:1:1
```

```
  |
1 | extern crate rand;
  | ^^^^^^^^^^^^^^^^^^^ can't find crate
```

Technically, you can type `rustc -help` and start looking around for the right way to link external code. But nobody does this when building programs with Rust because there is a package manager and build tool called Cargo that takes care of all of this. Cargo uses `rustc` to compile, too; it automates the process to make it a nearly painless experience.

One note about the name: it's called `cargo` because when you put crates together, you get cargo. A crate is a wooden box that you see on ships or trucks (figure 18.1), but you remember that every Rust project is also called a crate. When you put them together you get the whole cargo. So cargo comes from the idea of putting all the crates together to make a full project.

Figure 18.1 You can think of Cargo as this ship holding all of the external crates together in the same place.

You can see this when you use Cargo to run a project. To start a project in Cargo, type `cargo new` and its name. For example, you could type `cargo new my_project`. A directory will be created with the same name, inside of which is Cargo.toml and a directory called /src for the code. Inside this directory is `main.rs`, which is where you start writing your code. If you want to write a library (i.e., code that is meant for others to use), add `--lib` to the end of the command. Then Rust will create a `lib.rs` instead of `main.rs` in the /src directory.

With a new project started, let's add `rand = "0.8.5"` to Cargo.toml, as we learned previously, and write some code to randomly choose between eight letters:

```
use rand::seq::SliceRandom;          This is a blanket trait that lets us use a
                                     method called .choose() for slices, so
fn main() {                          we need to bring it into scope to use it.
    let my_letters = vec!['a', 'b', 'c', 'd', 'e', 'f', 'g', 'h'];
    let mut rng = rand::thread_rng();
    for _ in 0..6 {
        print!("{} ", my_letters.choose(&mut rng).unwrap());
    }
}
```

This will print something like `b c g h e a`. But let's first see what Cargo does before the program starts running. To use Cargo to both build and run a program, type `cargo run`. But there is quite a bit of output during compiling, too. It will look something like this:

```
Compiling rand_core v0.6.4
Compiling rand_chacha v0.3.1
Compiling rand v0.8.5
Compiling random_test v0.1.0 (C:\rust\random_test)
 Finished dev [unoptimized + debuginfo] target(s) in 2.61s
  Running `target\debug\random_test.exe`
```

It looks like Cargo didn't just bring in a single crate called `rand`, but some others, too. That's because we need `rand` for our crate, but `rand` also has code that needs other crates, too. Cargo will find all the crates we need and put them together. In our case, we only had a few, but on other projects, you may have 200, 600, or sometimes even more crates to bring in. In this case, the program took 2.61 seconds to compile, but this time will, of course, vary.

18.1.2 *Using Cargo and what Rust does while it compiles*

Compiling time is where you can see the tradeoff for Rust: compiling ahead of time is one reason why Rust is so fast, but you have to wait while Rust compiles your code. However, Rust does use *incremental compilation*. Incremental compilation means that when you make a change to your code, Rust will only recompile the changes, not the whole program. In our case, imagine that we add the letter `i` to my_letters and type `cargo run` again:

```
let my_letters = vec!['a', 'b', 'c', 'd', 'e', 'f', 'g', 'h', 'i'];
```

In this case, the crates such as `rand_core` are already brought in so they don't get recompiled, and the whole process is a lot quicker:

```
Compiling random_test v0.1.0 (C:\rust\random_test)
 Finished dev [unoptimized + debuginfo] target(s) in 0.55s
  Running `target\debug\random_test.exe`
f h i d e d
```

This time, it only took 0.55 seconds. So, to speed up your development time, try typing `cargo build` every time you add an external crate as you work on your code. Rust will compile your code in the background as you work, and every `cargo build` or `cargo run` thereafter will be a faster incremental compilation.

Rust optimizes (speeds up) its code in a number of ways, such as by turning generic functions and types into concrete ones. For example, here is some simple generic code that you might write:

```
use std::fmt::Display;

fn print_and_return<T: Display>(input: T) -> T {
    println!("You gave me {input} and now I will give it back.");
    input
}

fn main() {
    let my_name = print_and_return("Windy");
    let small_number = print_and_return(9.0);
}
```

This function can take anything with `Display`, so we gave it a `&str` and next gave it an `f64`, both of which implement `Display`. However, (unseen to us) the compiler changes generic functions to concrete ones for each type that it will use, which allows the program to be faster at run time.

So when it looks at the first part with `"Windy"` (a `&str`), it doesn't just produce a `fn print_and_return<T: Display>(input: T) -> T` to use at run time. Instead, it turns it into something like `fn print_and_return_str(input: &str) -> &str`. It does the same on the next line with the input `9.0`, turning the function into something like `fn print_and_return_f64(input: f64) -> f64`. All this is done during compile time. This is why generic functions take (slightly) longer to compile because the compiler generates a concrete function for each different type to be used at run time.

You'll sometimes see this called a *specialized definition* or *monomorphization*. That is, when the compiler turns the generic function above into something like `fn print_ and_return_f64(input: f64) -> f64`, it has turned the generic function into a function that is *specialized* to the `f64` type. And *monomorphism*, which is a Greek term for "single form-ism," means that the function is now concrete and only has a single form. When we write a generic function, it is *polymorphic* ("multiple form") because it can take on a lot of different forms in practice. The compiler then takes these generic functions, *specializing* them to the input type, and turns them into *monomorphic* ("single form") functions.

Thankfully, you don't have to think about any of this to write your code—the compiler does it all without showing you. But it's nice to know some of the reasons why Rust takes a while to compile but runs really fast once the compiling is done.

One more thing: the makers of Rust work hard on lowering compile time because compile time is one of Rust's largest pain points. However, almost every version of Rust compiles a bit faster than the previous version, and Rust today compiles much faster than it did a few years ago. If you are curious about some of these details, check out this blog by a Rust developer who writes about recent compiler improvements in a pretty readable way: https://nnethercote.github.io/.

Here are the most basic commands about Cargo to know:

- `cargo build` will build your program as an executable so you can run it. You'll find the executable inside the `/target` folder.
- `cargo run` will build your program and run it.
- `cargo build --release` and `cargo run --release` will do the same but in release mode. You will usually use release mode when your code is finally done and you want it to be as optimized as possible. In release mode, Rust will take even longer to compile, but it is worth it because the compiler uses everything it knows to make it faster. Release mode is actually a *lot* faster than regular mode, which is called `Debug` mode because it compiles quicker and has more debug information. The regular `cargo build` is called a "debug build" and `cargo build --release` is called a "release build." A debug build will go inside the `/target/debug` folder and release build inside the `/target/release` folder.

- `cargo check` is the fastest way to check your code. It's like compiling, except that it won't actually build the program, which is why it doesn't take as long. If you are in the middle of some coding and just curious whether your program will compile, use `cargo check`.

The best way to see the difference between debug and release mode is to look at a small function like this that uses a loop that runs 1,000 times:

```rust
pub fn add() -> i32 {
    let mut sum = 0;
    for _ in 0..1000 {
        sum += 1
    }
    sum
}
```

You'll notice that the code is asking the computer to do a lot of work (looping 1,000 times), but the code is pretty simple. Even humans can look at this and know what the final output will be. Rust can do this sometimes, too.

In `Debug` mode, the compiler will quickly put the code together to run this loop at run time, as well as add some debug info. The focus in debug mode is on compiling quickly and helping the developer. You can see this if you paste this function into the website Godbolt (https://rust.godbolt.org/), which shows the assembly code generated. For this function, you'll see 100+ lines of code generated. Even if you don't know any assembly, you'll notice that the compiler is generating the code needed to run the loop. Figure 18.2 shows there are a lot of terms like `Iterator`, `Range`, `into_iter`, `PartialOrd`, and so on, so quite a bit of code relating to iterators and comparing numbers.

```
rustc 1.71.0 (Editor #1)  ✎ ✕

rustc 1.71.0          ▼   ☐  ✓      Compiler options...

  ▼  ⚙ Output... ▼  ▼ Filter... ▼  ▤ Libraries  ✦ Overrides  + Add new... ▼  ✦ Add t

  1    <i32 as core::iter::range::Step>::forward_unchecked:
  2            mov     eax, esi
  3            add     edi, eax
  4            mov     dword ptr [rsp - 4], edi
  5            mov     eax, dword ptr [rsp - 4]
  6            ret
  7
  8    core::iter::range::<impl core::iter::traits::iterator::Iterator for
  9            push    rax
 10            mov     rax, qword ptr [rip + <core::ops::range::Range<T> as
 11            call    rax
 12            pop     rcx
 13            ret
 14
 15    <I as core::iter::traits::collect::IntoIterator>::into_iter:
 16            mov     edx, esi
 17            mov     eax, edi
```

Figure 18.2
Compiling in debug mode takes less time but the code itself ends up doing more work.

You can see the debug info at the end of the file, too, such as an error message in case the number overflows and the program needs to panic (figure 18.3).

```
rustc 1.71.0 (Editor #1)  ✎  ✕

  rustc 1.71.0              ▼   ☑   ✓   Compiler options...

  ▾   ✿ Output... ▾   ▼ Filter... ▾   ▤ Libraries   ✦ Overrides   + Add new... ▾   ✦ Add t

  78          lea      rdi, [rip + str.0]
  79          lea      rdx, [rip + .L__unnamed_1]
  80          mov      rax, qword ptr [rip + core::panicking::panic@GOTPCRE
  81          mov      esi, 28
  82          call     rax
  83          ud2
  84
  85    .L__unnamed_2:
  86          .ascii   "/app/example.rs"
  87
  88    .L__unnamed_1:
  89          .quad    .L__unnamed_2
  90          .asciz   "\017\000\000\000\000\000\000\000\004\000\000\000\t\
  91
  92    str.0:
  93          .ascii   "attempt to add with overflow"
```

Figure 18.3   And some parts of the compiled code in debug mode are easily readable.

Now, here comes the fun part: release mode. Click on the triangle on the top right next to Compiler Options, select `-C opt-level=val`, and change `val` to `3` (3 is the optimization level for release builds). The compiler will then try to optimize as much as possible (figure 18.4)—and now the assembly is only three lines long!

The compiler has spent some extra time in release mode to analyze the loop and sees that it will always return 1,000. So why bother adding any extra code at run time?

```
rustc 1.71.0 (Editor #1)  ✎  ✕                                      ☐ ⟩

  rustc 1.71.0              ▼   ☑   ✓   -C opt-level=3               ▼

  ▾   ✿ Output... ▾   ▼ Filter... ▾   ▤ Libraries   ✦ Overrides   + Add new... ▾   ✦ Add tool... ▾

  1    example::add:
  2          mov      eax, 1000
  3          ret
```

Figure 18.4   Release mode takes a lot longer, but the compiled code is most efficient.

That is essentially how optimization at compile time works. If you choose to spend the extra time to compile in release mode, the compiler will have the extra time to analyze the code and shorten it as much as possible.

Here are some more Cargo commands:

- `cargo clippy` will run `clippy`. It takes less time than `cargo run` and has all the opinions from `clippy` on how to improve your code.
- `cargo build --timings` (or `cargo run --timings`) will generate a nice report in HTML that shows you how long each crate took when compiling.

By the way, the `--release` part of the command is called a "flag." That means extra information in a command.

Let's finish up this section with a few more useful Cargo commands:

- `cargo clean` removes everything that was generated during the previous times that you compiled your code. When you add crates to Cargo.toml, the computer will download all the files it needs, which can take a lot of space (often a few gigabytes). If you don't want them on your computer anymore, type `cargo clean`. This also cleans up any artifacts (the binaries and related files) generated when compiling your code. You can see this in action, as the /target folder will disappear when you type `cargo clean`.
- `cargo add` followed by a crate name will add the latest version of an external crate to your Cargo.toml file (you can add it to Cargo.toml directly too).
- `cargo doc` will build the documentation for your code. We'll learn about `cargo doc` in just a few pages.

18.2 Working with user input

Now that we have Rust installed, we can work with user input. Generally, there are two ways to do this: while the program is running through `stdin` (that is, through the user's keyboard) and before the program runs through command line arguments.

18.2.1 User input through stdin

The easiest way to take input from the user is with `std::io::stdin`. This is pronounced "standard in," which in this case is the input from the keyboard. With the `stdin()` function, you can get a `Stdin` struct, which is a handle to this input and has a method called `.read_line()` that lets you read the input to a `&mut String`. Here is a simple example of that, which is a loop that continues forever until the user presses the x key. It sort of works, but not quite in the right way. If you are feeling adventurous, try running the code yourself on your computer and think about why it doesn't *quite* work as expected:

```
use std::io;

fn main() {
    println!("Please type something, or x to escape:");
    let mut input_string = String::new();
```

```
    while input_string != "x" {
        input_string.clear();
        io::stdin().read_line(&mut input_string).unwrap();
        println!("You wrote {input_string}");
    }
    println!("See you later!");
}
```

> ◁———————————◁——┐ **First, clear the**
> **String during**
> **every loop.**
> **Then use read_line to** **Otherwise, it will**
> **read the input from the** **just get longer**
> **user into read_string.** **and longer.**

Here is some possible output:

```
Please type something, or x to escape:
something
You wrote something

Something else
You wrote Something else

x
You wrote x

x
You wrote x
```

It takes our input and gives it back, and it even knows that we typed x. But it doesn't exit the program. The only way to get out is by closing the window or by typing Ctrl + C to shut the program down. Did you notice the space after the output that says, "You wrote x"? That's a hint. Let's change the {} to {:?} in println!() to see whether there is any more more information. Doing this shows us what is going on:

```
Please type something, or x to escape:
something
You wrote "something\r\n"
Something else
You wrote "Something else\r\n"
x
You wrote "x\r\n"
x
You wrote "x\r\n"
```

Ah ha! This is because the keyboard input is actually not just something; it is something and the Enter key. When pressing Enter, Windows will add a \r\n (a carriage return and a new line), while other operating systems will add a \n (new line). In either case, we aren't getting a simple x output when we press x to exit the program.

There is an easy method to fix this called .trim(), which removes all the whitespace. Whitespace, by the way, is defined as any of these characters (https://doc.rust-lang.org/reference/whitespace.html):

```
U+0009 (horizontal tab, '\t')
U+000A (line feed, '\n')
U+000B (vertical tab)
U+000C (form feed)
U+000D (carriage return, '\r')
```

```
U+0020 (space, ' ')
U+0085 (next line)
U+200E (left-to-right mark)
U+200F (right-to-left mark)
U+2028 (line separator)
U+2029 (paragraph separator)
```

Using .trim() will turn x\r\n (or x\n) into just x. Now it works:

```
use std::io;

fn main() {
    println!("Please type something, or x to escape:");
    let mut input_string = String::new();

    while input_string.trim() != "x" {
        input_string.clear();
        io::stdin().read_line(&mut input_string).unwrap();
        println!("You wrote {input_string}");
    }
    println!("See you later!");
}
```

Now it will print

```
Please type something, or x to escape:
something
You wrote something

Something
You wrote Something

x
You wrote x

See you later!
```

The std::io module has a lot of other structs (https://doc.rust-lang.org/std/io/index.html#structs) and methods if you need finer control over user input and program output.

With that quick introduction to user input done, let's take a look at another type of user input: input that happens before the program even starts.

18.2.2 *Accessing command-line arguments*

Rust has another kind of user input called std::env::Args. This Args struct holds what the user types when starting the program, known as command-line arguments. There is actually always at least one Arg in a program, no matter what the user types. Let's write a program that only prints them using std::env::args() to see what it is:

```
fn main() {
    println!("{:?}", std::env::args());
}
```

If we type cargo run, it prints something like this:

```
Args { inner: ["target\\debug\\rust_book.exe"] }
```

You can see that Args will always give you the name of the program, no matter what.

Let's give it more input and see what it does. Try typing cargo run but with some extra words. It gives us

```
Args { inner: ["target\\debug\\rust_book.exe", "but", "with", "some",
➡"extra", "words"] }
```

So it looks like every word after cargo run is recognized and can be accessed via this args() method. When we look at the documentation for Args (https://doc.rust-lang.org/std/env/struct.Args.html), we see that it implements IntoIterator, which is quite convenient. So we can just put it in a for loop:

```
use std::env::args;

fn main() {
    let input = args();
    for entry in input {
        println!("You entered: {}", entry);
    }
}
```

Now it says

```
You entered: target\debug\rust_book.exe
You entered: but
You entered: with
You entered: some
You entered: extra
You entered: words
```

Since the first argument is always the program name, you will often want to skip it. We can do that with the .skip() method that all iterators have:

```
use std::env::args;

fn main() {
    let input = args();
    input.skip(1).for_each(|item| {
        println!(
            "You wrote {item}, which in capital letters is {}",
            item.to_uppercase()
        );
    })
}
```

The code will print

```
You wrote but, which in capital letters is BUT
You wrote with, which in capital letters is WITH
You wrote some, which in capital letters is SOME
```

```
You wrote extra, which in capital letters is EXTRA
You wrote words, which in capital letters is WORDS
```

We can do more with these command line arguments inside our program besides print them. They are just strings, so it is easy enough to check to see if any arguments have been entered, and match on them if an argument is found. Here's a small example that either makes letters big (capital) or small (lowercase):

```
use std::env::args;

enum Letters {
    Capitalize,
    Lowercase,
    Nothing,
}

fn main() {
    let mut changes = Letters::Nothing;
    let input = args().collect::<Vec<_>>();

    if let Some(arg) = input.get(1) {
        match arg.as_str() {
            "capital" => changes = Letters::Capitalize,
            "lowercase" => changes = Letters::Lowercase,
            _ => {}
        }
    }

    for word in input.iter().skip(2) {
      match changes {
        Letters::Capitalize => println!("{}", word.to_uppercase()),
        Letters::Lowercase => println!("{}", word.to_lowercase()),
        _ => println!("{}", word)
      }
    }
}
```

Let's look at some examples of input. Try to imagine what will be printed out.

Input: `cargo run please make capitals`:
In this case, it will look at index 1, which is `please`. This input `please` doesn't match `capital` or `lowercase`, so it will print out the remaining words without any change:

```
make capitals
```

Input: `cargo run capital`

In this case, it will match as before, but there is nothing after index 1 to print out, so there is no output.

Now, let's look at some arguments from a user who is starting to figure out how the program works:

Input: `cargo run capital I think I understand now`

```
I
THINK
I
```

```
UNDERSTAND
NOW
```

Input: `cargo run lowercase Does this work too?`

```
does
this
work
too?
```

In practice, command-line arguments are used in a pretty similar way for most command-line interfaces (CLIs). An example of this is `cargo run --help`, which Cargo recognizes as a request to print out a menu to help the user know which commands are available. The main crate used by Rust users to work with command-line arguments is known as clap (CLAP = Command Line Argument Parser; https://docs.rs/clap/latest/clap/), which is highly recommended if you are putting together a CLI that needs to take in a lot of different types of arguments and flags.

18.2.3   *Accessing environment variables*

Besides `Args`, there are also `Vars`, which are environment variables. Those can be seen when using `std::env::args()` and are the basic settings for the operating system and program that the user didn't type in. These variables will include information like URLs.

Even the simplest program will have a lot of environment variables that vary by computer. Using `std::env::vars()` allows you to see them all as a `(String, String)` (a key and a value). Let's take a look at what the `Vars` on the Rust Playground look like:

```rust
fn main() {
    for (key, value) in std::env::vars() {
        println!("{key}: {value}");
    }
}
```

There's quite a bit!

```
CARGO: /playground/.rustup/toolchains/stable-x86_64-unknown-linux-gnu/bin/cargo
CARGO_HOME: /playground/.cargo
CARGO_MANIFEST_DIR: /playground
CARGO_PKG_AUTHORS: The Rust Playground
CARGO_PKG_DESCRIPTION:
CARGO_PKG_HOMEPAGE:
CARGO_PKG_LICENSE:
CARGO_PKG_LICENSE_FILE:
CARGO_PKG_NAME: playground
CARGO_PKG_REPOSITORY:
CARGO_PKG_VERSION: 0.0.1
CARGO_PKG_VERSION_MAJOR: 0
CARGO_PKG_VERSION_MINOR: 0
CARGO_PKG_VERSION_PATCH: 1
CARGO_PKG_VERSION_PRE:
DEBIAN_FRONTEND: noninteractive
HOME: /playground
HOSTNAME: 637927f45315
```

```
LD_LIBRARY_PATH: /playground/target/debug/build/libsqlite3-sys-
➡7c00a5831fa0c673/out:/playground/target/debug/build/ring-
➡c92344ea3efaac76/out:/playground/target/debug/deps:/playground/target
➡/debug:/playground/.rustup/toolchains/stable-x86_64-unknown-linux-
➡gnu/lib/rustlib/x86_64-unknown-linux-gnu/lib:/playground
➡/.rustup/toolchains/stable-x86_64-unknown-linux-gnu/lib
➡PATH: /playground/.cargo/bin:/usr/local/sbin:/usr/local/bin:/usr
➡/sbin:/usr/bin:/sbin:/bin
PLAYGROUND_EDITION: 2021
PLAYGROUND_TIMEOUT: 10
PWD: /playground
RUSTUP_HOME: /playground/.rustup
RUSTUP_TOOLCHAIN: stable-x86_64-unknown-linux-gnu
RUST_RECURSION_COUNT: 1
SHLVL: 1
SSL_CERT_DIR: /usr/lib/ssl/certs
SSL_CERT_FILE: /usr/lib/ssl/certs/ca-certificates.crt
USER: playground
_: /usr/bin/timeout
```

Environment variables can also be set while a program is running using `std::env::set_var()`. The following code will add an extra key and value for each existing key and value, except with an exclamation mark at the end:

```
fn main() {
    for (mut key, mut value) in std::env::vars() {
        key.push('!');
        value.push('!');
        std::env::set_var(key, value);
    }
    for (key, value) in std::env::vars() {
        println!("{key}: {value}");
    }
}
```

The output will show that there are now twice as many environment variables, half of which have exclamation marks everywhere. Here is part of the output:

```
CARGO!: /playground/.rustup/toolchains/stable-x86_64-unknown-linux-gnu/bin/
    cargo!
CARGO_HOME!: /playground/.cargo!
CARGO_MANIFEST_DIR!: /playground!
CARGO_PKG_AUTHORS!: The Rust Playground!
```

Now, let's take a look at a more real example of `set_var()`.

Programs often send logging information to an external service that displays the data in a nice format that makes it easy to understand. Most logging in Rust uses the RUST_LOG environment variable to keep track of how detailed logs should be. The five main logging levels are

- TRACE (maximum level of detail)
- DEBUG (detailed information)
- INFO (general information)

- WARN (something to keep an eye on)
- ERROR (actual errors)

You can see these logging levels in crates like `env_logger` (https://docs.rs/env_logger/latest/env_logger/).

Services are generally first deployed to a Dev environment for developers to work on and test, in which case RUST_LOG will be set to DEBUG, or maybe even TRACE. Then, when the developers are more confident in the service, they will move it to Prod (production), which will probably use a quieter logging level like INFO—but not always.

The following code represents a case where an app starting up will first check for RUST_LOG, and if nothing is set, will check to see if some other environment variable (we'll call it "LOGGER_URL") shows a url to send logging information to. If the LOGGER_URL matches the dev url, it will assume that the logging level is DEBUG, and if LOGGER_URL matches the prod url, it will assume that the logging level is INFO. And if neither of these can be found, then RUST_LOG will be set to INFO:

```
use std::env;
const DEV_URL: &str = "www.somedevurl.com";
const PROD_URL: &str = "www.someprodurl.com";

fn main() {
    match std::env::var("RUST_LOG") {
        Ok(log) => println!("Logging at {log} level"),
        Err(_) => match std::env::var("LOGGER_URL") {
            Ok(url) if url == DEV_URL => {
                println!("Dev url indicated, defaulting to debug");
                env::set_var("RUST_LOG", "DEBUG");
            }
            Ok(url) if url == PROD_URL => {
                println!("Prod url indicated, defaulting to info");
                env::set_var("RUST_LOG", "INFO");
            }
            _ => {
                println!("No valid url indicated, defaulting to info");
                env::set_var("RUST_LOG", "INFO");
            }
        },
    }
}
```

If run on the Playground, you will see this output, showing that the environment variable hasn't been set:

```
No valid url indicated, defaulting to info
```

You probably didn't find this section particularly difficult. Working with user input usually involves more thinking about how your software works than writing code that you need to work hard at to compile. There are, of course, many other forms of user input. The last two chapters of the book include working with instantaneous user input (e.g., keyboard presses), so feel free to take a look at those chapters if you are curious and want to know now.

18.3   *Using files*

With Rust installed on the computer, we can now start working with files. You will notice that a lot of this code involves working with Results. This makes sense, as many things can go wrong when it comes to working with files. A file might not even exist, maybe the computer can't read it, or you might not have permission to access it. All of these possible things that can go wrong make the ? operator really handy when working with files.

18.3.1   *Creating files*

Let's try working with files for the first time. The `std::fs` module contains methods for working with files, and with the `std::io::Write` trait in scope, you can write to them. With that, we can use `.write_all()` to write into the file. Here is a simple example that creates a file and writes some data to it:

```
use std::fs;
use std::io::Write;

fn main() -> std::io::Result<()> {
    let mut file = fs::File::create("myfilename.txt")?;
    file.write_all(b"Let's put this in the file")?;
    Ok(())
}
```

Creates a file with this name. Be careful! If you have a file with this name already, it will be deleted.

Files take bytes, so don't forget the b in front.

Then, if you click on the new file `myfilename.txt`, you can see the `Let's put this in the file` text inside.

We don't even need to use two lines to do this, though, thanks to the question mark operator. It will pass on the result we want if it works, kind of like when you chain methods on an iterator:

```
use std::fs;
use std::io::Write;

fn main() -> std::io::Result<()> {
    fs::File::create("myfilename.txt")?
        .write_all(b"Let's put this in the file")?;
    Ok(())
}
```

In fact, there is also a function that does both of these things together. It's called `std::fs::write()`. Inside it, you give it the file name you want and the content you want to put inside. Again, careful! It will delete everything in that file if it already exists. It even lets you write a `&str` without b in front because `write()` takes anything that implements `AsRef<[u8]>` and `str` implements `AsRef<[u8]>`:

```
pub fn write<P: AsRef<Path>, C: AsRef<[u8]>>(path: P, contents: C) -> Result<()>
```

This makes it very simple:

```
use std::fs;

fn main() -> std::io::Result<()> {
    fs::write("calvin_with_dad.txt",
```

```
"Calvin: Dad, how come old photographs are always black and white? Didn't
    they have color film back then?
Dad: Sure they did. In fact, those photographs are in color. It's just the
    world was black and white then.")?;
    Ok(())
}
```

18.3.2   *Opening existing files*

Opening a file is just as easy as creating one. You just use open() instead of create(). After that (if the program finds your file), you can use methods like read_to_ string(), which lets you read the contents of a file into a String. It looks like this:

```
use std::fs;
use std::fs::File;                  ┐  This is to use the function
use std::io::Read;       ◁───────┘  .read_to_string().

fn main() -> std::io::Result<()> {
    fs::write("calvin_with_dad.txt",
"Calvin: Dad, how come old photographs are always black and white? Didn't
➥they have color film back then?
Dad: Sure they did. In fact, those photographs are in color. It's just the
➥world was black and white then.")?;                      ┐ Opens the file
                                                           │ we just made
    let mut calvin_file = File::open("calvin_with_dad.txt")?;  ◁──┘
    let mut calvin_string = String::new();          ◁────────◁──── ┐ This String
    calvin_file.read_to_string(&mut calvin_string)?;              │ will hold the
    calvin_string.split_whitespace().for_each(|word| print!("{} ",│ contents of
        word.to_uppercase()));          ◁─────┐                   │ the file.
    Ok(())            ┌──────────────────────┐ │  Reads the file into the
}            Now that we have it as a String, we'll │   String using the
          capitalize the whole thing just for fun. │  read_to_string method
```

That will print

```
CALVIN: DAD, HOW COME OLD PHOTOGRAPHS ARE ALWAYS BLACK AND WHITE? DIDN'T
➥THEY HAVE COLOR FILM BACK THEN? DAD: SURE THEY DID. IN FACT, THOSE
➥PHOTOGRAPHS ARE IN COLOR. IT'S JUST THE WORLD WAS BLACK AND WHITE
➥THEN.
```

18.3.3   *Using OpenOptions to work with files*

What if we only want to create a file if there is no other file with the same name? This would let us avoid deleting any existing files when trying to make a new one. The std::fs module has a struct called OpenOptions that lets us do this, along with other custom behavior.

Interestingly, we've been using OpenOptions all this time and didn't even know it. The source code for File::open() shows us the OpenOptions struct being used to open a file:

```
pub fn open<P: AsRef<Path>>(path: P) -> io::Result<File> {
        OpenOptions::new().read(true).open(path.as_ref())
    }
```

That looks familiar! It's the builder pattern that we learned in chapter 15. The same pattern shows up inside the File::create() method:

```
pub fn create<P: AsRef<Path>>(path: P) -> io::Result<File> {
    OpenOptions::new().write(true).create(true).truncate(true).open(path.as_ref
    ➦())
    }
```

So, it looks like OpenOptions has a lot of methods to set whether to carry out certain actions when working with files. If you go to the documentation page for OpenOptions (https://doc.rust-lang.org/std/fs/struct.OpenOptions.html), you can see all the methods that you can choose from. Most take a bool:

- .append()—To add to the content that's already there instead of deleting.
- .create()—This lets OpenOptions create a file.
- .create_new()—Only creates a file if it's not there already, failing otherwise.
- .read()—Set this to true if you want it to be able to read a file.
- .truncate()—Set this to true if you want to cut the file content to 0 (delete the contents) when you open it.
- .write()—Allows writing to a file.

Then, at the end, you use .open() with the filename, and that will give you a Result.

Since Rust 1.58, you can access this OpenOptions struct directly from File through a method called options(). In the next example, we will make an OpenOptions with File::options(). Then we will give it the ability to write. After that, we'll set .create_new() to true and try to open the file we made. It won't work, which is what we want:

```
use std::fs::{write, File};

fn main() -> std::io::Result<()> {
    write("calvin_with_dad.txt",
"Calvin: Dad, how come old photographs are always black and white? Didn't
➦they have color film back then?
Dad: Sure they did. In fact, those photographs are in color. It's just the
➦world was black and white then.")?;

    let calvin_file = File::options()
        .write(true)
        .create_new(true)
        .open("calvin_with_dad.txt")?;
    Ok(())
}
```

The error shows us that the file already exists, so the program exits with an error:

```
Error: Os { code: 80, kind: AlreadyExists, message: "The file exists." }
```

Next, let's try using .append() so we can write to an existing file. We'll also use the write! macro this time, which is yet another option available to us. We saw this macro before when implementing Display for our structs:

```
use std::fs::{read_to_string, write, File};
use std::io::Write;

fn main() -> std::io::Result<()> {
```

```
    write("calvin_with_dad.txt",
"Calvin: Dad, how come old photographs are always black and white? Didn't
➡they have color film back then?
Dad: Sure they did. In fact, those photographs are in color. It's just the
➡world was black and white then.")?;

    let mut calvin_file = File::options()
        .append(true)
        .read(true)
        .open("calvin_with_dad.txt")?;
    calvin_file.write_all(b"Calvin: Really?\n")?;
    write!(&mut calvin_file, "Dad: Yep. The world didn't turn color until
➡sometime in the 1930s...\n")?;
    println!("{}", read_to_string("calvin_with_dad.txt")?);
    Ok(())
}
```

Thanks to the ability to append, the file now holds a bit more of the conversation between Calvin and his dad:

```
Calvin: Dad, how come old photographs are always black and white? Didn't
➡they have color film back then?
Dad: Sure they did. In fact, those photographs are in color. It's just the
➡world was black and white then.
Calvin: Really?
Dad: Yep. The world didn't turn color until sometimes in the 1930s...
```

Finally, Rust has a convenient macro called `include_str!` that simply pulls the contents of a file into a `&'static str` at compile time—right into the binary. If the file can't be found, the program won't compile. This next sample will simply take the contents of `main.rs` and print it out:

```
fn main() {
    // Text, text, text
    let main = include_str!("main.rs");
    println!("Here's what main.rs looks like:\n\n{main}");
}
```

So the `include_str!` macro not only gives compile-time checking and a file conveniently located in memory but also increases the size of the binary. For example, try copying the contents of Bram Stoker's *Dracula* (https://www.gutenberg.org/files/345/345-h/345-h.htm) into a file, use `include_str!()`, and then type `cargo build`. The file size inside the `target/debug` directory should be about 999 KB. But if you use `std::fs::read_to_string()` instead, you will have to access the file and handle the error (or unwrap) at run time, but the file size should be a much smaller 166 KB. In other words, the `include` part of the name of the macro refers to including the content inside the binary:

```
fn main() {
    let content = include_str!("dracula.txt");        ⟵┤ 999 KB
    // let content = std::fs::read_to_string("dracula.txt").unwrap();   ⟵┤ 166 KB
}
```

As you can see, opening and writing to files isn't particularly difficult. Just be careful that you don't end up deleting existing files when creating a new one. Starting with `File::options()` is good default behavior to make sure that you are reviewing how you want your program to react when it comes across files with the same name.

18.4   *cargo doc*

You might have noticed that Rust documentation looks almost the same whether the code is from the standard library or someone else's external crate. The left side of the documentation shows structs and traits, code examples are on the right, and so on in pretty much every crate you can find. This is because you can automatically make documentation just by typing `cargo doc`, and this convenience leads to almost everyone using it.

Even making a project with just a simple struct or two can help you learn about traits in Rust. For example, here are two structs that do almost nothing and nothing else:

```
pub struct DoesNothing {}
pub struct PrintThing {}

impl PrintThing {
    pub fn prints_something() {
        println!("I am printing something");
    }
}
```

With just two empty structs and one method, you would think that `cargo doc` would generate just the struct names and one method. But if you type `cargo doc --open` (`--open` will open up the documentation in your browser once it is done), you can see a lot more information than you expected. The front page looks like figure 18.5, which does look fairly empty.

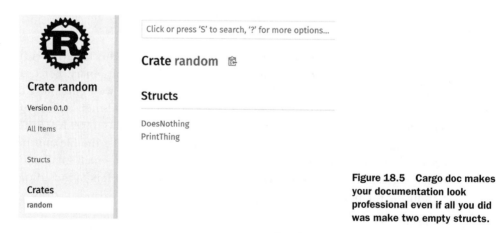

Figure 18.5   Cargo doc makes your documentation look professional even if all you did was make two empty structs.

But if you click on one of the structs, it will show you a lot of traits that you didn't think were there. If you click on the `DoesNothing` struct, it will show us quite a few traits even though we didn't type a single word of code to implement them. First, we see a number of traits that are automatically implemented:

```
Auto Trait Implementations
impl RefUnwindSafe for DoesNothing
impl Send for DoesNothing
impl Sync for DoesNothing
impl Unpin for DoesNothing
impl UnwindSafe for DoesNothing
```

And after that come some blanket implementations, which we learned about in the last chapter:

```
Blanket Implementations
impl<T> Any for T where T: 'static + ?Sized,
impl<T> Borrow<T> for T where T: ?Sized,
impl<T> BorrowMut<T> for T where T: ?Sized,
impl<T> From<T> for T
impl<T, U> Into<U> for T where U: From<T>,
impl<T, U> TryFrom<U> for T where U: Into<T>,
impl<T, U> TryInto<U> for T where U: TryFrom<T>
```

Then, if we add some documentation comments with `///` you can see them when you type `cargo doc`. Here is the same code with a few comments above each struct and method:

```
/// This is a struct that does nothing
pub struct DoesNothing {}

/// This struct only has one method.
pub struct PrintThing {}

impl PrintThing {
    /// This function just prints a message.
    pub fn prints_something() {
        println!("I am printing something");
    }
}
```

These comments will now show up in the documentation (figure 18.6).

Figure 18.6 Structs with comments added

When you click on `PrintThing`, it will show this struct's methods as well (figure 18.7).

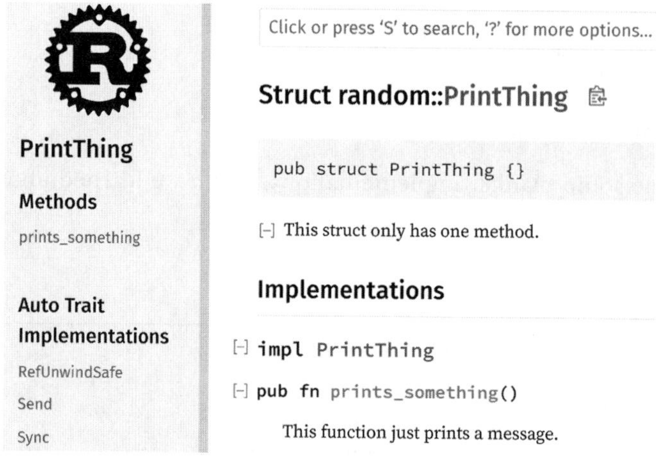

PrintThing

Methods

prints_something

Auto Trait Implementations

RefUnwindSafe

Send

Sync

Click or press 'S' to search, '?' for more options...

Struct random::PrintThing 📋

```
pub struct PrintThing {}
```

[-] This struct only has one method.

Implementations

[-] `impl PrintThing`

[-] `pub fn prints_something()`

This function just prints a message.

Figure 18.7   Showing methods via `PrintThing`

`cargo doc` is particularly nice when using a lot of external code. Because these crates are all on different websites, it can take some time to search them all. But if you use `cargo doc`, you will have them all in the same place on your hard drive. If you don't want to document all the external code, you can pass in a `--no-deps` (no dependencies) flag, which will only compile your code.

Cargo is one of the main reasons for Rust's popularity as a language, and after this chapter, you can probably see why. It allows you to start a project, build your code, document it, check it, add external crates, and much more. With Rust and Cargo installed by now, we were also able to take in user input and command-line arguments for the first time and work with files.

With Rust installed, we can also start to do HTTP requests, and in the next chapter, we will do just that with the `reqwest` crate that we first saw in the last chapter. Not only will we learn how the crate works, but it will also give us our first introduction to async Rust: Rust code that doesn't block its thread while doing some work. We'll also learn how to use feature flags to only take in part of an external crate, allowing us to shorten compile time a little.

Summary

- Use `cargo check` when building your code to see if it compiles, and `cargo run` to test it out. Don't forget that it won't be optimized for speed unless you build with the `--release` flag!
- If you are curious whether code is being optimized, try using Godbolt on different optimization levels. Even without knowing assembly, you can get a general sense of what is happening on a lower level.

- Debug printing a `String` will give more insight into what actual input is being passed in when working with user input. Display output looks cleaner but may hide some important information.
- `Args` are arguments passed in on the command line, while `Vars` are the environment variables that have to do with overall configuration. An example of an argument is `--open` for `cargo doc`, and an example of an environment variable is `RUST_BACKTRACE` that we saw in chapter 14.
- Be sure to take extra care when working with files, and use `File::options()` unless you are absolutely sure that no files will be unknowingly deleted when creating a new one.
- Make use of the `cargo doc --open` command a lot if you are writing open source code for other people to use. This will show you right away how well documented your code is to someone reading it for the first time.

19

More crates and
async Rust

This chapter covers

- Another external crate: `reqwest`
- Using feature flags to compile part of a crate
- Using async Rust for code that doesn't block

In this chapter, we will finally get around to using the `reqwest` crate. As you read through this chapter, you'll soon see why we didn't learn it until now: it's because the `reqwest` crate is the first one we have encountered that involves async Rust! Well, sort of. Read on to find out.

While we're at it, we'll also learn about feature flags, which let you bring in just part of an external crate and thereby help keep compilation time down.

19.1 The reqwest crate

Back in chapter 17, we had a code sample that included a Client (http://mng.bz/mjv4) from the `reqwest` crate in one of our structs. We didn't use it at the time because (among other reasons) the Rust Playground doesn't allow you to make HTTP requests. The code looked like this:

```
use reqwest::Client;

struct Logger {
    logs: Vec<Log>,
    url: String,
    client: Client,
}
```

Let's simplify this even more by removing the `Logger` struct and just creating a `Client`:

```
use reqwest::Client;

fn main() {
    let client = Client::default();
}
```

That was easy. So how do we use it? We can use our Client to `.post()` data, `.get()` it, `.delete()`, and so on. The easiest method to use is `.get()`. With this, we can ask a server to give you the HTML for a website or a response in a form like JSON from a server. The `.get()` method is pretty simple:

```
pub fn get<U: IntoUrl>(&self, url: U) -> RequestBuilder
```

This `IntoUrl` trait is one that the `reqwest` crate made, not the standard library, so you don't have to remember it. But you can guess from the name that `IntoUrl` means anything that can become a URL, and it's implemented for both `&str` and `String`. In other words, we can use `.get()` and stick a website URL inside. The `.get()` method gives us a `RequestBuilder`, which is a struct that has a lot of configuration methods like `.timeout()`, `.body()`, `.headers()`, and so on. But one of them is called `.send()`, and since we don't need to configure anything in particular to use it, that's the one we want.

Let's give it a try:

```
use reqwest::Client;

fn main() {
    let client = Client::default();
    client.get("https://www.rust-lang.org").send().unwrap();
}
```

Surprisingly, we get a cryptic error!

```
no method named `unwrap` found for opaque type `impl Future<Output =
➥Result<Response, reqwest::Error>>` in the current scope
  --> src\main.rs:5:52
   |
5  |         client.get("https://www.rust-lang.org").send().unwrap();
   |                                                         ^^^^^^ method not
   ➥found in `impl Future<Output = Result<Response, reqwest::Error>>`
```

```
 |
help: consider `await`ing on the `Future` and calling the method on its
➡ `Output`
 |
5 |        client.get("https://www.rust-lang.org").send().await.unwrap();
 |                                                          ++++++
```

It seems to be returning a type called `impl Future<Output = Result<Response,` `reqwest::Error>>`! The `Future` trait is used in async Rust, which we haven't learned yet. We'll learn about this return type in the next section and see what `Future` and async mean. But in the meantime, let's go back to the main page of `reqwest` and see if it can help. On the page, we see the following information:

The `reqwest::Client` is asynchronous. For applications wishing to only make
➡ a few HTTP requests, the `reqwest::blocking` API may be more convenient.

Okay, so it looks like there is a so-called "blocking" Client that isn't async. We still have no idea what async is, but the documentation suggests a blocking Client as an option, so we'll go with that. The blocking Client can be found at `reqwest::blocking::Client`, so we'll give it a try.

However, the message here has given us a hint about what async is because we have seen the word *blocking* in places like the `.lock()` method for `Mutex`, which "acquires a mutex, blocking the current thread until it is able to do so" (http://mng.bz/5o7a). So it's reasonable to assume that blocking means blocking the current thread. And if regular Rust is *blocking* (operations block the thread until they are done), then async Rust must be *non-blocking* (they don't block the thread). But more on that later. Let's try the blocking `Client`:

```
fn main() {
    let client = reqwest::blocking::Client::default();
    client.get("https://www.rust-lang.org").send();
}
```

What? Another cryptic error!

```
error[E0433]: failed to resolve: could not find `blocking` in `reqwest`
 --> src\main.rs:2:37
 |
2 |        let client = reqwest::blocking::Client::default();
 |                               ^^^^^^ not found in
➡ `reqwest::blocking`
 |
help: consider importing this struct
 |
1 | use reqwest::Client;
 |
help: if you import `Client`, refer to it directly
 |
2 -        let client = reqwest::blocking::Client::default();
2 +        let client = Client::default();
 |
```

Now, this is certainly odd. The blocking Client is right there in the documentation (http://mng.bz/5oda), clear as day. But why can't the compiler find it? To find out, we'll take a very short detour and learn what feature flags are.

19.2   Feature flags

Rust code can sometimes take a while to compile. To try to reduce this as much as possible, a lot of crates use something called feature flags, which let you compile just a part of the crate. Crates that use flags have some code enabled by default, and if you want to add more functionality, you have to indicate them inside `Cargo.toml`.

We didn't need to do this in the Playground because the Playground has all features enabled for every crate. But in our own projects, we don't want to spend time compiling things we won't use and must be more selective when it comes to which features we want to enable.

This is where the problem came up in the previous section: as far as Rust is concerned, if a feature flag isn't enabled, the code doesn't exist. When we tried to create a blocking `Client`, there simply wasn't any code for the compiler to look at, which is why there was no nice error message suggesting that we enable the feature flag. Because for the compiler to give a nice error message, it would first need to pull in the code, and if it pulled in the code, that would increase compile time, which nobody wants. The end result is that Rust users sometimes need to look at the source code directly to see whether a feature is hidden behind a feature flag.

Let's try using the command `cargo add reqwest` again. This command adds the `reqwest` crate but also shows which features are enabled, which is particularly useful here. The features that are enabled by default have a + to the left, and those that aren't enabled have a - instead. One of them is called `blocking`:

```
Adding reqwest v0.11.18 to dependencies.
        Features:
        + __tls
        + default-tls
        + hyper-tls
        + native-tls-crate
        + tokio-native-tls
        - __internal_proxy_sys_no_cache
        - __rustls
        - async-compression
        - blocking
        - brotli
        - cookie_crate
        - cookie_store
        - cookies
        - deflate
        - gzip
        - hyper-rustls
        - json
        - mime_guess
        - multipart
        - native-tls
```

```
- native-tls-alpn
- native-tls-vendored
- proc-macro-hack
- rustls
- rustls-native-certs
- rustls-pemfile
- rustls-tls
- rustls-tls-manual-roots
- rustls-tls-native-roots
- rustls-tls-webpki-roots
- serde_json
- socks
- stream
- tokio-rustls
- tokio-socks
- tokio-util
- trust-dns
- trust-dns-resolver
- webpki-roots
```

Now you can see why most features aren't enabled by default. All we want to do is make a simple HTTP request, and we certainly don't want to bring in code for `cookies`, `gzip`, `cookie_store`, `socks`, and so on.

To see feature flags in the documentation, click on the Feature Flags button on the top near the center. The page begins as follows:

```
reqwest
This version has 42 feature flags, 5 of them enabled by default.

default:
default-tls

default-tls:
hyper-tls
native-tls-crate
__tls
tokio-native-tls
... (and many others)
```

It has a flag called `default-tls` that enables four other flags. Fine, but how do we get the blocking Client? With `cargo add`, it's pretty easy. Change `cargo add reqwest` to `cargo add reqwest --feature blocking`, and now it will be there. Or, inside Cargo .toml, you can manually change it from

```
reqwest = "0.11.22"
```

to

```
reqwest = { version = "0.11.22", features = ["blocking"] }
```

Besides looking at the documentation, you can also find out whether a feature is behind a feature flag by looking through the source code for the attribute `#[cfg(feature = "feature_name")]`. You'll usually find this in a crate's lib.rs file where the module declarations are. A sample from the `reqwest` crate (http://mng.bz/vPy4) shows the exact location where the blocking feature is being hidden behind a feature flag:

```
async_impl;
cfg(feature = "blocking")]
mod blocking;
connect;
cfg(feature = "cookies")]
mod cookie;
mod dns;
proxy;
mod redirect;
cfg(feature = "__tls")]
mod tls;
util;
```

In short, if Rust can't find something, check to see whether there's a feature flag for it.

Armed with this knowledge, we can get back to the blocking Client. With the feature enabled, this code no longer gives an error:

```
fn main() {
    let client = reqwest::blocking::Client::default();
    client.get("https://www.rust-lang.org").send();
}
```

The compiler warns us that there is a `Result` we haven't used. We'll just unwrap for now. That gives us a struct called a `Response`—the response to our `.get()`. The `Response` struct (http://mng.bz/6n8A) has its own methods, too, like `.status()`, `.content_length()`, and so on, but the one we are interested in is `.text()`: it gives a `Result<String>`. Let's unwrap that and print it out:

```
fn main() {
    let client = reqwest::blocking::Client::default();
    let response = client.get("https://www.rust-lang.org").send().unwrap();
    println!("{}", response.text().unwrap());
}
```

Success! Our output starts with this:

```
<!doctype html>
<html lang="en-US">
  <head>
    <meta charset="utf-8">
    <title>


            Rust Programming Language

        </title>
    <meta name="viewport" content="width=device-width,initial-scale=1.0">
    <meta name="description" content="A language empowering everyone to
➥build reliable and efficient software.">
```

And much, much more. It gave us the text of the whole home page.

If you are using `reqwest`, you probably already know what you want to use it for, so take a look around the documentation to see what fits your needs. If you want to post something in JSON format, for example, you can use a method called `.json()` (http://mng.bz/orQp). At least here, it lets us know that it is behind a feature flag:

```
Available on crate feature json only.
```

So, that was `reqwest`, or at least part of it. However, the Client on `reqwest` is async by default, so it looks like it's time to learn what `async` is about.

19.3 Async Rust

We saw that regular Rust code will block the thread it is in while waiting. Async Rust is the opposite of regular Rust code because it doesn't block. The `reqwest` crate is the perfect example of why async Rust is often used: What if you send a `get` or a `post` that takes a long time? Rust code is extremely fast, but if you have to wait around for a server somewhere to respond, you aren't getting the full benefits of the speed Rust offers. One of the solutions to that is `async`, namely allowing other parts of the code to take care of other tasks while you wait. Let's see how this is done.

19.3.1 Async basics

async Rust is possible through a trait called `Future`. (Some languages have something similar and call it a "promise," but the underlying structure is different.) The `Future` trait is well named as it refers to a value that will be available *at some time in the future*. The "future" might be 1 microsecond away (in other words, basically instantaneous), or it might be 10 seconds away.

The `Future` trait is interesting as it looks sort of like `Option`. If a `Future` is `Ready`, it will have a value inside, and if it's still `Pending` (not ready), there will naturally be no value to access:

```
pub enum Poll<T> {
    Ready(T),
    Pending,
}
```

Here is the signature for the trait:

```
pub trait Future {
    type Output;
    fn poll(self: Pin<&mut Self>, cx: &mut Context<'_>) ->
    ➥Poll<Self::Output>;
}
```

`Pin` is used to pin the memory in place, the reasons for which are explained quite well in the book *Asynchronous Programming in Rust* (http://mng.bz/n1m2). But a deep understanding of `Pin` isn't necessary to use `async` in Rust, so feel free to ignore it for the time being unless you are really curious.

What is important is that there is an associated type called `Output` and that the main method in `async` is called `poll`—in other words, to check whether it's ready. We'll look at `poll` in more detail shortly.

The first big difference you'll notice in `async` is that functions begin with `async fn` instead of `fn`. Interestingly, though, the return types look the same!

```
fn give_8() -> u8 {
    8
}

async fn async_give_8() -> u8 {
    8
}
```

Both functions return a `u8` but in different ways. The `fn` function returns one right away, but the `async fn` returns something that *will* be a `u8` when it's done. Maybe it'll be done right away, or maybe it won't. And because it's `async`, if it's not done yet, your code can do other work as it waits.

Rust is actually hiding something here. An `async_give_8() -> u8` is not returning just a `u8`. Let's use our trusty method to see the true type by making the compiler mad via a method that doesn't exist:

```
async fn async_give_8() -> u8 {
    8
}

fn main() {
    let y = async_give_8();
    y.thoethoe(); //
}
```

Gets the output from async_give_8

Makes up a method that doesn't exist to see the error

Here's the error:

```
error[E0599]: no method named `thoethoe` found for opaque type `impl
Future<Output = u8>` in the current scope
  --> src/main.rs:12:7
   |
12 |     y.thoethoe();
   |       ^^^^^^^^ method not found in `impl Future<Output = u8>`
```

So there's the type. It's not a `u8`, it's an `impl Future<Output = u8>`! That's the actual type signature that Rust hides from us. The makers of async Rust decided that this would be better than making people type `impl Future<Output = u8>` all the time.

19.3.2 *Checking whether a Future is ready*

Now comes the `poll` method. Poll means to ask whether a `Future` is ready and, if it's not ready, to come back later to check again. The main way to poll a future in Rust is by adding the `.await` keyword, which gets the *run time* to handle the polling. (More on what an `async` run time is in the next section.) And every time a future is polled, it will return one of two things:

- `Poll::Pending`—if it's not ready
- `Poll::Ready(val)`—if it's ready

This is the part that looks like `Option`:

- `Option` has `None` if there's nothing, while `poll` has `Pending` if there's nothing yet. `None` isn't holding a value, and neither is `Pending`.
- `Option` has `Some(T)` if there's something, while `poll` has `Ready(T)` if the `Future` is ready. `Some` holds a value and so does `Pending`.

Okay, let's give it a try. We'll add `.await` to try to turn this `impl Future<Output = u8>` into an actual `u8`. There's no complex code inside the function, so the `poll` should resolve right away:

```
async fn async_give_8() -> u8 {
    8
}

fn main() {
    let some_number = async_give_8().await;
}
```

It doesn't work yet! This is why:

```
error[E0728]: `await` is only allowed inside `async` functions and blocks
  --> src/main.rs:6:37
   |
5  | fn main() {
   |    ---- this is not `async`
6  |     let some_number = async_give_8().await;
   |                                      ^^^^^^ only allowed inside `async`
   ➥functions and blocks
```

Ah, so `.await` can only be used inside a function or block that has the `async` keyword. And since we are trying to use `.await` in `main`, which is a function, `main` should be an `async fn`, too. Let's try it again. Change `fn main()` to `async fn main()`:

```
error[E0752]: `main` function is not allowed to be `async`
  --> src/main.rs:5:1
   |
5  | async fn main() {
   | ^^^^^^^^^^^^^^^^ `main` function is not allowed to be `async`
```

What?!

On second thought, this sort of makes sense because main can only return a `()`, a `Result`, or an `ExitStatus` (http://mng.bz/n152). But an `async fn` returns a `Future`, which is not one of those three return types. Plus, if main returned a `Future`, wouldn't that mean that something else would have to call `.await` on that `Future`? Where does it end?

On top of this, remember how `.await` polls a future and then comes back later to ask again if it's not ready yet? Who decides this? The answer to both of these is that you need an `async` run time, something that takes care of all of this. Rust doesn't have an official `async` run time, but as of 2023, almost everything uses a crate called Tokio (https://tokio.rs/). It's not the official run time, but everybody uses it, and it can be thought of as Rust's default `async` run time.

19.3.3 *Using an async run time*

After all this explaining, fortunately, the solution is quite simple: you can make `main` into an `async main` through Tokio by adding `#[tokio::main]` above it. Do this, and the code will work:

```
use tokio;

async fn async_give_8() -> u8 {
    8
}

#[tokio::main]
async fn main() {
    let some_number = async_give_8().await;
}
```

The Playground enables all feature flags by default automatically so this code will run as is, while on your computer, you need to enable two feature flags: "macros" to bring in the macro above main and "rt-multi-thread" to enable Tokio's multithreaded run time. All together, adding this to Cargo.toml will make the code compile: tokio = { version = "1.35.0", features = ["macros", "rt-multi-thread"]}.

Now `some_number` ends up as a regular `u8`, and the program finishes.

So how does `async` suddenly, magically work without needing to poll `main`? Tokio does this by invisibly making a scope inside `main` where it does all of its `async` work. After it's done, it exits and goes back into the regular main function, and the program exits. It's sort of a fake `async main`, but for our purposes it's real.

In fact, we can see this in the Playground by clicking on Tools > Expand Macros. Let's see what this `async fn main()` actually is! We'll use almost the same code but add an extra `.await` and print out the result:

```
use tokio;

async fn async_give_8() -> u8 {
    8
}

#[tokio::main]
async fn main() {
    let some_number = async_give_8().await;
    let second_number = async_give_8().await;
    println!("{some_number}, {second_number}");
}
```

Here is the expanded code (with unrelated parts removed):

```
use tokio;

async fn async_give_8() -> u8 {
    8
}
```

```
                         ┌─── Look here—async fn is a lie! It's actually just a
                         │    regular fn main(). As far as Rust is concerned,
fn main() {    ◁─────────┘    the main() function is not async at all.
    let body = async {                          ◁──┐
        let some_number = async_give_8().await;    │  First, everything gets enclosed inside a
        let second_number = async_give_8().await;  │  big async block called body. The .await
        {                                          │  keyword can be used inside here.
            ::std::io::_print(format_args!("{0}, {1}\n", some_number,
            ⮑second_number));
        };
    };
                                                Now the Tokio run time starts.
                                                It uses the builder pattern to
    {                                              set some configuration.
        return tokio::runtime::Builder::new_multi_thread()
            .enable_all()                                       ◁──┐
            .build()                                               │
            .expect("Failed building the Runtime")                 │
            .block_on(body);                        ◁──────────┐
    }                         And, finally, the part that matters: a method
}                                  called block_on(). Tokio is actually just
                                 blocking until everything has been resolved!
```

So, at the end of the day, an `async fn main()` is just a regular `fn main()` that Tokio manages by blocking until everything inside has run to completion. And when it's done, it returns whatever the output of the `async` block is, and `fn main()`, along with the entire program, is also done.

These are the main points when getting started with `async`:

- You need to be inside an `async fn` or an `async` block to use the `.await` keyword.
- Type `.await` to turn output into a concrete type again. (You don't need to manually use the `poll` method.)
- You need a run time to manage the polling, which usually means adding `#[tokio::main]`.
- Regular functions can't await `async` functions, so if you have a regular function that needs to call an `async` function, it will become async, too. So once you start to use `async` you'll see a lot of your other functions becoming async, too.
- `async` functions can call regular functions. This is usually no problem, but remember that regular functions will block the thread until they are done.

Knowing this, let's try `reqwest` again. This time, we are finally using the default Client, which is `async`. Knowing what we know, it's now pretty easy:

```
use reqwest;
use tokio;

#[tokio::main]
async fn main() {
    let client = reqwest::Client::default();
    let response = client
        .get("https://www.rust-lang.org")
        .send()
```

```
        .await
        .unwrap();
    println!("{}", response.text().await.unwrap());
}
```

See the difference? Each async function has an `.await` after it. And here we are just unwrapping, but in real code, you would want to handle errors properly, which usually means using the `?` operator. That's why you see `.await?` everywhere in async code.

19.3.4 *Some other details about async Rust*

You might have noticed that we still haven't used async Rust in a very async way just yet. So far, our code has just used `.await` to resolve values before moving on to the next line. Technically, this isn't a problem, as the code still compiles and works just fine. But to take advantage of async Rust, we'll need to set up our code to poll many futures at the same time. One of the ways to do this is by using the `join!` macro.

First, let's look at an example that doesn't use this macro. We'll make a function that uses `rand` to wait a bit and then return a u8. Inside `tokio` is an async function called `sleep()` that results in a non-blocking sleep—in this case, between 1 and 100 milliseconds. (We'll learn about `sleep()` and `Duration` in the next section.) After the sleep is over, it gives the number. Then we'll get three numbers and see what order we get them in:

```
use std::time::Duration;
use rand::*;
use tokio::time::sleep;                    ◄————————    This function is behind another
                                                        feature flag called "time," so add
async fn wait_and_give_u8(num: u8) -> u8 {              that to Cargo.toml if you are
    let mut rng = rand::thread_rng();                   running this code on your computer.
    let wait_time = rng.gen_range(1..100);
    sleep(Duration::from_millis(wait_time)).await;
    println!("Got a number! {num}");
    num
}

#[tokio::main]
async fn main() {
    let num1 = wait_and_give_u8(1).await;
    let num2 = wait_and_give_u8(2).await;
    let num3 = wait_and_give_u8(3).await;

    println!("{num1}, {num2}, {num3}");
}
```

When you run this, it will always be the same:

```
Got a number! 1
Got a number! 2
Got a number! 3
1, 2, 3
```

So we await one value, get it, and then call the next function, await it, and so on. It will always be 1, then 2, and then 3.

Now, let's change it a bit by joining them. Instead of `.await` on each, we'll use `join`, which will poll them all at the same time. Change the code to this:

```
use rand::*;
use tokio::join;
use std::time::Duration;

async fn wait_and_give_u8(num: u8) -> u8 {
    let mut rng = rand::thread_rng();
    let wait_time = rng.gen_range(1..100);
    tokio::time::sleep(Duration::from_millis(wait_time)).await;
    println!("Got a number! {num}");
    num
}

#[tokio::main]
async fn main() {

    let nums = join!(
        wait_and_give_u8(1),
        wait_and_give_u8(2),
        wait_and_give_u8(3)
    );

    println!("{nums:?}");
}
```

Here, too, the numbers (inside the `nums` variable) will always be `(1, 2, 3)`, but the `println!` shows us that it is now polling in an `async` way. Sometimes it will print this:

```
Got a number! 1
Got a number! 2
Got a number! 3
(1, 2, 3)
```

But other times, it might print this:

```
Got a number! 1
Got a number! 3
Got a number! 2
(1, 2, 3)
```

That's because each time the function waits for a random length of time, and one might finish before the other. As soon as they finish, they print out the number, and the polling is done. So this `join!` is what you want to use if you want to get the most speed out of your `async` code as possible.

As you use `async` code you might want to do more things than just using `.await` and the `join!` macro. For example, what if you have multiple functions that you want to poll at the same time and just take the first one that finishes? You can do that with a macro called `select!`. This macro uses its own syntax that looks like this:

```
name_of_variable = future => handle_variable
```

In other words, you first assign a name to the future you are polling and then add a =>
and decide what to do with the output. This is particularly useful when polling futures
that don't return the same type because you can modify the output to return the same
type, which will allow the code to compile.

This is best understood with an example. Here, we will poll four futures at the
same time. Three of them sleep for very similar lengths of time, so the output will differ depending on which one finishes first. The fourth future has no name and simply
returns after 100 milliseconds have passed, indicating a timeout. Try changing the
sleep time to see different results, such as lowering the timeout duration:

```rust
use std::time::Duration;
use tokio::{select, time::sleep};

async fn sleep_then_string(sleep_time: u64) -> String {
    sleep(Duration::from_millis(sleep_time)).await;
    format!("Slept for {sleep_time} millis!")
}

async fn sleep_then_num(sleep_time: u64) -> u64 {
    sleep(Duration::from_millis(sleep_time)).await;
    sleep_time
}

#[tokio::main]
async fn main() {
    let num = select!(
        first = sleep_then_string(10) => first,
        second = sleep_then_string(11) => second,
        third = sleep_then_num(12) => format!("Slept for {third} millis!"),
        _ = sleep(Duration::from_millis(100)) =>
            format!("Timed out after 100 millis!")
    );
    println!("{num}");
}
```

This async function sleeps and returns a String.

But this async function sleeps and returns a u64.

The first three futures in this select! sleep for almost the same length of time, so it's not certain which one will return first.

The variable num has to be a String, so we can't just pass on the variable third here. But with a quick format!, it is now a String, too.

Finally, we'll add a timeout to the select. If neither of the first three return before 100 milliseconds have passed, the select will finish with a timeout message.

There are many other similar macros, such as `try_join!`, which joins unless one of
the futures fails, in which case it returns an `Err`. Here is a quick example of the `try_join!` macro:

```rust
use tokio::try_join;

async fn wait_then_u8(num: u8, worked: bool) -> Result<u8, &'static str> {
    if worked {
        Ok(num)
    } else {
        Err("Oops, didn't work")
    }
}

#[tokio::main]
async fn main() {
```

```
    let failed_join = try_join!(
        wait_then_u8(1, true),
        wait_then_u8(2, false),
        wait_then_u8(3, true)
    );

    let successful_join = try_join!(
        wait_then_u8(1, true),
        wait_then_u8(2, true),
        wait_then_u8(3, true)
    );

    println!("{failed_join:?}");
    println!("{successful_join:?}");
}
```

The output for this will be

```
Err("Oops, didn't work")
Ok((1, 2, 3))
```

Async is a large subject in Rust, but hopefully this has made it less mysterious. The async ecosystem in Rust is still somewhat new, so a lot of it takes place in external crates (the main one is the `futures` crate; https://docs.rs/futures/latest/futures/). The `futures_concurrency` crate (http://mng.bz/or6p) is another convenient crate that contains traits to deal with joining, chaining, merging, zipping, and other such methods on futures. And, of course, Tokio (https://docs.rs/tokio/latest/tokio/ index.html) is filled to the brim with ways to work with async code.

Much of the async ecosystem is slowly moving into the standard library. For example, the `Stream` trait in the `futures` crate showed up as an experimental `AsyncIterator` trait in the standard library in 2022 (http://mng.bz/6nBA). One other example is the `async_trait` crate (https://docs.rs/async-trait/latest/async_trait/), which contains a macro that allows traits to be async. This crate was needed because async traits simply weren't possible until Rust 1.75, which was released just a few days before the end of 2023. As the only way to make async traits in Rust before version 1.75, you will still see the `async_trait` crate in a lot of code. So, by the time you read this book, some of the macros or traits inside the `async` external crates might be in the standard library!

With this introduction to async Rust out of the way, we are going to relax a bit by spending the next two chapters on a quick tour of the standard library. There are a lot of modules and types in there that we haven't come across yet, plus more methods and internal details about types we already know.

Summary

- If the compiler can't find a type for no good reason, check to see whether you need a feature flag to enable it.
- The most important thing to remember about async is that it doesn't block threads. Regular functions block them.

- An async function just returns a `Future`, which doesn't do anything. You have to `.await` it to get some actual usable output.
- There are many ways of working with multiple futures. You can `join!` them together, `select!` to race them against each other and take the first that completes, and so on.
- Much of this functionality in the `async` ecosystem is found in external crates. These often work as staging grounds for testing out new functionality to stabilize and add to the standard library.

20

A tour of the standard library

This chapter covers

- A more in-depth look at familiar types
- Associated constants
- A summary of the three associated items in Rust
- Recently added functions such as `from_fn` and `then_some`
- New types, such as `OsString` and `CString`

Good work! You're almost through the book—there are only five chapters left. For this chapter and the next, we are going to sit back and relax and go on a short tour of the standard library, including further details on some of the types we already know. You will certainly end up encountering these modules and methods as you continue to use Rust, so we might as well learn them now so that they are already familiar to you. Nothing in this chapter will be particularly difficult to learn, and we'll keep things pretty brief and run through one type per section.

20.1 Arrays

Arrays have become easier to work with over time, as we saw in the chapter on const generics. Some other nice changes have taken place that we'll take a look at now.

20.1.1 Arrays now implement Iterator

In the past (before Rust 1.53), arrays didn't implement Iterator, and you needed to use methods like .iter() on them in for loops. (Another method was to use & to get a slice in for loops). So, the following code didn't work in the past:

```
fn main() {
    let my_cities = ["Beirut", "Tel Aviv", "Nicosia"];

    for city in my_cities {
        println!("{}", city);
    }
}
```

The compiler used to give the following message:

```
error[E0277]: `[&str; 3]` is not an iterator
 --> src\main.rs:5:17
  |
  |                     ^^^^^^^^^^ borrow the array with `&` or call `.iter()`
  ➡ on it to iterate over it
```

Luckily, that isn't a problem anymore! If you see any old Rust tutorials that mention that arrays can't be used as iterators, remember that this isn't the case anymore. So all three of these work:

```
fn main() {
    let my_cities = ["Beirut", "Tel Aviv", "Nicosia"];

    for city in my_cities {
        println!("{city}");
    }
    for city in &my_cities {
        println!("{city}");
    }
    for city in my_cities.iter() {
        println!("{city}");
    }
}
```

This prints

```
Beirut
Tel Aviv
Nicosia
Beirut
Tel Aviv
```

```
Nicosia
Beirut
Tel Aviv
Nicosia
```

20.1.2 *Destructuring and mapping arrays*

Destructuring works with arrays as well. To pull out variables from an array, you can put their names inside `[]` to destructure it in the same way as in a tuple or a named struct. This is the same as using a tuple in `match` statements or to get variables from a struct:

```
fn main() {
    let my_cities = ["Beirut", "Tel Aviv", "Nicosia"];
    let [city1, _city2, _city3] = my_cities;
    println!("{city1}");
}
```

This prints `Beirut`.

Here's an example of some more complex destructuring, which pulls out the first and last variable in an array:

```
fn main() {
    let my_cities = [
        "Beirut", "Tel Aviv", "Calgary", "Nicosia", "Seoul", "Kurume",
    ];
    let [first, .., last] = my_cities;
    println!("{first}, {last}");
}
```

The output this time will be `Beirut, Kurume`.

Arrays have a `.map()` method as well that lets you return an array of the same size but of a different type (or the same type, if you wish). It's like the `.map()` method for iterators, except you don't have to call `.collect()` because it already knows the array length and type. Here is a quick example:

```
fn main() {
    let int_array = [1, 5, 9, 13, 17, 21, 25, 29];
    let string_array = int_array.map(|i| i.to_string());
    println!("{int_array:?}");
    println!("{string_array:?}");
}
```

The output is no surprise, but note that the original array is not destroyed:

```
[1, 5, 9, 13, 17, 21, 25, 29]
["1", "5", "9", "13", "17", "21", "25", "29"]
```

And here is an example of the same method that is a bit more interesting. We'll make an `Hours` enum that implements `From<u32>` to determine whether an hour is a working hour, a non-working hour, or an error (an hour greater than 24):

```
#[derive(Debug)]
enum Hours {
```

```
        Working(u32),
        NotWorking(u32),
        Error(u32),
}
```

```
impl From<u32> for Hours {
    fn from(value: u32) -> Self {
        match value {
            hour if (8..17).contains(&hour) =>
            ➡Hours::Working(value),
            hour if (0..=24).contains(&hour) =>
            ➡Hours::NotWorking(value),
            wrong_hour => Hours::Error(wrong_hour),
        }
    }
}
```

> Here, we will use an exclusive range (up to, but not including, 17) because if you work until 5 pm, and it's 5 pm, you're already going home and not working anymore.

> For the rest of the numbers, we will make the range inclusive. We already checked for working hours, so we are safe to match on anything between 0 and 24.

```
fn main() {
    let int_array = [1, 5, 9, 13, 17, 21, 25, 29];
    let hours_array = int_array.map(Hours::from);
    println!("{hours_array:?}");
}
```

Here is the output:

```
[NotWorking(1), NotWorking(5), Working(9), Working(13), NotWorking(17),
➡NotWorking(21), Error(25), Error(29)]
```

Knowing this `.map()` method will come in handy for the next method, called `from_fn()`.

20.1.3 Using from_fn to make arrays

The `from_fn()` method was released fairly recently in the summer of 2022 with Rust 1.63; it allows you to construct an array on the spot. The `from_fn()` method was introduced with the following code sample. Don't worry if it doesn't make much sense because a lot of people felt the same way when they first saw it:

```
fn main() {
    let array = std::array::from_fn(|i| i);
    assert_eq!(array, [0, 1, 2, 3, 4]);
}
```

You can imagine that there was a lot of discussion about this sample. How does it even work? How can you just write (`|i| i`) and get `[0, 1, 2, 3, 4]`? This sample was later improved to reduce confusion, but let's take a look on our own to see why the code works. First, we'll look at the code inside `from_fn()`:

```
pub fn from_fn<T, const N: usize, F>(mut cb: F) -> [T; N]
where
    F: FnMut(usize) -> T,
{
    let mut idx = 0;
```

```
    [(); N].map(|_| {
        let res = cb(idx);
        idx += 1;
        res
    })
}
```

The first lines tell us that this method makes an array of type T and a length of N and that it takes a closure. The closure is called cb (for callback), but it could be called anything: f, my_closure, and so on. Then, inside the function, it starts with a variable called idx (the index), which starts at 0. Then it quickly makes an array of unit types (the () type) of the same length as N and uses .map() to make the new array. For each item, it carries out the instructions inside, which include increasing the index by 1 each time before returning the value under the variable name res.

In other words, when you call from_fn, you have the option to use the index number. If you don't want to, you can write |_| instead. Here's an example:

```
fn main() {
    let array = std::array::from_fn(|_| "Don't care about the index");
    assert_eq!(
        array,
        [
            "Don't care about the index",
            "Don't care about the index",
            "Don't care about the index",
            "Don't care about the index",
            "Don't care about the index"
        ]
    );
}
```

We could take the index for the array we are creating, but we don't care about it.

So far, so good. But how did it know the length? Here, this is because of type inference. An array can only be compared to an array of the same type and length, so when you add an assert_eq!, the compiler will know that the array to compare will also have to be the same type and length. And that means that if you take out the assert_eq!, the code won't compile!

```
fn main() {
    let array = std::array::from_fn(|_| "Don't care about the index");
}
```

The error message shows us that the compiler was able to determine the type of the array but not its length:

```
error[E0282]: type annotations needed for `[&str; _]`
 --> src\main.rs:2:9
  |
2 |     let array = std::array::from_fn(|_| "Don't care about the index");
  |         ^^^^^
  |
help: consider giving `array` an explicit type, where the the value of
➡const parameter `N` is specified
```

```
2 |      let array: [&str; _] = std::array::from_fn(|_| "Don't care about
 ➡the index");
  |                           +++++++++++
```

And because it was able to determine the type, we can either write [&str; 5] or [_;
5], and that will be enough information. So the next two arrays will work just fine:

```
fn main() {
    let array: [_; 5] = std::array::from_fn(|_| "Don't need the index");
    let array: [&str; 5] = std::array::from_fn(|_| "Don't need the index");
}
```

To sum up:

- When using from_fn() for an array, you can pull in the index of each item if
  you want to use it or use |_| if you don't need it.
- Most of the time, you will have to tell the compiler the length of the array.
- If you are comparing one array to another, you won't need to tell the compiler
  the length. But you might want to write out the length anyway for the benefit of
  anyone else reading your code.

20.2 char

Our old friend char is pretty familiar by now, but let's take a look at a few neat things
that we might have missed.

You can use the .escape_unicode() method to get the Unicode number for a
char:

```
fn main() {
    let korean_word = "청춘예찬";
    for character in korean_word.chars() {
        print!("{} ", character.escape_unicode());
    }
}
```

This prints \u{ccad} \u{cd98} \u{c608} \u{cc2c}.

You can get a char from u8 using the From trait. However, to make a char from a
u32, you have to use TryFrom because it might not work. There are many more numbers in u32 than characters in Unicode. We can see this with a simple demonstration.
We will first print a char from a random u8, and then try 100,000 times to make a char
from a random u32:

```
use rand::random;

fn main() {
    println!("This will always work: {}", char::from(100));
    println!("So will this: {}", char::from(random::<u8>()));

    for _ in 0..100_000 {
        if let Ok(successful_character) = char::try_from(random::<u32>()) {
```

**The only implementation of From for char is
From<u8>, so Rust will automatically choose a u8.
It won't compile if the number is too large for a u8.**

```
        print!("{successful_character}");
      }
    }
  }
}
```

The output will be different every time, but even after 100,000 tries, the number of successful characters will be very small. And most of them will end up being Chinese characters, because there are so many of them:

```
This will always work:  D
So will this: Ñ
```

魼　嶄　　　　　　　　　　　　　圁　貯　橡

This makes sense because, at present, Unicode has a total of 149,186 characters, while a u32 can go up to 4,294,967,295. So, the chance of having a random u32 that is 149186 or less is extremely low. There is also a high chance that the character won't show on your screen if you don't have the fonts installed for the language of the character.

   We learned near the beginning of the book that all chars are 4 bytes in length. If you want to know how many bytes a char would be if it were a &str, you can use the len_utf() method. Let's put some greetings in and see how many bytes each character would be:

```
fn main() {
    "Hi, привіт, 안녕, ｻﾞｨﾝ"
        .chars()
        .for_each(|c| println!("{c}: {}", c.len_utf8()));
}
```

Here is the output:

```
H: 1
i: 1
,: 1
 : 1
п: 2
р: 2
и: 2
в: 2
і: 2
т: 2
,: 1
 : 1
안: 3
녕: 3
,: 1
 : 1
ｻ: 4
ﾞ: 4
ｨ: 4
```

There are a ton of convenience methods for char that are pretty easy to understand by their name, such as .is_alphanumeric(), .is_whitespace(), and .make_ascii_uppercase(). There's a good chance that a convenience method already exists if you need to validate or modify a char in your code.

20.3   *Integers*

There are a lot of math methods for these types, like multiplying by powers, Euclidean modulo, logarithms, and so on, that we don't need to look at here. But there are some other methods that are useful in our day-to-day work.

20.3.1   *Checked operations*

Integers all have the methods `.checked_add()`, `.checked_sub()`, `.checked_mul()`, and `.checked_div()`. These are good to use if you think you might produce a number that will overflow or underflow (i.e., be greater than the type's maximum value or less that its minimum value). They return an `Option` so you can safely check that your math works without making the program panic.

You might be wondering why Rust would even compile if a number overflows. It's true that the compiler won't compile if it knows at compile time that a number will overflow—for example:

```
fn main() {
    let some_number = 200_u8;
    println!("{}", some_number + 200);
}
```

This is pretty obvious (even to us) that the number will be 400, which won't fit into a `u8`, and the compiler knows this as well:

```
error: this arithmetic operation will overflow
  --> src/main.rs:3:20
   |
3  |     println!("{}", some_number + 200);
   |                    ^^^^^^^^^^^^^^^^^^ attempt to compute `200_u8 +
   200_u8`, which would overflow
   |
   = note: `#[deny(arithmetic_overflow)]` on by default
```

However, if a number isn't known at compile time, the behavior will be different:

- `Debug` mode—The program will panic.
- `Release` mode—The number will overflow.

Let's trick the compiler into making this happen. First, we will make a `u8` with a value of `255`, the highest value for a `u8`. Then we will use the `rand` crate to add 10 to it:

```
use rand::{thread_rng, Rng};

fn main() {
    let mut rng = thread_rng();
    let some_number = 255_u8;
    println!("{}", some_number + rng.gen_range(10..=10));
}
```

> We know that a range of 10..=10 will only return 10, but the Rust compiler doesn't know this at compile time, so it will let us run the program.

In `Release` mode, the number will overflow, and the program will print `10` without panicking. But in `Debug` mode, we will see this:

```
      Running `target/debug/playground`
thread 'main' panicked at 'attempt to add with overflow', src/main.rs:6:20
note: run with `RUST_BACKTRACE=1` environment variable to display a backtrace
```

We certainly don't want to panic, and we also don't want to add 10 to 255 and get 10. So let's use `.checked_add()` instead. Now we will never overflow or panic:

```
use rand::random;

fn add_numbers(one: u8, two: u8) {
    match one.checked_add(two) {
        Some(num) => println!("Added {one} to {two}: {num}"),
        None => println!("Error: couldn't add {one} to {two}"),
    }
}

fn main() {
    for _ in 0..3 {
        let some_number = random::<u8>();
        let other_number = random::<u8>();
        add_numbers(some_number, other_number);
    }
}
```

The output will be different every time, but it will look something like this:

```
Error: couldn't add 199 to 236
Added 34 to 97: 131
Added 61 to 109: 170
```

Environments that silently ignore integer overflows have been to blame for all kinds of crashes and security problems over the years, which is what makes methods like `.checked_add()` particularly nice for a systems programming language. Be sure to use the `.checked_` methods whenever you think an overflow could take place! And if you are often working with numbers that are larger than any integer in the standard library, take a look at the `num_bigint` crate (https://docs.rs/num-bigint/latest/num_bigint/).

20.3.2 *The Add trait and other similar traits*

You might have noticed that the methods for integers use the variable name `rhs` a lot. For example, the documentation on the method `.checked_add()` starts with this:

```
pub const fn checked_add(self, rhs: i8) -> Option<i8>
Checked integer addition. Computes self + rhs, returning None if overflow
occurred.
```

The term *rhs* means "right-hand side"— in other words, the right-hand side when you do some math. For example, in `5 + 6`, the number `5` is on the left and `6` is on the right, so `6` is the `rhs`. It is not a keyword, but you will see `rhs` a lot in the standard library, so it's good to know.

While we are on the subject, let's learn how to implement Add, which is the trait used for the + operator in Rust. In other words, after you implement Add, you can use + on a type that you create. You need to implement Add yourself (you can't just use #[derive(Add)]) because it's impossible to guess how you might want to add one type to another type. Here's the example from the page in the standard library:

```
use std::ops::Add;                          ◁──────       Add is found inside the std::ops
                                                          module, which has all the traits used
#[derive(Debug, Copy, Clone, PartialEq)]    ◁──────       for operations. You can probably
struct Point {                                            guess that the other traits have
    x: i32,                 PartialEq is probably the most names like Sub, Mul, and so on.
    y: i32,                 important part here. You want
}                           to be able to compare numbers.

impl Add for Point {
    type Output = Self;                     ◁──────       Remember, this is called an
                                                          associated type—a type that "goes
    fn add(self, other: Self) -> Self {                   together" with a trait. In this case,
        Self {                                            it's another Point.
            x: self.x + other.x,
            y: self.y + other.y,
        }
    }
}
```

Now let's implement Add for our own type just for fun. Let's imagine that we have a Country struct that we'd like to add to another Country. As long as we tell Rust how we want to add one to the other, Rust will cooperate, and then we will be able to use + to add them. It looks like this:

```
use std::fmt;
use std::ops::Add;

#[derive(Clone)]
struct Country {
    name: String,
    population: u32,            Size of the
    gdp: u32,            ◁──── economy
}

impl Country {
    fn new(name: &str, population: u32, gdp: u32) -> Self {
        Self {
            name: name.to_string(),
            population,
            gdp,
        }
    }
}

impl Add for Country {
    type Output = Self;
```

```
    fn add(self, other: Self) -> Self {
        Self {
            name: format!("{} and {}", self.name, other.name),
            population: self.population + other.population,
            gdp: self.gdp + other.gdp,
        }
    }
}
```

We decide that add means to concatenate the names, combine the population, and combine the GDP. It's entirely up to us what we want Add to mean.

```
impl fmt::Display for Country {
    fn fmt(&self, f: &mut fmt::Formatter<'_>) -> fmt::Result {
        write!(
            f,
            "In {} are {} people and a GDP of ${}",
            self.name, self.population, self.gdp
        )
    }
}

fn main() {
    let nauru = Country::new("Nauru", 12_511, 133_200_000);
    let vanuatu = Country::new("Vanuatu", 219_137, 956_300_000);
    let micronesia = Country::new("Micronesia", 113_131, 404_000_000);

    println!("{}", nauru);
    let nauru_and_vanuatu = nauru + vanuatu;
    println!("{nauru_and_vanuatu}");
    println!("{}", nauru_and_vanuatu + micronesia);
}
```

This prints

```
In Nauru are 12511 people and a GDP of $133200000
In Nauru and Vanuatu are 231648 people and a GDP of $1089500000
In Nauru and Vanuatu and Micronesia are 344779 people and a GDP of
$1493500000
```

The three others are called Sub, Mul, and Div, and they are basically the same to implement. There are quite a few other operators in the same module, such as +=, -=, *=, and /=, which use traits that start with the name Assign: AddAssign, SubAssign, MulAssign, and DivAssign. You can see the full list of such traits here: http://mng.bz/ 468j. They are all named in a pretty predictable fashion. For example, % is called Rem, - is called Neg, and so on.

Two other convenient traits, PartialEq (http://mng.bz/JdwK) and PartialOrd, (http://mng.bz/PRwY), are used to compare and order one variable with another. After these traits are implemented, you will be able to use signs like < and == for your type in the same way that implementing Add lets you use the + sign.

Because comparing for equality and order are done among variables of the same type, these traits are easier to implement and are usually done using #[derive], as we saw in chapter 13. But you can also manually implement them if you want. As always, the standard library contains some simple examples implementing these traits that you can copy and paste and then change to suit your own type if you want to manually implement them.

20.4 Floats

`f32` and `f64` have a very large number of methods that you use when doing math. We won't look at those, but here are some methods that you might use. They are: `.floor()`, `.ceil()`, `.round()`, and `.trunc()`. All of these return an `f32` or an `f64` that is like an integer (i.e., a whole number). They do the following:

- `.floor()`—Gives you the next lowest integer.
- `.ceil()`—Gives you the next highest integer.
- `.round()`—Gives you a higher number if 0.5 or more or the same number is less than 0.5. This is called *rounding* because it gives you a "round" number (a number that has a short, simple form).
- `.trunc()`—Cuts off the part after the period. Truncate means "to cut off."

Here is a simple sample that prints them:

```
fn four_operations(input: f64) {
    println!(
"For the number {}:
floor: {}
ceiling: {}
rounded: {}
truncated: {}\n",
        input,
        input.floor(),
        input.ceil(),
        input.round(),
        input.trunc()
    );
}

fn main() {
    four_operations(9.1);
    four_operations(100.7);
    four_operations(-1.1);
    four_operations(-19.9);
}
```

This prints

```
For the number 9.1:
floor: 9
ceiling: 10
rounded: 9
truncated: 9
```
                    Because it's
                    less than 9.5

```
For the number 100.7:
floor: 100
ceiling: 101
rounded: 101
truncated: 100
```
                    Because it's
                    more than 100.5

```
For the number -1.1:
floor: -2
ceiling: -1
rounded: -1
truncated: -1

For the number -19.9:
floor: -20
ceiling: -19
rounded: -20
truncated: -19
```

f32 and f64 have a method called .max() and .min() that gives you the higher or the lower of two numbers. (For other types, you can use the std::cmp::max() and std::cmp::min() functions.)

These .max() and .min() methods are a good opportunity to show again that the .fold() method for iterators isn't just for adding numbers. In this case, you can use .fold() to return the highest or lowest number in a Vec or anything else that implements Iterator:

To get the highest number, start with the lowest possible f64 value.

```
fn main() {
    let nums = vec![8.0_f64, 7.6, 9.4, 10.0, 22.0, 77.345, -7.77, -10.0];
    let max = nums
        .iter()
        .fold(f64::MIN, |num, next_num| num.max(*next_num));        ◄─────┐
    let min = nums
        .iter()
        .fold(f64::MAX, |num, next_num| num.min(*next_num));        ◄─────┐
    println!("{max}, {min}");
}
```

Conversely, start with the highest possible f64 value to get the lowest number.

With this, we get the highest and the lowest values: 77.345 and −10.0.

On the left side of the documentation for Rust's float types, you might notice that there are a lot of consts, known as "associated constants": DIGITS, EPSILON, INFINITY, MANTISSA_DIGITS, and so on. Plus, in the previous sample, we've used MIN and MAX, which we've also used with other types such as integers. How are these consts made anyway? Let's take a quick look at that.

20.5 Associated items and associated constants

Rust has three types of associated items. We are already familiar with the first two and are now going to learn the third one, so this is a good time to sum up all three. Associated items are connected to the type or trait they are associated with by the :: double colon. Let's start with the first one, which we know *very* well: functions.

20.5.1 Associated functions

When you implement a method on a type or a trait, you are giving it an associated function. Most of the time, we see it in variable_name.function() format when there is a

self parameter. But this is just a convenience instead of using forms like `TypeName::`
`function(&variable_name)` or `TypeName::function(&mut variable_name)`. When
you use the dot operator (a period) to call a method, Rust is actually just using the `::`
syntax, unseen to you, to call the function. Let's look at a quick example:

```
struct MyStruct(String);

impl MyStruct {                          ◁———┐  MyStruct has two methods;
    fn print_self(&self) {                    │  99.9% of the time, we
        println!("{}", self.0);               │  would use the dot operator
    }
    fn add_exclamation(&mut self) {
        self.0.push('!')
    }
}                                                        We are calling .print_self().
                                                         On this line, we use the dot
fn main() {                                              operator, but on the
    let mut my_struct = MyStruct("Hi".to_string());      following line, we use the
                                                         associated item syntax. It's
    my_struct.print_self();                         ◁——  exactly the same thing!
    MyStruct::print_self(&my_struct);

    my_struct.add_exclamation();                ◁——  The same thing happens here, too.
    MyStruct::add_exclamation(&mut my_struct);       my_struct.add_exclamation() takes a
                                                     &mut my_struct without us needing
    MyStruct::print_self(&my_struct);                to specify that. But if we want, we
}                                                    can use the full associated item
                                                     syntax like we do on the next line.
```

This sample is pretty easy, with an output of `Hi`, `Hi`, and `Hi!!`.

20.5.2 *Associated types*

The next item we've seen is an associated type, which is the type you define when
implementing a trait. We saw this most recently with the `Add` trait:

```
pub trait Add<Rhs = Self> {
    type Output;
                                                       Required
    fn add(self, rhs: Rhs) -> Self::Output;    ◁——┘    method
}
```

Here, `type Output` is defined when you implement the trait, and this also gets
attached to the type with the `::` double colon. Here, as well, we can use the full associated type signature. Let's use a really simple example: adding 10 to 10. This time, we
will start with the full signature and work backward:

```
use std::ops::Add;

fn main() {
    let num1 = 10;                                 The i32 type implements Add,
    let num2 = 10;                                 which gives it the add function:
                                                   i32::add(). This function takes
    print!("{} ", i32::add(num1, num2));    ◁——    self plus another number.
}
```

```
print!("{} ", num1.add(num2));
print!("{}", num1 + num2);
}
```

Since we have a self parameter, we can use the dot operator as well.

This last step is built into the language: if you implement Add, you can use + to add. This makes sense: nobody would want to use Rust if they had to type use std::ops::Add and 10.add(10) all the time just to add 10 and 10 together.

On each line, we are doing the same operation, so the output is just 20 20 20.

Now let's look at a simple example of our own. This time, we'll have a trait that just requires that a type destroy itself and turn into another form. This is defined by whoever implements the trait and can be anything:

```
trait ChangeForm {
    type SomethingElse;
    fn change_form(self) -> Self::SomethingElse;
}

impl ChangeForm for String {
    type SomethingElse = char;
    fn change_form(self) -> Self::SomethingElse {
        self.chars().next().unwrap_or(' ')
    }
}

impl ChangeForm for i32 {
    type SomethingElse = i64;
    fn change_form(self) -> Self::SomethingElse {
        println!("i32 just got really big!");
        i64::MAX
    }
}

fn main() {
    let string1 = "Hello there!".to_string();
    println!("{}", string1.change_form());

    let string2 = "I'm back!".to_string();
    println!("{}", String::change_form(string2));

    let small_num = 1;
    println!("{}", small_num.change_form());

    let also_small_num = 0;
    println!("{}", i32::change_form(also_small_num));
}
```

The type is called SomethingElse and can be anything.

Note the signature here: it's associated with Self and attached with the :: double colon.

We'll implement it for String and char. It's our own trait, so we can implement it on external types, too.

Here, as well, there are two ways to call the function: the method signature with the dot operator or the full associated type signature.

Here's the output:

```
H
I
i32 just got really big!
```

```
9223372036854775807
i32 just got really big!
9223372036854775807
```

The associated function and type signature with the `::` should look pretty familiar by now!

And with that, we are now at the last associated item: associated consts.

20.5.3 *Associated consts*

Associated consts are actually incredibly easy to use. Just start an `Impl` block, type `const CONST_NAME: type_name = value`, and you're done! Here's a quick example:

```
struct SizeTenString(String);

impl SizeTenString {
    const SIZE: usize = 5;
}

fn main() {
    println!("{}", SizeTenString::SIZE);
}
```

With this associated const, our `SizeFiveString` can pass on this `SIZE` const to whatever needs it.

Here is a longer yet still simple example of this associated const. In this example, we can use the associated const to ensure that this type will always be 10 characters in length:

```
#[derive(Debug)]
struct SizeTenString(String);

impl SizeTenString {
    const SIZE: usize = 10;
}

impl TryFrom<&'static str> for SizeTenString {
    type Error = String;
    fn try_from(input: &str) -> Result<Self, Self::Error> {
        if input.chars().count() == Self::SIZE {
            Ok(Self(input.to_string()))
        } else {
            Err(format!("Length must be {} characters!", Self::SIZE))
        }
    }
}

fn main() {
    println!("{:?}", SizeTenString::try_from("This one's long"));
    println!("{:?}", SizeTenString::try_from("Too short"));
    println!("{:?}", SizeTenString::try_from("Just right"));
}
```

An associated const can be used with traits, too, in a similar way to functions on traits. A type can override these associated consts, too, in the same way that you can write your own trait method even if there is a default method:

The value of the const **SET_NUMBER** is 10, so you don't need to decide the value when implementing the trait.

This other const, however, is unknown. You have to choose its value when implementing this trait.

```
trait HasNumbers {
    const SET_NUMBER: usize = 10;
    const EXTRA_NUMBER: usize;
    // fn set_number() -> usize { 10 }
    // fn extra_number() -> usize;
}

struct NothingSpecial;

impl HasNumbers for NothingSpecial {
    const EXTRA_NUMBER: usize = 10;
    // const SET_NUMBER: usize = 20;
}

fn main() {
    print!("{} ", NothingSpecial::SET_NUMBER);
    print!("{}", NothingSpecial::EXTRA_NUMBER);
}
```

These two commented-out functions are similar in behavior to the consts. One has a default implementation, while the other only shows the return type and has to be written out by anyone implementing the trait.

If you uncommented this, the struct NothingSpecial would have a value of 20 for SET_NUMBER instead of 10.

So this code will print 10 10, but if you uncomment the one line out, it will print 20 10.

That was a long enough detour, so let's get on to our next standard library type!

20.6   *bool*

Booleans are pretty simple in Rust but are quite robust compared to some other languages. (For comparison, one example of the difficulties of working with booleans in C can be found at http://mng.bz/1J51.) There are a few ways to use a bool that we haven't come across yet, so let's look at them now.

In Rust, you can turn a bool into an integer if you want because it's safe to do that. But you can't do it the other way around. As you can see, true turns to 1, and false turns to 0:

```
fn main() {
    let true_false = (true, false);
    println!("{} {}", true_false.0 as u8, true_false.1 as i32);
}
```

This prints 1 0. Or you can use .into() if you tell the compiler the type:

```
fn main() {
    let true_false: (i128, u16) = (true.into(), false.into());
    println!("{} {}", true_false.0, true_false.1);
}
```

This prints the same thing.

As of Rust 1.50 and 1.62, there are two methods, `.then()` and `.then_some()`, that turn a `bool` into an `Option`. With `.then()`, you write a closure, and the closure is called if the item is `true`. Whatever is returned from the closure gets wrapped in an `Option`. Here's a small example:

```
fn main() {
    let (tru, fals) = (true.then(|| 8), false.then(|| 8));
    println!("{:?}, {:?}", tru, fals);
}
```

This prints `Some(8)`, `None`.

These methods can be pretty nice for error handling. The following code shows how a simple `Vec<bool>` can be turned into a `Vec` of `Results` with some extra info as it is handled.

```
use std::time::{SystemTime, UNIX_EPOCH};

fn timestamp() -> f64 {                    A small function to generate a
    SystemTime::now()                      timestamp as an f64 to make the
        .duration_since(UNIX_EPOCH)        following code easier to read
        .unwrap()
        .as_secs_f64()
}
                                           This function is empty, but pretend that
                                           it sends the users of our system some
fn send_data_to_user() {}                  data in case it comes across as true.

fn main() {
    let bool_vec = vec![true, false, true, false, false];

    let result_vec = bool_vec
        .into_iter()
        .enumerate()
        .map(|(index, b)| {                We turn the bool into an Option<f64>
            b.then(|| {                    (the timestamp), sending the user the
                let timestamp = timestamp();   data before passing it on.
                send_data_to_user();
                timestamp                  With ok_or_else(), we turn the Option
            })                             into a Result and add some error info
            .ok_or_else(|| {               (the index number that failed).
                let time = timestamp();
                format!("Error with item {index} at {time}")
            })
        })
        .collect::<Vec<_>>();
    println!("{result_vec:#?}");
}
```

The output at the end will look something like this:

```
    Ok(
        1685149117.2468076,
    ),
    Err(
        "Error with item 1 at 1685149117.246808",
```

```
    ),
    Ok(
        1685149117.246833,
    ),
    Err(
        "Error with item 3 at 1685149117.2468333",
    ),
    Err(
        "Error with item 4 at 1685149117.2468338",
    ),
]
```

20.7   *Vec*

Vec has a lot of methods that we haven't looked at yet. Let's start with .sort(). The .sort() method is not surprising at all. It uses a &mut self to sort a vector in place (nothing is returned):

```
fn main() {
    let mut my_vec = vec![100, 90, 80, 0, 0, 0, 0, 0];
    my_vec.sort();
    println!("{:?}", my_vec);
}
```

This prints [0, 0, 0, 0, 0, 80, 90, 100]. But there is one more interesting way to sort called .sort_unstable(), and it is usually faster. It can be faster because it doesn't care about the order of items if they are the same value. In regular .sort(), you know that the last 0, 0, 0, 0, 0 will be in the same order after .sort() is performed. But .sort_unstable() might move the last zero to index 0, then the third last zero to index 2, and so on. The documentation in the standard library explains it pretty well:

> *It is typically faster than stable sorting, except in a few special cases, e.g., when the slice consists of several concatenated sorted sequences.*

.dedup() means "de-duplicate." It will remove items that are the same in a vector, but only if they are next to each other. This next code will not just print "sun", "moon":

```
fn main() {
    let mut my_vec = vec!["sun", "sun", "moon", "moon", "sun", "moon",
    ➥ "moon"];
    my_vec.dedup();
    println!("{:?}", my_vec);
}
```

Instead, it only gets rid of "sun" next to the other "sun", then "moon" next to one "moon", and again with "moon" next to another "moon". The result is: ["sun", "moon", "sun", "moon"].

So, if you want to use .dedup() to remove every duplicate, just .sort() first:

```
fn main() {
    let mut my_vec = vec!["sun", "sun", "moon", "moon", "sun", "moon",
    ➥ "moon"];
```

```
    my_vec.sort();
    my_vec.dedup();
    println!("{:?}", my_vec);
}
```

The result is `["moon", "sun"]`.

You can split a `Vec` with `.split_at()`, while `.split_at_mut()` lets you do the same if you need to change the values. These give you two slices while leaving the original `Vec` intact:

```
fn main() {
    let mut big_vec = vec![0; 6];
    let (first, second) = big_vec.split_at_mut(3);

    std::thread::scope(|s| {
        s.spawn(|| {
            for num in first {
                *num += 1;
            }
        });
        s.spawn(|| {
            for num in second {
                *num -= 5;
            }
        });
    });
    println!("{big_vec:?}");
}
```

The output is `[1, 1, 1, -5, -5, -5]`.

The `.drain()` method lets you pull a range of values out of a `Vec`, giving you an iterator. This iterator keeps a mutable borrow on the original `Vec` so doing something like collecting it into another `Vec` or outright using the `drop()` method will let you access the original `Vec` again:

```
fn main() {
    let mut original_vec = ('A'..'K').collect::<Vec<_>>();
    println!("{original_vec:?}");

    let drain = original_vec.drain(2..=5);
    println!("Pulled these chars out: {drain:?}");
    drop(drain);
    println!("Here's what's left: {original_vec:?}");

    let drain_two = original_vec.drain(2..=4).collect::<Vec<_>>();
    println!("Original vec: {original_vec:?}\nSecond drain: {drain_two:?}");
}
```

Here's the output:

```
['A', 'B', 'C', 'D', 'E', 'F', 'G', 'H', 'I', 'J']
Pulled these chars out: Drain(['C', 'D', 'E', 'F'])
Here's what's left: ['A', 'B', 'G', 'H', 'I', 'J']
```

```
Original vec: ['A', 'B', 'J']
Second drain: ['G', 'H', 'I']
```

20.8 *String*

We learned before that a String is kind of like a Vec, because it holds one (a Vec<u8>). A String isn't just a simple smart pointer over a Vec<u8>, but sometimes it almost feels like one because so many of the methods are exactly the same.

One of these is String::with_capacity(). This method can help avoid too many allocations if you are pushing chars to it with .push() or pushing &strs to it with .push_str(). Here's an example of a String that has too many allocations:

```
fn main() {
    let mut push_string = String::new();

    for _ in 0..100_000 {
        let capacity_before = push_string.capacity();
        push_string.push_str("I'm getting pushed into the string!");
        let capacity_after = push_string.capacity();
        if capacity_before != capacity_after {
            println!("Capacity raised to {capacity_after}");
        }
    }
}
```

> We check the capacity before and after the &str is pushed and print out the new capacity if it has changed.

This prints

```
Capacity raised to 35
Capacity raised to 70
Capacity raised to 140
Capacity raised to 280
Capacity raised to 560
Capacity raised to 1120
Capacity raised to 2240
Capacity raised to 4480
Capacity raised to 8960
Capacity raised to 17920
Capacity raised to 35840
Capacity raised to 71680
Capacity raised to 143360
Capacity raised to 286720
Capacity raised to 573440
Capacity raised to 1146880
Capacity raised to 2293760
Capacity raised to 4587520
```

We had to reallocate (copy everything over) 18 times. But now we know the final capacity. So we'll give it the capacity right away, and we don't need to reallocate—just one String capacity is enough:

> We know the exact number in this case. Even if you only have a general idea (like "at least 10,000"), you could still use with_capacity() to avoid too many allocations.

```
fn main() {
    let mut push_string = String::with_capacity(4587520);
```

```
    for _ in 0..100_000 {
        let capacity_before = push_string.capacity();
        push_string.push_str("I'm getting pushed into the string!");
        let capacity_after = push_string.capacity();
        if capacity_before != capacity_after {
            println!("Capacity raised to {capacity_after}");
        }
    }
}
```

And this prints nothing. Perfect! We never had to reallocate.

Of course, the actual length is certainly smaller than the final 4,587,520, which is simply a doubling of the previous capacity when it was 2,293,760. We can shrink it, though, with .shrink_to_fit(), which is another Vec method. But only do this once you are sure of the final length because the capacity will double again even if you push a single extra char to the Vec:

```
fn main() {
    let mut push_string = String::with_capacity(4587520);

    for _ in 0..100_000 {
        push_string.push_str("I'm getting pushed into the string!");
    }
    println!("Current capacity as expected: {}", push_string.capacity());
    push_string.shrink_to_fit();
    println!("Actual needed capacity: {}", push_string.capacity());
    push_string.push('a');
    println!("Whoops, it doubled again: {}", push_string.capacity());
    push_string.shrink_to_fit();
    println!("Shrunk back to actual needed capacity: {}",
     push_string.capacity());
}
```

This prints

```
Current capacity: 4587520
Actual needed capacity: 3500000
Whoops, it doubled again: 7000000
Shrunk back to actual needed capacity: 3500001
```

The .pop() method works for a String, just like for a Vec:

```
fn main() {
    let mut my_string = String::from(".daer ot drah tib elttil a si gnirts
    ➥sihT");
    while let Some(c) = my_string.pop() {
        print!("{c}");
    }
}
```

Try reading the String backward to see what the output will be for this sample.

By the way, look at how readable the .pop() method is: there's no magic to it. At this point in the book, you could easily write this method yourself!

```
pub fn pop(&mut self) -> Option<char> {
    let ch = self.chars().rev().next()?;
    let newlen = self.len() - ch.len_utf8();
    unsafe {
        self.vec.set_len(newlen);
    }
    Some(ch)
}
```

One convenient method for String is `.retain()`, which is a little bit like the `.filter()` method we know for iterators. This method passes in a closure that we can use to evaluate whether to keep each character or not. The following code keeps only the characters inside a `String` that are letters or spaces:

```
fn main() {
    let mut my_string = String::from("Age: 20 Height: 194 Weight: 80");
    my_string.retain(|ch| ch.is_alphabetic() || ch == ' ');
    dbg!(my_string);
}
```

This prints

```
[src\main.rs:4] my_string = "Age  Height  Weight "
```

20.9   *OsString and CString*

The `std::ffi` module of the standard library is the one that helps you use Rust with other languages or operating systems. This module includes types like `OsString` and `CString`, which are like `String` for the operating system or `String` for the language C. They each have their own `&str` type, too: `OsStr` and `CStr`. The three letters `ffi` stand for *foreign function interface*.

You can use `OsString` when you have to work with an operating system that doesn't use UTF-8. All Rust strings are UTF-8, but certain operating systems express strings in different ways. Here is a simplified version of the page in the standard library on why we have `OsString`:

- A string on Unix (Linux, etc.) might be a sequence of bytes together that don't have zeros, and sometimes you read them as Unicode UTF-8.
- A string on Windows might be made of sequences of 16-bit values that don't have zeros.
- In Rust, strings are always valid UTF-8, which may contain zeros.

So an `OsString` is made to be read by all of them.

You can do all the regular things with an OsString like `OsString::from("Write something here")`. It also has an interesting method called `.into_string()` that tries to make it into a regular `String`. It returns a `Result`, but the `Err` part is just the original `OsString`:

```
pub fn into_string(self) -> Result<String, OsString>
```

So if it doesn't work, you just get the previous `OsString` back. You can't call `.unwrap()` because it will panic, but you can use `match` to get the `OsString` back. We can quickly prove that the `Err` value is an `OsString` by calling methods that don't exist:

```
use std::ffi::OsString;

fn main() {
    let os_string = OsString::from("This string works for your OS too.");
    match os_string.into_string() {
        Ok(valid) => valid.thth(),
        Err(not_valid) => not_valid.occg(),
    }
}
```

Then the compiler tells us exactly what we want to know:

```
error[E0599]: no method named `thth` found for struct `std::string::String`
in the current scope
 --> src/main.rs:6:28
  |
6 |          Ok(valid) => valid.thth(),
  |                             ^^^^ method not found in `std::string::String`

error[E0599]: no method named `occg` found for struct `std::ffi::OsString`
in the current scope
 --> src/main.rs:7:37
  |
7 |          Err(not_valid) => not_valid.occg(),
  |                                      ^^^^ method not found in
  `std::ffi::OsString`
```

This book doesn't get into any FFI for Rust, but this module is a good place to start.

And with that, we are halfway through the tour! Hopefully, it has been pretty relaxing and enlightening so far, with nothing particularly difficult. The tour will finish up in the next chapter as we learn a lot of the methods related to memory, how to set up panic hooks and view backtraces, and some of the other convenient macros that we haven't learned yet.

Summary

- Even everyday types like `bool` and `char` have new methods added to them all the time, so keep an eye on the release notes for every new version of Rust to see what has been made available.
- Be sure to use checked operations if you ever think any of your numeric types may overflow. They require a bit more typing, but the extra guarantees are worth it.
- With associated consts, we now know all three associated items. The other two are associated functions and associated types.

- Despite the long name, associated items are not that intimidating: associated functions are just functions, associated types are just types declared inside a trait, and associated constants are just const values on a type or a trait.
- Try doing your own tour as well by taking a look at the methods and traits for the types you use the most in Rust. There is a lot in the standard library that we have only scratched the surface of.

Continuing the tour

This chapter covers

- The `mem` module
- The `std` library prelude
- Setting panic hooks and viewing backtraces
- Other macros

This is the second of two chapters touring the standard library, with a lot of new (but not difficult) types that you'll find useful to know. Near the end, we will look at some macros we haven't encountered before, which will lead into the next chapter, where you will learn how to write your own!

21.1 std::mem

As the name implies, the `std::mem` module has types and functions for dealing with memory. The functions inside this module are particularly interesting (and convenient). We have seen some of them already, such as `size_of()`, `size_of_val()`, and `drop()`:

437

```
use std::mem;

fn main() {
    println!("Size of an i32: {}", mem::size_of::<i32>());
    let my_array = [8; 50];
    println!("Size of this array: {}", mem::size_of_val(&my_array));
    let some_string = String::from("Droppable because it's not Copy");
    drop(some_string);
    // some_string.clear();
}
```

◁───┐ **If we uncommented this,
it wouldn't compile.**

This prints

```
Size of an i32: 4
Size of this array: 200
```

Note that in the previous code we didn't need to write `mem::drop()`, just `drop()`, because this function is part of the *prelude*. We will look at the prelude shortly.

Technically, you can call `drop()` on a `Copy` type, but it will have no effect. As the function documentation states:

> *This effectively does nothing for types which implement `Copy`, e.g., integers. Such values are copied and then moved into the function, so the value persists after this function call. (https://doc.rust-lang.org/std/mem/fn.drop.html)*

Let's look at some other functions in `std::mem`.

The `swap()` function lets you switch the values between two variables. You use a mutable reference for each to do it. This is particularly helpful when you have two things you want to switch and Rust doesn't let you because of borrowing rules or because the parameter isn't an `Option` that you could use `take()` to replace with `None`. (More on the `take()` function in a moment.)

Let's use this function to do some owner swapping of the One Ring from *Lord of the Rings*:

```
use std::mem;

#[derive(Debug)]
struct Ring {
    owner: String,
    former_owners: Vec<String>,
}

impl Ring {
    fn switch_owner_to(&mut self, name: &str) {
        if let Some(position) = self.former_owners.iter().position(|n| n ==
          name) {
            mem::swap(&mut self.owner, &mut self.former
              _owners[position])
        } else {
            println!("Nobody named {name} found in former_owners, sorry!");
        }
    }
}
```

This method will try to find a character inside former_owners that matches the search key and, if so, switch owners. We could return a Result or Option here, but to keep it simple, we'll print an error message if no matching character is found.

Directly accessing a Vec through an index can be risky, so we'll use the position method to ensure that we found a String that matches the name we are searching for.

```
fn main() {
    let mut one_ring = Ring {
        owner: "Frodo".into(),
        former_owners: vec!["Gollum".into(), "Sauron".into()],
    };

    println!("Original state: {one_ring:?}");
    one_ring.switch_owner_to("Gollum");
    println!("{one_ring:?}");
    one_ring.switch_owner_to("Sauron");
    println!("{one_ring:?}");
    one_ring.switch_owner_to("Billy");
    println!("{one_ring:?}");
}
```

For most of the book, the owner of the ring is Frodo, while both Gollum and Sauron are looking for it.

Now let's do some owner switching.

This will print

```
Original state: Ring { owner: "Frodo", former_owners: ["Gollum", "Sauron"] }
Ring { owner: "Gollum", former_owners: ["Frodo", "Sauron"] }
Ring { owner: "Sauron", former_owners: ["Frodo", "Gollum"] }
Nobody named Billy found in former_owners, sorry!
Ring { owner: "Sauron", former_owners: ["Frodo", "Gollum"] }
```

The next function inside `std::mem` is called `replace()`. It is similar to `.swap()` and actually uses `swap()` inside. The function is extremely simple:

```
pub fn replace<T>(dest: &mut T, mut src: T) -> T {
    swap(dest, &mut src);
    src
}
```

So, `replace()` does a swap and then returns the other item—that's all there is to it. In other words, `.replace()` replaces the value with what you put in and returns the old value, which makes it useful with a `let` binding to create a variable. Here's a quick example:

```
use std::mem;

struct City {
    name: String,
}

impl City {
    fn change_name(&mut self, name: &str) {
        let former = mem::replace(&mut self.name, name.to_string());
        println!("{former} is now called {new}.", new = self.name);
    }
}

fn main() {
    let mut capital_city = City {
        name: "Constantinople".to_string(),
    };
    capital_city.change_name("Istanbul");
}
```

This code prints `Constantinople is now called Istanbul`.

Now, let's get to the function `take()` that we previously mentioned. As the name implies, this function outright takes the value from something and returns it. But `take()` doesn't drop the existing variable; instead, it leaves its default value in its place. And that's why this function requires the type we are `take()`-ing from to implement `Default`:

```
pub fn take<T>(dest: &mut T) -> T
where
    T: Default,
```

So you can do something like this:

```
use std::mem;

fn main() {
    let mut number_vec = vec![8, 7, 0, 2, 49, 9999];
    let mut new_vec = vec![];

    number_vec.iter_mut().for_each(|number| {
        let taker = mem::take(number);
        new_vec.push(taker);
    });
    println!("{:?}\n{:?}", number_vec, new_vec);
}
```

As you can see, it replaced all the numbers with `0`: no index was deleted:

```
[0, 0, 0, 0, 0, 0]
[8, 7, 0, 2, 49, 9999]
```

Of course, for your own type you can implement `Default` to whatever you want. The following code shows a bank in a country called Klezkavania that gets robbed all the time. Every time it gets robbed, it replaces the money at the front with 50 credits (the default):

```
use std::mem;

#[derive(Debug)]
struct Bank {
    money_inside: u32,
    money_at_desk: DeskMoney,
}

#[derive(Debug)]
struct DeskMoney(u32);

impl Default for DeskMoney {
    fn default() -> Self {
        Self(50)        ⟵┐ default is always
    }                    │ 50, not 0.
}
```

```
fn main() {
    let mut bank_of_klezkavania = Bank {
        money_inside: 5000,                          Sets up our bank
        money_at_desk: DeskMoney(500),
    };

    let money_stolen = mem::take(&mut bank_of_klezkavania.money_at_desk);
    println!("Stole {} Klezkavanian credits", money_stolen.0);
    println!("{bank_of_klezkavania:?}");
}
```

This will print

```
Stole 500 Klezkavanian credits
Bank { money_inside: 5000, money_at_desk: DeskMoney(50) }
```

You can see that there is always $50 at the desk.

In practice, the `take()` function is often used as a convenience method to quickly turn a `Some` into a `None` without having to do any pattern matching. The following example shows just how short your code can be when using this function:

```
use std::time::Duration;

struct UserState {
    username: String,
    connection: Option<Connection>,     ◁   We could have the Connection struct hold
}                                           the state of the connection, but another
                                            way to do it is to wrap it in an Option. In
struct Connection {                         this case, Some represents a connected
    url: String,                            state, and None, a nonconnected state.
    timeout: Duration,
}

impl UserState {
    fn is_connected(&self) -> bool {        A real connect method would
        self.connection.is_some()           be more complicated than
    }                                       this, but you get the idea.
    fn connect(&mut self, url: &str) {   ◁
        self.connection = Some(Connection {
            url: url.to_string(),
            timeout: Duration::from_secs(3600),
        });
    }
    fn disconnect(&mut self) {
        self.connection.take();      ◁   To disconnect, just take() the
    }                                    value and do nothing with it,
}                                        leaving None in its place.

fn main() {
    let mut user_state = UserState {
        username: "Mr. User".to_string(),
        connection: None,
    };
    user_state.connect("someurl.com");
```

```
        println!("Connected? {}", user_state.is_connected());
        user_state.disconnect();
        println!("Connected? {}", user_state.is_connected());
}
```

The output is pretty simple:

```
Connected? true
Connected? false
```

21.2 *Setting panic hooks*

We learned back in chapter 5 that a panic in Rust is actually not very panicky. A panic is simply the program seeing that there is a problem that it can't deal with, so it gives up. For example, there is nothing a program can do when it sees this code:

```
println!("{}", vec![1, 2][3]);
```

The programmer here is telling the program to access the fourth item of a Vec that has two items, and that isn't allowed, so the only option is to give up. The program then prints a message and unwinds the stack, which cleans up the memory for the thread. And if the thread is the main thread, then the program is over. (Maybe it was named *panic* because the developer is the one who panics when it happens!)

In any case, because a panic is an orderly process, we can modify its behavior a bit. There is a module in the standard library that is also called `std::panic` that lets us modify what happens when a panic takes place.

First, let's review the output we see whenever a program panics. We'll start by just using the `panic!` macro, which is the easiest way to do it:

```
fn main() {
    panic!();
}
```

The output is

```
thread 'main' panicked at 'explicit panic', src\main.rs:2:5
note: run with `RUST_BACKTRACE=1` environment variable to display a
➥backtrace
```

The `panic!` macro can take a message, which will change the output somewhat:

```
fn main() {
    panic!("Oh man, something went wrong");
}
```

Now the output contains our message instead of just `'explicit panic'`:

```
thread 'main' panicked at 'Oh man, something went wrong', src\main.rs:2:5
note: run with `RUST_BACKTRACE=1` environment variable to display a
➥backtrace
```

Now let's take a look at what happens with a panic that happens outside of the `panic!` macro. First, we will try to parse a number without unwrapping, which will generate a

`Result` with the error info. After that, we'll unwrap and compare the panic info to what we printed out:

```
fn main() {
    let try_parse = "my_num".parse::<u32>();
    println!("Error output: {try_parse:?}");
    let my_num = try_parse.unwrap();
}
```

We can see that when a panic happens, it first tells us which thread panicked, why it panicked, any error info, the location in the code where the panic happened, and a note about how to display a backtrace:

```
Error output: Err(ParseIntError { kind: InvalidDigit })
thread 'main' panicked at 'called `Result::unwrap()` on an `Err` value:
➡ParseIntError { kind: InvalidDigit }', src/main.rs:4:28
note: run with `RUST_BACKTRACE=1` environment variable to display a
➡backtrace
```

So, that's the default behavior. But we can change all of this if we want by using a method called `set_hook()`. This sets up a global panic hook, which will be called instead of the default panic hook. Inside this method is a closure in which we can do whatever we like when a panic happens. Let's make a really simple one that prints out a message or two when a panic happens—one in English and another in Korean:

```
fn main() {
    std::panic::set_hook(Box::new(|_| {
        println!("Oops, that didn't work.");
        println!("앗 뭔가 잘못 됐네요.");        ⟵   Korean for "Oops,
    }));                                              something's gone wrong."

    panic!();
}
```

The panic hook does exactly what we told it to do, and even the location and error information is gone. This is all we see now when we run the program:

```
Well, that didn't work.
앗 뭔가 잘못 됐네요.
```

Where does the default information in a panic message come from? It would be nice if we could display that as well.

You might have noticed that inside `set_hook()` is a closure with an argument that we ignored by using `|_|`. If we give the argument a name, we can see that it is a struct called `PanicInfo`, which implements both `Debug` and `Display`. Let's print it out:

```
fn main() {
    std::panic::set_hook(Box::new(|info| {
        println!("Well, that didn't work: {info}");
    }));
    panic!();
}
```

This will print

```
Well, that didn't work: panicked at 'explicit panic', src\main.rs:6:5
```

The `PanicInfo` struct itself is fairly interesting, as it has a parameter called `payload` that implements `Any`:

```
pub struct PanicInfo<'a> {
    payload: &'a (dyn Any + Send),
    message: Option<&'a fmt::Arguments<'a>>,
    location: &'a Location<'a>,
    can_unwind: bool,
}
```

Back in chapter 13 we learned that the `Error` trait has methods that let us try to downcast it into a concrete type. The `Any` trait is another trait that includes methods for downcasting and is automatically implemented on any type unless it contains a non-`'static` reference. In other words, the `payload` parameter will hold a trait object behind, which technically could be almost anything.

However, the documentation for the `.payload()` method for the `PanicInfo` struct tells us which type the payload will usually be:

```
Returns the payload associated with the panic.
This will commonly, but not always, be a &'static str or String.
```

Let's give this downcasting a try:

```
fn main() {
    std::panic::set_hook(Box::new(|info| {
        if let Some(payload) = info.payload().downcast_ref::<&str>() {
            println!("{payload}");
        } else {
            println!("No payload!");
        }
    }));
    panic!("Oh no");
}
```

The `.downcast_ref::<&str>()` method returns a `Some`, so this will simply print `Oh no`.

This brings us to an important point: `.downcast_ref()` is a method that can fail, so we made sure to use `if let` to ensure that a panic did not occur. Avoiding panics is important in any case, but when setting a panic hook, it is especially important because a panic during a panic will lead to an *abort*, which means it won't unwind the stack and just hand everything over to the operating system to clean up.

The output for an abort will depend on your operating system, but it can look pretty ugly. On the Playground, a panic inside a panic (in other words, an abort) looks like this:

```
thread panicked while processing panic. aborting.
timeout: the monitored command dumped core
/playground/tools/entrypoint.sh: line 11:     8 Aborted
➥timeout --signal=KILL ${timeout} "$@"
```

And on Windows it will look something like this:

```
thread panicked while processing panic. aborting.
error: process didn't exit successfully: `target\release\rmol.exe` (exit
➥code: 0xc0000409, STATUS_STACK_BUFFER_OVERRUN)
```

So, be sure to be extra careful when setting a panic hook.

This does bring up an interesting point, though: sometimes people will choose to abort by default instead of panicking because that can reduce the size of the binary by a bit. The smaller size is because there will now be no cleanup code inside the binary. You don't want to set a panic inside a panic hook to do this, though. Instead, just add this to your Cargo.toml file:

```
[profile.release]
panic = 'abort'
```

Then run or build the binary in release mode (`cargo run -release` or `cargo build -release`), and it will be a little smaller. But the vast majority of the time, you won't want to abort when a panic happens.

Let's finish up this section with a somewhat larger (but imaginary) example of where we might want to use a panic hook. Here, we are running some sort of software that accesses a database. We want to make sure that the database gets shut down properly even if there is a panic, before the stack unwinds and the program stops. We'll also add some pretend types and functions that demonstrate how our system is working and what sometimes goes wrong:

```
use rand::Rng;

struct Database {
    data: Vec<String>,
}

fn get_hour() -> u32 {
    let mut rng = rand::thread_rng();
    rng.gen_range(0..=30)
}

fn shut_down_database(hour: u32) -> Result<(), String> {
    match hour {
        h if (6..18).contains(&h) => {

            Ok(())
        }
        h if h > 24 => Err(format!("Internal error: hour {h} shouldn't
➥exist")),
        h => Err(format!("Hour {h} is not working hours, can't shut down")),
    }
}

fn main() {
    std::panic::set_hook(Box::new(|info| {
```

Uh oh, someone made a mistake, and sometimes the hour of the day is greater than 24. We'll represent this with a simple function that returns a number up to 30.

Do some database shutting down stuff.

This method will only shut down the database during working hours. Outside of working hours, it will leave it running and log a message; it also checks for incorrect hours of the day.

```
        println!("Something went wrong / 문제가 생겼습니다!");
        println!("Panic info: {info}");
        let hour = get_hour();
        match shut_down_database(hour) {
            Ok(()) => println!("Shutting down database at {hour}
            ➡o'clock!"),
            Err(e) => println!("Couldn't shut down database before panic
            ➡finished: {e}"),
        }
    }));
    let mut db = Database { data: vec![] };
    db.data.push("Some data".to_string());
    panic!("Database broke");
}
```

The output will always include this:

```
Something went wrong / 문제가 생겼습니다!
Panic info: panicked at 'Database broke', src\main.rs:38:5
```

The rest of the output will be one of these three lines, depending on the hour of the day returned by get_hour():

```
Couldn't shut down database before panic finished: Internal error: hour 27
➡shouldn't exist
Shutting down database at 17 o'clock!
Couldn't shut down database before panic finished: Hour 1 is not working
➡hours, can't shut down
```

Finally, what if you want to undo the panic hook? That's easy, just use the take_hook() method. It looks something like this:

```
fn main() {
    std::panic::set_hook(Box::new(|_| {
        println!("Something went wrong / 문제가 생겼습니다!");
    }));

    let _ = std::panic::take_hook();
    panic!();
}
```

This will just print out the regular thread 'main' panicked at 'explicit panic', src\main.rs:8:5 panic message. We are using let _ because take_hook() returns the PanicInfo struct that was set in set_hook() in the previous example, and we don't need it here. But if you do need it, you can give it a variable name and use it however you like.

Before we finish this section, let's take a quick look at the take_hook() method. Don't worry about all the details inside, but do you notice a method that we learned in this chapter? There it is—our old friend mem::take()! You can see that it's being used to grab the old panic hook, after which it returns it to us:

```
pub fn take_hook() -> Box<dyn Fn(&PanicInfo<'_>) + 'static + Sync + Send> {
    if thread::panicking() {
```

```
        panic!("cannot modify the panic hook from a panicking thread");
    }
    let mut hook = HOOK.write().unwrap_or_else(PoisonError::into_inner);
    let old_hook = mem::take(&mut *hook);
    drop(hook);
    old_hook.into_box()
}
```

And since `mem::take()` leaves a default value behind, let's take a look at the `Hook` mentioned here to see what it looks like and what its default value is. It's pretty simple, just an enum that represents either a default panic hook or a custom panic hook.

```
enum Hook {
    Default,
    Custom(Box<dyn Fn(&PanicInfo<'_>) + 'static + Sync + Send>),
}
```

So, at this point in the book, there's not much code in the standard library that you can't understand.

The next part of the standard library is very closely related: backtraces.

21.3 *Viewing backtraces*

We learned about backtraces in chapter 14 in the section on testing our code. Viewing backtraces when a panic occurs has been a feature of Rust since the language began. However, being able to view a backtrace at run time is fairly new: it was added with Rust 1.65 in November 2022. Before this, the only way to see backtraces at run time was through a crate called `backtrace`.

But now it can be done without any external code, and viewing a backtrace is pretty simple: just use a function called `Backtrace::capture()`, which is located in the `std::backtrace` module. There is one thing to keep in mind, though. Try running this code on the Playground or your computer and see what happens:

```
use std::backtrace::Backtrace;

fn main() {
    println!("{}", Backtrace::capture());
}
```

This only prints out the following:

```
disabled backtrace
```

The documentation explains that this method will look for either a `RUST_BACKTRACE` or a `RUST_LIB_BACKTRACE` environment variable. Interestingly, the source code shows us that it only cares if the environment variables are set to `0` or not:

```
let enabled = match env::var("RUST_LIB_BACKTRACE") {
    Ok(s) => s != "0",
    Err(_) => match env::var("RUST_BACKTRACE") {
        Ok(s) => s != "0",
```

```
        Err(_) => false,
    },
};
```

In other words, this code will still just print `disabled backtrace` even though we have a `RUST_BACKTRACE` environment variable:

```
use std::backtrace::Backtrace;

fn main() {
    std::env::set_var("RUST_BACKTRACE", "0");
    println!("{:#?}", Backtrace::capture());
}
```

But anything else will print a backtrace at run time. This will work:

```
use std::backtrace::Backtrace;

fn main() {
    std::env::set_var("RUST_BACKTRACE", "1");
    println!("{}", Backtrace::capture());
}
```

Setting it to literally anything else will enable capturing a backtrace:

```
use std::backtrace::Backtrace;

fn main() {
    std::env::set_var("RUST_BACKTRACE", "Hi I'm backtraceㅎㅎㅎ");
    println!("{}", Backtrace::capture());
}
```

Now that it is enabled, the output will look something like what we see in the following example. (It will depend on your operating system, of course.) Here is what the Playground displays:

```
0: playground::main
          at ./src/main.rs:5:20
1: core::ops::function::FnOnce::call_once
          at /rustc/d5a82bbd26e1ad8b7401f6a718a9c57c96905483/library
       ➥/core/src/ops/function.rs:507:5
2: std::sys_common::backtrace::__rust_begin_short_backtrace
          at /rustc/d5a82bbd26e1ad8b7401f6a718a9c57c96905483/library/std/
       ➥src/sys_common/backtrace.rs:121:18
3: std::rt::lang_start::{{closure}}
          at /rustc/d5a82bbd26e1ad8b7401f6a718a9c57c96905483/library/std/
       ➥src/rt.rs:166:18
4: core::ops::function::impls::<impl core::ops::function::FnOnce<A> for
➥&F>::call_once
          at /rustc/d5a82bbd26e1ad8b7401f6a718a9c57c96905483/library
       ➥/core/src/ops/function.rs:606:13
5: std::panicking::try::do_call
          at /rustc/d5a82bbd26e1ad8b7401f6a718a9c57c96905483/library/std
       ➥/src/panicking.rs:483:40
```

```
 6: std::panicking::try
            at /rustc/d5a82bbd26e1ad8b7401f6a718a9c57c96905483/library/std
            ➥/src/panicking.rs:447:19
 7: std::panic::catch_unwind
            at /rustc/d5a82bbd26e1ad8b7401f6a718a9c57c96905483/library/std
            ➥/src/panic.rs:137:14
 8: std::rt::lang_start_internal::{{closure}}
            at /rustc/d5a82bbd26e1ad8b7401f6a718a9c57c96905483/library/std
            ➥/src/rt.rs:148:48
 9: std::panicking::try::do_call
            at /rustc/d5a82bbd26e1ad8b7401f6a718a9c57c96905483/library/std
            ➥/src/panicking.rs:483:40
10: std::panicking::try
            at /rustc/d5a82bbd26e1ad8b7401f6a718a9c57c96905483/library/std
            ➥/src/panicking.rs:447:19
11: std::panic::catch_unwind
            at /rustc/d5a82bbd26e1ad8b7401f6a718a9c57c96905483/library/std
            ➥/src/panic.rs:137:14
12: std::rt::lang_start_internal
            At /rustc/d5a82bbd26e1ad8b7401f6a718a9c57c96905483/library/std
            ➥/src/rt.rs:148:20
13: std::rt::lang_start
            at /rustc/d5a82bbd26e1ad8b7401f6a718a9c57c96905483/library/std
            ➥/src/rt.rs:165:17
14: main
15: __libc_start_main
16: _start
```

That was pretty easy. Now let's finish up with an example that combines both a panic hook and a backtrace.

The `Backtrace` struct also has a method called `status()` that returns an enum called a `BacktraceStatus`. Instead of just printing out the `Backtrace` struct, we can also match on the `BacktraceStatus` enum. The enum is quite simple but is interesting for two reasons:

- It has the `#[non_exhaustive]` attribute, meaning that it may be added to later. That means that you have to match on any extra possible variants after the three listed in the enum, just in case new variants get added later on.
- One of the variants is `Unsupported`, since some architectures don't support backtraces:

```
#[non_exhaustive]
pub enum BacktraceStatus {
    Unsupported,
    Disabled,
    Captured,
}
```

Here is the example:

```
use std::{
    backtrace::{Backtrace, BacktraceStatus::*},
```

```
            panic,
    };

    fn main() {
        panic::set_hook(Box::new(|_| {
            println!("Panicked! Trying to get a backtrace...");
            let backtrace = Backtrace::capture();
            match backtrace.status() {
                Disabled => println!("Backtrace isn't enabled, sorry"),
                Captured => println!("Here's the backtrace!!\n{backtrace}"),
                Unsupported => println!("No backtrace possible, sorry"),
                // Do some database shutting down stuff
            }
        }));

        std::env::set_var("RUST_BACKTRACE", "0");
        panic!();
    }
```

The code matches on the BacktraceStatus enum to see whether a backtrace has been enabled.

When a panic happens, we'll try to capture a backtrace.

It's pretty rare to find an architecture that wouldn't support a backtrace, but if so, we would see this message.

Finally, we enable or disable the backtrace.

And the output is

```
Panicked! Trying to get a backtrace...
Backtrace isn't enabled, sorry
```

Rust's precise error handling means that backtraces aren't used as much as backtraces (also known as stack traces) in other languages because you don't usually have to sift through a backtrace to find out what has gone wrong in your code. But the option is always there if you need the extra insight.

21.4   *The standard library prelude*

The prelude in the standard library is the reason why you don't have to write things like use std::vec::Vec to use a Vec or std::result::Result::Ok() instead of Ok(). You can see all the items in the documentation (http://mng.bz/2768) and will already know almost all of them.

There is an attribute called #![no_implicit_prelude] that disables the prelude. Let's give it a try and watch just how hard it becomes to write even the simplest of code:

```
#![no_implicit_prelude]
fn main() {
    let my_vec = vec![8, 9, 10];
    let my_string = String::from("This won't work");
    println!("{my_vec:?}, {my_string}");
}
```

Now Rust has no idea what you are trying to do:

```
error: cannot find macro `println` in this scope
 --> src/main.rs:5:5
  |
5 |     println!("{:?}, {}", my_vec, my_string);
  |     ^^^^^^^
```

```
error: cannot find macro `vec` in this scope
 --> src/main.rs:3:18
  |
3 |     let my_vec = vec![8, 9, 10];
  |                  ^^^


error[E0433]: failed to resolve: use of undeclared type or module `String`
 --> src/main.rs:4:21
  |
4 |     let my_string = String::from("This won't work");
  |                     ^^^^^^ use of undeclared type or module `String`


error: aborting due to 3 previous errors
```

For this simple code, you need to tell Rust to use the `extern` (external) crate called `std` and then the items you want. Here is everything we have to do just to create a `Vec` and a `String` and print it:

```
#![no_implicit_prelude]

extern crate std;          ◁────
use std::convert::From;


fn main() {                ◁────
    let my_vec = std::vec![8, 9, 10];
    let my_string = std::string::String::from("This won't work");
    std::println!("{my_vec:?}, {my_string}");
}
```

> We told Rust with #![no_implicit_prelude] that we won't be bringing in anything from std, so we have to let the compiler know again that we will use it.

> To write even this simple code, we need the vec! macro, String, From (to convert from a &str to a String), and println! to print.

Now it finally works, printing `[8, 9, 10]`, `This won't work`. So you can see why Rust has a prelude—it would be a horrible experience without it.

You might be wondering why we haven't see the `extern` keyword before. It's because you don't need it that much anymore. Up until 2018, you had to use this keyword when bringing in an external crate. So, to use `rand` in the past, you had to write `extern crate rand;`, followed by `use` statements for whatever else you wanted to bring into scope. But the Rust compiler doesn't need this help anymore; you can just use `use`, and it knows where to find it. So you almost never need `extern crate` anymore. But in other people's Rust code, you might still see it from time to time.

21.5   *Other macros*

We are getting close to the next chapter, where we will learn to write our own macros. But there are still quite a few macros inside the standard library that we haven't taken a look at yet, so let's learn them first. As is the case with the other macros we have used, they are all extremely easy to use and have a bit of a magical feel to them (until we learn in the next chapter how they work internally, that is).

21.5.1   *unreachable!*

The unreachable! macro is kind of like todo! except it's for code that will never be executed. Maybe you have a match in an enum that you know will never choose one of the arms, so the code can never be reached. If that's so, you can write unreachable! so the compiler knows that it can ignore that part.

For example, let's say you are using an external crate for a financial tool, and it includes a big enum with all the major banks. We're going to do a match on it, but as we look at the list we notice something:

```
enum Bank {
    BankOfAmerica,
    Hsbc,
    Citigroup,
    DeutscheBank,
    TorontoDominionBank,
    SiliconValleyBank
    // And so on...
}
```

Silicon Valley Bank is no more! We are 100% sure that customers will never choose it, so we don't want to mark this variant as todo! or unimplemented!. We're never going to implement it. This is definitely a case for the unreachable! macro:

```
enum Bank {
    BankOfAmerica,
    Hsbc,
    Citigroup,
    DeutscheBank,
    TorontoDominionBank,
    SiliconValleyBank
    // And so on...
}


fn get_swift_code(bank: &Bank) -> &'static str {
    use Banks::*;
    match bank {
        BankOfAmerica => "BOFAUS3N",
        Hsbc => "HSBCHKHHXXX",
        Citigroup => "CITIUS33XXX",
        DeutscheBank => "DEUTINBBPBC",
        TorontoDominionBank => "TDOMCATTTOR",
        SiliconValleyBank => unreachable!()
    }
}
```

Another case for unreachable! is when the compiler can't see something that we can. The following example shows a function that gives a random number from 0 to 3 as a usize, followed by another one called human_readable_rand_num() that gives a human-readable version of the output: zero instead of 0, one instead of 1, and so on. We are 100% certain that the function will never see any number that isn't in the range of 0..=3, but the compiler doesn't know this. The unreachable! macro is perfect in this situation:

```
use rand::{thread_rng, Rng};

fn zero_to_three() -> usize {
    let mut rng = thread_rng();
    rng.gen_range(0..=3)
}

fn human_readable_rand_num() -> &'static str {
    match zero_to_three() {
        0 => "zero",
        1 => "one",
        2 => "two",
        3 => "three",
        _ => unreachable!(),
    }
}
```

unreachable! is nice for others reading your code as a reminder of how code works: it's an assertion that something will never happen. You have to be sure that the code is actually unreachable, though. If the compiler ever calls unreachable!, the program will panic. Just like todo!, the responsibility is on us to make sure that the macro is never called.

On a related note, you'll see the word *unreachable* (not the macro unreachable!) when the compiler can determine that some code will never be run. Here is a quick example:

```
fn main() {
    let true_or_false = true;

    match true_or_false {
        true => println!("It's true"),
        false => println!("It's false"),
        true => println!("It's true"),
    }
}
```

Here, the compiler knows that the match will never reach the third line because it has already checked for both of the possible patterns: true and false.

```
warning: unreachable pattern
  --> src/main.rs:7:9
   |
7  |            true => println!("It's true"),
   |            ^^^^
   |
```

You'll see this "unreachable pattern" warning unexpectedly sometimes. The following code creates an enum representing the four seasons and a function that matches on each season. Take a close look at the code and see whether you can tell why the compiler is going to warn us that there are unreachable parts of the code:

```
pub enum Season {
    Spring,
    Summer,
    Autumn,
    Winter
}

pub fn handle_season(season: Season) {
    use Season::*;
    match season {
        Spring => println!("Spring"),
        summer => println!("Summer"),
        Autumn => println!("Autumn"),
        Winter => println!("Winter")
    }
}
```

Now let's take a close look at the output:

```
warning: unreachable pattern
  --> src/lib.rs:13:9
   |
12 |            summer => println!("Summer"),
   |            ------ matches any value
13 |            Autumn => println!("Autumn"),
   |            ^^^^^^ unreachable pattern
   |
   = note: `#[warn(unreachable_patterns)]` on by default

warning: unreachable pattern
  --> src/lib.rs:14:9
   |
12 |            summer => println!("Summer"),
   |            ------ matches any value
13 |            Autumn => println!("Autumn"),
14 |            Winter => println!("Winter")
   |            ^^^^^^ unreachable pattern
```

Can you see it? We made a typo when we tried to match on `Summer`, writing `summer` instead. Instead of matching on an enum variant, we created a wildcard variable called `summer` that will match on anything. And since it matches on anything, the code will never reach the `Summer` and `Winter` parts of the match statement.

21.5.2 *column!, line!, file!, and module_path!*

These four macros are incredibly easy and are just used to display the current location in the code. Here they are together:

- `column!` gives you column number where the macro is called.
- `file!` gives the filename in which the macro is called.

- `line!` gives the line number in which the macro is called.
- `module_path!` gives the path to the module.

These can be useful when generating error input or even just to print out hints for yourself that there are oddities to check out in the code. We'll use the previous `Bank` enum example again to illustrate this. In the following code, we are starting to put some modules together to handle bank customers, and this time, we think there might be some Silicon Valley Bank customers still somewhere in the system. Instead of panicking, though, we'll print out a warning and give the location in the code to make it easy to find and devise a fix:

```
pub mod input_handling {

    pub struct User {
        pub name: String,
        pub bank: Bank,
    }

    #[derive(Debug, Clone, Copy)]
    pub enum Bank {
        BankOfAmerica,
        Hsbc,
        Citigroup,
        DeutscheBank,
        TorontoDominionBank,
        SiliconValleyBank,
    }

    pub mod user_input {
        use crate::input_handling::{Bank, User};
        pub fn handle_user_input(user: &User) -> Result<(), ()> {
            match user.bank {
                Bank::SiliconValleyBank => {
                    println!(
                        "Darn it, looks like we have to handle this variant
                        even though Silicon Valley Bank doesn't exist
                        anymore: {}:{}:{}:{}",
                        module_path!(),
                        file!(),
                        column!(),
                        line!()
                    );
                    Ok(())
                }
                other_bank => {
                    println!("{other_bank:?}, no problem");
                    Ok(())
                }
            }
        }
    }
}
```

```
use crate::input_handling::{user_input::handle_user_input, Bank, User};

fn main() {
    let user = User {
        name: "SomeUser".to_string(),
        bank: Bank::SiliconValleyBank,
    };
    handle_user_input(&user).unwrap();

    let user2 = User {
        name: "SomeUser2".to_string(),
        bank: Bank::TorontoDominionBank,
    };
    handle_user_input(&user2).unwrap();
}
```

It prints

```
Darn it, looks like we have to handle this variant even though Silicon
➡Valley Bank doesn't exist anymore: playground::input_handling::user
➡_input:src/main.rs:25:28
TorontoDominionBank, no problem
```

21.5.3 *thread_local!*

This macro is similar to the `lazy_static!` macro that we saw in the `lazy_static` crate, except that the global content is local to the thread in which it is contained. Or rather, it might be more accurate to say that `lazy_static!` is similar to `thread_local!` because `thread_local!` is much, much older—it was released along with Rust version 1.0.0!

In any case, when this macro is used, you can create a `static` that will have the same initial value in every thread in which it is used. The value can then be accessed with a method called `.with()` that gives access to the value inside within a closure.

The easiest way to see how this works is with a simple example that compares it with the `lazy_static` behavior that we already know. The following code contains some test functions and should be run with `cargo test -- --nocapture` so that you can see the output. Remember: each test runs on its own thread!

```
use std::cell::RefCell;
use std::sync::Mutex;

lazy_static::lazy_static! {
    static ref INITIAL_VALUE: Mutex<i32> = Mutex::new(10);
}

thread_local! {
    static LOCAL_INITIAL_VALUE: RefCell<i32> = RefCell::new(10);
}
```

This INITIAL_VALUE is accessible to all threads. We have to wrap it in a thread-safe Mutex or RwLock.

However, LOCAL_INITIAL_VALUE is a static that is local to each thread— no need for a Mutex! A regular RefCell or Cell works just fine.

```
#[test]
fn one() {
    let mut lock = INITIAL_VALUE.lock().unwrap();
    println!("Test 1. Global value is {lock}");
    *lock += 1;
    println!("Test 1. Global value is now {lock}");

    LOCAL_INITIAL_VALUE.with(|cell| {
        let mut lock = cell.borrow_mut();
        println!("Test 1. Local value is {lock:?}");
        *lock += 1;
        println!("Test 1. Local value is now {lock:?}\n");
    });
}

#[test]
fn two() {
    let mut lock = INITIAL_VALUE.lock().unwrap();
    println!("Test 2. Global value is {lock}");
    *lock += 1;
    println!("Test 2. Global value is now {lock}");

    LOCAL_INITIAL_VALUE.with(|cell| {
        let mut lock = cell.borrow_mut();
        println!("Test 2. Local value is {lock:?}");
        *lock += 1;
        println!("Test 2. Local value is now {lock:?}\n");
    });
}

#[test]
fn three() {
    let mut lock = INITIAL_VALUE.lock().unwrap();
    println!("Test 3. Global value is {lock}");
    *lock += 1;
    println!("Test 3. Global value is now {lock}");

    LOCAL_INITIAL_VALUE.with(|cell| {
        let mut lock = cell.borrow_mut();
        println!("Test 3. Local value is {lock:?}");
        *lock += 1;
        println!("Test 3. Local value is now {lock:?}\n");
    });
}
```

Now, we have three tests, each of which does the exact same thing. Each test increments INITIAL_VALUE by 1 and prints it and then increments LOCAL_INITIAL_VALUE by 1 and prints it.

Each test is running on its own thread, so the order will always be different, but the output will look something like this:

```
running 3 tests
Test 3. Global value is: 10
Test 3. Global value is now: 11
Test 3. Local value is 10
Test 3. Local value is now 11

Test 1. Global value is: 11
Test 1. Global value is now: 12
```

```
Test 1. Local value is 10
Test 1. Local value is now 11

Test 2. Global value is: 12
Test 2. Global value is now: 13
Test 2. Local value is 10
Test 2. Local value is now 11
```

As you can see, by the end of all three tests, the INITIAL_VALUE (the global value) is now 13. But the LOCAL_INITIAL_VALUE (the thread-local value) starts at 10 inside each thread, and the other tests don't affect it.

If you check the documentation for LocalKey (the type created by the macro; https://doc.rust-lang.org/std/thread/struct.LocalKey.html), you'll see a lot of methods that look like the methods for Cell and RefCell. These methods were experimental for quite some time, but were stabilized shortly before the publication of this book in Rust 1.73!

21.5.4 *cfg!*

We know that you can use attributes like #[cfg(test)] and #[cfg(windows)] to tell the compiler what to do in certain cases. When you have the #[test] attribute, Rust will run the code when running a test. And when you use windows, it will run the code if the user is using Windows. But maybe you just want to change one tiny bit of code depending on the configuration. That's when this macro is useful. It returns a bool:

```
fn main() {
    let helpful_message = if cfg!(target_os = "windows") {
        "backslash"
    } else {
        "slash"
    };
    println!("...then type the directory name followed by a
    {helpful_message}. Then you...");
}
```

This will print differently, depending on your system. The Rust Playground runs on Linux, so it will print

```
...then in your hard drive, type the directory name followed by a slash.
Then you...
```

The cfg! macro works for any kind of configuration. Here is an example of a function that runs differently when you use it inside a test. We have a UserFile enum that can hold either real data (a File) or test data (a String). If this code is run inside main(), the open_file() function will open up the main.rs file and pass it on. If run inside a test, though, it will simply create a dummy String and pass that on instead. Try running this code with Run and with Test in the Playground (or cargo run and cargo test on your computer) to see the difference in behavior:

```
use std::fs::File;
use std::io::Read;

#[derive(Debug)]
enum UserFile {
    Real(File),
    Test(String),
}

fn open_file() -> UserFile {
    if cfg!(test) {
        UserFile::Test(String::from("Just a test file"))
    } else {
        UserFile::Real(File::open("src/main.rs").unwrap())
    }
}

fn get_file_content() -> String {
    let mut content = String::new();
    let file = open_file();
    match file {
        UserFile::Real(mut f) => {
            f.read_to_string(&mut content).unwrap();
            content
        }
        UserFile::Test(s) => s,
    }
}

#[test]
fn test_file() {
    let content = get_file_content();
    println!("Content is: {content}");
    assert_eq!(content, "Just a test file");
}

fn main() {
    let content = get_file_content();
    println!("{content}");
}
```

When this code is run with `cargo run`, it will print the entire content of the `main.rs` file, but during a test with `cargo test -- --nocapture`, it will simply print the following:

```
running 1 test
Content: Just a test file
test test_file ... ok
```

Hopefully, you found this tour of the standard library relaxing and fruitful. There are a lot of hidden gems in the standard library that even experienced Rust users haven't used before, so feel free to do your own tour and see what you can find. There are also a lot of experimental methods that might be stabilized one day, so check the tracking problems to see what work is being done if you find a method that you like in particular.

And remember, experimental doesn't mean unsafe! An experimental method is just a method that might be stabilized one day or might be thrown out if it doesn't make sense to stabilize it.

After these two relaxing chapters, there is only one difficult chapter left to go, and it's the next one: making your own macros!

Summary

- The functions in the `std::mem` module are really convenient for writing shorter code and getting around lifetime problems.
- With a panic hook, you can create your own behavior when a panic happens.
- You can shrink your binary size a bit by setting the panic behavior to abort instead of unwinding the stack.
- A backtrace is now easy to capture at run time without needing an external crate to do it. You will probably see the `backtrace` crate in a lot of external code, though, since the backtrace module is a recent addition to the standard library.
- The `cfg!` macro is a quick way to write code that reacts differently depending on the operating system or any other configuration.
- The `thread_local!` macro lets you create static values that don't get shared between threads.

Writing your own macros

This chapter covers

- Why macros exist
- Understanding and writing basic macros
- Learning to read macros written by others
- Using macros to reduce code duplication

It's now time to learn how to write your own macros. Writing macros can be pretty complicated, which is why they are here near the very end of the book. You very rarely need to write them, but sometimes you might want to because they are very convenient—they essentially write code for you. They have a syntax that is pretty different from normal Rust, and they take some getting used to. Well, a lot of getting used to.

Indeed, the book *Programming Rust* (O'Reilly, 2021) finishes its chapter on macros with a conclusion that sums up the feeling pretty well: "Perhaps, having read all this, you've decided that you hate macros." Hopefully, that's not the case with you, but we'll see! Macros offer a power that nothing else can, and they begin to feel friendlier as you use them more and more. We'll start out with the case for macros and why they even exist in the first place.

22.1   *Why macros exist*

Macros are extremely common in Rust, as we have already noticed since the beginning of the book. Even `println!` itself is a macro. But we haven't learned yet about what they are, besides mentioning in chapter 1 that a macro is like a function that writes code for you. This is actually a more important point than it might seem: a macro produces code before the compiler has even started looking at it.

Back in chapter 16, we looked at const generics, which removed a lot of pain for Rust users when it came to using arrays (and many other things). The chapter cites a Reddit user back in 2018 before const generics was stabilized and how macros had to be used instead:

> *By far the single biggest pain point is const_generics. It can't be implemented and stabilized fast enough. I wrote an elaborate system of macros to solve the issue for our particular system. (http://mng.bz/eE8V)*

So, for this user and his team, there was so much manual typing that needed to be done that they had to resort to macros to solve the task. The team needed something that takes some input from the user and produces code that the compiler can then start looking at.

For tasks like this, a regular function simply can't get the job done. Imagine that we need to create 100 structs. Each has a different name, and each has some parameters that need names. If we tried to make a function to make these structs, we would immediately run into problems, as the following example shows:

```
fn create_struct(struct_names: ???, struct_parameters: Vec<???>) -> ???? {
    struct struct_name {
        struct_parameters.into_iter()???
    }
}
```

You can see the problem already. What is the type of `struct_names`? It can't be a `String` because a `String` is a `Vec<u8>`, which has memory allocated to it and later gets dropped. And the parameters would be a `Vec` of what? But that doesn't work either because, once again, a `Vec` has memory allocated to it and is dropped. And what does the function even return? Same problem. We have no way to just return a bunch of code from a function.

Everything we write inside a regular function lives inside the Rust compiler's world. There's no way that anything we write inside this function would compile, and in fact, we don't even want it to compile: we want to generate something that can *then* be compiled.

The compiler wants to turn our code into machine code, but we don't want the compiler to evaluate what we are typing just yet. We need to take a step back before the Rust compiler takes a look at the code. That's what macros are for.

22.2 *Writing basic macros*

Interestingly enough, to write a macro in Rust you use a macro called `macro_rules!`. After this, you add your macro name and open a `{}` block. Inside is sort of like a `match` statement.

Here's a macro that only takes `()` and returns 6:

```
macro_rules! give_six {
    () => {
        6
    };
}

fn main() {
    let six = give_six!();
    println!("{}", six);
}
```

But it's not the same as a `match` statement because nothing here is being checked and compiled—the macro simply takes an input and gives an output. (Technically, it's called a *token parser*.) And only afterward the compiler checks to see whether it makes sense.

In fact, we can make a macro that doesn't make any sense at all to prove that macros work before the compiler takes a look at any code. The following macro only takes an output of `Hi Calvin.` and produces an interesting output:

```
macro_rules! pure_nonsense {
    (Hi Calvin.) => {
        GRITTINGS. MA NAM IS KAHLFIN. HEERYOR LUNBOKS. HOFFA GUT TAY ASKOOL.
    };
}

fn main() {

}
```

But if you hit Run, the code compiles! In fact, there isn't any code because we haven't called the macro anywhere.

Now, if we call the macro, that's when we have a problem:

```
macro_rules! pure_nonsense {
    (Hi Calvin.) => {
        GRITTINGS. MA NAM IS KAHLFIN. HEERYOR LUNBOKS. HOFFA GUT TAY ASKOOL.
    };
}

fn main() {
    let x = pure_nonsense!(Hi Calvin.);
}
```

The compiler tells us that it has no idea what GRITTINGS is supposed to be and helpfully lets us know that it's probably the macro's fault:

```
error[E0425]: cannot find value `GRITTINGS` in this scope
 --> src/main.rs:3:9
  |
3 |          GRITTINGS. MA NAM IS KAHLFIN. HEERYOR LUNBOKS. HOFFA GUT TAY
  ⇒ASKOOL.
  |          ^^^^^^^^^ not found in this scope
...
8 |      let x = pure_nonsense!(Hi Calvin.);
  |              ----------------------- in this macro invocation
  |
  = note: this error originates in the macro `pure_nonsense` (in Nightly
  ⇒builds, run with -Z macro-backtrace for more info)
```

A macro is only similar to a match statement in appearance. We know that a true match statement needs to return the same type, so this won't work:

```
fn main() {
    let my_number = 10;
    match my_number {
        10 => println!("You got a ten"),
        _ => 10,
    }
}
```

It will complain that you want to return () in one case and an i32 in the other:

```
error[E0308]: `match` arms have incompatible types
 --> src\main.rs:5:14
  |
3 | /      match my_number {
4 | |          10 => println!("You got a ten"),
  | |          ----------------------- this is found to be of type
  ⇒`()`
5 | |          _ => 10,
  | |               ^^ expected `()`, found integer
6 | |      }
  | |_____- `match` arms have incompatible types
```

But as we saw previously, a macro has nothing to do with code compilation, so it is fine with producing a completely different output from a different match arm. So, the following code works:

```
macro_rules! six_or_print {
    (6) => {
        6
    };
    () => {
        println!("You didn't give me 6.");
    };
}

fn main() {
    let my_number = six_or_print!(6);
    six_or_print!();
}
```

This is just fine and prints You didn't give me 6.. Another way that we can see that a macro is not a match statement is that there is no _ wildcard. We can only give it (6) or (). Anything else will make an error. Let's give the macro the input six_or_print!(66) and see what the error looks like:

```
error: no rules expected the token `66`
  --> src/main.rs:11:35
   |
1  | macro_rules! six_or_print {
   | ----------------------- when calling this macro
...
11 |     let my_number = six_or_print!(66);
   |                                   ^^ no rules expected this token in
   ➥macro call
   |
note: while trying to match `6`
  --> src/main.rs:2:6
   |
2  |     (6) => {
   |      ^
```

You will see this no rules expected the token a lot when making your macros.

This is another interesting point: the 6 this macro can take as input isn't even an i32; it's just the number 6—a token. A token doesn't have to be just ascii or numbers either:

```
macro_rules! might_print {
    (THis is strange input 하하はは哈哈 but it still works) => {
        println!("You guessed the secret message!")
    };
    () => {
        println!("You didn't guess it");
    };
}

fn main() {
    might_print!(THis is strange input 하하はは哈哈 but it still works);
    might_print!();
}
```

This macro only responds to two things: () and (THis is strange input 하하はは哈哈 but it still works). Nothing else. But the output is correct Rust code, so the code above compiles, and we get the following output:

```
You guessed the secret message!
You didn't guess it
```

So, it's pretty clear that a macro isn't exactly Rust syntax. However, a macro doesn't just match on raw tokens and nothing else. It can also do something similar to declaring variables in regular Rust code if you indicate what type of token it can expect to see. For example, you can tell a macro that it will receive an *expression*, a *type name*, an *identifier*, and so on. (We will learn what all of these mean shortly.) Here is a simple example of a macro that expects an expression:

```
macro_rules! might_print {
    ($input:expr) => {
        println!("You gave me: {}", $input);
    }
}

fn main() {
    might_print!(6);
}
```

This will print You gave me: 6. The $input:expr part is important. With this, you can give the macro any expression, which can then be used inside the macro code block with any name we choose, which, in this case, we decided to call $input. In macros, variables (technically, they are called *arguments*) start with a $. In this macro, if you give it one expression, it will print it. Let's try it out some more using Debug print instead of Display:

```
macro_rules! might_print {
    ($input:expr) => {
        println!("You gave me: {:?}", $input);
    }
}

fn main() {
    might_print!(());
    might_print!(6);
    might_print!(vec![8, 9, 7, 10]);
}
```

This will print

```
You gave me: ()
You gave me: 6
You gave me: [8, 9, 7, 10]
```

Note that we wrote {:?}, but the macro won't check to see whether &input implements Debug. Fortunately, the compiler will check when we try to compile the code that includes the macro output.

We can see that the macro is parsing as expected if we tell it to expect an expression but give it a statement:

```
macro_rules! wants_expression {
    ($input:expr) => {
        println!("You matched the macro input!");
    };
}

fn main() {
    wants_expression!(let x = 9);
}
```

The error output shows us clearly that it looked at the input but didn't find a match from what it expected to see:

```
error: no rules expected the token `let`
 --> src/main.rs:8:23
  |
1 | macro_rules! wants_expression {
  | ---------------------------- when calling this macro
...
8 |     wants_expression!(let x = 9);
  |                       ^^^ no rules expected this token in macro call
note: while trying to match meta-variable `$input:expr`
 --> src/main.rs:2:6
  |
2 |     ($input:expr) => {
  |      ^^^^^^^^^^^
```

But if we now tell it to expect a statement and give it the same input, it will match:

```
macro_rules! wants_statement {
    ($input:stmt) => {                          ◁──┐  We change expr to stmt,
        println!("You matched the macro input!");  │  instructing the macro to
    };                                             │  expect a statement.
}

fn main() {
    wants_statement!(let x = 9);
}
```

So what can a macro see besides `expr` and `stmt`? Here is the full list—give it a read, but don't worry about memorizing it:

```
block | expr | ident | item | lifetime | literal  | meta | pat | path
➡| stmt | tt | ty | vis.
```

NOTE The words in the list are officially known as *fragment specifiers*. But you don't need to know that to understand and write macros.

This is the complicated part. The documentation explains what each fragment specifier means (http://mng.bz/Rmwj). Let's go over them quickly:

- `block`—A block expression inside { }
- `expr`—An expression
- `ident`—An identifier, such as a variable name
- `item`—A struct, module, etc.
- `lifetime`—'a, 'static, etc.
- `literal`—"hello", 9, etc
- `meta`—The information that goes inside attributes
- `pat`—A path (like `std::vec::Vec`)
- `stmt`—A statement (like `let x = 9`), without the semicolon
- `tt`—A token tree, which matches almost anything

- ty—A type name
- vis—A visibility modifier like pub

There is another good site called cheats.rs (https://cheats.rs/#macros-attributes) that explains them and gives examples for each.

However, for most macros, you will probably use expr, ident, and tt. tt means token tree, which sort of means any type of input. Let's try a simple macro with a simple macro using two of them:

```
macro_rules! check {
    ($input1:ident, $input2:expr) => {
        println!(
            "Is {:?} equal to {:?}? {:?}",
            $input1,
            $input2,
            $input1 == $input2
        );
    };
}

fn main() {
    let x = 6;
    let my_vec = vec![7, 8, 9];
    check!(x, 6);
    check!(my_vec, vec![7, 8, 9]);
    check!(x, 10);
}
```

This will take one ident (such as a variable name) and an expression and see whether they are the same. It prints

```
Is 6 equal to 6? true
Is [7, 8, 9] equal to [7, 8, 9]? true
Is 6 equal to 10? false
```

Here's one macro that takes a tt and prints it. It uses a macro called stringify! to make a string first:

```
macro_rules! print_anything {
    ($input:tt) => {
        let output = stringify!($input);
        println!("{}", output);
    };
}

fn main() {
    print_anything!(ththdoetd);
    print_anything!(87575oehq75onth);
}
```

This prints

```
ththdoetd
87575oehq75onth
```

But it won't print if we give it something with spaces, commas, etc. The macro will think that we are giving it more than one token or extra information and will get confused.

This is where macros start to get difficult. To give a macro more than one item at a time, we have to use a different syntax. Instead of `$input`, it will be `$($input1),*`. The `*` means "zero or more," while the comma before the `*` means that the tokens have to be separated by commas. If you want to match on one or more tokens, use `+` instead of `*`.

Now our macro looks like this:

```
macro_rules! print_anything {
    ($($input1:tt),*) => {
        let output = stringify!($($input1),*);
        println!("{}", output);
    };
}


fn main() {
    print_anything!(ththdoetd, rcofe);
    print_anything!();
    print_anything!(87575oehq75onth, ntohe, 987987o, 097);
}
```

So it takes any token tree separated by commas and uses `stringify!` to make it into a String. Then it prints the String:

```
ththdoetd, rcofe

87575oehq75onth, ntohe, 987987o, 097
```

If we used `+` instead of `*`, it would give an error because one time we gave it no input. So `*` is a bit more flexible. Also, try changing the comma in `($($input1:tt),*)` to a semicolon to see what happens. The macro will generate an error, but only because it is expecting the tokens we give it to be separated by a semicolon now. So, if we change the way we call this macro by entering semicolons instead of commas, it will compile again:

```
macro_rules! print_anything {
    ($($input1:tt);*) => {                          ◁── The only difference between the macro
        let output = stringify!($($input1),*);          now and before is that it expects tokens
        println!("{}", output);                         to be separated by a semicolon.
    };
}

                                                    If we change the commas to
                                                    semicolons here, it will
fn main() {                                         accept our input as before.
    print_anything!(ththdoetd; rcofe);       ◁──┘
    print_anything!();
    print_anything!(87575oehq75onth; ntohe; 987987o; 097);
}
```

In this next example, we will make a macro that writes a simple function for us. First, it will match on a single identifier using `$name:ident`, after which it checks for repeating tokens using `$($input:tt),+` and then prints them all out:

```
macro_rules! make_a_function {
    ($name:ident, $($input:tt),+) => {
        fn $name() {
            let output = stringify!($($input),+);
            println!("{}", output);
        }
    };
}
```

It makes everything else into a string.

First, you give it one name for the function, and then it checks the rest of the input until there are no tokens left to check.

```
fn main() {
    make_a_function!(print_it, 5, 5, 6, I);
    print_it();
    make_a_function!(say_its_nice, this, is, really, nice);
    say_its_nice();
}
```

We want a function called print_it() that prints everything else we give it.

Same here, but we change the function name.

This prints

```
5, 5, 6, I
this, is, really, nice
```

In chapter 19, we learned that the Rust Playground has an Expand button that expands macros to show us the actual generated output. Let's click on that to see what the functions. The relevant part is here:

```
macro_rules! make_a_function {
    ($name:ident, $($input:tt),+) => {
        fn $name() {
            let output = stringify!($($input),+);
            println!("{}", output);
        }
    };
}
fn main() {
    fn print_it() {
        let output = "5, 5, 6, I";
        { ::std::io::_print(format_args!("{0}\n", output)); };
    }
    print_it();
    fn say_its_nice() {
        let output = "this, is, really, nice";
        { ::std::io::_print(format_args!("{0}\n", output)); };
    }
    say_its_nice();
}
```

The macro matched on a single identifier here called print_it, which it uses for the name of the function it generates. As you can see, it looks like any other function.

Next, it looks at the remaining tokens (separated by commas) and stringifies them on this line.

Since the function exists in this scope we can call it here.

Finally, it prints them out. This part is a bit ugly as it shows the internals of the println! macro.

22.3 *Reading macros from the standard library*

Let's use what we know now to see whether we can understand other macros. Some of the macros we've already been using in the standard library are pretty simple to read. Let's take a look at the write! macro that we used in chapter 18:

```
macro_rules! write {
    ($dst:expr, $($arg:tt)*) => ($dst.write_fmt($crate::format_args!($($arg)*)))
}
```

So, to use it, you enter this:

- An expression (expr) that is given the name $dst.
- Everything after that. If the macro had written $arg:tt, it would have only taken one argument, but because it wrote $($arg:tt)*, it takes zero, one, or any number.

Then it takes $dst (which stands for "destination") and uses a method called write_fmt on it. Inside that, it uses another macro called format_args! that takes $($arg)*, or all the arguments we put in, and passes them on to another macro. The format_args! macro is used internally quite a bit:

```
macro_rules! format_args {
    ($fmt:expr) => {{ /* compiler built-in */ }};
    ($fmt:expr, $($args:tt)*) => {{ /* compiler built-in */ }};
}
```

Unfortunately, this macro uses "compiler magic" to work so we can't look any deeper than this. The standard library has a lot of macros with this /* compiler built-in */ message. But, in any case, format_args! is an internal macro that allows us to use {} to capture arguments and format them.

Now let's take a look at the todo! macro. That's the one you use when you want the program to compile but haven't written your code yet. It looks like this:

```
macro_rules! todo {
    () => (panic!("not yet implemented"));
    ($($arg:tt)+) => (panic!("not yet implemented: {}",
    $crate::format_args!($($arg)+)));
}
```

This one has two options: you can enter () or a number of token trees (tt):

- If you enter (), it just uses panic! with a message. So you could actually just write panic!("not yet implemented") instead of todo! and it would be the same.
- If you enter some arguments, it will try to make them into a String. You can see the same format_args! macro inside again.

Having read the code for todo!, we can now see that this macro can take the same format we use for the println! macro. Let's give that a try:

If you write this, it will work, too:

```
fn not_done() {
    let time = 8;
    let reason = "lack of time";
    todo!("Not done yet because of {reason}. Check back in {time} hours");
}

fn main() {
    not_done();
}
```

This will print

```
thread 'main' panicked at 'not yet implemented: Not done yet because of
lack of time. Check back in 8 hours', src/main.rs:4:5
```

So, even if a macro is complex or obscure, we can at least take a look at the possible inputs it can take to get an idea of how to use it.

One interesting thing about macros is that they can even call themselves! Let's give this a try. See whether you can guess what the output will be for this macro:

```
macro_rules! my_macro {
    () => {
        println!("Let's print this.");
    };
    ($input:expr) => {
        my_macro!();
    };
    ($($input:expr),*) => {
        my_macro!();
    }
}

fn main() {
    my_macro!(vec![8, 9, 0]);
    my_macro!(toheteh);
    my_macro!(8, 7, 0, 10);
    my_macro!();
}
```

This one takes `()`, one expression, or many expressions. But take a look at what happens when it receives an expression: it ignores it and calls itself with `my_macro!()`. And when `my_macro!` gets the input `()`, it will print a message. So the output for the previous code is `Let's print this`, four times.

You can see the same thing in the `dbg!` macro, which also calls itself:

```
macro_rules! dbg {
    () => {
        $crate::eprintln!("[{}:{}]", $crate::file!(), $crate::line!());
    };
    ($val:expr) => {
        match $val {
            tmp => {
                $crate::eprintln!("[{}:{}] {} = {:#?}",
                    $crate::file!(), $crate::line!(),
    $crate::stringify!($val), &tmp);
                tmp
            }
        }
    };
    ($val:expr,) => { $crate::dbg!($val) };
    ($($val:expr),+ $(,)?) => {
        ($($crate::dbg!($val)),+,)
    };
}
```

We can try this out ourselves:

```
fn main() {
    dbg!();
}
```

With no particular input, it matches the first arm:

```
() => {
    $crate::eprintln!("[{}:{}]", $crate::file!(), $crate::line!());
};
```

So, it will print the filename and line name with the `file!` and `line!` macros. On the Playground, it prints `[src/main.rs:2]`.

Let's try it with this:

```
fn main() {
    dbg!(vec![8, 9, 10]);
}
```

This will match the next arm because it's one expression:

```
($val:expr) => {
    match $val {
        tmp => {
            $crate::eprintln!("[{}:{}] {} = {:#?}",
                $crate::file!(), $crate::line!(), $crate::stringify!
                ($val), &tmp);
            tmp
        }
    }
};
```

So, it looks like the macro grabs the expression given to it, prints the filename and line number, stringifies the tokens making up the expression, and then prints out the expression itself. For our input, it will write this:

```
[src/main.rs:2] vec![8, 9, 10] = [
    8,
    9,
    10,
]
```

And for other inputs, we can see that it calls `dbg!` on itself, even if you put in an extra comma. We know a trailing comma is allowed because of the the `$(,)?` inside.

Hold on, how exactly does `$(,)?` mean that there might be a trailing comma? Let's break it down bit by bit. First is the `?`, which is the third of the three repetition operators that can be used in a macro. We already know two of them, so let's summarize them together:

- Use * to signify any number of repetitions.
- Use + to signify any number of repetitions (but at least one).
- Use ? to signify zero or one occurrence.

A `?` inside a macro is sort of like an `Option` in regular Rust code. In this case, the `dbg!` macro allows a match to happen when there is a trailing comma but doesn't do anything with it.

We can practice this with our own macro:

```
macro_rules! comma_check {
    () => {
        println!("Got nothing!");
    };
    ($input:expr) => {
        println!("One expression!")
    };
    ($input:expr $(,)?) => {
        println!("One expression with a comma at the end!")
    };
    ($input:expr $(,)? $(,)?) => {
        println!("One expression with two commas at the end!")
    };
    ($input:expr $(;)? $(,)?) => {
        println!("One expression with a semicolon and a comma!")
    };
}

fn main() {
    comma_check!();
    comma_check!(8);
    comma_check!(8,);
    comma_check!(8,,);
    comma_check!(8;,);
}
```

Not too hard to read, is it? Here is the output:

```
Got nothing!
One expression!
One expression with a comma at the end!
One expression with two commas at the end!
One expression with a semicolon and a comma!
```

Now let's finish by looking at the `matches!` macro, which uses the ? operator quite a bit. This macro is used somewhat frequently in Rust, but we haven't seen it yet in this book. Let's look at the code first to see whether we can figure it out:

```
macro_rules! matches {
    ($expression:expr, $pattern:pat $(if $guard:expr)? $(,)?) => {
        match $expression {
            $pattern $(if $guard)? => true,
            _ => false
        }
    };
}
```

It looks like it takes an expression and a pattern and matches the expression against the pattern. After that, it has two optional items, but since they are optional, let's remove them for a moment to make it really easy to read:

```
macro_rules! matches {
    ($expression:expr, $pattern:pat) => {
```

```
        match $expression {
            $pattern => true,
            _ => false
        }
    };
}
```

Okay, let's match a few expressions against a few patterns:

```
fn main() {
    println!("{}", matches!(9, 9));
    println!("{}", matches!(9, 0..=10));
    println!("{}", matches!(9, 100..=1000));
}
```

Easy! This prints `true`, `true`, and `false`.

Now let's look at the optional items again. The one at the end is `$(,)?`, which allows a trailing comma. This code will work and produce the same output:

```
fn main() {
    println!("{}", matches!(9, 9,));
    println!("{}", matches!(9, 0..=10,));
    println!("{}", matches!(9, 100..=1000,));
}
```

Finally comes the other optional item:

```
$(if $guard:expr)?
```

This lets us add an `if` clause and an expression. It calls this expression `$guard` and uses it as follows:

```
$pattern $(if $guard)? => true,
```

Let's give this a quick try:

```
const ALLOWS_TRUE: bool = false;

fn main() {
    println!("{}", matches!(9, 9 if ALLOWS_TRUE));
}
```

This code will output `false` even though 9 matches 9 because the guard returns `false`.

Hopefully, this has made macros a bit less intimidating. To finish up, let's look at a small yet more real example of where a macro might come in handy.

22.4 Using macros to keep your code clean

Let's imagine that we have three structs that hold a `String`. One should be able to hold only small `Strings`, the next should be able to hold medium-sized `Strings`, and the last should be able to hold larger ones. Here they are:

```
struct SmallStringHolder(String);
struct MediumStringHolder(String);
struct LargeStringHolder(String);
```

The best way to make sure that these types take a `String` that is small enough is to use the `TryFrom` trait. We'll start with `SmallStringHolder` and make sure that it can only accept a `String` that is up to five characters in length:

```
#[derive(Debug)]
struct SmallStringHolder(String);
#[derive(Debug)]
struct MediumStringHolder(String);
#[derive(Debug)]
struct LargeStringHolder(String);

impl TryFrom<&str> for SmallStringHolder {
    type Error = &'static str;

    fn try_from(value: &str) -> Result<Self, Self::Error> {
        if value.chars().count() > 5 {
            Err("Must be no longer than 5")
        } else {
            Ok(Self(value.to_string()))
        }
    }
}

fn main() {
    println!("{:?}", SmallStringHolder::try_from("Hello"));
    println!("{:?}", SmallStringHolder::try_from("Hello there"));
}
```

This works well! Here is the output:

```
Ok(SmallStringHolder("Hello"))
Err("Must be no longer than 5")
```

Now, it's time to do the same for the others. But hold on, this is going to be a lot of repetitive code. This is where you might begin to feel the temptation to use a macro. In this case, a simple macro is pretty easy. We'll take a type name and a length and implement the trait:

```
macro_rules! derive_try_from {
    ($type:ident, $length:expr) => {
        impl TryFrom<&str> for $type {
            type Error = String;

            fn try_from(value: &str) -> Result<Self, Self::Error> {
                let length = $length;
```

> **We change the error type from `&str` to `String` because we want to format the error message now.**

> **The `format!` macro won't recognize {$length} (that's macro syntax, not regular Rust syntax), so here we declare a variable called length that is equal to $length. Now, we can put this into format!, and it will recognize the length.**

```
            if value.chars().count() > length {
                Err(format!("Must be no longer than {length}"))
            } else {
                Ok(Self(value.to_string()))
            }
        }
    }
};
}
```

Now we are able to implement `TryFrom` for all three types without having to repeat ourselves over and over. The code now looks like this:

```
macro_rules! derive_try_from {
    ($type:ident, $length:expr) => {
        impl TryFrom<&str> for $type {
            type Error = String;

            fn try_from(value: &str) -> Result<Self, Self::Error> {
                let length = $length;
                if value.chars().count() > length {
                    Err(format!("Must be no longer than {length}"))
                } else {
                    Ok(Self(value.to_string()))
                }
            }
        }
    };
}

#[derive(Debug)]
struct SmallStringHolder(String);
#[derive(Debug)]
struct MediumStringHolder(String);
#[derive(Debug)]
struct LargeStringHolder(String);

derive_try_from!(SmallStringHolder, 5);
derive_try_from!(MediumStringHolder, 8);
derive_try_from!(LargeStringHolder, 12);

fn main() {
    println!("{:?}", SmallStringHolder::try_from("Hello there"));
    println!("{:?}", MediumStringHolder::try_from("Hello there"));
    println!("{:?}", LargeStringHolder::try_from("Hello there"));
}
```

The code works and the output is

```
Err("Must be no longer than 5")
Err("Must be no longer than 8")
Ok(LargeStringHolder("Hello there"))
```

Since we are using a macro, why stop here? We can declare the types themselves inside the macro, too. Now we can shrink the code some more:

```
macro_rules! make_type {
    ($type:ident, $length:expr) => {
        #[derive(Debug)]
        struct $type(String);

        impl TryFrom<&str> for $type {
            type Error = String;

            fn try_from(value: &str) -> Result<Self, Self::Error> {
                let length = $length;
                if value.chars().count() > length {
                    Err(format!("Must be no longer than {length}"))
                } else {
                    Ok(Self(value.to_string()))
                }
            }
        }
    };
}
```

> Now, we declare the types themselves inside the macro, so derive_try_from! will both create the types and implement TryFrom for them.

```
make_type!(SmallStringHolder, 5);
make_type!(MediumStringHolder, 8);
make_type!(LargeStringHolder, 12);

fn main() {
    println!("{:?}", SmallStringHolder::try_from("Hello there"));
    println!("{:?}", MediumStringHolder::try_from("Hello there"));
    println!("{:?}", LargeStringHolder::try_from("Hello there"));
}
```

If you are feeling up for a challenge, take a look at chapter 16 again, where we looked at const generics. If Rust didn't have const generics, how would you use a macro to build an array of various sizes and implement some traits like `TryFrom` or `Display` for each?

```
#[derive(Debug)]
struct Buffers<T, const N: usize> {
    array_one: [T; N],
    array_two: [T; N],
}

fn main() {
    let buffer_1 = Buffers {
        array_one: [0u8; 3],
        array_two: [0; 3],
    };

    let buffer_2 = Buffers {
        array_one: [0i32; 4],
        array_two: [10; 4],
    };
}
```

As you can see, macros are pretty complicated! Usually, you only want a macro to automatically do something that a simple function can't do very well. The best way to learn about macros is to look at other macro examples until you get used to the syntax and try modifying them on your own. Macros are frequently used but rarely written, so very few people can sit down and write a complicated macro that works on the first try. Hopefully, this chapter has gotten you comfortable enough with them that you might want to start trying them on your own.

We have now reached the very last section of the book called "Unfinished Projects," which starts in the next chapter. Over the next two chapters, we will take a look at six small projects that work on their own but that you will probably want to expand yourself. See you there!

Summary

- Macros are used a lot but rarely written. Very few people are macro experts, but learning to read them is important.
- A macro can take any input, but if you tell the macro the kind of input (an expression, statement, etc.), you can give the input a name and use it in a similar way to a variable.
- Macros can call other macros and even call themselves.
- A lot of the macros in the standard library are built into the compiler, and their details can't be seen.
- Most people turn to macros for the first time to save time and reduce code duplication.

Unfinished projects: Projects for you to finish

This chapter covers

- Making a typing tutor
- Making a Wikipedia article searcher
- Making a clock and stopwatch

You made it to the last part of the book, well done! J.R.R. Tolkien, the author of *Lord of the Rings*, wrote quite a few stories that he never finished during his lifetime. These were completed by his son and published under the name *Unfinished Tales*.

These last two chapters are a sort of *Unfinished Tales* for you, the developer, to pick up and develop on your own. Each chapter contains three unfinished projects for you to pick up yourself and keep developing. They are finished in the sense that they all work: you can just type `cargo run` and start using them. But they are meant to be as short as possible, and that means they only have the most basic functionality. After that, it's up to you to keep working on them if you feel like it.

These two chapters also use quite a few new crates because the crates used for command-line interfaces (CLIs) and graphical user interfaces (GUIs) are best learned through real use on a computer. The crates used in this chapter won't work on the Playground because they require access to system resources and the ability to do things like take user input in real time and open new windows.

23.1 Setup for the last two chapters

Each of the working code samples for these six unfinished projects will be about 75 to 100 lines long. While short, that's still a bit too long for us to look at the entire code every time a new line is added. Instead, the code development will be divided into four steps:

- In step 1, we will set up the project and write some code.
- Step 2 will involve developing the code and will have most of the work.
- Step 3 will finish up with some further development and cleanup of the code.
- Finally, step 4 will contain some ideas for you to develop the projects further.

23.2 Typing tutor

The first unfinished project is a typing tutor. It takes a text file and displays it, and the user's job is to type the text that is displayed. The user will be able to see where the text has been typed wrong, and the typing tutor will display how well the user did after the test is over. You can do a search for "typing test" online to see what sort of functionality this small app will aim for.

23.2.1 Setup and first code

This first project uses Crossterm (https://docs.rs/crossterm/latest/crossterm/), a crate that lets you detect and react to user input as it happens. The user input that Crossterm lets you see includes keyboard, mouse, screen resizing, and more, but we only need to monitor the keyboard input. Another nice thing about Crossterm is its size, as it only brings in 22 dependencies and will compile in just a few seconds.

The name Crossterm, by the way, comes from the fact that Rust crates used to be built almost exclusively for Unix/Linux back when the language was still small. Crossterm was the first terminal library that was a *crossover*, containing support for both Unix and Windows.

The dependencies for this project are pretty simple. Just add this to your Cargo.toml file:

```
[dependencies]
crossterm = "0.26.1"
```

Crossterm has a function called `read()` that is used to see user input, so let's put it in a loop and see what happens. Try running this code and typing `Hi!`:

```
use crossterm::event::read;

fn main() {
    loop {
```

```
        println!("{:?}", read().unwrap());
    }
}
```

The output includes both pressing keys and releasing keys, so it will depend somewhat on how you type, but it will probably look something like this:

```
Key(KeyEvent { code: Char('H'), modifiers: SHIFT, kind: Press, state: NONE
⮡ })
Key(KeyEvent { code: Char('i'), modifiers: NONE, kind: Press, state: NONE
⮡ })
Key(KeyEvent { code: Char('h'), modifiers: NONE, kind: Release, state: NONE
⮡ })
Key(KeyEvent { code: Char('i'), modifiers: NONE, kind: Release, state: NONE
⮡ })
Key(KeyEvent { code: Char('!'), modifiers: SHIFT, kind: Press, state: NONE
⮡ })
Key(KeyEvent { code: Char('1'), modifiers: NONE, kind: Release, state: NONE
⮡ })
```

Here, the user pressed 'H' with shift, then pressed 'i'. Then the user released 'h' (no shift anymore), then released 'i', then pressed '!', and then released '1' (that is, the ! but without the shift).

If you type more slowly and deliberately, it will look like this:

```
Key(KeyEvent { code: Char('H'), modifiers: SHIFT, kind: Press, state: NONE
⮡ })
Key(KeyEvent { code: Char('h'), modifiers: NONE, kind: Release, state: NONE
⮡ })
Key(KeyEvent { code: Char('i'), modifiers: NONE, kind: Press, state: NONE
⮡ })
Key(KeyEvent { code: Char('i'), modifiers: NONE, kind: Release, state: NONE
⮡ })
Key(KeyEvent { code: Char('!'), modifiers: SHIFT, kind: Press, state: NONE
⮡ })
```

23.2.2 *Developing the code*

A look through the documentation shows that `Key` seen in the previous output comes from an enum called `Event`, which includes events such as `Key`, `Mouse`, and `Resize`:

```
pub enum Event {
    FocusGained,
    FocusLost,
    Key(KeyEvent),
    Mouse(MouseEvent),
    Paste(String),
    Resize(u16, u16),
}
```

We only care about `Key` events, so we can use an `if let` to react to `Key` events and ignore the rest.

The `Key` variant inside `Event` contains a `KeyEvent` struct:

```
pub struct KeyEvent {
    pub code: KeyCode,
    pub modifiers: KeyModifiers,
    pub kind: KeyEventKind,
    pub state: KeyEventState,
}
```

Let's see which parameters in the `KeyEvent` struct we care about:

- `code`—This contains information on which key was pressed. We definitely want to use this to `.push()` to or `.pop()` to our `String`, which keeps track of what the user has typed so far.
- `modifiers`—This refers to whether the user is pressing keys such as Shift, CTRL, and so on. But the `code` parameter gives us the correct capital or lowercase character on its own, so we don't need to think about `modifiers`.
- `kind`—We definitely care about `kind` because `KeyEventKind` includes `Press` and `Release`. We don't want to add or pop every time the character *releases* a key, just when the user presses one.
- `state`—This parameter holds a lot of extra possible state information (like whether caps lock is on) that we don't need to worry about.

Now it's time to pull in a file for the user to try to type. Make a file called `typing.txt` and put some text—any text—in there. For our output, we'll assume that the file says `"Hi, can you type this?"`. We can use the `read_to_string()` function that we learned in chapter 18 to read the file and put the contents into a `String`, and we'll make a `String` called `user_input` that holds everything the user has typed. And then we'll print out both `String`s one after another. The code is now as follows:

```
use crossterm::{
    event::{read, Event, KeyCode, KeyEventKind},
};
use std::fs::read_to_string;

fn main() {
    let file_content = read_to_string("typing.txt").unwrap();
    let mut user_input = String::new();

    loop {
        println!("{file_content}");                  ⎤ The underscore shows the
        println!("{user_input}_");          ⟵──┘ user where the cursor is.
        if let Event::Key(key_event) = read().unwrap() {
            if key_event.kind == KeyEventKind::Press {
                match key_event.code {
                    KeyCode::Backspace => {
                        user_input.pop();           ⎤ This allows the user to
                    }                                 │ escape the program without
                    KeyCode::Esc => break,   ⟵──┘ having to do an ugly Ctrl-C.
                    KeyCode::Char(c) => {
                        user_input.push(c);
                    }
```

```
                    _ => {}
                  }
                }
              }
            }
          }
        }
```

The output looks pretty good! As the user types away, the `String` to type against and the current input are both showing up. The output now looks like this as you type:

```
Hi, can you type this?
_
Hi, can you type this?
H_
Hi, can you type this?
Hi_
Hi, can you type this?
Hi_
Hi, can you type this?
Hi_
Hi, can you type this?
Hi,_
Hi, can you type this?
Hi,_
Hi, can you type this?
Hi, _
Hi, can you type this?
Hi, _
Hi, can you type this?
Hi, c_
```

So far, so good, but the output quickly fills up the screen and makes it look messy pretty quickly. And you can probably imagine how much worse it would look if we had to type a longer text. Let's do something about that!

23.2.3 Further development and cleanup

The next steps are as follows:

1. We want to clear the screen each time a key is pressed. Crossterm has a macro called `execute!` that takes a writer (like `stdout`) and a command. Crossterm commands are simple structs named after what they do: `Clear`, `ScrollDown`, `SetSize`, `SetTitle`, `EnableLineWrap`, and so on. We will use `Clear`, which holds an enum called `ClearType` that offers a number of ways to clear the screen. We want to clear the whole screen, so we will pass in a `Clear(ClearType::All)`. Putting all this together, the whole line will look like this:

   ```
   execute!(stdout(), Clear(ClearType::All));
   ```

2. Instead of just printing out the user input, we can use what we learned in chapter 8 to `.zip()` together an iterator of the content to type and another iterator of the user's output. With that, we can compare each character against the

other. If they are the same, we will print out the letter, and if they are different (in other words, if the user types the wrong key), we will print out a * instead.

3 We can calculate the letters typed correctly when the user presses enter to finish the typing test. This is pretty easy and involves another .zip() as previously discussed.

4 We can replace some .unwrap() calls with the question mark operator.

5 Finally, we'll put together a quick App struct that will hold the two strings. This will make main() a bit nicer to read.

The final code is as follows:

```rust
use crossterm::{
    event::{read, Event, KeyCode, KeyEventKind},
    execute,
    terminal::{Clear, ClearType},
};
use std::{fs::read_to_string, io::stdout};

struct App {
    file_content: String,
    user_input: String,
}

impl App {
    fn new(file_name: &str) -> Result<Self, std::io::Error> {
        let file_content = read_to_string(file_name)?;
        Ok(Self {
            file_content,
            user_input: String::new(),
        })
    }
}

fn main() -> Result<(), std::io::Error> {
    let mut app = App::new("typing.txt")?;

    loop {
        println!("{}", app.file_content);
        for (letter1, letter2) in
        app.user_input.chars().zip(app.file_content.chars()) {
            if letter1 == letter2 {
                print!("{letter2}");
            } else {
                print!("*");
            }
        }
        println!("_");
        if let Event::Key(key_event) = read()? {
            if key_event.kind == KeyEventKind::Press {
                match key_event.code {
                    KeyCode::Backspace => {
                        app.user_input.pop();
                    }
```

```
                KeyCode::Esc => break,
                KeyCode::Char(c) => {
                    app.user_input.push(c);
                }
                KeyCode::Enter => {
                    let total_chars = app.file_content.chars().count();
                    let total_right = app
                        .user_input
                        .chars()
                        .zip(app.file_content.chars())
                        .filter(|(a, b)| a == b)
                        .count();
                    println!("You got {total_right} out of
{total_chars}!");
                    return Ok(());
                }
                _ => {}
            }
        }
        execute!(stdout(), Clear(ClearType::All))?;
    }
    Ok(())
}
```

The output now when using the typing app should look pretty simple—something
like this:

```
Hi, can you type this?
Hi, can**** type thi_
```

In this case, the user has typed the first characters correctly, made four mistakes, and
is now two characters away from finishing the test. The output is pretty clean, but
there's a lot you might want to add to the app now.

23.2.4 *Over to you*

Now that the basic functionality for the typing tutor works, here are some ideas to continue developing it:

- Check the time it took to pass the test and give the user the typing speed in
  words per minute. Chapter 17 should help you out here if you are unsure where
  to start.
- Use a crate like `ansi_term` (https://crates.io/crates/ansi_term) to show incorrect entries in red instead of just an asterisk.
- Right now, `user_input` still increases in length if the user keeps typing after
  reaching the end of the test. The extra characters aren't displayed, but if, for
  example, you are 10 characters over, you will need to hit backspace 10 times to
  see the output change again. How would you keep `user_input` from getting
  longer than the `file_content` string?

- Implement accented characters. What if you have a typing test in another language? Can you set up the test so that the character can use dead keys (like e + ' to show é) instead of needing to switch keyboard layouts?
- Add more text samples. Maybe use the functionality in the next project to bring in Wikipedia article summaries to use as typing tests.
- The French novel *La Disparition* is a book without a single instance of the letter *e*. To help someone else do the same, could you remake the typing tutor into an app that removes any word that contains the letter *e* as the user types?

23.3 *Wikipedia article summary searcher*

The second unfinished project quickly pulls up the summary of a Wikipedia article. Getting started on this project is pretty easy because Wikipedia has an API that doesn't require registration or a key to use. One of the endpoints on the Wikipedia API gives a summary and some other information for any article, which should be perfect for us. The output from that API is a bit too messy to paste into this book, but you can see a sample output by pasting the following link into your browser and changing PAGE_NAME_HERE to any article name you can think of:

```
https://en.wikipedia.org/api/rest_v1/page/summary/PAGE_NAME_HERE
```

23.3.1 *Setup and first code*

The dependencies for this project are pretty easy because we already know how to use crossterm, and we learned to use reqwest in chapter 19. Putting these two together gives us 105 compiling units. Compiling shouldn't take too long, but if you want to reduce compiling time, you can choose a crate called ureq (https://docs.rs/ureq/latest/ureq/), which is smaller and simpler than reqwest. Here are the dependencies:

```
[dependencies]
reqwest = { version = "0.11.16", features = ["blocking"] }
crossterm = "0.26.1"
```

We can start with something similar to the code in the typing tutor. We'll have an App struct with a string called user_input that grows and shrinks as before, except that pressing Enter will search Wikipedia. The first code looks like this:

```
use crossterm::{
    event::{read, Event, KeyCode, KeyEventKind},
    execute,
    terminal::{Clear, ClearType},
};
use reqwest::blocking::get;
use std::io::stdout;

#[derive(Debug, Default)]
struct App {
    user_input: String
}
```

```
const URL: &str = "https://en.wikipedia.org/api/rest_v1/page/summary";

fn main() {
    let mut app = App::default();

    loop {
        if let Event::Key(key_event) = read().unwrap() {
            if key_event.kind == KeyEventKind::Press {
                execute!(stdout(), Clear(ClearType::All)).unwrap();
                match key_event.code {
                    KeyCode::Backspace => {
                        app.user_input.pop();
                        println!("{}", app.user_input);
                    }
                    KeyCode::Esc => app.user_input.clear(),
                    KeyCode::Enter => {
                        println!("Searching Wikipedia...");
                        let req = get(format!("{URL}/{}", app.user_input))
                        .unwrap();
                        let text = req.text().unwrap();
                        println!("{text}");
                    }
                    KeyCode::Char(c) => {
                        app.user_input.push(c);
                        println!("{}", app.user_input);
                    }
                    _ => {}
                }
            }
        }
    }
}
```

Easy enough! If we type a nonsense word and press Enter, we get a nice error message:

```
{"type":"https://mediawiki.org/wiki/HyperSwitch/errors/not_found","title":"
Not found.","method":"get","detail":"Page or revision not found.",
"uri":"/en.wikipedia.org/v1/page/summary/Nthonthoe"}
```

And if we type a real word like *Calgary*, we get a massive JSON response that is a little too big to fit here. The response from Wikipedia's servers is definitely coming in, but we should tidy it up somehow.

23.3.2 *Developing the code*

The JSON response has a lot of properties that we don't need like `"thumbnail"`, `"wikibase_item"`, and `"revision"`, but three properties inside it look useful to us: `title`, `description`, and `extract`. Let's make a struct with those three properties. Then, to deserialize into the struct as we learned in chapter 17, we are going to want to bring in the `serde` and `serde_json` crates.

Now, the dependencies are

```
[dependencies]
reqwest = { version = "0.11.16", features = ["blocking"] }
```

```
crossterm = "0.26.1"
serde = { version = "1.0.160", features = ["derive"] }
serde_json = "1.0.96"
```

By giving our struct the `Deserialize` trait and using `serde_json::from_str()` function to convert from JSON, we have a much nicer output:

```
use crossterm::{
    event::{read, Event, KeyCode, KeyEventKind},
    execute,
    terminal::{Clear, ClearType},
};
use serde::Deserialize;
use std::io::stdout;

#[derive(Debug, Deserialize, Default)]
struct App {
    user_input: String
}

#[derive(Debug, Deserialize, Default)]
struct CurrentArticle {
    title: String,
    description: String,
    extract: String
}

const URL: &str = "https://en.wikipedia.org/api/rest_v1/page/summary";

fn main() {
    let mut app = App::default();

    loop {
        if let Event::Key(key_event) = read().unwrap() {
            if key_event.kind == KeyEventKind::Press {
                execute!(stdout(), Clear(ClearType::All)).unwrap();
                match key_event.code {
                    KeyCode::Backspace => {
                        app.user_input.pop();
                        println!("{}", app.user_input);
                    }
                    KeyCode::Esc => app.user_input.clear(),
                    KeyCode::Enter => {
                        println!("Searching Wikipedia...");
                        let req = get(format!("{URL}/{}", app.user_input))
                            .unwrap();
                        let text = req.text().unwrap();
                        let as_article: CurrentArticle =
                            serde_json::from_str(&text).unwrap();
                        println!("{as_article:#?}");
                    }
                    KeyCode::Char(c) => {
                        app.user_input.push(c);
                        println!("{}", app.user_input);
                    }
                }
```

```
                    _ => {}
                }
            }
        }
    }
}
```

Okay, let's type `Interlingue` (that's the name of a language) and hit Enter. Quite readable! The output will now look like this:

```
Searching Wikipedia...
CurrentArticle {
    title: "Interlingue",
    description: "International auxiliary language created 1922",
    extract: "Interlingue, originally Occidental, is an international
    ➡auxiliary language created in 1922 and renamed in 1949. Its creator,
    ➡Edgar de Wahl, sought to achieve maximal grammatical regularity and
    ➡natural character. The vocabulary is based on pre-existing words from
    ➡various languages and a derivational system which uses recognized
    ➡prefixes and suffixes.",
}
```

23.3.3 *Further development and cleanup*

Now, let's improve the output and do some refactoring. The easiest place to start is by removing the calls to `.unwrap()` and replacing them with the question mark operator. We could use the `anyhow` crate, but let's practice the `Box<dyn Error>` method that we learned in chapter 13. We can move some code out of `main` into a method for our `App` called `.get_article()`, which will return a `Result<(), Box<dyn Error>>`, which means that `main()` will return a `Result<(), Box<dyn Error>>`, too, because it is also using the question mark operator. Also, implementing `Display` for our `App` struct will make the output look much nicer.

The code after these changes is as follows:

```
use crossterm::{
    event::{read, Event, KeyCode, KeyEventKind},
    execute,
    terminal::{Clear, ClearType},
};
use reqwest::blocking::get;
use serde::{Deserialize, Serialize};
use std::{error::Error, io::stdout};

#[derive(Debug, Serialize, Deserialize, Default)]
struct CurrentArticle {
    title: String,
    description: String,
    extract: String,
}

#[derive(Debug, Default)]
struct App {
    current_article: CurrentArticle,
    search_string: String,
```

```rust
}

impl App {
    fn get_article(&mut self) -> Result<(), Box<dyn Error>> {
        let text = get(format!("{URL}/{}", self.search_string))?.text()?;
        if let Ok(article) = serde_json::from_str::<CurrentArticle>(&text) {
            self.current_article = article;
        }
        Ok(())
    }
}

impl std::fmt::Display for App {
    fn fmt(&self, f: &mut std::fmt::Formatter<'_>) -> std::fmt::Result {
        write!(
            f,
            "
                Searching for: {}

Title: {}
------------
Description: {}
------------
{}",
            self.search_string,
            self.current_article.title,
            self.current_article.description,
            self.current_article.extract
        )
    }
}

const URL: &str = "https://en.wikipedia.org/api/rest_v1/page/summary";

fn main() -> Result<(), Box<dyn Error>> {
    let mut app = App::default();

    loop {
        println!("{app}");
        if let Event::Key(key_event) = read()? {
            if key_event.kind == KeyEventKind::Press {
                match key_event.code {
                    KeyCode::Backspace => {
                        app.search_string.pop();
                    }
                    KeyCode::Esc => app.search_string.clear(),
                    KeyCode::Enter => app.get_article()?,
                    KeyCode::Char(c) => {
                        app.search_string.push(c);
                    }
                    _ => {}
                }
            }
        }
        execute!(stdout(), Clear(ClearType::All))?;
    }
}
```

Now the output looks pretty clean!

```
                    Searching for: Interlingue

Title: Interlingue
------------
Description: International auxiliary language created 1922
------------
Interlingue, originally Occidental, is an international auxiliary language
➥created in 1922 and renamed in 1949. Its creator, Edgar de Wahl,
➥sought to achieve maximal grammatical regularity and natural
➥character. The vocabulary is based on pre-existing words from various
➥languages and a derivational system which uses recognized prefixes and
➥suffixes.
```

23.3.4 *Over to you*

Let's think about what could be developed with this app now that the basic functionality works:

- The output is pretty clean now, but nothing is displayed when the user searches for a page that doesn't exist. What error info should be displayed to help the user know what to do when something goes wrong? What about other errors like a broken internet connection?
- You will be able to make the output even nicer after we finish the next project, which uses a crate that lets you put together terminal interfaces that look almost graphical.
- Wikipedia is available in more languages than just English. How could you add an option to let the user switch languages?

23.4 *Terminal stopwatch and clock*

The third project we will make is a text- or terminal-based user interface (TUI) that holds a stopwatch and a clock. In the previous examples, we used Crossterm on its own, which worked well enough. But there are crates that allow you to put together a terminal-based app that looks surprisingly nice. These are fairly popular because they are quick to compile, extremely responsive, and run inside the same terminal window we use to `cargo run` our programs.

23.4.1 *Setup and first code*

The main crate for TUIs in Rust is called `ratatui` (https://docs.rs/ratatui/latest/ratatui/), which, in fact, uses `crossterm` on its backend. To be precise, the main crate is/was known as `tui`, but the owner of the crate ran out of time to maintain the crate (real life will do that to you sometimes; https://github.com/fdehau/tui-rs/issues/654), and it was forked under the new name `ratatui`. The original `tui` works just fine, but `ratatui` is being actively maintained and has new features added, so we will go with `ratatui`.

> **NOTE** We will use version 0.21 of `ratatui`, which is more or less the same as the original `tui` crate, but at the time of publication `ratatui` has reached

version 0.24 with quite a few new features added! By the time you read this book, there may be even more.

Every GUI and TUI crate has its own preferred method for building user interfaces, meaning that the quickest way to get started is to look for a working example. Inside ratatui is a Terminal that holds a backend, such as the crossterm backend. There is also a method called .draw() to draw the output on the screen, which we will run in a loop. Inside this method is a closure, which provides a struct on which we can use methods to create widgets and then call .render_widget() to display them.

Inside every loop, we will create a Layout, give it a direction (horizontal or vertical), set the size of each part of the layout by giving them constraints, and then split the layout into parts based on the total screen size. We want a simple horizontal app split 50% each way, so it will be set up as follows. Note the builder pattern here:

```
let layout = Layout::default()
    .direction(Direction::Horizontal)
    .constraints([Constraint::Percentage(50), Constraint::Percentage(50)])
    .split(f.size());
let stopwatch_area = layout[0];
let utc_time_area = layout[1];
```

The f is a struct called a Frame that the closure gives us access to. The f is a variable name and could be any other name as well.

With this code, we have split up the layout, but we haven't made anything to display yet. To display something, we can choose among some of the widgets that ratatui offers, such as BarChart, Block, Dataset, Row, Table, Paragraph, and so on. A Paragraph lets us display some text, and we can put it inside a Block, which is the base widget used to give other widgets a border. All together it looks like this:

```
let stopwatch_block =
    Block::default().title("Stopwatch").borders(Borders::ALL);
stopwatch_text = Paragraph::new("First block").block(stopwatch_block);
```

And then finally comes the .render_widget() method, which takes a widget and an area:

```
f.render_widget(stopwatch_text, stopwatch_area);
```

That was quite a bit of typing, but nothing too complex: we are just instructing the TUI what to display. Let's put it all together now:

```
use std::io::stdout;
use ratatui::{
    backend::CrosstermBackend,
    layout::{Constraint, Direction, Layout},
    widgets::{Block, Borders, Paragraph},
    Terminal,
};

fn main() {
    let stdout = stdout();
    let backend = CrosstermBackend::new(stdout);
    let mut terminal = Terminal::new(backend).unwrap();
```

The ratatui Terminal takes a crossterm backend.

```
loop {
    terminal
        .draw(|f| {
            let layout = Layout::default()
                .direction(Direction::Horizontal)
                .constraints([Constraint::Percentage(50), Constraint::
                ➡Percentage(50)])
                .split(f.size());
            let stopwatch_area = layout[0];
            let utc_time_area = layout[1];

            let stopwatch_block =
Block::default().title("Stopwatch").bord
➡ers(Borders::ALL);
            let utc_time_block = Block::default().title("UTC time").bord
                ➡ers(Borders::ALL);

            let stopwatch_text = Paragraph::new("I'm a stopwatch").block
                ➡(stopwatch_block);
            let utc_text = Paragraph::new("Hi I'm in London").block(utc_
                ➡time_block);

            f.render_widget(stopwatch_text, stopwatch_area);
            f.render_widget(utc_text, utc_time_area);

        })
        .unwrap();
    std::thread::sleep(std::time::Duration::from_millis(20));        ◀────────┐
    terminal.clear().unwrap();   ◀─────┐                                      │
}                                      │                                      │
}                                      │                                      │
```

Ratatui has a convenience method called	The terminal is going to loop as fast as it
.clear(), so we don't need to use a crossterm	possibly can, so let's put it to sleep each
command to clear the screen anymore.	time to keep the screen from flickering.
	Using .sleep() can be a bad idea in complex
	and async code, but we are just running a
	little terminal app on a single thread.

If you run the code now, you should see a pretty nice-looking terminal interface (figure 23.1). It isn't doing anything at the moment, but you can resize the window and watch how the display changes. This is a lot slicker than just using `crossterm`!

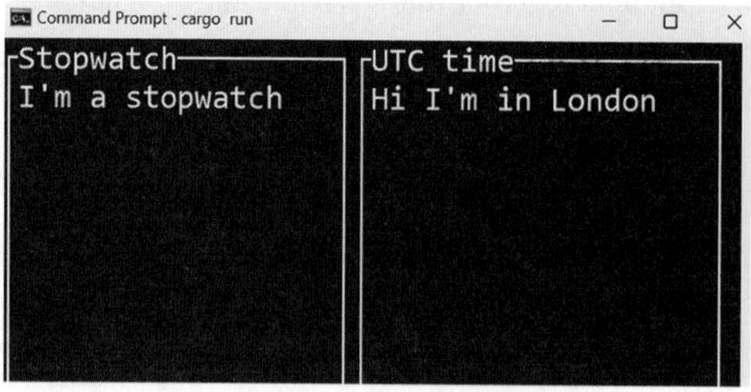

Figure 23.1   Terminal interface

23.4.2 *Developing the code*

It's now time to start implementing the clock and stopwatch. We've used the `chrono` crate before in chapter 17, so this should not be too hard. Getting the current UTC datetime is quite easy:

```
chrono::offset::Utc::now();
```

Printing this out will look something like this:

```
2023-06-10T04:13:05.169920165Z
```

That output isn't too readable. Fortunately, the `DateTime` struct in chrono has a method called `.format()` that lets us specify how we want it to look. This method takes a `&str` that recognizes tokens after a `%` sign, such as `%Y` to display the year, `%H` to display the hour, and so on (http://mng.bz/A8Gp). Let's give it a try:

```
chrono::offset::Utc::now().format("%Y/%m/%d %H:%M:%S")
```

Now the output is much better:

```
2023/06/10 04:18:46
```

For the stopwatch, we are going to have to think a bit. A stopwatch should have three states:

- *Not started*—In this state, it should display 0:00:00.
- *Running*—In this state, we should see the time passing as the seconds and milliseconds go by.
- *Stopped*—In this state, we should see the seconds and milliseconds that passed when we stopped it.

That sounds like an enum with three variants. Fortunately, the state changes are easy: if the user presses a key, the stopwatch starts running. Another key press stops it, and the stopwatch shows the time that passed. Finally, another key resets it, bringing it back to a "not started" state.

The last thing to figure out is how to display the time. This isn't too hard either, thanks to the `Instant` struct we learned to use in chapter 17. When the stopwatch starts, it should hold an `Instant::now()`, and as it runs or it has stopped, it should use `.elapsed().millis()` on the `Instant` to see how much time has passed in milliseconds.

Following this, all we need to do is to "pull off" the minutes, the seconds, and the milliseconds—in that order. For example, if the stopwatch stops and 70,555 milliseconds have passed, the code should do the following steps:

1. One minute has 60,000 milliseconds. See how many minutes have passed: 70,555 / 60,000 = 1 minute.
2. Subtract the minutes in milliseconds: 70,555 − 1 * 60,000 = 10,555 milliseconds left.
3. One second has 1,000 milliseconds. See how many seconds have passed: 10,555 / 1,000 = 10 seconds.

4 Subtract the seconds in milliseconds: $10,555 - 10 * 1,000 = 555$ milliseconds left.

5 Finally, divide the milliseconds by 10 to get the split seconds (hundredths of a second).

When you put all that together, our `Stopwatch` struct will handle the logic like this:

```
fn new() -> Self {
    Self {
        now: Instant::now(),
        state: StopwatchState::NotStarted,
        display: String::from("0:00:00"),
    }
}
fn get_time(&self) -> String {
    use StopwatchState::*;
    match self.state {
        NotStarted => String::from("0:00:00"),
        Running => {
            let mut elapsed = self.now.elapsed().as_millis();
            let minutes = elapsed / 60000;
            elapsed -= minutes * 60000;
            let seconds = elapsed / 1000;
            elapsed -= seconds * 1000;
            let split_seconds = elapsed / 10;
            format!("{minutes}:{seconds}:{split_seconds}")
        }
        Done => self.display.clone(),
    }
}
```

Here, we see how many full minutes there are to display.

Then we subtract these minutes in milliseconds from the total time elapsed.

Then we repeat with the next largest unit, seconds. And so on.

With the stopwatch logic out of the way, we now have a working clock and stopwatch to play around with.

The last new entry to the code is the `poll()` method inside `crossterm`, which we will use instead of `read()`. Using `read()` waits until a user event takes place, but we want the stopwatch to run even if nobody is pressing any keys. The `poll()` method lets you specify a `Duration` to wait for an event. In our case, we will enter `0` for the `Duration`. Doing so will let us quickly check for a key event every loop, followed by redrawing the screen.

Here is the code we have so far:

```
use std::{
    io::stdout,
    time::Instant,
};

use crossterm::event::{poll, read, Event, KeyCode, KeyEventKind};
use ratatui::{
    backend::CrosstermBackend,
    layout::{Constraint, Direction, Layout},
    widgets::{Block, Borders, Paragraph},
    Terminal,
};
```

```rust
struct Stopwatch {
    now: Instant,
    state: StopwatchState,
    display: String,
}

enum StopwatchState {
    NotStarted,
    Running,
    Done,
}

impl Stopwatch {
    fn new() -> Self {
        Self {
            now: Instant::now(),
            state: StopwatchState::NotStarted,
            display: String::from("0:00:00"),
        }
    }
    fn get_time(&self) -> String {
        use StopwatchState::*;
        match self.state {
            NotStarted => String::from("0:00:00"),
            Running => {
                let mut elapsed = self.now.elapsed().as_millis();
                let minutes = elapsed / 60000;
                elapsed -= minutes * 60000;
                let seconds = elapsed / 1000;
                elapsed -= seconds * 1000;
                let split_seconds = elapsed / 10;
                format!("{minutes}:{seconds}:{split_seconds}")
            }
            Done => self.display.clone(),
        }
    }
    fn next_state(&mut self) {
        use StopwatchState::*;
        match self.state {
            NotStarted => {
                self.now = Instant::now();
                self.state = Running;
            }
            Running => {
                self.display = self.get_time();
                self.state = Done;
            }
            Done => self.state = NotStarted,
        }
    }
}

fn main() {
    let stdout = stdout();
    let backend = CrosstermBackend::new(stdout);
    let mut terminal = Terminal::new(backend).unwrap();
    let mut stopwatch = Stopwatch::new();
```

```
    loop {
        if poll(std::time::Duration::from_millis(0)).unwrap() {
            if let Event::Key(key_event) = read().unwrap() {
                if let (KeyCode::Enter, KeyEventKind::Press) = (key_event.co
                ➥de, key_event.kind) {
                    stopwatch.next_state();
                }
            }
        }

        terminal
            .draw(|f| {
                let layout = Layout::default()
                    .direction(Direction::Horizontal)
                    .constraints([Constraint::Percentage(50), Constraint::Pe
                    ➥rcentage(50)])
                    .split(f.size());
                let stopwatch_area = layout[0];
                let utc_time_area = layout[1];

                let stopwatch_block = Block::default().title("Stopwatch").bo
                ➥rders(Borders::ALL);
                let utc_time_block = Block::default()
                    .title("UTC time")
                    .borders(Borders::ALL);

                let stopwatch_text = Paragraph::new(stopwatch.get_time()).bl
                ➥ock(stopwatch_block);
                let utc_text = Paragraph::new(chrono::offset::Utc::now().for
                ➥mat("%Y/%m/%d %H:%M:%S").to_string())
                    .block(utc_time_block);

                f.render_widget(stopwatch_text, stopwatch_area);
                f.render_widget(utc_text, utc_time_area);
            })
            .unwrap();
        std::thread::sleep(std::time::Duration::from_millis(20));
        terminal.clear().unwrap();
    }
}
```

The output on your screen should now look like figure 23.2.

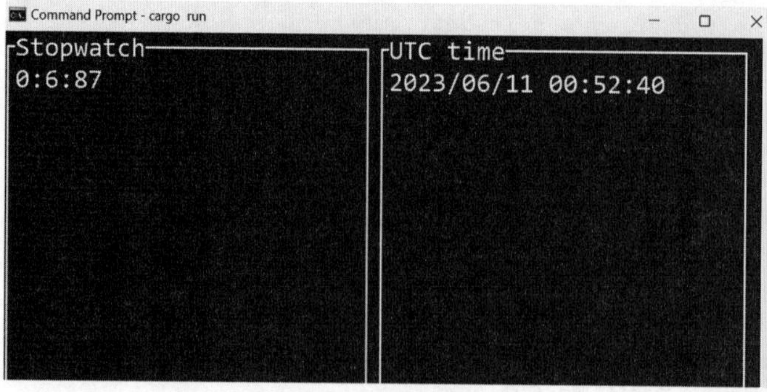

Figure 23.2   Updated terminal interface

23.4.3 *Further development and cleanup*

The code is working quite well, so let's focus on cleaning it up. As always, we can replace calls to .unwrap() with the question mark operator. Let's practice with anyhow this time by returning a Result<(), anyhow::Error> inside main(). The dependencies inside Cargo.toml should now look like this:

```
[dependencies]
anyhow = "1.0.71"
chrono = "0.4"
crossterm = "0.26.1"
ratatui = "0.21"
```

So what else should we clean up?

The builder pattern in ratatui makes it easy to set up an app, but it is also quite wordy. Let's do some general readability cleanup, too, while we are at it. Instead of calling Block::default().title and so on twice inside main, we can put together a quick helper function that takes a &str and returns a Block. The same will go for the call to generate a formatted UTC time, which makes the line in main really long. This can be a helper function, too.

This sort of readability cleanup is a personal decision, but a good general rule is that helper functions can be good for readability as long as the important information can be seen in the first function. However, too many helper functions can be bad for readability. Writing a helper function that calls another helper function and then *another* helper function can help each function be nice and small, but it will take a lot of clicking for the reader of your code to finally find out exactly what is being done. Imagining yourself reading your own code one year later is a good way to decide how to refactor your code for readability.

In any case, here is what our code looks like now with some cleanup done:

```
use std::{io::stdout, thread::sleep, time::Duration, time::Instant};
use chrono::offset::Utc;
use crossterm::event::{poll, read, Event, KeyCode, KeyEventKind};
use ratatui::{
    backend::CrosstermBackend,
    layout::{Constraint, Direction, Layout},
    widgets::{Block, Borders, Paragraph},
    Terminal,
};

struct Stopwatch {
    now: Instant,
    state: StopwatchState,
    display: String,
}

enum StopwatchState {
    NotStarted,
    Running,
    Done,
}
```

```
impl Stopwatch {
    fn new() -> Self {
        Self {
            now: Instant::now(),
            state: StopwatchState::NotStarted,
            display: String::from("0:00:00"),
        }
    }
    fn get_time(&self) -> String {
        use StopwatchState::*;
        match self.state {
            NotStarted => String::from("0:00:00"),
            Running => {
                let mut elapsed = self.now.elapsed().as_millis();
                let minutes = elapsed / 60000;
                elapsed -= minutes * 60000;
                let seconds = elapsed / 1000;
                elapsed -= seconds * 1000;
                let split_seconds = elapsed / 10;
                format!("{minutes}:{seconds}:{split_seconds}")
            }
            Done => self.display.clone(),
        }
    }
    fn next_state(&mut self) {
        use StopwatchState::*;
        match self.state {
            NotStarted => {
                self.now = Instant::now();
                self.state = Running;
            }
            Running => {
                self.display = self.get_time();
                self.state = Done;
            }
            Done => self.state = NotStarted,
        }
    }
}

fn block_with(input: &str) -> Block {
    Block::default().title(input).borders(Borders::ALL)
}

fn utc_pretty() -> String {
    Utc::now().format("%Y/%m/%d %H:%M:%S").to_string()
}

fn main() -> Result<(), anyhow::Error> {
    let stdout = stdout();
    let backend = CrosstermBackend::new(stdout);
    let mut terminal = Terminal::new(backend)?;
    let mut stopwatch = Stopwatch::new();

    loop {
        if poll(Duration::from_millis(0))? {
```

```
            if let Event::Key(key_event) = read()? {
                if let (KeyCode::Enter, KeyEventKind::Press) = (key_event
                ➥.code, key_event.kind) {
                    stopwatch.next_state();
                }
            }
        }

        terminal.draw(|f| {
            let layout = Layout::default()
                .direction(Direction::Horizontal)
                .constraints([Constraint::Percentage(50), Constraint::Percen
                ➥tage(50)])
                .split(f.size());

            let stopwatch_area = layout[0];
            let utc_time_area = layout[1];

            let stopwatch_block = block_with("Stopwatch");
            let utc_time_block = block_with("Time in London");

            let stopwatch_text = Paragraph::new(stopwatch.get_time()).block(
            ➥stopwatch_block);
            let utc_text = Paragraph::new(utc_pretty()).block(utc_time_block
            ➥);

            f.render_widget(stopwatch_text, stopwatch_area);
            f.render_widget(utc_text, utc_time_area);
        })?;
        sleep(Duration::from_millis(20));
        terminal.clear()?;
    }
}
```

23.4.4 *Over to you*

There's quite a bit that you might want to add to this app. Here are some ideas:

- The stopwatch outputs numbers like 0:9:1 but also numbers like 0:10:14, which is two characters longer. Can you make the display look cleaner than this?
- Add some more cities in different time zones and line them up underneath the time in London.
- The ratatui crate lets you build other widgets, such as charts. You could try using a free API like open-meteo (https://open-meteo.com/) to get the weather information for a location, displayed in a nice chart form.
- The stopwatch continues to run even if the window is not visible, so it is using system resources even when you aren't looking at it. The Event enum inside crossterm includes events called FocusGained and FocusLost that could let you avoid redrawing the screen when the user isn't looking at the app.
- The stopwatch returns a String every time the app loops, but much of the time, it is only showing the default time or the time when it was stopped. Could it be worth it to find a way to not allocate memory when the stopwatch is in a NotStarted or Done state?

Hopefully, you enjoyed these first three projects! Ideally, they should give you both a sense of satisfaction and a desire to keep working on and improving them. The next chapter is the very last chapter of the book and will continue with another three projects for you to keep developing. See you there!

Summary

- Crates to make CLI apps are a great way to start making your own projects. They are responsive and quick to compile, and not much can go wrong.
- GUIs and TUIs have structs with a lot of configuration options, which makes them an ideal place to use `Default` and the builder pattern.
- Even a simple CLI can use a lot of system resources if it is set up to loop and check for user input. Solutions to this include short sleeps and monitoring user events (like `FocusLost` and `FocusGained`), only redrawing when the visual state has changed, and so on.
- The Rust ecosystem is still fairly new. New crates pop up all the time, while older crates sometimes stop being maintained and are forked under new names.

24

Unfinished projects,
continued

This chapter covers

- Making a web server–based word-guessing game
- Making a laser pointer for your cat
- Making a directory and file navigator
- Saying goodbye!

You've reached the very last chapter of the book. Congratulations! In this chapter, we will continue with three more unfinished projects so that you'll have something to work on once you have finished reading the book. The first project in this chapter will be a simple guessing game, except that we'll set up a web server to do it. The second project is a laser pointer that runs away when you try to touch it. And, finally, we will finish up with a GUI to navigate and view the files on your computer. Let's get started!

24.1 Web server word-guessing game

The fourth unfinished project is a word-guessing game. A regular word-guessing game on the command line is extremely simple, and at this point, you could probably make one of those in your sleep. So, to make things more interesting, we are going to make a guessing game that takes place over a web server instead.

To make this, we will need to use one of Rust's web frameworks. Rust has three main web frameworks as of 2023, although there are many more out there. Let's quickly summarize the main three:

- *Rocket*—One of the first web frameworks, Rocket is quite slick and uses a lot of macro magic. The documentation is also especially nice.
- *Actix Web*—Lots of features and maintainers and extremely fast. Generally, the larger the project, the more likely that Actix is the right choice.
- *Axum*—The newest of the three but part of the Tokio project so there is a lot of collaboration between Axum and Tokio.

For us, the decision is simple. We are making a small project, so let's see which of the three is the quickest to compile:

- `rocket = "0.5"`—174 compilation units
- `actix-web = "4.4""`—161 compilation units
- `axum = "0.72""`—87 compilation units

Axum has the smallest number of compilation units by far, so we will use it.

24.1.1   *Setup and first code*

For our first code, we will put together a server with a few paths and see whether they work as expected. After typing `cargo run` for this code, the server will begin running locally, and you can go to `http://localhost:8080/` to see the responses it gives. A full explanation of how Axum works is impossible in a small amount of space, but here is how to quickly start a project with Axum:

- First, use `axum::Router::new()` to start a router, which handles the paths that will be used to take requests.
- Add `.route()` to give the router a path, followed by an HTTP method (such as `get`) and then an `async` function to handle the request.
- So, if you type `.route("/", get(function_name))`, it will create a route at `http://localhost:8080/` that takes a `get`. A `get` is the most basic HTTP request; it is the request used whenever you view a webpage. You probably make hundreds of `get` requests through your browser and phone every day.
- Another example of a route is `.route("/guessing_game", get(function_name))`, which would take `get` requests at `http://localhost:8080/guessing_game`. But if this server were hosted at `http://yourwebsite.com` instead, it would take requests at `http://yourwebsite.com/guessing_game`.
- After the routes are set, put the router inside another method that binds the router to an address, which, in our case, is `127.0.0.1:8080`. In our address, `127.0.0.1` is called the *localhost* and represents your own computer on your own network, and `8080` is a port number.

- After this, you call the async `.serve()` method, which returns a `Future` that holds a `Server`, but the `Future` doesn't return until the server shuts down. In other words, it runs forever by default.

And two more things to know before we get to the code:

- Axum uses types called *extractors* that are used to handle requests. In our case, we will use the simplest one called a `Path<String>`. A `Path<String>` holds a `String` of the path it is given after the router address. So, if we access the server at `127.0.0.1:8080/guessing_game/my_guess` and there is a route at `127.0.0.1:8080/guessing_game`, the `Path<String>` extractor will give us a `String` that holds `"my_guess"`.
- Handling a route in Axum requires an `async fn`, which includes async closures. We'll try both.

That was a lot of information! Everything will make much more sense once we look at some code. Let's put together a really simple server now. First, let's add some dependencies inside Cargo.toml:

```
[dependencies]
axum = "0.7.2"
fastrand = "2.0.1"
tokio = { version = "1.35", features = ["macros", "rt-multi-thread"] }
```

The `fastrand` crate is similar to `rand` but a bit smaller and simpler, so we'll give it a try here.

And now for the code:

```
use axum::{extract::Path, routing::get};

async fn double(Path(input): Path<String>) -> String {
    match input.parse::<i32>() {
        Ok(num) => format!("{} times 2 is {}!", num, num * 2),
        Err(e) => format!("Uh oh, weird input: {e}")
    }
}

#[tokio::main]
async fn main() {
    let app = axum::Router::new()
        .route("/", get(|| async { "The server works!" }))
        .route(
            "/game/:guess",
            get(|Path(guess): Path<String>| async move { format!("The guess
            is {guess}") }),
```

The signature here may look a bit odd, but it is just deconstructing the input inside the function signature. Axum uses this syntax a lot, so we'll copy it.

Nothing else in this function is particularly surprising: it tries to parse a string into an i32 and doubles it if it can.

This first route just lets us know that the server works, and we handle the response inside an async closure.

For the second route, we will also use an async function. The colon in :guess means to pass in whatever is after /game/ to the function under the variable name guess. This time, we need async move because we want the function to take ownership of guess. Then we will return the guess to the user.

```
        )
        .route("/double/:number", get(double));    ◄────────────────┐

    axum::Server::bind(&"127.0.0.1:8080".parse().unwrap())
        .serve(app.into_make_service())
        .await                          For the third route, we will use the previous
        .unwrap();                      doubling function. Here, as well, we pass in the
                                        path as the variable number, but inside the
}                                       function itself, it will have a different name.
```

Now let's run the server and test some of its output. If you try the following paths in your browser, you should see the following output:

- Response from path: http://localhost:8080

  ```
  The server works!
  ```

- Response from path: http://localhost:8080/thththth

```
This localhost page can't be found
No webpage was found for the web address: http://localhost:8080/thththth
HTTP ERROR 404
```

- Response from path: http://localhost:8080/double/10

  ```
  10 times 2 is 20!
  ```

- Response from path: http://localhost:8080/double/TEN

  ```
  Uh oh, weird input: invalid digit found in string
  ```

- Response from path: http://localhost:8080/double/9879879879879

  ```
  Uh oh, weird input: number too large to fit in target type
  ```

- Response from path: http://localhost:8080/game/MyGuess

  ```
  The guess is MyGuess
  ```

So far, so good. The server recognizes the routes we give it and is handling our input property at the `/double` path. The next task is to put together the guessing game.

24.1.2 *Developing the code*

To stay focused on one task at a time, let's forget about Axum for a moment, put our guessing game together, and run it on the command line. Nothing in the following code will be difficult for you, so you won't need any preparation to understand. One good read through the code with notes on the side should do it:

```
const RANDOM_WORDS: [&str; 6] =
    ["MB", "Windy", "Gomes", "Johnny", "Seoul", "Interesting"];    ◄────────┐

                                        Six random words: the author's
                                        four cats, city of residence, and
                                        a final random word
```

```
#[derive(Clone, Debug, Default)]
struct GameApp {
    current_word: String,
    right_guesses: Vec<char>,
    wrong_guesses: Vec<char>,
}
```

> The game app is pretty simple, too. Later on, we'll be able to make it a static because both Vec::new() and String::new() are const functions, as we learned in chapter 16.

```
enum Guess {
    Right,
    Wrong,
    AlreadyGuessed,
}
```

> Three things can happen when a letter is chosen: it can be right, wrong, or already guessed.

```
impl GameApp {
    fn start(&mut self) {
        self.current_word =
    RANDOM_WORDS[fastrand::usize(..RANDOM_WORDS.len())].to_lowercase();
        self.right_guesses.clear();
        self.wrong_guesses.clear();
    }
```

> Every time .start() is called, the app will choose a new word and clear its data. The fastrand::usize(..RANDOM_WORDS.len())] part will choose a random usize index up to the length of RANDOM_WORDS. Note that we also made the word lowercase.

```
    fn check_guess(&self, guess: char) -> Guess {
        if self.right_guesses.contains(&guess) ||
    self.wrong_guesses.contains(&guess) {
            return Guess::AlreadyGuessed;
        }
        match self.current_word.contains(guess) {
            true => Guess::Right,
            false => Guess::Wrong,
        }
    }
```

> The check_guess() function lets us know what sort of guess has been given. If the letter is already in right_guesses or wrong_guesses, it has been guessed already. If not, it is either a right guess or a wrong guess.

```
    fn print_results(&self) {
        let output = self
            .current_word
            .chars()
            .map(|c| {
                if self.right_guesses.contains(&c) {
                    c
                } else {
                    '*'
                }
            })
            .collect::<String>();
        println!("{output}");
    }
```

> This method just prints the character if the letter is within right_guesses or a * otherwise. If the random word is "school" and the user has guessed l and o, it will print ***ool.

```
    fn take_guess(&mut self, guess: String) {
        match guess.chars().count() {
            0 => println!("What are you doing? Please guess something."),
            1 => {
                let the_guess = guess.chars().next().unwrap();

                match self.check_guess(the_guess) {
                    Guess::AlreadyGuessed => {
                        println!("You already guessed {the_guess}!")
                    }
                    Guess::Right => {
```

> Finally, we have the main method that handles a guess from the user. If the guess is one character in length, it is a letter guess; if it is more than one character in length, it assumes that the user is trying to guess the whole word.

```
                            self.right_guesses.push(the_guess);
                            println!("Yes, it contains a {the_guess}!")
                        }
                        Guess::Wrong => {
                            self.wrong_guesses.push(the_guess);
                            println!("Nope, it doesn't contain a {the_guess}!")
                        }
                    }
                    self.print_results();
                    println!(
                        "Already guessed: {}",
                        self.wrong_guesses.iter().collect::<String>()
                    );
                }
                _ => {
                    if self.current_word == guess {
                        println!("You guessed right, it's {}!",
                            self.current_word);
                    } else {
                        println!(
                            "Bzzt! It's not '{guess}', it's {}.\nTime to move
                            on to another word!",
                            self.current_word
                        );
                    }
                    self.start();
                }
            }
        }
    }
}
```

We have already checked to see whether the length is 0 or 1, so anything else will have to be longer. When this happens, the stakes are higher: either the user wins or loses right away.

Since the user either wins or loses, the game will reset no matter what.

```
fn main() {
    let mut app = GameApp::default();
    app.start();

    loop {
        println!("Guess the word!");
        let mut guess = String::new();
        std::io::stdin().read_line(&mut guess).unwrap();
        app.take_guess(guess.trim().to_lowercase());
    }
}
```

Finally, don't forget to .trim() the user's guess and make it lowercase.

Now we have two things:

- The knowledge of how to make a simple web server
- A simple guessing game that runs locally

Now, it's time to join these two together. How do we do this? Because, at the moment, the guessing game is inside `main()`, and our functions to handle requests only provide us a `Path<String>`, not a reference to any app:

```
async fn handle_request(Path(input): Path<String>) -> String {
}
```

All we have is a variable called input that holds a String. How do we get to the app from here?

The proper way on Axum to get access to a struct like our GameApp is through a method called .with_state() (http://mng.bz/xjZ8) that allows functions inside Axum's router to access structs like our game app. Besides the Axum documentation, Axum's version 0.6 announcement in 2022 (http://mng.bz/Jd9z) also has some simple examples.

For our quick example, however, we can make our GameApp into a static. One reason is that we don't have the space in this chapter to get into Axum's internal details; also, our game app is so simple that everything is on one screen.

If you decide to continue developing the example into a server for real work, one good place to start would be doing away with the global static and replacing it with the .with_state() method. Doing so makes a project much easier to test as it begins to grow.

24.1.3 *Further development and cleanup*

So let's make our app into a static item. That's pretty easy because (as we learned in chapter 16) all of the following methods are const fn and thus don't require an allocation:

```
static GAME: Mutex<GameApp> = Mutex::new(GameApp {
    current_word: String::new(),
    right_guesses: vec![],
    wrong_guesses: vec![]
});
```

And then when a guess comes in on the server, we'll pick it up through a new function called get_res_from_static() that will pass on the String to the GameApp, which will do its work and finally return a String as the route's output:

```
let app = axum::Router::new()
    .route("/", get(|| async { "The server is running well!" }))
    .route("/game/:guess", get(get_res_from_static));
```

And what does the get_res_from_static() function look like? It's extremely simple. It locks the Mutex to gain mutable access to static GAME and calls its .take_guess() method:

```
fn get_res_from_static(guess: String) -> String {
    GAME.lock().unwrap().take_guess(guess)
}
```

Finally, the only changes we have left to make are for the println! statements to be replaced with format! so that a String can be returned that will be the response from the server. Instead of printing each piece of information as we get it, we'll have to build a String and use .push_str() to add the information every step of the way, which will finally return the String at the end so that the user can see it.

The full code now looks like this:

```
use axum::{extract::Path, routing::get};
use std::sync::Mutex;

const RANDOM_WORDS: [&str; 6] =
    ["MB", "Windy", "Gomes", "Johnny", "Seoul", "Interesting"];

static GAME: Mutex<GameApp> = Mutex::new(GameApp {
    current_word: String::new(),
    right_guesses: vec![],
    wrong_guesses: vec![],
});

#[derive(Clone, Debug)]
struct GameApp {
    current_word: String,
    right_guesses: Vec<char>,
    wrong_guesses: Vec<char>,
}

enum Guess {
    Right,
    Wrong,
    AlreadyGuessed,
}

async fn get_res_from_static(Path(guess): Path<String>) -> String {
    GAME.lock().unwrap().take_guess(guess)
}

impl GameApp {
    fn restart(&mut self) {
        self.current_word =
        ➥RANDOM_WORDS[fastrand::usize(..RANDOM_WORDS.len())]
            .to_lowercase();
        self.right_guesses.clear();
        self.wrong_guesses.clear();
    }
    fn check_guess(&self, guess: char) -> Guess {
        if self.right_guesses.contains(&guess) ||
        ➥self.wrong_guesses.contains(&guess) {
            return Guess::AlreadyGuessed;
        }
        match self.current_word.contains(guess) {
            true => Guess::Right,
            false => Guess::Wrong,
        }
    }
    fn results_so_far(&self) -> String {
        let mut output = String::new();
        for c in self.current_word.chars() {
            if self.right_guesses.contains(&c) {
                output.push(c)
            } else {
                output.push('*')
            }
```

```
        }
        output
    }
    fn take_guess(&mut self, guess: String) -> String {
        let guess = guess.to_lowercase();
        let mut output = String::new();
        match guess {
            guess if guess.chars().count() == 1 => {
                let the_guess = guess.chars().next().unwrap();

                match self.check_guess(the_guess) {
                    Guess::AlreadyGuessed => {
                        output.push_str(&format!("You already guessed
                        ➥{the_guess}!\n"));
                    }
                    Guess::Right => {
                        self.right_guesses.push(the_guess);
                        output.push_str(&format!("Yes, it contains a
                        ➥{the_guess}!\n"));
                    }
                    Guess::Wrong => {
                        self.wrong_guesses.push(the_guess);
                        output.push_str(&format!("Nope, it doesn't contain
                        ➥a {the_guess}!\n"));
                    }
                }
                output.push_str(&self.results_so_far());
            }
            guess => {
                if self.current_word == guess {
                    output.push_str(&format!("You guessed right, it's {}!
                    ➥Let's play again!", self.current_word));
                } else {
                    output.push_str(&format!(
                        "Bzzt! It's not {guess}, it's {}.\nTime to move on
                        ➥to another word!",
                        self.current_word
                    ));
                }
                self.restart();
            }
        }
        output
    }
}

#[tokio::main]
async fn main() {
    GAME.lock().unwrap().restart();

    let app = axum::Router::new()
        .route("/", get(|| async { "The server is running well!" }))
        .route("/game/:guess", get(get_res_from_static));

    axum::Server::bind(&"127.0.0.1:8080".parse().unwrap())
        .serve(app.into_make_service())
```

```
        .await
        .unwrap();
}
```

This has been our longest example so far, but a basic web server and a game in just 105 lines of code isn't too bad!

24.1.4 Over to you

What are some possible next steps now that the guessing game is done?

- As previously mentioned, replace the global static with `.with_state()` as recommended by Axum. You'll notice that the method will pass on the struct immutably, so you will have to use an `Arc<Mutex>` on the parameters to change their values.
- Try implementing the same thing with one of the two other web frameworks to see whether you have a preferred style. The three main web frameworks feel pretty similar to each other much of the time. For example, Rocket also allows accessing a struct through a type called `State` (https://api.rocket.rs/v0.5/rocket/struct.State.html).
- Try deploying the app online! Deployment is beyond the scope of this book, but a search for "deploy axum server" shows a lot of possibilities.
- Right now, the server holds a single game, so if more than one person accesses the server at the same time, they will get some pretty confusing output. You could try a crate like `axum_sessions` (https://docs.rs/axum-sessions/latest/axum_sessions/) to create a proper session per user. Or, for something quick and hacky, you could have the main route at `"/"` give a random suffix to the URL for the user to play the game that only lasts for a short period of time. For example, a user who visits the main address would get a URL like `http://localhost:8080/w8ll2/game/` that only they would know. Or you might have a better idea to make this work.
- Combine the server with the graphical interface that we will learn in the very next section!

24.2 Laser pointer

Thus far, this book has only focused on making code for humans to use, but it's time to make something for our cats (or other pets?). Making a moving red dot that looks like a laser pointer should be enough to entertain them. This can be done through the `egui` crate, which is a GUI that allows us to add buttons, graphics, charts, and more. Making the dot move in random directions and at random speeds will be the key to making this laser pointer interesting.

24.2.1 Setup and first code

`egui` is pretty straightforward after learning `ratatui`, as drawing widgets on the screen is pretty similar: you draw them by calling methods on a struct that is passed into a closure. But let's start one step at a time, starting with the dependencies in Cargo.toml:

```
[dependencies]
egui = "0.21.0"
eframe = "0.21.3"
fastrand = "2.0.0"
```

The `eframe` crate is the crate used to compile and run `egui` apps. You will almost always use `egui` and `eframe` together in this way.

Here is the minimum you will need to run an `egui` app on your computer:

- Create a struct to hold your state: numbers, strings, whatever you need to access when the app is running.
- Implement the eframe `App` trait (https://docs.rs/eframe/latest/eframe/trait.App.html) for your app struct. This trait has a required method called `update()` that is called continuously when running an `egui` app. This method is essentially the same as the loop we used in the `ratatui` example in the last chapter.
- Inside `main()`, use the `eframe::run_native()` method, which runs the app on your computer (which is why it is called *native*). Into this, you pass in a `Box<dyn FnOnce(&CreationContext<'_>) -> Box<dyn App>>;`. The `Box<dyn App>` is the app struct that we implemented the `App` trait for. The `CreationContext` part can be accessed once the app starts up and can be used for long-term settings like adding fonts or anything you don't want to happen every loop.

To get a sense of what all that means when put together, let's build a quick app that displays a few widgets:

```
#[derive(Default)]
struct NothingApp {
    number: i32,
    text: String,
    code: String,
}
```

This app will hold a number that can be increased or decreased by clicking on buttons, some text for a text editor widget, plus more text for a code text editor widget. All of these widgets are built into egui.

```
impl NothingApp {
    fn new(_cc: &eframe::CreationContext<'_>) -> Self {
        Self {
            number: 0,
            text: String::from("Put some text in here!"),
            code: String::from(
                r#"fn main() {
    println!("Hello, world!");
}"#,
            ),
        }
    }
}
```

Here, we make a method that creates our app, and to follow the eframe::run_native() method, it needs to take a CreationContext. We don't have any need for it, though.

And now for the App trait, which is where all of the update logic goes. This is where you spend the majority of your time when developing an egui app.

```
impl eframe::App for NothingApp {
    fn update(&mut self, ctx: &egui::Context, _frame: &mut eframe::Frame) {
        egui::CentralPanel::default().show(ctx, |ui| {
```

App layouts start with a panel such as a CentralPanel or SidePanel. Inside the panel, we have access to the ui struct (https://docs.rs/egui/latest/egui/struct.Ui.html), which has a ton of methods to create widgets.

```
        if ui.button("Counter up").clicked() {
            self.number += 1
        }
        if ui.button("Counter down").clicked() {
            self.number -= 1
        }

        ui.label(format!("The counter is: {}", self.number));

        ui.text_edit_multiline(&mut self.text);
        ui.code_editor(&mut self.code);
    });
}
}
fn main() {
    let native_options = eframe::NativeOptions::default();
    let _ = eframe::run_native(
        "My egui App",
        native_options,
        Box::new(|cc| Box::new(NothingApp::new(cc))),
    );
}
```

And now we call some methods on the ui struct to create some widgets. First, we will make two buttons that change the number when they are clicked, then a label to display some text, and then a text editor area and a code editor area.

Finally comes the main() function, on which we call the run_native() method and add our app.

Now if you type `cargo run`, the code will start compiling. Once the compiling is done, a screen similar to figure 24.1 should suddenly pop up! You should be able to click the buttons to change the value of the counter and type inside the two boxes.

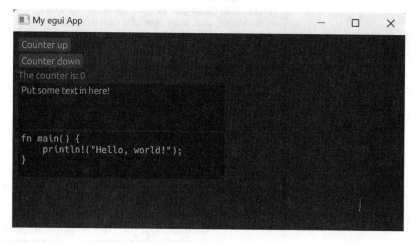

Figure 24.1 An incredibly basic egui app

24.2.2 *Developing the code*

Now that we have some understanding of egui, it's time to put together our laser pointer. To do this, first we have to visualize the screen that the laser will be floating around on. The screen is a rectangle with an *x*-axis and a *y*-axis. If we have a screen that is 500.0 pixels by 500.0 pixels, the edge of the *x*-axis goes from top left at 0.0 to the top right at 500.0. And the edge of the *y*-axis starts at the top left at 0.0 to the bottom left at 500.0.

`egui` has two structs here called a `Pos2` and a `Rect` that help us work with the screen dimensions. A `Pos2` is simply a point in space:

```
pub struct Pos2 {
    pub x: f32,
    pub y: f32,
}
```

And a `Rect` holds two points: the point at the top left and the point at the bottom right. These are inclusive ranges, as can be seen by the `RangeInclusive` struct on the documentation (https://docs.rs/egui/latest/egui/struct.Rect.html) for `Rect`.

```
pub struct Rect {
    pub min: Pos2,
    pub max: Pos2,
}
```

If you put these all together, you get a setup like figure 24.2. You can see where *x* and *y* start and end, as well as a `Pos2` located 100.0 pixels to the right and 400.0 pixels down.

`egui` also has a struct called a `Vec2`, which looks exactly like a `Pos2`. But instead of representing a single point, the *x* in `Vec2` represents how many pixels to the right, and the *y* represents how many pixels down:

```
pub struct Vec2 {
    pub x: f32,
    pub y: f32,
}
```

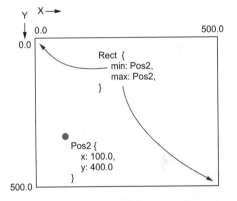

Figure 24.2   A laser pointer dot 100 pixels across and 400 pixels down

With that in our minds, let's start building the laser pointer!

```
use eframe::egui;
use egui::{Vec2, Color32, Sense, Pos2};

#[derive(Default)]
struct LaserPointer {
    position: Pos2
}

impl LaserPointer {
    fn new(_cc: &eframe::CreationContext<'_>) -> Self {
        Self {
            position: Pos2 { x: 0.0, y: 0.0 }
```

The LaserPointer is just a dot, so all we need is a Pos2 to represent it.

We'll put it at the top left corner to begin with.

```
            }
        }
    }

impl eframe::App for LaserPointer {
    fn update(&mut self, ctx: &egui::Context, _frame: &mut eframe::Frame) {
        egui::CentralPanel::default().show(ctx, |ui| {

            let rect = ctx.screen_rect();
            let screen_size = Vec2 {
                x: rect.width(),
                y: rect.height()
            };
            let (response, painter) =
        ui.allocate_painter(screen_size, Sense::hover());
            if response.hovered() {
                let Pos2 {x, y} = self.position;
                let Pos2 {x: x2, y: y2} =
        ctx.pointer_hover_pos().unwrap_or_default();
```

The ctx variable lets us work with the context of our app, which includes information like screen size. The screen_rect() method gives us a Rect.

And now we'll make a Vec2 out of the Rect because the next method is going to need it.

This next method is pretty interesting. It takes in a screen size (a Vec2) as well as a Sense. Sense is an enum that lets it know what sort of user input to react to, such as clicking, dragging, hovering, and so on. Let's go with hover. The method returns two things: a Response and a Painter.

Now we can tell the app what to do when the Response notices that the mouse is hovering. Here is where we add the laser pointer logic!

First, we're going to try to make the laser pointer run away when the mouse arrow gets too close. To do that, we get the position of the laser pointer and then use the pointer_hover_pos() method to get the position of the mouse arrow.

```
                if (x - x2).abs() < 10.0 && (y - y2).abs() < 10.0 {
                    if fastrand::bool() {
                        self.position.x += fastrand::f32() * 20.0;
                    } else {
                        self.position.x -= fastrand::f32() * 20.0;
                    }
                    if fastrand::bool() {
                        self.position.y += fastrand::f32() * 20.0;
                    } else {
                        self.position.y -= fastrand::f32() * 20.0;
                    }
                }
            }
            self.position.x += 0.5;
            self.position.y += 0.5;
            let radius = 10.0;
            painter.circle_filled(self.position, radius, Color32::RED);
        });
    }
}
```

Then we'll move the laser pointer across and down by 0.5 pixels per loop. We'll develop this in the next section.

And then, in these lines, we'll instruct the laser pointer to move in a random direction if the mouse pointer is within 10.0 pixels. The fastrand::bool() method randomly returns true or false, and based on that, it will go either forward or backward by up to 20.0 pixels.

Finally, we'll draw the actual laser pointer, which is a circle. It gets a radius of 10.0 and a color of Red.

```
fn main() {
    let native_options = eframe::NativeOptions::default();
    let _ = eframe::run_native(
        "My egui App",
        native_options,
        Box::new(|cc| Box::new(LaserPointer::new(cc))),
    );
}
```

Once all this is done, you should see something that looks like figure 24.3. The laser pointer will move steadily across and down whenever you hover the mouse over the screen, and if the mouse pointer gets too close, it will jump away. At this point, your cat might already be entertained by it, but we can make it better!

Figure 24.3   Your laser pointer

24.2.3 Further development and cleanup

Our next task is to make the laser pointer move without needing the mouse pointer to hover over the screen and to move as randomly as possible. Without the random movement, a cat will quickly get bored with it.

Here are some of the changes we will make:

- *Speed*—The laser pointer will have a few speeds that will change randomly. Sometimes it will be still, other times it will move slowly, and other times it will move fast or `CrazyFast`.
- *Random movement*—How do we make the pointer move in random directions? There are many ways to do it, but one easy way to do it is to give the pointer an invisible target that it heads toward every time it moves. The target will change from time to time as well.
- *Looping without mouse hover*—At the moment, our app only loops whenever a hover event is detected, which means we would have to keep moving our mouse around to get the laser pointer to do anything. Fortunately, `egui` has a method called `request_repaint()` that lets the app logic loop without needing to detect an event from the user. All we have to do is stick this method into the `.update()` method.
- *Moving random movement logic*—Moving a lot of the random movement logic over to the LaserPointer's methods so that the code doesn't look so cluttered.

With all these changes made, the code now looks like the following:

```rust
use eframe::egui;
use egui::{Color32, Pos2, Rect, Sense, Vec2};

#[derive(Default, Clone, Copy)]
struct LaserPointer {
    x: f32,
    y: f32,
    speed: Speed,
    imaginary_target: Pos2,
}
```

We could have kept the Pos2 struct to represent the laser pointer's position, but holding an x and a y instead of a Pos2 makes the code a bit cleaner.

```rust
#[derive(Clone, Copy, Default)]
enum Speed {
    #[default]
    Still,
    Slow,
    Fast,
    CrazyFast,
}
```

Nothing about this enum is too difficult. Note the #[default] attribute, though, which was added fairly recently to Rust!

Implementing From here isn't essential, but it helps the following code be a bit cleaner.

```rust
impl From<LaserPointer> for Pos2 {
    fn from(pointer: LaserPointer) -> Self {
        Pos2 {
            x: pointer.x,
            y: pointer.y,
        }
    }
}
```

This method now handles the random laser pointer movement when the mouse arrow gets too close.

```rust
impl LaserPointer {
    fn random_movement(&mut self, amount: f32) {
        if fastrand::bool() {
            self.x += fastrand::f32() * amount;
        } else {
            self.x -= fastrand::f32() * amount;
        }
        if fastrand::bool() {
            self.y += fastrand::f32() * amount;
        } else {
            self.y -= fastrand::f32() * amount;
        }
    }
    fn try_change_speed(&mut self) {
        use Speed::*;
        if fastrand::f32() > 0.98 {
            self.speed = match fastrand::u8(0..3) {
                0 => Still,
                1 => Slow,
                2 => Fast,
                _ => CrazyFast,
            }
        }
    }
}
```

We don't want the speed to change too frequently (cats get bored when a laser pointer moves too quickly), so we'll use a random f32 from 0.0 to 1.0 and only change when the number is greater than 0.98. In practice, this will mean a speed change every few seconds. The following try_change_target() changes the invisible target for the pointer in the same way.

Note that we used _ here because the compiler doesn't know that the random number will only go up to 3. Alternatively, we could have used 3 on this line and then added _ below and the unreachable! macro.

```
    fn try_change_target(&mut self, rect: Rect) {
        let bottom_right = rect.max;
        if fastrand::f32() > 0.98 {
            self.imaginary_target = Pos2 {
                x: fastrand::f32() * bottom_right.x,
                y: fastrand::f32() * bottom_right.y,
            }
        }
    }
    fn change_speed(&self) -> f32 {
        match self.speed {
            Speed::Still => 0.0,
            Speed::Slow => 0.05,
            Speed::Fast => 0.1,
            Speed::CrazyFast => 0.3,
        }
    }
    fn move_self(&mut self) {
        let x_from_target = self.imaginary_target.x - self.x;
        let y_from_target = self.imaginary_target.y - self.y;
        self.x += fastrand::f32() * x_from_target * self.change_speed();
        self.y += fastrand::f32() * y_from_target * self.change_speed();
    }
}

impl LaserPointer {
    fn new(_cc: &eframe::CreationContext<'_>) -> Self {
        Self {
            x: 50.0,
            y: 50.0,
            speed: Speed::default(),
            imaginary_target: Pos2 { x: 50.0, y: 50.0 },
        }
    }
}

impl eframe::App for LaserPointer {
    fn update(&mut self, ctx: &egui::Context, _frame: &mut eframe::Frame) {
        ctx.request_repaint();
        egui::CentralPanel::default().show(ctx, |ui| {
            self.try_change_speed();
            self.try_change_target(rect);
            self.move_self();

            let rect = ctx.screen_rect();
            let screen_size = Vec2 {
                x: rect.width(),
                y: rect.height()
            };
            let (_, painter) = ui.allocate_painter(screen_size,
                Sense::hover());
            let LaserPointer { x, y, .. } = self;
            let Pos2 { x: x2, y: y2 } =
                ctx.pointer_hover_pos().unwrap_or_default();
```

Finally, we have this method to move the laser pointer once every loop. One of the speeds is 0.0, though, so it will stay absolutely still in that case.

With all of these methods added, the final code is much cleaner.

The laser pointer moves on its own now, and we are checking to see whether the mouse arrow is close to the laser pointer or not, so we don't need to use the response returned from allocate_painter() anymore.

```
            if (*x - x2).abs() < 20.0 && (*y - y2).abs() < 20.0 {
                self.random_movement(50.0);
            }
            painter.circle_filled(Pos2::from(*self), 20.0, Color32::RED);
        });
    }
}

fn main() {
    let native_options = eframe::NativeOptions::default();
    let _ = eframe::run_native(
        "Awesome laser pointer",
        native_options,
        Box::new(|cc| Box::new(LaserPointer::new(cc))),
    );
}
```

With these changes made, the laser pointer should now make some pretty erratic movements. Sometimes it will stay still, other times it will move slowly, and other times it will suddenly jump across the screen. See whether your cat or other pet likes it!

24.2.4 *Over to you*

The laser pointer is probably the most complete of the six unfinished projects in these last two chapters, but here are a few ideas for further development:

- The laser pointer uses an invisible random target to move. Why not draw that as well? Not only would it look interesting, but it could also help you test and refine the laser pointer's movement.
- Cats react differently to different types of laser pointers. Some enjoy a pointer that stays still for a while because it lets them imagine the thrill of catching it before they pounce. Others, usually kittens, prefer a wild pointer that moves as fast as possible. Could you add some settings to the laser pointer to allow the user to pick between different types of movement?
- The next project also uses egui to make a directory and file navigator. Why not stick the laser pointer inside that app, too, so that your cat can try to catch it while you work with the files on your computer?
- Try checking out some other popular GUI crates at https://www.areweguiyet .com/. Some popular crates include Yew, Iced, and Dioxus.
- Check out the egui web demo (https://www.egui.rs/#demo) to get a feel for all of the possibilities that egui offers. The page includes a link to the source code, so you can copy and paste what you need to get started.

24.3 *Directory and file navigator*

The last unfinished project in the book will be a simple navigator that lets you look through the directories on your computer and view the files inside. This project will also use egui because we still have only made some simple graphics with egui but haven't tried making a more complete UI with it.

24.3.1 *Setup and first code*

Before we begin working with egui again, first we need to take a look at a few types and methods in the standard library that we haven't seen yet for working with directories and files:

- std::env::current_dir(), which gives you the current directory. It returns the directory in the form Result<PathBuf>.
- PathBuf, which is similar to a String but is made for working with file and directory paths. A PathBuf has both .push() and .pop() methods, but they work with parts of a path instead of a char. For example, if we are inside the directory "/playground" and use the .pop() method, the directory will now be "/".
- std::fs::read_dir(), which returns a Result<ReadDir>. A ReadDir is an iterator over the contents inside a directory.
- Each entry inside a ReadDir is an io::Result<DirEntry>. A DirEntry holds the information that we are finally looking for that can be accessed through methods like .file_name(), path(), .file_type(), and .metadata().

Let's put this all together in a quick example that takes a look at the directories inside the Playground:

Let's take a look at the second item inside the directory. Note the two unwraps here: the .nth() method might return None, while inside is an io::Result<DirEntry>. Some of the information we can get includes the path name and filename, so let's print them out and see.

```
fn main() {
    let mut current_dir = std::env::current_dir().unwrap();
    println!("Current directory: {current_dir:?}");

    let mut read_dir = std::fs::read_dir(&current_dir).unwrap();
    println!("{read_dir:?}");
    let first = read_dir.nth(1).unwrap().unwrap();          // ←
    println!("Path: {:?} Name: {:?}", first.path(), first.file_name());

    current_dir.pop();                                      // ←
    println!("Now moved back to: {current_dir:?}");         // Use .pop() to move
                                                            // back a directory.
    let mut read_dir = std::fs::read_dir(&current_dir).unwrap();
    println!("{read_dir:?}");
    let first = read_dir.nth(1).unwrap().unwrap();          // ←
    println!("Path: {:?} Name: {:?}", first.path(), first.file_name());
}
```

We'll do the same for the second item inside the root directory.

The output should look like this:

```
Current directory: "/playground"
ReadDir("/playground")
Path: "/playground/.bashrc" Name: ".bashrc"
Now moved back to: "/"
ReadDir("/")
Path: "/mnt" Name: "mnt"
```

None of this code was probably all that surprising: it's just a lot of methods for working with directories and files. These methods all return `Results` because they all have the possibility of failure.

24.3.2 Developing the code

Now that we know how to work with directories and directory entries, let's try putting the app together. We learned how to add buttons on egui during the last section, so we can add a button for each item we find inside a directory and `.push()` to the `PathBuf` whenever it is clicked. And on the top, we can add another button that holds `".."` that will move back one directory. This part is easy: just `.pop()` from the `PathBuf` whenever it is clicked.

We will also use a struct called `RichText`, which in egui allows you to create text with extra formatting options such as color.

Putting all this together gives us the following code:

```
use std::{
    env::current_dir,
    fs::read_dir,
    path::PathBuf,
};

use eframe::egui;
use egui::{Color32, RichText};
```

> RichText is used in egui if you want to change the text of a widget, and Color32 allows us to choose a color.

```
struct DirectoryApp {
    current_dir: PathBuf,
}
```

> The app so far holds a PathBuf that we will use .push() and .pop() on.

> This is a good example of where we might want to keep .unwrap()—or turn it into .expect()—because if there is a problem getting the current directory on startup, the whole app should crash to allow us to try to fix what's wrong.

```
impl DirectoryApp {
    fn new(_cc: &eframe::CreationContext<'_>) -> Self {
        Self {
            current_dir: current_dir().unwrap(),
        }
    }
}
```

> Now we are going to work through the directory information. Look at all the unwraps! Each one of these methods returns a Result.

```
impl eframe::App for DirectoryApp {
    fn update(&mut self, ctx: &egui::Context, _frame: &mut eframe::Frame) {
        egui::CentralPanel::default().show(ctx, |ui| {
            if ui.button(" .. ").clicked() {
                self.current_dir.pop();
            }
            let read_dir = read_dir(&self.current_dir).unwrap();
            for entry in read_dir.flatten() {
                let metadata = entry.metadata().unwrap();
                let name = entry.file_name().into_string().unwrap();
```

> **This part is pretty easy! Make a button and .pop() when it is clicked.**

> **We get the metadata and file/directory name. With the metadata we can see whether we have a file or a directory.**

> **Note that here we are using .flatten() to ignore anything inside the read_dir() method that returns an Err.**

We'll make buttons with different text depending on whether we have a file or a directory. If we have a directory, clicking the button will .push() to the PathBuf and move us into that directory.

If we have a file, we should print it out. But let's think about that in the next section.

If the entry isn't a file or a directory, let's print out a label to show what it is.

```
                              if metadata.is_dir() {
                                  if ui
                                      .button(RichText::new(&name).color(Color32::GRAY))
                                      .clicked()
                                  {
                                      self.current_dir.push(&name);
                                  }
                              } else if metadata.is_file() {
                                  if ui
                                      .button(RichText::new(&name).color(Color32::GOLD))
                                      .clicked()
                                  {}
                              } else {
                                  ui.label(name);
                              }
                          }
                      });
                  }
              }

fn main() {
    let native_options = eframe::NativeOptions::default();
    let _ = eframe::run_native(
        "File explorer",
        native_options,
        Box::new(|cc| Box::new(DirectoryApp::new(cc))),
    );
}
```

Running this code, you should see an app like the one in figure 24.4. Directories show up in gray letters, and clicking on them will show you the content inside. Clicking on .. will take you up a directory. But the files themselves in gold lettering don't do anything when you click on them.

Figure 24.4 Your file explorer app

And since we are still using .unwrap() everywhere, sometimes when you click a button the program will crash with some sort of system error. Here's one error that you might see:

```
thread 'main' panicked at 'called `Result::unwrap()` on an `Err` value: Os
{ code: 5, kind: PermissionDenied, message: "Access is denied." }',
src\main.rs:112:56
```

But so far so good! Now let's develop the app a little bit more and make sure that it can never crash.

24.3.3 *Further development and cleanup*

We need to clean up most of the unwraps in the code and add the option to display the content of files that the user clicks on. When a file is clicked on, the app will need to know the address of the file, but we don't want to change the `current_dir` to do that. One way would be to create a clone of `current_dir` and then push the filename in the next line, but there is a quicker way to do it: a `PathBuf` can be built from an array or Vec. The `PathBuf` documentation gives an example of this:

```
let path: PathBuf = [r"C:\", "windows", "system32.dll"].iter().collect();
```

After that comes the `TextEdit` that we saw in the last example. We can set the app to hold a `String` called `file_content` and then check whether it's empty. If it's not, we'll pull up a `SidePanel` (in addition to the existing `CentralPanel`) to display it there. egui tends to change the size of panels when the app is being used, so to prevent this from happening, we'll use the same `screen_rect()` method from the last example to get the size of the screen. This can then be passed into the panel with a method called `.min_width()` and then again to the `TextEdit` with its method called `.desired_width()`.

Here is the final code after all of these changes have been made:

```
use std::{
    env::current_dir,
    fs::{read_dir, read_to_string},
    path::PathBuf,
};

use eframe::egui;
use egui::{Color32, RichText, TextEdit};

struct DirectoryApp {
    file_content: String,
    current_dir: PathBuf,
}

impl DirectoryApp {
    fn new(_cc: &eframe::CreationContext<'_>) -> Self {
        Self {
            file_content: String::new(),
            current_dir: current_dir().unwrap(),
        }
    }
}
```

```
impl eframe::App for DirectoryApp {
    fn update(&mut self, ctx: &egui::Context, _frame: &mut eframe::Frame) {
        egui::CentralPanel::default().show(ctx, |ui| {
            if ui.button(" .. ").clicked() {
                self.current_dir.pop();
            }
            if let Ok(read_dir) = read_dir(&self.current_dir) {
                for entry in read_dir.flatten() {
                    if let Ok(metadata) = entry.metadata() {
                        if metadata.is_dir() {
                            if let Ok(dir_name) =
                              entry.file_name().into_string() {
                                if ui
                                    .button(RichText::new(&dir_name)
                                    .color(Color32::GRAY))
                                    .clicked()
                                {
                                    self.current_dir.push(&dir_name);
                                }
                            }
                        } else if metadata.is_file() {
                            if let Ok(file_name) =
                              entry.file_name().into_string() {
                                if ui
                                    .button(RichText::new(&file_name)
                                    .color(Color32::GOLD))
                                    .clicked()
                                {
                                    if let Some(current_dir) =
                                      self.current_dir.to_str() {
                                        let file_loc: PathBuf =
                                            [current_dir,
                                              &file_name].iter().collect();
                                        let content =
                                          read_to_string(file_loc)
                                            .unwrap
                                            _or_else(|e| e.to_string());
                                        self.file_content = content;
                                    }
                                }
                            }
                        } else {
                            ui.label(format!("{:?}", metadata.file_type()));
                        }
                    }
                }
            }
        });

        let width = ctx.screen_rect().max.x / 2.0;
        if !self.file_content.is_empty() {      #C
            egui::SidePanel::right("Text viewer")
                .min_width(width)
                .show(ctx, |ui| {
```

The unwraps have been removed, but egui's update() method doesn't return a Result, so we can't use the question mark operator. The if let syntax is helpful here.

Here is the part with the new PathBuf to get the contents of the file if a file button has been clicked. We then use read_to_string() to create a String to hold the file content. If there is an error, it will show the error information instead of the file content.

Finally, this part displays a new panel on the side if the app holds any file content.

```
                    ui.add(TextEdit::multiline(&mut
                  ⮡self.file_content).desired_width(width));
                });
            }
        }
    }

fn main() {
    let native_options = eframe::NativeOptions::default();
    let _ = eframe::run_native(
        "File explorer",
        native_options,
        Box::new(|cc| Box::new(DirectoryApp::new(cc))),
    );
}
```

With this code, we now have a crash-free app that runs exceptionally fast. It might even be faster than the file explorer on your computer. Figure 24.5 shows a screenshot of the app showing the same code being used to run it.

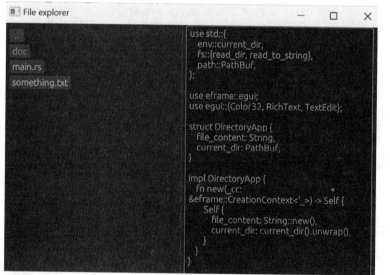

Figure 24.5   Your now crash-free file explorer app

24.3.4 *Over to you*

You probably have a few ideas of your own for how to develop this app further. But here are some other ideas to think about:

- If a directory has a lot of files in it, you will see buttons go well past the height of the screen, but no scroll bar appears. Can you find out how to add a scroll bar in egui?

- The panel on the right appears when a file is clicked, but there is no way to remove it again. You could use a regular button, a radio button, a selectable label, or something else to allow the user to make the text on the right disappear.
- The typing area in the panel on the right lets you copy the whole text to allow you to save it separately, but there is no way to save the content. You could add a way to do this, as well as keep track of whether text has been changed. You could also keep track of whether a file has been changed to ask the user whether the changes should be saved or not.
- The code uses a lot of `if let`. This is good for error handling when you can't return a `Result`, but the indentation in the code is pretty deep. You could reduce the indentation by making a method for the app to do some of this work. For example, the method could look through the current directory and return a Vec of an enum called something like `DirectoryContent` that has `Dir`, `File`, and `Other` variants.
- Errors are being handled, but error information isn't being displayed in most places. Most users might not care to know about this, but you could add a check box to open a panel that displays error info for users who want to keep a close watch on the output of every method that returns a Result.

And with that, we have reached the end of the sixth unfinished project.

And we have also reached the end of *Learn Rust in a Month of Lunches*! Hopefully, your month of lunches was a pleasant one that has given you the knowledge and confidence to start writing your own tools and projects in Rust. It will be interesting to see what further developments happen with these unfinished projects by you, the reader, or what else you end up creating on your own.

Finally, hopefully you have come to see Rust as a language that is complex in a good way, a language that is always watching your back to make sure that problems are taken care of before you run your code, not after.

Summary

- Rust is used in enterprise software and even inside Windows and the Linux kernel, but it is a fantastic language for small tools like these as well. It only takes 50 to 100 lines of code to put a tool together that is quite usable, and Rust's type correctness and error handling can guarantee that crashes will not happen.
- As of 2024, Rust has a lot of impressive web frameworks, and no one framework is the One Framework to Rule Them All. Be sure to find the right one that fits your needs and preferences as a developer.
- The same goes with Rust's GUI frameworks, which are already quite impressive but without one single crate that stands above the rest.
- Rust has a few websites that track the progress of crates in certain domains, all of which have the form "Are we ... yet?" Some examples are https://

arewegameyet.rs for game development, https://www.arewewebyet.org for web development, and https://www.arewelearningyet.com for machine learning. The full list of these tracking web pages can be seen at https://wiki.mozilla.org/ Areweyet.

- Curious which Rust version is coming next and when? Check out http:// whatrustisit.com.
- You are awesome for having read all the way to the end of the book!!!

index

Code Like a Pro in Rust
by Brenden Matthews

ISBN 9781617299643
264 pages (estimated), $59.99
March 2024 (estimated)

Rust in Action
by Tim McNamara

ISBN 9781617294556
456 pages, $59.99
June 2021

Rust Web Development
by Bastian Gruber

ISBN 9781617299001
400 pages, $49.99
December 2022

Rust Servers, Services, and Apps
by Prabhu Eshwarla

ISBN 9781617298608
328 pages, $59.99
July 2023

For ordering information, go to www.manning.com

MANNING

A new online reading experience

liveBook, our online reading platform, adds a new dimension to your Manning books, with features that make reading, learning, and sharing easier than ever. A liveBook version of your book is included FREE with every Manning book.

This next generation book platform is more than an online reader. It's packed with unique features to upgrade and enhance your learning experience.

- Add your own notes and bookmarks
- One-click code copy
- Learn from other readers in the discussion forum
- Audio recordings and interactive exercises
- Read all your purchased Manning content in any browser, anytime, anywhere

As an added bonus, you can search every Manning book and video in liveBook—even ones you don't yet own. Open any liveBook, and you'll be able to browse the content and read anything you like.*

Find out more at www.manning.com/livebook-program.

*Open reading is limited to 10 minutes per book daily